CONSTITUTIONALISM IN AMERICA

A Blaisdell Book in Political Science

Robert G. McCloskey, *Harvard University, Consulting Editor*

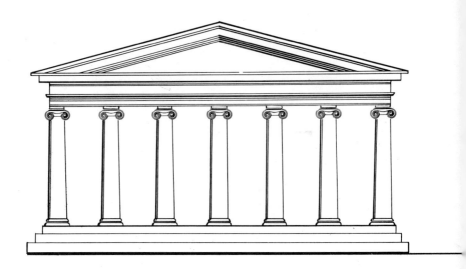

Arthur E. Sutherland
HARVARD UNIVERSITY

CONSTITUTIONALISM IN AMERICA

Origin and Evolution of its Fundamental Ideas

BLAISDELL PUBLISHING COMPANY
A DIVISION OF GINN AND COMPANY
NEW YORK · TORONTO · LONDON

FOR
Arthur Eugene Sutherland
AND
Eleanor Reed Sutherland
1862–1949
remembering many lessons
they taught their children

*Custodi igitur temetipsum et animam tuam,
ne obliviscaris verborum quae viderunt oculi tui.
Docebis ea filios ac nepotes tuos.*

PREFACE

Only a resolute man will undertake a book on American Constitutional theory. The subject is commonly thought to be perpetually mobile, fluid beyond seizing. One hesitates to write in water. Continuous development of this system can make temperamental difficulties for the scholar.

There are also practical problems. The sheer mass of materials increases at a rate that overmatches whatever acquisitive powers man's intellect may summon. The traditional literature of American constitutionalism consists of Supreme Court opinions. When Story finished his Commentaries in 1833 he had only 31 volumes of Supreme Court reports to systematize.[1] Cooley, in 1868, had to scan 73.[2] When Willoughby put out his first edition in 1910, the last of the United States Reports was No. 218.[3] The Burdicks, publishing in 1922, must have studied 259 volumes.[4] Willoughby in his second edition of 1929 covered 277 volumes.[5] Rottschaefer in 1939 had to know 307.[6]

[1] Joseph Story, *Commentaries on the Constitution of the United States with a Preliminary Review of the Constitutional History of the Colonies and States, Before the Adoption of the Constitution* (3 vols.; Boston: Hilliard, Gray and Co., 1833).
[2] Thomas M. Cooley, *A Treatise on the Constitutional Limitations Which Rest Upon the Legislative Power of the States of the American Union* (Boston: Little, Brown & Co., 1868).
[3] Westel Woodbury Willoughby, *The Constitutional Law of the United States* (2 vols.; New York: Baker Voorhis & Co., 1910).
[4] Charles K. and Francis M. Burdick, *The Law of the American Constitution. Its Origin and Development* (New York and London: G. P. Putnam's Sons, 1922).
[5] Westel Woodbury Willoughby, *The Constitutional Law of the United States* (2nd ed.; 2 vols.; New York: Baker Voorhis & Co., 1929).
[6] Henry Rottschaefer, *Handbook of American Constitutional Law* (St. Paul: West Publishing Co., 1939).

Corwin's monumental annotated constitution of 1953 contains in its notes material from 343 volumes of the United States Reports,[7] far more than ten times Story's material from the Supreme Court alone. In 1964, as this manuscript is at length completed, the last published volume of United States Reports is the 378th. Because opinions of the Supreme Court constitute the classic source of modern constitutional doctrine, a book which purported to include every relevant reference would certainly proceed toward obsolescence each year at the rate of three volumes or so, a thousand or more pages of Supreme Court reports.

But the Supreme Court is by no means the only source of our constitutional theory. Lower federal courts decide important questions that never go above the Courts of Appeal. Analysis of many issues requires study of State cases: constitutional doctrines which would seem, from federal opinions, to have died a generation ago may still have a flourishing life in State Supreme Courts, often sheltered by "adequate state grounds"[8] which preclude review in the Supreme Court of the United States. And non-judicial writings are much relied on by courts in deciding such mingled questions of policy and law as those of due process, or equal protection, or the validity of State action in the presence of the Commerce Clause.[9] For a book undertaking to marshal all this material, a corps of indexers would be needed more than an author.[10]

So a writer on American constitutionalism can be appalled and discouraged by his inevitable choice between superficiality and omission. He is continually reminded, by references in opinions of the Supreme Court, that a study of our constitutional law is, in one aspect, a part of the study of our people's history. He must know and write something of the development of our nation and its government since 1789; but to do this he must write of the formation of the Union, and of the Revolution of 1776. For its theoretical justification, the American War of Independence depended much on the Revolution

[7] Edward S. Corwin, *The Constitution of the United States of America* (82nd Cong., 2d Sess; Sen. Doc. 170) Washington, D.C., Government Printing Office, 1953.

[8] See *Central Savings Bank* v. *City of New York*, 279 N.Y. 266, 280 N.Y. 9 (1939); c.d. 306 U.S. 661 (1939); and see A. M. Horn, *Judicial Power over Policies under State Constitutions*, VI Public Policy 47 (1955).

[9] See, for example, *Youngstown Sheet & Tube Co.* v. *Sawyer*, 343 U.S. 579 (1952); *Brown* v. *Board of Education*, 347 U.S. 483 (1954); 349 U.S. 294 (1955).

[10] See, for examples, *The Federal Digest*, continuously edited by West Publishing Co.; The *Digest of the Supreme Court Reports*, Lawyers' Edition, published by Lawyers' Cooperative Publishing Co.; and the *Index to Legal Periodicals*, published by H. W. Wilson Co. in cooperation with the American Association of Law Libraries.

of 1688; an author must, then, try to know and explain the constitutional controversies that led to Cromwell's Commonwealth, and to the restoration and final downfall of the Stuarts. But Coke and Parliament are part of this history; and Coke's use of medieval materials in his arguments with James and Charles, is hardly comprehensible without some understanding of medieval England. Whoever would write on the American constitution must make himself to a certain extent a historian of England in the Middle Ages and in the Renaissance; and of Puritan times in England and America. He must write some account of the political, social, economic and military development of the United States through nearly two centuries. If he is to do his work as well as he would wish, he must take all knowledge of English history to be his province, and he must be at home in every part of our own country's story. This is more than any man can do in his allotted years.

For good or ill, therefore, here is no encyclopaedic work, purporting to explore all the original sources of constitutional history. I have tried to present a condensed account of only so much English history as contributes some main themes to an understanding of American Constitutional theory. I have not attempted to arrange in purported order the entire mass of American judicial and political precedent. I have instead tried to be wisely selective, discussing those American materials which illustrate the theories of our constitutional system. In 1932 Mr. Justice Brandeis made a suggestion which, to the discerning, should have taught that principles of constitutional law are comparatively few, remaining fairly constant despite social, political and judicial change, while confusion and multiplicity arise rather from the infinite number of differing fact situations, different "cases," in which accepted constitutional standards are applied. Justice Brandeis wrote,

> . . . In the cases which now come before us there is seldom any dispute as to the interpretation of any provision [of the Constitution]. The controversy is usually over the application to existing conditions of some well-recognized constitutional limitation. This is strikingly true of cases under the due process clause when the question is whether a statute is unreasonable, arbitrary or capricious; of cases under the equal protection clause when the question is whether there is any reasonable basis for the classification made by a statute; and of cases under the commerce clause when the question is whether an admitted burden laid by a statute upon interstate commerce is so substantial as to be deemed direct. These issues resemble, fundamentally, that of reasonable care in negligence cases, the determination of which is ordinarily left to the verdict of the jury. In every such case the decision, in the first instance, is dependent upon the determination of

what in legal parlance is called a fact, as distinguished from the declaration of a rule of law. When the underlying fact has been found, the legal result follows inevitably. The circumstance that the decision of that fact is made by a court, instead of by a jury, should not be allowed to obscure its real character.[11]

The title of this book describes its limited undertaking. Here is proposed a statement of constitutional theory in the United States, in its origins long ago and in our own times, illustrated by what seem the principal decisions of courts and other relevant public actions. For the studious, published digests, cyclopedias and such tools of research as "Shepard's Citations" will soon expand these leading authorities.

The plan is simple. Essentially it is an account of the development, through more than seven centuries, of five aspirations in human government—majority rule; government subject to justice; equality of man; diffusion of governmental power lest it be too strong for liberty; and statement in a written compact of fundamentals of decent rule.

Without the learning and wisdom of my colleagues at Harvard, Paul Freund, Mark De Wolfe Howe and Ernest Brown, three authors of a casebook on Constitutional Law in which they let me join, accumulation of the material for this book would have been beyond my powers. My indebtedness to these scholars is obvious and unlimited.

And, finishing such a book as this, one is conscious of a lifetime's unpayable debts to a host of others; students alert, critical, and yet tolerant; kindly and careful teachers in Universities at home and abroad, in youth and later; judicial friends; companions at the Bars of New York, Massachusetts, and of the Supreme Court.

Two men, now great shades, I must mention particularly: Oliver Wendell Holmes, proud soldier, wise judge, gentle friend to a one-time Secretary; and first and finally, a justice of the New York Supreme Court in whose house as a child I first came to know the high intolerance of sham and oppression, a strong trait in our best judges, which has moved our people to entrust so much to their courts.

ARTHUR E. SUTHERLAND

Cambridge, Massachusetts
August 1964

---

[11] Dissenting in *Burnet* v. *Coronado Oil & Gas Co.*, 285 U.S. 393–413 (1932).

CITATION

An arduous campaign produces heroes who well earn Mention in Despatches. So does the making of a book; this one should not appear without mention of the Aides. My old friend Geoffroy Billo of Baker, Voorhis and Company first suggested that I write the book, and I drew on his long experience for wise advice, particularly advice about indexing. Typing the manuscript required far more than nimble fingers; to this task Nan Emery, Elizabeth Johnson, and Rosemary Wilson contributed vigilant and literate understanding. Joseph Cheavens, correcting proofs, saved me from grievous errors; he also compiled a major part of the bibliography. Mary Catherine Kopko carefully performed the exacting work of preliminary indexing. Mary Kirk Sutherland went through the entire book in page proofs, completing the bibliography and accomplishing the essential detailed work of preparing the Table of Cases. Without these and other well-deserving friends there could have been no book.

A.E.S.

CONTENTS

CONSTITUTIONALISM IN AMERICA

1. ELEMENTS OF CONSTITUTIONAL THEORY

. . . Theory is the most important part of the dogma of the law, as the architect is the most important man who takes part in the building of a house. . . . It is not to be feared as unpractical, for, to the competent, it simply means going to the bottom of the subject. For the incompetent, it sometimes is true, as has been said, that an interest in general ideas means an absence of particular knowledge. I remember in army days reading of a youth who, being examined for the lowest grade and being asked a question about squadron drill, answered that he never had considered the evolutions of less than ten thousand men. But the weak and foolish must be left to their folly. The danger is that the able and practical minded should look with indifference or distrust upon ideas the connection of which with their business is remote. I heard a story, the other day, of a man who had a valet to whom he paid high wages, subject to deduction for faults. One of his deductions was, "For lack of imagination, five dollars." The lack is not confined to valets.[1]

To DESCRIBE the constitutional aspirations of the people of the United States is not easy. The elements of our governing theory can not be stated by listing the more conspicuous clauses of the Constitution; nor by enumerating the public issues raised by notable constitutional litigation. Constitutional clauses, and judicial opinions on constitutional matters, are evidences of underlying principles; they are rarely statements of the principles themselves. The task of the theorist is to discern, behind the specific and the occasional, those hopes for human government that are so general, so abiding, as to be parts of "the very idea of a government of limited powers set up by a free people."[2]

[1] O. W. Holmes, "The Path of the Law," 10 *Harv. L. Rev.* 45 (1897); reprinted in *Collected Legal Papers* (New York: Peter Smith, 1952) p. 200.
[2] See Roscoe Pound, *An Introduction to Philosophy of Law* (New Haven: Yale University Press, 1922) p. 51.

1

Five such underlying principles[3] have been conspicuous in the development of American constitutionalism. The most fundamental is freedom of men, acting through an organized majority, to control their own political and economic fate.[4] This should not be dismissed as a proposition tiresomely obvious and universally accepted. Many nations, through many generations, accepted the doctrine that certain families were divinely ordained to rule; and although this idea of hereditary rule by divine right now seems generally extinct, there persists, half-acknowledged in many minds, another and more perennially plausible ideal, that the strong, able, and wise should rule the multitude; should rule when possible in kindness, and ultimately for the multitude's benefit; but should nevertheless rule; should rule because, so this theory goes, the multitude lacks ability and wisdom to provide for itself. The Divine Right of Kings we rejected once and for all in 1776; the continually recurring concept of a benign élite we have often considered, and, thus far, have rejected. We reject because we have kept much of the optimism that ran through our nation when it was new. Without embarrassing ourselves by too much cruel thought we cling to our trust in man's perfectibility, which persuades us that "education is perhaps the most important function of state and local governments."[5] Our First and Fourteenth Amendments, and the Courts which apply them, have promised to each of our people freedom to speak and to publish even statements which, to the overwhelming majority of us, seem silly, unjust, and cruel. We aspire to allow every man to convert his fellows to new religions and new political creeds. And despite this promise of optional heterodoxy we have stubbornly maintained institutions designed to assure majoritarian rule, rule by the unconverted many, regardless of their wisdom or momentary unwisdom, their impatience or vulgarity. The first constitutional principle of our people is their right to make, and ultimately (one hopes) to correct, their own mistakes.

Our second great aspiration—a principle sometimes irreconcilable with the first—is that government shall be righteous and just, and shall

[3] No taxonomy is wholly satisfactory; and here at the outset, I gladly concede that there are many ways to divide and arrange men's ideas of a just and wise governmental order. Each man may prefer his own. In deference to the fallibility of human judgment I have not used the definite article before the words "Five . . . underlying principles."

[4] I do not here yield to the seductive temptation to discuss what a people's political and economic fate should ideally be. This inquiry, not wholly novel, transcends even the elastic limits of this book. Howard Mumford Jones' charming and witty lectures at Michigan *The Pursuit of Happiness* (Cambridge: Harvard University Press, 1953) would offer a good place to start.

[5] Warren, C. J., in *Brown* v. *Board of Education of Topeka*, 347 U.S. 483 (1954) at page 493.

establish sound institutions for the correction of its own injustices. This is a doctrine independent of majorities. It turns on the concept that governmental action may be unjust even if willed by most of the people. It postulates an ascertainable standard of rightness, distinct from majority will. Its great difficulty lies in the perception and statement of general principles of justice; and in devising means to compel a government, powerful enough to rule effectively, to act in a manner contrary to the will of its rulers. This ancient dilemma, theoretical and practical, becomes most difficult when the rulers are the people themselves. *Quis custodiet ipsos custodes?*

Not infrequently just rule has been an ideal for autocracies as well as for popular governments. Medieval kings were told that they must govern under God; but philosophers found no means of obliging kings to be just when they were powerful.[6] In our turn we have found comparable difficulty in discovering devices to ascertain and to correct injustices of a ruling majority. None the less we persist in believing that a majority can be wrong, and that a law, though made and applied with all due procedures, can be an unjust law which ought not to bind the citizen.

This is an uneasy doctrine. In any state where no man would obey a law unless he thought it just, there would be anarchy, ". . . perpetual Disorder and Mischief, Tumult, Sedition and Rebellion . . ."[7] Renouncing this intolerable state of affairs, but still holding to our aspiration for government under a rule of justice, we have sought to compromise by empowering judicial officers, less exposed than others to majoritarian pressures, to declare inoperative any governmental action inconsistent with such sweeping concepts as "due process of law," and other like standards of constitutional justice.

Formulation of such standards is a difficult task, whether formulation falls to courts or to constitution-makers. Courts, to be sure, ordinarily limit their efforts to specific cases; they only declare standards interstitially, bit by bit, as occasion arises in the incidents of litigation. They have only to pronounce the just or the unjust in one set of circumstances, explaining it as logically as possible, comforted perhaps by remembering that judicial precedents can be confined to their particular facts. Draftsmen of Constitutions, who undertake the more difficult task of formulating a generally applicable and practically useful definition of justice, will find success impossible unless they are wiser than any man who has gone before us. Rules can well be stated for narrowly defined situations. Such are the prohibitions of bills of

---

[6] See André Tunc, "The Royal Will and the Rule of Law," in *Government Under Law*, Arthur E. Sutherland, ed. (Cambridge: Harvard University Press, 1956).

[7] John Locke, *Second Treatise of Civil Government*, Chapter I, Paragraph 1.

attainder and *ex post facto* laws in the first Article of the federal Constitution, and the exemption from self-incrimination in the Fifth Amendment. Looser in terms, but still not statements of universal scope, are such limitations as the "establishment of religion" clause in the First Amendment, and the "punishment clause" of the Eighth Amendment. The difficulty comes with the attempt at a universal formula; it comes in seeking a constitutional standard of general application, defining all the unjust governmental action which the constitution purports to renounce. The vagueness inherent in words, the hopelessness of the search for some phrase which will happily reconcile the endless multiplicity of conflicts between the necessity of human rule and the eternal human desire not to be ruled, drive the constitutionalist, hunting for a characterization of just government, to use such phrases as "due process of Law" or "equal protection of the laws"[8] though these formulas are only nominally constitutional standards. They prescribe no specific governmental action or forbearance; questions arising under them can not be answered by scrutinizing dictionary definitions. We are moved by aspirations of general constitutional theory not inherent in the words of any constitutional text. We have thought the governing norms,

> . . . principles of natural law 'running back of all constitutions' and inherent in the very idea of a government of limited powers set up by a free people.[9]

A third underlying principle of American constitutionalism is the fundamental equality of all men before government. This has always been a difficult conception. Human beings are not alike; and government has always necessarily differentiated men from women, soldiers from civilians, children from adults, the sick from the well, citizens from strangers, the able from the incompetent, the guilty from the innocent. Men tend to redefine equality as "equality of opportunity"[10] which appears to mean absence of impediments in the way of each man's attaining the best that his individual traits permit.[11] Equation

[8] Cromwell's Army Council attempted such a definition in the "Agreement of the People" of January 15, 1649, See page 77 *infra*.

[9] See Roscoe Pound, *An Introduction to the Philosophy of Law*, p. 51; cf. the dissenting opinion of Black, J. in *Adamson v. California*, 332 U.S. 46 (1947) p. 68.

[10] On this well-meaning misnomer I have made some comment in *The Law and One Man Among Many* (Madison: University of Wisconsin Press, 1956) p. 23 *et seq.*

[11] President Kennedy on June 9, 1963 told the Conference of Mayors, meeting in Hawaii, "I do not say that all men are equal in their ability, character and motivation. I do say that every American should be given a fair chance to develop in full whatever talents he has and to share equally in the American dream." See *N.Y. Times*, June 10, 1963, p. 1, Col. 8.

thus of equality with individualism is another instance of the wide-spread desire to call something by a palatable misdescription. "Equality of opportunity" is not equality at all; it is inequality institutionalized according to innate talent.

The idea of equality can be stated in another way—that all men shall be equal save in those respects in which they are justly unequal. Justice being insusceptible of definition, this formula for equality under law is not easy to apply, as experience with the Equal Protection Clause of the Fourteenth Amendment has shown. Still we have gone on eliminating "artificial" or "arbitrary" inequalities, those arising in different governmental treatment of different races or religions, for example, without being driven to state the criteria of that differentiation which is just.

In 1776 the United States abandoned English hereditary distinctions of personal rank, but until after the Civil War the federal constitution still permitted the States to distinguish the civil status of negroes from that of whites. And, of course, to this day we have maintained the legally protected institution of inheritable property, which by birth gives some men an economic advantage over others. Despite these distinctions the concept of human equality is a cherished one, explicit since 1868 in the Equal Protection clause of the Fourteenth Amendment. To this half-understood ideal of equality men will assert devotion, and perhaps will often feel it, notwithstanding inequalities they tolerate, or insistently impose on their neighbors.

These three aspirations, government by majority; the subordination of government to a standard of justice transcending even its enacted law; the fundamental equality of men; these are the underlying substantive principles of our constitutionalism. A fourth principle concerns structure. Government must not be monolithic lest it be too strong for our liberties. Under the Constitution, power to rule is segmented. We have deliberately sacrificed,

> . . . complete, all-embracing, swiftly moving authority . . . 'not to promote efficiency but to preclude the exercise of arbitrary power.'[12]

By conscious provision in 1789, adapted and modified by practice and by constitutional amendment, we divided governmental power between the nation and the component states. Within the central government, we have divided power between three organs, legislative, executive, and judicial, each in original theory separate from the other. This principle of form, that government should be segmented, is not

[12] Frankfurter, J., In the Steel Seizure Case, 343 U.S. 541, 613 (1952). The internal quotation is from the dissent of Brandeis, J., in *Myers* v. *U.S.* 272 U.S. 52, 293 (1926).

less important than those principles called substantive. Limitation of governmental power by segmentation postulates a belief that men do best if let alone by government, not by any means a universally accepted idea, but still strong in the United States. Without the separation of powers, without the institution of an independent judiciary, without a champion furnished by government against government, constitutional rights would become "ghosts that are seen in the law, but that are elusive to the grasp."[13] And without the semi-independence of the States, diminished though it is in today's United States, we should lack a large part of the opportunity for participation in government, which assures the citizen a hand in the control of his political and economic fate.

A fifth idea, deeply rooted in our constitutional theory, is the reduction of the fundamentals of our constitutional system to a written statement. Here is logical application of an ancient theory, that the basis of governmental power is a contract between governor and governed. The immense prestige that Magna Carta has acquired over the centuries furnishes one illustration. The existence of this contractual concept in the mind of American colonists is evident from the Mayflower Compact, and from the early prestige of our colonial charters. John Locke, theorist of the "Glorious Revolution of 1688," whom we Americans borrowed eighty-eight years later, wrote "Of the Beginning of Political Society,"

> Men being, as has been said, by Nature, all free, equal and independent, no one can be put out of this Estate, and subjected to the Political Power of another, without his own Consent. The only Way whereby any one devests himself of his natural Liberty, and puts on the Bonds of Civil Society is by agreeing with other Men to joyn and unite into a Community, for their comfortable, safe and peaceable Living one amongst another, in a secure Enjoyment of their Properties, and a greater Security against any, that are not of it.[14]

The idea of reducing to writing such a compact is part of the concept of government of laws and not of men; it goes with a suspicious watchfulness lest government treat one man better than another without a generally agreed reason for the difference. For us the fundamental writing[15] has a mystique greater than its words can explain by themselves. Some terms of our written Constitution are so inconclusive that

[13] Holmes, J., in *The Western Maid* (*United States* v. *Thompson*) 257 U.S. 419, 433 (1922).

[14] *Second Treatise*, Ch. VIII, Paragraph 95.

[15] C. H. McIlwain, *The High Court of Parliament and Its Supremacy* (New Haven: Yale University Press, 1910) Chap. II.

meaning has to be attributed to them by judges, who for this purpose necessarily have recourse to general doctrines derived from diverse sources often not conventionally "legal." The process of interpretation draws criticism whenever for the moment its results are inconvenient to the adverse critics.[16] But few rail at a written constitution as an institution. One of the assembly points of national sentiment is the great writing itself.

Each of these five ideas—popular control of government;[17] government subject to justice; government applied equally to men; government with diffused and segmented powers; government by written compact—has had a long history. Some survey of their different origins and development is necessary for understanding.

> . . . The provisions of the Constitution are not mathematical formulas having their essence in their form; they are organic, living institutions transplanted from English soil. The significance is vital, not formal; it is to be gathered not simply by taking the words and a dictionary, but by considering their origin and the line of their growth.[18]

Such a historical survey, unavoidable summary, omitting much, is the content of this book.

Note

Historians often date events in English history by reference to the reign in which they occurred. Thus Sir Frederick Pollock and Professor F. W. Maitland called their monumental joint work *The History of English Law Before the Time of Edward I*. The convenience of American readers may be served by a chronological table of English reigns from the Conquest to the accession of William and Mary.

[16] See for example, certain congressional reactions to the "School Segregation Cases in 100 *Congressional Record* Part 5 (2nd Session of the 83rd Congress) May 18, 1954, pp. 6742, 6777, 6778. Note particularly the remarks of Messrs. Forrester & Wheeler (Ga.) of the House of Representatives, pp. 6777–6778. See also "Charles River Bridge Case," 11 Peters 420 (1837) and Associate Justice Baldwin's pamphlet entitled, "A General View of the Origin and Nature of the Constitution and Government" Philadelphia, 1837, reprinted in 9 Lawyers' Edition of the Supreme Court Reports 873. Justice Baldwin's separate but concurring opinion in "The Charles River Bridge Case" is set out at p. 938.

[17] "Popular sovereignty" would be a useful term for the people's control of government, for rule by majority. But Stephen O. Douglas at one time gave to "popular sovereignty" an undeserved bad reputation, by using it as a favorable name for local-option to retain negro slavery.

[18] Holmes, J., in *Gompers v. U.S.* 233 U.S. 604, 610 (1914).

Reigns of English Kings from the Conquest
to the Revolution of 1688
with some notable
events helpful for mnemonic cross-reference.

Norman Kings

William the Conqueror	1066–1087	Domesday Book, 1086.
William Rufus	1087–1100	Westminster Hall built.
Henry I	1100–1135	Henry I issues "Charter of Liberties" on his coronation.
Stephen	1135–1154	Anarchic state of war with Matilda, wife of Count Geoffrey of Anjou.

Plantagenets or Angevins

Henry II (Henry Plantagenet, Count of Anjou, Matilda's son)	1154–1189	Murder in the Cathedral of Archbishop Thomas à Becket 1170. Development of central court system and growth of Common Law.
Richard I	1189–1199	"Coeur de Lion" away on Crusade. Hubert Walter, Archbishop of Canterbury and Justiciar, fosters growth of town liberties.
John	1199–1216	Magna Carta, 1215.
Henry III	1216–1272	Simon de Montfort, Earl of Leicester, most influential of Barons in 1265, summons a notable Parliament in which chartered boroughs, "communities" or "commons" were represented.
Edward I	1272–1307	Edward "The English Justinian" promotes statutory form of law. Statutes *De Donis Conditionalibus*, 1285 and *Quia Emptores*, 1290 restate and alter feudal tenures and become ancestors of modern land law. "Year Books" begin.
Edward II	1307–1327	Baronial tumult and increased significance of Parliament.

Edward III	1327–1377	Hundred Years' War 1337–1453, Crécy 1346. Black Death 1348–1349. Battle of Poitiers 1356. Chaucer 1340–1400.
Richard II	1377–1399	Peasants' Rising 1381.

Lancastrian and Yorkist Kings

Henry IV	1399–1413	House of Lancaster seized throne.
Henry V	1413–1422	Agincourt 1415.
Henry VI	1422–1461	Joan of Arc's career, 1429–1431. Hundred Years' War ends, 1453. Wars of the Roses break out, 1455.
Edward IV (York)	1461–1483	Caxton establishes first printing press in England, 1474.
Edward V	1483	
Richard III	1483–1485	Murder of the "Princes in the Tower," 1483. Richard killed in battle at Bosworth Field, 1485.

Tudors

Henry VII	1485–1509	End of Wars of Roses. Firm and efficient government for England. Statute later called *Pro Camera Stellata*, 1487, strengthened use of Council as a central organ of government. John Cabot with a British crew visits America, 1497.
Henry VIII	1509–1547	Reformation Parliament, 1529–1536. Act of Supremacy of Henry over *Anglicana Ecclesia*, 1534.
Edward VI	1547–1553	Archbiship Cranmer's Prayer Book in English, 1549–1552. Acts of Uniformity, 1549, 1552.
Mary I	1553–1558	Queen Mary marries Philip of Spain, 1554. Reunion with Rome, 1555.

Elizabeth I	1558–1603	New Act of Uniformity, 1559, restored Prayer Book of 1552. Mary Queen of Scots executed, 1587. Armada defeated, 1588.
Stuarts		
James I	1603–1625	Virginia Charter, 1606. Coke dismissed as Chief justice after offending James, 1616. Mayflower Compact, 1620.
Charles I	1625–1649	Petition of Right, 1628. Charles beheaded 30 January 1649.

Commonwealth and Protectorate 1649–1660.

Charles II	[1649] 1660–1685	Charles grants what is now New York to "our dearest Brother James Duke of York," 1664. Col. Nicolls takes New York from the Dutch for James, 1664.
James II	1685–1688	The Glorious Revolution, the accession of William and Mary, and the Bill of Rights 1688–1689.

2. THE GREAT CHARTER
OF 1215

[POPULAR CONTROL of government is complex, like all social arrange-ments. The democratic system in the United States was not struck off in 1787 by the brain and purpose of man. As in England, so in America, the institution grew with the procession of history.[1] In England it was foreshadowed by struggles between the king and great magnates, long before elective parliaments existed. After centuries Englishmen turned to contests between an elected Parliament and the Crown, which finally ended in Parliamentary victory when James II abandoned his throne in the revolution of 1688. In America, contests for power between elective assemblies and royal governors lasted nearly a century longer, until the War of Independence ended the tenure of all royal officers. Executive power in today's England is exercised by a cabinet ordinarily composed of elected members of the Commons. The position of the American executive branch was stated in the second Article of the Constitution; the years have demonstrated the difficulty of confining government in a definition.

Legislative supremacy has been only one objective of the struggle toward popular control of government. Another and later object was popular instead of oligarchic control of legislatures. In the United States still another, and a still later objective was to make the President himself a popularly elective officer, who should compete for democratic support with the popularly elected Congress. Yet another

[1] A misconception produced Gladstone's celebrated pronouncement "As the British Constitution is the most subtle organism which has proceeded from progressive history, so the American Constitution is the most wonderful work ever struck off at a given time by the brain and purpose of man." See his "Kin Beyond the Sea," in *The North American Review* for Sept. 1878, p. 179.

aspiration was freedom of political expression and of other political
activity, by which popular will may transmit itself to organs of
government.

Subjection of the executive to an elected legislature deserves the
first account: in this feature modern majoritarian government first
emerged from medieval feudalism.

Movement toward constitutional privilege in any people is a slow
and general process; it does not happen in a single bound; there is no
one triumph, no one conclusive compact. Nevertheless, from time to
time great events stand out as markers on the road. In England three
such episodes particularly marked progress toward subjection of kings
to parliamentary will. Each was signalized by a notable and revered
document. The first was John's yielding of Magna Carta in 1215; another was the contest between Parliament and the first two Stuarts,
documented in the Petition of Right of 1628 and signalized, sadly and
dramatically, by Charles' death on a Whitehall scaffold twenty-one
years later. The third was the Glorious Revolution of 1688, marked by
the ouster of the restored Stuarts, and the passage of an Act of Parliament called the Bill of Rights.

Magna Carta has become so revered during its seven centuries and
more of life that one tends to think not so much of the document's
actual provisions as of its symbolic essence as a muniment of our
constitutionalism. In writing of the past there is always danger that
today's word used to describe something centuries old may suggest
that the ancient thing so described was the thing of our day we now
describe by the old word.

> We must not be in a hurry to get to the beginning of the long history
> of law. Very slowly we are making our way towards it. The history of
> law must be a history of ideas. It must represent not merely what men
> have done and said, but what men have thought in bygone ages. The
> task of reconstructing ancient ideas is hazardous, and can only be
> accomplished little by little. If we are in a hurry to get to the begin-
> ning we shall miss the path. Against many kinds of anachronism we
> now guard ourselves. We are careful of costume, of armour and archi-
> tecture, of words and forms of speech. But it is far easier to be careful
> of these things than to prevent the intrusion of untimely ideas. In
> particular there lies a besetting danger for us in the barbarian's use
> of a language which is too good for his thought. Mistakes then are
> easy, and when committed they will be fatal and fundamental mis-
> takes. If, for example, we introduce the *persona ficta* too soon, we
> shall be doing worse than if we armed Hengest and Horsa with
> machine guns or pictured the Venerable Bede correcting proofs for the
> press; we shall have built upon a crumbling foundation. The most

efficient method of protecting ourselves against such errors is that of reading our history backwards as well as forwards, of making sure of our middle ages before we talk about the "archaic," of accustoming our eyes to the twilight before we go out into the night.[2]

The "law of the land" when promised by King John in Magna Carta carried little connotation of modern "due process of law." One must read Magna Carta or any other great document with consciousness of the context of its time.

The grant of the Charter was not a parliamentary victory. There was no "parliament" in 1215; the gathering of Barons that overbore John could not be so termed without distorting today's meaning. English society in 1215 was, of course, feudal; the political thought of the Middle Ages was not that of today's parliamentary state. The king was from time to time advised, supported, or controlled by a group of notables whom he could, or might be compelled to, summon to his aid. This was no legislative body in any modern sense; our concept of "legislation" was not in men's minds in the England of King John. The division of governmental functions between lawmaking, executive action, and adjudication, so much an unexpressed premise of all American constitutional discussion, could not have been stated in medieval language. It would have had no meaning for John's baronage. Magna Carta belongs in a discussion of parliamentary supremacy not because it stood for a victory by a parliament, but because it stood for defeat of a king.

The irritation and disgust that brought the barons to revolt came from John's ineptitude and indecisiveness in war, and from his larger than customary demands for money. Financial grievances were to occasion later constitutional crises, in Stuart England and in America. One thinks of Hampden and the "ship money," and of "no taxation without representation."[3]

John granted the Charter in the course of intricate moves and reverses, unsuccessful military campaigns in France, financial exigencies, quarrels with his magnates in England, many of whom refused either to follow him to war across the Channel or to pay the war's cost. Quarrels with the Church further complicated his difficulties.

These controversies began long before 1215. In 1205 Hubert Walter,

[2] F. W. Maitland, *Domesday Book and Beyond*, (Cambridge: Cambridge University Press, 1897) p. 356.

[3] On March 22, 1775, speaking "On Conciliation with the Colonies," Edmund Burke (1729–1797) told the House of Commons: "It happened you know, sir, that the great contests for freedom in this country were from the earliest times chiefly upon the question of taxing." See *Burke's Speeches & Letters on American Affairs*, Ernst Rhys, ed. (London: J. M. Dent & Co., 1908) p. 91.

Archbishop of Canterbury died; his death gave John a chance to appoint in his place the Bishop of Norwich, one of the royal supporters. The canons of the Cathedral at Canterbury, dissatisfied with the King's choice, elected their own Sub-Prior as Archbishop. The Papal Curia set aside both elections in favor of a third nominee, Cardinal Stephen Langton, who was destined to play a leading part in the events leading up to the drama at Runnymede in June, 1215.

John, annoyed at papal opposition to his royal will, refused to acknowledge Langton. In March, 1208, Innocent III placed England under interdict, a papal prohibition limiting the rites of the Church available in that Kingdom. In 1209 the King was declared excommunicated. John, by way of riposte, confiscated certain property of the great clergy, refilling his treasury with the proceeds. He hoped thus to conciliate disaffected northern barons by financing his French campaigns out of confiscated church estates, so, for a time, doing without the annual "scutage" payments he had been exacting from his feudal tenants. But the baronage continued hostile. In 1211 Innocent declared, through envoys, that unless the King would submit, the Pope would issue a bull absolving John's subjects from their allegiance, would depose him, and would commit the execution of this mandate to Philip of France.

Religious sanctions and the menace of attack from abroad were not all of King John's worries. In 1212 his son-in-law Llywelyn raised an armed revolt in Wales; John reacted quickly and cruelly. "Before he either ate or drank"[4] he hanged twenty-eight hostages, boys of noble Welsh families, and was preparing to move his forces to Wales when he heard that English barons were preparing to revolt. He was obliged to let Wales simmer while he prepared for other hazards in England. Across the channel during the winter of 1212–1213 Philip of France was collecting forces for invasion of England. The aggregate of all these opposing pressures was too great for King John to sustain. In the spring of 1213 he capitulated to Rome; he agreed to restore confiscated church estates; he surrendered the Crowns of England and Ireland into the hands of the papal representative, to receive them back as the Pope's vassal; and he accepted the papal appointment of Stephen Langton as Archbishop of Canterbury. This submission satisfied Innocent III, who remained John's supporter during the short remainder of the King's life. On July 20, 1213, Archbishop Langton

---

[4] Roger of Wendover, *Flowers of History*, Giles Tr (1849), Vol. II, p. 257. The author of *Flores Historiarum*, probably named for his Buckinghamshire birthplace, was a monk of St. Albans, and for a time Prior at Belvoir. His book begins at the Creation and extends to 1235; it gives a dark and sinister account of King John. Roger died in 1236.

absolved him from the excommunication under which he had labored.[5]

Thinking his troubles reasonably lightened, John began preparation for Channel crossing and another attempt on Poitou. Many of his barons refused to go along; the King spent the rest of 1213 in unavailing efforts to persuade or force these feudatories to undertake his French war. Meantime the Archbishop of Canterbury and the Justiciar, Geoffrey FitzPeter, Earl of Essex, on August 4, 1213, held a general assembly at St. Albans, attended not only by the bishops and barons, but also by the reeve and four "legales homines" from each township on the royal demesne. Nominally summoned by the King, to determine the sums due to despoiled bishops, the council discussed much wider issues, including the laws of Henry I as the standard of good customs which ought to be restored. This gathering might perhaps be called the earliest national representative assembly on record. To it was submitted the first draft of the reforms afterward embodied in the Charter.[6] Later, in the same month, on the 25th of August, another council convened in London at St. Paul's. Old accounts tell that a charter of Henry I was there produced and that the assembled notables at once saw that it furnished a formula for their desired reforms.[7]

Despite these stirrings at home[8] John crossed the channel in the early spring of 1214, relying for conquest mainly on mercenary troops and continental allies. To finance the expedition, he issued writs in May 1214, for collection of scutage from the English barons, at the high rate of three marks on a knight's fee. The great tenants who sailed with him to attempt Poitou were excused from the payment. On July 2, 1214,[9] Pope Innocent lifted the six-year old interdict from his newly submissive vassal. But the northern barons, who had already refused to follow John to Poitou, also refused to pay the scutage. On July 27, 1214, John's continental allies suffered a calamitous military defeat at

---

[5] T. P. Taswell-Langmead, *English Constitutional History* (9th ed.; London: Sweet & Maxwell, 1929) p. 202; see also W. E. Lunt, *History of England* (New York: Harper & Brothers, 1957) p. 136.

[6] Stubbs, William, *The Constitutional History of England* (Oxford: Clarendon Press, 1874) I, p. 567.

[7] Matthew Paris, II, 552, whom Bishop Stubbs accepts. *Const. Hist.* I, 566. Matthew Paris spent most of his life as a monk at St. Albans, writing his voluminous accounts of contemporary events. In addition to other writings, he continued Roger Wendover's *Flores Historiarum* from 1235 to 1259. He died in 1259.

[8] "At home" assumes that John thought of himself as more English than French.

[9] ". . . *die Sanctorum Processi et Martiniani* . . ." Ralph of Coggeshall, *Chronicon Anglicanum*, (Stevenson ed. 1875), p. 169. The editor in a footnote explains this as July second. Ralph was a monk who in 1207 became Abbott of the Cistercian monastery of Coggeshall in Essex. His chronicle extends from 1066 to 1224.

Bouvines, and in September he was obliged to sign a five-year's truce with King Philip of France. This was the end of John's disastrous efforts to reconquer continental domains. Humiliated, he returned to England in October.

Through the autumn and winter the barons continued preparations for civil war. They refused the King's renewed demands for money, and toward the close of 1214 a group of them met at Bury St. Edmund's, probably on November 20, St. Edmund's day,[10] under pretence of devotions. They formed a league, swore on the high altar to withdraw from fealty to John, and to make war on him until by charter under his seal, he should confirm the liberties they demanded. Shortly after Christmas they went in a body to present their demands to the King. John, playing for time, finally got from the barons a truce until Easter. In the meantime both parties had gone on with their maneuvers. The barons sent a deputation to Pope Innocent III, seeking his favorable intervention; for their pains they obtained only a rebuke from Innocent who was supporting his repentant royal vassal. John, on the other hand, by a charter originally issued on November 21, and reissued January 15, 1215, sought to win Church support in England by extending to all monasteries and cathedrals greater freedom to elect their prelates. On February 2, he sought immunity from baronial violence by "taking the cross," vowing an expedition against the infidels in the Holy Land, a vow which supposedly made profane and irreligious any violence against the heroic votary or his property. The barons were not impressed by John's gesture of knightly piety. Archbishop Langton was secretly on their side. After the truce expired the barons assembled their forces at Stamford; John sent the Archbishop and the faithful Marshal, William Earl of Pembroke, to ask what the insurgents' terms were. When the King heard the report of his emissaries he cried out "Why not ask me for my kingdom?" The barons marched south toward the Thames with "no less than two thousand Knights." On May 5, 1215, they formally renounced allegiance to the King.

London was a military strong-point, perhaps decisive. On May 9, John hoping to win the support of its citizens granted them a new city charter with the long-sought right to elect a Mayor annually. The Londoners were no more won over than the barons had been. On May 12, John, desperate, issued to his Sheriffs a futile order to overcome the rebels. London opened its gates to them on May 17. On June 15, John came from Windsor with his few remaining followers to parley

[10] See Blackstone's *Great Charter*, in his *Law Tracts* (Oxford: Clarendon Press, 1762) II, p. xv.

at Runnymede on the Thames with the much larger number of insurgents. Archbishop Stephen Langton, a number of bishops, and some barons intervened and brought about a settlement[11] under which John conceded most of the barons' demands. A preliminary memorandum of the agreement referred to as the Articles of the Barons, dated June 15, and sealed by the King[12] was drawn up on the spot. For several days more the parties argued over details and agreed on some amendments. Subsequent versions of the Great Charter containing these final alterations were engrossed at more leisure; they are all dated June 15.

Magna Carta[13]

JUNE 15, 1215

John, by the Grace of God, king of England, lord of Ireland, duke of Normandy and Aquitaine, and count of Anjou: to the archbishops, bishops, abbots, earls, barons, justiciars, foresters, sheriffs, stewards, servants, and to all his bailiffs and liege subjects, greeting. Know ye that, in the presence of God, and for the salvation of our soul, and those of all our ancestors and our heirs, and unto the honour of God and the exaltation of Holy Church, and for the betterment of our realm, on the advice of our venerable fathers, Stephen, archbishop of Canterbury, primate of all England and cardinal of the Holy Roman Church, Henry archbishop of Dublin, William of London, Peter of Winchester, Jocelyn of Bath and Glastonbury, Hugh of Lincoln, Walter of Worcester, William of Coventry, Benedict of Rochester, bishops; of master Pandulf, subdeacon and member of the household of our lord the Pope, of brother Aymeric, master of the Knights-Templars in England, and of the illustrious men William Marshal, earl of Pembroke, William, earl of Salisbury, William, earl of Warenne,

---

[11] *"Intervenientibus itaque archiepiscopo Cantuariensi cum pluribus coepiscopis et baronibus non nullis, quasi pax inter regem et barones formata est . . ."* Ralph of Coggeshall, *Chronicon Anglicanum* (Stevenson Ed. 1875), p. 172.

[12] The Articles are printed in Blackstone's *Great Charter*, p. 1 *et seq.* They are headed *"Articuli Magne Carte Liberatum sub sigillo Regis Johannis. Ista sunt capitula que barones petunt et dominus rex concedit."*

[13] An account of the original versions of the Charter, and of later printed editions and commentaries, appears in Professor William Sharp McKechnie's *Magna Carta* (2nd ed.; Glasgow: J. Maclehose & Sons, 1914), Part V. McKechnie relies on four "original" sealed copies of the Charter; (1) The British Museum Magna Carta No. 1 formally cited as "Cotton, Charter XIII 31 A" named for its 17th century owner, Cotton. (2) The British Museum Magna Carta, No. 2, "Cotton, Augustus, II 106," its name similarly derived. (3) The Lincoln Magna Carta, in

William, earl of Arundel, Alan of Galloway, Constable of Scotland, Warin Fitz-Gerald, Peter Fitz-Herbert, Hubert de Burgh, Seneschal of Poitou, Hugh de Nevil, Matthew Fitz-Herbert, Thomas Basset, Alan Basset, Philip d'Aubigny, Robert of Roppesley, John Marshal, John Fitz Hugh, and others, our liegemen;

[1] We have in the first place granted to God, and by this our present charter have confirmed, for us and for our heirs for ever, that the English church shall be free, and shall have her rights unimpaired, and her liberties inviolate; and it is our will that this be observed in such a manner that from it may be evident that freedom of elections, reckoned most important and very essential to the English church, we did grant, of our pure and unconstrained will, and we did confirm by our charter and thereof did obtain ratification from our lord, Pope Innocent III, before discord arose between us and our barons: and this we have observed, and it is our will that this be observed, in good faith by our heirs forever.

We have also granted for us and our heirs forever to all freemen of our kingdom, all the following liberties, to have and to hold, to them and their heirs, of us and our heirs, forever

[2] If any of our earls, or barons, or others who hold of us in chief by military service, shall die, and at the time of his death his heir shall be of full age and shall owe a relief, he shall have his inheritance on payment of the established relief; that is to say, the heir or heirs of an earl, 100 pounds for a whole earl's barony; the heir or heirs of a baron, 100 pounds for a whole barony; the heir or heirs of a knight, 100 shillings at most for a whole knight's fee; and whoever owes less let him give less, according to the established custom of fiefs.

---

custody of the Dean and Chapter of Lincoln Cathedral; and (4) The Salisbury Magna Carta, preserved in the archives of Salisbury Cathedral. Coke's *Second Institute* (London: Flesher and Young, 1642) contains a Latin version of the Charter (not actually John's, but an early reissue, McKechnie thought) with Coke's commentary in English. Sir William Blackstone's *The Great Charter and the Charter of the Forest,* first published in 1759, contains a Latin version, collated from the two Cottonian copies which are now in the British Museum; of which at least one probably bore John's seal. See Blackstone, *Law Tracts*. Richard Thomson's *An Historical Essay on the Magna Charta of King John* (London, 1829) contains the Latin text and an English translation on opposite pages. Bishop Stubbs prints the Magna Carta in Latin in his *Select Charters* and gives a classic commentary in his *Constitutional History of England*. McKechnie prints the Latin of each "Chapter," followed by his English text. There are many English translations in collections of historical documents; for example, Carl Stephenson and Frederic George Marcham's *Sources of English Constitutional History* (New York: Harper & Brothers, 1937). A translation with commentary appears in Perry and Cooper, *Sources of Our Liberties* (Chicago: American Bar Foundation, 1959).

After all this work by enlightened scholars, a late-comer does well to step carefully in translation; the instant version contains few innovations. The division of the Charter into a preamble and sixty-three chapters is not warranted by anything in the "original" texts, but it has become a conventional convenience for reference.

[3] If, however, the heir of any one of the aforesaid be under age and in wardship, let him have his inheritance without relief and without fine when he comes of age.

[4] The guardian of the land of an heir who is thus under age, shall take from the land of the heir nothing but reasonable yield, reasonable customs, and reasonable services, and this without destruction or waste of men or goods. And if we commit the wardship of the lands of anyone to a sheriff, or to any other who is responsible to us for its yield, and he has made destruction or waste of what he holds in wardship, we will take amends from him, and the land shall be entrusted to two lawful and discreet men of that fief, who shall be responsible for the yield to us or to him to whom we shall assign them. And if we give or sell the wardship of any such land to anyone, and he has therein made destruction or waste, he shall forfeit that wardship, and it shall be transferred to two lawful and discreet men of that fief, who shall be responsible to us in like manner as aforesaid.

[5] The guardian, moreover, so long as he has the wardship of the land, shall out of the issues of the land keep up the houses, parks, fishponds, pools, mills, and other things pertaining to the land; and he shall restore to the heir, when he has come to full age, all his land, stocked with ploughs and other implements, according as the season of husbandry shall require, and the issues of the land can reasonably afford.

[6] Heirs shall be married without disparagement, provided that before the marriage takes place notice be given to the heir's next of kin.

[7] A widow, after the death of her husband, shall forthwith and without difficulty have her marriage portion and inheritance; nor shall she be required to pay anything for her dower, or for her marriage portion, or for the inheritance which her husband and she held on the day of her husband's death; and she may remain in her husband's house for forty days after his death, within which time her dower shall be allotted to her.

[8] No widow shall be compelled to marry, if she prefers to live without a husband; provided that she give security not to marry without our consent, if she holds of us; or, if she holds of another, without the consent of the lord of whom she holds.

[9] Neither we nor our bailiffs shall seize any land or rent for any debt, so long as the chattels of the debtor are sufficient to repay the debt; nor shall the sureties of the debtor be distrained so long as the principal debtor is able to satisfy the debt; and if the principal debtor shall fail to pay the debt, having nothing whereby to pay it, then the sureties shall answer for the debt; and, if they wish, they may have the lands and rents of the debtor, until they are repaid for the debt which they have paid for him, unless the principal debtor can show proof that he is discharged against those sureties.

[10] If one who has borrowed from the Jews any sum, great or small, die before that loan be repaid, the debt shall not bear interest while the heir is under age, of whomsoever he may hold; and if the debt fall into our hands, we will not take anything except the principal sum nominated in the bond.

[11] And if anyone die indebted to the Jews, his wife shall have her dower and pay nothing of that debt; and if any children of the deceased are left under age, necessaries shall be provided for them in keeping with the holding of the deceased; and out of the residue the debt shall be paid, reserving, however, service due to feudal lords; in like manner let it be done respecting debts due to others than Jews.

[12] No scutage nor aid shall be imposed on our kindom, unless by common counsel of our kingdom, except for ransoming our person, for making our eldest son a knight, and for once marrying our eldest daughter; and for these there shall not be levied more than a reasonable aid. In like manner it shall be done concerning aids from the city of London.

[13] And the city of London shall have all its ancient liberties and free customs, as well by land as by water; furthermore, we decree and grant that all other cities, boroughs, towns, and ports shall have all their liberties and free customs.

[14] And for obtaining the common counsel of the kingdom as to the assessing of an aid (except in the three cases aforesaid) or of a scutage, we will cause to be individually summoned the archbishops, bishops, abbots, earls, and greater barons, by our letters; and we will moreover cause to be summoned generally, through our sheriffs and bailiffs, all others who hold of us in chief, for a day certain, namely, after the expiry of at least forty days, and at a fixed place; and in all letters of such summons we will specify the reason for the summons. And when the summons has thus been made, the business shall proceed on the day appointed, according to the counsel of such as are present, although not all who were summoned have come.

[15] We will not for the future grant to any one licence to take an aid from his own free tenants, except to ransom his body, to make his eldest son a knight, and once to marry his eldest daughter; and for these there shall be levied only a reasonable aid.

[16] No one shall be distrained for performance of greater service for a knight's fee, or for any other free tenement, than is due therefrom.

[17] The Court of Common Pleas shall not follow our court, but shall be held in some fixed place.

[18] Inquests of *novel disseisin,* of *mort d'ancestor,* and of *darrein presentment,* shall not be held elsewhere than in their own county-courts, and that in manner following,—We, or, if we should be out of the realm, our chief justiciar, will send two justiciars through every county four times a year, who shall, along with four knights of the county chosen by the county court, hold the said assizes in the county, on the day and in the place of meeting of that court.

[19] And if any of the said assizes cannot be held on the day of the county court, let there remain of the knights and freeholders, who were present at the county court on that day, as many as may be required for the efficient making of judgments, according as the business be more or less.

[20] A freeman shall not be amerced for a slight offence, except in accordance with the gravity of the offence, yet saving always to him a suitable means of livelihood;[14] and a merchant in the same way, saving his stock in trade; and a villein shall be amerced in the same way, saving his implements of tillage—if they have fallen into our mercy: and none of the aforesaid amercements shall be imposed except by the oath of honest men of the neighborhood.

[21] Earls and barons shall not be amerced except through their peers, and only in accordance with the degree of the offence.

[22] A clerk shall not be amerced in respect of his lay holding except after the manner of the others aforesaid; further, he shall not be amerced in accordance with the extent of his ecclesiastical benefice.

[23] No village nor man shall be compelled to build bridges over rivers, except those obliged to do so by custom and by law.

[24] No sheriff, constable, coroners, or others of our bailiffs, shall hold pleas of our Crown.

[25] All counties, hundreds, wapentakes, and trethings[15] (except our demesne manors) shall remain at the old rents, and without any additional payment.

[26] If any one holding of us a lay fief shall die, and our sheriff or bailiff shall exhibit our letters patent of summons for a debt which the deceased owed to us, it shall be lawful for our sheriff or bailiff to attach and inventory chattels of the deceased, found upon the lay fief, to the value of that debt, on a view by law-worthy men, provided always that nothing whatever be thence removed until the debt which is evident shall be fully paid to us; and the residue shall be left to the executors to fulfil the will of the deceased; and if there be nothing due from him to us, all the chattels shall go to the deceased, saving to his wife and children their reasonable shares.

[27] If any freeman shall die intestate, his chattels shall be distributed by the hands of his nearest kinsfolk and friends, under supervision of the church, saving to every one the debts which the deceased owed to him.

---

[14] See Coke's *Second Institute*, Cap. XIV, which indicates that even in the early 17th century the Latin expression "contenemento suo," here rendered as the freeman's "suitable means of livelihood," were puzzling to lawyers. Coke concluded that "contenement" was the same as "countenance," adding "the armor of a Souldior is his countenance, the books of a Scholler his countenance, and the like." One is reminded of modern statutory exemptions from execution on money-judgments.

[15] McKechnie explains what the Charter calls "trethingii," and what McKechnie calls "trithings" as the "ridings" in the Counties of York and Lincoln, three in each.

[28] No constable or other bailiff of ours shall requisition corn or other supplies from any one without immediately paying money therefor, unless the seller voluntarily consents to deferred payment.

[29] No constable shall compel any knight to give money in lieu of castle-guard, when he is willing to perform it in his own person, or (if he himself cannot do it from any reasonable cause) then by another responsible man. Further, if we have led or sent him upon military service, he shall be relieved from guard in proportion to the time during which he has been on duty under our orders.

[30] No sheriff or bailiff of ours, or other person, shall take the horses or carts of any freeman for transport duty, against the will of said freeman.

[31] Neither we nor our bailiffs shall take, for our castles or for any other work of ours, timber which is not ours, against the will of the owner of the timber.

[32] We will not retain beyond one year and one day, the lands of those who have been convicted of felony, and the lands shall thereafter be handed over to the lords of the fiefs.

[33] For the future all fish-traps shall be removed altogether from Thames and Medway, and throughout all England, except upon the sea shore.

[34] The royal writ called *praecipe* shall not for the future be issued to anyone, regarding any tenement, whereby a freeman may be deprived of a trial in his manorial court.[16]

[35] Let there be one measure of wine throughout our whole realm; and one measure of ale; and one measure of corn, to wit, the London quarter; and one width of cloth whether dyed, or russet, or halberget,[17] to wit, two ells within the selvedges; of weights also let it be as of measures.

[36] Nothing in future shall be paid or taken for a writ of inquisition of life or limbs,[18] but freely it shall be granted, and never denied.

[37] If anyone holds of us by fee-farm, by socage, or by burgage, and holds also land of another lord by knight's service, we will not (by reason of that fee-farm, socage, or burgage) have the wardship of the heir, or of such land of his as is of the fief of that other; nor shall we have wardship of that fee-farm, socage, or burgage, unless such fee-farm owes knight's service. We will not by reason of any petty serjeanty which anyone may hold of us by the service of rendering to us knives, arrows, or the like, have wardship of his heir or of the land which he holds of another lord by knight's service.

[16] I.e. whereby a baron or other freeholder may lose jurisdiction of his man. See Stephenson and Marcham, *Sources of English Constitutional History*, p. 120, fn. 30.

[17] "Halbergectorum," a puzzle today. Professor McKechnie suggests thick cloth worn under a coat-of-mail or hauberk.

[18] Roughly a writ granting trial by jury instead of by combat.

[38] No bailiff for the future shall, upon his own unsupported complaint, put anyone to his law,[19] without creditable witnesses brought for this purpose.

[39] No freeman shall be taken or imprisoned or disseised or exiled or in any way destroyed, nor will we go upon him nor send upon him, except by the lawful judgment of his peers and by the law of the land.

[40] To no one will we sell, to no one will we refuse or delay, right or justice.

[41] All merchants shall have the right to safe and secure departure from England, and entry into England, and sojourn and travel within England, both by land and by water, for buying and selling by the ancient and right customs, free from all evil tolls, except in time of war such merchants as are of the enemy land. And if such are found in our land at the beginning of the war, they shall be detained, without injury to their bodies or goods, until information be received by us, or by our chief justiciar, how the merchants of our land found in the land at war with us are treated; and if our men are safe there, the others shall be safe in our land.

[42] It shall be lawful in the future for any person to leave our kingdom and to return, safe and secure by land and water,—reserving always the allegiance due to us,—except for a short period in time of war, for the common good of the realm, excepting always those imprisoned or outlawed in accordance with the law of the kingdom, and natives of any country at war with us, and merchants, who shall be treated as is above provided.

[43] If anyone holding of an escheat such as the honour of Wallingford, Nottingham, Boulogne, Lancaster, or of other escheats which are in our hands and are baronies, shall die, his heir shall give no other relief, and perform no other service to us than he would have done to the baron, if that barony had been in the baron's hand; and we shall hold it in the same manner in which the baron held it.

[44] Men who dwell without the forest need not henceforth come before our justiciars of the forest upon a general summons,[20] except those who are impleaded, or who have become sureties for any person or persons attached, for forest offences.

[45] We will appoint as justices, constables, sheriffs, or bailiffs only such as know the law of the realm and mean to observe it well.

[46] All barons who have founded abbeys, concerning which they hold charters from the kings of England, or of which they have long-continued tenurial rights, shall have the wardship of them, when vacant, as they ought to have.

[47] All forest that have been made in our time shall forthwith be

[19] The nature of this oppression by bailiffs is now uncertain.

[20] A summons nominally calling in all men of the four adjoining townships concerning offenses committed during a past interval. See McKechnie's comment.

disafforested; and a similar course shall be followed with regard to river-banks that have been made hawking preserves[21] by us in our time.

[48] All evil customs connected with forests and warrens, foresters and warreners, sheriffs, and their officers, river-banks and their wardens, shall immediately be inquired into in each county by twelve sworn knights of the same county chosen by the honest men of the same county, and shall, within forty days of the said inquest, be utterly abolished by them,[22] so as never to be restored, provided always that we previously have notice thereof, or our justiciar, if we should not be in England.

[49] We will immediately restore all hostages and charters delivered to us by Englishmen, as sureties of the peace or of faithful service.

[50] We will entirely remove from their offices, the relations of Gerard of Athee (so that in the future they shall have no office in England); namely, Engelard of Cigogne, Peter, Guy, and Andrew of Chanceaux, Guy of Cigogne, Geoffrey of Martigny with his brothers, Philip Mark with his brothers and his nephew Geoffrey, and all their followers.

[51] As soon as peace is restored, we will banish from the kingdom all foreign-born knights, cross-bowmen, serjeants, and mercenary soldiers, who have come with horses and arms to the kingdom's hurt.

[52] If any one has been dispossessed or removed by us, without the lawful judgment of his peers, from his lands, castles, franchises, or from his rights, we will immediately restore them to him; and if a dispute arise over this, then let it be decided by the five-and-twenty barons of whom mention is made below in the clause for securing the peace. Moreover, for all those possessions, from which any one has, without the lawful judgment of his peers been disseised or removed, by our father, King Henry, or by our brother, King Richard, and which we retain in our hands (or which are possessed by others, to whom we are bound to warrant them) we shall have respite during the usual term of crusaders;[23] excepting those matters about which legal proceedings were begun, or an inquest was made by our order, before our taking of the cross; but as soon as we return from our expedition (or if perchance we desist from the expedition) we will immediately grant full justice therein.

[53] We shall have, moreover, the same respite and in the same manner in rendering justice concerning the disafforestation or reten- tion of those forests which Henry our father and Richard our brother afforested, and concerning the wardship of lands which are of the fief of another (namely, such wardships as we have hitherto had by reason of a fief which anyone held of us by knight's service) and concerning abbeys founded on other fiefs than our own, in which the

---

[21] *"posite sunt in defenso."*
[22] I.e. by the twelve knights.
[23] Three years.

lord of the fee claims to have right; and when we have returned, or if we desist from our expedition, we will immediately grant full justice to all who complain of such matters.

[54] No one shall be arrested or imprisoned upon the appeal of a woman, for the death of any other than her husband.

[55] All fines made with us unjustly and against the law of the land, and all amercements imposed unjustly and against the law of the land,[24] shall be entirely remitted; or else such cases shall be disposed of according to the decision of the five-and-twenty barons of whom mention is made below in the clause for securing peace, or according to the judgment of the majority of the same, along with the aforesaid Stephen, archbiship of Canterbury, if he can be present, and such others as he may wish to bring with him for this purpose; and if he cannot be present the business shall nevertheless proceed without him, provided always that if any one or more of the aforesaid five-and-twenty barons are in a similar particular judgment, others being substituted in their places after having been selected by the rest of the same five-and-twenty for this purpose only, and after having been sworn.

[56] If we have disseised or removed Welshmen from lands or liberties, or other things, in England or in Wales, without the legal judgment of their peers, they shall be immediately restored to them; and if a dispute arise over this, then let it be decided in the marches by the judgment of their peers; for tenements in England according to the law of England, for tenements in Wales according to the law of Wales, and for tenements in the marches according to the law of the marches. Welshmen shall do the same to us and ours.

[57] Further, for all those possessions from which any Welshman has, without the lawful judgment of his peers, been disseised or removed by King Henry our father, or King Richard our brother, and which we retain in our hand (or which are possessed by others, to whom we are bound to warrant them) we shall have respite during the usual term of crusaders; excepting those things about which legal proceedings were begun or an inquest was made by our order before we took the cross; but as soon as we return (or if perchance we desist from our expedition), we will immediately grant full justice in accordance with the laws of the Welsh, and appropriately for the aforesaid regions.[25]

[24] McKechnie describes a sharp difference between "amercement" and "fine." The former was like a modern criminal fine; the thirteenth century "fine" was a volunteer offering to the King to obtain favor or avert punishment. "The Bishop of Winchester paid a tun of good wine for not reminding the King (John) to give a girdle to the countess of Albemarle; and Robert de Vaux five best palfreys, that the same King might hold his peace about Henry Pinel's wife. Another paid four marks 'for leave to eat.'" Hallam, *Middle Ages,* II, 438. *View of the State during the Middle Ages* (London: J. Murray, 1841).

[25] The marches and so on? See 56.

[58] We will immediately give up the son of Llywelyn and all the hostages of Wales, and the charters delivered to us as security for the peace.

[59] We will do towards Alexander, King of Scots, concerning the return of his sisters and his hostages, and concerning his franchises, and his rights, in the same manner as we shall do towards our other barons of England, unless it ought to be otherwise according to the charters which we hold from William his father, formerly King of Scots; and this shall be according to the judgment of his peers in our court.

[60] Moreover, all these aforesaid customs and liberties, the observance of which we have agreed shall be observed in our kingdom by us towards our men, shall be observed by all men of our kingdom, as well clergy as laymen, in relations between them and their own men.

[61] Since, moreover, for the love of God and the amendment of our kingdom and for the better allaying of the quarrel that has arisen between us and our barons, we have granted all these concessions, desirous that they should enjoy them in complete and firm endurance for ever, we give and grant to them the underwritten security, namely, that the barons choose five-and-twenty barons of the kingdom, whomsoever they will, who shall be bound with all their might, to observe and hold, and cause to be observed, the peace and liberties we have granted and confirmed to them by this our present Charter; so that if we, or our justiciar, or our bailiffs or any one of our officers, shall break any one of the articles of the peace or of this security, and, notice of the offence be given to four barons of the aforesaid five-and-twenty, the said four barons shall repair to us (or our justiciar, if we are out of the realm) and, laying the transgression before us, petition to have that transgression redressed without delay. And if we shall not have corrected the transgression (or, in the event of our being out of the realm, if our justiciar shall not have corrected it) within forty days, reckoning from the time it has been intimated to us (or to our justiciar, if we should be out of the realm), the four barons aforesaid shall refer that matter to the rest of the five-and-twenty barons, and those five-and-twenty barons shall, together with the community of the whole land,[26] distrain and distress us in all possible ways, namely, by seizing our castles, lands, possessions, and in any other way they can, until redress has been obtained according to their judgment, saving however our own person, and our Queen and children; and when redress has been made they shall resume their old relations towards us. And let whoever in the country desires it, swear to obey

---

[26] "Few words of medieval Latin offer a more tempting field to enquirers than this *communa*, which, with its English and French equvalents, holds the key to many problems of constitutional origins . . . to the barons at Runnymede it may have meant either the entire body of feudal tenants or only the magnates; but medieval analogies make it impossible that the word could embrace the free peasantry, still less the villeins of England." McKechnie, pp. 471, 472.

the orders of the said five-and-twenty barons for the execution of all the aforesaid matters, and along with them, to molest us to the utmost of his power; and we publicly and freely grant leave to every one who wishes to swear, and we shall never forbid anyone to swear. All those, moreover, in the land who of themselves and of their own accord are unwilling to swear to the twenty-five barons to help them in constraining and molesting us, we shall by our command compel them to swear, as aforesaid. And if any one of the five-and-twenty barons shall have died or departed from the land, or be incapacitated in any other manner which would prevent the aforesaid provisions being carried out, those of the said twenty-five barons who are left shall choose another in his place according to their own judgment, and he shall be sworn in the same way as the others. Further, in all matters, the execution of which is intrusted to these twenty-five barons, if perchance these twenty-five are present and disagree among themselves about anything, or if some of them, after being summoned, are unwilling or unable to be present, that which the majority of those present ordain or command shall be held as fixed and established, exactly as if the whole twenty-five had concurred in this; and the said twenty-five shall swear that they will faithfully observe all that is aforesaid, and cause it to be observed with all their might. And we shall procure nothing from anyone, directly or indirectly, whereby any part of these concessions and liberties might be revoked or diminished; and if any such thing has been procured, let it be void and null, and we shall never use it personally or by another.

[62] And all the ill-will, hatred, and rancors that have arisen between us and our men, clergy and lay, from the date of the quarrel, we have completely remitted and pardoned to everyone. Moreover, all acts of misconduct occasioned by the said quarrel, from Easter in the sixteenth year of our reign till the restoration or peace, we have fully remitted to all, both clergy and laymen, and completely forgiven, as far as pertains to us. And furthermore, we have caused to be made for them letters testimonial patent, of the lord Stephen, archbishop of Canterbury, of the lord Henry, archbishop of Dublin, of the bishops aforesaid, and of Master Pandulf, respecting this security and the concessions aforesaid.

[63] Wherefore it is our Will, and we firmly enjoin, that the English Church be free, and that the men in our kingdom have and hold all the aforesaid liberties, rights, and concessions, well and peaceably, freely and quietly, fully and wholly, for themselves and their heirs, of us and our heirs, in all respects and in all places for ever, as is aforesaid. An oath, moreover, has been sworn alike on our part and on the part of the barons, that all these conditions aforesaid shall be kept in good faith and without evil intent. Given under our hand— the above-named and many others being witnesses—in the meadow which is called Runnymede, between Windsor and Staines, on the fifteenth day of June, in the seventeenth year of our reign.

The specific demands made by the barons are apparent in the terms of the Charter conceded by the overmatched King. Its specific promises evidence grievances of the men who exacted it; the Charter was a practical document, intended to correct crying wrongs. Great inclusive guarantees, generalizations like those in the Declaration of Independence, are rare in it; and those few gained their general effect only by gradual and long subsequent attributions of meaning. The first and the sixty-third chapters demonstrate that despite Innocent III's support of the King, the Church in England considered John an oppressor. The general guarantee that the Church shall be "free," and the specification of free elections, reasonably autonomous choice of church dignitaries by English ecclesiastical authorities, reflect the irritation of the clergy at John's intervention in appointments, and at foreigners thrust into English benefices. The fiftieth and fifty-first chapters call for the ejection of foreign laymen, a number of magnates listed by name, and all foreign-born knights, crossbow men, serjeants, and mercenaries who have come with horses and arms for the injury of the realm. A number of chapters specify feudal payments which the King thereafter would not wrongfully exact; the Charter here, perhaps more than in any of its other provisions, reflects the circumstances which brought it about. There are several detailed guarantees of judicial procedure (e.g. Chapters 17, 22, and 24). London was rewarded for siding with the barons by a promise that it should have "all its ancient liberties and free customs, as well by land as by water." The Barons remembered John's hanging of the Welsh boy-hostages in retaliation for Llywelyn's revolt; the King agreed to give back, immediately, Llywelyn's son and several other Welsh hostages he still held. (Chapters 56 to 58). Such provisions for the times would not have made the Charter long memorable; others, still more specific, are now no more than reminders of medieval conditions; they relieve some burdens of debts due to "the Jews," they abolish fish weirs, they limit the duty to maintain bridges, they provide uniform measures for wine, ale, grain, and cloth. But there were other clauses, set in nobler terms, which men were to remember centuries later in controversies with other kings. John made his promises for all time,

> We have also granted to all freemen of our kingdom, for us and our heirs forever, all the liberties written below, to be had and held by them and their heirs, of us and our heirs.

Succeeding centuries have given substance to the thirty-ninth and fortieth chapters. The Fortieth,

Nulli vendemus nulli negabimus aut differemus rectum vel iusticiam.

expressed an aspiration to justice which has heartened righteous lawyers and judges of all ages. For a twentieth century constitutionalist
the thirty-ninth chapter is the heart of the Charter,

> *Nullus liber homo capiatur vel imprisonetur, aut disseisiatur, aut*
> *utlagetur, aut exuletur, aut aliquo modo destruatur, nec super eum*
> *ibimus, nec super eum mittemus, nisi per legale judicum parium suorum*
> *vel per legem terre.*

> No freeman shall be taken or (and) imprisoned or disseised or out-
> lawed or exiled or in any way destroyed, nor will we go upon him nor
> send upon him, except by the lawful judgment of his peers or (and)
> by the law of the land.[27]

And of these promises, John's agreement to rule "per legem terrae"
has been the most influential.[28] At the time it guaranteed the "good
laws" of a better time past; men paint old days in colors brighter than
those of a degenerate present. The idea so formulated lived and developed in a series of paraphrases. The Parliament of 1350 paraphrased
"per legem terrae" as "par voie de la lei"; the Parliament of 1354
rendered it "par due process de lei" whence, probably through Coke's
Institutes, we get the language of our Fifth and Fourteenth Amendments and various State due-process clauses; centuries have added
generality to the concept.[29] In the fourteenth century there was still
strong in men's mind an idea of time-honored justice from which
rulers should not depart. So the Parliament of 1368 called the legal
order to which they aspired "l'auncien leye de la terre.[30]

The Charter did forecast a doctrine which was not to have a name
for centuries afterward—the separation of powers. The idea is not
strange, after all. If any effective limit, short of revolution, is ever to
be set on any unjust rule, some institutionalized power of government
must be chartered to restrain government's own unjust power. The bad
ruler must be lawfully opposed by powerful good men, whose opposition must be acknowledged in advance of the event as legitimate, as
"constitutional." Chapter 61 granted this function to a committee of
twenty-five barons. Under the fifty-second and fifty-fifth articles the
twenty-five were to be judges of the merits of controversies with the

[27] McKechnie's translation omits "or outlawed"; *Magna Carta*, p. 375.
[28] See C. H. McIlwain, "Due Process of Law in Magna Carta," 14 *Colum. L.
Rev.* 27 (1914).
[29] See C. H. McIlwain, "Due Process of Law in Magna Carta," 14 *Colum. L.
Rev.* 27 (1914).
[30] *Ibid.*, p. 49. See for 1350, 25 Edw. III, Stat. 5, c. 4; for 1354, 28 Edw. III,
c. 3; for 1368, 42 Edw. III, c. 3.

king and were to award what are in effect judgments. The barons were chartered to enforce these awards by their might, by "distressing and distraining" the king in every way save for hurt to his person, his queen, and his children. John accepts the process; by the sixty-first chapter he not only legitimates adherence to the twenty-five by any others who may come to their aid, but undertakes to constrain all in the land to take oath thus to enforce justice against the King.

The Great Charter failed of its immediate purpose. The twenty-five were not effective; John at once began military preparations against them. On August 16, 1215, he sent word to two gatherings, of bishops and barons, respectively, that the barons had broken their promises made in Magna Carta. On August 25, the Pope declared the Charter void for duress. Some powerful earls returned to John's side. The opposing barons, despairing of victory without foreign aid, offered the crown to Louis, son of the King of France. John still had at his disposal in England tough paid French soldiers under French professional mercenary officers, and with these were barons who sided with him, notably his justiciar Hubert de Burgh and faithful William the Marshal, Earl of Pembroke. With such help John took the field against his baronial enemies in the autumn and winter of 1215. But a September storm had ruined John's fleet, the opposing French began to land, and in May, 1216, prince Louis of France himself came to England. Civil war became bitter and indecisive. John's last success was at Lynn in Norfolk which he entered in mid-October, 1216. Immediately thereafter he rashly lost his baggage-train and treasure trying to cross the watery sands of "the river Wellester."[31] He managed himself to reach the far side, but was taken with a violent illness aggravated by a surfeit of peaches and new cider.[32] He struggled on to Newark where, sick to death, he gave for his soul's sake ten pounds to a monastery and died on October 19, 1216. He has been much condemned; but in the strange complex of historic cause and effect, constitutionalism is much in his debt.

John's son Henry III, then only nine years old, succeeded to his father's throne. William the Marshal became his guardian, and at once, in the child King's name made the first of many reissues of the Charter. In 1217 young Henry's party, which had continued John's war with considerable success, arranged a peace. Prince Louis returned to

[31] The Welland, today.

[32] The story is told by the chronicler Roger of Wendover in his *Flowers of History*; see L. A. Giles' translation from the Latin (1849) Vol. II, p. 378. A standard and much respected modern account is Bishop Stubbs, *Constitutional History of England* (Oxford: Clarendon Press, 1880) II; see Chapter XIV "The Struggles for the Charters."

France. England had an English king and the Charter belonged to the English-speaking people.

There had been other and earlier royal charters of liberties before Magna Carta. It may trace its ancestry back through the Charter of Liberties of Henry II (1154) and the like charters of Stephen (1135) and Henry I (1100), to the Charter of Cnut (1020).[33] But John's Great Charter is the one men remember. It was repeatedly confirmed by Henry III (1216–1272) and by Edward I (1272–1307). A recent study finds 44 confirmations between 1327 and 1422.[34] The Great Charter was obviously a cherished standard, a welcome assurance that people could set some limitation on the arbitrary powers of the king.

As a guarantee of popular liberties in the Middle Ages the Charter had little perceivable effect. It did promise some protection to all freemen, that is to say, to everyone above the status of villein, but certainly at the time it was exacted from King John it could not have been conceived as any guarantee of what would be thought "the people's rights" today. The Charter was a hard feudal bargain, forced on a dictatorial king by strong and rough men who resented his independence. But its importance is not to be judged solely by its original limited diffusion of power in a medieval society. During the next three centuries all Englishmen became freemen, and so came within its terms.[35] Magna Carta has been a central theme of English constitutional history.[36] It was remembered in hard days; its forty reissues, despite some modifications, all signalized control over the single ruler by the concerted power of many men.[37] Coke revived it in the early 17th century to serve as a needed political theory in his contest with James I. Its great promise not to apply the force of government to

[33] R. Pound, *Development of Constitutional Guarantees of Liberty* (New Haven: Yale University Press, 1957) p. 19; These charters can be found in Stubbs, *Select Charters* (8th ed.; Oxford: Clarendon Press, 1895), the charter of Henry II at p. 135; of Stephen at p. 120; of Henry I at p. 100; of Canute at p. 75.

[34] Faith Thompson, *Magna Carta, Its Role in the Making of the English Constitution, 1300–1629* (Minneapolis: University of Minnesota Press, 1948) p. 10.

[35] G. M. Trevelyan *A Shortened History of England* (London: Longmans, Green & Co., 1942) p. 131.

[36] "The Whole of the Constitutional History of England is a commentary on this charter, the illustration of which must be looked for in the documents that precede and follow." Bishop Stubbs in *Select Charters* (9th ed.; Oxford: Clarendon Press, 1913) p. 291. Zechariah Chafee writes of ". . . the three basic English documents, each of which guaranteed several human rights at one time—the Bill of Rights of 1689, the Petition of Right in 1628, and Magna Carta in 1251." *How Human Rights Got into the Constitution* (Boston: Boston University Press, 1952) p. 43.

[37] McIlwan, "Due Process of Law in Magna Carta," 14 *Colum. L. Rev.* 27 (1914).

any free man . . . *"nisi per legale judicium parium suorum vel per legem terre"* are still quoted in our own times.[38] The Great Charter has acquired a life of its own which has little to do with its original significance. For centuries it has been a symbol of limitation on arbitrary rule, in a doubtful day a brave standard to rally free men.

[38] Corwin, "Due Process of Law Before the Civil War" 24 *Harv. L. Rev.* 366 (1911); Coke Second Inst. Cap. XXIX; Wilkins, C. J., in *Pugliese* v. *Commonwealth,* 335 Mass. 471 (1957), where, quoting Article 12 of the Massachusetts Declaration of Rights, he says, ". . . the words 'the law of the land' in Art. 12 which were taken from Magna Carta embrace all that is comprehended in the words 'due process of law' in the Fourteenth Amendment." In February 1963 the Supreme Court held unconstitutional an Act of Congress which purported to deprive of United States nationality a man who left the country to evade military service. *Kennedy* v. *Mendoza-Martinez,* 372 US 144. The Court's opinion culminated in these words, "Dating back to Magna Carta . . . it has been an abiding principle governing the lives of civilized men that 'no freeman shall be taken or imprisoned or disseised or outlawed or exiled . . . without the judgment of his peers or by the law of the land . . .' What we hold is only that, in keeping with this cherished tradition, punishment cannot be imposed 'without due process of law.' Any lesser holding would ignore the constitutional mandate upon which our essential liberties depend."

3. ELEMENTS OF FUTURE
CONSTITUTIONAL THEORY: 1603

AT THE BEGINNING of this book there was proposed some survey of five great theses of American constitutional theory; majoritarian control of government; government subject to justice; equality of men; diffusion of power lest power prove too strong for liberty; and a revered written statement, widely accepted, assuring the essentials of just government. Those who retravel the road of British and American men across the centuries would do well to pause, now and then, on a bit of high ground to see what has been the progress. Surely such a vantage-point is the end of Elizabeth's reign, with England's government ordered and competent, with her dominance of the seas attained, and with English colonies projected on the American seaboard.[1]

Political change is not easy to locate in time. Great developments in the fundamentals of government come gradually; their nature and magnitude are often unperceived even by those active in effecting them. An episode of change in mode of rule, evidence of some drastic and lasting evolution occurring in men's habits, may at the moment appear as a minor expedient, as a momentary adjustment to transient exigency, which will be left off as soon as the occasion passes; or as restoration of some cherished institution which for a time had been

[1] Elizabeth died in 1603. In the preceding year an Englishman named Bartholomew Gosnold had landed with thirty-two men on a sandy headland about latitude 42 North, longitude 70 West. Offshore they found codfishing good. They named the promontory Cape Cod, and sailed west on the south side of the Cape, past a large island they called Martha's Vineyard, to a row of smaller islets which for their great Queen they named the Elizabeth Islands. On the southernmost of these, called by the Indian name Cuttyhunk, Gosnold and his men tried to found a settlement, grew discouraged after a month, and sailed back to England where they told the tale. The first English settlers in New England, then, came when Elizabeth was Queen.

regrettably disestablished. And man's preference for continuity of nomenclature tends to conceal constitutional change. Men tend to feel at ease with what is habitual, and so, desiring to believe in continuity of institutions, give new political devices old familiar names. Constitutional change sometimes, perhaps often, is thus brought about under the aspect of old forms, not because rulers wish to gull the unperceiving plebs, but because people want it so.

All this makes difficult an appraisal of the stage of constitutional development reached in Elizabeth's England. What of the major premise of the present-day United States, majoritarian government, rule by the most? Perhaps there was more of it than Elizabeth realized. She was greatly loved by her people, and this is a useful form of majoritarianism. True, the electorate choosing her parliaments was still narrow by our standards; a forty-shilling freehold was a substantial holding, and a large class of voters depended on that qualification. "Rotten boroughs" had already come into existence. Three years after Elizabeth's death, James I was to direct his Sheriffs not to send any precept to any borough town,

> . . . being so utterly ruined and decayed that there are not sufficient residents to make such choice, and of whom lawful election may be made.[2]

But a Queen kept in office by the love of her subjects is a majoritarian ruler. Elizabeth's successors, less loved, had a difficult time; Parliamentary dominance, obscured by affectionate relations with Elizabeth, became evident as soon as the country had trouble with James and Charles.

Some examination of the origins and the development of the Parliament that so became the dominant element in English government is well worth the time.

By the end of Elizabeth's reign nearly four centuries after Magna Carta, the assembled baronage of John's day had come to be a Parliament in form much like the Parliament of the mid-20th century, with a House of Peers, and with a separate House of Commons, which was to demonstrate its effective dominance over Elizabeth's two Stuart successors. But subordination of the executive branch of government, to laws made by a legislative body, is only one step toward popular control of government. Another is popular control of the lawmaking assembly. The magnates who got the Charter from John would not have recognized the concept of a popularly elected legislature; but by the time of James I (1603–1625) the House of Commons had come to

[2] H. of C. Journals, I, 477, quoted in E. and A. Porritt, *The Unreformed House of Commons* (Cambridge: Cambridge University Press, 1903) I, pp. 379–380.

be something like such an institution. Although the Commons of Stuart England was chosen by no such universal suffrage as is today's House, or as the House of Representatives in the United States, still by Elizabeth's day men were familiar with the concept of "representation" of all Englishmen in the Commons. Sir Thomas Smyth in 1584 wrote of Parliament in his "Commonwealth of England,"

> For everie Englishman is entended to be there present, either in person or by procuration and attornies, of what preheminence, state, dignitie, or qualitie soever he be, from the Prince (be he King or Queene) to the lowest person of Englande. And the consent of the Parliament is taken to be everie mans consent.[3]

Coke once told the Commons that each of its members represented a thousand Englishmen.[4]

This progress toward popular representation deserves an explanation, as an introduction to the story of Coke's conflict with James I and Charles I during the first three decades of the seventeenth century. Coke began the contest as a judge; he ended it as a House of Commons man. One way to dramatize the change in English life between the Charter of 1215 and the Petition of Right of 1628 is to point out that John's adversaries were medieval barons in armor, while Charles' opponents were comparatively modern parliamentarians.

Elective representation in England first grew up from the grass roots in the shires. Under Henry I, townships were represented in the local courts by "the priest, the reeve, and four of the best men."[5] In June 1215, shortly after John granted the Great Charter, he directed that twelve knights be chosen in each shire at the next county court, to inquire into the evil customs to be abolished.[6] The county courts, be it remembered, were undifferentiated organs of general county administration. Under the sheriff's guidance the court attended to all shire matters, judicial, fiscal, military and other.[7] Here in each shire was a prototype Parliament.

During the long reign of Henry III (1216–1272) the practice of summoning to the "Parliament" two or more knights elected in each

---

[3] *De Republica Anglorum* (Printed by Henrie Midleton for Gregorie Seton, 1584) p. 35.

[4] See Catherine Drinker Bowen, *The Lion and the Throne: The Life and Times of Sir Edward Coke* (Boston: Little, Brown and Co., 1957) p. 44.

[5] Stubbs, *Select Charters* (8th ed.; Oxford: Clarendon Press, 1895) p. 105; Maitland, *Constitutional History of England* (Cambridge: Cambridge University Press, 1909) p. 71. Bishop Stubbs dates between 1108 and 1118 the compilation of "Leges Henrici Primi," from which the quoted words are drawn.

[6] Stubbs, *The Constitutional History of England* (Oxford: Clarendon Press, 1880) II, p. 231; Stubbs, *Select Charters* 8th ed., p. 307.

[7] Stubbs, *The Constitutional History of England*, II, p. 227.

shire Court to represent the county came to be occasional though not invariable.[8] At the time this delegation did not seem an extraordinary innovation. In "the medieval world the representation of communities was a normal way of getting business done."[9]

In 1254 Henry in Gascony needed money. His wife and brother, acting as regents, summoned to Westminster, by writ directed to his Sheriffs, from each county, two "lawful and discreet knights . . ., whom the county shall have chosen for this purpose . . . to provide . . . what aid they will give to us in this our great necessity."[10] The writ prescribed no limits on how the county court should choose its representative knights; the absence of restriction is suggestive. The power of choice was not limited to tenants-in-chief or knights. No one was excluded who customarily participated in county court resolves.

Borough members of Parliament date from 1265. Tensions rising between King Henry and the barons, for reasons not dissimilar to those at the time of Magna Carta, brought about renewed civil war in 1261. On May 14, 1264 the forces of the confederated barons under Simon de Montfort, Earl of Leicester, brother-in-law of the king, defeated the king's army at Lewes. Henry III and his son Edward surrendered; and for a few months Earl Simon was in effect master of England. That brief tenure of power has caused men to remember him as "founder of the House of Commons." For his government he sought the support not only of the shires but also of the towns, whose resources he needed if he was to prevail over dissident elements in the baronage. Necessity to grant concessions in order to get tax-money has brought many governments to change their ways. De Montfort on December 14, 1264 issued writs in the name of the captive Henry III, calling a parliament to meet in London on January 20, 1265. His innovation was issuance of the writs to boroughs, towns or cities, as well as to counties. The writs ordered the sheriffs to send to Parliament not only the familiar Knights of the Shires, but from each of the boroughs of England ". . . *duos de discretioribus, legalioribus et probioribus tam civibus quam burgensibus.*"[11] "This summons," wrote Taswell-Langmead in 1875, "completed

---

[8] The development is described by Taswell-Langmead, in his *English Constitutional History* (9th ed.; London: Sweet and Maxwell, 1929) Chapter XII.

[9] G. M. Trevelyan, *History of England* (Garden City, N.Y.: Doubleday Anchor, 1953) I, p. 237.

[10] F. W. Maitland, *Constitutional History of England,* p. 72; Stubbs, *Select Charters,* 8th ed., p. 374. The Latin writ reproduced in the *Select Charters* is confusing. Maitland says four knights were called from each shire. Stubbs and Taswell-Langmead say two. See the latter's *English Constitutional History,* 9th ed., p. 204.

[11] Stubbs, *Select Charters* 8th ed., p. 415.

the formation of the national parliament on substantially the basis which it has ever since retained."[12] Such a sweeping statement can mislead the American reader. By Taswell-Langmead's time the franchise in England had of course been greatly widened, and has since been still further widened to include substantially all adults. But Simon de Montfort's innovation was to summon not only knights— noblemen they would have been called on the Continent—but also commoners, representatives of "communes" or communities. After Simon de Montfort's time the Commons consisted of two different categories, county representatives, two for each English shire; and "corporation" members, two (or more rarely one) from each City; each town or borough to which the privilege had been extended; the Cinque Ports; and the universities.

Civil War did not end with the Parliament of 1265. Barons hostile to Simon marched against him, defeated his army at Evesham on August 4, 1265, and killed him in the battle. But popular representation, once granted, is not easily withdrawn. Money to support a government must come from great numbers of reasonably willing contributors; in the long run the cost of forcible confiscation consumes its product. Much of the growth of Anglo-American popular legislative representation, through many centuries, can be explained by this fact of practical political life.

The lower English House, the Commons, since it became a separate body has always contained the only popular representation. The Lords' House so far as not made up of an hereditary aristocracy, has throughout its history completed its membership by an élite with life tenure, an élite episcopal, judicial, and, since 1958 political.[13] No definite date can be set for the separation of Parliament into upper and lower Houses. The division probably occurred during the reign of the third Edward (1327–1377). When the King requested "aids" the Knights of the Shires and the Burgesses developed the practice of conferring separately on the requests. In time knights and burgesses came to meet together, but separately from the magnates of the Council. Thus the knights and burgesses came to form a House of Commons, replying through the Speaker to the King's requests, and through him asking that their common petitions be made statutes.[14]

---

[12] Taswell-Langmead, *English Constitutional History*, 9th ed., p. 210.

[13] See Dr. R. H. Maudsley's scholarly paper "The House of Lords," 15 *U. Miami L. Rev.* 174 (1960).

[14] A. F. Pollard, *The Evolution of Parliament* (London: Longmans, Green & Co., 1920) pp. 117–128; Hood Phillips, *Constitutional Law of Great Britain and the Commonwealth* (London: Sweet and Maxwell, 1952) p. 97 *et seq.*

The growth of popular representation in the medieval house of "communes"[15] is hard to follow because it grew up by custom in the boroughs and counties, not by sweeping national legislation. For one who looks backward from the middle of the twentieth century, it is difficult to estimate the effectiveness of popular representation in the House of Commons six hundred years ago.[16] The fifteenth century House must have had less than 300 members. During the first two centuries of parliamentary representation all free men may have had a part in electing Knights of the Shires. The text of an Act of Parliament of 1430[17] suggests that "people of small substance and of no value" had a hand in the county electorate and that elections of the time occasionally provoked brawls. This first national legislation concerning English electoral representation was a restriction, not an extension, of the franchise. It deserves quotation.

*What sort of Men shall be Choosers, and Who shall be chosen Knights of the Parliament

Item. Whereas the Elections of Knights of Shires to come to the Parliaments of our Lord the King, in many Counties of the Realm of England, have now of late been made by very great, outragious and excessive Number of People dwelling within the same Counties of the Realm of England, of the which most part was of People of small Substance, and of no Value, whereof every of them pretended a Voice equivalent, as to such Elections to be made, with the most worthy Knights and Esquires dwelling within the same Counties, whereby Manslaughters, Riots, Batteries and Divisions among the Gentlemen, and other People of the same Counties, shall very likely rise and be, unless convenient and due Remedy be provided in this behalf; our Lord the King, considering the Premisses, hath provided, ordained, and stablished by Authority of this present Parliament, that the Knights of the Shires to be chosen within the same Realm of England to come to the Parliaments of our Lord the King hereafter to be holden, shall be chosen in every County of the Realm of England, by

[15] F. W. Maitland points out that "commons" is a word which blends two different ideas. He suggests that "House of Commons" does not mean the House of ordinary men, but rather refers to communities, organized bodies of freemen of the shires and towns. See *Constitutional History of England*, p. 85; and see Stubbs, *Constitutional History of England*, II, p. 185.

[16] See generally, E. and A. Porritt, *The Unreformed House of Commons*, I; A. E. McKinley, *Suffrage Franchise in the Thirteen English Colonies in America* (Boston: Ginn and Co., 1905) chapter I; D. L. Keir, *The Constitutional History of Modern Britain* (3rd ed.; London: A. and C. Black, 1946) p. 40 *et seq.*

[17] 8 Henry VI, Chapter VII.

* I Statutes at Large, (W. Hawkins, 1734) p. 504.

People dwelling and resident in the same Counties, whereof every one of them shall have Land or Tenement to the value of forty Shillings by the Year at the least above all Charges; and that they which shall be so chosen shall be dwelling and resident within the same Counties; and such as have the greatest number of them that may expend Forty Shillings by Year and above, as afore is said, shall be returned by the Sheriffs of every County, Knights for Parliament, by Indentures sealed betwixt the said Sheriffs and the said Choosers so to be made. And every Sheriff of the Realm of England shall have Power, by the said Authority, to examine upon the Evangelists every such Chooser how much he may expend by the Year; and if any Sheriff return Knights to come to the Parliament contrary to the said Ordinance, the Justices of Assises in their Sessions of Assises shall have Power, by the Authority aforesaid, thereof to inquire; and if by Inquest the same be found before the Justices, and the Sheriff thereof be duly attainted, that then the said Sheriff shall incur the Pain of an hundred Pounds, to be paid to our Lord the King, and also that he have Imprisonment by a Year, without being let to Bail or Mainprise; and that the Knights for the Parliament returned contrary to the said Ordinance, shall lose their Wages.

Provided always, That he which cannot expend forty Shillings by Year, as afore is said, shall in no wise be Chooser of the Knights for the Parliament; and that in every Writ that shall hereafter go forth to the Sheriffs to choose Knights for the Parliament, mention be made of the said Ordinances.

The forty-shilling freehold provision so prescribed in 1430, which remained on the statute books for four centuries,[18] was a substantial property qualification when it was enacted five hundred years ago, though decline in the value of money came in time to diminish its effect. Any requirement that a county member live in the county for which he was elected gradually came to be disregarded. Coke was returned from various constituencies, regardless of his domicile. The boroughs came to return many more members of the House of Commons than the county constituencies. The number of boroughs varied from time to time, though in the fifteenth century there may have been more than 100 in all, each returning two members. The borough electoral franchise varied from borough to borough. All householders in a borough might be electors; or those householders who paid the local rates known as "scot and lot"; or those householders who had their own hearths, boiled their own dinners, described as "potwallopers";[19] or landholders who held by "burgage tenure." The mode

[18] Porritt, *The Unreformed House of Commons,* I, pp. 20–21.
[19] *Ibid.,* p. 31.

of election was largely in the discretion of the local authority. In 1621 the election for the City of Exford was "in the Mayor, fifteen more, called Magistrates, and Common-Council, making in all 48." In 1623 "the right of election of Barons for Town and Port of Dover in Kent, is in Freemen and Free Burgesses, inhabitants of Dover." In 1624, the Mayor, Bailiffs and Common Council elected for Newcastle in Staffordshire, while Pontefract in Yorkshire elected by "all the inhabitants, householders." In 1628 the Commons resolved that "the right of election for Warwick is in the Commonalty of the Town, paying to church and poor," while "the right of election of Burgesses to serve in Parliament for Boston, Lincolnshire, resteth in the Commonalty, and not in the Mayor, Alderman, and Common-Council."[20] Such resolutions evidently reflect a sturdy assertion, by ordinary ratepaying townsmen, that they, not merely a few notables, were entitled to a voice in choosing their Members of Parliament.[21]

Election procedures in medieval England are not easy to explore. The secret ballot is a recent development, dating from the Ballot Act of 1872.[22] One supposes that a medieval election was made by a show of hands, or by a voice vote, at a gathering of shire or borough electors. In 1406 the Parliament provided for a written record of votes at shire elections, by a statute of Henry IV entitled "The Manner of the Election of Knights of Shires for a Parliament." It provided,

> At the meeting of the next County Court, after delivery of the writ, proclamation shall be made of the day and place of holding the Parliament; and that all present shall attend the election of their Knights; and shall proceed to the election freely in full county.
>
> After Knights of the Shire be chosen, the names of the persons who chose them shall be written in indenture under their seals and tacked to the writ, which indenture shall be the return; and in the writs of Parliament this clause, 'and your election in your full County made, you shall without delay, distinctly and evenly, certify under your seal, and the seals of them who were concerned in that election, to us, in our Chancery, at the day and place in the writ contained.'[23]

[20] See Hood Phillips, *Constitutional Law*, p. 113.

[21] A number of such resolutions are collected in *A Concise Abstract of All the Laws Relating to Parliamentary Elections, by a Gentleman of the Inner Temple* (London: printed for J. Walker, n.d.).

[22] 35 & 36 Vict. c. 33; see also W. E. Lunt, *History of England* (New York: Harper and Brothers, 1957) p. 695.

[23] 7 Hen. 4, c. 15; E. C. Lodge and G. A. Thornton, *English Constitutional Documents, 1307–1485* (Cambridge: Cambridge University Press, 1935) p. 162; see also Taswell-Langmead, *English Constitutional History*, T. F. T. Plucknett, ed. (London: Sweet and Maxwell, 1960) pp. 200, 202.

As the seventeenth century began, Parliament, like other British institutions, was serving its people well despite its anomalies, and few worried about the theory of its representation. When the first James came to the throne the Commons contained four hundred sixty-seven members for England and Wales. About ninety of these represented counties; the rest were borough members elected in various ways, often by very few people. Elizabeth had added enough new boroughs to increase the membership of the House by sixty, most of whom were chosen by small electorates.[24]

The Commons was a large body in relation to the population,[25] which may have tended to make that House more representative than might be supposed from the manner of its choice. The solid gentry on its benches were often independent and courageous men, with a sense of public responsibility, and with able leadership. The Commons House that prevailed in its contest with the Stuarts did not lack statesmanship. Electoral reforms still in the distant future were necessary to give Englishmen a satisfactory sense of participation in their government, but no later House was more distinguished than that of Coke, Eliot, Hampden, and Cromwell.

What of subjection of rule to justice in 1603? Was government under law? Perhaps Elizabeth would have thought that as applied to her the question was impious and treasonous. One repeats, at the risk of wearying, that men of her day did not think of the problem as we now do. Their premises of political theory, their ideas of the nature of law, of the relation of religion to government, of wise arrangement of governmental institutions, are no longer taken for granted. Today's philosophical difficulty with the ideal of government under law no longer arises from any idea of a king chosen by God to rule, but because men rather generally have come to the conclusion that law is what the majority wants, formally expressed for the common governance. If majoritarian government, utilizing established forms of lawmaking, can proclaim any law it pleases, if government is thus the only source of law, what law shall government be under? But this dilemma is not universal. In all times some of the men who have thought about law, in some times many such men, perhaps in some times all men who gave it thought, have conceived of law as a system

[24] The figures here given are drawn from J. R. Tanner's note "Composition of Parliament" in his *Tudor Constitutional Documents, 1485–1603* (Cambridge: Cambridge University Press, 1922) p. 513 *et seq.*, and from the sources there cited.
[25] Gregory King's celebrated chart gives England five and a half millions in 1688. See G. N. Clark, *Later Stuarts, 1660–1714* (Oxford: Clarendon Press, 1934) p. 25; and Trevelyan, *Illustrated English Social History* (4 vols.; London: Longmans, Green & Co., 1949–1952) I, p. 135.

quite independent of men's ordinances, as a brooding omnipresence[26] somehow resting ". . . on a general principle, on the reason and nature of things . . ."[27] Elizabeth's Parliaments were not yet entirely sure whether they were making law or were finding and declaring it as "a thing fundamental and immutable, a subject of science, capable of being learnt by special study, but not capable of being altered by the mere will of government . . ."[28] And as to the Queen's own acts, she would scarcely have told her startled subjects that she was in doubt about the lawfulness of what she did. Probably (who can know?) she would not have acknowledged such doubts even to herself. Before Leviathan begins to worry about contriving a hook for his own jaw[29] he must first have recognized his own proclivity to evil courses. Wishing only the prosperity of her dominions, the great Queen may well have felt that any subject who opposed her was a bad man.[30] She can hardly have thought that her own rule might be so lawless as to require institutionalized restraints.

Medieval and early modern rulers did not think of the relation of religion to government in the way now generally the fashion. When justice was what God willed; when religious belief and its organized expression in a national Church were more evident premises of government than they have since become; when Church and temporal rule were not separate concepts as in today's theory, the question of government subject to law did not present itself as it now does. There

[26] This omnipresence Holmes disclaimed in his *Southern Pacific* v. *Jensen* dissent, 244 U.S. 205 (1917) p. 222. "The common law is not a brooding omnipresence in the sky, but the articulate voice of some sovereign or quasi sovereign that can be identified; although some decisions with which I have disagreed seem to me to have forgotten the fact." He reinforced this objection when dissenting in *Black and White Taxi Co.* v. *Yellow Taxi Co.*, 276 U.S. 518 (1928) p. 533.

[27] The words are quoted from the opinion of Mr. Justice Johnson in *Fletcher* v. *Peck*, 6 Cranch 87 (1810) p. 143. He added the comment that this was "a principle which will impose laws even on the Deity," thus presenting other problems which transcend even the scope of this book.

[28] A matter treated by C. H. McIlwain in *The High Court of Parliament and Its Supremacy* (New Haven: Yale University Press, 1910) p. 109 ff, from which the quotation is taken.

[29] Today's reader may forgive a reminder of Job 41:1 and of Thomas Hobbes.

[30] Surely Elizabeth was no less self-confident than her successor in 1782. On November 4 of that year, Lord North wrote George III that his friends in the House of Commons were "in general, well inclined to support His Majesty's Govt." To this qualified assurance the King replied, "The times certainly require the concurrence of all who wish to prevent anarchy. I have no wish but the prosperity of my dominions; therefore, must look on all who will not heartily assist me as bad men, as well as ungrateful subjects." See Lord Brougham's *Historical Sketches of Statesmen*, (London: Richard Griffin & Co., 1855) I, p. 164. George III's words are best known from W. M. Thackeray's comment in *The Four Georges* (New York: Doubleday-Dolphin, n.d.) p. 78.

were few to challenge Bracton's statement in the thirteenth century that the king must be under God and the law.[31] Men killed one another in quarrels over the question of rightful authority to declare God's will, and over what that will was in this or that juncture; but king and peasant avowed, and probably believed, that God's will ruled them both.

Our twentieth-century position is more complex. We have detached government from religious imperatives; these, we say, are for the citizen to take or leave as he will. And our law we no longer see as a brooding omnipresence, but as a set of imperatives designed by ourselves. Instead of assuming Godly government, as did our predecessors in medieval or renaissance Europe, or as did our Puritan forebears in New England, we postulate a government achieving justice through majority control. Our justice is lay justice, in which we find not only all the theoretical difficulties of defining rightness which troubled medieval religious theorists, but also the added practical dilemma involved in finding means to constrain a majority to a course it finds distasteful. Our thought is devoted to devising mechanisms of government—presently our Supreme Court—which can defer the effectiveness of hasty, intemperate, and arbitrary acts of rule until they are replaced by more settled and more just policy. But the Elizabethans and their predecessors did not spend much thought devising schemes by which a majoritarian government might restrain itself from working injustice. "Tyranny of the majority" is no problem until the majority takes charge; and in Elizabeth's day the idea that the many should decide for themselves what their government should do was itself a radical speculation for the future. Majorities under Elizabeth's successors were still to have enough trouble to get their way; her subjects were not yet faced with their descendants' problem of devising means to stop themselves from doing wrong.

What of equality of men at the end of Elizabeth's reign? One could more easily ask what of inequality, which was taken for granted. Grievous difference in the status of men seemed "natural" during the Middle Ages and the Renaissance. The acceptance of startling contrasts in human condition largely obscured for a time theoretical problems which would arise in later centuries, when the governmental assumption was to be human equality, and the difficulty would be choice of those human inequalities which should justly call for differences in government. In the feudal England of 1215 men were

[31] See Professor André Tunc's "The Royal Will and the Rule of Law," in *Government Under Law*, A. E. Sutherland, ed. (Cambridge: Harvard University Press, 1956) pp. 401 *et seq.*

classified in lay and religious rankings, from the villeins or serfs each tied to a plot of land,[32] up to the great overlords, earls and dukes, bishops and abbots, and finally the King himself. The most obvious difference between classes was in their manner of life. Villeins or small free cultivators lived in squalor and hunger; great lords fed themselves grossly, living in drafty and uncomfortable splendor until war, pestilence or dysentery laid them in ornate tombs.[33]

In John's England and for long after, much governmental power lay in the hands of local petty tyrants. Even if a man was a free peasant, not a serf, the lord of the manor or his bailiff must still have had an inordinate control of the small man's life.

But several forces were bit by bit moving the lowly toward a better status, toward more freedom. One impulse was economic. Men were in demand, as the Middle Ages moved on, and this demand became acute in 1348 and 1349 when the calamitous pestilence called the Black Death in sixteen months killed a third or more of the English, reducing the population from, perhaps, four million to two and a half million. The value of labor (which in that day was largely agricultural labor) doubled at once. The villein found it tempting to go over the hill, or more likely several hills, and hire out as a free laborer with no questions asked and with some chance that he could not be traced. Laborers who were already free struck for better pay. The Statutes of Laborers reflect the shock felt by the ruling classes at this sudden demonstration of their inferiors' self-assertion. The disruption caused by the Black Death must have been appalling.

The violence of the pestilence of 1348–1349 inhibited the call of a Parliament until 1351, but in the meantime the King's Council in 1349 promulgated the famous "Ordinance of Labourers."[34] In the King's name it recited that,

> . . . as a great part of the populace and especially of workmen and servants is dead in the pestilence, not a few, seeing the straits of their masters and the small number of servants, refuse to work unless they receive excessive pay, and others prefer to beg in idleness rather than to seek their bread by work; we, considering the grave hardships which can result from the dearth especially of farm workers and laborers, have deliberated about this matter with our prelates and

[32] See Vinogradoff, *Villainage in England* (Oxford: Clarendon Press, 1892).

[33] See G. M. Trevelyan, *Illustrated English Social History*, I, Chapter i, *passim*.

[34] Close Rolls, 23 Edw. III, pt. I, m. 8d: Statutes of the Realm of the same year cc 1–7. The Ordinance is quoted by Dr. Bertha Haven Putnam in her essay "The Enforcement of the Statutes of Labourers During the First Decade after the Black Death, 1349–1359," XXXII *Columbia University Studies in History, Economics and Public Law* (1908) Appendix p. 8 *et seq.*

nobles and other experienced persons, and with their unanimous advice we have determined to ordain . . .

the ordinance goes on to institute a detailed code of wage and price controls. A parliament held two years later enacted a statute with similar provisions. "Justices of Labourers" and other magistrates enforced these provisions, and the fines served as a much-needed source of public revenue.[35] The records of these proceedings tell much about the social conditions of the time. A man, though in the status of villein to his own lord, might nevertheless be heard to complain in court that some other lord had "eloigned" the villein's plowmen in violation of the Statute of Labourers, which suggests that villeinage was not inconsistent with enough prosperity to be an employer.[36]

Despite these enactments and their successors, the Black Death hastened the upward movement of small Englishmen and accelerated the decline of servile status. Among other changes, the pestilence which had so diminished the number of farmhands, brought many large proprietors to abandon cultivation of crops and turn instead to raising sheep, which required fewer laborers. But peasants, too, took to raising sheep, came up in the world, became proprietors themselves in a small way, and shared in the prosperity that came with the wool-trade.

Then, too, the Hundred Years' War (1337–1453) had its effect. A man gained a new sense of self-confidence and self-respect by serving in a campaign or two in France, or even by training at home to handle a long bow or other arm. Free archers, who had shot down French mailed knights at Crecy, came home to England in 1346 with less patience to stand oppression from English nobles. The same spirit stirred villeins. A Statute of 1377[37] provides,

> . . . VI. ITEM, At the grievous Complaint of the Lords and Commons of the Realm, as well Men of Holy Church as other, made in the Parliament, of that in many Signories and Parts of the Realm of England, the Villaines and Landtenants in Villenage, who Services and Customs to their said Lords, have now late withdrawn, and do daily

[35] Dr. Putnam demonstrated from contemporary records that many "labourers" in the mid-fourteenth century to which the Statutes were applied were artisans, people in the cloth trades, millers, tapsters, household servants, etc. Some laborers she found unidentifiable from their recorded descriptions; and I should be less than wise to venture a guess where she would not, at the trade of an "aquebanilatrix," a "membranator," a "schuppestre" or a "sunyere." *Ibid.*, p. 81.

[36] *Ibid.*, p. 95. In the instance Professor Putnam mentions, the villein's complaint was dismissed because he could not sue the lord who "owned" him; the villein had asserted that he was not the defendant's villein, but the King's.

[37] I Ric II Chapter 6; II Statutes of the Realm, p. 2 *et seq.*

withdraw their Services and Customs due to their said Lords, by Comfort and Procurement of other their Counsellors, Maintainers, and Abettors in the Country, which hath taken Hire and Profit of the said Villaines and Landtenants, by Colour of certain Exemplifications made out of the Book of Domesday of the Manors and Towns where they have been dwelling, and by virtue of the same Exemplifications, and their evil Interpretations of the same, they affirm them to be quite and utterly discharged of all Manner Servage, due as well of their Body as of their said Tenures, and will not suffer any Distress or other Justice to be made upon them; but do menace the Ministers of their Lords of Life and Members, and, which more is, gather themselves together in great Routs, and agree by such Confederacy, that every one shall aid other to resist their Lords with strong Hand; and much other Harm they do in sundry Manner, to the great Damage of their said Lords, and evil Example to other to begin such Riots; so that if due Remedy be not the rather provided upon the same Rebels, greater Mischief, which God Prohibit, may thereof spring through the Realm: It is Ordained and stablished, that the Lords which feel themselves grieved, shall have special Commissions under the Great Seal to the Justices of Peace, or to other sufficient Persons, to enquire of all such Rebels, and of their Offences, and their Counsellors, Procurers, Maintainers and Abettors, and to imprison all those that thereof shall be endited before them, as well for the Time past, as for the Time to come, without delivering them out of Prison by Mainprise, Bail, or otherwise, without Assent of their Lords, till they thereof be attainted or acquit; and that the same Justices have Power to hear and determine as well at the King's Suit, as at the Suit of the Party. Provided always, That if the said Villaines or Landtenants, Rebels, be thereof attainted at the Suit of the said Lords, they shall in no wise be delivered, till they have made a Fine to the King, and also they have the assent of their Lords aforesaid; and as to the said Counsellors, Procurers, Maintainers and Abettors, such Process in like Manner shall be made of them, which thereof shall be attainted, so that they be in no wise delivered from Prison, till they have made a Fine to the King, and gree to the Lords so grieved, according as their Estate, and the Quantity of their Offence doth require, if the same Lords will sue against them by Writ or by Bill; saving always, as to the said Fines, the Franchises and Liberties of Lords, which have Fines and Amerciaments of their Tenants: And as to the said Exemplifications made and purchased as afore is said, which were caused to come in the Parliament, [and to be] declared in the said Parliament, that the same may not nor ought to avail or hold place to the said Villaines or Landtenants, as to the Franchise of their Bodies; nor to change the Condition of their Tenure and Customs of old Time due; nor to do Prejudice to the said Lords, to have their Services and Customs as they were wont of old Time; and It is ordained, that upon this

Declaration the said Lords shall have Letters Patents under the Great Seal, as many and such as they shall need, if they the same require.

In 1381 came the Rising and the capture of London which G. M. Trevelyan has called the most remarkable incident in English social history. It was a revolt centering in southeastern England, fomented by years of distress and hardship, and immediately set off by an ill-conceived poll-tax. There must have been some degree of preparatory organization. Word for the rising was passed 'round by local leaders in the name of John Ball, a noted popular preacher, "John Ball hath rungen your bell." The revolt spread to twenty-eight counties; sympathetic Londoners opened the city's gates to the rebels; the Tower itself surrendered. Young King Richard II, scarcely more than a boy, saved the situation by his boldness. The rebels harbored no grudge against their King; and he rode out in the face of their multitude, promising a commutation of all servile dues for payment of fourpence an acre, and a pardon for all. This satisfied most rebels, and a good many went off home. Some remained recalcitrant; at a later parley the Mayor of London, in the presence of the assembled rebels, killed their leader, Wat Tyler. The Rising dwindled away. As in many revolutions, it had proved easier to overthrow the dominant regime than to plan and effectuate a new one. Parliament revoked Richard's concessions as made by duress. Numbers of the rebels were executed in mockery of Richard's pardons. But when a mass of common men have once organized a revolt and have quite easily struck down their overlords, the many and the overlords both remember it, and matters are never again quite what they once were.

Villeinage in England did not end with the Rising, which was only one symptom of a process begun long before, and continued long after.[38] Villeinage never had been a completely abject status, for the English serf was a free man as against everybody but his lord.[39] The long war, the pestilence, the Rising, all accelerated emancipation. A farmer finds unwilling field-hands a poor reliance, and as the fifteenth century went forward most serfs bought their freedom; their late lords instead rented the land to farmers who hired free labor. By the end of the Tudor era villeinage, as a practical institution, was ended. About the time the English were starting to colonize what is now Massa-

---

[38] There are, of course, many excellent accounts of the Rising. Here I follow G. M. Trevelyan's *History of England*, I, p. 316 *et seq.*, and the same author's *Illustrated English Social History*, I, p. 11 *et seq.* A recent vivid account is found in H. F. Hutchinson's life of Richard II, *The Hollow Crown* (New York: John Day Co., 1961).

[39] See Vinogradoff, *Villainage in England*, p. 69.

chusetts there occurred the last English reported case—trespass for taking a horse—in which a defendant attempted to get the complaint dismissed on the ground that the plaintiff was the defendant's "villein regardant." The plea failed for lack of proof of villeinage. So villeinage ended in England, characteristically not with a great stroke like the American Emancipation Proclamation or the Thirteenth Amendment, but by slow development, finally marked by the judgment of a court, awarded on an issue of fact.[40]

Equality of men in their choice of religious belief and affiliation is another modern tenet which took a long time to put out roots and grow. That all religions stand alike before the law; that no man's religion or lack of it can affect his public status; these professions of our modern constitutionalism would have seemed strange or fantastic to an Elizabethan. Under the First and the Fourteenth Amendments we have come generally to think that acceptance of this or that religious belief, by many or by few, is a private matter, unrelated to the conduct of government; and while England still has the forms of Establishment, disabilities by reason of religion have there disappeared as they have in the United States.[41] But in Elizabeth's day, and long before and long after, Church was taken as an obvious part of the structure of government. The question was not whether Church was to influence State, and State influence Church; the question was which Church. If a belief was heretical and damnable according to State's Church, the State's business was to suppress the belief, which was apt to mean punishing the man who expressed it. In Elizabeth's England a Roman Catholic was not equal to the rest of the Queen's subjects; a Quaker was not equal to a Congregationalist in early Massachusetts. The Puritans came to New England to establish their own religion, not to welcome its competitors.

In our own time we have tried some experiments in religious equality by extending governmental favors to all religions equally. We have not been uniformly successful;[42] the difficulties involved have evoked, in the most quoted judicial gloss on the subject,[43] a statement that under our Constitution neither nation nor State can aid one religion

[40] See, on the dying-out of villeinage, Taswell-Langmead, *English Constitutional History,* 9th ed., p. 262 *et seq.* The case (cited Taswell-Langmead *ubi supra,* p. 266 fn z), is *Pigg* v. *Caley* (1618) Noy R. 27; 74 Eng. Rep. 997.

[41] See e.g. *Torcaso* v. *Watkins,* 367 U.S. 488 (1961).

[42] Compare tax exemptions for all religious schools, sustained in *Heisey* v. *County of Alameda,* 352 U.S. 921 (1956), with religious instruction in public schools for Protestants, Catholics, and Jews, these being all the religious groups involved, held unconstitutional at the suit of an avowed atheist parent in *Illinois* ex rel *McCollum* v. *Board of Education,* 333 U.S. 203 (1948).

[43] Mr. Justice Black's celebrated dictum in *Everson* v. *Board of Education,* 330 U.S. 1 (1947) at pages 15 and 16.

or all. But in 1603 and for centuries before, this idea would have seemed freakish and fantastic.

Nevertheless egalitarian religious ideas had already begun to quicken in the minds of some men as early as the fourteenth century. Itinerant preachers urged freedom and justice in God's name. In every era including the Middle Ages some firm believers have found difficulty in reconciling the divine right of State or Church magnates with the idea that man is but dust. John Wycliffe, born in Yorkshire in 1320, typifies these early stirrings of what long afterward was to become the Protestant Reformation. He was educated at Oxford, in time became a Fellow of Balliol, and later Master of that college. He was a compassionate man, with a resentment of vested privilege in the clergy; he criticized the splendor of the great Churchmen, urging their return to apostolic poverty; he taught that salvation depended on the faith of the individual believer. To help simple Englishmen follow this ideal he had the Bible translated into English, and founded an organization of "poor priests" to instruct the lowly in religion. His influence was obnoxious to the great clerics; but John of Gaunt, Edward the Third's son, found Wycliffe a convenient ally in one of the perennial controversies with Rome, and with this support the reforming preacher held his place at Oxford until 1381. Then, however, he lost favor with his powerful friend by denying the reality of transubstantiation; with loss of Gaunt's protection went the loss of Wycliffe's college living. Wycliffe was still Rector of Lutterworth, near Oxford, and from that parish he continued to publish pamphlets until he died in 1384.

Wycliffe's later followers, known to their enemies as "Lollards," combined religious individualism with tendencies to economic levelling. In 1401 Parliament passed the Act *"De Haeretico comburendo,"* aimed at lollardry; the statute directed the civil power to burn condemned heretics at the stake. Lollardry shrank in the face of such threats, but its ideas never entirely died out. They reappeared more than a century later in the separatist Protestant sects of England and Holland; some of their thoughts stirred in the Levellers of Cromwell's time, and some in the Puritans of New England. Human beings not addicted to fine distinctions do not readily split up egalitarianism according to subject matter. Religious equality and individual judgment in matters spiritual are close kin to political equality particularly in a society where lay rule and religious rule are thought properly to be one. And then, say levellers of all times, why economic disparity? Wycliffe's ideas had consequences in State as well as in Church, and ultimately in society generally.

At the opening of the seventeenth century, constitutional separation of the powers of government was not prominent in the minds of those who shaped and controlled England. A long contest was about to start, between Crown and Parliament; but men thought of the controversy between Stuarts and the Commons as a contest for control of a unified government, not as a development toward divided rule. Separation of powers is a theory that comes to the fore when the many come to have a dominant influence in government, and as Elizabeth's reign ended this dominance had still not been demonstrated.

The idea of a written governing compact was latent in 1603. Coke was to put new life into Magna Carta; the royal assent to the Petition of Right in 1628 was much like the acceptance that, with the accepted offer, forms a contract. The ideas which, half a century later, were to produce the brief constitutional experiments of the Cromwellian commonwealth must have been stirring long before. But the English people were about to start other greater, more portentous experiments. The various charters that defined rights of settlers in America, the explicit agreements made in the cabin of the *Mayflower* in 1620, and in Connecticut in 1639,[44] these were about to demonstrate that a new era was starting in man's government of himself. One can well be skeptical of sharp watersheds in history; one can fully recognize that change in human affairs is ordinarily gradual, coming little by little. Still in the light of retrospect, the beginning of the seventeenth century seems to have been one of the great moments in the unfolding history of constitutional ideas.

[44] See Clinton Rossiter, *Seedtime of the Republic* (New York: Harcourt, Brace and Co., 1953) p. 31 *et seq.*

4. THE PETITION OF RIGHT; FOREWORD TO THE CROMWELLIAN REVOLUTION

In the path of the law, as in other tracks of history, there are few sharp turnings. Man is constrained by habit; most developments in society and government are gradual, not eruptive. But sometimes, as changes are slowly occurring, great events may indicate to the perceptive that change is in progress. Probably the dramatic event more often demonstrates a change which has already occurred without many people becoming conscious of it. Such a dramatic evidence of accomplished change was the Petition of Right of 1628, marking the seniority of Parliament over Charles Stuart. This parliamentary episode was part of an old contest which had flared up in the early days of the rule of Charles' father. The long contest with the Crown was not clearly bilateral, with an elected parliament on one side and the king with his adherents on the other. Political events are not often so diagrammatical. The powers of James I and Charles I to rule England by the royal will were challenged not only by the increasingly confident and self-conscious Commons, but by increasingly independent judges under the leadership of that man of his time, Edward Coke.[1] This was a contest mainly between Parliament and Crown; but sometimes it presented itself as a struggle between Crown and Judges aligned with Parliament.

[1] Holdsworth gives an excellent short account of Coke's career and character in his *History of English Law* (Boston: Little, Brown and Co., 1927) V, p. 425 *et seq.* A recent vivid account in Catherine Drinker Bowen's *The Lion and the Throne* (Boston: Little, Brown and Co., 1957). Another, older but still useful history appears in Campbell's *Lives of the Chief Justices* (London: J. Murray, 1849) I, pp. 269 ff.

Coke opposed the Stuarts in both roles. He began as a parliamentarian under Elizabeth, went on to become a faithful and severe law officer of the Crown under James; but when he then became a Justice, he developed a streak of stubborn, proud independence that made him defy the royal prerogative power until defiance cost him his place on the Bench. Coke's people sent him back into the Commons, and there he continued resistance to the arbitrary powers asserted by James and by James' son, Charles. Sir Edward Coke personifies all resistance to unlimited Stuart power; he was a forerunner of James Otis, of John Adams, of Thomas Jefferson, when they waged another contest, with a later King, in a different land. Coke's stand against the first two Stuarts is part of the constitutional tradition of the United States.

To understand the merits and the progress of Coke's contest with the Crown, one must understand something about the status of the Commons during the reigns of James I and Charles I; about the position of the common-law courts; about the ideas of James and Charles concerning the powers and prerogatives of the Crown; and about the use these monarchs made of the Prerogative Courts, particularly the Star Chamber and the High Commission, to attempt to establish royal predominance over the other organs of Stuart government.

The four centuries between Magna Carta of 1215 and the reign of James I (1603–1625) had brought the government of England a long way toward its modern structure. By 1300 the three common-law courts, Kings Bench, Exchequer, and Common Pleas had grown into existence. A half century later the House of Commons had emerged as a separate part of the Parliament. By 1430 the Commons had become an elected representative body, chosen by an electorate narrow under today's standards, but still an electorate which was sometimes annoying to the great because the electors included "people of small substance and of no value." The statutes of Elizabeth show that by the late sixteenth century the law-making function of Parliament had come to be seen as separate from its residue of adjudicatory power.[2] By the time of James I of England, the House of Commons had become the permanently predominant governmental power in England, though neither James nor his descendants realized this until 1688 when James Stuart's grandson was obliged to flee the kingdom. Perhaps even then the Stuarts had not learned what was obvious to their country.

[2] See e.g. 13 Eliz. c. 5 (1558) 6 Pickering, *Statutes at Large* (Cambridge: Joseph Bentham, Printer to the University, 1763) p. 268. This was an act against fraudulent deeds, alienations, etc. made to avoid the debts or duty owed to others, declaring these transfers to be void. The statute is obviously new law, not a declaration of an existing rule.

From his accession in 1603 until his death in 1625, James held stubbornly to theories of royal absolutism which had become inconsistent with the realities of parliamentary power. As a practical matter he could not finance his government without the cooperation of the Commons; but like some other and later strong-minded men, James failed to perceive the slow changes of time. He continued to persuade himself that only temporary and avoidable annoyances, caused by his upstart subjects, kept his royal will from being absolute in England. Charles, James' son, struggled on burdened with this illusion until 1649 when he died on a scaffold at Whitehall.

Religious differences in Stuart times aroused governmental quarrels which, in the twentieth century, are difficult to sense. The Puritan movement, at first a reform enterprise within the Church of England, had begun before James' accession. In 1604, the year after James began to reign, some leading clergymen of the Establishment came to a conference at Hampton Court to attempt legalized acceptance of Puritans within the Church. They did not ask acceptance of congregationalism, or repudiation of the Episcopacy; they asked only a certain tolerance of variety in ritual and in parish work which would keep the Puritans lawfully within the Church of England. The Puritan influence on the Commons was powerful, and a wiser king might have seen that to put the religious reformers outside the established Church was to invite ultimate civil war. But this exile was exactly what James proclaimed and civil war was the ultimate result. He lectured the Conference on the theme "No Bishop, no King," and, closing the day's deliberations observed, "If this be all they have to say I shall make them conform themselves, or I will harry them out of the land, or else do worse."[3] His words were curiously prophetic. Four years later the Puritan congregation of Scrooby in Nottinghamshire fled to Holland. Twelve years thereafter that little group furnished a number of the passengers on the voyage of the *Mayflower* to Plymouth, first detachment of the Puritan exodus to New England.

James' insistence on religious orthodoxy was probably based on a sound judgment that the Puritan's individual judgment in religious matters would ultimately prove inconsistent with unquestioning acceptance of kingship. James' son and successor, Charles, followed the same line, identifying assured loyalty to the royal government with adherence to the Establishment. This stubbornness was to drive increasing thousands of Puritans into the ranks of Cromwell's regiments

[3] A brief account occurs in W. H. Frere, *History of the English Church in the Reigns of Elizabeth and James I, 1558–1625* (London: Macmillan, 1904) p. 297 *et seq.*

called Ironsides, which ultimately became the ruling governmental power in England.

Both James and Charles thought that they found in the Prerogative Courts, the Star Chamber, and the High Commission, useful royal devices for attempting to maintain supremacy over their opponents in government. These bodies[4] had by Tudor times become specialized judicial organs of the royal Council. Although the name Star Chamber has today become almost synonymous for judicial tyranny,[5] this evil reputation was originally neither deserved nor generally attributed. The Star Chamber's bad name is probably a legacy from Stuart abuses of a once-wholesome institution. The Star Chamber was popular at first; it started as a royal means of doing justice swiftly and efficiently, unhampered by the long and complex procedures which had grown up in the common-law courts, and free from lawless local influence which at times dominated common-law juries.[6] Thus the Star Chamber resembled the Court of Chancery, in that it could and did serve to mitigate evils in the administration of justice. But, as Stuart England discovered, swift informal procedure can easily be misused.

The Court of Star Chamber took its name from a room at Westminster where the King's Council sometimes met to transact judicial business: the ceiling is supposed to have been decorated with stars. In 1487 an Act of 3 Henry VII,[7] called "Pro Camera Stellata," recited corruption of sheriffs in making panels and returns, bribery of jurors, and other injustices perpetrated in common-law courts, and to correct these evils provided,

---

[4] Other Prerogative Courts were the Court of Requests, the Council of Wales, and the Council of the North. The Star Chamber is often mentioned today as a symbol of tyrannical behavior by those who only know its reputation. Few but scholars now mention the High Commission; the Requests and the other two prerogative Courts are almost forgotten.

[5] For example, in a 1949 opinion holding unconstitutional a confession obtained by undue questioning, Justice Frankfurter wrote,

> Ours is the accusatorial as opposed to the inquisitional system. Such has been the characteristic of Anglo-American criminal justice since it freed itself from practices borrowed by the Star Chamber from the Continent whereby an accused was interrogated in secret for hours on end.

Watts v. *Indiana*, 388 U.S. 49, 54; and see Justice Black's opinion in *Re Oliver*, 333 U.S. 257 (1948) at pp. 268-269, and his dissent in *Re Graham*, 352 U.S. 330 (1957) at p. 351.

[6] See J. R. Tanner, *Tudor Constitutional Documents, 1485–1603* (Cambridge: Cambridge University Press, 1922) p. 249 *et seq.*; Sir D. L. Keir, *The Constitutional History of Modern Britain*, (3rd ed.; London: A. and C. Black, 1946) p. 20 *et seq.*

[7] C. I.; II Statutes of the Realm 509. See Tanner, *Tudor Constitutional Documents, 1485–1603*, pp. 249, 258 *et seq.* for a description of the origins, jurisdiction and procedure of the Star Chamber.

. . . That the Chancellor and Treasurer of England for the time being and Keeper of the King's Privy Seal, or two of them, calling to them a bishop and a temporal lord of the King's most honourable Council and the two Chief Justices of the King's Bench and Common Pleas for the time being or other two Justices in their absence, upon bill or information put to the said Chancellor for the King or any other against any person for any misbehaving afore rehearsed, have authority to call before them by writ or privy seal the said misdoers, and them and other by their discretions to whom the truth may be known to examine, and such as they find therein defective to punish them after their demerits, after the form and effect of statutes thereof made, in like manner and form as they should and ought to be punished if they were thereof convict after the due order of the law. . . .

Today's lawyer, used to thinking of a tidy separation of civil from criminal jurisdiction, of judicial functions segregated from administrative, might be puzzled to classify the Star Chamber according to modern ideas. Private individuals could institute proceedings before it; so could the Attorney-General. The Court could issue orders like modern injunctions, enforceable by contempt proceedings; it could, in effect, award judgments for payment of money damages;[8] it could impose fines, sentence to prison, or direct corporal punishment short of death. It might make sweeping administrative orders, as in a decree of 1585 regulating printers.[9] In Elizabeth's day the Star Chamber used powers as drastic as it did later under James and Charles. But the two first Stuarts were monarchs quite different from the last of the Tudors; they reigned in changed times; and a Parliament quite different in temper from any called by Elizabeth ended the Star Chamber in 1641 and cut off Charles' head eight years later.

The High Commission had its beginnings in ecclesiastical commissions issued by Henry VIII and his immediate successors.[10] Religion had political connotations in the sixteenth century, and the occupant of the throne, whether a Protestant or a Roman Catholic, could use such devices to root out heretical opponents. Letters patent would issue under royal authority designating a group of able men acting under the general control of the Council, to inquire into whatever current heresy was troublesome. By 1580, certain Ecclesiastical Commissioners for the Province of Canterbury had evolved into a permanent Court, with something like an established procedure, in which a defendant could have the assistance of counsel called a Proctor, who

[8] See for example instances cited by Tanner, *Tudor Constitutional Documents, 1485–1603*, p. 278.
[9] Reprinted in J. R. Tanner's *Tudor Constitutional Documents, 1485–1603*, p. 279.
[10] A convenient brief account is in Tanner, *Tudor Constitutional Documents, 1485–1603*, p. 360.

might successfully urge somewhat technical defenses.[11] Like the Star Chamber, the High Commission initiated proceedings by bringing in the defendant and requiring him to take the "oath ex officio,"[12] by which he was sworn to speak truth as to any matters the Court might ask about. The object of the inquiry was not defined in advance by any such inconveniently technical procedure as an indictment, or the process of common-law pleading. The Commission thus started out as a sort of criminal court in ecclesiastical cases, but it so frequently started proceedings at the instance of an aggrieved subject claiming remedial redress against another in some matter vaguely connected with ecclesiastical jurisdiction, that in time the High Commission resembled an ordinary civil tribunal which in many ways duplicated the jurisdiction of the common-law courts. Here was a source of jealousy and mutual suspicion, a situation inviting writs of prohibition from common-law courts, and in turn resentful resistance by the High Commission and the Star Chamber.

During the 1630's Archbishop Laud and other high clergy who were supporting Charles against his Puritan opponents, found the High Commission a convenient device for prosecutions. And so in 1641 the Long Parliament by statute abolished the High Commission along with the Star Chamber. In 1645, partly because of his misuse of those courts, the unfortunate Laud was beheaded.

Writs of prohibition issued by the common-law courts, which purported to forbid proceedings in the prerogative courts, had become a subject of sharp dispute as early as the third year of James I's reign, even before Coke became a judge. Long afterward Coke, in his *Second Institute* wrote of a complaint ("Articuli Cleri") concerning prohibitions, lodged in 1605 by Richard Bancroft, Archbishop of Canterbury, on behalf of the whole English clergy before the lords of the Privy Council,[13]

> . . . articles Richard Bancroft, Archbishop of Canterbury exhibited in the name of the whole clergy in Michaelmas terme anno 3 Jacobi regis to the lords of the privie councell against the judges of the realm, intitled, Certain articles of abuses, which are desired to be reformed, in granting of prohibitions, and the answers thereunto, upon mature deliberations, and consideration, in Easter terme following, by all the

[11] An account of such a defense presented by a Puritan named Carew in 1583–84, appears in Roland G. Usher, *The Rise and Fall of the High Commission* (Oxford: Clarendon Press, 1913) p. 77 *et seq.*

[12] See Mary Hume Maguire, "The Oath Ex Officio," in *Essays in History and Political Theory in Honor of Charles H. McIlwain,* (Cambridge: Harvard University Press, 1936) p. 199.

[13] Coke, *Second Institute* (London: Flesher and Young, 1642), p. 599; Corbett, *State Trials* (London: Hansard, 1809) II; 3 James I, *1605, Articuli Cleri,* p. 131.

judges of England, and the barons of the exchequer with one unanimous consent under their hands (resolutions of highest authorities in law) which were delivered to the councell. And we for destinction sake (because we shall have occasion often to cite them) call them *Articuli Cleri* 3 *Jacobi*.

His Majesty hath power to reform abuses in prohibitions.

Objection The clergy well hoped, that they had taken a good course in seeking some redress at his majesties hands concerning Sundry abuses offered to his ecclesiasticall jurisdiction, by the over frequent and undue granting of prohibitions; for both they and we supposed (all jurisdiction, both ecclesiasticall and temporall being annexed to the imperiall crowne of this realme) that his highness had been held to have sufficient authority in himselfe, with the assistance of his said jurisdictions, and to have reformed the same accordingly; otherwise a wrong course is taken by us, if nothing may bee reformed that is now complained of, but what the temporall judges shall of themselves willingly yeeld unto. This is therefore the first point, which upon occasion lately offered before your lordships by some of the judges, we desire may be cleared, because we are strongly persuaded as touching the validity of his majesties said authorities, and doe hope we shall be able to justify the same, notwithstanding any thing that the judges, or any other can alledge to the contrary.

Answer of Judges No man maketh any question, but that both the jurisdictions are lawfully and justly in his majesty, and that if any abuses be, they ought to bee reformed: but what the law doth warrant in cases of prohibitions to keep every jurisdiction in his true limits, is not to be said an abuse, nor can be altered but by parliament.

Coke's discussion of the *Articuli Cleri* goes on for twenty-three pages of the Second Institute, but the essence of the judges' position in the controversy is in their first brief answer; it was to be Coke's position throughout his judgeship,

> . . . what the law doth warrant in cases of prohibitions to keep every jurisdiction in his true limits, is not to be said an abuse, nor can be altered but by parliament.

In 1605, common-law judges were thus asserting parliamentary supremacy over the royal power to "reform." Here, to use modern terms, was the theory of separation of powers; it was an assumption of judicial control of executive organs of government, suggestive of the Steel Seizure case of 1952.[14]

When James appointed Attorney General Sir Edward Coke to be Chief Justice of the Common Pleas in 1606, Coke promptly came into

[14] *Youngstown Sheet and Tube* v. *Sawyer*, 343 U.S. 579 (1952).

prominence as the king's most notable adversary. As Elizabeth's and James' Attorney General, Coke had been an arrogant and oppressive Crown prosecutor.[15] Now as Chief Justice, demonstrating the qualities of his defects, he became a boldly assertive protector of the subject's rights against the Crown's arrogance. He was particularly obnoxious to James and the royal partisans because he issued so many writs of prohibition forbidding litigation before the High Commission. The high standing of legality in English political life, even three centuries and a half ago, is evident from the annoyance this caused the king's party. An effective royal or ecclesiastical tyranny would have simply overridden Coke's writs, which had no armed force to make them effective and no other organized sanctions such as those of the medieval Church. Even in James' day, English judges had a standing essentially moral, in the face of which a king hesitated, with reason.

In 1607 Archbishop Bancroft again complained about prohibitions issued by common-law judges in the celebrated controversy Coke called "Prohibitions del Roy." Coke tells the story in his Reports,

> Note, upon Sunday the 10th of November in this same term, the King, upon complaint made to him by Bancroft, Archbishop of Canterbury, concerning prohibitions, the King was informed, that when the question was made of what matters the Ecclesiastical Judges have cognizance, either upon the exposition of the statutes concerning tithes, or any other thing ecclesiastical, or in any other case in which there is not express authority in law, the King himself may decide it in his Royal person; and that the King may take what causes he shall please to determine, from the determination of the Judges, and may determine them himself. And the Archbishop said, that this was clear in divinity, that such authority belongs to the King by the word of God in the Scripture. To which it was answered by me, in the presence, and with the clear consent of all the Judges of England, and Barons of the Exchequer, that the King in his own person cannot adjudge any case, either criminal, as treason, etc., felony, or betwixt party and party, concerning his inheritance, chattels, or goods, etc. but this ought to be determined and adjudged in some Court of Justice, according to the law and custom of England; . . . then the King said, that he thought the law was founded upon reason, and that he and others had reason, as well as the Judges; to which it was answered by me, that true it was, that God had endowed His Majesty with excellent science, and great endowments of nature; but His Majesty was not

[15] Against Sir Walter Raleigh on trial for his life for treason in 1603, Coke broke out, ". . . I will prove you to be the most notorious traitor that ever came to the bar! . . . Thou art a monster! Thou hast an English face but a Spanish heart. . . . I *thou* thee, thou traitor! I will prove thee the rankest traitor in all England. . . ." The story is told by Catherine Drinker Bowen in *The Lion and the Throne* p. 194 ff.

learned in the laws of his realm of England, and causes which concern the life, or inheritance, or goods, or fortunes of his subjects, are not to be decided by natural reason but by the artificial reason and judgment of law, which law is an art which requires long study and experience, before that a man can attain to the cognizance of it: that the law was the golden met-wand and measure to try the causes of the subjects; and which protected His Majesty in safety and peace: with which the King was greatly offended, and said, that then he should be under the law, which was treason to affirm, as he said; to which I said that Bracton saith, *quod Rex non debet esse sub homine, sed sub Deo et lege. . . .*[16]

James, according to one account of this celebrated interview, ". . . fell into that high indignation as the like was never known in him, looking and speaking fiercely with bended fist, offering to strike him."[17] Coke asked the King's pardon with decorous humility. Lord Treasurer Robert Cecil, Coke's uncle by marriage, interceded for him. James, somewhat mollified, went off to Royston for his customary deer-hunting. And next morning, Coke issued another prohibition to the High Commission.

In 1609 the President of York (head of a provincial Council which exercised in the north a power comparable to that of the Prerogative Courts in London) complained to James that "the Judges of the common law had, in contempt of the command of the King the last term, granted sixty, or fifty prohibitions to the President and Council of York. . . ." Coke explained the matter to James sufficiently for the moment, though the repetition of this assertion of authority can scarcely have been welcome to the already irritated King.[18] Indeed the failure of James to get rid of Coke earlier than he did is one of the most significant signs of the times. Assured tenure for judges was still far in the future; but James was evidently hesitant to turn off a judicial adversary.

In the long controversy between the common-law courts and those tribunals with more royal inclination, the *Prohibitions del Roy,* and the complaints of the Lord Presidents against writs of prohibition were not the only incidents. Other disputes arose over premature arrests by the High Commission: it used to send its officers,

[16] 12 Co. Rep. 63, Mich 5 Jacobi I (1607). 77 English Reprints, 1342, 1343. Mr. Justice Jackson quoted "The Case of the Prohibitions del Roy" in his concurring opinion in the Steel Seizure Case, *Youngstown Sheet & Tube Co.* v. *Sawyer,* 343 U.S. 579, 655 (1952).

[17] See a letter, Sir Rafe Boswell to Dr. Milborne, quoted in Bowen, *The Lion and the Throne,* p. 305.

[18] "Prohibitions," 13 Co. Rep. 30 (1609) The Lord President of Wales made a similar complaint in 1608. See "The Case of the Lords President of Wales and York," 12 Co. Rep. 50 (1608).

"pursuivants," to arrest defendants at the outset of litigation and bring them in to answer, instead of notifying the defendants in the manner usual in ecclesiastical courts, by "citation," requiring them to answer, with contempt proceedings and arrest following only if the citation were disregarded. In 1608 Coke and his brethren of the Common Bench held, in the case of one Allan Ball[19] that the High Commission could not so proceed; Coke's report cites another case holding it no murder to kill a pursuivant who should attempt such a tortious arrest. The procedure, says Coke, is in violation of a statute of 5 Elizabeth,

> which shall be in vain, if they may arrest him by a pursuivant before any answer or default made: and this will be against the Statute of Magna Charta, and all the ancient statutes. . . .[20]

As Coke does in some other cases in his Reports, he irritates the reader of Allan Ball's case by omitting a description of the procedure. We are left wondering if the Common Bench here too issued a writ of prohibition. But the substantive question in Ball's case was clear and important. The judges, relying on Magna Carta for inspiration, were resolved to enforce established procedures to protect individuals; "the history of liberty has largely been the history of observance of procedural safeguards."[21]

The constitutional history of Stuart England concerns contests with kings, carried on in many ways—at the worst in battles; in pamphleteering campaigns; in demonstrations of heroic endurance like that of John Lilburn walking behind a cart from Fleet Street to Westminster Palace Yard in 1638 while the executioner lashed his back raw under a sentence of the Court of Star Chamber;[22] in quiet resolution like that of the Scrooby congregation, leaving its Nottinghamshire home for Holland, and going thence to a stern New England. One can be surprised to see how often some phase of the contest became a legalistic one, a dispute in judicial form, over the rules for the ordering of society and government. The lawyers' controversies turned on differing

[19] 12 Co. Rep. 49 (1608) "The Case of the Lords President of Wales and York" apparently was decided in the same term as "Allan Ball"; it appears on the folio following "Allan Ball" in Coke's Reports.

[20] 12 Co. Rep. 50 (1608) See Campbell, *Lives of the Chief Justices* Chapter VIII, for an account of the case in question.

[21] The quoted words are from Mr. Justice Frankfurter's opinion in *McNabb* v. *U.S.*, 318 U.S. 332, 347 (1943); see for other examples in Coke's reports, Marmaduke Langdale's Case, 12 Co. Rep. 50; The Case of the Lords Presidents of Wales and York, 12 Co. Rep. 50; Prohibitions. Answer to the complaint of the President of York to the King, 13 Co. Rep. 30; the Case de Modo Decimandi, and of Prohibitions Debated before the King's Majesty, 13 Co. Rep. 37.

[22] An account is given in M. A. Gibb's *John Lilburne the Leveller* (London: L. Drummond, 1947) p. 47 *et seq.*

theories; sometimes common-law courts against newer prerogative courts speaking for King and Bishops; sometimes common-law precedents and acts of parliament against royal fiat.

Because in Stuart times Parliament was predominantly ranged with the elements opposing the Royal will, the courts gave little attention to a theme so prominent in American theory three centuries later, conflict between parliamentary legislation and a "higher law" which would make the statute void.

Tyranny of the majority had not developed in Stuart England where the majority was in no position to tyrannize. But some statements of Coke when he was Chief Justice of the Common Pleas suggest that he considered Acts of Parliament subordinate to a higher standard, subordinate to a natural law régime. His judgment may have been influenced by some after-memory of Parliament declaring law rather than making it; he may, like other much later judges, have entertained the concept that "Law was to an important extent conceived by both governors and governed as a subject of science, capable of being learnt by special study, but not capable of being altered by the mere arbitrary will of government, any more than the principles or conclusions of mathematics."[23]

The idea of a Higher Law, predominant over a statute, appears in Dr. Bonham's Case in 1610[24] where Coke refused to enforce against a physician an Act of Parliament purporting to empower the Royal College of Physicians to fine those who practiced without a license and to keep half the fine. Coke wrote,

> . . . The censors cannot be judges, ministers, and parties; judges to give sentence or judgment; ministers to make summons; and parties to have the moiety of the forfeiture, quia aliquis non debet esse Judex in propria causa, imo iniquum est aliquem suae rei esse judicem; and one cannot be Judge and attorney for any of the parties, . . . And it appears in our books, that in many cases, the common law will controul Acts of Parliament, and sometimes adjudge them to be utterly void: for when an Act of Parliament is against common right and reason, or repugnant, or impossible to be performed, the common law wil controul it, and adjudge such Act to be void; . . .[25]

[23] Sidgwick, *The Elements of Politics* (2nd ed., 1897) pp. 652–53, quoted in C. H. McIlwain, *The High Court of Parliament and Its Supremacy,* (New Haven: Yale University Press, 1910) p. 47.

[24] 8 Rep. 114 a, 2 Brown p. 255; 77 Engl. Rep. 647. The case is discussed in Corwin, "The Higher Law Background of American Constitutional Law," 42 *Harv. L. Rev.* 149, 365 (1928–1929); Plucknett, "Bonham's Case and Judicial Review," 40 *Harv. L. Rev.* 30 (1926); Thorne, "Dr. Bonham's Case" 54 *L. Q. Rev.* 543 (1938).

[25] See T. F. T. Plucknett, "Bonham's Case and Judicial Review," 40 *Harv. L. Rev.* 30 (1926).

Coke had stated the same theme in his report of Calvin's Case[26] decided one and one-half years before Dr. Bonham's Case,

> The law of nature is that which God at the time of creation of the nature of man infused into his heart, for his preservation and direction; and this is Lex aeterna, the moral law, called also the law of nature. And by this law, written with the finger of God in the Heart of man, where the people of God a long time governed before the law was written by Moses, who was the first reporter or writer of law in the world . . . and Aristotle, nature's Secretary Lib. 5 Ethic. saith that jus naturale est, quod apud omnes homines eandem habet potentiam. And herewith doth agree Bracton lib. 1 cap. 5. and Fortescue cap. 8. 12. 13. and 16. Doctor and Student, cap. 2. and 4.[27]

Bacon, arguing as counsel, had invoked the "law of nature."[28] Evidently a higher-law theory was an element in the thinking of Stuart lawyers. But Coke's doctrine in Bonham's Case never took deep root in England. In 1614 Chief Justice Hobart echoed it in a suit over a bag of nutmegs, *Day* v. *Savadge*.[29] He wrote,

> . . . even an Act of Parliament, made against natural equity, as to make a man judge in his own case, is void in itself, for jura naturae sunt immutabilia and they are leges legum.

The doctrine appears in scattered mentions thereafter.[30] But validity, not invalidity, of Parliamentary powers, was the principal concern of Coke as judge and as parliamentarian. Bonham's Case was to have its important influence over one and a half centuries later in America, when Otis was arguing against Writs of Assistance in Massachusetts and when judicial review of the constitutionality of statutes was developing in American courts under the Constitution of the United States.[31]

The recurring controversies, recounted in Coke's reports, over prohibitions and common-law precedents, were far more than lawyers' squabbles over individuals' claims. From the contest over jurisdictions emerged the great question of executive or legislative supremacy. The

[26] 7 Co. Rep. I, Trin 6 Jacobi I, 12b (1608).

[27] Professor Corwin discusses Bonham's Case and Calvin's Case in his celebrated essay, "The 'Higher Law' Background of American Constitutional Law," 42 *Harv. L. Rev.* 149 and 365 (1928–1929), reprinted in *Selected Essays on Constitutional Law* (Chicago: The Foundation Press, 1938) I, 1–66.

[28] Basil Montagu, ed., *The Works of Francis Bacon* (London: J. Murray, 1825–34) II, pp. 166, 176.

[29] Hobart 85, 80 Eng. Rep. 235.

[30] See Corwin's "Higher Law Background," *passim*.

[31] See page 126 *infra*.

common-law courts acknowledged that Parliament could alter the jurisdiction of tribunals; what the judges resisted was a claim of royal prerogative to do so, they held out against the contention of executive independence, a claim by the Crown that it could authorize officers to disregard enacted law. The frequency of the disputes demonstrates the prominence of the issue. In 1688 James' grandson and namesake lost his throne by asserting the same royal prerogative to issue dispensations from obedience to Acts of Parliament.

Despite Coke's irritating opposition, King James in 1613 appointed him Chief Justice of the King's bench and so Chief Justice of England. Perhaps the appointment, nominally a distinction, was intended less to honor Coke than to make a series of moves ultimately providing a place as Attorney-General, lower in the legal hierarchy, for Francis Bacon, a partisan of James.

Coke was not Chief Justice of England very long. In 1616 the King attempted to intervene in the "Case of Commendams," a controversy about the right to present to a vacant living; the King had given the living to a bishop, to be held "in commendam," that is temporarily but not for a defined period, to enjoy the revenues along with those of his bishopric. Colt and Glover, two persons who could have presented a candidate for the living, if the Bishop had not occupied the place, brought suit to challenge his rights.[32] James, who had no liking for judicial interference with distribution of royal patronage, had his Attorney-General write Coke and the other judges that it was

> . . . his Majesty's express pleasure that the day appointed for farther argument of the said cause be put off till his Majesty's farther pleasure be known upon consulting him.

This assertion of royal prerogative to delay pending litigation in the common-law courts appeared illegal to the judges. They proceeded to decide the case in defiance of the royal will, and notified the King in a respectful communication that the Attorney-General's letter was contrary to law, and that under their oaths of office they would not yield to it. On June 6, 1616, James in a fury summoned the judges and reprimanded them for their insubordination. They were decorously apologetic. Thereupon the King and the Council put to the judges the question whether in any future litigation concerning the King's power and profit they would stay the case if ordered by the King. All the judges but Coke agreed. Coke, less submissive, answered ". . . that

---

[32] Somewhat different versions of this controversy appear in Campbell's *Lives of the Chief Justices*, I, Ch. VIII, and Catherine Drinker Bowen's, *The Lion and the Throne*, Ch. 28. The substance is the same. A "living" is an ecclesiastical office or cure, the position of rector of a parish for example, with attached endowments.

when the case should be, he would do that which should be fit for a judge to do."[33]

Even this defiance did not at once bring immediate dismissal on the Chief Justice. But twenty days later he came to grief in another quarrel over patronage, the perennial interest of all politicians. Coke resisted the appointment of a protégé of the Duke of Buckingham as Chief Clerk of the King's Bench. The Chief Justice was thereupon suspended from the performance of his duties and by the King's direction, was required to spend this enforced leisure reviewing his Reports wherein "as his Majesty is informed, be many extravagant and exorbitant opinions set down and published for positive and good law." On October 6, 1616, Sir Francis Bacon, James' Attorney-General, prepared a declaration for the King to make to the Privy Council touching Lord Coke; it recited many of Coke's shortcomings including the objectionable Reports, "which after three months time he had entirely failed to explain or to justify." On November 16, 1616, the King removed Coke from the office of Chief Justice.[34] Nevertheless James thought well of his quondam Chief Justice. After removing him, James still said he was "uncorrupt and a good justice"; in December, 1616, James "graciously received" Coke and spent two hours with him.[35] With surprising patience the King restored Coke to the Privy Council[36] where he performed duties not unlike those of the present judicial Committee. He occasionally sat in the court of Star Chamber. In 1620, he was elected a member of Parliament for the borough of Liskeard in Cornwall;[37] he thereafter carried on his opposition to James' pretensions from his seat in the House of Commons.

One acute question was the freedom of Parliament to debate any public matters, even those which the King thought his own exclusive business. In Elizabeth's time a member was by no means at liberty to debate anything he pleased in the Commons. Peter Wentworth and a number of his fellow-members of the House had been sent to the Tower in 1587 for insisting that they could discuss religious reform, though perhaps their imprisonment was technically for agitating such

[33] Hobart 140 *sub nomine* Colt and Glover v. Bishop of Coventry. For other references and a discussion of the case, see Holdsworth, *History of English Law* (Boston: Little, Brown and Co., 1927) V, p. 439.

[34] The circumstances of Coke's dismissal are told by Holdsworth in *History of English Law*, V, p. 440 *et seq.* Campbell has an account in *Lives of the Chief Justices*, I, Ch. VIII. The story is also told in Bowen's *The Lion and the Throne*, Ch. 28.

[35] See for these evidences of James' reasonableness Holdsworth, *op. cit.*, pages 434–443.

[36] Holdsworth, *op. cit.*, p. 443.

[37] Holdsworth, *op. cit.*, p. 444, says Coke was so returned "by the King's command."

matters outside the House, and so their case concerns freedom of speech generally, rather than freedom of debate in Parliament.[38]

In 1621, King James, resenting an address from the Commons concerning the proposed marriage of his son to a Spanish princess, and concerning aid to the King of Bohemia, sent a command to the Speaker:

> Make known in our name unto the House, that none therein shall presume henceforth to meddle with any thing concerning our Government, or deep matters of State . . . we think ourself very free and able to punish any man's misdemeanours in Parliament, as well during their sitting, as after: which we mean not to spare hereafter, upon any occasion of any man's insolent behaviour there that shall be ministered unto us. . . .

Coke then drew, on behalf of the House, a "Protestation" urging that every member of the House had, and of right ought to have,

> . . . freedom of speech to propound, treat, reason, and bring to conclusion the same; and that the Commons in Parliament have the liberty and freedom to treat of those matters in such order as in their judgments shall seem fittest; And that every such Member of the said House hath like freedom from all Impeachment, Imprisonment, and Molestation (other than by censure of the House itself) for or concerning . . . any matter or matters touching the Parliament or Parliament-business; . . .[39]

The House adopted the Protestation and entered it on the journals. James immediately dissolved Parliament, sent for the journals,[40] declared the Protestation invalid, and with his own hands ripped the offending page out of the Journal and tore it to pieces. He directed that an entry be made in the Council Books that if allowed to remain:

> . . . it might have served for future times to invade most of the right and prerogatives annexed to the Imperial Crown of this Realm.

Coke with another leader of the opposition was committed to the Tower; his house and his papers were seized. He remained in the Tower for several months working on his "Littleton" until finally set free through the intercession of Prince Charles. His name was, however, struck from the list of Privy Councillors.

Nonetheless for James' last Parliament in 1624 Coke was again elected to the House of Commons, as a member for Coventry. When

---

[38] Chafee, *Three Human Rights in the Constitution of 1787* (Lawrence: University of Kansas Press, 1956) p. 40 citing J. E. Neale, in *Eng. Hist. Rev.* Mrs. Bowen tells the story in *The Lion and the Throne*, p. 453 ff.
[39] Chafee, *Three Human Rights in the Constitution of 1787*, pp. 58–59.
[40] *Ibid.*, p. 59.

Charles I came to the throne on James' death in 1625, he called a new Parliament, and Coke was yet again returned for Coventry. The issue now was a supply of funds for the King, and Coke moved for a committee to inquire into Crown expenditures. Edmund Burke rightly said in the Commons a century and a half later,[41] "It happened . . . that the great contests for freedom in this country were from the earliest times chiefly upon the question of taxing."

Coke's motion was carried, and the King, irritated by this and like evidences of independence, abruptly dissolved Parliament.[42] But royal funds were still necessary. In 1626 Charles called still another Parliament but, adopting a device he used with other members he found obnoxious, the King appointed Coke Sheriff of Buckinghamshire, attempting so to keep him out of the House on the theory that his duties as Sheriff disqualified him as a parliamentarian. Nevertheless without solicitation Coke was returned by his native county of Norfolk. He never took his seat at this parliament, which lasted only from February 10 to June 15, 1626; but a resolution on House business mentioned Coke as "standing *de facto* returned a member of that House."[43]

Unsuccessful war with France increased the needs of the Crown for revenue. Without Parliamentary authorization Charles undertook "forced loans and benevolences," and his Privy Council took severe measures with those who refused to "lend." Noblemen and members of the gentry went to prison; ordinary folk were impressed as soldiers.[44] Five respected landowners, knights who had refused to make loans and had been imprisoned as a result, applied to the King's Bench in 1627 for a Writ of *Habeas Corpus*.[45] After a warm argument, the Judges finally held that the five knights were not releasable on that writ, but the opinions of the judges showed much doubt about the matter, treating the King's power to imprison the subject as something exceptional, something fitted only to special crises. Though they were willing to allow the King the power to judge when such a crisis existed, they indicated that they regarded arbitrary imprisonment as no ordinary instrument of government. The Opinions roused much popular feeling against Charles. After a short stay in the Tower, the

[41] On March 22, 1775, speaking "On Conciliation with the Colonies." See *Burke's Speeches and Letters on American Affairs*, Ernst Rhys, ed. (London: J. M. Dent and Sons, 1908) p. 91.

[42] Campbell, *Lives of the Chief Justices*, I, p. 323.

[43] Campbell, *Lives of the Chief Justices*, I, p. 324.

[44] F. C. Montague, *Elements of English Constitutional History* (London: Longmans, Green, and Co., 1894) p. 118.

[45] See the Five Knights' Case, Frances Helen Relf, "The Petition of Right," *University of Minnesota Studies in the Social Sciences*, No. 8 (1917) p. 1 ff.

five knights were released, but their release came by royal command, not by order of any judge.[46]

Excessive use of military courts was another popular grievance. Soldiers back from the French Wars were billeted in private houses; and not only were the soldiers subjected to the discipline of courts martial, but upon the complaint of soldiers, civilians were tried the same way. English and American people have traditionally resented and feared extension of military justice beyond the strict necessities of the Services.[47]

Charles' third Parliament, called in 1628, immediately occupied itself with these discontents. There followed a struggle to gain royal assent to a Petition of Right which should assure the subject a redress of his grievances. The Commons had originally proposed to make their assertion of freedom by passing a statute declaring the rights of the subject, but Charles indicated strong resistance, and the Commons substituted a petition, seeking Charles' assent to its terms. This mode of proceeding sounds strange today, when executive respect for legislative bodies is confidently expected. But in 1628 the form of a petition, obsequious in terms, humbly beseeching royal generosity, was more likely to be acceptable to Charles.[48]

Like the American Declaration of Independence, the Petition of Right begins with a long recital of grievances, arising from abuses ascribed to royal officers.[49] It condemns forced loans as violating a statute of Edward I. It recites unlawful imprisonments made in the course of such exactions; it mentions Magna Carta, and the confirmation of the charter by Edward III;[50] it complains of failure to discharge men from unjust imprisonment on *habeas corpus;* it recites the billeting of great companies of soldiers on the people against their wills; it complains of courts martial against civilians who join with

[46] S. R. Gardiner, *Constitutional Documents of the Puritan Revolution, 1628–1660* (Oxford: Clarendon Press, 1889) pp. xxii–xxiii.

[47] See e.g. Ex parte Milligan 4 Wall. 2 (1866). The Supreme Court has recently decided, in a series of cases, that military jurisdiction must be strictly confined. Even when stationed abroad, civilian dependents of military personnel and civilian employees of the armed forces are not subject to trial by courts martial. See *Reid v. Covert,* 354 U.S. I (1957), and *Kinsella v. Krueger* 351 U.S. 470 (1957). See further, *McElroy v. Guagliardo, Wilson v. Bohlender,* 361 U.S. 281 (1959); and see also *Grisham v. Hagan,* 361 U.S. 278 (1960) and *Kinsella v. Singleton* 361 U.S. 234 (1960).

[48] Lord Campbell says that Coke "framed the famous Petition of Right, this small Magna Charta . . ." *Lives of the Chief Justices,* I, Chapter X.

[49] The text of the Petition of Right 3 Car. I, Ch. 1 can be found in 5 Statutes of the Realm 23; it is also set forth in Gardiner, *Constitutional Documents of the Puritan Revolution, 1628–1660,* p. 1.

[50] 28 Edw. III Ch. 3.

soldiers in misconduct, while other persons have escaped punishment for civilian offenses on the pretext, by royal officers, that they "were triable only by court-martial law."

The King's first response, given on June 2, 1628, was not in the customary form for assent to a statute; it gave to the Commons the impression that he was seeking by fair words to avoid categorical agreement to the Petition. He answered evasively:

> The King willeth that right be done according to the laws and customs of the realm; and that the statutes be put in due execution, that his subjects may have no cause to complain of any wrong or oppressions, contrary to their just rights and liberties, to the preservation whereof he holds himself as well obliged as of his prerogative.[51]

The Commons civilly but persistently allowed Charles to know that his answer was unsatisfactory. Finally on June 7, 1628 the Royal assent was given in the traditional form: *Soit droit fait comme il est désiré.* The news spread swiftly through London. The rejoicing people lit bonfires in the streets. It was a great day; Coke so ended his last service in a triumphant Parliament.[52]

The Petition of Right

JUNE 7, 1628

> The Petition exhibited to His Majesty by the Lords Spiritual and Temporal, and Commons in this present Parliament assembled, concerning divers Rights and Liberties of the Subjects, with the King's Majesty's Royal Answer thereunto in full Parliament.

> To the King's Most Excellent Majesty.

> Humbly show unto our Sovereign Lord the King, the Lords Spiritual and Temporal, and Commons in Parliament assembled, that whereas it is declared and enacted by a statute made in the time of the reign of King Edward the First, commonly called *Statutum de Tallagio non concedendo*,[53] that no tallage or aid shall be laid or levied by the King or his heirs in this realm, without the goodwill and assent of the Archbishops, Bishops, Earls, Barons, Knights, Burgesses,

---

[51] Gardiner's *Constitutional Documents of the Puritan Revolution, 1628–1660*, pp. 4–5.

[52] See C. D. Bowen, *The Lion and the Throne*, pp. 503–4.

[53] For a discussion of this curious "statute", see Stubbs, *The Constitutional History of England* (Oxford: Clarendon Press, 1880) II, p. 143; *Select Charters* (8th ed., Oxford: Clarendon Press, 1895) p. 87.

and other the freemen of the commonalty of this realm: and by authority of Parliament holden in the five and twentieth year of the reign of King Edward the Third,[54] it is declared and enacted, that from thenceforth no person shall be compelled to make any loans to the King against his will, because such loans were against reason and the franchise of the land; and by other laws of this realm it is provided, that none should be charged by any charge or imposition, called a Benevolence, or by such like charge,[55] by which the statutes before-mentioned, and other good laws and statutes of this realm, your subjects have inherited this freedom, that they should not be compelled to contribute to any tax, tallage, aid, or other like charge, not set by common consent in Parliament:

Yet nevertheless, of late divers commissions directed to sundry Commissioners in several counties with instructions have issued, by means whereof your people have been in divers places assembled, and required to lend certain sums of money unto your Majesty, and many of them upon their refusal so to do, have had an oath administered unto them, not warrantable by the laws or statutes of this realm, and have been constrained to become bound to make appearance and give attendance before your Privy Council, and in other places, and others of them have been therefore imprisoned, confined, and in sundry other ways molested and disquieted and divers other charges have been laid and levied upon your people in several counties, by Lords Lieutenants, Deputy Lieutenants, Commissioners for Musters, Justices of Peace and others, by command or direction from your Majesty or your Privy Council, against the laws and free customs of this realm:

And where also by the statute called, 'The Great Charter of the Liberties of England,'[56] it is declared and enacted, that no freeman may be taken or imprisoned or be disseised of his freeholds or liberties, or his free customs, or be outlawed or exiled; or in any manner destroyed, but by the lawful judgment of his peers, or by the law of the land:

And in the eight and twentieth year of the reign of King Edward the Third,[57] it was declared and enacted by authority of Parliament, that no man of what estate or condition that he be, should be put out of his lands or tenements, nor taken, nor imprisoned, nor disherited, nor put to death, without being brought to answer by due process of law:

Nevertheless, against the tenor of the said statutes,[58] and other the good laws and statutes of your realm, to that end provided, divers of your subjects have of late been imprisoned without any cause showed, and when for their deliverance they were brought before your Justices,

[54] Gardiner was unable to discover this statute.
[55] In 1484, I Ric. III, c. 2.
[56] 9 Hen. III. 29.
[57] 28 Ed. III. 3.
[58] 37 Ed. III. 18; 38 Ed. III. 9; 42 Ed. III. 3; 17 Ric. II. 6.

by your Majesty's writs of Habeas Corpus, there to undergo and receive as the Court should order, and their keepers commanded to certify the causes of their detainer; no cause was certified, but that they were detained by your Majesty's special command, signified by the Lords of your Privy Council, and yet were returned back to several prisons, without being charged with anything to which they might make answer according to the law:

And whereas of late great companies of soldiers and mariners have been dispersed into divers counties of the realm, and the inhabitants against their wills have been compelled to receive them into their houses, and there to suffer them to sojourn, against the laws and customs of this realm, and to the great grievance and vexation of the people:

And whereas also by authority of Parliament, in the 25th year of the reign of King Edward the Third,[59] it is declared and enacted, that no man shall be forejudged of life or limb against the form of the Great Charter, and the law of the land: and by the said Great Charter and other the laws and statutes of this your realm,[60] no man ought to be adjudged to death; but by the laws established in this your realm, either by the customs of the same realm or by Acts of Parliament: and whereas no offender of what kind soever is exempted from the proceedings to be used, and punishments to be inflicted by the laws and statutes of this your realm: nevertheless of late divers commissions under your Majesty's Great Seal have issued forth, by which certain persons have been assigned and appointed Commissioners with power and authority to proceed within the land, according to the justice of martial law against such soldiers and mariners, or other dissolute persons joining with them, as should commit any murder, robbery, felony, mutiny, or other outrage or misdemeanour whatsoever, and by such summary course and order, as is agreeable to martial law, and is used in armies in time of war, to proceed to the trial and condemnation of such offenders, and them to cause to be executed and put to death, according to the law martial:

By pretext whereof, some of your Majesty's subjects have been by some of the said Commissioners put to death, when and where, if by the laws and statutes of the land they had deserved death, by the same laws and statutes also they might, and by no other ought to have been, adjudged and executed:

And also sundry grievous offenders by colour thereof, claiming an exemption, have escaped the punishments due to them by the laws and statutes of this your realm, by reason that divers of your officers and ministers of justice have unjustly refused, or foreborne to proceed against such offenders according to the same laws and statutes, upon pretence that the said offenders were punishable only by martial law, and by authority of such commissions as aforesaid, which commissions,

[59] 25 Ed. III. 9.
[60] 9 Hen. III. 29; 25 Ed. III. 4; 28 Ed. III. 3.

and all other of like nature, are wholly and directly contrary to the said laws and statutes of this your realm:

They do therefore humbly pray your Most Excellent Majesty, that no man hereafter be compelled to make or yield any gift, loan, benevolence, tax, or such like charge, without common consent by Act of Parliament; and that none be called to make answer, or take such oath, or to give attendance, or be confined, or otherwise molested or disquieted concerning the same, or for refusal thereof; and that no freeman, in any such manner as is before-mentioned, be imprisoned or detained; and that your Majesty will be pleased to remove the said soldiers and mariners, and that your people may not be so burdened in time to come; and that the foresaid commissions for proceeding by martial law, may be revoked and annulled; and that hereafter no commissions of like nature may issue forth to any person or persons whatsoever, to be executed as aforesaid, lest by colour of them any of your Majesty's subjects be destroyed or put to death, contrary to the laws and franchise of the land.

All of which they most humbly pray of your Most Excellent Majesty, as their rights and liberties according to the laws and statutes of this realm: and that your Majesty would also vouchsafe to declare, that the awards, doings, and proceedings to the prejudice of your people, in any of the premises, shall not be drawn hereafter into consequence or example: and that your Majesty would also be graciously pleased, for the further comfort and safety of your people, to declare your royal will and pleasure, that in the things aforesaid all your officers and ministers shall serve you, according to the laws and statutes of this realm, as they tender the honour of your Majesty, and the prosperity of this kingdom. . . .

[On June 7 the answer was given in the accustomed form, *Soit Droit fait comme il est désiré.*]

The Petition of Right, like Magna Carta, "was the beginning, not the end of a struggle for the principles it enunciated."[61] The contest between Parliament and king went on for twenty years after the Petition had received the royal assent. Nonetheless, like Magna Carta, the Petition of Right acquired a life of its own, an influence much greater than at first appeared, greater than the words of the Petition literally prescribed. It became symbolic of successful resistance by the Commons against arbitrary royal power. Some clauses in the United States Constitution, and in our Bill of Rights, are obviously related to

[61] The phrase is G. M. Trevelyan's. See his *History of England* (Garden City, N.Y.: Doubleday Anchor, 1953) II, p. 164. For a similar reflection on the Supreme Court's "wall of separation" statement of Church-State relations, see Mr. Justice Frankfurter's opinion in *Illinois* ex rel *McCollum* v. *Board of Education* 333 U.S. 203, 212 (1948) ". . . This case . . . demonstrates anew that the mere formulation of a relevant Constitutional principle is the beginning of the solution of a problem, not its answer."

matters in the Petition, and to the controversies which brought it about. Article I, Section 6 of the Constitution guaranteeing freedom from arrest during attendance at sessions of the House of Representatives suggests episodes during the bitter quarrels between the first two Stuart kings and the Commons. The provisions of Article I, Section 7 of the Constitution concerning the origin of bills of revenue in the House of Representatives are related to the seventeenth century English controversies over forced loans; the prohibition in Article I, Section 9 of suspension of the writ of *habeas corpus,* save in cases of rebellion or invasion, harks back to the Five Knights' Case. The Third Amendment prohibition against quartering of soldiers on unwilling civilians, the Fifth Amendment insistence on indictment by grand jury and on the compensation for private property taken for public use, the careful procedural guarantees in the Sixth Amendment, all suggest the struggles that led up to the English Commonwealth. David Dudley Field cited the Petition of Right to the Supreme Court in his successful argument against the trial of Milligan by a Military Commission,[62] and in 1946 the Supreme Court in holding invalid military convictions of civilians in *Duncan* v. *Kahanamoku*[63] relied on the Petition of Right as an authority. So men still remember it in sorry moments.

The first great wave of migration from England to Massachusetts came during the two decades 1620–1640. When Parliament won supremacy over the crown, movement of people to New England slowed considerably. But the first comers were Puritans whose sympathies had been on the side of Parliament in its struggles against Charles I. The Five Knights' Case in 1627 and the Petition of Right that followed it in 1628, must have strongly affected the minds of the men and women who left home and moved to New England because for them old England had become intolerable. Their descendants in 1775 had not forgotten the controversies with the Stuarts in the reigns of James I and Charles I.

A few months after the Petition of Right, there was more trouble between King and Commons. In November 1628, Charles, at the suggestion of Bishop Laud,[64] undertook to quiet religious controversy by issuing a new edition of the Articles of Religion, with a prefatory declaration,

> . . . That therefore in these both curious and unhappy differences, which have for so many hundred years, in different times and places, exercised the Church of Christ, We will, that all further curious search

[62] See *Ex parte Milligan*, 4 Wall 2 (1866).

[63] 327 U.S. 304, at page 320.

[64] Then Bishop of London. Laud did not become Archbishop of Canterbury until 1633.

be laid aside, and the disputes shut up in God's promises, as they be generally set forth to us in the Holy Scriptures, and the general meaning of the Articles of the Church of England according to them. And that no man hereafter shall either print, or preach, to draw the Article aside any way, but shall submit to it in the plain and full meaning thereof; and shall not put his own sense or comment to be the meaning of the Article, but shall take it in the literal and grammatical sense.

That if any publick Reader in either of Our Universities, or any Head or Master of a College, or any other person respectively in either of them, shall affix any new sense to any Article, or shall publickly read, determine, or hold any publick Disputation, or suffer any such to be held either way, in either the Universities or Colleges respectively; or if any Divine in the Universities shall preach or print any theory either way, other than is already established in Convocation with Our Royal Assent; he, or they the Offenders, shall be liable to Our displeasure, and, the Church's censure in our Commission Ecclesiastical, as well as any other: and We will see there shall be due Execution upon them.[65]

At the same time the old question of taxation by royal fiat (at the moment in the form of "tonnage and poundage") was stirring. The Commons in the Parliamentary session of 1629 proposed to pass a "protestation" on taxes and religion. The proposal was obnoxious to Charles, and on March 7, 1629, the Speaker, Sir John Finch, told the House that the King required the House to adjourn. The House continued its proceedings; Finch arose, attempting to end the sessions by vacating his chair; two members thrust him down and held him in his seat; another locked the door of the House; the Commons passed the resolutions by acclamation and adjourned of their own motion.

The resolutions declared that introducers of innovation in religion or "popery" and all who should counsel levying tonnage and poundage, not granted by Parliament, should be reputed capital enemies to the kingdom and commonwealth; and that those who voluntarily paid the exactions should be reputed betrayers of the liberties of England, and her enemies.[66]

Charles hastened to punish the Members who had led in this affair. Nine were committed to prison. On March 10, 1629, when the House met again the King in person dissolved Parliament, referring to the "disobedient and seditious carriage of those ill-affected persons of the

[65] The royal declaration is prefixed to the Articles of Religion in the Book of Common Prayer; see also W. H. Hutton, A History of the Church of England from the Ascension of Charles to the Death of Anne (London: Macmillan, 1903) p. 34; Taswell-Langmead, English Constitutional History (9th ed.; London: Sweet and Maxwell, 1929); The King's Declaration is also set out in Gardiner, Constitutional Documents of the Puritan Revolution, 1628–1660, p. 7.

[66] Taswell-Langmead, English Constitutional History, 9th ed., p. 509.

House of Commons," and threatening to punish "these vipers amongst them."[67] No Parliament was held again until 1640. For what they had done in the House, three prominent members, Sir John Eliot and his friends Valentine and Strode, were kept in prison; Eliot, an unselfish and public-spirited man, died in the Tower, refusing to obtain release by acknowledging submission; his two friends remained in prison eleven years.

The differences between Charles and his adversaries continued through the 1630's. Coke died in retirement in 1634 but other stout-hearted Englishmen carried forward his cause. The King continued to press for the collection of "tonnage and poundage" and added exactions of "ship-money," memorable for Hampden's resistance.[68] Bitter religious disputes grew bitterer; civil war broke out; and ultimately the victorious Commons in 1649 set up a High Court of Justice to try Charles "for the crimes and treasons in this said Act mentioned." On January 27, 1649, that Court judged "Charles Stuart" to be "a tyrant, traitor, murderer, and public enemy to the good people of this nation," and directed that he "be put to death by the severing of his head from his body."[69] On January 30, a horror-struck crowd watched Charles die, with dignity and courage, on a scaffold in front of his own palace of Whitehall.

[67] *Ibid.*

[68] J. R. Tanner's *English Constitutional Conflicts of the Seventeenth Century, 1603–1689* is an excellent general survey. For *Hampden's Case*, see *State Trials*, III, 826 (1637).

[69] See S. R. Gardiner, *Constitutional Documents of the Puritan Revolution, 1628–1660*, p. 287. The death warrant of Charles I, decreeing the time and place of execution, was issued on January 29 by the High Court of Justice.

5. COMMONWEALTH AND PROTECTORATE, 1649-1660

ENGLISH GOVERNMENT between the execution of Charles I in 1649, and the restoration of his son Charles II in 1660, was filled with republican innovations.[1] One might expect that the governmental devices of that period would have been continuously cited by the founders of the American republic. But Madison in his journal of the Constitutional Convention gives only two references to Cromwell,[2] in neither instance on any matter of political theory. Except for this fleeting mention the members of the Convention of 1787 passed over the Commonwealth in silence. Not Cromwell and his puritan Commonwealth, but Locke and the Glorious Revolution of 1688 furnished the acknowledged political theory for the young United States. To be sure, every schoolboy has read or (a more cautious note would put it) should have read of Patrick Henry's speech in the Virginia House of Burgesses, "Tarquin and Caesar each had his Brutus, Charles the First his Cromwell, and George the Third . . . may profit by his example."[3]

---

[1] A convenient short account of the Commonwealth, and the text of the constitutional documents important in its history, can be found in Samuel Rawson Gardiner's *Constituitonal Documents of the Puritan Revolution, 1628–1660* (Oxford: Clarendon Press, 1889). The Introduction is a most useful historical outline. Gardiner's account and documents are the principal basis of what is here given; copies of the documents here mentioned are there reproduced. The work is cited hereafter as Gardiner, *Documents*. It has appeared in three editions, of which the latest is dated 1906. See also G. M. Trevelyan, *England Under the Stuarts*, (New York: G. P. Putnam's Sons, 1920).

[2] Max Farrand, ed., *Records of the Federal Convention of 1787* (New Haven: Yale University Press, 1911) II, pp. 370, 451.

[3] Henry was speaking on the Stamp Act, in a meeting of the House at Williamsburg on May 29, 1765. At the mention of the reigning King's name, the Speaker cried "Treason" but Henry continued, adding, "If this be treason, make the most of it."

But it may be that, in retrospect, the execution of Charles I seemed uncharacteristic to the English—something to be ashamed of. The guillotining of the King of France in 1793 ended any considerable English indulgence for the French Revolution. Execution of unsuccessful chiefs of state is not a procedure to which we give retrospective approval. But the Commonwealth nevertheless offered parallels to the American Revolution, and its precedents may well have had an unacknowledged influence, not only on the England of Locke, but on the America of Jefferson.

The power in Cromwell's England was the victorious army. Its principal officers, constituting the Council of the Officers on January 15, 1649, fifteen days before Charles was beheaded, approved a document known as the Agreement of the People.[4] This paper had been in the process of composition since October 1647.[5] It resembled in some respects a previous document produced by the Council of the Army in August 1647, called Heads of the Proposals,[6] containing the Army's earlier plan for the settlement of the kingdom. The Heads of the Proposals had contemplated a government with powers vested partly in a King, partly in Parliament; the draftsmen hoped that each would serve as a check on the other. By the time they settled on the final form of the Agreement of the People however, the Army's political theorists had turned against retention of the kingship; their problem was thus reduced to devising a check on possible parliamentary despotism. Like the Americans of 1787, the Puritan draftsmen turned to the idea of a written constitution predicated on the consent of the governed, which should control the Parliament.

The Agreement of the People, which in 1649 embodied this concept, was a sketch of a republican government, containing no reference to a King. The legislature, there called the "Representative," was to be supreme in most matters, but on its powers were six express "particulars" of limitation, making up a sort of Bill of Rights. There was a prohibition of a draft for military service abroad; there was a guaranty of immunity for those who had been anti-royalist partisans. There was to be no law impairing the obligation of public contract; no immunity by birth or privilege from subjection to law. There was to be no legislative "judgment upon any man's person or estate, where

---

[4] Gardiner, *Constitutional Documents of the Puritan Revolution, 1625–1660* (3rd ed.; Oxford: Oxford University Press, 1906) p. 359. Cited hereafter as Gardiner, *Documents,* 3rd ed.; see Gardiner, *History of the Great Civil War* (New York: Longmans, Green and Co., 1904–05) IV, p. 295.

[5] The evolution of the Agreement of the People is described by Gardiner in his *History of the Great Civil War,* III, Chapter IV.

[6] Gardiner, *Documents,* 3rd ed., pp. 316–326.

no law hath before provided . . .," and finally, the sixth Particular proclaimed,

> That no Representative [i.e. legislature] may in any wise render up, or give, or take away, any of the foundations of common right, liberty, and safety contained in this Agreement, nor level men's estates, destroy property, or make all things common and that, in all matters of such fundamental concernment there shall be a liberty to particular members of the said Representatives to enter their dissents from the major vote.

The Agreement of the People was not a naive document. It perceived perennial injustices of government, and recognized the indefinable nature of many of the public wrongs it undertook to renounce. The sixth "Particular" blends the ideas in the American due process clauses and in Dr. Bonham's Case,[7] curiously forecasting problems of constitutional theory which were still troublesome in the mid-twentieth century.[8]

The Agreement provided in detail for election of members of the new "Representative" by a broadened electorate, voting in reformed constituencies. This election was to be the people's acceptance of the proposed compact.

There was no provision for constitutional amendment. No mechanism was set up for rejecting unconstitutional statutes. There was a division of constitutional provisions; some were declared "fundamental to our common right, liberty, and safety."

> . . . Of the things expressed in this Agreement: the certain ending of this Parliament, as in the first Article; the equal or proportionable distribution of the number of the representers to be elected, as in the second; the certainty of the people's meeting to elect for Representatives biennial, and their freedom in elections; with the certainty of meeting, sitting and ending of Representatives so elected, as in the first and second particulars under the third Article; also the certainty of a number for passing a law or preparatory debates, provided for in the fourth Article; the matter of the fifth Article, concerning the Council of State, and of the sixth, concerning the calling, sitting and ending of Representatives extraordinary; also the power of Representatives to be, as in the eighth Article, and limited, as in the six reserves next following the same; likewise the second and third Par-

[7] 8 Co. Rep. 107, 118a Hill 7 Jacobi (1610). See page 61 above for a discussion of Bonham's Case.

[8] Compare the diverse views of the "natural law" content of the 14th Amendment due-process clause, emerging from the opinions of Justices Frankfurter and Black in *Adamson* v. *California* 332 U.S. 46 (1947) and *Rochin* v. *California*, 342 U.S. 165 (1952).

ticulars under the ninth Article concerning religion, and the whole matter of the tenth Article; all these we do account and declare to be fundamental to our common right, liberty, and safety: and therefore do both agree thereunto, and resolve to maintain the same, as God shall enable us.[9]

The rest of the provisions were, with less commitment, accounted only "useful and good for the public."

The Articles of Agreement never became effective in whole, but the Long Parliament (1640–1653) enacted parts as statutes. On February 13, 1649, the House of Commons appointed a Council of State;[10] nine days later, on February 22 the House drew up an "Engagement," to be taken by the councillors to defend Parliamentary resolutions for establishing a republic without King or House of Lords. On March 17, 1649 the Parliament abolished the office of King. Two days later it abolished the House of Lords and declared "the people of England, and of all the dominions and territories thereunto belonging" to be a Commonwealth and Free State, to be governed

. . . by the supreme authority of this nation, the representatives of the people in Parliament, and by such as they shall appoint and constitute as officers and ministers under them for the good of the people, and that without any King or House of Lords.

But Parliament delayed in launching the remainder of the new scheme of government, and in appointing a day for its own dissolution. The Army grew restless. On April 22, 1653 Cromwell as Lord General and his Council of Officers dissolved the Long Parliament;[11] in June 1653, he nominated and summoned an assembly nicknamed "the Barebones Parliament," or "Nomination Parliament," which on December 12, 1653 dissolved itself, leaving Cromwell in sole effective power. On December 16, 1653, Cromwell announced his intention to rule according to a constitutional document known as The Instrument of Government,[12] which named him Lord Protector for life.

[9] Gardiner, *Documents*, p. 270.

[10] Charles' execution had taken place two weeks before, on January 30, 1649. See for the documents here discussed Gardiner, *Documents*, Parts III, IV.

[11] Gardiner, *Documents*, p. 308. The Long Parliament had first met on November 7, 1640. *Ibid.*, Introduction, p. xxxi.

[12] Gardiner, *Documents*, p. 314. The procession from Heads of the Proposals to Instrument of Government is concisely described in Gardiner's *Documents*, Introduction, p. xlviii and following.

The Instrument of Government[13]

DECEMBER 16, 1653

The government of the Commonwealth of England, Scotland, and Ireland, and the dominions thereunto belonging.

I. That the supreme legislative authority of the Commonwealth of England, Scotland, and Ireland, and the dominions thereunto belonging, shall be and reside in one person, and the people assembled in Parliament: the style of which person shall be the Lord Protector of the Commonwealth of England, Scotland, and Ireland.

II. That the exercise of the chief magistracy and the administration of the government over the said countries and dominions, and the people thereof, shall be in the Lord Protector, assisted with a council, the number whereof shall not exceed twenty-one, nor be less than thirteen.

III. That all writs, processes, commissions, patents, grants, and other things, which now run in the name and style of the keepers of the liberty of England by authority of Parliament, shall run in the name and style of the Lord Protector, from whom for the future, shall be derived all magistracy and honours in these three nations; and have the power of pardons (except in case of murders and treason) and benefit of all forfeitures for the public use; and shall govern the said countries and dominions in all things by the advice of the council, and according to these presents and the laws.

IV. That the Lord Protector, the Parliament sitting, shall dispose and order the militia and forces, both by sea and land, for the peace and good of the three nations, by consent of Parliament; and that the Lord Protector, with the advice and consent of the major part of the council, shall dispose and order the militia for the ends aforesaid in the intervals of Parliament.

V. That the Lord Protector, by the advice aforesaid, shall direct in all things concerning the keeping and holding of a good correspondency with foreign kings, princes, and states; and also, with the consent of the major part of the council, have the power of war and peace.

VI. That the laws shall not be altered, suspended, abrogated, or repealed, nor any new law made, nor any tax, charge, or imposition laid upon the people, but by common consent in Parliament, save only as is expressed in the thirtieth article.

VII. That there shall be a Parliament summoned to meet at Westminster upon the third day of September, 1654, and that successively a Parliament shall be summoned once in every third year, to be accounted from the dissolution of the present Parliament.

[13] See for The Instrument of Government, Gardiner, *Documents*, p. 314.

VIII. That neither the Parliament to be next summoned, nor any successive Parliaments, shall, during the time of five months, to be accounted from the day of their first meeting, be adjourned, prorogued, or dissolved, without their own consent.

IX. That as well the next as all other successive Parliaments shall be summoned and elected in manner hereafter expressed; that is to say, the persons to be chosen within England, Wales, the Isles of Jersey, Guernsey, and the town of Berwick-upon-Tweed, to sit and serve in Parliament, shall be, and not exceed, the number of four hundred. The persons to be chosen within Scotland, to sit and serve in Parliament, shall be, and not exceed the number of thirty; and the persons to be chosen to sit in Parliament for Ireland shall be, and not exceed, the number of thirty.

X. That the persons to be elected to sit in Parliament from time to time, for the several counties of England, Wales, the Isles of Jersey and Guernsey, and the town of Berwick-upon-Tweed, and all places within the same respectively, shall be according to the proportions and numbers hereafter expressed: that is to say,

Bedfordshire	5
Bedford Town	1
Berkshire	5
Abingdon	1
Reading	1
Buckinghamshire	5
Buckingham Town	1

[Note:—The Instrument of Government listed 164 Counties and communities of England, Yorkshire (!) and Wales, dividing among them in stated numbers 400 seats in Parliament. The balance of the list is here omitted.]

The distribution of the persons to be chosen for Scotland and Ireland, and the several counties, cities, and places therein, shall be according to such proportions and number as shall be agreed upon and declared by the Lord Protector and the major part of the council, before the sending forth writs of summons for the next Parliament.

XI. That the summons to Parliament shall be by writ under the Great Seal of England, directed to the sheriffs of the several and respective counties, with such alteration as may suit with the present government, to be made by the Lord Protector and his council, which the Chancellor, Keeper, or Commissioners of the Great Seal shall seal, issue, and send abroad by warrant from the Lord Protector. If the Lord Protector shall not give warrant for issuing of writs of summons for the next Parliament, before the first of June, 1654, or for the Triennial Parliaments, before the first day of August in every third year, to be accounted as aforesaid; that then the Chancellor, Keeper, or Commissioners of the Great Seal for the time being, shall, without any warrant or direction, within seven days after the said first day of June, 1654, seal, issue, and send abroad writs of summons (changing therein what is to be changed as aforesaid) to the several and respective Sheriffs of England, Scotland and Ireland, for summoning the Parliament to meet at Westminster, the third day of September next; and shall likewise, within seven days after the said first day of August, in every third year, to be accounted from the dissolution of the precedent Parliament, seal, issue, and send forth abroad several writs of summons (changing therein what is to be changed) as aforesaid, for summoning the Parliament to meet at Westminster the sixth of November in that third year. That the said several and respective Sheriffs shall, within ten days after the receipt of such writ as aforesaid, cause the same to be proclaimed and published in every market-town within his county upon the market-days thereof, between twelve and three of the clock; and shall then also publish and declare the certain day of the week and month, for choosing members to serve in Parliament for the body of the said county, according to the tenor of the said writ, which shall be upon Wednesday five weeks after the date of the writ; and shall likewise declare the place where the election shall be made: for which purpose he shall appoint the most convenient place for the whole county to meet in; and shall send precepts for elections to be made in all and every city, town, borough, or place within his county, where elections are to be made by virtue of these presents, to the Mayor, Sheriff, or other head officer of such city, town, borough, or place, within three days after the receipt of such writ and writs; which the said Mayors, Sheriffs, and officers respectively are to make publication of, and of the certain day for such elections to be made in the said city, town, or place aforesaid, and to cause elections to be made accordingly.

XII. That at the day and place of elections, the Sheriff of each county, and the said Mayors, Sheriffs, Bailiffs, and other head officers within their cities, towns, boroughs, and places respectively, shall take view of the said elections, and shall make return into the chancery within twenty days after the said elections, of the persons elected by the greater number of electors, under their hands and seals, between him on the one part, and the electors on the other part; wherein shall be contained, that the persons elected shall not have power to alter the government as it is hereby settled in one single person and a Parliament.

XIII. That the Sheriff, who shall wittingly and willingly make any false return, or neglect his duty, shall incur the penalty of 2000 marks of lawful English money; the one moiety to the Lord Protector, and the other moiety to such person as will sue for the same.

XIV. That all and every person and persons, who have aided, advised, assisted, or abetted in any war against the Parliament, since the first day of January, 1641 (unless they have been since in the service of the Parliament, and given signal testimony of their good affection thereunto) shall be disabled and incapable to be elected, or to give any vote in the election of any members to serve in the next Parliament, or in the three succeeding Triennial Parliaments.

XV. That all such, who have advised, assisted, or abetted the rebellion of Ireland, shall be disabled and incapable for ever to be elected, or give any vote in the election of any member to serve in Parliament; as also all such who do or shall profess the Roman Catholic religion.

XVI. That all votes and elections given or made contrary, or not according to these qualifications, shall be null and void; and if any person, who is hereby made incapable, shall give his vote for election of members to serve in Parliament, such person shall lose and forfeit one full year's value of his real estate, and one full third part of his personal estate; one moiety thereof to the Lord Protector, and the other moiety to him or them who shall sue for the same.

XVII. That the persons who shall be elected to serve in Parliament, shall be such (and no other than such) as are persons of known integrity, fearing God, and of good conversation, and being of the age of twenty-one years.

XVIII. That all and every person and persons seised or possessed to his own use, of any estate, real or personal, to the value of 200 pounds, and not within the aforesaid exceptions, shall be capable to elect members to serve in Parliament for counties.

XIX. That the Chancellor, Keeper, or Commissioners of the Great Seal, shall be sworn before they enter into their offices, truly and faithfully to issue forth, and send abroad, writs of summons to Parliament, at the times and in the manner before expressed: and in case of neglect or failure to issue and send abroad writs accordingly, he or they shall for every such offence be guilty of high treason, and suffer the pains and penalties thereof.

XX. That in case writs be not issued out, as is before expressed, but that there be a neglect therein, fifteen days after the time wherein the same ought to be issued out by the Chancellor, Keeper, or Commissioners of the Great Seal; that then the Parliament shall, as often as such failure shall happen, assemble and be held at Westminster, in the usual place, at the times prefixed, in manner and by the means hereafter expressed; that is to say, that the Sheriffs of the several and respective counties, sheriffdoms, cities, boroughs and places aforesaid within England, Wales, Scotland, and Ireland, the Chancellor, Masters, and Scholars of the Universities of Oxford and Cambridge, and the Mayor and Bailiffs of the borough of Berwick-upon-Tweed, and other places aforesaid respectively, shall at the several courts and places to be appointed as aforesaid, within thirty days after the said fifteen days, cause such members to be chosen for their said several and respective counties, sheriffdoms, universities, cities, boroughs, and places aforesaid, by such persons, and in such manner, as if several and respective writs of summons to Parliament under the Great Seal had issued and been awarded according to the tenor aforesaid: that if the sheriff, or other persons authorised, shall neglect his or their duty herein, that all and every such sheriff and person authorised as aforesaid, so neglecting his or their duty, shall, for every such offence, be guilty of high treason, and shall suffer the pains and penalties thereof.

XXI. That the clerk, called the clerk of the Commonwealth in Chancery for the time being, and all others, who shall afterwards execute that office, to whom the returns shall be made, shall for the next Parliament, and the two succeeding triennial Parliaments, the next day after such return, certify the names of the several persons so returned, and of the places for which he and they were chosen respectively, unto the Council; who shall peruse the said returns, and examine whether the persons so elected and returned be such as is agreeable to the qualifications, and not disabled to be elected: and that every person and persons being so duly elected, and being approved of by the major part of the Council to be persons not disabled, but qualified as aforesaid, shall be esteemed a member of Parliament, and be admitted to sit in Parliament, and not otherwise.

XXII. That the persons so chosen and assembled in manner aforesaid, or any sixty of them, shall be, and be deemed the Parliament of England, Scotland, and Ireland; and the supreme legislative power to be and reside in the Lord Protector and such Parliament, in manner herein expressed.

XXIII. That the Lord Protector, with the advice of the major part of the Council, shall at any other time than is before expressed, when the necessities of the State shall require it, summon Parliaments in manner before expressed, which shall not be adjourned, prorogued, or dissolved without their own consent, during the first three months of their sitting. And in case of future war with any foreign State, a Parliament shall be forthwith summoned for their advice concerning the same.

XXIV. That all Bills agreed unto by the Parliament, shall be presented to the Lord Protector for his consent; and in case he shall not give his consent thereto within twenty days after they shall be presented to him, or give satisfaction to the Parliament within the time limited, that then, upon declaration of the Parliament that the Lord Protector hath not consented nor given satisfaction, such Bills shall pass into and become laws, although he shall not give his consent thereunto; provided such Bills contain nothing in them contrary to the matters contained in these presents.

XXV. That Henry Lawrence, Esq., . . . ,[14] or any seven of them, shall be a Council for the purposes expressed in this writing; and upon the death or other removal of any of them, the Parliament shall nominate six persons of ability, integrity, and fearing God, for every one that is dead or removed; out of which the major part of the Council shall elect two, and present them to the Lord Protector, of

[14] The names of fifteen members are given here.

which he shall elect one; and in case the Parliament shall not nominate within twenty days after notice given unto them thereof, the major part of the Council shall nominate three as aforesaid to the Lord Protector, who out of them shall supply the vacancy; and until this choice be made, the remaining part of the Council shall execute as fully in all things, as if their number were full. And in case of corruption, or other miscarriage in any of the Council in their trust, the Parliament shall appoint seven of their number, and the Council six, who, together with the Lord Chancellor, Lord Keeper, or Commissioners of the Great Seal for the time being, shall have power to hear and determine such corruption and miscarriage, and to award and inflict punishment, as the nature of the offence shall deserve, which punishment shall not be pardoned or remitted by the Lord Protector; and, in the interval of Parliaments, the major part of the Council, with the consent of the Lord Protector, may, for corruption or other miscarriage as aforesaid, suspend any of their number from the exercise of their trust, if they shall find it just, until the matter shall be heard and examined as aforesaid.

XXVI. That the Lord Protector and the major part of the Council aforesaid may, at any time before the meeting of the next Parliament, add to the Council such persons as they shall think fit, provided the number of the Council be not made thereby to exceed twenty-one, and the quorum to be proportioned accordingly by the Lord Protector and the major part of the Council.

XXVII. That a constant yearly revenue shall be raised, settled, and established for maintaining of 10,000 horse and dragoons, and 20,000 foot, in England, Scotland and Ireland, for the defence and security thereof, and also for a convenient number of ships for guarding of the seas; besides 200,000 pounds per annum for defraying the other necessary charges of administration of justice, and other expenses of the Government, which revenue shall be raised by the customs, and such other ways and means as shall be agreed upon by the Lord Protector and the Council, and shall not be taken away or diminished, nor the way agreed upon for raising the same altered, but by the consent of the Lord Protector and the Parliament.

XXVIII. That the said yearly revenue shall be paid into the public treasury, and shall be issued out for the uses aforesaid.

XXIX. That in case there shall not be cause hereafter to keep up so great a defence both at land or sea, but that there be an abatement made thereof, the money which will be saved thereby shall remain in bank for the public service, and not be employed to any other use but by consent of Parliament, or, in the intervals of Parliament, by the Lord Protector and major part of the Council.

XXX. That the raising of money for defraying the charge of the present extraordinary forces, both at sea and land, in respect of the present wars, shall be by consent of Parliament, and not otherwise: save only that the Lord Protector, with the consent of the major part of the Council, for preventing the disorders and dangers which might otherwise fall out both by sea and land, shall have power, until the meeting of the first Parliament, to raise money for the purposes aforesaid; and also to make laws and ordinances for the peace and welfare of these nations where it shall be necessary, which shall be binding and in force, until order shall be taken in Parliament concerning the same.

XXXI. That the lands, tenements, rents, royalties, jurisdictions and hereditaments which remain yet unsold or undisposed of, by Act or Ordinance of Parliament, belonging to the Commonwealth (except the forests and chases, and the honours and manors belonging to the same; the lands of the rebels in Ireland, lying in the four counties of Dublin, Cork, Kildare, and Carlow; the lands forfeited by the people of Scotland in the late wars, and also the lands of Papists and delinquents in England who have not yet compounded), shall be vested in the Lord Protector, to hold, to him and his successors, Lords Protectors of these nations, and shall not be alienated but by consent in Parliament. And all debts, fines, issues, amercements, penalties and profits, certain and casual, due to the Keepers of the liberties of England by authority of Parliament, shall be due to the Lord Protector, and be payable into his public receipt, and shall be recovered and prosecuted in his name.

XXXII. That the office of Lord Protector over these nations shall be elective and not hereditary; and upon the death of the Lord Protector, another fit person shall be forthwith elected to succeed him in the Government; which election shall be by the Council, who, immediately upon the death of the Lord Protector, shall assemble in the Chamber where they usually sit in Council; and having given notice to all their members of the cause of their assembling, shall, being thirteen at least present, proceed to the election; and, before they depart the said Chamber, shall elect a fit person to succeed in the Government, and forthwith cause proclamation thereof to be made in all the three nations as shall be requisite; and the person that they, or the major part of them, shall elect as aforesaid, shall be, and shall be taken to be, Lord Protector over these nations of England, Scotland and Ireland, and the dominions thereto belonging. Provided that none of the children of the late King, nor any of his line or family, be elected to be Lord Protector or other Chief Magistrate over these nations, or any of the dominions thereto belonging. And until the aforesaid election be past, the Council shall take care of the Government, and administer in all things as fully as the Lord Protector, or the Lord Protector and Council are enabled to do.

XXXIII. That Oliver Cromwell, Captain-General of the forces of England, Scotland and Ireland, shall be, and is hereby declared to be, Lord Protector of the Commonwealth of England, Scotland and Ireland, and the dominions thereto belonging, for his life.

XXXIV. That the Chancellor, Keeper or Commissioners of the Great

Seal, the Treasurer, Admiral, Chief Governors of Ireland and Scotland, and the Chief Justices of both the Benches, shall be chosen by the approbation of Parliament; and, in the intervals of Parliament, by the approbation of the major part of the Council, to be afterwards approved by the Parliament.

XXXV. That the Christian religion, as contained in the Scriptures, be held forth and recommended as the public profession of these nations; and that, as soon as may be, a provision, less subject to scruple and contention, and more certain than the present, be made for the encouragement and maintenance of able and painful teachers, for the instructing of the people, and for discovery and confutation of error, [t]hereby, and whatever is contrary to sound doctrine; and until such provision be made, the present maintenance shall not be taken away or impeached.

XXXVI. That to the public profession held forth none shall be compelled by penalties or otherwise; but that endeavours be used to win them by sound doctrine and the example of a good conversation.

XXXVII. That such as profess faith in God by Jesus Christ (though differing in judgment from the doctrine, worship or discipline publicly held forth) shall not be restrained from, but shall be protected in, the profession of the faith and exercise of their religion; so as they abuse not this liberty to the civil injury of others and to the actual disturbance of the public peace on their parts: provided this liberty be not extended to Popery or Prelacy, nor to such as, under the profession of Christ, hold forth and practise licentiousness.

XXXVIII. That all laws, statutes and ordinances, and clauses in any law, statute or ordinance to the contrary of the aforesaid liberty, shall be esteemed as null and void.

XXXIX. That the Acts and Ordinances of Parliament made for the sale or other disposition of the lands, rents and hereditaments of the late King, Queen, and Prince, of Archbishops and Bishops, &c., Deans and Chapters, the lands of delinquents and forest-lands, or any of them, or of any other lands, tenements, rents and hereditaments belonging to the Commonwealth, shall nowise be impeached or made invalid, but shall remain good and firm; and that the securities given by Act and Ordinance of Parliament for any sum or sums of money, by any of the said lands, the excise, or any other public revenue; and also the securities given by the public faith of the nation, and the engagement of the public faith for satisfaction of debts and damages, shall remain firm and good, and not be made void and invalid upon any pretence whatsoever.

XL. That the Articles given to or made with the enemy, and afterwards confirmed by Parliament, shall be performed and made good to the persons concerned therein; and that such appeals as were depending in the last Parliament for relief concerning bills of sale of delinquents' estates, may be heard and determined the next Parliament, any thing in this writing or otherwise to the contrary notwithstanding.

XLI. That every successive Lord Protector over these nations shall take and subscribe a solemn oath, in the presence of the Council, and such others as they shall call to them, that he will seek the peace, quiet and welfare of these nations, cause law and justice to be equally administered; and that he will not violate or infringe the matters and things contained in this writing, and in all other things will, to his power and to the best of his understanding, govern these nations according to the laws, statutes and customs thereof.

XLII. That each person of the Council shall, before they enter upon their trust, take and subscribe an oath, that they will be true and faithful in their trust, according to the best of their knowledge; and that in the election of every successive Lord Protector they shall proceed therein impartially, and do nothing therein for any promise, fear, favour or reward.

The Instrument of Government set up a constitutional régime with a unicameral legislature, with members elected for Counties by persons owning at least 200 pounds in real or personal property.[15] The single executive, in the first instance Cromwell, was called Lord Protector; after Cromwell the Protector was to be elected by a Council, which also had other important governing duties, particularly when Parliament was not in session.

The Instrument of Government could have given England a good rule. It failed of its purposes because of the unwillingness of the first Parliament summoned under it to work within its system.[16] The Parliament, instead, undertook to be a constituent as well as a legislative body, and brought forward new plans of its own. The last seven years of the Commonwealth were occupied with successive schemes of government, with futile debates on political theory, and with wrangles between Parliament and Army. Revival of a "Second House" proved an unsuccessful measure. Oliver Cromwell, who had refused a proffer of the title of King, died on September 3, 1658.[17] His son Richard, acknowledged as Protector by the Army, proved an insignificant figure. Army factions took arms against each other. The residue

---

[15] P. xviii. The Boroughs were to continue their representation as it was, varying *inter sese*. See S. R. Gardiner, *Documents*, Introduction pp. lvi, lvii.

[16] This estimate is S. R. Gardiner's. "It was not, however, in consequence of its merits or demerits as a constitutional settlement that the Instrument of Government failed. It broke down because the first Parliament summoned under it refused to acknowledge its binding force, and claimed to be a constituent as well as a legislative body." See his *Documents*, Introduction, p. lx. And see Sir D. Lindsay Keir, *The Constitutional History of Modern Britain*, (3rd ed.; London: A. and C. Black, 1946) pp. 222–229.

[17] See generally Professor C. H. Firth's, *The Last Years of the Protectorate, 1656–1658* (London: Longmans, Green and Co., 1909) for a scholarly continuation of S. R. Gardiner's *History of the Commonwealth and Protectorate*.

or "rump" of the Long Parliament revived. In this chaos England felt the need for traditional royal rule. General Monk, commanding a force in Scotland, marched into England, sent an emissary to Holland to negotiate with Charles II and on April 4, 1660, obtained from Charles the Declaration of Breda[18] in which he promised, with certain exceptions, freedom of conscience and pardon for revolutionary offenses,

> . . . desiring and ordaining that henceforth all notes of discord, separation and difference of parties be utterly abolished among all our subjects, whom we invite and conjure to a perfect union among themselves, under our protection, for the re-settlement of our just rights and theirs in a free Parliament, by which, upon the word of a King, we will be advised.

A "Convention Parliament," elected without the king's writ, restored Charles to the throne in May 1660; in theory his kingship dated from the death of Charles I. Monk was made Duke of Albemarle; he determined with Charles' assent to leave the details of the restoration to a free Parliament. Despite a proclamation by the restored King that he held the throne by inherent birthright, "the Restoration was from the first a restoration of parliamentary monarchy rather than of personal government."[19]

[18] S. R. Gardiner, *Documents*, p. 351.
[19] C. H. Firth, "Anarchy and the Restoration, 1659–60," *Cambridge Modern History* (New York: Macmillan, 1908) IV, p. 559; see also the introduction to Gardiner's *Documents*, and W. A. Shaw, "The Commonwealth and the Protectorate," *Cambridge Modern History* (New York: Macmillan, 1908) IV, chapter XV; F. W. Maitland's *Constitutional History of England* (Cambridge: Cambridge University Press, 1909) p. 282, discusses the constitutional theory of the Restoration, under which various governmental acts during the revolutionary period were ignored as void.

6. THE "GLORIOUS REVOLUTION OF 1688" AND THE ENGLISH BILL OF RIGHTS

THE RETURN OF Charles II gave great satisfaction to the people of England; they were tired of revolution and regimental rule, and as Charles ·rode from Dover to Whitehall, where the parliamentarians had beheaded his father, village girls strewed flowers in his path. But the nation which had tried and executed one king could never think of another in quite the same way as before. Any later English king who wished to keep his throne would have to be careful to keep reasonably within the limits of the Constitution.[1] The restoration Parliament, no subservient body, was quite ready to pass measures opposed to known royal desires. The political traditions of puritanism still lived among the London nonconformists and in the other towns, and here were the materials for a Whig party, with aristocratic leaders but with democratic composition, which was to prove capable of political opposition.[2] The Habeas Corpus Act of 1679 made it impossible to keep a political opponent of the King indefinitely in prison; it was passed chiefly through the efforts of the Earl of Shaftesbury, the Whig leader. When Charles died in 1685, his brother, the Duke of York,[3] succeeded him as James II. Religious feelings ran high, as James was a Roman Catholic. By "Declarations of Indulgence," royal decrees issued in 1687 and 1688, James purported to suspend the operation of statutory

---

[1] F. C. Montague, *Elements of English Constitutional History* (London: Longmans, Green and Co., 1894) p. 135.

[2] Sir D. L. Keir, *Constitutional History of Modern Britain* (3rd ed.; London: A. and C. Black, 1946) p. 243.

[3] New York land titles derive from a grant by Charles II, in 1664, to "our dearest Brother James Duke of Yorke," for whom the State is named.

disabilities on Catholics and nonconformist Protestants, and so to open their way to governmental preferment. Such decrees, abrogating parliamentary enactments, amounted to royal assertions that the law did not bind the King; that the King could in effect repeal parliamentary legislation. The first Declaration of Indulgence was bitterly resented, and resentment grew still hotter when James issued a royal order that the second Declaration of Indulgence should be read aloud in every church in the Kingdom. The Archbishop of Canterbury and six bishops signed a petition to the King remonstrating against the order, whereupon James directed that the petitioners be prosecuted for seditious libel. Their trial is the celebrated "Case of the Seven Bishops."[4]

The accused bishops were popular. Michael Arnold, royal brewer, when drawn for the jury uttered a famous complaint. "Whatever I do," said he, "I am sure to be half ruined. If I say 'not guilty' I shall brew no more for the King; if I say 'guilty' I shall brew no more for anybody else." The unhappy brewer held out all night for conviction, but finally joined the rest of the jurors in a verdict for acquittal.[5] At this victory of the bishops, Lord Halifax waved his hat in the face of the Court like a schoolboy, and the exulting people of London cheered around bonfires in the streets.

James' daughter, Mary, a zealous Protestant, was the wife of William, Prince of Orange. English Protestants hoped that she would succeed to the throne when James should come to die. But in 1688 a son was born to James, a Catholic male heir ready for the throne, and hope waned that by inheritance Mary would succeed on James' death. A group of prominent Englishmen wrote to the Protestant Prince of Orange inviting him to come to England. William accepted and landed with an army. James attempted to escape to France, dropping the Great Seal in the Thames as he went. To William's embarrassment some fishermen of Sheerness recognized the fugitive Stuart and brought him back to London. The Prince of Orange wisely afforded James a welcome opportunity to escape again, this time successfully, making plausible the contention that when he left the kingdom for France, James abdicated of his own accord. So within forty years England got rid of two Stuart kings, the first by a headsman, the second by a sort of exile.

---

[4] 3 Mod 212 (1688).

[5] 87 English Rep. 136, 12 How St., Tr. 183; See 12 How St. Tr. 201 and Macaulay, *History of England* (London: Longmans, Green and Co., 1862); H. W. V. Temperley, "The Revolution and the Revolution Settlement in England," *Cambridge Modern History*, V, p. 242. The question of jurors who are government servants appears in *U.S. v. Wood*, 299 U.S. 123 (1937), *Frazier v. U.S.*, 335 U.S. 497 (1949) and *Dennis v. U.S.*, 339 U.S. 162 (1950).

William, on the advice of an assembly of peers, of former members of the Commons, and others, summoned a Convention,[6] which on February 13, 1688/9, passed a Declaration of Right reciting James' abdication and condemning as unlawful the principal acts by which he had offended England. The Convention tendered the crown to William and Mary, which they accepted, so accomplishing the "Glorious Revolution of 1688."[7] The Convention turned itself into a Parliament on February 24, 1688/9, and on December 16, 1689, repassed the Declaration of Right, somewhat redrafted, as the Bill of Rights. The Bill of Rights, with the Magna Carta of 1215 and the Petition of Right of 1628 is one of the three great documents of British Constitutional Liberty.[8]

Sessio Secunda
Anno Regni *Gulielmi & Mariae* primo

CAP. II. DECEMBER 16, 1689

An act for declaring the rights and liberties of the subject, and settling the succession of the crown.

WHEREAS the lords spiritual and temporal, and commons, assembled at Westminster, lawfully, fully, and freely representing all the estates of the people of this realm, did upon the thirteenth day of February, in the year of our Lord one thousand six hundred eighty eight, present unto their Majesties, then called and known by the names and stile of William and Mary, prince and princess of Orange, being present in their proper persons, a certain declaration in writing, made by the said lords and commons, in the words following; viz.

WHEREAS the late King James the Second, by the assistance of divers evil counsellors, judges, and ministers employed by him, did endeavour to subvert and extirpate the protestant religion, and the laws and liberties of this kingdom.

1. By assuming and exercising a power of dispensing with and sus-

---

[6] T. C. Hansard, *Parliamentary History of England* (London: Hansard, 1809) V, p. 24.

[7] See F. W. Maitland, *Constitutional History of England* (Cambridge: Cambridge University Press, 1909) p. 283 *et seq.* for a discussion of the revolutionary character of these events.

[8] Should I have mentioned four, counting as the fourth the Act of Union with Scotland in 1607? My Scots friends might say so; and might point to the opinion of Lord President Cooper in *MacCormick* v. *Lord Advocate*, 1953 Session Cases 364, which suggests the possibility that in a proper case the Act of Union would prevail over an Act of Parliament inconsistent with it.

pending of laws, and the execution of laws, without consent of parliament.

2. By committing and prosecuting divers worthy prelates, for humbly petitioning to be excused from concurring to the said assumed power.

3. By issuing and causing to be executed a commission under the great seal for erecting a court called, *The court of Commissioners for ecclesiastical causes.*

4. By levying money for and to the use of the crown, by pretence of prerogative, for other time, and in other manner, than the same was granted by parliament.

5. By raising and keeping a standing army within this kingdom in time of peace, without consent of parliament, and quartering soldiers contrary to law.

6. By causing several good subjects, being protestants, to be disarmed, at the same time when papists were both armed and employed, contrary to law.

7. By violating the freedom of election of members to serve in parliament.

8. By prosecutions in the court of King's bench, for matters and causes cognizable only in parliament; and by divers other arbitrary and illegal courses.

9. And whereas of late years, partial, corrupt, and unqualified persons have been returned and served on juries in trials, and particularly divers jurors in trials for high treason, which were not freeholders.

10. And excessive bail hath been required of persons committed in criminal cases, to elude the benefit of the laws made for the liberty of the subjects.

11. And excessive fines have been imposed; and illegal and cruel punishments inflicted.

12. And several grants and promises made of fines and forfeitures, before any conviction or judgment against the persons, upon whom the same were to be levied.

All which are utterly and directly contrary to the known laws and statutes, and freedom of this realm.

And whereas the said late King James the Second having abdicated the government, and the throne being thereby vacant, his highness the prince of Orange (whom it hath pleased Almighty God to make the glorious instrument of delivering this kingdom from popery and arbitrary power) did (by the advice of the lords spiritual and temporal, and divers principal persons of the commons) cause letters to be written to the lords spiritual and temporal, being protestants; and other letters to the several counties, cities, universities, boroughs, and cinque-ports, for the choosing of such persons to represent them, as were of right to be sent to parliament, to meet and sit at Westminster upon the two and twentieth day of January, in this year one thousand six hundred eighty and eight, in order to such an establishment, as that their religion, laws, and liberties might not again be in danger of being subverted: upon which letters, elections have been accordingly made,

And thereupon the said lords spiritual and temporal, and commons, pursuant to their respective letters and elections, being now assembled in a full and free representative of this nation, taking into their most serious consideration the best means for attaining the ends aforesaid; do in the first place (as their ancestors in like case have usually done) for the vindicating and asserting their ancient rights and liberties, declare;

1. That the pretended power of suspending of laws, or the execution of laws, by regal authority, without consent of parliament, is illegal.

2. That the pretended power of dispensing with laws, or the execution of laws, by regal authority, as it hath been assumed and exercised of late, is illegal.

3. That the commission for erecting the late court of commissioners for ecclesiastical causes, and all other commissions and courts of like nature are illegal and pernicious.

4. That levying money for or to the use of the crown, by pretence of prerogative, without grant of parliament, for longer time, or in other manner than the same is or shall be granted, is illegal.

5. That it is the right of the subjects to petition the King, and all committments and prosecutions of such petitioning are illegal.

6. That the raising or keeping a standing army within the kingdom in time of peace, unless it be with consent of parliament, is against law.

7. That the subjects which are protestants, may have arms for their defense suitable to their conditions, and as allowed by law.

8. That election of members of parliament ought to be free.

9. That the freedom of speech, and debates or proceedings in parliament, ought not to be impeached or questioned in any court or place out of parliament.

10. That excessive bail ought not to be required, nor excessive fines imposed; nor cruel and unusual punishments inflicted.

11. That jurors ought to be duly impanelled and returned, and jurors which pass upon men in trials for high treason ought to be freeholders.

12. That all grants and promises of fines and forfeitures of particular persons before conviction, are illegal and void.

13. And that for redress of all grievances, and for the amending, strengthening, and preserving of the laws, parliaments ought to be held frequently.

And they do claim, demand, and insist upon all and singular the premises, as their undoubted rights and liberties; and that no declarations, judgments, doings or proceedings, to the prejudice of the people in any of the said premises, ought in any wise to be drawn hereafter into consequence or example.

To which demand of their rights they are particularly encouraged by the declaration of his highness the prince of Orange, as being the only means for obtaining a full redress and remedy therein.

Having therefore an entire confidence, That his said highness the prince of Orange will perfect the deliverance so far advanced by him, and will still preserve them from the violation of their rights, which they have here asserted, and from all other attempts upon their religion, rights, and liberties.

II. The said lords spiritual and temporal, and commons, assembled at Westminster, do resolve, That William and Mary prince and princess of Orange be, and be declared, King and Queen of England, France and Ireland, and the dominions thereunto belonging, to hold the crown and royal dignity of the said kingdoms and dominions to them the said prince and princess during their lives, and the life of the survivor of them; and that the sole and full exercise of the regal power be only in, and executed by the said prince of Orange, in the names of the said prince and princess, during their joint lives; and after their deceases, and said crown and royal dignity of the said kingdoms and dominions to be to the heirs of the body of the said princess; and for the default of such issue to the princess Anne of Denmark, and the heirs of her body; and for default of such issue to the heirs of the body of the said prince of Orange. And the lords spiritual and temporal, and commons, do pray the said prince and princess to accept the same accordingly.

III. And that the oaths hereafter mentioned be taken by all persons of whom the oaths of allegiance and supremacy might be required by law, instead of them; and that the said oaths of allegiance and supremacy be abrogated.

I A.B. do sincerely promise and swear, That I will be faithful, and bear true allegiance, to their Majesties King William and Queen Mary:
So help me God.

I A.B. do swear, That I do from my heart abhor, detest, and abjure as impious and heretical, that damnable doctrine and position, That princes excommunicated or deprived by the pope, or any authority of the see of Rome, may be deposed or murdered by their subjects, or any other whatsoever. And I do declare, That no foreign prince, person, prelate, state, or potentate hath, or ought to have any jurisdiction, power, superiority, pre-eminence, or authority ecclesiastical or spiritual, within this realm:
So help me God.

IV. Upon which their said Majesties did accept the crown and royal dignity of the kingdoms of England, France, and Ireland, and the dominions thereunto belonging, according to the resolution and desire of the said lords and commons contained in the said declaration.

V. And thereupon their Majesties were pleased, That the said lords spiritual and temporal, and commons, being the two houses of parliament, should continue to sit, and with their Majesties royal concurrence make effectual provision for the settlement of the religion, laws and liberties of this kingdom, so that the same for the future might not be in danger again of being subverted; to which the said lords spiritual and temporal, and commons, did agree and proceed to act accordingly.

VI. Now in pursuance of the premises, the said lords spiritual and temporal, and commons, in parliament assembled, for the ratifying, confirming and establishing the said declaration, and the articles, clauses, matters, and things therein contained, by the force of a law made in due form by authority of parliament, do pray that it may be declared and enacted, That all and singular the rights and liberties asserted and claimed in the said declaration, are the true, ancient, and indubitable rights and liberties of the people of this kingdom, and so shall be esteemed, allowed, adjudged, deemed, and taken to be, and that all and every the particulars aforesaid shall be firmly and strictly holden and observed, as they are expressed in the said declaration; and all officers and ministers whatsoever shall serve their Majesties and their successors according to the same in all times to come.

VII. And the said lords spiritual and temporal, and commons, seriously considering how it hath pleased Almighty God, in his marvellous providence, and merciful goodness to this nation, to provide and preserve their said Majesties royal persons most happily to reign over us upon the throne of their ancestors, for which they render unto him from the bottom of their hearts their humblest thanks and praises, do truly, firmly, assuredly, and in the sincerity of their hearts think, and do hereby recognize, acknowledge and declare, That King James the Second having abdicated the government, and their Majesties having accepted the crown and royal dignity as aforesaid, their said Majesties did become, were, are, and of right ought to be, by the laws of this realm, our sovereign liege lord and lady, King and Queen of England, France, and Ireland, and the dominions thereunto belonging, in and to whose princely persons the royal state, crown, and dignity of the said realms, with all honours, stiles, titles, regalities, prerogatives, powers, jurisdictions and authorities to the same belonging and appertaining, are most fully, rightfully, and intirely invested and incorporated, united and annexed.

VIII. And for preventing all questions and divisions in this realm, by reason of any pretended titles to the crown, and for preserving a certainty in the succession thereof, in and upon which the unity, peace, tranquillity, and safety of this nation doth, under God, wholly consist and depend, The said lords spiritual and temporal, and commons, do beseech their Majesties that it may be enacted, established and declared, That the crown and regal government of the said kingdoms and dominions, with all and singular the premisses thereunto belonging and appertaining, shall be and continue to their said Majesties, and the survivor of them, during their lives, and the life of the survivor of them: And that the intire, perfect, and full exercise of the regal power and government be only in, and executed by his Majesty, in the names of both their Majesties during their joint lives; and after their deceases the said crown and premisses shall be and remain to the heirs of the body of her Majesty; and for default of such issue, to her royal highness the princess Anne of Denmark, and the heirs of her body; and for default of such issue, to the heirs of the body of his said Majesty: And thereunto the said lords spiritual and temporal, and commons, do, in the name of all the people aforesaid, most humbly and faithfully submit themselves, their heirs and posterities for ever; and do faithfully promise, That they will stand to, maintain, and defend their said Majesties, and also the limitation and succession of the crown herein specified and contained, to the utmost of their powers, with their lives and estates, against all persons whatsoever, that shall attempt any thing to the contrary.

IX. And whereas it hath been found by experience, that it is inconsistent with the safety and welfare of this protestant kingdom, to be governed by a popish prince, or by any King or Queen marrying a papist; the said lords spiritual and temporal, and commons, do further pray that it may be enacted, That all and every person and persons that is, are or shall be reconciled to, or shall hold communion with, the see or church of Rome, or shall profess the popish religion, or shall marry a papist, shall be excluded, and be for ever incapable to inherit, possess, or enjoy the crown and government of this realm, and Ireland, and the dominions thereunto belonging, or any part of the same, or to have, use, or exercise any regal power, authority, or jurisdiction within the same; and in all and every such case or cases the people of these realms shall be, and are hereby absolved of their allegiance; and the said crown and government shall from time to time descend to, and be enjoyed by such person or persons, being protestants, as should have inherited and enjoyed the same, in case the said person or persons so reconciled, holding communion, or professing, or marrying as aforesaid, were naturally dead.

X. And that every King and Queen of this realm, who at any time hereafter shall come to and succeed in the imperial crown of this kingdom, shall on the first day of the meeting of the first parliament, next after his or her coming to the crown, sitting in his or her throne in the house of peers, in the presence of the lords and commons therein assembled, or at his or her coronation, before such person or persons who shall administer the coronation oath to him or her, at the time of his or her taking the said oath (which shall first happen) make, subscribe, and audibly repeat the declaration mentioned in the statute made in the thirtieth year of the reign of King Charles the Second, intituled, An act for the more effectual preserving the King's person and government, by disabling papists from sitting in either house of Parliament. But if it shall happen, that such King or Queen, upon his or her succession to the crown of this realm, shall be under the age of twelve years, then every such King or Queen shall make, subscribe, and audibly repeat the said declaration at his or her coronation, or the first day of the meeting of the first parliament as aforesaid, which shall first happen after such King or Queen shall have attained the said age of twelve years.

XI. All which their Majesties are contented and pleased shall be declared, enacted, and established by authority of this present parliament, and shall stand, remain, and be the law of this realm for ever; and the same are by their said Majesties, by and with the advice and consent of the lords spiritual and temporal, and commons, in parliament assembled, and by the authority of the same, declared, enacted, and established accordingly.

XII. And be it further declared and enacted by the authority aforesaid, That from and after this present session of parliament, no dispensation by *non obstante* of or to any statute, or any part thereof, shall be allowed, but that the same shall be held void and of no effect, except a dispensation be allowed of in such statute, and except in such cases as shall be specially provided for by one or more bill or bills to be passed during this present session of parliament.

XIII. Provided that no charter, or grant, or pardon, granted before the three and twentieth day of October, in the year of our Lord one thousand six hundred eighty nine shall be any ways impeached or invalidated by this act, but that the same shall be and remain of the same force and effect in law, and no other than as if this act had never been made.[9]

The Bill of Rights, like the Petition of Right, suggests by its form the Declaration of Independence. Like the Declaration of Independence, the Bill of Rights is a recital of termination of one government and the establishment of another. As in the Declaration, there is first a recital of grievances, followed by the dispositive part of the document.

Some clauses of the Bill of Rights of 1688 strikingly suggest the provisions of the American Bill of Rights of 1791. The right of petition in Clause 5 is echoed in the First Amendment. The restriction, in Clause 6, on keeping a standing army in time of peace unless by parliamentary consent suggests Article 1, Section 8, Clause 12 of United States Constitution, limiting appropriations of money to support an army to two-year terms. The allowance of arms to Protestant subjects suggests the Second Amendment. It somewhat ominously suggests Madison's argument in the 46th Federalist Paper that state militia

---

[9] Pickering, *Statutes at Large, 1 Will. & Mary to 8 Will. 3* (Cambridge: Bentham, Printer to the University, 1764) IX, pp. 67–73.

would be an effective defense against tyranny attempted by the federal government and by its regular standing army. The idea of equipping the people of England, or the several American States with arms for resistance to their government, is enough to make today's Englishman or American feel properly horrified. In 1688, when the last Stuart king had just been sent on his travels, this appeared in quite a different light. Hamilton and Madison evidently thought it would appeal to the people of the United States, who were jealous of the central government proposed for them by the convention of 1787.

Free speech in Parliament guaranteed by Clause 9 of the Bill of Rights is reflected in Article 1, Section 6 of the federal Constitution. The 10th clause of the English Bill of Rights concerning excessive bail, fines, and punishments is reproduced almost word for word in the Eighth Amendment to the United States Constitution, a fact sufficient in itself to demonstrate that the draftsmen of 1789 remembered what was known in England as the Glorious Revolution of 1688.

The Bill of Rights of 1689 decided in the people's favor all the principal issues which Parliament had contested against the Stuarts. After 1688, parliamentary leaders were the governors of England. They governed in the forms and with the phrases of monarchial rule, but the power was theirs; after 1688 whatever influence a king exerted on the course of English policy, he accomplished through persuasion of the Parliament. Parliament could be influenced; but even kings knew where lay the ultimate mastery.[10]

[10] See the eloquent fifteenth and sixteenth chapters of Hallam's *Constitutional History of England* (London: J. Murray, 1827).

7. CONSTITUTIONAL
THEORY: 1688

THE REVOLUTION OF 1688 marks at once a resting-place and a new
departure in the story of English constitutionalism. Magna Carta;
valiant resistance by Coke and Commons against Stuart absolutism;
the Commonwealth's tragedy and aspiration; Restoration and its invited King; the Glorious Revolution which dismissed one king and
accepted his two successors only on their

> . . . distinct and solemn assertion of the fundamental principles of the
> constitution and of the ancient franchises of the English nation; so
> that the right of king to his crown and of the people to their liberties
> might rest upon one and the same title-deed,[1]

all these are part of the constitutional tradition held in common by
the people of the British Commonwealth and by the people of the
United States.

This book is primarily an account of the constitutional theory of
the United States; and after 1688 our constitutional theory developed
on the western side of the Atlantic. 1688 is a good moment for a survey
of the ground. The Thirteen Colonies in 1775 chose to take the

---

[1] The quoted words are from Taswell-Langmead's *English Constitutional History*
(9th ed.; London: Sweet and Maxwell, 1929) pp. 596–597. At the risk of boring,
one reminds American readers that the same word often has different overtones
for different users, and that when an Englishman speaks of "the Constitution" he
thinks of his system of government as established by long and respected usage.
The functions of the Supreme Court of the United States as arbiter of the conformity, *vel non*, of federal legislation with the written Constitution; and as arbiter
of the relation of the States to the federal government and to one another, which
come to an American's mind when he speaks of "Constitutional Law," are not
apt to be in the Englishman's thoughts when he uses the same words.

Glorious Revolution as a theoretical precedent for their own self-determination. As nations measure time, the move for American independence came not long after the accession of William and Mary. A man born before James' dismissal by his disaffected subjects, could have greeted the American Declaration of Independence at the age of eighty-eight.[2] John Locke's *Second Treatise of Government, an Essay Concerning the True Original, Extent, and End of Civil Government* probably written during several years ending in 1689[3] gave a satisfying sense of legality to many of those Englishmen who had turned out James Stuart and in his place put William and Mary. Eighty-eight years after, read in a new continent by later men, Locke's book served to furnish Thomas Jefferson with much of the theory, and even with some of the phrases, of the Declaration of Independence. As this review turns to American matter, then, the English Revolution of 1688 invites appraisal of English constitutional theory at the moment when the Prince of Orange and his consort came to the throne. What was the status in 1689 of those premises which underlie today's American constitutionalism? Of majoritarian rule? Of the higher law? Of the equality of man? Of the diffusion of governmental power the better to secure liberty? Of the reduction of the fundamentals of government to a great, senior writing, immune from hasty, intemperate change?

Here Locke tempts the analyst. The significant fact concerning his Second Treatise is less the purpose of its author than the acceptance of his work, the use made of it by others. Magna Carta has had a comparable history; it was not written to help the opponents of James I and Charles I; but in time it served Coke well.

And in a true sense the Revolution of 1688 did not occur only in 1688. Great political episodes are not instantaneous; they develop through considerable spans of time; they consist of changes in the thinking of many men; they grow in volume; acceptance is slower than

[2] The first Earl of Bathurst was born in 1684 and died in 1775. Burke, in his Conciliation speech told the Commons that a farsighted angel might have said to Bathurst in 1704, "Young man, there is America, which at this day serves for little more than to amuse you with stories of savage men and uncouth manners, yet shall, before you taste of death, show itself equal to the whole of that commerce which now attracts the envy of the world. Whatever England has been growing to by a progressive increase of improvement, brought in by varieties of people, by succession of civilizing conquests and civilizing settlements in a series of seventeen hundred years, you shall see as much added to her by America in the course of a single life!"

[3] The textually inexpert has no business attempting judgment of the time when Locke wrote; I here rely on the fourth chapter of Peter Laslett's scholarly edition of the *Two Treatises of Government* (Cambridge: Cambridge University Press, 1960).

crisis. Political advocacy is bilateral; it includes not only the advocate but also the one who is persuaded. The Second Treatise was a process as well as a publication.

Locke's book, by acceptance in two great episodes of constitution-making,[4] one on each side of the Atlantic, has acquired a mystique of its own. To take it as a statement of English theory in 1688 would be easy and satisfying. But a *pièce justificative* is rarely a reliable source of observed political fact. Locke's book can properly stand for what a number of people (one can not say how many) probably liked to persuade themselves was English constitutionalism at and shortly after the time of the Glorious Revolution. What the greater part of the governing people in England actually considered a just frame of government one can only guess. The Anglo-American habit of government is distrustful of theory; we are practical rather than doctrinaire. The common-law tradition of deciding each case only as it arises extends far beyond the technique of the judiciary. We develop our constitutions piecemeal, political case by political case. No matter what John Locke says, he does not clearly demonstrate what a majority of those who in his day reconstituted their governmental structure thought a proper relation between government and the governed. The best evidence of what they thought is not any treatise; the best evidence is what they did.

Government by consent of the governed was a theory Locke clearly stated and in 1788 the exchange of an unwelcome king for two other more acceptable monarchs was evidently a transaction which would not have occurred unless the people in effective control of English politics had so willed it. "Of the Beginning of Political Societies" Locke wrote in his eighth chapter of his Second Treatise,

> Men being, as has been said, by Nature, all free, equal, and inde-
> pendent, no one can be put out of this Estate, and subjected to the
> Political Power of another, without his own Consent. The only Way
> whereby any one devests himself of his Natural Liberty, and puts on
> the Bonds of Civil Society is by agreeing with other Men to joyn and
> unite into a Community, for their comfortable, safe, and peaceable
> Living one amongst another, in a secure Enjoyment of their Properties,
> and a greater Security against any, that are not of it. This any num-
> ber of Men may do, because it injures not the Freedom of the rest;
> they are left as they were in the Liberty of the state of Nature. When
> any number of Men have so consented to make one Community or
> Government, they are thereby presently incorporated, and make one

[4] This statement was phrased with care, and in the light of Peter Laslett's statement in the foreword to his 1960 edition, "Locke did not write in 1689 to justify the Revolution of 1688."

Body politick, wherein the Majority have a Right to act and conclude the rest.[5]

There were in this explanation certain small difficulties. For one thing, comparatively few men sign articles of membership in a Commonwealth. In place of express consent, Locke posits tacit consent,

> And thus the Consent of Freemen, born under Government, which only makes them Members of it, being given separately in their Turns, as each comes to be of Age, and not in a Multitude together; People take no Notice of it, and thinking it not done at all,[6] or not necessary, conclude they are naturally Subjects as they are Men.[7]

And why should a majority have constitutional power to bind, by majority consent, a non-consenting minority? This the theoretician of the Glorious Revolution explains satisfactorily, at least to a ruling majority, by reference to the necessities of practical existence and the Law of Nature and Reason,

> For when any number of Men have, by the consent of every individual, made a Community, they have thereby made that Community one Body, with a Power to act as one Body, which is only by the will and determination of the Majority. For that which acts any Community, being only the consent of the individuals of it, and it being necessary to that which is one Body to move one way; it is necessary the Body should move that way whither the greater force carries it, which is the consent of the Majority: Or else it is impossible it should act or continue one Body, one Community, which the consent of every individual that united into it, agreed that it should; and so every one is bound by that consent to be concluded by the Majority.[8]

Majority rule, he reasons, obtains in assemblies generally by that useful norm, the Law of Nature and Reason,

> . . . the Act of the Majority passes for the Act of the whole, and of course determines, as having by the Law of Nature and Reason, the Power of the whole.[9]

But in 1688 some further theory was required to justify James' *congé*. The English people had already "consented" to the restored

[5] Chapter VIII, Section 95.

[6] One hesitates to write an irreverent footnote to John Locke; but is there not something odd about a consent given by one who takes no notice of the giving and thinks it not done at all? Would it be too obvious to suggest that, consent or not, a national state must of necessity treat those under it, of all ages, as if they had consented?

[7] Chapter VIII, Section 117.

[8] Chapter VIII, Section 96.

[9] *Ibid.*

Stuarts in 1660. Must consent to be governed, once given, be irrevocable? Legitimists felt as much intellectual necessity for a theory to justify the dismissal of the last Stuart, as they did for the call to William and Mary. To explain the retraction of once-granted governing power they could find a formula as good as another in Locke's chapter "Of the Dissolution of Government,"

> . . . The Power that every Individual gave the Society, when he entered into it, can never revert to the Individuals again, as long as the Society lasts, but will always remain in the Community; because without this, there can be no Community, no Commonwealth, which is contrary to the original Agreement: So also when the Society hath placed the Legislative in any Assembly of Men, to continue in them and their Successors, with Direction and Authority for providing such Successors, the Legislative can never revert to the People whilst that Government lasts: Because having provided a Legislative with Power to continue for ever, they have given up their Political Power to the Legislative, and cannot resume it. But if they have set Limits to the Duration of their Legislative, and made this supreme Power in any Person, or Assembly, only temporary: Or else, when by the Miscarriages of those in Authority, it is forfeited; upon the Forfeiture, or at the Determination of the Time set, it reverts to the Society, and the People have a Right to act as Supreme, and continue the Legislative in themselves; or erect a new Form, or under the old Form place it in new Hands, as they think good.[10]

There is, to be sure, the matter of prescribing a means of deciding between the undoubtedly differing views, entertained by ruler and ruled, as to the ruler's miscarriages in authority and consequent forfeiture of his rule. Few rulers, be they princes or modern politicians, consider that their ways have been anti-social, or evil. "I have no wish but the prosperity of my dominions"; said George III, aggrieved by the Opposition in 1782, "therefore, must look upon all who would not heartily assist me as bad men, as well as ungrateful subjects."[11]

How resolve this impasse between the ruler who feels himself righteous and the ruled who feel themselves outraged? Locke, theorizing on Dissolution of Government, has small trouble. "The People" are to decide, and Locke does not tarry to explain who constitute the deciding people; nor the arrangements for ascertaining their desires,

[10] Chapter VIII, Section 96.

[11] The statement is found in a reprint of some autograph notes of George III appended by Lord Brougham to his biographical sketch of Lord North; *Works* (Edinburgh: A. and C. Black, 1872–73) III, p. 164. Thackeray, quoting this statement in *The Four Georges* (New York: Doubleday-Dolphin, n.d.) follows it by a paraphrase: "I wish nothing but good, therefore every man who does not agree with me is a traitor and a scoundrel." See Doubleday-Dolphin reprint, p. 78.

. . . 'tis like, the common Question will be made, Who shall be Judge, whether the Prince or Legislative act contrary to their Trust? This, perhaps, ill affected and factious Men may spread amongst the People, when the Prince only makes use of his due Prerogative. To this I reply; The People shall be Judge; for who shall be Judge whether his Trustee or Deputy acts well, and according to the Trust reposed in him, but he who deputes him, and must, by having deputed him, have still a Power to discard him, when he fails in his Trust?[12]

The political evolution of nearly three centuries has made the cogency of Locke's latter question and the adequacy of his answer largely academic in Great Britain and in the United States. Here, by constitutions (in either British or American sense), we have set limits to the duration of the legislative and made temporary this supreme power, in any person or assembly. In the England of 1688, the Glorious Revolution firmly established the great principle that executive government did not subsist by will of the executive. True, the majoritarian character of the power that dethroned James was debatable. The parliament that replaced him with the House of Orange represented mostly influential landowners,[13] not small men. Some members came from rotten boroughs, such as Locke condemned,

. . . we see the bare Name of a Town, of which there remains not so much as the Ruines, where scarce so much Housing as a Sheep-coat, or more Inhabitants than a Shepherd is to be found, sends as many Representatives to the grand Assembly of Law-makers, as a whole County numerous in People, and powerful in Riches.[14]

One can hardly call England of 1688 a popular democracy. The great significance of the events of that year lies in the dismissal of James and the conditioned call of William and Mary, not in a majoritarian character of the groups that compelled the change. The Parliament of the Glorious Revolution had what today seems a narrow electoral foundation, but that Parliament was in charge of political power, and William and Mary held the Crown by Parliament's will. Time would give that will a broader popular base. What counted in 1688 was accession of the Prince and Princess of Orange on the invitation of an elected body, which in writing prescribed terms on which the new monarchs were pleased to come. This royal contract of employment

[12] Chapter XIX, Section 240.

[13] A brief discussion of the reluctance to change parliamentary representation at the time of the Glorious Revolution occurs in Professor G. N. Clark's *Later Stuarts, 1660–1714* (Oxford: Clarendon Press, 1934) p. 124. Gregory King's estimate of the incomes and numbers of various classes of England's population in 1688 is reprinted at page 25 of Professor Clark's book.

[14] Chapter XIII, Section 157.

was the significant symbol of the change in constitutional theory which had come about since James I came to the throne in 1603, and which explained the dismissal of his namesake eighty-five years later.

What of the higher law? For the American this most conspicuously appears in review of the constitutionality of legislation, a judicial function which has few examples in England. Dr. Bonham's Case,[15] decided in 1610, had little influence in late English theory. After the Commons had gained the upper hand, judges did not care to contest with Parliament. In 1653 one Captain Streater petitioned the Court of the Upper Bench for release from the Gate House Prison by *habeas corpus*. He asserted invalidity of an order for his commitment made by the Barebones Parliament without any cause stated in its order. The judge told him,

> Mr. Streater, one must be above another, and the inferior must submit to the superior; and in all justice, an inferior court cannot controul what the Parliament does. If the parliament should do one thing, and we do the contrary here, things would run round. We must submit to the legislative power: for if we should free you, and they commit you again, why here would be no end: and there must be an end in all things. . . .[16]

A generation later, in 1688, Englishmen had the same view of Parliamentary power unrestricted by judicial supremacy. Locke cited the law of Nature and Reason to justify a parliamentary majority—not to contradict it. Diffusion of political power among an electorate then appeared sufficient guarantee of popular liberty, without dividing that power between organs of government so that one might protect the people from the others. Hamilton phrased the same theory in 1788 when he argued against the necessity of an American Bill of Rights in the eighty-fourth Federalist paper.

> It has been several times truly remarked that bills of rights are, in their origin, stipulations between kings and their subjects, abridgments of prerogative in favour of privilege, reservations of rights not surrendered to the prince. Such was Magna Carta, obtained by the barons, sword in hand, from King John. Such were the subsequent confirmations of that charter by succeeding princes. Such was the Petition of Right assented to by Charles I, in the beginning of his reign. Such, also, was the Declaration of right presented by the Lords and Commons to the Prince of Orange in 1688, and afterwards thrown into the form of an act of parliament called the Bill of Rights. It is evident, therefore, that, according to their primitive signification they have no application to constitutions professedly founded upon the power

---

[15] 8 Co. Rep. 107, discussed at page 61.
[16] V State Trials 365, 386.

of people, and executed by their immediate representatives and servants. Here, in strictness, the people surrender nothing; and as they retain everything they have no need of particular reservations. 'We the people of the United States, to secure the blessings of liberty to ourselves and our posterity, do ordain and establish this Constitution for the United States of America.' Here is a better recognition of popular rights than volumes of those aphorisms which make the principal figure in several of our State bills of rights, and which would sound much better in a treatise of ethics than in a constitution of government.

What of equality between man and man? Locke is comfortably generous in his assurances. He starts his second chapter with a discussion "Of the State of Nature," in which men enjoyed

> . . . a State of perfect Freedom to order their Actions, and dispose of their Possessions, and Persons as they think fit, within the bounds of the Law of Nature without asking leave, or depending upon the Will of any other Man.

> A State also of Equality, wherein all the Power and Jurisdiction is Reciprocal, no one having more than another; there being nothing more evident, than that Creatures of the same species and rank, promiscuously born to all the same advantages of Nature, and the use of the same Faculties, should also be equal one amongst another without Subordination or Subjection, . . .[17]

John Locke was a thoughtful man, whose influence during close to three centuries has been on the side of liberty and decency; of few men can as much be said. We are much in his debt. But Carl Lotus Becker reminded us[18] that Locke was not describing an "actual pre-social state of history, but an imaginative state rationally constructed." Locke was not really "concerned to know how governments had come to be what they were; what he wanted to know was whether there was any justification for their being what they were." So, like other writers who have penned magnificent generalizations about ideal conditions, Locke had uneasy afterthoughts, and hedged with a qualification his discourse about natural equality. Men in the State of Nature were equal one to another without subordination or subjection,

> . . . unless the Lord and Master of them all, should by any manifest Declaration of his Will set one above another, and confer on him, by an evident and clear Appointment, an undoubted Right to Dominion and Sovereignty.[19]

[17] Chapter II, Section 4.
[18] In his charming essay, *The Declaration of Independence: A Study in the History of Political Ideas* (New York: Alfred A. Knopf, 1942) p. 65.
[19] Chapter II, Section 4.

In 1688 there were a number of evident and clear appointments which by undoubted right modified any state of equality wherein all power and jurisdiction being reciprocal, no one in that happy State of Nature had more than another. There was the royal family to be hereditarily established by a constituent convention. There was a House of Lords, hereditarily participating in the Legislative. Most conspicuously unequal of all unequal circumstances, there was the institution of property. It so naturally set one man above another, its unequal effect seemed so inevitable, that thinkers did not at all class the institution of inheritable riches with, say, inheritable nobility. The brief 'Leveller' movement[20] of Lilburn, Walwyn, Overton, and their friends in the Cromwellian era, with a mild enough political and economic egalitarian program judged by mid-twentieth-century standards, finally came to nothing. The Agreement of the People, origination among Levellers, when finally presented to the Commons by the Council of the Officers repudiated any economic levelling in one of the irrevocable provisions,

> 6. That no Representative may in any wise render up, or give, or take away, any of the foundations of common right, liberty and safety contained in this Agreement, nor level men's estates, destroy property, or make all things common; . . .[21]

One risks accusation of restating what is obvious by pointing out that neither Commonwealth, nor Restoration, nor Revolution of 1688 were movements consciously directed toward economic egalitarianism. For Locke, the institution of property was a basic premise; government he wrote, "has no other end but the preservation of property."[22] The late seventeenth century brought a new scientific spirit to England, a stirring which would ultimately work deep change in the development of her resources, in the nature and location of her wealth, in the life of her cities and farms, in the classes of her society. Ingeniously powered machines, then dimly perceived; diffusion of literacy, then under way, had in them the seeds of distant future levelling no one could foresee.[23] But in 1688 landed proprietors ruled England. Equality of man could be found in Locke's imaginary ac-

---

[20] The literature on the Levellers is scantier than one would expect. See Joseph Frank, *The Levellers* (Cambridge: Harvard University Press, 1955) and C. V. Wedgwood's *Cromwell* (London: Duckworth, 1939).

[21] Gardiner, *Constitutional Documents of the Puritan Revolution, 1625–1660* (3rd ed.; Oxford: Clarendon Press, 1906) p. 369.

[22] Chapter VIII, Section 94.

[23] In 1664 the Royal Society was investigating atmospheric pressure. Charles II laughed at the scientists "for spending time only in the weighing of Ayre . . ." See G. N. Clark, *Later Stuarts, 1660–1714*, p. 42.

count of a long-past State of Nature, but not in the daily affairs of practical people.

Religious equality was little further advanced in 1700 than it had been a century earlier. The toleration James II showed for Catholics was a strong factor in rousing the antagonism that finally drove him out. The Bill of Rights of 1689 cautiously guaranteed "That the subjects which are protestants may have arms for their defence . . ." The "Toleration Act" of the same year[24] relaxed some but by no means all of the restrictions against nonconformists, and the statute excepted Roman Catholics and Unitarians from its benefits. In 1700, an Act of Parliament[25] offered a reward of 100 pounds for the discovery of any Roman Catholic priest exercising his office; the priest was to be imprisoned for life. The same statute disabled every Roman Catholic from inheriting or purchasing land unless he abjured his religion, and it forbade any Roman Catholic to send his children abroad for education. Equal treatment of men holding every sort of religious belief was still a long way ahead.

Separation of Powers in late seventeenth-century England was in process of developing, not by any such entrenched arrangement as that in the Constitution of the United States, but by habit of government. Locke in his twelfth chapter writes "Of the Legislative, Executive and Federative Power of the Commonwealth," explaining that the 'federative' is the power to manage foreign affairs.[26] He comments that "the Legislative and Executive Power come often to be separated," but at the outset of chapter thirteen he states,

> . . . there can be but one Supream Power, which is the Legislative, to which all the rest are and must be Subordinate, yet the Legislative being only a Fiduciary Power to act for certain ends, there remains still in the People a Supream Power to remove or alter the Legislative, when they find the Legislative act contrary to the trust reposed in them. . . .

He suggests no institutionally independent judiciary, which is such a conspicuous feature of American theory.

The governing constitutional fact in Locke's England was a "supream" Parliament, though the Kings were to assert vestiges of what had been Stuart independency for another century, while actual executive power was gradually coming to center in the developing

---

[24] I Will. & Mary, c. 18; C. Grant Robertson, *Select Statutes, Cases and Documents to Illustrate English Constitutional History, 1660–1832* (6th ed.; London: Methuen and Co., 1935).

[25] II Will. III, c. 4; see 13 Will. III, c. 6.

[26] Chapter XII, Section 146.

Cabinet, a Parliamentary organ. The Act of Settlement[27] provided for a judiciary holding office ". . . *quamdiu se bene gesserint,*" removable only on address of both Houses of Parliament, but this provision for tenure only legislated what was already the practice under William. The Parliament remained supreme in theory; in practice as the seventeenth century ended, Crown, Parliament, and Bench came to operate much as though their functions were constitutionally set apart.

The separation of powers thus did quite well without entrenched constitutional status. Similarly, the ideal of a written Compact of Government, of a great reassuring Document, which was later to be influential in America, had in England the effect without the formal institution. Names of constitutional statutes are significant—the Act of Settlement is actually "An Act for the further Limitation of the Crown and better securing the Rights and Liberties of the Subject."[28] The words are lawyers' words; the draftsmen might have been preparing a conveyance in trust of family estates, safeguarding the interests of parents and children's children. Of this Hallam wrote in 1827,

> The act of settlement was the seal of our constitutional laws, the complement of the revolution itself and the bill of rights, the last great statute which restrains the power of the crown, and manifests in any conspicuous degree, a jealousy of parliament in behalf of its own and the subject's privileges. The battle had been fought and gained; . . .[29]

The Parliament of William and Mary's time and thereafter had the nominal power to repeal the Bill of Rights, or to repeal Magna Carta itself; in practical politics this would have been as unlikely as the repeal by the American people of their Bill of Rights and Fourteenth Amendment in 1964.

[27] 12 & 13 Will. III, C 2 (1701), VII Statutes of the Realm 636.

[28] 12 & 13 Will. III. c. 2 (1701) VII Statutes of the Realm, vii 636–638.

[29] These are the opening words of the sixteenth chapter of Hallam's *Constitutional History of England* (London: J. Murray, 1827).

8. CONSTITUTIONAL THEORY
IN THE THIRTEEN COLONIES

ONE WHO READS the Supreme Court's constitutional opinions may be struck by the relatively infrequent reference to colonial experience. Stuart struggles with Commons or common-law courts are often cited; the English Bill of Rights is not rare in our judicial writing; but colonial America has furnished our judges comparatively few precedents.[1] The colonists thought proudly of themselves as Englishmen; up to the eve of the War of Independence, their grievances were expressed as denials of an Englishman's rights;[2] their claims were

[1] Colonial material is conspicuous in Chief Justice Marshall's opinion in *Johnson and Graham's Lessee* v. *M'Intosh*, 8 Wheat. 543 (1823); he reviews the origins of colonial settlements, and the land titles derived from colonial authority. The opinion is extensively quoted in "History of the Colonies," the first Book of Story's *Commentaries on the Constitution of the United States* (2nd ed., Boston: Little, Brown and Co., 1851) I, pp. 3–136. Another noted opinion making use of colonial precedent is that of Chief Justice Morgan Lewis of the New York Supreme Court, written but never delivered, in the criminal libel prosecution against Harry Croswell; the Chief Justice, arguing that truth is not admissible in defense of a prosecution for criminal libel, discusses John Peter Zenger's case of 1735. See *People* v. *Croswell*, 3 Johnson's Cases 337; 3 Wheeler's Criminal Cases 330 (1804). Mr. Justice Frankfurter refers to early territorial representation in colonial assemblies to support his dissenting opinion in *Baker* v. *Carr*, 369 U.S. 186 (1962). One could cite a fair number of other examples of colonial precedent. But references to seventeenth-century English precedents are much more frequent. They are copious in *Baker* v. *Carr*, the Tennessee redistricting case just cited. For a few other instances see *U.S.* v. *Wong Kim Ark*, 169 U.S. 649 (1898); *Twining* v. *New Jersey*, 211 U.S. 78 (1908); *Tumey* v. *Ohio* 273 U.S. 510 (1927); *Youngstown Sheet & Tube Co.* v. *Sawyer*, 343 U.S. 579 (1952). The list could be extended indefinitely. The *Youngstown* opinion demonstrates that controversies with the first two Stuart kings are still prominent in American judicial memory.

[2] See C. L. Rossiter *Seedtime of the Republic* (New York: Harcourt, Brace & Co. 1953) p. 315. Professor Rossiter's book is a most valuable source of material on pre-Revolutionary origins of American constitutionalism.

documented by English precedent. Our judges have used similar documentation.

Nevertheless in colonial America arose the prototypes of most constitutional controversies that later came to trouble the United States. Asserted sovereignty of the people is conspicuous in wrangles between elected Assemblies and Royal Governors, and in such related episodes as John Peter Zenger's trial in 1735 for seditious libel of Governor Cosby of New York. The ideal of government subject to a justice which exists apart from enacted law, was a general aspiration among colonial thinkers, whether they were clergy of the early Puritan theocracy, or later followers of the eighteenth-century concept of an immutable natural order, divinely arranged. Equality was a natural feeling on the frontier; a man who had cut out a clearing for himself, and with the same gun had fought wolves, Indians and Frenchmen, was unlikely to pay much or long deference to any tidewater aristocracy. But two sorts of inequality were accepted as normal in most of colonial America: one was establishment of a favored religion, with associated intolerance of certain types of dissent; the other was Negro slavery. The former has disappeared; the difficult legacy of the latter still plagues us.

The federal structure of what in time became the United States had its origins in the scattered settlement of the North American seaboard by thirteen different groups, under different colonial governments. And the Charters of the several colonies, defining the modes of their government, and delimiting their powers, accustomed Americans to the idea of a written, controlling law, unalterable by companies, proprietors, or colonial assemblies.[3] As the colonial period progressed, colonial political experience increasingly resembled that which was later to characterize the United States. The preview became clearly evident in the last years before the Revolution.

A compact but inclusive account of constitutional evolution in British colonial America would be a difficult undertaking. Virginia's formal origin differs from that of Massachusetts. New York's story differs from both. The scattered up-country pioneers were more radical in their political ideas than were the tidewater traders.[4] England, from time to time, changed the manner of her governmental relation to this or that colony. With such discrete political beginnings there can be no easy and confident description of British America as though it were a single homogeneous unit.

Some colonies originated with grants of corporate charters. The

[3] See C. L. Rossiter *Seedtime of the Republic,* p. 32.
[4] See Carl Lotus Becker, *Beginnings of the American People* (Boston: Houghton Mifflin Company, 1915) Chapter V.

Second Charter of Virginia, of 1609, named the corporation "The Treasurer and Company of Adventurers and Planters of the City of London for the first Colony in Virginia."[5] Connecticut and Rhode Island governed themselves under their colonial charters until well into the nineteenth century. Other colonies, beginning as chartered companies were converted into royal colonies with no corporate intermediary. Virginia so became a royal colony in 1624 when James annulled her previous charter. In other instances the Crown granted vast tracts by instruments like modern conveyances of real property; these conferred on the favored Proprietors not only title to the land, but governing authority. So Pennsylvania came to William Penn; so Maryland came to Cecil, Lord Baltimore. New York began under a charter to the Dutch West India Company, granted by the Netherlands. Charles II of England in 1663, anticipating victory in the war with Holland, granted what was then the New Netherlands and is now New York, with other great tracts, to his brother James. Colonel Richard Nicolls in 1664 took New Amsterdam for James, when the prudent burghers persuaded fiery Peter Stuyvesant to surrender. The Dutch recaptured New York in July, 1673. England regained it by Treaty in 1674; Charles thereupon made a confirmatory grant to his "Dearest Brother James Duke of York, his Heirs and Assigns." Such early corporate charters and patents mingled concepts of government and ownership, ideas so clearly distinguished in modern minds, so intertwined in the minds of our predecessors who were closer to feudal concepts than we are.

Formal differences in the beginnings of the Colonies should not obscure their fundamental likenesses. In their constitutional structure they came more and more to resemble one another as the hazardous plantations of James I became the settled and comparatively thriving

[5] A comparable charter created the Hudson's Bay Company which still exists, a reminder of much Canadian history. A number of early colonial charters and other constitutional documents are printed in Professor William MacDonald's, *Documentary Source Book of American History* (New York: Macmillan, 1920). The origins of the Thirteen Colonies are described in Book I of Story's *Commentaries on the Constitution of the United States*. Professor Rossiter presents a remarkable analytical summary in "Colonial Government and the Rise of Liberty," the first chapter of his *Seedtime of the Republic*. The development of political institutions in the colonies is described in H. L. Osgood's two great works, *The American Colonies in the Seventeenth Century* (3 vols.; New York: Macmillan, 1904–07), and *The American Colonies in the Eighteenth Century* (4 vols.; New York: Macmillan, 1924). For government in the eighteenth century, there is no better summary than C. P. Nettels, *The Roots of American Civilization* (New York: Crofts, 1938). A study of great merit is Louise Kellogg's "The American Colonial Charter," in *American Historical Association Annual Report* (1903) I, pp. 185–341.

colonies of 1700. Every English colony held under the Crown; the colonists felt a pride in this ancestral allegiance which the irritated literature of revolutionary war days should not obscure. All the Colonies were subjected to a common minimum of English administration. Various official bodies in England exerted over all of them a measure of control, which became firmer when the Cromwellian controversies ceased to preoccupy English attention. In 1696 the Lords Commissioners of Trade, replacing the less effective Lords of Trade, acquired some supervision of royal Governors. The Privy Council, charged with judicial oversight, heard some appeals from colonial judgments.[6]

In every colony a Governor represented the Crown. The mode of selection varied; in royal colonies the king appointed a sort of viceroy;[7] in the proprietary colonies the Proprietor designated a dignitary to act in his stead; in Connecticut and Rhode Island the local legislature designated an executive. However this official was chosen, he was a dignified chief magistrate, commanding the colony's military forces, exercising a veto power over legislation of the colonial assembly, making appointments to office, and, where the colony had an established church, exercising some leadership of it. The Governor was a person of pomp and circumstance. When a stamp-act mob in November 1765 destroyed the coach of Cadwallader Colden, Lieutenant-Governor of New York, his London coach-makers submitted an itemized bill for its replacement. The carriage epitomizes the Governor's status,

A New Post Chariot made of the Best Seasoned timber lin'd with a light colourd Cloth trimmd with a Near Coffoy laice & a Handsome folding Hammock cloth with 2 rows of fringe 2 fore Glasses Door Glasses and a sett of mahogany shutters with rose lights the Glass [doors?] . . . & Holders Coffoy & pockets to the fore end & Doors lin'd with leather a Nett to the roof an Additional seat with iron work to take off or on a Wainscoat Box with a lock a Carpet to the bottom steps to slide under with brass handles, Painted a fine Glaizd Crimson with light Crimson flowers on silver all over the Panels & Gold Ciphers with proper colourd flowers twisting round them and Gilding the Ogees and Beads and Varnished—and a Neat Carriage with iron Axletrees and Good Seasond Wheels a Post Budget a sett of Bow Ess steel springs & Colourd and Varnishd Vermillion and a New Pair of Harness Bridles & ranes sewd white & Ornamented with Brass pieces

[6] See J. H. Smith, *Appeals to the Privy Council from the American Plantations* (New York: Columbia University Press, 1950).

[7] The term is Rossiter's; see *Seedtime of the Republic*, p. 14. The title "Viceroy," one says at the risk of the obvious, does not occur in colonial documents of appointment.

& Ciphers engravd on the Howsings and all things Completed to the Chariot & Harness in the Best manner . . . 90 pounds.[8]

Associated with the Governor was a Council—ordinarily made up of a small number of colonial gentlemen of property and prestige who served the Governor as advisors. The Council might act as an upper legislative House, passing on Acts of the colonial assembly. It might have judicial functions as a senior colonial court of appeals.[9] The Governor's Council was generally appointed by the Crown on the Governor's recommendation; but in Massachusetts the lower House, the General Court, chose Councillors annually, subject to the Governor's veto.

The colonial Assemblies (by whatever name known) are the ancestors of present American legislatures. In them developed a measure of popular representation which opposed the Governor's élitism. Much constitutional history in the Colonies can be told in annals of controversy between Assemblies and Governors. In time the Assemblies won out in these contests; their victory resulted from the same forces which ultimately brought independence from Great Britain, and which guided the evolution of the Constitution of the United States. Of five great principles of American constitutionalism discussed in this book, the first and greatest—popular control of the people's political and economic fate—is exemplified by the story of colonial Assemblies. They deserve study.

Measured by modern standards, a comparatively small proportion of the total colonial population took part in Assembly elections. Women had no vote; and some adult males were excluded by the requirement, in effect in most Colonies, that an elector must be a freeholder of real property,[10] though acquisition of land was easy and the freehold qualification was not the obstacle it would be today. Massachusetts, to be sure, had early required full membership in a church congregation as a condition of the electoral franchise. Until the original rigors of this restriction broke down, it occasioned much irritation.[11]

[8] See W. E. Abbott, *New York in the American Revolution* (New York: Charles Scribner's Sons, 1929), p. 60.

[9] In New York, Senators and high judicial officers formed the Court of Errors, the highest appellate tribunal in the State, until the constitutional revision of 1846 which created the present Court of Appeals.

[10] Robert E. Brown, in his study *Middle Class Democracy and the Revolution in Massachusetts, 1691–1780* (Ithaca, N.Y.: Cornell University Press, 1955) pp. 51–52, estimates that 20% of Massachusetts residents were adult males, of whom 80% were freeholders. For property qualifications in the various Colonies, see Chilton Williamson, *American Suffrage from Property to Democracy* (Princeton: Princeton University Press, 1960) pp. 12, 13.

[11] See Perry Miller, *From Colony to Province* (Cambridge: Harvard University Press, 1953) Chapter XXII.

In all Colonies the proportion of the population which actually took part in elections was very small. In Virginia, between 1744 and 1772, about 9% voted; in New York City at about the same time, 8%. In Pennsylvania the qualified (as distinguished from actual) voters were about 8% of the rural population and 2% of the population of the City of Philadelphia. In New England the actual voters seemed to have been proportionally less than those in the middle and southern colonies. In Massachusetts immediately before the War of Independence, only about 2% of the population took part in elections; Connecticut had about the same proportion. Potential voters in the Rhode Island area totalled only 9% of the total population. Property qualifications, difficulty of travel in large election districts, and the absence of party organization all combined to make colonial electorates much narrower than they have become by the middle of the twentieth century.[12] Still, to an Englishman, it appeared that in America the people ruled themselves. Edmund Burke on March 22, 1775, told the House of Commons concerning the American Colonies,

> Their governments are popular in an high degree; some are merely popular; in all, the popular representative is the most weighty; and this share of the people in their ordinary government never fails to inspire them with lofty sentiments, and with a strong aversion from whatever tends to deprive them of their chief importance.[13]

In the Thirteen Colonies, whether for the moment under charters, under proprietary grants, or under more direct government from London, the demand for legislative supremacy over royal governors grew increasingly urgent until the War of Independence ended all British rule.[14] The people of the Colonies tended to resent the application of British statutes; they were eager to assert supremacy of their own colonial Parliaments.[15] As elective assemblies became more and more solidly established the Crown's executive power simultaneously diminished. It was replaced, in fact if not in theory, by the sovereignty

[12] For the voting privilege in the Thirteen Colonies, see Albert E. McKinley *Suffrage Franchise in the Thirteen English Colonies in America* (Boston: Ginn and Co., 1905); Robert Brown, in *Middle Class Democracy and the Revolution in Massachusetts, 1691–1780,* pp. 51–52 agrees generally with McKinley's figures for Massachusetts, but complains of his neglect to stress the difference between the numbers qualified to vote and those actually voting. *Gentlemen Freeholders,* by Charles S. Sydnor, (Chapel Hill: University of North Carolina Press, 1952) gives a lively picture of Virginia practical politics in Washington's day.

[13] "On Conciliation with the Colonies," in *Burke's Speeches and Letters on American Affairs,* Ernst Rhys, ed. (London: J. M. Dent and Sons, 1908) p. 92.

[14] See generally A. B. Keith, *Constitutional History of the First British Empire* (Oxford: Clarendon Press, 1930); and Sir D. L. Keir, *The Constitutional History of Modern Britain* (3rd ed.; London: A. and C. Black, 1946).

[15] D. L. Keir, *The Constitutional History of Modern Britain,* p. 347 *et seq.*

of the colonial assemblies. Although the active electorate was only a small proportion of the population, the Crown had little control over this oligarchic electoral minority, and no means of acquiring control. Aggressive assemblies asserted authority over the system of elections, and over the frequency and duration of legislative sessions. The Governors tended to be unsuccessful in initiating legislation, and in withholding their assent from acts of colonial assemblies. In several colonies the careers of Governors degenerated into quarrelsome disputes, in which the probabilities of success favored the legislatures. During the French and Indian War the dependence of Governors on their assemblies for supplies of money and men showed where political power lay.[16] One recalls John, vainly trying to raise scutages and soldiers for an earlier French war.

By the outbreak of the War of Independence, the people of the Thirteen Colonies had come to consider election of their own colonial legislatures as a vested right, and the assemblies had learned the art of controlling royal Governors. When the Colonies undertook national independence they had no practical difficulty in continuing their legislative assemblies; they were thoroughly familiar with this institution. And when the Continental Congress drafted the Articles of Confederation in 1777, the members at first felt neither need nor desire for an executive chief to replace the King. They provided no separate executive whatever.

Casting of votes for election of legislators is only one part of majoritarian control of government. Popular self-government is intimately connected with the capability of political expression, individual or organized; with the right to petition for the redress of grievances; with an opportunity to persuade otherwise indifferent neighbors that grievances exist. Fear of future elections influences officeholders more effectively than gratitude for those past; mobilization of opinion in political parties, using massive communications devices, can swiftly produce governmental action by threats of reprisal at the polls.[17] Free expression thus becomes an integral part of popular government. In modern states aspiration to liberty of expression about politics tends to be mingled with the claim to liberty of expression on all subjects. Freedom from moral and religious censorship is discussed in the same terms as freedom from censorship of political dissent, although the latter has an extra claim for it includes

[16] Corwin, *The President: Office and Powers* (3rd ed.; New York: New York University Press, 1948) p. 4.

[17] See John F. Kennedy, *Profiles in Courage* (New York: Harper & Brothers, 1956) *passim*.

the means to all freedoms. A man may resent being forbidden to buy *Ulysses*,[18] or to see *La Ronde*,[19] simply because he is irked by governmental interference; he is in a worse case if he is forbidden to express a political protest, for his chance to turn the censors out of office is then similarly forbidden; he is barred from ". . . those political processes which can ordinarily be expected to bring about repeal of undesirable legislation. . . ."[20]

Practical operation of government, however, may require substantially equal tolerance of expression without distinction between that which advocates political change and that which does not. Freedoms have a way of being interdependent. When Church and State were united, dissent logically became sin; and the force of moral condemnation was turned against an opponent of the governmental regime. Decline of the religio-political State, rise of popular assemblies, an increasingly preferred position of the right to political organization and expression, all came gradually, and came together. Freedom of expression became a habit before it became a law; freedom of debate in Parliament was established before there was any legal formulation of a general freedom of expression for everybody, whether in Parliament or out. Libels were common matter for criminal prosecution in seventeenth- and eighteenth-century England. And the greater the truth, the greater was the libel. The Star Chamber decided the famous case of *Libellis Famosis* in the third year of James I's reign,

> In the case of L.P. in the Star-Chamber this term, against whom the Attorney-General proceeded *ore tenus* on his own confession, for composing and publishing an infamous libel in verse, by which John Archbishop of Canterbury (who was a prelate of singular piety, gravity, and learning, now dead) by descriptions and circumlocutions, and not in express terms; and Richard Bishop of Canterbury who now is, were traduced and scandalized: in which these points were resolved:
>
> 1. Every libel (which is called *famosus libellus, seu infamatoria scriptura*), is made either against a private man, or against a magistrate or public person. If it be against a private man it deserves a severe punishment, for although the libel be made against one, yet it

[18] U.S. v. *One Book Entitled Ulysses by James Joyce*, 5 Fed. Supp. 182 (DCSDNY 1933); 72 F. 2d 705, (CA 2 1934).

[19] *Commercial Pictures Corporation* v. *Regents etc., of New York*, 346 U.S. 587 (1954).

[20] The quoted words occur in Mr. Justice Stone's celebrated Footnote 4, in his opinion in *United States* v. *Carolene Products Company*, 304 U.S. 144 (1938) at p. 152; he suggested that freedom to influence political action is the cardinal constitutional liberty, on which all others turn.

incites all those of the same family, kindred, or society to revenge, and so tends *per consequens* to quarrels and breach of the peace, and may be the cause of shedding of blood, and of great inconvenience: if it be against a magistrate, or other public person, it is a greater offence; for it concerns not only the breach of the peace, but also the scandal of Government; for what greater scandal of Government can there be than to have corrupt or wicked magistrates to be appointed and constituted by the King to govern his subjects under him? And greater imputation to the State cannot be, than to suffer such corrupt men to sit in the sacred seat of justice, or to have any meddling in or concerning the administration of justice.

2. Although the private man or magistrate be dead at the time of the making of the libel, yet it is punishable; for in the one case it stirs up others of the same family, blood, or society, to revenge, and to break the peace, and in the other the libeller traduces and slanders the State and Government, which dies not.

3. A libeller (who is called *famosus defamator*) shall be punished either by indictment at the common law, or by bill, if he deny it, or *ore tenus* on his confession in the Star-Chamber, and according to the quality of the offence he may be punished by fine or imprisonment; and if the case be exorbitant, by pillory and loss of his ears.

4. It is not material whether the libel be true, or whether the party against whom it is made, be of good or ill fame; for in a settled state of Government the party grieved ought to complain for every injury done him in an ordinary course of law, and not by any means to revenge himself, either by the odious course of libelling, or otherwise: he who kills a man with his sword in fight is a great offender, but he is a greater offender who poisons another; for in the one case he, who is openly assaulted, may defend himself, and knows his adversary, and may endeavour to prevent it: but poisoning may be done so secretly that none can defend himself against it; for which cause the offence is the more dangerous, because the offender cannot easily be known; . . .[21]

Free expression was not widely accorded in seventeenth-century English America. Massachusetts exiled Anne Hutchinson and Roger Williams because they expressed religious opinions irreconcilable with Puritan theocracy—exiled them logically enough, if the premises of the early Puritans were to be accepted. In 1660 the Boston Puritans hanged a persistent Quakeress named Mary Dyer for stubbornly asserting her religion.[22] Printers, too, could be troublemakers; the

[21] *The Case de Libellis Famosis, or of Scandalous Libels*, Pasch. 3 Jac. 1 (1605), 5 Co. Rep. 125 a; 77 E.R. 250.
[22] Now, after three centuries, Mary Dyer, sculptured in bronze, sits quietly in front of the State House in Boston looking across the Common where she died.

authorities regarded them accordingly. In 1671 Governor Berkeley wrote to the Lords Commissioners of his Virginia,

> . . . I thank God, there are no free schools nor printing, and I hope we shall not have these hundred years; for learning has brought disobedience, and heresy, and sects into the world, and printing has divulged them, and libels against the best government. God keep us from both![23]

Governor Berkeley's views were orthodox. They anticipated what became a habitual royal command to Governors through the first third of the eighteenth century,

> Forasmuch as great inconveniences may arise by the liberty of printing in our said province, you are to provide by all necessary order that no person keep any press for printing, nor that any book, pamphlet, or other matters whatsover be printed without your especial leave and license first obtained.[24]

Decline of theocracy, the rise of elective assemblies, and the general influence of the conditions of a sparsely populated primitive country, where English governmental controls were loosened, may all have contributed to the rise in freedom of expression in the early eighteenth century. Newspapers increased in the Colonies as the century grew older. Probably free expression in the new world, as in the old, was a habit before it was a right.

The famous New York trial of John Peter Zenger in 1735 showed the increasing political power of the press, the absence of effective prior censorship, and the inability of a hostile Governor to shut up a critical newspaper. On August 1, 1732, Colonel William Cosby, lately the unpopular Governor of Minorca, arrived in New York as its new Governor. He was imperious and grasping, and made himself political enemies, who thought that an anti-administration paper would awaken enough general criticism to bring about Cosby's recall. They turned to a printer named Zenger and perhaps subsidized him financially in the production of the "New York Weekly Journal," containing the "Freshest Advices, Foreign and Domestic." The 'administration' paper, the Gazette, exchanged editorial counterblows with Zenger's Journal. By order of the Council, a number of issues of the Journal were burnt under the Sheriff's direction. Though Zenger was imprisoned, and his bail fixed at an amount he could not raise, he continued to publish his paper with the help of his wife, passing his instructions to her through

---

[23] W. W. Hening, *Statutes at Large* (Virginia) Vol. II (1823) p. 517 quoted in C. L. Rossiter, *Seedtime of the Republic*, p. 29.

[24] Labaree, *Royal Instructions,* II, 495–496, quoted in Rossiter, *Seedtime of the Republic*, p. 29.

a hole in his cell door. The Attorney-General of the Province filed an information in the New York Supreme Court,[25]

> . . . That John Peter Zenger, late of the City of New York, Printer, 'being a seditious Person, and a frequent Printer and Publisher of false News and seditious Libels, and wickedly and maliciously devising the Government of Our said Lord the King of this His Majesty's Province of New York under the Administration of His Excellency William Cosby, Esq., Captain General and Governour in Chief of the said Province, to traduce, scandalize and vilify, and His Excellency the said Governour, and the Ministers and Officers of Our said Lord the King . . . did falsely, seditiously and scandalously print and publish . . . a certain . . . Libel in which Libel (of and concerning His Excellency the said Governour, and the Ministers and Officers of our said Lord the King of and for the said Province) . . . among other Things . . . are these Words,
>
>> 'Your appearance in print at last, gives a Pleasure to many, tho' the most wish you had come fairly into the open Field, and not appeared behind Retrenchments made of the supposed Laws against Libelling, and of what other Men have said and done before: these Retrenchments, Gentlemen, may soon be shewn to you and all men to be weak, and to have neither Law nor Reason for their Foundation, so cannot long stand you in stead: Therefore, you had much better as yet leave them, and come to what the People of this City and Province (the City and Province of New York meaning) think are the Points in Question (to witt) They (the People of the City and Province of New York meaning) think as matters now stand, that their LIBERTIES and PROPERTIES are precarious, and that SLAVERY is like to be intailed on them and their Posterity, if some past Things be not amended, and this they collect from many past Proceedings." (Meaning many of the past Proceedings of His Excellency the said Governour, and of the Ministers and Officers of our said Lord the King, of and for the said Province.)'

There were other libels alleged against Zenger; one was a story told in the Journal, of a Jerseyman who tried to get a New Yorker to move to New Jersey, at which the New Yorker said that such a move would only be jumping from the frying pan into fire, "for, says he, we both are under the same Governour." Another concerned a quotation ascribed to a New Yorker about to move to Pennsylvania,

> We (the People of the Province of New-York meaning) see mens deeds destroyed, judges arbitrarily displaced, new courts erected without consent of the legislature (within the Province New-York, mean-

[25] An account of the Zenger case, from which are quoted the excerpts here given, appears in Livingston Rutherford, *John Peter Zenger, His Press, His Trial, and a Bibliography of Zenger Imprints* (New York: Dodd, Mead and Co., 1904).

ing) by which it seems to me, tryals by juries are taken away when a governour pleases, (His Excellency the said Governour meaning) men of known estates denied their votes, contrary to the received practice, the best expositor of any law: . . .

James Alexander and William Smith, counsel for Zenger, proceeded to move before the Court that Chief Justice DeLancey and Justice Philips of the New York Supreme Court be disqualified on the ground that their commissions were irregularly issued. The Chief Justice replied,

> . . . you have brought it to that Point, That either, We must go from the Bench or you from the Barr: Therefore We exclude you and Mr. Alexander from the Barr.

Thereupon the court entered a formal order

> . . . that for the said Contempt, the said James Alexander and William Smith, be excluded from any farther Practice in this Court, and that their Names be struck out of the Roll of Attornies of this Court.

A young man named John Chambers was then assigned as counsel for Zenger; but Alexander and Smith looked about for more experienced counsel, and obtained Andrew Hamilton of Philadelphia, one of the leaders of the Bar in the Colonies. Hamilton had been Attorney-General and Speaker of the Assembly in Philadelphia, and had been to London to probate William Penn's will. He was obviously a great advantage to Zenger's cause.

At Zenger's trial, after the jury was empanelled, Hamilton conceded the publication of the articles, whereupon the Attorney-General stated that the jury must find a verdict for the King; even if the publications were true, he argued, they would be none the less libellous, for their being true was only an aggravation of the crime. The Court agreed with the Attorney-General. Hamilton had now no recourse but the jury. The interest of the case today turns largely on his argument made to the court but evidently for the jury's benefit, and on his summation to the jury itself. It was a bold argument, contending for free expression, for free criticism of government, for truth as a justification, and for the right of the jury to pass on the law as well as the facts. Hamilton repeatedly referred to the evils of the Court of Star Chamber, to Coke's Institutes, to the great controversies concerning public liberty under the Stuarts in England. He cited the argument of counsel for the defendants in the trial of the Seven Bishops. He showed no awe of Governor or Court—

> It is true in times past it was a crime to speak truth, and in that terrible Court of Star Chamber, many worthy and brave men suffered

for so doing; and yet even in that Court, and in those bad times, a great and good man durst say, what I hope will not be taken amiss of me to say in this place, to wit, the practice of informations for libels is a sword in the hands of a wicked King, and an arrant coward, to cut down and destroy the innocent; the one cannot, because of his high station, and the other dares not, because of his want of courage, revenge himself in another manner.

Here the Attorney-General interrupted—

Pray Mr. Hamilton, have a care what you say, don't go too far neither, I don't like those liberties.

Mr. Hamilton continued—

Sure, Mr. Attorney, you won't make any applications; all men agree that we are governed by the best of kings, and I cannot see the meaning of Mr. Attorney's caution; my well known principles, and the sense I have of the blessings we enjoy under His present Majesty, makes it impossible for me to err, and I hope, even to be suspected, in that point of duty to my King. May it please your Honour, I was saying, that notwithstanding all the duty and reverence claimed by Mr. Attorney to men in authority, they are not exempt from observing the rules of common justice, even in their private or public capacities; the laws of our mother country know no exemption. It is true, men in power are harder to be come at for wrongs they do, either to a private person, or to the publick; especially a Governor in the Plantations, where they insist upon an exemption from answering complaints of any kind in their own Government. We are indeed told, and it is true they are obliged to answer a suit in the King's Courts at Westminster, for a wrong done to any person here: But do we not know how impracticable this is to most men among us, to leave their families (who depend upon their labour and care for their livelihood) and carry evidences to Britain, and at a great, nay, a far greater expense than almost any of us are able to bear, only to prosecute a Governour for an injury done here. But when the oppression is general, there is no remedy even that way, no, our Constitution has (blessed be God) given us an opportunity, if not to have such wrongs redressed, yet by our prudence and resolution we may in a great measure prevent the committing of such wrongs, by making a Governour sensible that it is to his interest to be just to those under his care; for such is the sense that men in general (I mean freemen) have of common justice, that when they come to know that a chief magistrate abuses the power with which he is trusted for the good of the people and is attempting to turn that very power against the innocent whether of high or low degree, I say, mankind in general seldom fail to interpose, and as far as they can, prevent the destruction of their fellow subjects. And has it not often been seen (and I hope it will always be seen) that when the representatives of a free people are by just representations or remonstrances, made sensible of the sufferings of their fellow-subjects, by the abuse of power in the hands of a Governour, they have declared (and loudly too) that they were not obliged by any law to support a Governour who goes about to destroy a province or colony, or their priviledges, which by His Majesty he was appointed, and by the law he is bound to protect and encourage. But I pray it may be considered of what use is this mighty priviledge, if every man that suffers must be silent? And if a man must be taken up as a libeller, for telling his sufferings to his neighbor?

When Hamilton had finished, the Attorney-General spoke only briefly, and the Chief Justice charged the jury, using almost the identical instruction Chief Justice Holt in 1704 had given in *Tutchin's Case*,[26]

> To say that corrupt Officers are appointed to administer Affairs, is certainly a Reflection on the Government. If People should not be called to account for possessing the People with an ill Opinion of the Government, no Government can subsist for it is very necessary for all Governments that the people should have a good Opinion of it. And nothing can be worse to any Government, than to endeavor to procure Animosities; as to the Management of it, this has always been look'd upon as a Crime, and no Government can be safe without it be punished.

The jury promptly found Zenger not guilty, "upon which there were three huzzas in the Hall which was crowded with People. . . ."[27] The Common Council of the City of New York voted Hamilton the Freedom of the City, engrossed in a certificate, presented with the City seal enclosed in a gold box provided by "sundry of the members of the Corporation and gentlemen of the City."

John Peter Zenger's case is probably the most famous single episode in the history of free political expression in what is now the United States. His trial and acquittal popularized the idea that the jury should be judges of both law and fact in cases of criminal libel; should return, that is to say, a general verdict of "guilty" or "not guilty." The jury, persuaded by Hamilton's eloquence and by their sympathies, arrived at the position reached by Fox's Libel Act in England in 1792,[28] and by many of the present State constitutions in the United States.[29] Chief Justice Lewis of the New York Supreme Court cited *Zenger's Case* in

[26] R. V. Tutchin (1704) as reported in 14 State Trials 1095; *sub. nom. Tuchin's Case*, Holt, K.B. 424; 90 E.R. 1133–4.

[27] Rutherford, *John Peter Zenger*, p. 125.

[28] 32 Geo. III. c. 60.

[29] See also *Beauharnais* v. *Illinois*, 343 US 250, at 295, 296 (1952).

1804, in *People* v. *Croswell,* a celebrated prosecution of an editor for "publishing a scandalous, malicious and seditious libel upon Thomas Jefferson, the President of the United States."[30] *Zenger's Case* has become a symbol of the legal right of a free press to express political protest.[31]

The War of Independence broke out only forty years after Zenger's trial. By that time free discussion and publication had become a habit in British America. Burke's celebrated words in the Speech on Conciliation delivered on March 22, 1775, are relevant here. He spoke of the great share of the "popular representative" in the provincial legislative assemblies; of the influence of dissenting religious sects in the northern Colonies; of the widespread literacy in America, of the export to that country of English lawbooks and the printing of lawbooks in America, of the sale in America of nearly as many copies of Blackstone as in England. Law was common learning.

> This study renders men acute, inquisitive, dexterous, prompt in attack, ready in defence, full of resources. In other countries, the people, more simple, and of a less mercurial cast, judge of an ill principle in government only by an actual grievance; here they anticipate the evil, and judge of the pressure of the grievance by the badness of the principle. They augur misgovernment at a distance, and snuff the approach of tyranny in every tainted breeze. . . .[32]

> You cannot persuade them to burn their books of curious science, to banish their lawyers from their courts of laws, or to quench the lights of their assemblies by refusing to choose those persons who are best read in their privileges. It would be no less impracticable to think of wholly annihilating the popular assemblies in which these lawyers sit.[33]

Blackstone's words on the free press must have been studied by thousands of American law students during the last few years before the War of Independence. He wrote (Book IV, Ch. 11),

> The liberty of the press is indeed essential to the nature of a free state: but this consists in laying no previous restraints upon publications, and not in freedom from censure for criminal matter when published. Every freeman has an undoubted right to lay what sentiments he pleases before the public: to forbid this, is to destroy the freedom

[30] 3 Wheeler's Criminal Cases 330, 368.

[31] See Thayer, *Legal Control of the Press* (Chicago: The Foundation Press, 1944) pp. 18–22; C. Rossiter, *Seedtime of the Republic,* pp. 27 ff.; see also Report of the New York Law Revision Commission, for 1948; p. 15 and ff. See p. 258, below, for a fuller account of Croswell's Case.

[32] "On Conciliation with the Colonies," in *Burke's Speeches and Letters on American Affairs,* p. 95.

[33] *Ibid.,* p. 102.

of the press; but if he publishes what is improper, mischievous, or illegal, he must take the consequences of his own temerity.

Much of the development of law under the principle of the First Amendment has consisted in fixing limits to Blackstone's last clause. But certainly by 1775 the Colonies had outgrown a censored press. On October 14, 1774, the First Continental Congress had declared,

> That the Inhabitants of the English Colonies in North-America by the immutable Laws of Nature, the Principles of the English Constitution, and the several Charters or Compacts, have the following RIGHTS. . . .
>
> *Resolved*, N.C.D. 8. That they have a Right peaceably to assemble, consider of their Grievances, and petition the king; and that all Prosecutions, prohibitory Proclamations, and Commitments for the same, are illegal.[34]

There was to be no renewal of the case of the Seven Bishops.

Substantive judicial review of federal statutes under the United States Constitution has led to much scholarly search of colonial records in an effort to find American origins for the doctrine that statutes are invalid when they conflict with a Higher Law, when they are inconsistent with a canon of "common right and reason," when they depart from "the immutable laws of nature." The search has turned up little established doctrine effective in the Colonies. Colonials were generally satisfied when they could achieve power for their assemblies to legislate in the teeth of Governor and Council; they felt small need for theory to show that their own enactments might be invalid. There was a homey quality in these colonial legislatures elected by the few pioneers who cared to vote. The laws they made were not imperial enactments of a distant, aristocratic Parliament; they were "our" laws, not "theirs." If the colonial members legislated in a way that displeased their hardy constitutents, there was no trouble in turning the legislators out. But the British Parliament was far off, beyond colonial influence. When Acts of Parliament galled the colonials they sought exemption on a theory that curiously anticipates later constitutional claims of entrenched "States' rights." The Continental Congress of 1774 resolved on October 14

> 4. That the Foundation of English Liberty, and of all free Government, is a Right in the People to participate in their legislative Council: and as the English Colonists are not represented, and from their local and other Circumstances cannot properly be represented in the British Parliament, they are entitled to a free and exclusive Power of

[34] 1 Journal of Congress (1777) pp. 28, 29; MacDonald, *Documentary Source Book of American History*, (New York: Macmillan, 1920) pp. 358, 360. See Levy, *Freedom of Speech and Press in Early American History* (New York: Harper and Row, 1963).

Legislation in their several provincial Legislatures, where their Right of Representation can alone be preserved, in all Cases of Taxation and internal Polity, subject only to the Negative of their Sovereign, in such manner as has been heretofore used and accustomed: But from the Necessity of the Case, and a Regard to the mutual Interests of both Countries, we cheerfully consent to the Operation of such Acts of the British Parliament, as are *bona fide*, restrained to the regulation of our external Commerce, for the Purpose of securing the commercial Advantages of the whole Empire to the mother Country, and the commercial Benefits of its respective Members; excluding every Idea of Taxation internal or external, for raising a Revenue on the Subjects in *America* without their Consent.[35]

Here is doctrine suggestive of the Tenth Amendment. Certain matters—here "external commerce"—remained in Parliament's power. "Taxation and internal polity" were for colonial Assemblies alone, subject only to a royal veto. This was not so much a doctrine of Higher Law as a forecast of future federal-state division of powers.[36]

While the Higher Law theory, exemplified by Coke in Bonham's Case, played no great effective part in actually upsetting colonial legislation, men never wholly forgot it. It became a convenient theoretical resource for the colonials as the quarrels of approaching Revolution became more and more heated.

In 1761 the Higher Law became identified with the colonial cause in the matter of "writs of assistance"—general search warrants, authorizing the King's customs officers to enter and ransack a citizen's house on suspicion of smuggling. In that year an officer named Paxton moved for such a writ in the Massachusetts Superior Court of Judicature, and James Otis of the Boston Bar appeared in opposition. John Adams, then a law student, heard the argument and made notes of Otis' words; his notes happily are still preserved. The writ, Otis argued, was "against the fundamental principles of law." Young Adams hastily wrote,

As to Acts of Parliament.
An Act against the Constitution is void: an act against natural Equity is void: and if an Act of Parliament should be made, in the very words of this petition, it would be void. The executive Courts must pass such Acts into disuse. 8 Rep. 118 from Viner—Reason of ye Com. Law to control an Act of Parliament.[37]

[35] Journal of Congress 29, R. Aitken, Philadelphia, 1777; William MacDonald, *Documentary Source Book of American History, 1606–1775*, pp. 356, 359.

[36] See the U.S. Constitution Art. I, S 8, Clause 3, and the Tenth Amendment.

[37] See for the Case of the Writs of Assistance Quincy's Report (Mass. 1865), especially pp. 51, 56 and fn. (17). The quotation from Adams' notes occurs in an appendix to Quincy's Report, pp. 471–474. The citation to Coke's 8th Report, which young Adams noted, refers to *Dr. Bonham's Case.* The use of Coke's doc-

The case was argued twice. Chief Justice Hutchinson finally ruled against Otis and issued the writ; but Otis' fiery argument that an unjust law had no force struck the imagination of the irritated colonials. Paxton's Case has been remembered ever since as one of the opening dramas of the American Revolution. An idealized mural painting of the courtroom scene covers one side of the entrance hall of the Massachusetts State House, rightly reminding an occasional one of the busy citizens hurrying to and fro under it that their country came into being with great aspirations, held by great men.

The colonial period in some small degree familiarized Americans with the theory of a Higher Law. It also gave them an example of procedural arrangements for reviewing the validity of colonial enactments. At this distance in time, when the political controversies of the eighteenth century have cooled, review by the Privy Council seems inevitable. The several colonies not only had some organic limits in their charters; they were necessarily subject to the overall rule of the Parliament at Westminster. When Holmes, in 1913, spoke of "how often a local policy prevails with those who are not trained to national views"[38] he might *mutatis mutandis* have been arguing for some control of colonial legislation and adjudication in the Privy Council.

Appeals to the Privy Council were not frequent. They moved slowly—inevitably so, not only because of the leisured pace of the time, but because of the sheer distances involved. Chief Justice Wait Still Winthrop, of Massachusetts, died intestate in 1717 leaving Connecticut real property. In 1725–26, the Connecticut Superior Court held that under an Act of the Connecticut General Assembly the decedent's daughter inherited part of his lands. A son, claiming that under English law he would inherit all the realty, and that the conflicting Connecticut Act, benefiting the daughter, was void, carried an appeal to the Privy Council. He was there upheld on February 15, 1727–28,[39] by a decree made over ten years after Wait Still died. In the case of the *Moheagan Indians, Appellants,* v. *The Colony of Connecticut and Others, Respondents,* entries in the Colony's Bill of Costs in the Privy

---

trine in *Paxton's Case* is described in a valuable note by Horace Gray, Jr., later a Justice of the Supreme Court of the United States, printed in J. B. Thayer's *Cases on Constitutional Law,* (Cambridge: George H. Kent, 1895) I, p. 48. An account of the case, and a copy of a writ of assistance, appears in MacDonald, *Select Charters and other Documents Illustrative of American History, 1606–1775* (New York: Macmillan, 1904) p. 258.

[38] "The Law and the Court," *Collected Legal Papers* (New York: Peter Smith, 1952) p. 296.

[39] *Winthrop v. Lechmere,* Thayer, *Cases on Constitutional Law* I, p. 34; Wambaugh, *Cases on Constitutional Law* (Cambridge: Harvard University Press, 1914) Book I, p. 7.

Council begin on May 15, 1765, and do not end until June 11, 1771. The costs of the Colony were 1049 pounds, 19 shillings, one pence; those of certain landholders, also respondents, were 619 pounds, 13 shillings, 2 pence.[40] Appeals were thus expensive as well as slow and inconvenient; they must have been available only in extraordinary cases. Joseph Henry Smith's *Appeals to the Privy Council from the American Plantations* gives a total of 795 American appeals in the 87 years preceding the end of the War of Independence in 1783. 157 resulted in affirmances; 336 in reversals. 147 were dismissed for want of prosecution. The high proportion of reversals suggests that circumstances did not encourage speculative appeals on doubtful grounds. There were, on an average, about 7.5 American appeals each year, but a number of these came from colonies or plantations other than the Thirteen—the Bahamas, Barbados, Bermuda, Dominica, East Florida, West Florida, Jamaica, the Leeward Islands, Newfoundland, Quebec, Nova Scotia, Tobago, and Tortola. Among the Thirteen Colonies, Rhode Island was most fertile in filing appeals. During the 87 years in question, 78 Rhode Island appeals reached the Privy Council. Twenty-seven of these were dismissed for lack of prosecution. Virginia originated fewer appeals but finished proportionally more; of 54 only six were not prosecuted to a decision, and twenty-four resulted in reversals.[41]

Thus the Thirteen Colonies had available a central court which exercised an appellate jurisdiction suggesting the present Supreme Court's review of State court judgments. But appeal to the Privy Council was inconvenient, slow, and expensive. For most litigants it must have been only a theoretical resource. Neither the substantive constitutional law nor the judicial institutions, available to the colonists, furnish much more than suggestive precedents for later constitutional theory in the United States.

"Equality" for white men in the Thirteen Colonies derived from pioneer conditions in a new country, more than from development of constitutional theory. Colonials were knighted, but not many. When they were, the distinction came from achievement by energy and intelligence, not from accident of birth. Indentured servants or "redemptioners," who had sold a part of their lives for a miserable carriage to the New World, could see ahead possible prosperity at the end of their term of servitude. They could reasonably hope to become landowning farmers or independent artisans in the colonies. Criminals, sometimes convicted and "transported" to America for re-

[40] The Bills of Costs are reproduced in Joseph Henry Smith's *Appeals to the Privy Council from the American Plantations*, pp. 672–684.

[41] These statistics are derived from the tables in Appendix A of J. H. Smith's book.

ligious or political offenses, could find a new chance for a decent life[42] on the western side of the Atlantic.

But America was no place for levelers. Opportunity, a *carrière ouverte aux talents*, a society that let a man rise if he was able, and that asked few questions about his antecedents or his early missteps; these contemplated an opportunity for inequality according to certain abilities, not a system of equality of condition imposed on unequal mankind. And for one increasing sort of colonial inhabitants there was little opportunity for advancement of any kind, few careers open either for talented or untalented. The Negro in colonial America saw little equality between himself and the white. Negro population in the Thirteen Colonies began in 1619 when a Dutch naval vessel brought "20 negars" for sale in Jamestown. In 1672, Parliament chartered the Royal African Company, giving it a monopoly of British colonial slave trade. By 1698 American shipowners were in the business. By 1760 there were in the colonies north of Maryland 87,000 Negroes among a population of 878,000 colonists. In the more southerly colonies there were 299,000 Negroes in a population of 718,000.[43] A few American Negroes were free men, but the great bulk were slaves; the sequels of that slavery still plague the descendants of the masters who brought it about.

The existence of Negro slavery in the American colonies was inconsistent with the law in England—curiously, where in many respects colonial charters provided and Privy Council judgments had held that colonial laws must not be inconsistent with the law of England. Lord Holt had ruled in 1705 that a slave became a free man as soon as he set foot in England.[44] Blackstone, whose *Commentaries* sold widely in America,[45] told his hearers and readers,

> . . . this spirit of liberty is so deeply implanted in our constitution, and rooted in our very soil, that a slave or a negro, the moment he lands in England, falls under the protection of the laws and so far becomes a freeman; though the master's right to his services may probably still continue.[46]

[42] H. J. Carman and H. C. Syrett, in their *History of the American People* (2 vols.; New York: Alfred A. Knopf, 1952) I, p. 35 *et seq.* give an account of these elements of colonial population.

[43] E. Channing, *History of the United States* (New York: Macmillan, 1924) II, p. 491.

[44] *Smith* v. *Brown and Cooper*, Salkeld 666, 2 Ld. Raym. 1274; 91 Engl. Rep. 566.

[45] Burke so states, in his speech on conciliation. *Burke's Speeches and Letters on American Affairs*, Ernst Rhys, ed., p. 94.

[46] Blackstone, *Commentaries* (2nd ed., Oxford: Clarendon Press, 1766) p. 127. The Vinerian Professor did not explain how the English master might enforce the right to services.

But for the Negro slave, in America the spirit of liberty was not to prevail until a century after Blackstone wrote.

Institutional diffusion of governmental power in order to ensure liberty for the citizen was understood as sound political theory in the later colonial days. Montesquieu's *De L'Esprit des Loix,* which appeared in 1748, reflected the French author's admiration for Locke, and praised a separation of powers which Montesquieu thought he perceived in the England of his own time. He wrote,

> When the legislative and executive powers are united in the same person, or in the same body of magistrates, there can be no liberty, because apprehensions may arise lest the same monarch or senate should enact tyrannical laws, to execute them in a tyrannical manner.
>
> Again, there is no liberty if the judiciary power be not separated from the legislative and executive. Were it joined with the legislative, the life and liberty of the subject would be exposed to arbitrary control; for the judge would be then the legislator. Were it joined to the executive power, the judge might behave with violence and oppression.[47]

In the late colonial period Montesquieu was favored reading for American intellectuals. Jefferson copied extracts in his notebook.[48] Madison in the 47th Federalist quotes Montesquieu on the separation of powers,[49] and points to the incorporation of the doctrine—"this fundamental article of liberty," he calls it, in the Massachusetts constitution of 1780 which directed—and still directs—

> . . . the legislative department shall never exercise the executive and judicial powers, or either of them: the executive shall never exercise the legislative and judicial powers, or either of them: the judicial shall never exercise the legislative and executive powers, or either of them: to the end it may be a government of laws and not of men.[50]

The provision for separation of powers in early State constitutions and in the Constitution of the United States indicates a widespread readiness to accept the theory. Diffusion of governmental power was already an established aspiration in America when the Revolution made it a practical way of governing.

The idea of a great document, a charter, compact, fundamental law,

[47] Montesquieu, *De L'Esprit des Loix,* translated by Nugent and Prichard (New York: Appleton and Co., 1900) I, p. 182.
[48] See Dumas Malone, *Jefferson the Virginian* (Boston: Little, Brown and Co., 1948) p. 176.
[49] Hamilton and Madison use Montesquieu repeatedly in the Federalist papers. See Nos. 9, 43, 47, 78.
[50] Constitution of Massachusetts, Declaration of Rights, Pt. 1, Art. XXX.

constitution, wherein are clearly stated the fundamentals of just government, had also become ready for practical use when the colonial period ended. The Great Charter with its many reissues; the Petition of Right wrung from Charles I; the Revolution of 1688 and its agreement with the House of Orange engrossed in the Bill of Rights and the Act of Settlement; the colonial charters which set up frames of government for the new plantations; the Mayflower Compact of 1620; the Fundamental Orders of Connecticut, adopted by a convention of the three towns of Windsor, Hartford, and Wethersfield on January 14, 1639, called by some the first written constitution in the modern sense; the Declaration of Rights of 1765, adopted by the delegates of nine colonies who met in New York on October 7 of that year, in what has come to be called the Stamp Act of Congress;[51] all these had become part of the political theory of the Thirteen Colonies when in the later eighteenth century tensions with Great Britain became intolerable. When the leaders of American opinion undertook to achieve independence and to construct a constitution for themselves, the underlying theories, and a great deal of essential practical experience, were ready in the traditions of the people.

[51] Copies of the last three documents can be found in many places: a convenient source is Vol. 43 of the "Harvard Classics," *American Historical Documents* (New York: Collier, 1910) pp. 62, 63, and 157. They may also be found in MacDonald's *Select Charters and Other Documents, 1606–1775* (New York: Macmillan Company, 1920) pp. 33, 60, and 313; and in Commager's *Documents of American History* (5th ed.; New York: Appleton-Century-Crofts, 1949) pp. 15, 22, and 57.

9. MAKING THE AMERICAN CONSTITUTION

Federalism

To be quotable, a statement must have a certain inclusive sweep, And because no generalization can be completely true, every epigram is thus doomed in advance to some measure of error. So it is with William Ewart Gladstone's great phrase, written in 1878 for the North American Review[1]—

> . . . as the British Constitution is the most subtile organism which has proceeded from . . . the long gestation of progressive history, so the American Constitution is . . . the most wonderful work ever struck off at a given time by the brain and purpose of man.

In one way this is a true saying, worthy of all men to be received. The founding fathers, working in Philadelphia through the summer of 1787, did write out a plan of government that must bring wonder to the mind of any thoughtful man. Their work served to keep together the thirteen discrete little republics whose four million[2] people, looking anxiously to the north and south, were scattered along the Atlantic seaboard from Canada to the Florida border. The ten amendments of 1791 were precautionary, confirming old immunities, rather than novel. The three amendments adopted between 1865 and 1870 did effect a profound change in the balance of power between nation and States. But except for these alterations, the Constitution today retains essentially what men devised a century and two thirds ago as the frame of government for a nation numbering in 1964 more than a

[1] In an essay "Kin Beyond Sea."
[2] 16th Census, "Population" (1940) Vol. I, Number of Inhabitants, gives 3,929,214.

hundred and ninety millions, drawn from every part of the world, peopling the breadth of a continent, and undertaking the major burdens of the whole family of free nations. This plan of government was no mere happy chance, no fortunate strike by facile random improvisers. A remarkable stock of practical political wisdom and political theory of government was held in common by the eighteenth-century landowners, merchants, and lawyers who worked in Philadelphia through the summer of 1787. The Federalist papers of 1787–1788 were not naïve productions, nor were they intended for naïve readers. The founding fathers knew what they were about, and Gladstone's words deserve their frequent quotation.

But the Constitution has its roots deep in English and American history; this agreement of the people, like most political devices, shows more adaptation than invention. Long before Locke's Second Treatise, the Mayflower Compact was a practical contract by the governed concerning the manner of their governing. Colonial charters acquired some of the high esteem we give the Constitution; the very documents themselves seemed to have a virtue separate from the rights they recited. The story that the Connecticut colonials hid their Charter in a hollow oak to keep it from seizure by Governor Andros in 1687, may well be apocryphal. But the popularity of the tale shows the strength of the compact theory in people's minds, the durability of the idea that government is consensual, the abiding appeal of the concept of a contract defining the rights of government and governed, and the power of the very paper embodying that agreement.

Actual plans for union of the Thirteen Colonies began long before the Revolution. Like all governments, that of the United States began in necessity. In the mid-eighteenth century the English colonies faced war waged against them by the French and Indians to the north; and no single colony was strong enough to cope with it alone. From this necessity came the first move toward the present federal government.

The Albany Congress of 1754

In one sense the drafting of the Constitution began at the Albany Congress of 1754 with Benjamin Franklin's plan for a union of the Colonies. Then, as later, foreign affairs were the major worry, though the enemy was not yet England. Delegates came to Albany representing the New England Colonies, and New York, Pennsylvania, and Maryland, to take thought for defense against the French and their Indian allies on the northern frontier. The delegates unanimously voted that a plan for permanent union of the Colonies was "abso-

lutely necessary for their preservation."[3] The scheme they adopted
after debate was Franklin's—it contemplated a chief executive ("President-General"); a legislature ("Grand Council") of forty-eight members, chosen by the several colonial assemblies. The Grand Council
was to maintain an army and navy, control Indian affairs, make laws
to carry out joint policies, and finance its undertakings by taxes. Its
statutes would be subject to veto first by the President-General, then
by the Crown.[4]

Franklin's plan came to nothing because the colonial legislatures
were unwilling to ratify it. The views of the Colonies were still too
local. As 1754 closed Franklin wrote to Peter Collinson in London,

> Every Body cries, a Union is absolutely necessary, but when they
> come to the Manner and Form of the Union, their weak Noddles are
> presently distracted.[5]

The Stamp-Act Congress of 1765

But when sufficiently aroused the Colonies could act together.
Eleven years after the Albany Congress, in 1765, the French had
been beaten, and Americans had become irritated with the English
instead. Taxation seemed tyrannical when levied by the English Parliament in which the Colonists were not represented. On October 7,
1765, delegates of nine colonies met in New York in what became
known as the "Stamp-Act Congress," and passed, among other matters, a series of resolutions which have been called the Declaration
of Rights and Grievances.

[3] H. J. Carman and H. C. Syrett, *History of the American People* (New York:
Alfred A. Knopf, 1952) I, pp. 118 ff.

[4] A copy of the plan appears in H. S. Commager, *Documents of American History*
(7th ed.; New York: Appleton-Century-Crofts, 1963) p. 43; and in W. Mac-
Donald, *Documentary Source Book of American History, 1606–1775* (New
York: Macmillan, 1899) p. 253.

[5] Leonard W. Labaree, ed., *The Papers of Benjamin Franklin* (New Haven:
Yale University Press, 1962) p. 454.

Resolutions of the Stamp Act Congress

OCTOBER 19, 1765

The members of this Congress, sincerely devoted, with the warmest sentiments of affection and duty to his Majesty's person and government, inviolably attached to the present happy establishment of the Protestant succession, and with minds deeply impressed by a sense of the present and impending misfortunes of the British colonies on this continent; having considered as maturely as time will permit, the circumstances of the said colonies, esteem it our indispensible duty to make the following declarations of our humble opinion, respecting the most essential rights and liberties of the colonists, and of the grievances under which they labour, by reason of several late acts of parliament.

I. That his Majesty's subjects in these colonies, owe the same allegiance to the crown of Great Britain, that is owing from his subjects born within the realm, and all due subordination to that august body the parliament of Great-Britain.

II. That his Majesty's liege subjects in these colonies, are intitled to all the inherent rights and liberties of his natural born subjects, within the kingdom of Great-Britain.

III. That it is inseparably essential to the freedom of a people, and the undoubted right of Englishmen, that no Taxes be imposed on them but with their own consent, given personally, or by their representatives.

IV. That the people of these colonies are not, and, from their local circumstances, cannot be, represented in the House of Commons in Great-Britain.

V. That the only representatives of the people of these colonies are persons chosen therein by themselves, and that no taxes ever have been, or can be constitutionally imposed on them, but by their respective legislatures.

VI. That all supplies to the crown being free gifts of the people, it is unreasonable and inconsistent with the principles and spirit of the British constitution, for the people of Great-Britain to grant to his Majesty the property of the colonists.

VII. That trial by jury, is the inherent and invaluable right of every British subject in these colonies.

VIII. That the late act of parliament, entitled An act for granting and applying certain stamp duties, and other duties, in the British colonies and plantations in America, &c. by imposing taxes on the inhabitants of these colonies, and the said act, and several other acts, by extending the jurisdiction of the courts of admiralty beyond its ancient limits, have a manifest tendency to subvert the rights and liberties of the colonists.

IX. That the duties imposed by several late acts of parliament, from the peculiar circumstances of these colonies, will be extremely burthensome and grievous; and from the scarcity of specie, the payment of them absolutely impracticable.

X. That as the profits of the trade of these colonies ultimately center in Great-Britain, to pay for the manufactures which they are obliged to take from thence, they eventually contribute very largely to all supplies granted there to the crown.

XI. That the restrictions imposed by several late acts of parliament on the trade of these colonies, will render them unable to purchase the manufactures of Great-Britain.

XII. That the increase, prosperity and happiness of these colonies, depend on the full and free enjoyments of their rights and liberties, and an intercourse with Great-Britain mutually affectionate and advantageous.

XIII. That it is the right of the British subjects in these colonies to petition the king, or either house of parliament.

Lastly, That it is the indispensible duty of these colonies, to the best of sovereigns, to the mother country, and to themselves, to endeavour by a loyal and dutiful address to his Majesty, and humble applications to both houses of parliament, to procure the repeal of the act for granting and applying certain stamp duties, of all clauses of any other acts of parliament, whereby the jurisdiction of the admiralty is extended as aforesaid, and of the other late acts for the restriction of American commerce.[6]

One hears echoes of 1628, and the Petition of Right. The country was moving toward the American Revolution and the great names begin to appear. John Dickinson of Pennsylvania[7] drafted the Declaration of Rights and Grievances; he was later to sign the Articles of Confederation, and in 1787 was to take a prominent part in the Philadelphia convention that drafted the Constitution of the United States.

[6] The Declaration of Rights appears at page 27 and following of the "Journal of the First Congress of the American Colonies in opposition to the Tyrannical Acts of the British Parliament." It is reprinted in Commager's *Documents of American History,* 7th ed., p. 57; in MacDonald, *Select Charters and Other Documents Illustrative of American History, 1606–1775* (2nd ed.; New York: Macmillan, 1904) p. 313.

[7] Commager, in his *Documents of American History,* 7th ed., p. 58, says that the Declaration of Rights was probably drafted by John Dickinson, but that some ascribe it to John Cruger of New York.

The Continental Congress

Relations between America and England continued to deteriorate. Radicals thought the English were tyrants; English reactionaries thought the colonists were rebels. On May 17, 1774, a Providence town meeting proposed an intercolonial congress to discuss the troubles.[8] "Committees of Correspondence" from New York and Philadelphia, and the Virginia House of Burgesses made the same proposal. On June 17, the Massachusetts Assembly, prompted by Samuel Adams, invited the other colonies to send delegates to a Continental Congress in Philadelphia the following September—

> to consult upon . . . wise and proper measures to be by them recommended to all the colonies, for the recovery and establishment of their just rights and liberties, civil and religious, and the restoration of union and harmony between Great Britain and the colonies. . . .

The Massachusetts House suggested to the other colonies choice of delegates ". . . either by their respective houses of Congresses or representatives, or by convention, or by the Committees of Correspondence . . ." The Continental Congress met on September 5, 1774,[9] with representatives from every colony except Georgia. Resounding pronouncements expressed their present discontents. On October 14, 1774, the Congress agreed to a Declaration of American Rights, denouncing as unjust and unconstitutional the Parliamentary "Intolerable Acts," passed in response to the Boston Tea Party and other

[8] Carman and Syrett, *History of the American People*, I, p. 143.

[9] *Journals of the Continental Congress* (34 vols.; Washington: U.S. Government Printing Office, 1904–1937) I, p. 13; MacDonald, *Select Charters and Other Documents, 1606–1775*, p. 356; Carman and Syrett, *History of the American People*, p. 139. The session of the Continental Congress from Sept. 5 to Oct. 26, 1774, is commonly called the "First Continental Congress"; that from May 10, 1775, to Dec. 12, 1776, is often called the "Second Continental Congress." There were fifteen sessions in all; the exigencies of war moved the meeting place, from time to time: the Congress sat in Philadelphia, Baltimore, Lancaster (a session of one day, September 27, 1777), York, Princeton, Annapolis, Trenton, and New York. Perhaps these peregrinations and the brevity of some sessions have discouraged reference by ordinal numbers to the sessions after the Second. After the Articles of Confederation took effect, on March 1, 1781, when Maryland furnished the thirteenth ratification, the assembly should properly be called the Congress of the Confederation. However the edition of the Journals prepared by the Library of Congress from its original records refers to the body from 1774 to 1789 as the Continental Congress. It was superseded by the Congress of the United States on March 4, 1789, when the present Constitution began its operation.

colonial resistance to the Crown.[10] The Colonists, said the Declaration, were "entitled to life, liberty and property & . . . had never ceded to any sovereign power whatever, a right to dispose of either without their consent."[11]

Here was the language of Locke; here was a hint of the future Declaration of Independence. In the Declaration of American Rights was language suggestive of the Constitution of 1789, of the Bill of Rights of 1791, and of the Fourteenth Amendment of 1868. The seeds of the Constitution were growing. The Continental Congress, extra-legally called together, was the direct ancestor of today's national legislature.

Those who write history are accustomed to mark changes in national development by dramatic events, as though mankind from time to time turned sharp corners. Conventionally, the origin of the United States has been considered the Declaration of Independence, but like most human institutions, the United States came about in slow growth. If some one moment had to be chosen for the Union's beginning, perhaps the calling of the First Continental Congress is a better point than any other. The Congress in an "Address to the People of Great Britain" of October 21, 1774,[12] speaks of "friends" and "fellow-subjects"; but it speaks of America as "This unhappy country." Congress speaks to the British of "your Parliament"—not "our Parliament." There was independence in the phrase, "Let justice and humanity cease to be the boast of your nation!"

The Continental Congress was originally an extralegal, a revolutionary body. It had only one House, in which each State had only a single vote, no matter how large the State's delegation. The Congress managed in some way to sever the Colonies from England, to run the United States, and to carry on the war of independence, all without a formal constitution, until 1781. It governed without any carefully organized governmental structure. But the embryonic origins of a national government operating directly on individuals, not through the governments of the Colonies, may be seen in the "Association" of October 20, 1774.[13] This was an attempt to apply economic sanctions against England. Measures were to commence by nonimportation on December 1, 1774: If this did not bring the British to terms, exports to Great Britain, Ireland, and the West Indies "except rice

---

[10] Carman and Syrett, *History of the American People*, I, p. 144; *Journals of the Continental Congress*, I, p. 63.

[11] *Journals of the Continental Congress*, I, p. 67; MacDonald, *Select Charters and Other Documents, 1606–1775*, p. 356.

[12] *Journals of the Continental Congress*, I, p. 82 *et seq.*

[13] *Journals of the Continental Congress,* I, p. 75 *et seq.*; Carman and Syrett, *History of the American People*, I, p. 145.

to Europe" were to cease on September 10, 1775.[14] One would have to understand the contemporary theories of economics and colonial trade to comprehend the reasons why men thought this project could strengthen the troubled Colonies by excluding goods they needed. Perhaps the Congress thought the Colonies were less dependent on overseas trade than Great Britain, and so embargoes could be an effective means of pressure on the mother-country. At any rate, the existence of the Association scheme, not its soundness, is here the point. To enforce it, some local machinery was essential, and the Congress recommended "Committees of Safety and Inspection" in every county, city and town, supposedly chosen by persons qualified to vote for members of the colonial legislatures. When any person should violate the Association, the appropriate Committee was to "cause the truth of the case to be published in the Gazette; to the end, that all such foes to the rights of British-America may be publicly known and universally continued as the enemies of American liberty." Denunciation would bring about boycotts of the violators. Such committees, mostly made up of radical elements in the population, quickly appeared in every colony but Georgia. They functioned vigorously, and imports to the Colonies fell radically. Here was a mechanism of government, revolutionary in its origin like the Continental Congress, which furthermore could operate on individuals. After actual warfare with England had broken out at Lexington and Concord on April 19, 1775, the patriot troops, gathered in Cambridge, were collected for the most part by these radical Committees appointed to enforce the Association.

Meantime revolutionary movements were well under way. By 1774, every colony except New York and Georgia had some form of revolutionary government in the form of a Provincial Congress, Convention or Conference. On May 10, 1775, the Second Continental Congress assembled in Philadelphia. By the autumn of 1775, the old colonial governments had largely disappeared.

A basic weakness of the United States under the Continental Congress was its powerlessness to compel States to comply with national policies. The Congress in a contest for predominance depended on local cooperation; unless compliance with some national policy could be obtained in all States, a divergence from it in one or a few States tended to destroy the policy even in those States which attempted to comply with it. This phenomenon has appeared in much more recent times. Mr. Justice Holmes, dissenting in 1918 in the Child Labor case[15] wrote of the necessity for a central government to in-

---

[14] *Journals of the Continental Congress*, I, p. 77.
[15] *Hammer* v. *Dagenhart*, 247 U.S. 251 at p. 281.

hibit economic parochialism in the States, lest the least wise depreciate the best. Just as it was difficult in 1918 for one State which wished to eliminate child labor to do so in the face of competition from States having a less humane and so less immediately expensive policy, so in 1778 it was difficult for any State seeking to control inflation during the War of Independence to do so when neighboring States were unwilling to control prices. On November 22, 1777, the Congress recommended to the legislatures of New Hampshire, Massachusetts, Rhode Island, Connecticut, New York, New Jersey, Pennsylvania, and Delaware that they appoint commissioners to convene at New Haven on January 15[16] to regulate prices. These commissioners met and agreed to a general advance of not more than 75% over prices in 1774.

New York by Chapter 34 of its first session, on April 3, 1778, accordingly set prices for various goods and services:

> Seventhly. That the price of the following articles at the first port of delivery or place of manufacture within the respective States shall not exceed the rates to them affixed respectively viz. Good West-India rum three dollars per gallon, by wholesale, best Muscovado sugar, thirty three dollars and one third of a dollar per hundred, gross weight and all other sugars in usual proportion according to quality; best molasses one dollar and an half per gallon, by wholesale; coffee three fourths of a dollar per pound by the hundred weight; good merchantable geneva two dollars per gallon. Good merchantable brandy two dollars per gallon. Good merchantable whiskey, one dollar and one sixth of a dollar per gallon. All other distilled spirits, not therein enumerated, not to exceed two dollars per gallon. . .
>
> Ninthly. That innholders be not allowed more than fifty per centum advance on the wholesale prices of all liquors or other foreign articles therein stated and by them sold in small quantities allowing aforesaid for charges of transportation, and for all other articles of entertainment refreshment and forage not exceeding seventy five per centum advance on the prices which the same were sold at in the same places in the year one thousand seven hundred and seventy four. . .
>
> Tenthly. Best grass fed beef with hide and tallow two pounds six shillings and eight pence for every hundred pounds weight and so in proportion for that of inferior quality. Best stall fed beef with the hide and tallow three pounds four shillings for every hundred pounds weight and so in proportion for that of inferior quality. Good butter by the firkin or cask one shilling and eight pence per pound and by

---

[16] *Journals of the Continental Congress*, IX, p. 956. Commissioners from Virginia, Maryland and North Carolina were to meet at Fredericksburg, Va., on the same day; those from South Carolina and Georgia, at Charleston a month later.

the single pound or small quantity one shilling and nine pence half penny. . .

> . . . Common sort of mens shoe made of neat leather sixteen shillings per pair. Mens calf skin shoes of the best quality twenty shillings per pair; and womens and childrens shoes in due proportion. . .

This war-time price-fixing effort was temporarily suspended during part of the summer of 1778, and finally collapsed because of the neglect or refusal of some of the other States to pass similar legislation. At the second session of the New York Legislature in Chapter 2, that body recited on October 28, 1778:

> Inasmuch as the act entitled 'An act to regulate the wages of mechanicks and labourers, the prices of goods and commodities and the charges of innholders within this State; and for other purposes therein mentioned,' passed on the third day of April last, has not answered the salutary purposes for which it was intended by reason of the neglect or refusal of some of the other United States to pass similar laws.
>
> Be it therefore enacted by the People of the State of New York represented in Senate and Assembly. . . That the said act, . . . and every clause, article and thing therein contained, shall be, and is hereby repealed and made void, to all intents, constructions and purposes whatever.

By February 26, 1780[17] the New York Legislature pursuant to a new recommendation of the Congress dated November 19, 1779, was trying to limit prices to twenty times those current in 1774. The statute made sale obligatory upon tender of the statutory price to anyone having a surplus of goods; but rather pathetically provided that the statute would not take effect until the legislatures of Massachusetts, Connecticut, and Pennsylvania should pass similar measures. The laws of New York contain nothing to indicate the subsequent fate of this well-meaning legislation.

In any country engaged in a serious war, the prospect of monetary inflation presents a grave threat. The Continental Congress lacked the formal power and the popular backing to achieve what was easily attained in 1948 when the Congress as part of the aftermath of the Second World War successfully set a limit on the rentals of residential real property in Cleveland, Ohio.[18]

The Constitution of the United States, between 1774 and 1781, was whatever the Continental Congress decided to attempt. And

[17] See Chapter 43, third session, Laws of New York.
[18] *Woods* v. *Miller Co.*, 333 U.S. 138 (1948).

despite a dearth of means to give effect to its policies, the Congress accomplished astonishing successes. It contracted an offensive and defensive alliance with France in 1778; it financed the war of independence, raised and organized a continental army, built and administered a navy, and made war against England by land and sea. That Congress and the system under which it operated had serious shortcomings; but its accomplishments were amazing. Our present government evolved from it. It set going the United States of America.

One is struck by the detail of the Congress' concerns. Its journal discloses that one day in July, 1776 it decided to apply to the Committee of Safety of Pennsylvania for a supply of gunflints; it requested "the colony of Maryland and Delaware" to send troops to Philadelphia; it told off a couple of members to determine the proper payment for the hire of a Mr. Walker's vessel employed by Commodore Hopkins; it arranged to send a man to Orange county for a sample of flintstone; it ordered that an express who brought despatches from Trenton be paid "27/= 3 54/90ths dollars," a sum now rather incomprehensible, but doubtless no more than his due who brought good news from Trenton. Amid these and other like preoccupations the Congress on the same day approved a formal declaration that all political connection between the United States and Great Britain was and ought to be totally dissolved.[19]

The Declaration of Independence

The Declaration of July 4, 1776, was actually a formal announcement of a *fait accompli,* long in the making. The ultimate preceding step had occurred two days earlier, on July 2.

On June 7, 1776, Richard Henry Lee had moved in the Continental Congress a resolution[20] "that these united colonies are, and of right ought to be free and independent states . . ." and further moved that alliances be negotiated and that there be prepared a plan of confederation. John Adams seconded the motion. After final decision had been postponed for three weeks, a committee consisting of Thomas Jefferson, Benjamin Franklin, John Adams, Roger Sherman, and Robert R. Livingston was appointed to prepare a declaration of national independence. Nine colonies voted for the declaration when it again came before Congress on July 1. Pennsylvania and South

[19] *Journals of the Continental Congress,* V, Transactions of July 4, 1776, p. 509 *et seq.*

[20] *Journals of the Continental Congress,* V, p. 425.

Carolina were opposed; the Delaware delegation was tied; New York was excused from voting as its delegates had no instructions. On the following day, July 2, 1776, when the final vote was taken, all colonies but New York voted for independence.[21] The Resolution of Independence[22] was thus actually adopted[23] two days earlier than the day we celebrate. The action of the Continental Congress on July 4 was adoption of the final draft of the Declaration.[24]

The Declaration is not a piece of legislation in the same sense as the Constitution. It is a statement of political theory, justifying the break with England, and expressing an egalitarian philosophy common among the less conservative elements in the Continental Congress. It is a Lockean statement, reciting the right of the people to end one government and institute another, taking as the premises of the new government so created the "self-evident truth" that all men are created equal; that they are endowed by their Creator with certain inalienable rights; that among these are life, liberty, and the pursuit of happiness. The Declaration states that governments are instituted among men to secure these rights, and that their just powers are derived from the consent of the governed. Its Lockean flavor is not at all extraordinary; Jefferson was its primary draftsman and he knew and respected Locke. He wrote of Locke's as one of the "elementary books of public right," and he cited Chapter 11 of the Second Treatise in his Commonplace Book.[25] The style as well as the substance of the Declaration are evidence that the theorist and apologist of the Glorious Revolution of 1688 had an influence nearly a century later consciously felt by the theorist and apologist of the American Revolution. There was a sort of laying on of hands.

Like other constituent documents in English-American constitutional history, the Declaration has acquired an influence far greater than its legal effect. Its long recital of grievances against George III seems to a modern reader a little contrived, as indeed it was. The

[21] A readable account is John Fiske, *The American Revolution* (Boston: Houghton Mifflin and Co. 1891) Chapter V.

[22] Carl Becker's term. See his *Declaration of Independence* (New York: Alfred A. Knopf, 1942) p. 3

[23] *Journals of the Continental Congress*, V, p. 57.

[24] See Carl Becker's *Declaration of Independence* and Carman and Syrett, *History of the American People*, I, pp. 147–152.

[25] See a letter from Jefferson to Henry Lee, quoted in Chinard, *The Commonplace Book of Thomas Jefferson* (Baltimore: Johns Hopkins Press, 1926) p. 44; the reference to Chapter 11 of the *Second Treatise of Government* occurs at page 214. Jefferson also abstracted part of the Letter Concerning Toleration. See Chinard's appendix. See also Carl Lotus Becker, *Declaration of Independence*, p. 27.

Declaration was intended to rally faint hearts. The strange beauty of its style, Jefferson's "felicitous, haunting cadence"[26] which makes quotation so appealing, the wistful aspiration to equality in its philosophy, have struck the imagination of many generations. What other political document of the eighteenth century is still reprinted annually in American newspapers?[27]

The Declaration of Independence

In Congress JULY 4, 1776

THE UNANIMOUS DECLARATION OF THE THIRTEEN UNITED STATES OF AMERICA

When, in the course of human events, it becomes necessary for one people to dissolve the political bands which have connected them with another, and to assume, among the powers of the earth, the separate and equal station to which the laws of nature and of nature's God entitle them, a decent respect to the opinions of mankind requires that they should declare the causes which impel them to the separation.

We hold these truths to be self-evident: that all men are created equal; that they are endowed, by their Creator, with certain unalienable rights; that among these are life, liberty, and the pursuit of happiness. That, to secure these rights, governments are instituted among men, deriving their just powers from the consent of the governed; that whenever any form of government becomes destructive of these ends, it is the right of the people to alter or to abolish it, and to institute a new government, laying its foundation on such principles, and organizing its powers in such form, as to them shall seem most likely to effect their safety and happiness. Prudence, indeed, will dictate, that governments long established, should not be changed for light and transient causes; and accordingly all experience hath shown, that mankind are more disposed to suffer, while evils are sufferable, than to right themselves by abolishing the forms to which they are accustomed. But when a long train of abuses and usurpations, pursuing invariably the same object, evinces a design to reduce them under absolute despotism, it is their right, it is their duty, to throw off such government, and to provide new guards for their future security. Such has been the patient sufferance of these colonies, and such is now the necessity which constrains them to alter their former systems of government. The history of the present King of Great Britain is a history

[26] Becker, *Declaration of Independence*, p. 5.
[27] See for example, the *N.Y. Times*, July 4, 1964, p. 6. The text which follows is that printed in United States Statutes at Large, I, p. 1.

of repeated injuries and usurpations, all having in direct object the establishment of an absolute tyranny over these states. To prove this, let facts be submitted to a candid world: —

He has refused his assent to laws the most wholesome and necessary for the public good.

He has forbidden his governors to pass laws of immediate and pressing importance, unless suspended in their operation till his assent should be obtained; and when so suspended, he has utterly neglected to attend to them.

He has refused to pass other laws for the accommodation of large districts of people, unless those people would relinquish the right of representation in the legislature; a right inestimable to them, and formidable to tyrants only. He has called together legislative bodies at places unusual, uncomfortable, and distant from the depository of their public records, for the sole purpose of fatiguing them into compliance with his measures.

He has dissolved representative houses repeatedly, for opposing, with manly firmness, his invasions on the rights of the people.

He has refused for a long time, after such dissolutions, to cause others to be elected; whereby the legislative powers, incapable of annihilation, have returned to the people at large for their exercise; the state remaining, in the meantime, exposed to all the danger of invasion from without, and convulsions within.

He has endeavored to prevent the population of these States; for that purpose obstructing the laws for naturalization of foreigners; refusing to pass others to encourage their migration hither, and raising the conditions of new appropriations of lands.

He has obstructed the administration of justice, by refusing his assent to laws for establishing judiciary powers.

He has made judges dependent on his will alone, for the tenure of their offices, and the amount and payment of their salaries.

He has erected a multitude of new offices, and sent hither swarms of officers, to harass our people, and eat out their substance.

He has kept among us, in time of peace, standing armies, without the consent of our legislatures.

He has affected to render the military independent of, and superior to the civil power.

He has combined with others to subject us to a jurisdiction foreign to our constitution, and unacknowledged by our laws; giving his assent to their acts of pretended legislation:

For quartering large bodies of armed troops among us:

For protecting them, by a mock trial, from punishment for any murders which they should commit on the inhabitants of these States;

For cutting off our trade with all parts of the world;

For imposing taxes on us without our consent;

For depriving us, in many cases, of the benefit of trial by jury;

For transporting us beyond seas to be tried for pretended offenses;

For abolishing the free system of English laws in a neighboring province, establishing therein an arbitrary government, and enlarging its boundaries, so as to render it at once an example and fit instrument for introducing the same absolute rule into these colonies;

For taking away our charters, abolishing our most valuable laws, and altering fundamentally the powers of our governments;

For suspending our own legislatures, and declaring themselves invested with power to legislate for us in all cases whatsoever.

He has abdicated government here, by declaring us out of his protection, and waging war against us.

He has plundered our seas, ravaged our coasts, burnt our towns, and destroyed the lives of our people.

He is at this time transporting large armies of foreign mercenaries to complete the works of death, desolation, and tyranny, already begun with circumstances of cruelty and perfidy, scarcely paralleled in the most barbarous ages, and totally unworthy the head of a civilized nation.

He has constrained our fellow citizens, taken captive on the high seas, to bear arms against their country, to become the executioners of their friends and brethren, or to fall themselves by their hands.

He has excited domestic insurrections amongst us, and has endeavored to bring on the inhabitants of our frontiers the merciless Indian savages, whose known rule of warfare is an undistinguished destruction of all ages, sexes, and conditions.

In every stage of these oppressions, we have petitioned for redress, in the most humble terms. Our repeated petitions have been answered only by repeated injury. A prince, whose character is thus marked by every act which may define a tyrant, is unfit to be the ruler of a free people.

Nor have we been wanting in attentions to our British brethren. We have warned them, from time to time, of attempts by their legislature to extend an unwarrantable jurisdiction over us. We have reminded them of the circumstances of our emigration and settlement here. We have appealed to their native justice and magnanimity, and we have conjured them by the ties of our common kindred to disavow these usurpations, which would inevitably interrupt our connexions and correspondence. They too have been deaf to the voice of justice and of consanguinity. We must, therefore, acquiesce in the necessity which denounces our separation, and hold them, as we hold the rest of mankind, enemies in war, in peace friends.

We, therefore, the representatives of the UNITED STATES OF AMERICA, in General Congress assembled, appealing to the Supreme Judge of the world for the rectitude of our intentions, do, in the name, and by the authority of the good people of these colonies, solemnly publish and declare, that these United Colonies are, and of right ought to be, FREE and INDEPENDENT STATES; that they are absolved from all allegiance to the British Crown, and that all political connexion between them and the state of Great Britain is, and ought to be, totally dissolved; and that, as FREE and INDEPENDENT STATES, they have full power to levy war, conclude peace, contract alliances, establish commerce, and to do all other acts and things which INDEPENDENT STATES may of right do. And, for the support of this declaration, with a firm reliance on the protection of DIVINE PROVIDENCE, we mutually pledge to each other our lives, our fortunes, and our sacred honor.

John Hancock

New Hampshire.—Josiah Bartlett, William Whipple, Matthew Thornton.

Massachusetts Bay.—Samuel Adams, John Adams, Robert Treat Paine, Elbridge Gerry.

Rhode Island, &c.—Stephen Hopkins, William Ellery.

Connecticut.—Roger Sherman, Samuel Huntington, William Williams, Oliver Wolcott.

New York.—William Floyd, Philip Livingston, Francis Lewis, Lewis Morris.

New Jersey.—Richard Stockton, John Witherspoon, Francis Hopkinson, John Hart, Abraham Clark.

Pennsylvania.—Robert Morris, Benjamin Rush, Benjamin Franklin, John Morton, George Clymer, James Smith, George Taylor, James Wilson, George Ross.

Delaware.—Cæsar Rodney, George Read, Thomas M'Kean.

Maryland.—Samuel Chase, William Paca, Thomas Stone, Charles Carroll of Carrollton.

Virginia.—George Wythe, Richard Henry Lee, Thomas Jefferson, Benjamin Harrison, Thomas Nelson, Jun., Francis Lightfoot Lee, Carter Braxton.

North Carolina.—William Hooper, Joseph Hewes, John Penn.

South Carolina.—Edward Rutledge, Thomas Hayward, Jun., Thomas Lynch, Jun., Arthur Middleton.

Georgia.—Button Gwinnett, Lyman Hall, George Walton.

The Articles of Confederation

Some kind of union had existed between the American States ever since the first Continental Congress assembled in 1774.[28] Indeed some

---

[28] This account is largely drawn from Chapter III of John Fiske's *Critical Period of American History* (Boston: Houghton Mifflin, 1888). Fiske's book, intended rather for the general reader than for the critical scholar, is still a vivid and effective story of the difficulties of the Confederation which led to the Constitutional Convention of 1787. Mr. Justice Jackson cited Fiske's fourth chapter, "Drifting Toward Anarchy," in his opinion in *Independent Warehouses* v. *Scheele*, 331 U.S. 70, 91 (1947), and again in *Hood* v. *Du Mond*, 336 U.S. 525 (1949)

sort of community action had existed ever since the French War. At the time of the Declaration of Independence, Maryland and South Carolina, without any crying grievances of their own, joined from a feeling that union was desirable. The Declaration was itself a sort of act of union. It was more than an announcement by which a series of independent republics severally split off from England; it was the manifesto of a new aggregate nation, a statement of common ideals and united action, made together by colonies formerly somewhat separate. Its form was significant; it was a "Declaration by the Representatives of The United States of America in General Congress Assembled."

Nevertheless, even before the Declaration was drawn, the necessity for a better defined government was already present in the minds of the members of Congress. On July 21, 1775, Franklin had presented to the Congress a draft of Articles of Confederation.[29] Three weeks before the adoption of the Declaration of Independence, the Congress had appointed a committee to draw up "Articles of Confederation and Perpetual Union." The work of the committee was done in secret and has never been reported, and no one now knows just how the Articles were produced. John Dickinson is supposed to have been their principal author. The committee finished its work by the 12th day of July, 1776,[30] but the Articles were not adopted by Congress until November 15, 1777. Ratification by the several States took over three years more. The Articles had an odd omission: in them is no statement (as there is in the last Article of the Constitution of 1789) prescribing the number of State ratifications which will render the Articles effective. The Congress assumed that this would occur only when all thirteen States should have accepted the new instrument of union.

Maryland, on March 1, 1781, became the thirteenth and final State to approve the Articles. Nearly twenty-two months had passed since the twelfth State, Delaware, had signed. Maryland had held out until she was sure that the unoccupied western lands, expected as a gain if the war should be won, and claimed by a number of the States, would become an asset of the nation and not of any one State. In the Journal of the Continental Congress, immediately before the note of

---

p. 533. Mr. Justice Black cited Fiske's *Critical Period* in the prevailing opinion in *Engel* v. *Vitale*, 370 U.S. 421 (1962) pp. 428 and 429. For an adverse judgment of Fiske, see Merrill Jensen, *The New Nation* (New York: Alfred A. Knopf, 1962).

[29] *Journals of the Continental Congress*, II, p. 195.

[30] *Journals of the Continental Congress*, V, p. 546. The Committee's draft is in Dickinson's handwriting.

Maryland's ratification, is recorded an Act of Cession by which New York quit-claimed ". . . for the only use, and benefit of such of the states as are or shall become parties to the Articles of Confederation," lands west of a north-south line through the most westerly "bent" of Lake Ontario or, if farther west, a north-south line twenty miles west of the most westerly "bent" of the Niagara River; and all lands north of the forty-fifth degree of north latitude.[31]

Between March 1, 1781 and the first Wednesday in March, 1789, when the Continental Congress called the meeting of the first Congress under the Constitution, the Articles defined the Government of the United States—

Articles of Confederation and Perpetual Union

To all to whom these Presents shall come, we the undersigned Delegates of the States affixed to our Names, send greeting. Whereas the Delegates of the United States of America, in Congress assembled, did, on the fifteenth day of November, in the Year of our Lord One Thousand Seven Hundred and Seventy Seven, and in the Second Year of the Independence of America, agree to certain articles of Confederation and perpetual Union between the States of New-hampshire, Massachusetts-bay, Rhode-island and Providence Plantations, Connecticut, New York, New Jersey, Pennsylvania, Delaware, Maryland, Virginia, North-Carolina, South-Carolina and Georgia in the words following, viz. "Articles of Confederation and perpetual Union between the states of New-hampshire, Massachusetts-bay, Rhode-island and Providence Plantations, Connecticut, New-York, New-Jersey, Pennsylvania, Delaware, Maryland, Virginia, North-Carolina, South-Carolina and Georgia.

Art. I. The Stile of this confederacy shall be "The United States of America."

Art. II. Each state retains its sovereignty, freedom, and independence, and every Power, Jurisdiction and right, which is not by this confederation expressly delegated to the United States, in Congress assembled.

Art. III. The said states hereby severally enter into a firm league of friendship with each other, for their common defence, the security of their Liberties, and their mutual and general welfare, binding themselves to assist each other, against all force offered to, or attacks made upon them, or any of them, on account of religion, sovereignty, trade, or any other pretence whatever.

Art. IV. The better to secure and perpetuate mutual friendship and intercourse among the people of the different states in this union, the

[31] *Journals of the Continental Congress,* XIX, p. 208 *et seq.*

free inhabitants of each of these states, paupers, vagabonds and fugitives from justice excepted, shall be entitled to all privileges and immunities of free citizens in the several states; and the people of each state shall have free ingress and regress to and from any other state, and shall enjoy therein all the privileges of trade and commerce, subject to the same duties, impositions and restrictions as the inhabitants thereof respectively, provided that such restriction shall not extend so far as to prevent the removal of property imported into any state, to any other state, of which the Owner is an inhabitant; provided also that no imposition, duties or restriction shall be laid by any state, on the property of the united states, or either of them.

If any Person guilty of, or charged with treason, felony, or other high misdemeanor in any state, shall flee from Justice, and be found in any of the united states, he shall, upon demand of the Governor or executive power, of the state from which he fled, be delivered up and removed to the state having jurisdiction of his offence.

Full faith and credit shall be given in each of these states to the records, acts and judicial proceedings of the courts and magistrates of every other state.

Art. V. For the more convenient management of the general interests of the united states, delegates shall be annually appointed in such manner as the legislature of each state shall direct, to meet in Congress on the first Monday in November, in every year, with a power reserved to each state, to recal its delegates, or any of them, at any time within the year, and to send others in their stead, for the remainder of the Year.

No state shall be represented in Congress by less than two, nor by more than seven Members; and no person shall be capable of being a delegate for more than three years in any term of six years; nor shall any person, being a delegate, be capable of holding any office under the united states, for which he, or another for his benefit receives any salary, fees or emolument of any kind.

Each state shall maintain its own delegates in a meeting of the states, and while they act as members of the committee of the states.

In determining questions in the united states in Congress assembled, each state shall have one vote.

Freedom of speech and debate in Congress shall not be impeached or questioned in any Court, or place out of Congress, and the members of congress shall be protected in their persons from arrests and imprisonments, during the time of their going to and from, and attendance on congress, except for treason, felony, or breach of the peace.

Art. VI. No state, without the Consent of the united states in congress assembled, shall send any embassy to, or receive any embassy from, or enter into any conference, agreement, or alliance or treaty with any King, prince or state; nor shall any person holding any office of profit or trust under the united states, or any of them, accept of any present, emolument, office or title of any kind whatever from any king, prince or foreign state; nor shall the united states in congress assembled, or any of them, grant any title of nobility.

No two or more states shall enter into any treaty, confederation or alliance whatever between them, without the consent of the united states in congress assembled, specifying accurately the purposes for which the same is to be entered into, and how long it shall continue.

No state shall lay any imposts or duties, which may interfere with any stipulations in treaties, entered into by the united states in congress assembled, with any king, prince or state, in pursuance of any treaties already proposed by congress, to the courts of France and Spain.

No vessels of war shall be kept up in time of peace by any state, except such number only, as shall be deemed necessary by the united states in congress assembled, for the defence of such state, or its trade; nor shall any body of forces be kept up by any state, in time of peace, except such number only, as in the judgment of the united states, in congress assembled, shall be deemed requisite to garrison the forts necessary for the defence of such state; but every state shall always keep up a well regulated and disciplined militia, sufficiently armed and accoutred, and shall provide and constantly have ready for use, in public stores, a due number of field pieces and tents, and a proper quantity of arms, ammunition and camp equipage.

No state shall engage in any war without the consent of the united states in congress assembled, unless such state be actually invaded by enemies, or shall have received certain advice of a resolution being formed by some nation of Indians to invade such state, and the danger is so imminent as not to admit of a delay, till the united states in congress assembled can be consulted: nor shall any state grant commissions to any ships or vessels of war, nor letters of marque or reprisal, except it be after a declaration of war by the united states in congress assembled, and then only against the kingdom or state and the subjects thereof, against which war has been so declared, and under such regulations as shall be established by the united states in congress assembled, unless such state be infested by pirates, in which case vessels of war may be fitted out for that occasion, and kept so long as the danger shall continue, or until the united states in congress assembled, shall determine otherwise.

Art. VII. When land-forces are raised by any state for the common defence, all officers of or under the rank of colonel, shall be appointed by the legislature of each state respectively, by whom such forces shall be raised, or in such manner as such state shall direct, and all vacancies shall be filled up by the State which first made the appointment.

Art. VIII. All charges of war, and all other expences that shall be incurred for the common defence or general welfare, and allowed by the united states in congress assembled, shall be defrayed out of a common treasury, which shall be supplied by the several states in proportion to the value of all land within each state, granted to or surveyed for any Person, as such land and the buildings and improvements thereon shall be estimated according to such mode as the united states in congress assembled, shall from time to time direct and appoint. The taxes for paying that proportion shall be laid and levied by the authority and direction of the legislatures of the several states within the time agreed upon by the united states in congress assembled.

Art. IX. The united states in congress assembled, shall have the sole and exclusive right and power of determining on peace and war, except in the cases mentioned in the sixth article—of sending and receiving ambassadors—entering into treaties and alliances, provided that no treaty of commerce shall be made whereby the legislative power of the respective states shall be restrained from imposing such imposts and duties on foreigners, as their own people are subjected to, or from prohibiting the exportation or importation of any species of goods or commodities whatsoever—of establishing rules for deciding in all cases, what captures on land or water shall be legal, and in what manner prizes taken by land or naval forces in the service of the united states shall be divided or appropriated—of granting letters of marque and reprisal in times of peace—appointing courts for the trial of piracies and felonies committed on the high seas and establishing courts for receiving and determining finally appeals in all cases of captures, provided that no member of congress shall be appointed a judge of any of the said courts.

The united states in congress assembled shall also be the last resort on appeal in all disputes and differences now subsisting or that hereafter may arise between two or more states concerning boundary, jurisdiction or any other cause whatever; which authority shall always be exercised in the manner following. Whenever the legislative or executive authority or lawful agent of any state in controversy with another shall present a petition to congress stating the matter in question and praying for a hearing, notice thereof shall be given by order of congress to the legislative or executive authority of the other state in controversy, and a day assigned for the appearance of the parties by their lawful agents, who shall then be directed to appoint by joint consent, commissioners or judges to constitute a court for hearing and determining the matter in question: but if they cannot agree, congress shall name three persons out of each of the united states, and from the list of such persons each party shall alternately strike out one, the petitioners beginning, until the number shall be reduced to thirteen; and from that number not less than seven, nor more than nine names as congress shall direct, shall in the presence of congress be drawn out by lot, and the persons whose names shall be so drawn or any five of them, shall be commissioners or judges, to hear and finally determine the controversy, so always as a major part of the judges who shall hear the cause shall agree in the determination: and if either party shall neglect to attend at the day appointed, without showing reasons, which congress shall judge sufficient, or being present shall refuse to strike, the congress shall proceed to nominate three persons out of each state, and the secretary of congress shall strike in behalf of such party absent or refusing; and the judgment and sentence of the court to be appointed, in the manner before prescribed, shall be final and conclusive; and if any of the parties shall refuse to submit to the authority of such court, or to appear or defend their claim or cause, the court shall nevertheless proceed to pronounce sentence, or judgment, which shall in like manner be final and decisive, the judgment or sentence and other proceedings being in either case transmitted to congress, and lodged among the acts of congress for the security of the parties concerned: provided that every commissioner, before he sits in judgment, shall take an oath to be administered by one of the judges of the supreme or superior court of the state, where the cause shall be tried, "well and truly to hear and determine the matter in question, according to the best of his judgment, without favour, affection or hope of reward:" provided also, that no state shall be deprived of territory for the benefit of the united states.

All controversies concerning the private right of soil claimed under different grants of two or more states, whose jurisdictions as they may respect such lands, and the states which passed such grants are adjusted, the said grants or either of them being at the same time claimed to have originated antecedent to such settlement of jurisdiction, shall on the petition of either party to the congress of the united states, be finally determined as near as may be in the same manner as is before prescribed for deciding disputes respecting territorial jurisdiction between different states.

The united states in congress assembled shall also have the sole and exclusive right and power of regulating the alloy and value of coin struck by their own authority, or by that of the respective states—fixing the standard of weights and measures throughout the united states—regulating the trade and managing all affairs with the Indians, not members of any of the states, provided that the legislative right of any state within its own limits be not infringed or violated—establishing or regulating post-offices from one state to another, throughout all the united states, and exacting such postage on the papers passing thro' the same as may be requisite to defray the expences of the said office—appointing all officers of the land forces, in the service of the united states, excepting regimental officers—appointing all the officers of the naval forces, and commissioning all officers whatever in the service of the united states—making rules for the government and regulation of the said land and naval forces, and directing their operations.

The united states in congress assembled shall have authority to appoint a committee, to sit in the recess of congress, to be denominated "A Committee of the States," and to consist of one delegate from each state; and to appoint such other committees and civil officers as may be necessary for managing the general affairs of the united states under their direction—to appoint one of their number to preside, provided that no person be allowed to serve in the office of president more than one year in any term of three years; to ascertain the necessary sums of Money to be raised for the service of the united states, and to appropriate and apply the same for defraying the public expences—to borrow money, or emit bills on the credit of the united states, transmitting every half year to the respective states an account of the sums of money so borrowed or emitted—to build and equip a navy—to agree upon the number of land forces, and to make requisitions from each state for its quota, in proportion to the number of white inhabitants in such state; which requisition shall be binding, and thereupon the legislature of each state shall appoint the regimental officers, raise the men and cloath, arm and equip them in a soldier like manner, at the expence of the united states; and the officers and men so cloathed, armed and equipped shall march to the place appointed, and within the time agreed on by the united states in congress assembled: But if the united states in congress assembled shall, on consideration of circumstances judge proper that any state should not raise men, or should raise a smaller number than its quota, and that any other state should raise a greater number of men than the quota thereof, such extra number shall be raised, officered, cloathed, armed and equipped in the same manner as the quota of such state, unless the legislature of such state shall judge that such extra number cannot be safely spared out of the same, in which case they shall raise officer, cloath, arm and equip as many of such extra number as they judge can be safely spared. And the officers and men so cloathed, armed and equipped, shall march to the place appointed, and within the time agreed on by the united states in congress assembled.

The united states in congress assembled shall never engage in a war, nor grant letters of marque and reprisal in time of peace, nor enter into any treaties or alliances, nor coin money, nor regulate the value thereof, nor ascertain the sums and expences necessary for the defence and welfare of the united states, or any of them, nor emit bills, nor borrow money on the credit of the united states, nor appropiate money, nor agree upon the number of vessels of war, to be built or purchased, or the number of land or sea forces to be raised, nor appoint a commander in chief of the army or navy, unless nine states assent to the same: nor shall a question on any other point, except for adjourning from day to day be determined, unless by the votes of a majority of the united states in congress assembled.

The congress of the united states shall have power to adjourn to any time within the year, and to any place within the united states, so that no period of adjournment be for a longer duration than the space of six Months, and shall publish the Journal of their proceedings monthly, except such parts thereof relating to treaties, alliances or military operations, as in their judgment require secrecy; and the yeas and nays of the delegates of each state on any question shall be entered on the Journal, when it is desired by any delegate; and the delegates of a state, or any of them at his or their request shall be furnished with a transcript of the said Journal, except such parts as are above excepted, to lay before the legislatures of the several states.

Art. X. The committee of the states, or any nine of them, shall be authorised to execute, in the recess of congress, such of the powers of congress as the united states in congress assembled, by the consent of nine states, shall from time to time think expedient to vest them with; provided that no power be delegated to the said committee, for the exercise of which, by the articles of confederation, the voice of nine states in the congress of the united states assembled is requisite.

Art. XI. Canada acceding to this confederation, and joining in the measures of the united states, shall be admitted into, and entitled to all the advantages of this union: but no other colony shall be admitted into the same, unless such admission be agreed to by nine states.

Art. XII. All bills of credit emitted, monies borrowed and debts contracted by, or under the authority of congress, before the assembling of the united states, in pursuance of the present confederation, shall be deemed and considered as a charge against the united states, for payment and satisfaction whereof the said united states, and the public faith are hereby solemnly pledged.

Art. XIII. Every state shall abide by the determinations of the united states in congress assembled, on all questions which by this confederation are submitted to them. And the Articles of this confederation shall be inviolably observed by every state, and the union shall be perpetual; nor shall any alteration at any time hereafter be made in any of them; unless such alteration be agreed to in a congress of the united states, and be afterwards confirmed by the legislatures of every state.

And Whereas it hath pleased the Great Governor of the World to incline the hearts of the legislatures we respectively represent in congress, to approve of, and to authorize us to ratify the said articles of confederation and perpetual union. Know Ye that we the undersigned delegates, by virtue of the power and authority to us given for that purpose, do by these presents, in the name and in behalf of our respective constituents, fully and entirely ratify and confirm each and every of the said articles of confederation and perpetual union, and all and singular the matters and things therein contained: And we do further solemnly plight and engage the faith of our respective constituents, that they shall abide by the determinations of the united states in congress assembled, on all questions, which by the said confederation are submitted to them. And that the articles thereof shall be inviolably observed by the states we respectively represent, and that the union shall be perpetual. In Witness thereof we have hereunto set our hands in Congress. Done at Philadelphia in the state of Pennsylvania the ninth day of July, in the Year of our Lord one Thousand seven Hundred and Seventy-eight, and in the third year of the independence of America.

JOSIAH BARTLETT
JOHN WENTWORTH Junr
   August 8th 1778

On the part & behalf of the State of New Hampshire

JOHN HANCOCK
SAMUEL ADAMS
ELBRIDGE GERRY
FRANCIS DANA
JAMES LOVELL
SAMUEL HOLTEN

On the part and behalf of The State of Massachusetts Bay

WILLIAM ELLERY
HENRY MARCHANT
JOHN COLLINS

On the Part and Behalf of the State of Rhode-Island and Providence Plantations

ROGER SHERMAN
SAMUEL HUNTINGTON
OLIVER WOLCOTT
TITUS HOSMER
ANDREW ADAMS

On the part and behalf of the State of Connecticut

JA^s DUANE
FRA^s LEWIS
Wm DUER
GOUV MORRIS

On the Part and Behalf of the State of New York

JNO WITHERSPOON
NATH^l SCUDDER

On the Part and in Behalf of the State of New Jersey. Novr 26, 1778. —

ROB^t MORRIS
DANIEL ROBERDEAU
JON^a BAYARD SMITH
WILLIAM CLINGAN
JOSEPH REED   22^d July
   1778

On the part & behalf of the State of Pennsylvania

THO M:KEAN   Feby 12
   1779
JOHN DICKINSON   May 5th
   1779
NICHOLAS VAN DYKE

On the part & behalf of the State of Deleware

JOHN HANSON   March 1
   1781
DANIEL CARROLL d^o

On the part and behalf of the State of Maryland

RICHARD HENRY LEE JOHN BANISTER THOMAS ADAMS JN° HARVIE FRANCIS LIGHTFOOT LEE	On the Part and Behalf of the State of Virginia
JOHN PENN July 21st 1778 CORNs HARNETT JN° WILLIAMS	On the part and Behalf of the State of N° Carolina
HENRY LAURENS WILLIAM HENRY DRAYTON JN° MATHEWS RICHd HUTSON THOs HEYWARD Junr	On the part & behalf of the State of South-Carolina
JN° WALTON 24th July 1778 EDWd TELFAIR EDWd LANGWORTHY	On the part & behalf of the State of Georgia

The Congress on Friday, March 2, 1781, seemed to consider themselves a new body—they appointed a committee to revise the rules of "the late Congress."[32] Otherwise Congress' detailed conduct of the war went on.[33] The third of the Articles describes the Confederation thus established as a "firm League of Friendship" between the States "for their common defense, the security of their liberties, and their mutual and general welfare." Article II retains all residual powers in the States, as does the later Constitution: but the retaining language is stronger than that of the Tenth Amendment:

> Art. II. Each state retains its sovereignty, freedom and independence, and every Power, Jurisdiction and right, which is not by this confederation expressly delegated to the United States, in Congress assembled.

The Congress is of course continued, with one vote for each State no matter how many representatives it may send. A striking feature of the Articles is the lack of explicit commitment of legislative power to the Congress, despite the tasks imposed on that body which must have contemplated some federal law-making. Foreign relations, conducted by diplomacy or by war, are entrusted to Congressional control. The Congress is given charge of the currency, of the Indian trade, and of interstate postal services. But there was no power in

[32] *Journals of the Continental Congress*, XIX, p. 225.
[33] The war was coming to an end. Cornwallis surrendered at Yorktown the next October 19, and in effect this brought victory.

the Congress to impose federal taxation; Congress was to appropriate funds for federal purposes, but its common treasury was to be supplied with money by the several States, in proportion to the value of all land within each, provided by taxes levied "by the authority and direction of the legislatures of the several States." One is reminded of the difficulty of providing funds for the United Nations as this is written in 1964.

The entire lack of any provision for a separate executive in the Articles may come as a surprise to one steeped in the tradition of separate powers. The Congress is provided with a "Committee of the States" to sit when the Congress is in recess, and to manage the general affairs of the United States. The Committee has an officer to preside as "President," but he is the chairman of a committee of the Congress, not a separate President in the modern sense. The Continental Congress was its own Executive.

The Congress not only intermingled the executive with law-making functions; it also did certain judiciary work. The Articles made Congress the "last resort on appeal" in all disputes between States concerning boundary jurisdiction "or any other cause whatever." Congress was to exercise this power through "commissioners or judges to constitute a court," selected by the parties if they could agree, and if not, selected by the Congress. Congress was the office of record of such controversies. The Congress was also empowered to appoint "courts for the trial of piracies and felonies committed on the high seas," and to establish "courts for receiving and determining finally appeals in all cases of captures, provided that no member of congress" should be appointed to any such court.[34]

Some years before the ratification of the Articles the Congress had itself taken jurisdiction of appeals from the judgments of State Courts of Admiralty in prize cases; and about a year before ratification it created a court with a similar jurisdiction. The history of this court (ancestor of the Supreme Court of the United States) begins substantially before the Declaration of Independence. In 1889 its reporter and historian, J. C. Bancroft Davis, wrote in a Centennial Appendix to the U. S. Reports—

> The idea of a Federal Court, with a jurisdiction coextensive with the limits of what were then the United Colonies and Provinces of Great Britain in North America, originated with Washington some months before Congress put off British rule. On the 11th of November, 1775, he wrote from Cambridge, in Massachusetts, to the President of Congress, enclosing a copy of an act then just passed by the

[34] Article IX.

Council and House of Representatives of that Province[35] for the establishment of a Prize Court, and he added: 'Should not a court be established by authority of Congress, to take cognizance of prizes made by the Continental vessels? Whatever the mode in which they are pleased to adopt, there is an absolute necessity of its being speedily determined on.'

General Washington's letter was at once referred to a Congressional Committee—

to take into consideration as much of the General's letter as relates to the disposal of such vessels and cargoes belonging to the enemy, as shall fall into the hands of, or be taken by, the inhabitants of the United Colonies.

In practical effect the independence of the United Colonies was thus already asserted by the Commander in Chief and the Congress. England was "the enemy." Our judicial organs were to condemn English vessels as prize. The language of the Congress is not that of colonials referring to a mother country, but that of independent belligerents. Prizes were condemned in the first place by State courts of Admiralty, while a committee of the Congress acted as an appellate tribunal. The first such case, The Schooner Thistle, came before the Congress on August 5, 1776. Ultimately a standing committee was set up to hear such appeals.[36] On January 15, 1780, the Congress resolved to create a Court of Appeals for admiralty cases. The court functioned through the remaining years of the war and for a few years thereafter; it had trouble (not entirely unknown to the later Supreme Court of the United States) in persuading State courts to enforce its decrees.[37]

[35] This act is remarkable as having been the first which was passed by any of the colonies for fitting out vessels of marque and reprisal, and for establishing a court to try and condemn the captured vessels of the enemy. Jared Sparks, ed., *The Writings of George Washington* (12 vols.; Boston: Hilliard, Gray and Co., 1834–37) III, p. 154. See also George T. Curtis, *History of the Origin, Formation, and Adoption of the Constitution* (2 vols.; New York: Harper and Brothers, 1860–61) I, pp. 75–77. J. C. Bancroft Davis, "Federal Courts Prior to the Adoption of the Constitution," 131 U.S. Appendix xix (1889) [Footnote by J. C. B. Davis]

[36] See J. C. Bancroft Davis, "Federal Courts Prior to the Adoption of the Constitution," Appendix to 131 U.S. (1889) xix, xxiii.

[37] See *Doane* v. *Penhallow*, 1 Dallas 218 (1787), and *Penhallow* v. *Doane* 3 Dallas 54 (1795), discussed by Story in *Commentaries on the Constitution of the United States* (2nd ed.; Boston: Little, Brown and Co., 1851) I, p. 205 *et seq.* See also the account in J. C. Bancroft Davis' "Federal Courts Prior to the Adoption of the Constitution" in 131 U.S. Appendix xxix (1889). Mr. Davis there gives a table of cases decided by the Committee on Appeals, and those in the Court of Appeals

The Confederation deserved a higher regard than it has generally received. In England a committee of the House of Commons carries on the executive function; in America, under the Articles of Confederation, the Committee of the States might have become a Cabinet responsible to the Congress. The judicial machinery of the Continental Congress might have developed until the Committee on Appeals or a statutory Supreme Court gradually acquired detachment, independent status, and respectful acceptance, like that accorded to the Judicial Committee of the Privy Council. But the experiences of 1781–1787 were so discouraging, so much disillusionment spread concerning the capability of Congressional government, that in hope of better things we turned instead to rigid separation of powers.

Still it is unjust to forget the value of the Articles of Confederation, just as it is unfair to be toplofty over the shortcomings of the Continental Congress. The thirteen States would not have survived to join in the Constitution of 1789 unless the Confederation had provided a working government in the meantime. The fundamental trouble with the government provided by the Articles was not their draftsmanship; much of that went into the present Constitution. The trouble was the reluctance of the States to compromise their independence by joining in a novel union ruled from a far capital. Nothing like the United States had ever existed before. We had to learn by trial.

The Peace Treaty of 1783

If Americans were not so used to thinking of the Constitution as a single document, another of our great national premises would be the treaty of September 3, 1783,[38] which ended the war, established independence from Great Britain, ceded to the United States all British territory from the Great Lakes to Florida and from the Atlantic to the Mississippi, and guaranteed free navigation of that river. Even before the treaty, several States with conflicting claims to parts of the northwest territory had ceded the areas in question to the United States.[39] Such grants from England and from the States created a

---

not reported by Dallas. See page xxxv. He also gives an account of the controversies between States coming before the Congress or referred by Congress to "Courts." See also H. L. Carson, *The Supreme Court of the United States* (Philadelphia: J. Y. Huber Co., 1891) Chapters III, IV, and V.

[38] 8 U.S. Statutes at Large 80.

[39] Story wrote in 1833 that contentions between the States over the western territories had aroused such irritation as to threaten dissolution of the confederacy. See his *Commentaries on the Constitution of the United States*, 2nd ed., I, p. 159. In 1780 the Congress recommended to the States that they cede the disputed

great asset owned by the central government of the United States, a source of future States which had never been British colonies, and which so might find the federal government less remote and dangerous than did the original thirteen States. The treaty of 1783 guaranteed that there would be no State impediments to the collection of debts owed to British creditors; it was one of the first assertions of federal dominance over local policy.[40] A specific provision in the Constitution of 1789[41] made this and other preconstitutional treaties, as well as later ones, the "supreme law of the land."

Inadequacies of Confederation

The United States lived as a Confederation for fourteen years, from the outbreak of active war with Great Britain in 1775, until 1789 when government began under the new Constitution. The word "confederation" now carries overtones less favorable than terms used to describe some closer-knit political aggregate—"federation" for example. Usage of political theorists may suggest that "confederation" denotes a well-defined type of union having attributes easily understood by those adequately informed. But one searches for useful definitions without success. The criterion for distinguishing a confederation from some more firmly bonded concretion of States is one of degree as in most constitutional matters. A man despairs of verbally distinguishing much from little.

Each of the thirteen States lived too independently for the hard necessities of nationhood, during our first years of independence. This was true as well after as before the adoption of the Articles of Confederation. During the first fourteen years, our national minority, we were deficient in two essentials—one international, one internal. Neither in war nor in peace could we conduct our foreign affairs as we should. And we were unable so to govern our national economy

---

western areas to the national government. Between 1781 and 1787 New York, Virginia, Massachusetts and Connecticut made such cessions, Connecticut's subject to an excepted 6,000 square miles called the Western Reserve. On July 13, 1787, the Congress passed a measure for the government of these territories, now called the Northwest Ordinance, or Ordinance of 1787. Copies of the Ordinance and bibliographical references can be found in MacDonald, *Select Charters and Other Documents Illustrative of American History, 1776–1861*, p. 21; and in Commager, *Documents of American History*, 7th ed., at page 128.

[40] See Fairfax's *Devisee* v. *Hunter's Lessee*, 7 Cranch 603 (1813) and *Martin* v. *Hunter's Lessee* (1816). The cases are discussed in A. E. Sutherland, "Restricting the Treaty Power," 65 *Harv. L. Rev.* 1305 (1952); and see a note, reviewing the litigation, in 66 *Harv. L. Rev.* 1242 (1953).

[41] Article VI, Clause 2.

as to permit wholesome coexistence of our several States. This dual incapacity was the result of an illusion, of a vain belief that thirteen little republics, no one of them able alone to defend herself against foreign hostility or to maintain her own people in reasonable prosperity, could in a loose league somehow cooperate well enough to make war, and then live in peace, and could still each do quite as each pleased. Experience corrected this estimate.

During the War of Independence we had barely been able to keep Washington's small army in the field. The national government, without the form or the substance of power to conscript men, without tax resources to maintain its few troops, had to wheedle whatever soldiers and money it could out of thirteen more or less reluctant States. Probably all that saved our war was the help of France, by sea and by land. Even after the Peace of Paris had ended open hostilities with Great Britain in 1783, our international weakness invited disrespect. John Adams, Minister to England, had to attempt to carry out his duties in face of the "dry decency and cold civility" of official London. Despite treaty provisions, British troops continued for years to occupy our strategic frontier posts, thus retaining for British merchants a large part of the Indian fur trade. As a pretext for this occupation the British asserted, quite correctly, that our States were denying British loyalists their rights to American lands, and their rights to collect American debts which the treaty had promised them.[42] The Confederation lacked means to compel compliance, either by the British, or by our own States.

During the mid-1780's, several States began to impose their own duties on imports from foreign countries—a helter-skelter way to conduct an important part of the nation's foreign relations. These parochial tariff-barriers held possibilities of trouble abroad and at home. Experience has long since shown that foreign and domestic policies are not clearly separate. States having good ports, which sold much of their imports to States less favored, were in a position to raise needed revenue at the expense of their neighbors. Export duties levied by shipping States similarly took toll on the produce of States whose shippers, lacking harbors, were less able to send their own goods overseas.[43] Here was a threat of future domestic quarrels.

[42] See for litigation arising out of State legislation hostile to loyalists, *Rutgers* v. *Waddington,* Mayor's Court, New York (1784) Thayer, *Cases on Constitutional Law* (Cambridge, Mass.: George H. Kent and Co., 1895) I, p. 63; and see the proceedings which culminated in *Martin* v. *Hunter's Lessee,* 1 Wheat. 304, 4 L. Ed. 97 (1816).

[43] See the opinion of Mr. Justice Jackson in *Canton R.R. Co.* v. *Rogan,* 340 U.S. 511, 516 (1951), and T. R. Powell, "State Taxation of Imports," 58 *Harv. L. Rev.* 858 (1945).

James Madison wrote in the Preface to his *Debates in the Convention of 1787,*

> Besides the vain attempts to supply their respective treasuries by imposts, which turned their commerce in to the neighboring ports . . . the States having ports for foreign commerce, taxed and irritated the adjoining States, trading thro' them, as N.Y. Pena. Virga. and S-Carolina. Some of the States, as Connecticut, taxed imports as from Mass'tts higher than imports even from G.B. of wch Massts. complained to Virga. and doubtless to other States. . . In sundry instances of N.Y. N.J. Pa. and Maryd . . . the navigation laws treated the citizens of other States as aliens.[44]

Hamilton writing as a New Yorker, in the seventh "Federalist," told of the prospect before the country in 1787-8 if such centrifugal tendencies could not be checked by a stronger national government:

> The opportunities which some States would have of rendering others tributary to them by commercial regulations would be impatiently submitted to by the tributary States. The relative situation of New York, Connecticut, and New Jersey would afford an example of this kind. New York, from the necessities of revenue, must lay duties on her importations. A great part of these duties must be paid by the inhabitants of the two other States in the capacity of consumers of what we import. New York would neither be willing nor able to forego this advantage. Her citizens would not consent that a duty paid by them should be remitted in favour of the citizens of her neighbours; nor would it be practicable, if there were not this impediment in the way, to distinguish the customers in our own markets. Would Connecticut and New Jersey long submit to be taxed by New York for her exclusive benefit? Should we be long permitted to remain in the quiet and undisturbed enjoyment of a metropolis, from the possession of which we derived an advantage so odious to our neighbours, and, in their opinion, so oppressive? Should we be able to preserve it against the incumbent weight of Connecticut on the one side, and the cooperating pressure of New Jersey on the other? These are questions that temerity alone will answer in the affirmative.

Throughout the years, memories of this separatist drift, resulting from uncontrolled commercial rivalry between States during the Confederation, have had a powerful influence on the Supreme Court of the United States. Mr. Justice Jackson wrote[45] in 1947:

> The unedifying story of Colonial rivalry in preying upon commerce, which more than any one thing made our Federal constitution a neces-

[44] Quoted in Farrand, *Records of the Federal Convention of 1787,* III, p. 547.
[45] Dissenting in *Independent Warehouses, Inc.* v. *Scheele,* 331 U.S. 70 (1947) at 94.

sity, is too often told by historians to justify repetition. In 1787 New York was being supplied with firewood from Connecticut and much farm produce from New Jersey. It seized upon 'local incidents' to lay a tax. Every sloop which came down through Hell Gate, every cart of firewood entering the city, and every market boat rowed across the Hudson River had to pay heavy entrance duties. Then came retaliatory measures. See Fiske, *The Critical Period of American History*, Chapter IV. These chronic quarrels were destroying the trade of all the rivals, and it was sought by the Constitution to free trade from local burdens and controls.

He returned to the same theme two years later, writing for the Court in *Hood* v. *Du Mond*.[46]

When victory relieved the Colonies from pressure for solidarity that war had exerted, a drift toward anarchy and commercial warfare between states began. . . The desire of the Forefathers to federalize regulation of foreign and interstate commerce stands in sharp contrast to their jealous preservation of the state's power over its internal affairs. No other federal power was so universally assumed to be necessary, no other state power was so readily relinquished. There was no desire to authorize federal interference with social conditions or legal institutions of the states. Even the Bill of Rights amendments were framed only as a limitation upon the powers of Congress. The states were quite content with their several and diverse controls over most matters but, as Madison has indicated, 'want of a general power over Commerce led to an exercise of this power separately, by the States, which not only proved abortive, but engendered rival, conflicting and angry relations.' Farrand, *Records of the Federal Convention of 1787*, III, p. 547.

In 1913 Mr. Justice Holmes told the Harvard Law School Association of New York:

I do not think the United States would come to an end if we lost our power to declare an Act of Congress void. I do think the Union would be imperiled if we could not make that declaration as to the laws of the several States. For one in my place sees how often a local policy prevails with those who are not trained to national views and how often action is taken that embodies what the Commerce Clause was meant to end.[47]

Territorial rivalries, too, left bitterness. Fighting broke out in the Wyoming District of Western Pennsylvania between Connecticut and

[46] 336 U.S. 525 (1949) at page 533.
[47] In "The Law and the Court," *Collected Legal Papers* (New York: Peter Smith, 1952) pp. 295–296.

Pennsylvania settlers, who claimed the same lands. Quarrels over border lands arose between the independent republic of Vermont[48] and the State of New York.

Unless every State was to live by itself, currency and public finance had to be nationally regulated; but there was no constitutional basis for national regulation. The Articles gave the Confederation no power to control the national economy. Inflation was serious in any State which issued quantities of paper money; it was painful in Rhode Island and New Jersey. Rhode Island attempted by statute to make paper pass at the gold rate under penalty of a five hundred dollar fine and loss of suffrage, with half the fine going to an informer. When a man named Trevett attempted to enforce this law against a Newport butcher named Weeden who had refused to sell meat for paper money, the Rhode Island Supreme Court in 1786 held the statute "repugnant and unconstitutional," without specifying the constitution or the constitutional clause on which it relied.[49]

The post-war economic troubles came to a head in Massachusetts, where debt bore heavily on the rural population.[50] Legislation did not alleviate the farmers' burdens. The legislature refused to pass a soft-money bill supported by the debtor classes, and the refusal increased popular discontent with law, government and lawyers. Surly crowds hampered court sessions in various counties. A former revolutionary army captain named Daniel Shays organized and drilled an insurgent force of about 1200 men at Worcester for two months in the winter of 1786–87; his troops lived off the distressed country. To suppress them, Governor Bowdoin called out an "army" of 4400 men, equipped by contributions from well-to-do Bostonians, and commanded by General Lincoln, another Revolutionary veteran. Shays' forces increased; late in January 1787, hoping to seize the arms

[48] Vermont stood aloof from the Union until 1791.

[49] See *Trevett* v. *Weeden,* in Thayer's *Cases on Constitutional Law,* p. 73. Thayer cites an alternative reading of the Court's characterization of the law "unjust and unconstitutional." The organic law of Rhode Island was then the Charter granted by Charles II in 1663! Did the Rhode Island Court think of "unconstitutional" as meaning "so unlike our accustomed ways as to be intolerable," much like Coke's "against common right and reason" in Bonham's Case, 8 Co. Rep. 114A (C.P. 1610)?

[50] J. S. Bassett, *Short History of the United States* (New York: Macmillan, 1923) says Connecticut, Massachusetts, Delaware, Maryland, and Virginia resisted demands for paper money; (p. 235) "they all had conservative classes who were able to keep control of the situation." The Massachusetts trouble was deflation: Shays' rebellion was in part a protest against lack of paper money. See Andrew C. McLaughlin, *The Confederation and the Constitution, 1783–1789* (New York: Harper and Brothers, 1905) pp. 208–209, and Merrill Jensen, *The New Nation,* Chapter 16.

in the United States Arsenal, he marched on Springfield. A force under General Shepard repulsed him, and the insurgents fell back to Amherst. Lincoln moved up with his troops, and Shays' men straggled back through a night over the frozen hills until defeat and capture overtook them at Petersham. How many motorists, hastening through Amherst a century and three quarters later, notice Shays Street running northward out of the village, recognize the name, and spare a minute's pity for the Revolutionary captain and his desperate, beaten men on that last winter night?

Shays escaped to Vermont but the Massachusetts courts found a number of his men guilty of treason and sentenced them to death. This was not entirely easy for Boston gentlemen to explain to distressed farmers. Successful revolutionaries always have some logical difficulty in differentiating their late rebellion against a tyrannical government from new rebellion against their own power, which now intends only that which is wise and good. The first revolt was patriotism, the next treason; tyrannical measures which justified war against the old regime are necessary social disciplines of the new; but not everyone perceives the distinction. A movement arose to pardon the rebels. Samuel Adams, then President of the Massachusetts Senate, opposed the pardon for a reason which has appealed to more recent revolutionaries. He argued:

> In Monarchies the crime of treason and rebellion may admit of being pardoned or lightly punished; but the man who dares to rebel against the laws of a republic ought to suffer death.[51]

John Hancock, successor to Bowdoin in the Governorship, pardoned the lot, which well pleased most people in Massachusetts. But these depressions and disorders alarmed the whole country. In October, 1787, Congress called on the States for a new Continental force to replace that practically dissolved at the close of the war. An American army to fight Americans was distasteful; the pretext was an expedition against north-western Indians, but this cover-plan was itself a confession. Even in the face of local rebellion, the States would not tolerate successors to Gage's red-coat regiments. Propaganda has a way of recoiling on its operators, and the patriots of 'Seventy-Five had hammered home the story of the Boston Massacre of 1770. A standing army in time of peace had become a nightmare for a people

---

[51] A contemporary account of Shays' Rebellion is George Richards Minot's *History of the Insurrection in Massachusetts in the Year Seventeen Hundred and Eighty-Six and the Rebellion Consequent Thereon* (Worcester, Mass.: Isaiah Thomas, 1788). Minot was Secretary of the Massachusetts Convention that ratified the United States Constitution.

who had been indoctrinated with the Right of Revolution and who failed to recognize that sauce cooked up for the British goose would not do for our own gander.

Americans had been taught to distrust all distant effective authority, and change in this prepossession was to be a slow and complex business. It required change in the formal union of the United States; even more important, it required change in the spirits of men who still were mainly interested in their own States. A new writing could not by itself cure our troubles, though for a people accustomed to revere charters, a new written Constitution was essential to needed political reform. But to form a more perfect union, Americans had first to develop a consciousness that they must subject themselves to governmental authority—not only the authority of their own States, but of the United States. They had to develop the pride and the self-discipline involved in being citizens primarily of the United States, not of several touchy, suspicious semi-independent ex-colonies. This growth was to take time. It could not come to pass, happy and complete in 1789, though ratification of the new Constitution in that year was itself a symbol of union that stirred new pride in nationality. But as late as the war of 1812, Massachusetts was still showing jealous separatism in the use of her State forces. In 1861 officers of the regular services as high-minded as Robert E. Lee chose to go with what the North called the Rebellion because they thought of themselves primarily as Virginians or Georgians, whose duty it was to follow their States. Holmes was thinking of that war when he wrote[52] of the men who in 1787 formed the new Constitution, ". . . it has taken a century and has cost their successors much sweat and blood to prove that they created a nation."

Changing the Articles of Confederation presented formal difficulties. Article XIII provided,

> . . . the Articles of this confederation shall be inviolably observed by every state, and the union shall be perpetual; nor shall any alteration at any time hereafter be made in any of them; unless such alteration be agreed to in a congress of the united states, and be afterwards confirmed by the legislatures of every state.

Unanimous consent was an almost impossible condition of improvement. Would the small States consent to their own constitutional downgrading? If some refused their assent, but change still appeared necessary to the strong and populous States, would the strong States override the weak? This was the great problem of 1787.

[52] In *Missouri* v. *Holland*, 252 U.S. 416 (1920) at p. 433.

Making a Better Constitution

The first moves toward the Constitutional Convention were made in 1785, when early in that year the legislatures of Virginia and Maryland appointed commissioners to form a compact concerning navigation on the Potomac and the Pocomoke, and on Chesapeake Bay. The two States came to a working agreement without bothering to obtain the congressional consent required by Article VI. But as a practical matter they felt it necessary to ask the cooperation of Pennsylvania and Delaware. Clearly the United States needed new interstate arrangements wider in subject-matter and in participation than this local compact on navigation. In January 1786 the Virginia legislature resolved to designate commissioners "to meet such commissioners as may be appointed in the other states of the Union, at a time and place to be agreed on, to take into consideration the trade of the United States." The Virginia commissioners, two of whom were James Madison and Edmund Randolph, proposed a meeting on the first Monday in September 1786 at Annapolis. Delegations from only five States appeared—Virginia, Delaware, Pennsylvania, New Jersey, and New York. At least four other States had named Commissioners, but these had not got 'round to attend. Still an increased public interest in some better inter-State arrangement was evident and the five participating delegations, on September 14, 1786, made a common report to their respective legislatures, referring to "important defects in the System of the Federal Government" and recommending ". . . a Convention of Deputies from the different States" to investigate what the defects were, and to "digest" a plan to remedy them. They urged a meeting of representatives to convene at Philadelphia on the second Monday in May, 1787—

> . . . to take into Consideration the situation of the United States to devise such further Provisions as shall appear to them necessary to render the Constitution of the Federal Government adequate to the exigencies of the Union; and to report such an Act for that purpose to the United States in Congress Assembled, as when agreed to, by them and afterwards confirmed by the Legislatures of every State, will effectually provide for the same.[53]

New Jersey, Virginia, Pennsylvania, North Carolina, Delaware, and Georgia promptly named their delegations. On February 21, 1787,

[53] Gaillard Hunt and James Brown Scott, eds., *Debates in the Federal Convention of 1787* (New York: Oxford University Press, 1920) p. xlix.

while in the Berkshire hills Massachusetts troops were putting down Shays' Rebellion, Congress adopted a resolution in favor of a constitutional convention at the time and place recommended by the Annapolis report. Before the second Monday in May every State except New Hampshire and Rhode Island had appointed deputies; New Hampshire later did so, still in time for participating in a few important decisions. Rhode Island, to the regret of some of its merchants and other substantial people, never took any part in framing the Constitution.

The men who came together to devise a new plan of government for the United States were an extraordinary assemblage. Fifty-five delegates attended at least some of the Convention sessions. Thirty-four were lawyers or had at any rate studied law. Forty-six had been members of colonial or State legislatures. Two future Presidents, Washington and Madison, took important parts in the proceedings. Many other delegates were destined later to have important functions in State and national government. They were not really what Jefferson called them—"an assembly of demi-gods";[54] but they were highly able men, most of them well experienced in public affairs. As a group they proved sufficiently wise to save what was good in government under the Articles, and still to concede some of their States' independence which had to be limited if the government of the United States was to prosper.

Compromises were necessary if the States were to agree on a new and more effective Constitution. Small States were jealous of the great. Virginia, populous and powerful, had much to gain from a federal union controlled by herself and her dominant sisters. But what of Rhode Island and Delaware and New Jersey? What union, more perfect, would still leave the minor States the same ability to do as they wished? Earlier I have suggested (by no means as an innovation) that fragmentation of government, diffusion of power to assure liberty, has always been a constitutional ideal of our people. Men in the smaller States had their own governments, their own ways; they were prepared to be well-satisfied with the Confederation as it was if only foreign affairs and interstate trade could be better arranged, provided they could still be let alone to do as they saw fit. Many were reluctant, then as now, to realize that order and power have their cost. The Confederation was weak because too few people wanted union badly enough; the jealous separatism of their States produced the

[54] In a letter written from Paris on August 30, 1787 to John Adams in London: see Farrand, *Records of the Federal Convention of 1787*, III, p. 70. Jefferson was in Europe on a diplomatic mission throughout the Convention.

form of the Articles. The price they put on their consent to the Constitution drafted in 1787 was retention of equal voting power in the national Senate for every State, no matter how small. This compromise of 1787, this concession of ultranumerical power to the minority States, was unavoidable; the benefits it brought have sometimes cost serious disadvantages. Two-thirds of the way through the twentieth century a minority of stubborn Senators from small but defiant States can still block legislation the majority favors by using the filibuster, a parliamentary device deriving its power from the compromise of 1787 and from an abiding suspicion of national compulsion. But this compromise was not made heedlessly; it has brought benefits well worth the price. The necessity for a fairly wide consensus to support legislation in the Senate has resulted in ultimate general acceptance of measures that finally emerge.

Proceedings of the Convention called for May, 1787 are known mainly, though not exclusively, from James Madison's careful notes. He chose a seat in front of the President's chair and kept a record of whatever went on, using his own abbreviations and symbols, and writing up his notes during the hours of recess. The task was confining and unremitting and, Madison afterward wrote, almost killed him. But his records have been invaluable as our best source of information concerning the formation of the written Constitution.[55]

The Convention had been called for the second Monday in May, which fell on the 19th, but very few delegates were then in Philadelphia. By Friday, May 25, delegates had come in from seven States and these organized the Convention. It met, as everyone knows, in the State House, probably on the second floor. The delegates unanimously elected George Washington as President; his influence on the Convention was much greater than his few recorded words suggest. His unselfish service during the War of Independence, his complete integrity, his aloofness from personal ambition in political life, all reminded the delegates of their own obligations, and went far to gain acceptance in the Convention, and in the country afterward, for the

---

[55] A number of publications contain the records, such as we have, of the Convention. Probably the best known and most widely used is Professor Max Farrand's *Records of the Federal Convention of 1787*, published in 1911 and supplemented by an additional volume in 1937. The introductory material in the 1911 and 1937 volumes gives an account of many other useful publications of Convention papers. A government publication, Charles C. Tansill, ed., *Documents Illustrative of the Formation of the Union of American States* (Washington: Legislative Reference Service, 1927). Charles Warren's *Making of the Constitution* (Boston: Little, Brown and Co., 1928) and Professor Farrand's *Framing of the Constitution of the United States,* (New Haven: Yale University Press, 1913) give convenient accounts of the proceedings.

sacrifices of local interest that union entailed. Consciousness of high purpose is evident in Washington's attitude, early in the Convention, toward proposals of half-way measures of reform, put forward because some delegates feared that the American people would not accept the changes really needed. Gouverneur Morris much later[56] told of Washington's response—

> It is too probable that no plan we propose will be adopted. Perhaps another dreadful conflict is to be sustained. If, to please the people, we offer what we ourselves disapprove, how can we afterwards defend our work? Let us raise a standard to which the wise and the honest can repair. The event is in the hand of God.

Virginia had led in convoking the Convention, and now led in producing its constitutional reform. While the early delegates waited in Philadelphia for a quorum to assemble, the Virginians met regularly and prepared a set of fifteen resolutions which have come to be known as the Virginia Plan. On May 29, Governor Randolph presented this document to the assembled Convention.[57] The Plan proposed that the Articles of Confederation be "so corrected and enlarged" as to provide for the "common defense, security of liberty and general welfare," and set out a series of specific changes to attain these ends. The Articles of Confederation, modified by these Virginia proposals, which in their turn were modified by compromise during the Convention, make up the substance and much of the phrasing of the Constitution under which the United States has lived since 1789.

Virginia proposed to replace the unicameral Continental Congress by a new national legislature of two houses. It was to have new, additional powers to legislate directly over individuals, relying much less than the old Congress on exercise of government through the States. The new Congress, Virginia proposed, would have power to legislate ". . . in all cases to which the separate States are incompetent, or in which the harmony of the United States may be interrupted by the exercise of individual [State] legislation; . . ." The Plan proposed a national executive branch where the Confederation had none; it was to be chosen by the Congress for a term of years and might have consisted of one man or a group. A third innovation in the Virginia proposals was a national judiciary consisting of ". . . one or more supreme tribunals"; and of a system of lower national courts.

[56] In an oration Morris delivered Dec. 31, 1799, on Washington's death; see Farrand, *Records of the Federal Convention of 1787*, III, pp. 381–382.

[57] See Farrand, *Records of the Federal Convention of 1787*, I, pp. 20–22. A copy is printed in Farrand, *The Framing of the Constitution of the United States*, p. 225 et seq.

Two striking proposals of the Virginia Plan never gained effective support in the Convention. One, vainly pushed on the floor by Charles Pinckney of South Carolina and by Madison[58] was a grant of power to the national legislature to override almost any State statute; another was the creation of a Council of Revision, consisting of the executive and "a convenient number of the National Judiciary" empowered to impose a suspensory veto on national legislation. Though the Convention finally rejected this latter proposal, something like it finally emerged as the present Presidential veto; and Congressional power to negative State action has steadily increased as the Supreme Court, step by step, has come to recognize a wider and wider national legislative capability. By 1963 the Congress, under the expanded commerce and war powers, has acquired constitutional competence to legislate on a sweep of subjects which would have startled the delegates of 1787. And with this expanding power to enact national legislation has gone corresponding capability to negative State action. The Congress now has power approaching the substance of Madison's proposals for a general legislative veto on State laws. Today's Congress is restrained in prohibiting State action less by constitutional limitation than by political regard for State feelings.[59]

The most difficult and controversial proposal of the Virginia Plan would have made the voting power of both houses of the national legislature proportionate to the ". . . quotas of contribution, or to the number of free inhabitants, as the one or the other rule may seem best in different cases." The "first branch," as the delegates termed what is now the House of Representatives, would be elected by the people of the several States; the "second branch" (Senate, now), would be elected by the first branch. Under the Virginia Plan the populous and rich States (Virginia was then first in both respects) would have dominated the smaller. This naturally produced protests.

The first two active weeks of the Convention were spent in Committee of the Whole, debating the resolutions of the Virginia Plan, which made much progress despite opposition from certain delegations, or delegates (for State delegations not infrequently divided their vote). Brearly and Paterson of New Jersey were leaders in op-

---

[58] Farrand, *Records of the Federal Convention of 1787*, I, pp. 164 *et seq.*

[59] The Power of the Congress to inhibit State action either by implication or, more rarely, by express statutory provision, is always being demonstrated: e.g., *McCulloch* v. *Maryland*, 4 Wheat. 316 (1819); *New York Central R.R.* v. *Winfield*, 244 U.S. 147 (1917); *Pennsylvania* v. *Nelson*, 350 U.S. 497 (1956); *Guss* v. *Utah Labor Relations Board*, 353 U.S. 1 (1957); see also an Act relating to the power of the States to impose net income taxes on income derived from interstate commerce—15 U.S. Code 381 *et seq.* (1959).

position. Maryland, Connecticut, and New York opposed on some issues. Delaware opposed. To say that the Convention consistently split into two groups, of the largest and of the smallest States,[60] is an over-simplification. The three largest States, Virginia, Pennsylvania, and Massachusetts, together favored a strong central government with a national legislature controlled by the populous States. Connecticut, New York, New Jersey, Delaware, and Maryland generally cooperated in resisting this move, favoring instead a national legislature in which each State should keep the equal vote it had in the Confederation. Thus some States which opposed the Virginia Plan were substantial in size and influence. All agreed that the national power needed strengthening; the differences concerned the degree of strength, and the political forces which would control it.

The first two weeks of debate showed that the uncommitted States were tending toward the Virginia position, a tendency coming to a climax on June 11, when a majority of States voted for "proportional representation"[61] (that is, more votes in Congress for large than for small States) in the upper house as well as in the lower. But on June 15, William Paterson of New Jersey submitted a plan which he wished to substitute for Randolph's.[62] New Jersey, with her associates Connecticut, New York, Delaware and at least Luther Martin of Maryland, proposed to leave Congress as it was, a single house in which every State, large or small would have an equal vote. This plan would have increased the powers of Congress, however: it would be authorized "to pass acts for the regulation of trade and commerce as well with foreign nations as with each other," and to raise national revenue by import duties, stamp taxes, and postage charges. "Requisitions" on the States would be made proportionate to population (counting only three-fifths of the Negroes). New Jersey also proposed a plural national executive of unspecified numbers, and a national supreme judiciary whose chief function would be to hear appeals from State Supreme courts in a limited class of cases.

[60] At the time of the first census, in 1790, the populations of the thirteen States were (in round thousands)

Virginia	747,000	New York	340,000	New Hampshire	141,000
Massachusetts		Maryland	319,000	Georgia	82,000
(incl. Maine)	474,000	South Carolina	249,000	Rhode Island	68,000
Pennsylvania	434,000	Connecticut	237,000	Delaware	59,000
North Carolina	393,000	New Jersey	184,000		

[61] This term, of course, has now acquired a highly specialized meaning, quite different from the usage in the Convention debates.

[62] The New Jersey Plan is reproduced in Farrand's *Framing of the Constitution of the United States*, Appendix III.

The present Constitution derives its most fundamental form from the old Articles of Confederation; we are still a national union of partly independent States; we still act through a national legislature in which the States are represented, as we did under the Articles. To the Virginia Plan we owe the bicameral structure of the Congress, with its power to legislate directly on individuals; to it we owe the executive branch with general authority to effectuate the national laws; and the national judiciary with a Supreme Court and lower tribunals. But the New Jersey Plan also contributed to what we now have. What the Convention finally accepted was a compromise between the Virginia Plan and the much less centralized New Jersey Plan, a compromise traditionally ascribed to the efforts of Connecticut at the end of June, 1787. By that time two weeks of argument had followed New Jersey's proposals. Controversy had become harsh— Gouverneur Morris, who had a flair for dramatic statement, afterward said that the fate of America was suspended by a hair. On June 28, old Benjamin Franklin made a moving speech, urging prayers for the assistance of the Convention. He produced only a wrangle ended by adjournment for the day. Men were in no fit temper to make a Constitution.

But somehow overnight a plurality decided to compromise. Next day, Friday, June 29, the Convention voted, in a curiously negative form, for proportional representation in the lower House—"that the rule of suffrage in the first branch ought not to be according to that established by the articles of Confederation." The vote was six to four, with Maryland divided, and New Hampshire and Rhode Island not represented. Oliver Ellsworth of Connecticut then moved "That in the second branch each State have an equal vote," which, he frankly acknowledged, would "make the general government partly federal and partly national." He supported his motion eloquently, pointing out that proportional representation in the first branch would secure the large States against the small, while an equality of voices in the upper House would secure the small States against the large. He trusted that on this middle ground a compromise would take place. He did not see that it could on any other. The Convention argued Ellsworth's motion at length. Tempers still were sharp. Madison taunted Ellsworth, saying "Now the small [States] are the House of Lords requiring a negative to defend them against the more numerous Commons"[63]—not an amiable simile only five years after the close of a bitter war with Great Britain. Ellsworth answered for Connecticut—the muster rolls would show, he observed, that his State

63 Farrand, *Records of the Federal Convention of 1787*, I, p. 485.

had more troops in the field than even Virginia. Probably it was fortunate that July 1st was a Sunday and the Convention stood adjourned.

On Monday, July 2, the delegates voted on Ellsworth's compromise proposal for equal State suffrage in the Senate,[64] to counterbalance proportional representation in the lower House. The vote was a tie—Connecticut, New York, New Jersey, Delaware, and Maryland (represented that day by Luther Martin alone) voting for the Connecticut Compromise; Massachusetts, Pennsylvania, Virginia, North Carolina, and South Carolina voting against it. Georgia's two delegates divided their votes; New Hampshire and Rhode Island were not represented.

No one really knows, a century and three-quarters after the event, whether affairs were in fact as critical as the debates of July 2, 1787 suggest. What if the deadlock had continued? Suppose the Convention had broken up. Would the United States have broken up too? Would we, or part of us, have negotiated some sort of reunion with Great Britain, as Vermont was threatening?[65] That seems incredible, but at any rate the question involves only reconstruction of history contrary to the events. The Convention wisely adopted the mollifying device of reference to a committee.[66] On July 5, the Committee reported, recommending an implementation of the Connecticut Compromise; in the "first branch" each State should have one representative to every 40,000 inhabitants (counting three-fifths of the slaves); money bills should originate in the first branch; in the second branch each State should have an equal vote. Debate broke out again, with some remaining rancor. But on Monday, July 16, the Convention by a vote of five States to four adopted the substance of the Connecticut Compromise—Connecticut, New Jersey, Delaware, Maryland, and North Carolina voting in favor; Pennsylvania, Virginia, South Carolina, and Georgia against. Massachusetts divided her vote. New York's delegation had gone home. New Hampshire's had not come yet. And Rhode Island had appointed none.

That vote was the turning point. There were two more months of drafting and of debates; there were arguments about the quota of inhabitants to be allotted a representative in the House; there were disputes over the mode of election of the executive; over the establishment of the judiciary. There were other, easier compromises. But

[64] Madison's notes ascribe to himself the use of the term "Senate" in debate on June 30, to designate the upper House.

[65] How serious Vermont was, no one can now judge. She may have been posturing for effect.

[66] Made up of one man from each State.

after July 16, 1787, there was little doubt that the United States would have a new Constitution. For the moment a balance had been established between national power and States' rights.

On Wednesday, September 12, a Committee of Style submitted its final revised draft. We thus owe the present version of the Constitution to Dr. William Samuel Johnson of Connecticut, Alexander Hamilton, Gouverneur Morris of Pennsylvania, James Madison of Virginia, and Rufus King of Massachusetts. Morris seems to have applied the last touches. Madison wrote Jared Sparks in 1831 that the "finish given to the style and arrangement of the constitution fairly belongs to the pen of Mr. Morris." There were still a few small changes on September 13 and 14, but the delegates did little debating. The Convention appears to have been unconscious of the extent to which the commerce power might later expand the national government's capabilities; the delegates did not suspect the sweep of the "necessary and proper" clause, or of the power to spend for the "general welfare." On September 14, Dr. Franklin moved to vest in Congress a power to provide for cutting canals, which of course never became part of the Constitution. Madison and Pinckney[67] unsuccessfully moved to authorize a national university "in which no preference or distinctions should be allowed on account of Religion." Gouverneur Morris observed "It is not necessary. The exclusive power at the Seat of Government, will reach the object."

On Monday, September 17, 1787, the engrossed Constitution was read to the Convention. At that point, Dr. Franklin rose with a prepared statement in his hand. Only General Washington stood higher in the general prestige. In American eyes, for learning, for ripe scholarly wisdom, Franklin had no peer in the Convention, or in his country. His great age led him not to attempt to read his paper. His colleague Wilson read on his behalf—

"Mr. President.

"I confess that there are several parts of this constitution which I do not at present approve, but I am not sure I shall never approve them: For having lived long, I have experienced many instances of being obliged by better information or fuller consideration, to change opinions even on important subjects, which I once thought right, but found to be otherwise. It is therefore that the older I grow, the more apt I am to doubt my own judgment, and to pay more respect to the judgment of others. Most men indeed as well as most sects in Religion, think themselves in possession of all truth, and that wherever others differ from them it is so far error. Steele, a Protestant in a Dedication

[67] Charles Pinckney of South Carolina, whom Madison calls "Mr." Pinckney. His older colleague from the same State, Charles Cotesworth Pinckney, Madison calls "General." See e.g., Madison's notes for September 15, 1787.

tells the Pope, that the only difference between our Churches in their opinions of the certainty of their doctrines is, the Church of Rome is infallible and the Church of England is never in the wrong. But though many private persons think almost as highly of their own infallibility as of that of their sect, few express it so naturally as a certain french lady, who in a dispute with her sister, said 'I don't know how it happens, Sister but I meet with nobody but myself, that's always in the right'—'Il n'y a que moi qui a toujours raison.'

"In these sentiments, Sir, I agree to this Constitution with all its faults, if they are such; because I think a general Government necessary for us, and there is no form of Government but what may be a blessing to the people if well administered, and believe farther that this is likely to be well administered for a course of years, and can only end in Despotism, as other forms have done before it, when the people shall become so corrupted as to need despotic Government, being incapable of any other. I doubt too whether any other Convention we can obtain may be able to make a better Constitution. For when you assemble a number of men to have the advantage of their joint wisdom, you inevitably assemble with those men, all their prejudices, their passions, their errors of opinion, their local interests, and their selfish views. From such an Assembly can a perfect production be expected? It therefore astonishes me, Sir, to find this system approaching so near to perfection as it does; and I think it will astonish our enemies, who are waiting with confidence to hear that our councils are confounded like those of the Builders of Babel; and that our States are on the point of separation, only to meet hereafter for the purpose of cutting one another's throats. Thus I consent, Sir, to this Constitution because I expect no better, and because I am not sure, that it is not the best. The opinions I have had of its errors, I sacrifice to the public good—I have never whispered a syllable of them abroad—Within these walls they were born, and here they shall die— If every one of us in returning to our Constituents were to report the objections he has had to it, and endeavor to gain partizans in support of them, we might prevent its being generally received, and thereby lose all the salutary effects & great advantages resulting naturally in our favor among foreign Nations as well as among ourselves, from our real or apparent unanimity. Much of the strength & efficiency of any Government in procuring and securing happiness to the people, depends on opinion, on the general opinion of the goodness of the Government, as well as of the wisdom and integrity of its Governors. I hope therefore that for our own sakes as a part of the people, and for the sake of posterity, we shall act heartily and unanimously in recommending this Constitution (if approved by Congress & confirmed by the Conventions) wherever our influence may extend, and turn our future thoughts & endeavors to the means of having it well administered.

"On the whole, Sir, I cannot help expressing a wish that every member of the Convention who may still have objections to it, would with me, on this occasion doubt a little of his own infallibility—and to make manifest our unanimity, put his name to this instrument."[68]

Dr. Franklin then moved that the Constitution be signed. But even at this ultimate moment, one final change was made in the draft. Mr. Gorham of Massachusetts moved that the maximum number of Representatives, which, as the draft then stood, was not to exceed one for every forty thousand, be, instead, not over one to thirty thousand. Evidently demands for a fuller popular representation were still being heard. This, one notes was significantly, the only issue on which George Washington as President entered into Convention debate. On putting the question of the thirty thousand, he said that he could not forbear expressing his wish that the alteration proposed might take place. The smallness of the proportion of representatives had been considered by many members of the Convention an insufficient security for the rights and interests of the people. He thought it of so much consequence that it would give him much satisfaction to see it adopted. No one opposed Mr. Gorham's proposition, which was unanimously approved. All the States then answered "Aye" on a motion to agree to the Constitution as enrolled.[69]

The Convention deposited its journals and other papers in Washington's hands, subject to the order of the new Congress if it should ever be formed. All the delegates then signed the instrument, except Messrs. Randolph and Mason of Virginia and Mr. Gerry of Massachusetts.

> Whilst the last members were signing it Doctr. Franklin looking towards the Presidents Chair, at the back of which a rising sun happened to be painted, observed to a few members near him, that Painters had found it difficult to distinguish in their art a rising from a setting sun. I have, said he, often and often in the course of the Session, and the vicissitudes of my hopes and fears as to its issue, looked at that behind the President without being able to tell whether it was rising or setting: But now at length I have the happiness to know that it is a rising and not a setting Sun.[70]

Washington sent the signed document to the Congress; the Congress on September 28, 1787, sent it to the States for ratification by their own Conventions.

Delaware ratified first on December 7, 1787. Pennsylvania followed on December 12, then New Jersey on December 18, and Connecticut

[68] Farrand, *Records of the Federal Convention of 1787*, II, pp. 641–643.
[69] The text of the Constitution is set out at p. 204 *infra*.
[70] Farrand, *Records of the Federal Convention of 1787*, II, p. 648.

on January 9, 1788. All these had accepted the Constitution without comment, but Massachusetts, ratifying the sixth day of February, 1788, was the first of several States to recommend amendments to remove the fears of the people "against an undue administration of the Federal government." The Massachusetts Convention resolved:

And as it is the opinion of this Convention, that certain amendments and alterations in the said Constitution would remove the fears, and quiet the apprehensions, of many of the good people of this commonwealth, and more effectually guard against an undue administration of the federal government,—the Convention do therefore recommend that the following alterations and provisions be introduced into the said Constitution. —

I. That it be explicitly declared that all powers not expressly delegated by the aforesaid Constitution are reserved to the several states, to be by them exercised.

II. That there shall be one representative to every thirty thousand persons, according to the census mentioned in the Constitution, until the whole number of the representatives amounts to two hundred.

III. That the Congress do not exercise the powers vested in them by the 4th section of the 1st article, but in cases where a state shall neglect or refuse to make the regulations therein mentioned, or shall make regulations subversive of the rights of the people to a free and equal representation in Congress, agreeably to the Constitution.

IV. That Congress do not lay direct taxes but when the moneys arising from the impost and excise are insufficient for the public exigencies, nor then until Congress shall have first made a requisition, agreeably to the census fixed in the said Constitution, in such way and manner as the legislatures of the states shall think best; and in such case, if any state shall neglect or refuse to pay its proportion, pursuant to such requisition, then Congress may assess and levy such state's proportion, pursuant to such interest thereon at the rate of six per cent. per annum, from the time of payment prescribed in such requisition.

V. That Congress erect no company of merchants with exclusive advantages of commerce.

VI. That no person shall be tried for any crime by which he may incur an infamous punishment, or loss of life, until he be first indicted by a grand jury, except in such cases as may arise in the government and regulation of the land and naval forces.

VII. The Supreme Judicial Federal Court shall have no jurisdiction of causes between citizens of different states, unless the matter in dispute, whether it concerns the realty or personalty, be of the value of three thousand dollars at the least; nor shall the federal judicial powers extend to any actions between citizens of different states, where the matter in dispute, whether it concerns the realty or personalty, is not of the value of fifteen hundred dollars at least.

VIII. In civil actions between citizens of different states, every issue of fact, arising in actions at common law, shall be tried by a jury, if they or either of them, request it.

IX. Congress shall at no time consent that any person, holding an office of trust or profit under the United States, shall accept of a title of nobility, or any other title or office, from any king, prince, or foreign state.[71]

Such demands for a Bill of Rights, included in the recommendations of the ratifying Conventions in Massachusetts and in four other States, South Carolina, New Hampshire, Virginia, and New York, give an indication of what people in many parts of the Union felt were the important interests which might be invaded by the proposed new central government. The first Massachusetts recommendation appears as the present Tenth Amendment; the sixth Massachusetts paragraph is part of the Fifth Amendment; the eighth Massachusetts recommendation is incorporated in the Seventh Amendment. Throughout these Massachusetts cautionary proposals appears a distrust of central government, a feeling that the new powers granted might be used to diminish the stature and powers of the States. Georgia ratified January 2, 1788, without a stipulation for a Bill of Rights. Maryland followed on April 28, 1788, likewise without such a stipulation. South Carolina on May 23, 1788, however, proposed amendments reserving to the States the manner of election to the Congress, "exclusive of the general interference of the government except in cases where the Legislatures of the States shall refuse or neglect to perform and fulfill the same." South Carolina also recommended a provision like the Tenth Amendment; a provision like the Massachusetts fourth proposal concerning a postponement of federal taxing powers until the States shall have failed to pay requisitions; she also proposed that in Article 6, Clause 3, which prescribed an oath or affirmation to support the Constitution, the reading that no *other* religious test shall ever be required. On June 21, 1788, New Hampshire ratified the Constitution. In addition to a number of recommendations resembling those of Massachusetts, New Hampshire added some of her own—

X. That no standing army shall be kept up in time of peace, unless with the consent of three fourths of the members of each branch of Congress; nor shall soldiers, in time of peace, be quartered upon private houses, without the consent of the owners.

XI. Congress shall make no laws touching religion, or to infringe the rights of conscience.

[71] Jonathan Elliot, ed., *Debates in the Several State Conventions* (2nd ed.; 5 vols.; Washington: Elliot, 1836–1845) I, pp. 322–323.

XII. Congress shall never disarm any citizen, unless such as are or have been in actual rebellion.

And the Convention do in the name and in behalf of the people of this state, enjoin it upon their representatives in Congress, at all times until the alterations and provisions aforesaid have been considered agreeably to the fifth article of the said Constitution, to exert all their influence, and use all reasonable and legal methods to obtain a ratification of the said alterations and provisions, in such manner as is provided in the article.

And that the United States in Congress assembled may have due notice of the assent and ratification of the said Constitution by this Convention, it is Resolved, That the assent and ratification aforesaid be engrossed on parchment, together with the recommendation and injunction aforesaid, and with this resolution; and that John Sullivan, Esq., president of the Convention, and John Langdon, Esq., president of the state, transmit the same, countersigned by the secretary of the Convention, and the secretary of state, under their hands and seals to the United States in Congress assembled.[72]

The provision concerning the billeting of troops appears in the present Third Amendment; the prohibition of acts of Congress "touching religion" suggests the first Clause of the First Amendment; and the New Hampshire twelfth recommendation suggests the Second Amendment.

As New Hampshire was the ninth State to ratify, the Constitution, as its seventh Article provided, was thereupon established between the States so ratifying.

On June 27, 1788, six days after New Hampshire, Virginia ratified. Her Convention made the following recital:[73]

We . . . do in the name and in behalf of the people of Virginia, declare and make known that the powers granted under the Constitution being derived from the people of the United States may be resumed by them whensoever the same shall be perverted to their injury or oppression and that every power not granted thereby remains with them and at their will; that therefore no right of any denomination can be cancelled abridged restrained or modified by the Congress by the Senate or House of Representatives acting in any Capacity by the President or any Department or officer of the United States except in those instances in which power is given by the Constitution for those purposes; & that among other essential rights the liberty of Conscience and of the Press cannot be cancelled abridged restrained or modified by any authority of the United States. With these impressions with a solemn appeal to the Searcher of hearts for the purity of our intentions

[72] Elliot, *Debates in the Several State Conventions,* I, p. 326.
[73] Elliot, *Debates in the Several State Conventions,* I, p. 327.

and under the conviction that whatsover imperfections may exist in the Constitution ought rather to be examined in the mode prescribed therein than to bring the Union into danger by a delay with a hope of obtaining amendments previous to the Ratification, We the said Delegates—in behalf of the People of Virginia do by these presents—ratify the Constitution. . .

Congress received the New Hampshire ratification on July 2, 1788, and at once that day referred the nine ratifications to a committee to examine them, and to report to Congress an act for putting the Constitution into operation. On September 13, a resolution was adopted that the first Wednesday in the following January be the day for appointing electors in those States which by that day should have ratified the Constitution; that on the first Wednesday in the following February the electors should assemble in their States and vote for a President; and that on the first Wednesday in March, Congress should commence proceedings under the new Constitution.

While New Hampshire's acceptance was sufficient to set the new form of government going, and while Virginia's favorable action strengthened the Union immensely, ratification by New York was essential to the success of the Constitution. Her absence from the list of ratifying States would have made the United States unworkable, and friends of the new Constitution had seen from the first that New York's acceptance was not at all certain. From October 1787, to July 1788, the Constitution was debated in every prominent newspaper in the State. Of these publications, those now best remembered are, of course, the Federalist essays. They were written as tracts in support of ratification by Hamilton, Madison, and John Jay, all using the pen name "Publius." Hamilton, tradition has it, wrote the first of the series in the cabin of a sloop on his way from Albany to New York. This paper appeared in the New York *Independent Journal* on October 27, 1787; thereafter essays appeared either in that journal or in one of three others, the *New York Packet*, the *Daily Advertiser*, and the *New York Journal and Daily Patriotic Register*. The first 36 letters were published in book form on March 22, 1788.[74] The rest appeared in a second volume two months later.

The influence of the Federalist papers on New York's ratification has been doubted. There were able writers on both sides. General George Clinton, war Governor of New York and a strong opponent of ratification, wrote against ratification under the name of Cato; his popularity and persuasiveness may have convinced Hamilton that answering publication was necessary, and so may have induced the Federalist papers. The Federalist series is lofty and scholarly in style,

[74] Charles Warren, *The Making of the Constitution*, p. 767, fn. 1.

and would not be well adapted to swaying today's general public. On the other hand, the subject matter then held acute interest and the Federalist papers addressed prepared readers. In the autumn of 1787, debates about the wisdom or unwisdom of ratifying the proposed Constitution must have been at least as familiar to the ordinary man as the discussions of the United Nations which occupy so much space in newspapers while these pages are written. Whatever the influence of the Federalist papers on New York ratification, they have since become the best-known commentary on the Constitution. They continually furnish material for Supreme Court opinions; they have attained a status higher than that of an ordinary treatise—they have an institutional value of their own.[75]

The New York convention assembled in Poughkeepsie on June 17, 1788. Governor George Clinton was elected its President. The membership was distinguished. Among the delegates were John Jay, Alexander Hamilton, Robert R. Livingston, Isaac Roosevelt, James Duane, and Nicholas Low. From Albany came Robert Yeats and John Lansing, Jr., who in July 1787, had withdrawn from the Constitutional Convention on the ground that they had, as they explained

> been reduced to the disagreeable alternative of either exceeding the powers delegated to us, and giving assent to measures which we conceive destructive to the political happiness of the citizens of the United States, or opposing our opinions to that of the body of respectable men, to whom those citizens had given the most unequivocal proofs of confidence. Thus circumstanced under these impressions, to have hesitated would have been culpable. We therefore gave the principles of the Constitution which has received the sanction of the majority of the Convention, our decided and unreserved dissent; . . .[76]

The opponents of the new Constitution were said to have a two-thirds majority in the New York convention. Governor Clinton, its President, was a stout adversary. His ally, Melancthon Smith, one of the ablest debaters in the country, could hold his own with Hamilton. The country people, the "upstate" interest, saw the new central government as remote, potentially tyrannical, somehow aristocratic. To Hamilton belongs much of the credit for overcoming these formidable forces. He was able to convince some opponents of the Constitution by eloquent oratorical argument; others he persuaded by the logic of events, arranging for swift horse expresses to bring to Poughkeepsie tidings of the New Hampshire and Virginia conven-

[75] For the Scots "institutional" treatises which Scots cited as authorities, much as Americans now cite the Law Institute Restatements; see T. B. Smith, *The United Kingdom: Scotland* (London: Stevens and Sons, 1955) pp. 620 ff.
[76] Elliot, *Debates in the Several State Conventions*, I, pp. 344, 480.

tions. As New York hesitated and harangued, word came that New Hampshire had ratified, thus putting the Constitution in operation; then came the news that Virginia, far the most populous State, had also approved. New York was left with only North Carolina and Rhode Island. Governor Clinton, fearing that New York City and the lower counties would break off and form their own State, advised some of his allies to vote for the Constitution. Melancthon Smith had swung over. On July 26, the New York Convention voted to ratify, but it was a near thing; of fifty-seven votes cast, twenty-seven were adverse. Clinton did not vote. New York's resolution recited the "impressions" of the Convention that a long list of rights (some in much the same terms as those later adopted in Amendments I to X), could not be abridged or violated; that these "explanations" were consistent with the Constitution; and that the Convention had confidence that amendments would receive early and mature consideration.[77]

Without North Carolina and Rhode Island, the United States organized its new government in the spring of 1789. On August 1, 1788, North Carolina had demanded a Declaration of Rights and refused to ratify without it; but on November 21, 1789, she finally accepted the Constitution as it was. Rhode Island only ratified on May 29, 1790, when George Washington had been President more than a year.

Organizing the New Government

Among other measures of September 13, 1788, the Continental Congress resolved—

> . . . that the first Wednesday in March next be the time and the present seat of Congress[78] the place for commencing proceedings under the said constitution.

Meantime the Continental Congress was left to do whatever national governing was done. Attendance dwindled. On October 10, the Congress voted against a resolution imposing penalties on "officers of the late army" who had not fully settled their accounts, a result which

[77] An account of the New York Convention is given in D. S. Alexander's *Political History of the State of New York* (4 vols.; New York: H. Holt and Co., 1906) I, p. 32 *et seq.* Elliot's *Debates in the Several State Conventions* is a standard source for the proceedings in the several States. The resolutions of ratification with the texts of State demands for a Bill of Rights can be found conveniently in Charles C. Tansill, ed., *Documents Illustrative of the Formation of the Union of American States.*

[78] Then New York.

will have the approval of any ex-officer who has ever been tardily beset by financial officials long after he has misplaced his meager records. So, as it turned out, the Continental Congress cast its last vote. On November 3 began a new "federal year"; a few delegates attended the Congress from time to time. On Monday, March 2, 1789, with Mr. Philip Pell of New York alone recorded as present, the life of that remarkable body finally came to an end. It had governed the country during the War of Independence and the trying years that followed; to it the United States owes deep gratitude.

Of the eleven States which had ratified the Constitution, all except New York[79] chose presidential electors on the first Wednesday in January, 1789. On the first Wednesday in February the electors unanimously chose George Washington as President, and as Vice President chose John Adams,[80] just back from his diplomatic mission to England. On Wednesday, March 4, a handful of Senators and Congressmen appeared in New York to begin the new government. The House could not muster a quorum until April 1; the Senate was unable to start business until five days after the House. Finally on April 6, both Houses decided that George Washington and John Adams had been duly elected. On April 30, in Federal Hall at Wall and Nassau Streets, Chancellor Livingston of New York administered to Washington the first presidential oath and then shouted—

Long live George Washington, President of the United States!

Livingston's shout was echoed by an assembled multitude. The new Constitution was launched.

The First Work of Congress

The Congress at once faced several peremptory tasks. Without waiting for the inauguration of the President, both Houses adopted rules for the conduct of business, and the House immediately began work on a revenue bill. Money would be a prime requisite of the new government, which was no longer to be dependent on requisitions directed to the reluctant States. Executive departments had to be provided for a nation which never before had had an executive. A judiciary branch had to be constructed, and its jurisdiction defined; its proposed powers were certain to reawaken the States-rights irritation which two years before had heated the constitutional convention. As a wholly new mechanism of national government was set

[79] Which thus lost its chance to vote for Washington as first President.
[80] Not unanimously: John Jay, Adams' nearest competitor, had nine electoral votes.

going, endless details demanded attention. And besides all the rest, the new Senators and Congressmen remembered the urgent demands for a Bill of Rights made by ratifying conventions. Good faith (and political prudence) required that Congress at once propose a number of appropriate amendments.

On April 7, the day after a quorum finally assembled, the Senate appointed a committee of eight to draft a judiciary act, which as Senate Bill No. 1 was to be the basis of the present federal judicial system. Four of the eight committeemen had served in the Constitutional Convention of 1787, Oliver Ellsworth of Connecticut, William Paterson of New Jersey, William Few of Georgia, and Payne Wingate of New Hampshire. On April 13, Charles Carroll of Maryland, and Ralph Izard of South Carolina were added, thus providing one member from each State—half the Senate's membership.[81] The committee worked on the bill for two months; it was finally passed by both Houses in late September.

Judgment of the constitutional function of an organ of government is sometimes obscured by dramatic crises, which tend to divert attention from the daily round of duties. This has been true, for example, of the Supreme Court. The hasty reader of brief histories may have to be reminded that *Marbury* v. *Madison*[82] was only one episode in the Court's multiple duties. So, too, for the work of the first Congress; to understand its actuality, one has to turn over the leaves of the Annals from day to day to see what occupied its time. The Annals give only skeleton accounts of the Senate's early sessions, as that body habitually met behind closed doors until November 1794, but the House of Representatives held open debate from the start and the Annals give a vivid picture of its early weeks. The first impression one gets is the protracted attention given to revenue measures. Another is occasional preoccupation, even in that demanding period, with matters which today seem unimportant. The "style or title" by which the President should be addressed required the Senate's early attention. The first Act of Congress was a statute to regulate the time and manner of administering certain official oaths.

By July 4, however, pieces of major legislation had begun to emerge. On that day the President approved an act laying duty on certain imports—including, oddly enough, tea! On July 20, the President approved an act imposing a tonnage duty on ships. On July 27, he approved an act establishing the "Department of Foreign Affairs," ancestor of the present State Department, and on July 31, approved

[81] See Charles Warren, "New Light on the History of the Federal Judiciary Act of 1789," 37 *Harv. L. Rev.* 49 (1923). New York had not yet chosen Senators.
[82] 1 Cranch 137 (1803).

a long statute providing procedures for the collection of customs and tonnage duties. In August, the President approved several measures: a bill to continue the Board of Commissioners established by the late Congress in 1787 to settle the accounts between the United States and individual States; an act setting up the War Department; an act adapting the Northwest Ordinance of 1787 to the new Constitution; and one establishing and supporting lighthouses, beacons, buoys, and public piers. Another statute provided for the expenses of negotiating with Indian tribes. On September 1, came a statute for registering vessels and regulating the coasting trade. On September 2, the President signed a measure setting up the Treasury Department. Statutes fixing salaries of certain officers (including the President), safekeeping national records, further regulating the collection of customs, and temporarily setting up a Post Office, were approved between September 2 and September 24. On the latter day the President signed the Judiciary Act of 1789.[83] And on September 25, the Senate and the House agreed on twelve recommended Amendments to the Constitution, of which ten were ultimately ratified by the States.

On Sepember 29, the President approved a final list of statutes; one regulating process in the federal courts; one "amending and explaining" the statutes concerning shipping and the coasting trade; acts making appropriations of $639,000 for the cost of government; directing payment of pensions to disabled veterans; adapting the provisions of the Continental Congress concerning the Army to government under the Constitution; and lastly, an Act fixing the first Monday in January 1790 for the next meeting of Congress. Both Houses adjourned on the 29th. They had debated long and without result in an effort to select a site for the national capital. But by modern standards, they had accomplished a great deal, and perhaps the President did not mean to be stiff in a little note which he wrote to the Senate reminding it of various advices and consents it had not yet given.

The congressional session of 1789 provided the essentials of the new government—revenues, executive departments to dispatch the national business, and a system of courts. The development of constitutional theory during the next century and three-quarters has been so much a judicial task that the judiciary act of 1789 deserves particular discussion.

This first judiciary act[84] was remarkable in many respects—most notably, perhaps, because it created a set of lower federal courts

[83] Chapter 20 of the Laws of the First Session of the First Congress: "An Act to Establish the Judicial Courts of the United States."

[84] 1 U.S. Statutes at Large 72.

which could administer justice where federal questions were involved or where citizens of different States were parties. The Congress might have left all federal questions to be decided in the first instance by State courts, leaving the control of national justice to the Supreme Court on appellate review. The enforcement of federal policy in matters where strong local sentiments were involved, such as the racial desegregation cases of the mid-twentieth century, would have been far different without federal courts of first instance; and if the federal system had originally been set up without such courts, their later addition would have been much more difficult. Appellate review by the Supreme Court of State judgments on federal questions was itself a conspicuous new feature in 1789. The Congress had evidently determined to make the federal judiciary a strong part of the national government. The judiciary act created one District Court for each State,[85] and two more, one for Maine, then a part of Massachusetts, and one for Kentucky, still a part of Virginia. The District Courts were courts of first instance with rather restricted jurisdictions of cases involving federal questions. The judicial districts were grouped in three circuits; a Circuit Court would sit twice annually in each district; it would consist of two justices of the Supreme Court and the district judge of the district in question. The Circuit Courts had original jurisdiction of cases where the parties had diverse citizenship; the act also gave to the Circuit Courts jurisdiction of grave federal crimes, and an appellate jurisdiction to review District Court judgments.

To the Supreme Court the judiciary act gave original jurisdiction of certain civil suits where a State was a party, and jurisdiction of proceedings in which foreign diplomats or their "domestics or domestic servants" were involved. The statute provided some appellate review by the Supreme Court of judgments of lower federal courts, but its most controversial appellate function concerned review of State court determinations.

Section 25 of the act which provided for this review was destined to be a battleground.[86] It gave to the Supreme Court appellate jurisdiction over

> a final judgment or decree in any suit, in the highest court of law or equity of a State in which a decision in the suit could be had, where is drawn in question the validity of a treaty or statute of, or an authority exercised under the United States, and the decision is against their validity; or where is drawn in question the validity of a statute

[85] Except North Carolina and Rhode Island, which had not yet ratified the Constitution.

[86] See *Martin* v. *Hunter's Lessee*, 1 Wheat. 304 (1816).

of, or an authority exercised under any State, on the ground of their being repugnant to the constitution, treaties or laws of the United States, and the decision is in favour of such their validity, or where is drawn in question the construction of any clause of the constitution, or of a treaty, or statute of, or commission held under the United States, and the decision is against the title, right, privilege, or exemption specially set up or claimed by either party, under such clause of the said Constitution, treaty, statute or commission, . . .

Section 34 of the judiciary act provided:

And be it further enacted, That the laws of the several states, except where the constitution, treaties or statutes of the United States shall otherwise require or provide, shall be regarded as rules of decision in trials at common law in the courts of the United States in cases where they apply.[87]

The word "laws" in this famous section was to have a troubled history. The Court, in an opinion written by Mr. Justice Story in 1842,[88] held that section 34 applied only to "statute laws" of the States; this decision entrusted the federal judiciary with discretion to apply its own "general principles and doctrines of commercial jurisprudence" to questions of a general nature, even though the decisional law of the State in question might differ from the federal court doctrine so promulgated. Over the years the United States courts thus built up an important body of federal decisional law, quite different from that of the States in which the federal courts sat. In 1923 Charles Warren undermined the historical basis of this federal independence by an article in the *Harvard Law Review* under the title, "New Light on the History of the Federal Judiciary Act of 1789."[89] Mr. Warren asserted that "the laws of the several States" which section 34 required the federal courts to follow were intended to include the decisional as well as statute "laws" of the States. In 1938 the Supreme Court accepted Mr. Warren's views in its decision of *Erie Railroad Company* v. *Tompkins,*[90] thus ending ninety-six years of that court's independence of State decisional doctrines on questions of "general common law."

The First Ten Amendments

Madison was the principal author of the first Ten Amendments to the Constitution. The Annals of Congress in the spring and summer

[87] 1 Stat. at Large, p. 92.
[88] *Swift* v. *Tyson,* 16 Pet. 1.
[89] 37 *Harv. L. Rev.* 49.
[90] 304 U.S. 64.

of 1789, reporting his speeches in the House at all stages in the development of the Bill of Rights, show him wise, reasonable, patient, and courteous despite what must have been the maddening repetitiousness of his opponents. The Bill of Rights as it was finally accepted is surprisingly close to what Madison originally proposed. So great was his part that nearly two centuries later judicial commentary on the First Amendment occasionally sounds as if it depended on somewhat inconclusive guesses as to what Madison had in his mind in 1789.[91] Still the fact remains that the United States is indebted to James Madison for a substantial part of its written Constitution; his recorded ideas are rightly respected.

Madison's reasoned and reasonable advocacy of the Bill of Rights in the House demonstrates his genuine convictions; but his position was also essential to his Virginian political career. Patrick Henry, opponent of the Constitution, had so managed matters that Madison had not become a Senator. Anti-federalists, backing James Monroe against Madison for a seat in the new House of Representatives, put out the story that Madison was opposed to any amendments at all.[92] Henry was urging the Virginia House of Delegates to call on Congress for another constitutional convention; Madison and his associates saw in such a move the possible reopening of all the States-rights debates which had racked the Convention of 1787, and a threat to all progress toward effective national government. Amendments which would satisfy State suspicions of the new federal power, and thus abate State demands for a new convention, were essential to the political safety of the whole structure.

Fortunately for the United States, Madison succeeded in his candidacy for a seat in the House, but he was not able to propose amendments at once. Business in the House was delayed almost a month until a quorum assembled. Then came nearly another month of debate on import and tonnage duties. Money was obviously essential for any governmental activity, and indeed on April 8, 1789, the first day on which the House considered any legislation, Madison himself proposed a resolution for import and tonnage duties, a subject, he said in the House, "which appears to me to be of the greatest magnitude; a subject, sir, that requires our first attention, and our united exertions."

[91] See, e.g., the dissenting opinion of Mr. Justice Rutledge in *Everson* v. *Board of Education*, 330 U.S. 1 (1947) p. 31; the dissenting opinion of Mr. Justice Reed in *Illinois* ex rel. *McCollum* v. *Board of Education*, 333 U.S. 203 (1948) pp. 247, 248; see also the opinions of Clark, J. and Brennan, J. in *School District of Abington Township* v. *Schempp*, 374 U.S. 203 (1963).

[92] See Robert Allen Rutland, *The Birth of the Bill of Rights* (Chapel Hill: University of North Carolina Press, 1955) Chapter IX.

Nearly a month later, on Monday, May 4, they were still discussing duties on tonnage. At the close of that day Madison gave notice that he proposed to bring up the subject of constitutional amendments on the 4th Monday, which would be May 25. When the 25th came it was full of a number of things—contested New Jersey elections; salaries for the President, the Vice President, and the legislators; duties on tonnage; but nothing about Madison's amendments appears in that day's Annals. In the Annals of June 8, however, the proposal for amendments suddenly appears. Madison explained that because of other urgent business[93] he had moved for delay when his original day came. He now moved that the House in Committee of the Whole discuss the constitutional amendments he had in mind. Dilatory objections arose at once; amendments might be considered, but a select committee was the proper procedure; or else the amendments ought to be printed and laid on the table. The time was not ripe. The revenue business was not settled. One senses that the subject was faintly embarrassing.

Madison equably withdrew his motion for a Committee of the Whole, proposed instead a select committee, and went on to discuss his amendments, which, he suggested, should be incorporated in the several articles of the original Constitution instead of being placed in a list at the end where they now are. In nine proposals which he then brought forward appear the substance, and much of the wording of the first ten amendments ultimately adopted.[94] The extent of his contribution clearly appears from a parallel arrangement of the measures Madison put forward on June 8, 1789, and the actual text of the first ten amendments.

The First Ten Amendments As Adopted	Madison's Proposals Of June 8, 1789[95]
I	
Congress shall make no law respecting an establishment of religion, or prohibiting the free exercise thereof; or abridging the freedom of speech, or of the press; or the right	The civil rights of none shall be abridged on account of religious belief or worship, nor shall any national religion be established, nor shall the full and equal rights of con-

[93] *Annals of Congress,* I, p. 427.

[94] In Madison's fourth proposal can be seen the present First, Second, Third, Fourth, Fifth, Sixth, Eighth and Ninth Amendments, except for the present guarantees of grand and petit criminal juries found in the present Fifth and Sixth Amendments. These and the civil jury guarantees of our Seventh Amendment appear in Madison's sixth and seventh proposals. The present Tenth Amendment is included in Madison's eighth proposal.

[95] See the *Annals of Congress,* I, p. 433 *et seq.*

of the people peaceably to assemble, and to petition the Government for a redress of grievances.

science be in any manner, or on any pretext, infringed. [4th Proposal, 1st paragraph]

The people shall not be deprived or abridged of their right to speak, to write, or to publish their sentiments; and the freedom of the press, as one of the great bulwarks of liberty, shall be inviolable. [4th, 2d par.]

The people shall not be restrained from peaceably assembling and consulting for their common good; nor from applying to the Legislature by petitions, or remonstrances, for redress of their grievances. [4th, 3d par.]

II

A well regulated Militia, being necessary to the security of a free State, the right of the people to keep and bear Arms, shall not be infringed.

The right of the people to keep and bear arms shall not be infringed; a well-armed and well-regulated militia being the best security of a free country: but no person religiously scrupulous of bearing arms shall be compelled to render military service in person. [4th, 4th par.]

III

No Soldier shall, in time of peace be quartered in any house, without the consent of the Owner, nor in time of war, but in a manner to be prescribed by law.

No soldier shall in time of peace be quartered in any house without the consent of the owner; nor at any time, but in a manner warranted by law. [4th, 5th par.]

IV

The right of the people to be secure in their persons, houses, papers, and effects, against unreasonable searches and seizures, shall not be violated, and no Warrants shall issue, but upon probable cause, supported by Oath or affirmation, and particularly describing the place to be searched, and the persons or things to be seized.

The rights of the people to be secured in their persons, their houses, their papers, and their other property, from all unreasonable searches and seizures, shall not be violated by warrants issued without probable cause, supported by oath or affirmation, or not particularly describing the places to be searched, or the persons or things to be seized. [4th, 8th par.]

V

No person shall be held to answer for a capital, or otherwise infamous crime, unless on a presentment or indictment of a Grand Jury, except in cases arising in the land or naval forces, or in the Militia, when in actual service in time of War or public danger; nor shall any person be subject for the same offence to be twice put in jeopardy of life or limb; nor shall be compelled in any criminal case to be a witness against himself, nor be deprived of life, liberty, or property, without due process of law; nor shall private property be taken for public use, without just compensation.

No person shall be subject, except in cases of impeachment, to more than one punishment or one trial for the same offence; nor shall be compelled to be a witness against himself; nor be deprived of life, liberty, or property, without due process of law; nor be obliged to relinquish his property, where it may be necessary for public use, without a just compensation. [4th, 6th par.] . . . and in all crimes punishable with loss of life or member, presentment or indictment by a grand jury shall be an essential preliminary. . . [7th, 2d par.]

VI

In all criminal prosecutions, the accused shall enjoy the right to a speedy and public trial, by an impartial jury of the State and district wherein the crime shall have been committed, which district shall have been previously ascertained by law, and to be informed of the nature and cause of the accusation; to be confronted with the witnesses against him; to have compulsory process for obtaining witnesses in his favor, and to have the Assistance of Counsel for his defense.

In all criminal prosecutions, the accused shall enjoy the right to a speedy and public trial, to be informed of the cause and nature of the accusation, to be confronted with his accusers, and the witnesses against him; to have a compulsory process for obtaining witnesses in his favor; and to have the assistance of counsel for his defense. [4th, 9th par.]

The trial of all crimes (except in cases of impeachments, and cases arising in the land or naval forces, or the militia when on actual service, in time of war or public danger) shall be by an impartial jury of freeholders of the vicinage, with the requisite of unanimity for conviction, of the right of challenge, and other accustomed requisites; . . . [7th, 2d par.]

In cases of crimes committed not within any county, the trial may by law be in such county as the laws shall have prescribed. . . [7th, 3d par.]

VII

In suits at common law, where the value in controversy shall exceed twenty dollars, the right of trial by jury shall be preserved, and no fact tried by jury, shall be otherwise re-examined in any Court of the United States, than according to the rules of the common law.

In suits at common law, between man and man, the trial by jury, as one of the best securities to the rights of the people, ought to remain inviolate. [7th, 3d par.] . . . nor shall any fact triable by jury, according to the course of common law, be otherwise re-examinable than may consist with the principles of common law. [6th, 2d par.]

VIII

Excessive bail shall not be required, nor excessive fines imposed, nor cruel and unusual punishments inflicted.

Excessive bail shall not be required, nor excessive fines imposed, nor cruel and unusual punishments inflicted. [4th, 7th par.]

IX

The enumeration in the Constitution, of certain rights, shall not be construed to deny or disparage others retained by the people.

The exceptions here or elsewhere in the Constitution, made in favor of particular rights, shall not be so construed as to diminish the just importance of other rights retained by the people, or as to enlarge the powers delegated by the Constitution; but either as actual limitations of such powers, or as inserted merely for greater caution. [4th, 10th par.]

X

The powers not delegated to the United States by the Constitution, nor prohibited by it to the States, are reserved to the States respective, or to the people.

The powers not delegated by this Constitution, nor prohibited by it to the States, are reserved to the States respectively. [8th, 3d par.]

The Congress, and ultimately the several State legislatures, accepted the great majority of Madison's June 8th proposals. Even his unaccepted ideas still have historical interest. He would first have prefixed to the Constitution a statement of political theory, reminiscent of the Declaration of Independence, affirming that—

> . . . all power is originally vested in, and consequently derived from, the people.

That Government is instituted and ought to be exercised for the benefit of the people; which consists in the enjoyment of life and liberty, with the right of acquiring and using property, and generally of pursuing and obtaining happiness and safety.

That the people have an indubitable, unalienable, and indefeasible right to reform or change their Government, whenever it be found adverse or inadequate to the purposes of its institution.

Madison's second and third proposals reflected a substantial popular feeling that there should be more members in the lower House. He would have changed the provision of Article I, Section 2, Clause 2 which fixes as a top limit on membership of the House one representative for every thirty thousand inhabitants; he would, instead, have made this maximum a minimum, and have provided at least one representative for every thirty thousand people. He would have guaranteed to each State at least two members of the House, after the first census, in place of the single representative provided by Article I. And to guard against legislative self-indulgence, Madison would have deferred the effective date of any measure raising Congressional salaries until a succeeding House election had furnished an opportunity for aroused popular indignation to turn the rascals out.

Madison's amendments were almost all limits on the national government, but his fifth proposal would have placed restrictions on certain State action—

No State shall violate the equal rights of conscience, or the freedom of the press, or the trial by jury in criminal cases.

Prophetically he told the House—

I think there is more danger of those powers being abused by the State Governments than by the Government of the United States.

A federal guarantee of State jury trials has never come; but the Supreme Court's twentieth-century construction of the Fourteenth Amendment of 1868 has read the substance of the rest of Madison's fifth proposal into the Constitution.[96]

In his sixth proposal Madison suggested a money limit on cases appealable to the Supreme Court. This has never come about; but the present $10,000 jurisdictional limit for many federal court causes of action in the first instance has a somewhat comparable overall effect.[97] The Supreme Court's appellate jurisdiction has mainly been limited by the device of optional review on certiorari,[98] without a dollar limit.

[96] See, e.g., *Near* v. *Minnesota*, 283 U.S. 697 (1931) for freedom of the press; and *Cantwell* v. *Connecticut*, 310 U.S. 296 (1940) for "equal rights of conscience."
[97] See 28 U.S. Code Sec. 1331 and 1332.
[98] See 28 U.S. Code Sec. 1254 and 1257.

The first part of Madison's eighth proposal may have been drawn from Article XXX of the Declaration of Rights of the Massachusetts Constitution of 1780; or perhaps both stemmed from a common root. Both reflect a devotion to Montesquieu's separation of powers, a literal belief in that concept to which the United States has since paid more verbal than functional compliments. Madison suggested this language—

> The powers delegated by this Constitution are appropriated to the departments to which they are respectively distributed: so that the Legislative Department shall never exercise the powers vested in the Executive or Judicial, nor the Executive exercise the powers vested in the Legislative or Judicial, nor the Judicial exercise the powers vested in the Legislative or Executive Departments.

This ideal is inherent in the separate description of functions in the first three Articles of the Constitution, but probably we have got on at least as well without Madison's clause; the history of independent regulatory commissions has demonstrated that hermetic sealing-off of governmental functions is impossible in practice.

After Madison had explained his proposed amendments, debates over the procedure to follow in considering them occupied what was left of the day. At length the House voted, after all, to refer the matter to a Committee of the Whole, and adjourned for the day. Somewhat relieved, it returned next morning to considering means of raising national revenue. Six weeks passed; the House debated a Department of Foreign Affairs, the pay of the President, western lands. On July 21, Madison moved that the House go into the Committee of the Whole in which six weeks earlier it had resolved to discuss amendments. Fisher Ames of Massachusetts then moved to reverse the vote of the 8th of June and refer the amendments to a select committee.

One reads these dilatory discussions with a feeling that the subject was irksome, that excuses to put it off were welcome. At the end of the 21st day of July the House voted to refer Madison's proposals, and also those proposed by the States, to a select committee of one member from each State. Thus constitutional amendments again disappear from the Annals, this time until August 13, when Mr. Lee of Virginia moved to go into Committee of the Whole to consider the report of the committee of eleven. Madison urged this. Further dilatory argument arose; the House, some said, should debate the judiciary act first. Finally, after some members became impatient, the House did go into Committee of the Whole, and debated amendments until August 22. Then at length a committee of three[99] was appointed

[99] Benson, Sherman, and Sedgwick.

to "arrange" the amendments which the Whole had approved. Two days later their report came in; the House sent it over to the Senate whose ideas evidently differed. The Amendments were not adjusted between the two Houses until September 25; on that day both agreed on twelve proposed amendments, to be referred to the legislatures of the several States, to be valid when three-fourths should ratify.[100] On December 5, 1791, the last ten articles of the twelve so proposed became the first ten amendments to the Constitution.[101] The first two proposals, which never obtained the necessary ratifications, would have increased representation in the House and would have restricted the right of Congress to raise its own pay,[102] as Madison had moved on June 8, 1789.

On March 1, 1792, Thomas Jefferson, Secretary of State, announced the acceptance of the first ten amendments. Massachusetts, Connecticut, and Georgia had not ratified any of them, and did not get around to it for a century and a half. Then, as part of their celebration of the sesquicentennial of the Constitution in 1939, all three States finally approved the Bill of Rights.

1791 saw the completion of the Constitutional structure of the United States. 1787 had been occupied with the drafting of the Constitution; 1788 with its ratification in the States, 1789 with organization of the new government, and with formulating the amendments which in effect had been conditions of acceptance of the Constitution by the States. Perhaps more important, the first months and years under the new Constitution passed with no signs of the federal tyranny which men like Governor Clinton had feared. The States found that in practice they had plenty of power left; ratification of the amendments gave them formal reassurance.

[100] The twelve are printed in 1 U.S. Statutes at Large, pp. 97–98.

[101] On that day Virginia ratified all twelve; this made her the eleventh State to ratify what are now amendments I-X; several States had rejected proposals I and II. By 1791 fourteen States were members of the Union; pursuant to an Act of Congress approved February 18, 1791, Vermont had become the fourteenth State on March 4, 1791. Eleven ratifications were then required to make three-fourths of fourteen.

[102] Article I. After the first enumeration required by the first article of the Constitution, there shall be one Representative for every thirty thousand, until the number shall amount to one hundred, after which the proportion shall be so regulated by Congress, that there shall be not less than one hundred Representatives, nor less than one Representative for every forty thousand persons, until the number of Representatives shall amount to two hundred; after which the proportion shall be so regulated by Congress, that there shall not be less than two hundred Representatives, nor more than one Representative for every fifty thousand persons. Article II. No law varying the compensation for the services of the Senators and Representatives shall take effect, until an election of Representatives shall have intervened.

If the Albany Convention of 1754 were to be taken as the first step in the creation of the United States, Virginia's ratification of the first ten amendments in 1791, thirty-seven years later, can be thought of as the completion of the Revolution. There were to be other times of swift constitutional change. One occurred during the five years after the Civil War, when the Thirteenth, Fourteenth and Fifteenth Amendments made the national government the guarantor of tolerable government by the States. Another, coming not by constitutional amendment but by judicial reconsideration, occurred between 1937 and 1942 when the Supreme Court extended the national power to include control of the entire national economy, and notably reduced judicial restriction of economic legislation. Another occurred in 1954 and the following few years, when the Supreme Court's changed construction of the post-Civil War amendments produced new national protection for the Negro against State wrongs. Another occurred in 1962–1964 when the Supreme Court held that States must follow a basic standard of equality among voters in the apportionment of seats in both houses of their own legislatures, and in creating districts for elections to the federal House of Representatives. The Constitution has always grown and changed, but most growth, most change, has been interstitial, gradual. Sudden advances have been comparatively few since 1791.

The adoption of the Bill of Rights provides an appropriate breathing-space for travelers to view the ground. This book undertakes to survey the development in America, and in its English predecessor-nation, of five underlying constitutional principles; popular control of government despite the fallibility of majorities; aspiration to justice in government despite the uncertainty of determining what is just; equality of mankind, with all the difficulties that go with the difference between every man and every other; diffusion of governmental power the better to secure liberty against government, with acceptance of the governmental ineptitude that this diffusion connotes; and definition in a written charter of restrictions on governmental powers, despite the short range of human foresight, despite the difficulty of finding words to provide for the unexpected, despite the ancient unwillingness of stubborn Leviathan to submit to self-capture with his own hook.[103] What progress had these difficult ideals made by 1791?

That "the people" should govern themselves was a doctrine living not so much in the written Constitution as in the American spirit. The draftsmen of 1787, some of them suspicious of the unbridled

[103] One can only wonder what Thomas Hobbes, naming his book, thought about the forty-first chapter of Job.

multitudes, rather yielded to majoritarianism than welcomed it; but Washington understood its force when he intervened for the only time in convention debate, just at the end, supporting the demand for increased popular representation in the House. The effectiveness of the call for a Bill of Rights was another demonstration that government had come to follow the wishes and the fears of the people. The War of Independence had been fired by much oratory and much pamphleteering about liberty and tyranny. Men can take such exhortation to heart; the men of 1789 applied it to their own rulers as well as to George the Third. America would see no peasants rising like England's in 1381. There were no peasants. No matter what the percentage of voters was, no matter what were the guarantees of democratic rule in constitutions or statutes, by 1789 popular will ruled the United States. Our problems of political practice and theory were still difficult and persistent, but in one form or another the problems arose from majority wrong done to assertive minorities. Majority rule had come to be the premise of thought and argument, the datum from which political theory started.

Rightness of government—an idea that there was in men's affairs an ascertainable natural right which even majority will could not transcend—this too was a concept more widespread in men's minds than in the careful words of the Constitution. The late eighteenth century was impressed with order in the universe, and looked for this order in human affairs as it was observable in celestial mechanics. Blackstone's introductory lecture—he was read in America as in England[104]—explained man's actions as subject to the law of nature, just as a clock's motion is prescribed by the will of the master clockmaker. In 1792 two of the Judges of the State of South Carolina, sitting in its Common Pleas, wrote of a statute purporting to divest one man of his title to lands and to vest the title in another,

> . . . it was against common right, as well as against *magna charta*, to take away the freehold of one man and vest it in another. . .[105]

In 1798 four justices of the Supreme Court delivered opinions in *Calder* v. *Bull*;[106] two of them, Chase and Paterson, referred to the "principles of the social compact" as clashing with retrospective legislation.

Evidently during the last decade of the eighteenth century there was current in some men's thinking some theory that a general higher

---

[104] See the well-known passage in Burke's speech on Conciliation with America; Ernest Rhys, ed., *Burke's Speeches and Letters on American Affairs* (London: J. M. Dent and Sons, 1908) page 94.
[105] *Bowman* v. *Middleton*, 1 Bay (So. Car.) 252, 254.
[106] 3 Dallas 387.

law should control unjust acts of legislation and administration even if that law was unspecified in the prescriptions of the Constitution. Religious impulses still worked strongly in men's minds as bore witness the Preamble of the Massachusetts Constitution of 1780,[107] and religious ideas are closely akin to the theory of a higher law in human governing. But this higher law was not destined to much immediate effect. It was only one of the cross-currents of thought in that time of many political theories. It ran counter to a desire to circumscribe by writings the powers of those who governed; the same Massachusetts Constitution by the thirteenth article of its Declaration of Rights testified to a popular wish for government of laws and not of men. But, still and all, underlying the federal Constitution of 1789 was a necessary theory that constitutional provisions would prevail over conflicting acts of government. In 1795, Mr. Justice Paterson, sitting as Circuit Justice in Pennsylvania, charged the jury in *Vanhorne's Lessee* v. *Dorrance*—[108]

> What is a Constitution? It is the form of government, delineated by the mighty hand of the people, in which certain first principles of fundamental laws are established. The Constitution is certain and fixed; it contains the permanent will of the people, and is the supreme law of the land; it is paramount to the power of the Legislature and can be revoked or altered only by the authority that made it. . . . What are Legislatures? Creatures of the Constitution; they owe their existence to the Constitution; they derive their powers from the Constitution. It is their commission; and, therefore, all their acts must be comformable to it, or else they will be void.

What of the doctrine that all eighteenth-century men were created equal? Here parted company the Declaration of Independence of 1776 and the Constitution of 1787–89. Despite the magnificent announcement of self-evident equality ascribed to Jefferson (who allotted what he deemed suitable places for his slaves in his charming hilltop house at Monticello), the new Constitution prescribed inequalities between Negroes and whites. Its first Article gave representation to all

[107] ". . . We, therefore, the people of Massachusetts, acknowledging, with grateful hearts, the goodness of the great Legislator of the universe, in affording us, in the course of His providence, an opportunity, deliberately and peaceably, without fraud, violence or surprise, of entering into an original, explicit, and solemn compact with each other; and of forming a new constitution of civil government, for ourselves and posterity; and devoutly imploring His direction in so interesting a design, do agree upon, ordain and establish the following *Declaration of Rights, and Frame of Government*, as the CONSTITUTION OF THE COMMONWEALTH OF MASSACHUSETTS." 1 Massachusetts General Laws Annotated.

[108] 2 Dallas 304, 308.

"free Persons" but as to "all other Persons" (meaning Negro slaves) the Constitution counted each Negro as only three-fifths of one Person. There were already, in the United States of 1787, many men who opposed the slave-trade; there were, on the contrary, men who would lose by its abolition. This conflict was resolved by a cautiously phrased compromise, inserted in the Constitution—[109]

> The . . . Importation of Such Persons as any of the States now existing shall think proper to admit, shall not be prohibited by the Congress prior to the Year one thousand eight hundred and eight. . .

But already the urgings were stirring that brought war in 1861. In 1794 the Congress enacted a cautiously phrased statute penalizing American shipmasters who, without importation of Negroes, still engaged in the slave-trade overseas.[110] During the next twenty years this prohibitory legislation was progressively stiffened. Importing of slaves was forbidden as soon as the Constitutional clause permitted.[111] By 1820 the Congress had branded as piracy overseas slave trade by Americans and had prescribed for it the penalty of death.[112]

Personal equality of white men in America[113] was a different matter. The Constitution had no great proclamation of faith like Jefferson's declaration that all men were created equal, but as to white men none was needed. The efforts of Rensselaers and Livingstons in New York to preserve a landed élite sustained by a grateful, respectful, and perpetual tenantry[114] had a wistful quality, an unreality, a reaching backward for something gone forever. The frontier was too close, America was too unpeopled, to sustain these remains of a medieval society already disappearing in England. When the Black Death had partly depopulated English farms in 1348–9, villein laborers had easily moved a county or two away and hired out as free cultivators, reasonably safe from pursuit. In the America of 1791 there were no white villeins, and there was a whole continent almost empty for the taking. And there was a vigorous tradition of revolutionary egalitarianism which had made it difficult to maintain military subordination during

---

[109] Article I, § 9.

[110] Act of March 22, 1794, 1 U.S. Statutes at Large 347.

[111] Act of March 2, 1807, 2 U.S. Statutes at Large 426, effective January 1, 1808. Almost simultaneously Great Britain forbade the slave trade.

[112] Act of May 15, 1820, 3 U.S. Statutes at Large 609.

[113] To Americans of nations other than the United States, I apologize for the use of "America" and "American" with an over-exclusive meaning. The usage is not here adopted in arrogance but out of a desire to avoid repetition of "United States." Tocqueville provides a precedent.

[114] See A. E. Sutherland, "The Tenantry on the New York Manors," 41 Cornell L. Q. 620 (1956).

the War of Independence. On paper the voting franchise was often restricted, but by the toil of his own hands a man could become a substantial landowner and so a voter, provided only he had the initiative to move himself and his family to the Hampshire Grants, to the Genesee country, or to the Ohio valley. Furthermore so much of government was local that voting in State elections, or voting for congressmen, cannot have meant nearly as much as having a voice in town affairs. A man who in 1791 for a few cents an acre bought a farm in the Phelps and Gorham Purchase in western New York must then have had his part in most of what to him counted in government. Equality of men was more an actuality of frontier life than it was a legal right dependent on an enforceable Constitution. There were no American cities in the modern dimension. Poor men and defeated men there were then as now; but in a sense truer than it has been since, the energetic and assertive could go West, or go to sea, and better themselves. In such a society one who tried to set himself up as ranking above his fellows was apt to be laughed at.

Diffusion of governmental power was so much taken as a premise in 1791 that one can wonder at the successful ratification of the Constitution, essential as was the added power it gave to the central government of the United States. The first ten amendments were all limits on the national power, cautiously added by States nervous at what they had created. The original concept of the delegated powers, as specified in Article I, Section 8, proved to be impracticable, but Washington in 1791 hesitated to approve the charter of the first Bank of the United States. Randolph, his Attorney-General, and Jefferson, his Secretary of State, advised him that the federal government had no delegated power to charter a bank; and only on Hamilton's urging did he finally approve the measure.[115] A multitude of service functions which all governments now perform for their people were in 1791 very largely carried out by nongovernmental entities, or were not performed at all. The Constitution added much to the powers of the federal government, but still added grudgingly and cautiously. The whole federal structure, our whole "constitution" in the British use of the term, our habit of governing ourselves, was premised on minimal public activity, on most things being done individually, or by nongovernmental groups. If services were performed by public entities, these were apt to be local governments, the town or the school-district. This left much scope for individual energy and initiative, uncontrolled by the public political process. Such nonpublic governments were

[115] See Bray Hammond, *Banks and Politics in America* (Princeton: Princeton University Press, 1957) p. 118; and see *McCulloch* v. *Maryland*, 4 Wheat. 316 (1819).

then, as now, repositories of much social power.[116] Our Constitution of 1791 left much room for their operation, and in this permissive diffusion was much unexpressed political theory, much vaguely conceived conviction that man, if left alone, would do right. This was a simple and comforting creed. During the next century and a half little in our politics was to assure us of its truth.

Perhaps the greatest affirmation of the Constitution-makers of 1787 was belief in the Writing. The thoughtful Americans of those years (and we shall not soon see their betters) were confident that by carefully making phrases they could describe their theory of governmental wisdom in a few well-chosen words, leaving unsaid the things that ought not to be said, and saying those things that ought to be said. In this they greatly succeeded; but probably for a reason they did not foresee. To prescribe the Constitution[117] of a nation of four millions destined to grow to more than one hundred ninety millions during the next century and three-quarters, more foresight is required than has been granted even to the wisest men of any generation. Half seeing this in the mists of the future, the Founding Fathers established the Supreme Court. So in many ways the Constitution has been what that Court has declared it to be,[118] and necessarily so. Few statutes, and no document as general in terms as a Constitution, can speak with enough specifics to meet the emerging needs of a complex society. The amending process is too inflexible to serve the needs of adaptation and change; but the Court has been able to accomplish both. The provision against Bills of Attainder in Article I, Section 9, has served to invalidate a "rider" on an appropriation bill denying future pay to three federal employees,[119] and what was equal protection by a State in 1896 had ceased to be so by 1954.[120] The success of the Constitution as a symbol has been possible only by the functioning of the Supreme Court.

[116] See A. E. Sutherland, "Private Government and Public Policy," 41 *Yale Review* 405 (1952).

[117] Whoever writes footnotes risks boring by repetition. In the English usage constitution (with a small "c") means the British habit of governing. In our usage, Constitution (capitalized) means the document accepted by the States in 1789.

[118] As Charles Evans Hughes pointed out in 1907, "I reckon him one of the worst enemies of the community who will talk lightly of the dignity of the bench. We are under a Constitution, but the Constitution is what the judges say it is, and the judiciary is the safeguard of our liberty and of our property under the Constitution." Speech before the Elmira Chamber of Commerce, May 3, 1907, in Charles Evan Hughes, *Addresses and Papers* (New York: G. P. Putnam's Sons, 1908) pp. 133, 139.

[119] *United States* v. *Lovett*, 328 U.S. 303 (1946).

[120] *Plessy* v. *Ferguson*, 163 U.S. 537 (1896); *Brown* v. *Board of Education*, 347 U.S. 438 (1954).

The Constitution of the United States

We the People of the United States, in Order to form a more perfect Union, establish Justice, insure domestic Tranquility, provide for the common defence, promote the general Welfare, and secure the Blessings of Liberty to ourselves and our Posterity, do ordain and establish this Constitution for the United States of America.

ARTICLE I

Section 1. All legislative Powers herein granted shall be vested in a Congress of the United States, which shall consist of a Senate and House of Representatives.

Section 2. The House of Representatives shall be composed of Members chosen every second Year by the People of the several States, and the Electors in each State shall have the Qualifications requisite for Electors of the most numerous Branch of the State Legislature.

No Person shall be a Representative who shall not have attained to the Age of twenty-five Years, and been seven Years a Citizen of the United States, and who shall not, when elected, be an Inhabitant of that State in which he shall be chosen.

Representatives and direct Taxes shall be apportioned among the several States which may be included within this Union, according to their respective Numbers, which shall be determined by adding to the whole Number of free Persons, including those bound to Service for a Term of Years, and excluding Indians not taxed, three fifths of all other Persons. The actual Enumeration shall be made within three Years after the first Meeting of the Congress of the United States, and within every subsequent Term of ten Years, in such Manner as they shall by Law direct. The Number of Representatives shall not exceed one for every thirty Thousand, but each State shall have at Least one Representative; and until such enumeration shall be made, the State of New Hampshire shall be entitled to chuse three, Massachusetts eight, Rhode-Island and Providence Plantations one, Connecticut five, New-York six, New Jersey four, Pennsylvania eight, Delaware one, Maryland six, Virginia ten, North Carolina five, South Carolina five, and Georgia three.

When vacancies happen in the Representation from any State, the Executive Authority thereof shall issue Writs of Election to fill such Vacancies.

The House of Representatives shall chuse their Speaker and other Officers; and shall have the sole Power of Impeachment.

Section 3. The Senate of the United States shall be composed of two Senators from each State, chosen by the Legislature thereof, for six Years; and each Senator shall have one Vote.

Immediately after they shall be assembled in Consequence of the first Election, they shall be divided as equally as may be into three Classes. The Seats of the Senators of the first Class shall be vacated at the Expiration of the second Year, of the second Class at the Expiration of the fourth Year, and of the third Class at the Expiration of the sixth Year, so that one third may be chosen every second Year; and if Vacancies happen by Resignation, or otherwise, during the Recess of the Legislature of any State, the Executive thereof may make temporary Appointments until the next Meeting of the Legislature, which shall then fill such Vacancies.

No Person shall be a Senator who shall not have attained to the Age of thirty Years, and been nine Years a Citizen of the United States, and who shall not, when elected, be an Inhabitant of that State for which he shall be chosen.

The Vice President of the United States shall be President of the Senate, but shall have no Vote, unless they be equally divided.

The Senate shall chuse their other Officers, and also a President pro tempore, in the absence of the Vice President, or when he shall exercise the Office of President of the United States.

The Senate shall have the sole Power to try all Impeachments. When sitting for that Purpose, they shall be on Oath or Affirmation. When the President of the United States is tried, the Chief Justice shall preside: And no Person shall be convicted without the Concurrence of two thirds of the Members present.

Judgment in Cases of Impeachment shall not extend further than to removal from Office, and disqualification to hold and enjoy any Office of honor, Trust or Profit under the United States: but the Party convicted shall nevertheless be liable and subject to Indictment, Trial, Judgment and Punishment, according to Law.

Section 4. The Times, Places and Manner of holding Elections for Senators and Representatives, shall be prescribed in each State by the Legislature thereof; but the Congress may at any time by Law make or alter such Regulations, except as to the Places of chusing Senators.

The Congress shall assemble at least once in every Year, and such Meeting shall be on the first Monday in December unless they shall by Law appoint a different Day.

Section 5. Each House shall be the Judge of the Elections, Returns and Qualifications of its own Members, and a Majority of each shall constitute a Quorum to do Business; but a smaller Number may adjourn from day to day, and may be authorized to compel the Attendance of absent Members, in such Manner, and under such Penalties as each House may provide.

Each House may determine the Rules of its Proceedings, punish its Members for disorderly Behaviour, and, with the Concurrence of two thirds, expel a Member.

Each House shall keep a Journal of its Proceedings, and from time to time publish the same, excepting such Parts as may in their Judgment require Secrecy; and the Yeas and Nays of the Members of either House on any question shall, at the Desire of one fifth of those Present, be entered on the Journal.

Neither House, during the Session of Congress, shall, without the Consent of the other, adjourn for more than three days, nor to any other Place than that in which the two Houses shall be sitting.

Section 6. The Senators and Representatives shall receive a Compensation for their Services, to be ascertained by Law, and paid out of the Treasury of the United States. They shall in all Cases, except Treason, Felony and Breach of the Peace, be privileged from Arrest during their Attendance at the Session of their respective Houses, and in going to and returning from the same; and for any Speech or Debate in either House, they shall not be questioned in any other Place.

No Senator or Representative shall, during the Time for which he was elected, be appointed to any civil Office under the Authority of the United States, which shall have been created, or the Emoluments whereof shall have been encreased during such time; and no Person holding any Office under the United States, shall be a Member of either House during his Continuance in Office.

Section 7. All Bills for raising Revenue shall originate in the House of Representatives; but the Senate may propose or concur with Amendments as on other Bills.

Every Bill which shall have passed the House of Representatives and the Senate, shall, before it become a Law, be presented to the President of the United States; if he approve he shall sign it, but if not he shall return it, with his Objections to that House in which it shall have originated, who shall enter the Objections at large on their Journal, and proceed to reconsider it. If after such Reconsideration two thirds of that House shall agree to pass the Bill, it shall be sent, together with the Objections, to the other House, by which it shall likewise be reconsidered, and if approved by two thirds of that House, it shall become a Law. But in all such Cases the Votes of both Houses shall be determined by yeas and Nays, and the Names of the Persons voting for and against the Bill shall be entered on the Journal of each House respectively. If any Bill shall not be returned by the President within ten Days (Sundays excepted) after it shall have been presented to him, the Same shall be a Law, in like Manner as if he had signed it, unless the Congress by their Adjournment prevent its Return, in which Case it shall not be a Law.

Every Order, Resolution, or Vote to which the Concurrence of the Senate and House of Representatives may be necessary (except on a question of Adjournment) shall be presented to the President of the United States; and before the Same shall take Effect, shall be approved by him, or being disapproved by him, shall be repassed by two thirds of the Senate and House of Representatives, according to the Rules and Limitations prescribed in the Case of a Bill.

Section 8. The Congress shall have Power To Lay and collect Taxes, Duties, Imposts and Excises, to pay the Debts and provide for the common Defence and general Welfare of the United States; but all Duties, Imposts and Excises shall be uniform throughout the United States;

To borrow Money on the credit of the United States;

To regulate Commerce with foreign Nations, and among the several States, and with the Indian Tribes;

To establish an uniform Rule of Naturalization, and uniform Laws on the subject of Bankruptcies throughout the United States;

To coin Money, regulate the Value thereof, and of foreign Coin, and fix the Standard of Weights and Measures;

To provide for the Punishment of counterfeiting the Securities and current Coin of the United States;

To establish Post Offices and post Roads;

To promote the Progress of Science and useful Arts, by securing for limited Times to Authors and Inventors the exclusive Right to their respective Writings and Discoveries;

To constitute Tribunals inferior to the supreme Court;

To define and punish Piracies and Felonies committed on the high Seas, and Offenses against the Law of Nations;

To declare War, grant Letters of Marque and Reprisal, and make Rules concerning Captures on Land and Water;

To raise and support Armies, but no Appropriation of Money to that Use shall be for a longer Term than two Years;

To provide and maintain a Navy;

To make Rules for the Government and Regulation of the land and naval Forces;

To provide for calling forth the Militia to execute the Laws of the Union, suppress Insurrections and repel Invasions;

To provide for organizing, arming, and disciplining the Militia, and for governing such Part of them as may be employed in the Service of the United States, reserving to the States respectively, the Appointment of the Officers, and the Authority of training the Militia according to the discipline prescribed by Congress;

To exercise exclusive Legislation in all Cases whatsover, over such District (not exceeding ten Miles square) as may, by Cession of particular States, and the Acceptance of Congress, become the Seat of the Government of the United States, and to exercise like Authority over all Places purchased by the Consent of the Legislature of the State in which the Same shall be, for the Erection of Forts, Magazines, Arsenals, dock-Yards, and other needful Buildings;—And

To make all Laws which shall be necessary and proper for carrying into Execution the foregoing Powers, and all other Powers vested by this Constitution in the Government of the United States, or in any Department or Officer thereof.

Section 9. The Migration or Importation of such Persons as any of the States now existing shall think proper to admit, shall not be prohibited by the Congress prior to the Year one thousand eight hundred and eight, but a Tax or duty may be imposed on such Importation, not exceeding ten dollars for each Person.

The privilege of the Writ of Habeas Corpus shall not be suspended, unless when in Cases of Rebellion or Invasion the public Safety may require it.

No Bill of Attainder or ex post facto Law shall be passed.

No Capitation, or other direct, Tax shall be laid, unless in Proportion to the Census or Enumeration herein before directed to be taken.

No Tax or Duty shall be laid on Articles exported from any State.

No Preference shall be given by any Regulation of Commerce or Revenue to the Ports of one State over those of another: nor shall Vessels bound to, or from, one State be obliged to enter, clear, or pay Duties in another.

No Money shall be drawn from the Treasury, but in Consequence of Appropriations made by Law; and a regular Statement and Account of the Receipts and Expenditures of all public Money shall be published from time to time.

No Title of Nobility shall be granted by the United States: And no Person holding any Office of Profit or Trust under them, shall, without the Consent of the Congress, accept of any present, Emolument, Office, or Title, of any kind whatever, from any King, Prince, or foreign State.

Section 10. No State shall enter into any Treaty, Alliance, or Confederation; grant Letters of Marque and Reprisal; coin Money; emit Bills of Credit; make any Thing but gold and silver Coin a Tender in Payment of Debts; pass any Bill of Attainder, ex post facto Law, or Law impairing the Obligation of Contracts, or grant any Title of Nobility.

No State shall, without the Consent of the Congress, lay any Imposts or Duties on Imports or Exports, except what may be absolutely necessary for executing its inspection Laws: and the net Produce of all Duties and Imposts, laid by any State on Imports or Exports, shall be for the Use of the Treasury of the United States; and all such Laws shall be subject to the Revision and Control of the Congress.

No State shall, without the Consent of Congress, lay any duty of Tonnage, keep Troops, or Ships of War in time of Peace, enter into any Agreement or Compact with another State, or with a foreign Power, or engage in War, unless actually invaded, or in such imminent Danger as will not admit of delay.

ARTICLE II

Section 1. The executive Power shall be vested in a President of the United States of America. He shall hold his Office during the Term of four Years, and, together with the Vice President, chosen for the same Term, be elected, as follows:

Each State shall appoint, in such Manner as the Legislature thereof may direct, a Number of Electors, equal to the whole Number of Senators and Representatives to which the State may be entitled in the Congress: but no Senator or Representative, or Person holding an Office of Trust or Profit under the United States, shall be appointed an Elector.

The Electors shall meet in their respective States, and vote by Ballot for two Persons, of whom one at least shall not be an Inhabitant of the same State with themselves. And they shall make a List of all the Persons voted for, and of the Number of Votes for each; which List they shall sign and certify, and transmit sealed to the Seat of the Government of the United States, directed to the President of the Senate. The President of the Senate shall, in the Presence of the Senate and House of Representatives, open all the Certificates, and the Votes shall then be counted. The Person having the greatest Number of Votes shall be the President, if such Number be a Majority of the whole Number of Electors appointed; and if there be more than one who have such Majority, and have an equal Number of Votes, then the House of Representatives shall immediately chuse by Ballot one of them for President; and if no Person have a Majority, then from the five highest on the List the said House shall in like Manner chuse the President. But in chusing the President, the Votes shall be taken by States, the Representation from each State having one Vote; A quorum for this Purpose shall consist of a Member or Members from two thirds of the States, and a Majority of all the States shall be necessary to a Choice. In every Case, after the Choice of the President, the Person having the greatest Number of Votes of the Electors shall be the Vice President. But if there should remain two or more who have equal Votes, the Senate shall chuse from them by Ballot the Vice President.

The Congress may determine the Time of chusing the Electors, and the Day on which they shall give their Votes; which Day shall be the same throughout the United States.

No person except a natural born Citizen, or a Citizen of the United States, at the time of the Adoption of this Constitution, shall be eligible to the Office of President; neither shall any Person be eligible to that Office who shall not have attained to the Age of thirty five Years, and been fourteen Years a Resident within the United States.

In Case of the removal of the President from Office, or of his Death, Resignation, or Inability to discharge the Powers and Duties of the said Office, the Same shall devolve on the Vice President, and the Congress may by Law provide for the Case of Removal, Death, Resignation or Inability, both of the President and Vice President, declaring what Officer shall then act as President, and such Officer shall act accordingly, until the Disability be removed, or a President shall be elected.

The President shall, at stated Times, receive for his Services, a Compensation, which shall neither be encreased nor diminished during the Period for which he shall have been elected, and he shall not receive within that Period any other Emolument from the United States, or any of them.

Before he enter on the Execution of his Office, he shall take the following Oath or Affirmation:—"I do solemnly swear (or affirm) that I will faithfully execute the Office of President of the United States, and will to the best of my Ability, preserve, protect and defend the Constitution of the United States."

Section 2. The President shall be Commander in Chief of the Army and Navy of the United States, and of the Militia of the several States, when called into the actual Service of the United States; he may require the Opinion, in writing, of the principal Officer in each of the executive Departments, upon any Subject relating to the Duties of their respective Offices, and he shall have Power to grant Reprieves and Pardons for Offenses against the United States, except in Cases of Impeachment.

He shall have Power, by and with the Advice and Consent of the Senate, to make Treaties, provided two thirds of the Senators present concur; and he shall nominate, and by and with the Advice and Consent of the Senate, shall appoint Ambassadors, other public Ministers and Consuls, Judges of the supreme Court, and all other Officers of the United States, whose Appointments are not herein otherwise provided for, and which shall be established by Law; but the Congress may by Law vest the Appointment of such inferior Officers, as they think proper, in the President alone, in the Courts of Law, or in the Heads of Departments.

The President shall have Power to fill up all Vacancies that may happen during the Recess of the Senate, by granting Commissions which shall expire at the End of their next Session.

Section 3. He shall from time to time give to the Congress Information of the State of the Union, and recommend to their Consideration such Measures as he shall judge necessary and expedient; he may, on extraordinary Occasions, convene both Houses, or either of them, and in Case of Disagreement between them, with Respect to the Time of Adjournment, he may adjourn them to such Time as he shall think proper; he shall receive Ambassadors and other public Ministers; he shall take Care that the Laws be faithfully executed, and shall Commission all the Officers of the United States.

Section 4. The President, Vice President and all civil Officers of the United States, shall be removed from Office on Impeachment for, and Conviction of, Treason, Bribery, or other high Crimes and Misdemeanors.

ARTICLE III

Section 1. The judicial Power of the United States, shall be vested in one supreme Court, and in such inferior Courts as the Congress may from time to time ordain and establish. The Judges, both of the supreme and inferior Courts, shall hold their Offices during good Behaviour, and shall, at stated Times, receive for their Services a Compensation which shall not be diminished during their Continuance in Office.

Section 2. The judicial Power shall extend to all Cases, in Law and Equity, arising under this Constitution, the Laws of the United States, and Treaties made, or which shall be made, under their Authority;— to all Cases affecting Ambassadors, other public Ministers and Consuls; —to all Cases of admiralty and maritime Jurisdiction;—to Controversies to which the United States shall be a Party;—to Controversies between two or more States;—between a State and Citizens of another State;— between Citizens of different States;—between Citizens of the same State claiming Lands under Grants of different States, and between a State, or the Citizens thereof, and foreign States, Citizens or Subjects.

In all Cases affecting Ambassadors, other public Ministers and Consuls, and those in which a State shall be Party, the supreme Court shall have original Jurisdiction. In all the other Cases before mentioned, the supreme Court shall have appellate Jurisdiction, both as to Law and Fact, with such Exceptions, and under such Regulations as the Congress shall make.

The trial of all Crimes, except in Cases of Impeachment, shall be by Jury; and such Trial shall be held in the State where the said Crimes shall have been committed; but when not committed within any State, the Trial shall be at such Place or Places as the Congress may by Law have directed.

Section 3. Treason against the United States, shall consist only in levying War against them, or in adhering to their Enemies, giving them Aid and Comfort. No Person shall be convicted of Treason unless on the Testimony of two Witnesses to the same overt Act, or on Confession in open Court.

The Congress shall have power to declare the Punishment of Treason, but no Attainder of Treason shall work Corruption of Blood, or Forfeiture except during the Life of the Person attainted.

ARTICLE IV

Section 1. Full Faith and Credit shall be given in each State to the public Acts, Records, and judicial Proceedings of every other State.

And the Congress may by general Laws prescribe the Manner in which such Acts, Records and Proceedings shall be proved, and the Effect thereof.

Section 2. The Citizens of each State shall be entitled to all Privileges and Immunities of Citizens in the several States.

A Person charged in any State with Treason, Felony, or other Crime, who shall flee from Justice, and be found in another State, shall on demand of the executive Authority of the State from which he fled, be delivered up, to be removed to the State having Jurisdiction of the Crime.

No Person held to Service or Labour in one State, under the Laws thereof, escaping into another, shall, in Consequence of any Law or Regulation therein, be discharged from such Service or Labour, but shall be delivered up on Claim of the Party to whom such Service or Labour may be due.

Section 3. New States may be admitted by the Congress into this Union; but no new State shall be formed or erected within the Jurisdiction of any other State; nor any State be formed by the Junction of two or more States, or Parts of States, without the Consent of the Legislatures of the States concerned as well as of the Congress.

The Congress shall have Power to dispose of and make all needful Rules and Regulations respecting the Territory or other Property belonging to the United States; and nothing in this Constitution shall be so construed as to Prejudice any Claims of the United States, or of any particular State.

Section 4. The United States shall guarantee to every State in this Union a Republican Form of Government, and shall protect each of them against Invasion; and on Application of the Legislature, or of the Executive (when the Legislature cannot be convened) against domestic Violence.

ARTICLE V

The Congress, whenever two thirds of both Houses shall deem it necessary, shall propose Amendments to this Constitution, or, on the Application of the Legislatures of two thirds of the several States, shall call a Convention for proposing Amendments, which, in either Case, shall be valid to all Intents and Purposes, as part of this Constitution, when ratified by the Legislatures of three fourths of the several States, or by Conventions in three fourths thereof, as the one or the other Mode of Ratification may be proposed by the Congress; Provided that no Amendment which may be made prior to the Year One thousand eight hundred and eight shall in any Manner affect the first and fourth Clauses in the Ninth Section of the first Article; and that no State, without its Consent, shall be deprived of its equal Suffrage in the Senate.

ARTICLE VI

All Debts contracted and Engagements entered into, before the Adoption of this Constitution shall be as valid against the United States under this Constitution, as under the Confederation.

This Constitution, and the Laws of the United States which shall be made in Pursuance thereof; and all Treaties made, or which shall be made, under the Authority of the United States, shall be the supreme Law of the Land; and the Judges in every State shall be bound thereby, any Thing in the Constitution or Laws of any State to the Contrary notwithstanding.

The Senators and Representatives before mentioned, and the Members of the several State Legislatures, and all executive and judicial Officers, both of the United States and of the several States, shall be bound by Oath or Affirmation, to support this Constitution; but no religious Test shall ever be required as a Qualification to any Office or public Trust under the United States.

ARTICLE VII

The Ratification of the Conventions of nine States shall be sufficient for the Establishment of this Constitution between the States so ratifying the Same.

Articles in Addition to, and Amendment of, the Constitution of the United States of America, Proposed by Congress and Ratified by the Several States, Pursuant to the Fifth Article of the Original Constitution.

AMENDMENT I

Congress shall make no law respecting an establishment of religion, or prohibiting the free exercise thereof; or abridging the freedom of speech, or of the press, or the right of the people peaceably to assemble, and to petition the Government for a redress of grievances.

AMENDMENT II

A well regulated Militia, being necessary to the security of a free State, the right of the people to keep and bear Arms, shall not be infringed.

AMENDMENT III

No Soldier shall, in time of peace be quartered in any house, without the consent of the Owner, nor in time of war, but in a manner to be prescribed by law.

AMENDMENT IV

The right of the people to be secure in their persons, houses, papers, and effects, against unreasonable searches and seizures, shall not be violated, and no Warrant shall issue, but upon probable cause, supported by Oath or affirmation, and particularly describing the place to be searched, and the persons or things to be seized.

AMENDMENT V

No person shall be held to answer for a capital, or otherwise infamous crime, unless on a presentment or indictment of a Grand Jury, except in cases arising in the land or naval forces, or in the Militia, when in actual service in time of War or public danger; nor shall any person be subject for the same offence to be twice put in jeopardy of life or limb, nor shall be compelled in any criminal case to be a witness against himself, nor be deprived of life, liberty, or property, without due process of law; nor shall private property be taken for public use without just compensation.

AMENDMENT VI

In all criminal prosecutions, the accused shall enjoy the right to a speedy and public trial, by an impartial jury of the State and district wherein the crime shall have been committed, which district shall have been previously ascertained by law, and to be informed of the nature and cause of the accusation; to be confronted with the witnesses against him; to have compulsory process for obtaining witnesses in his favor; and to have the Assistance of Counsel for his defence.

AMENDMENT VII

In suits at common law, where the value in controversy shall exceed twenty dollars, the right of trial by jury shall be preserved, and no fact tried by jury, shall be otherwise re-examined in any Court of the United States, than according to the rules of the common law.

AMENDMENT VIII

Excessive bail shall not be required, nor excessive fines imposed, nor cruel and unusual punishments inflicted.

AMENDMENT IX

The enumeration in the Constitution, of certain rights, shall not be construed to deny or disparage others retained by the people.

AMENDMENT X

The powers not delegated to the United States by the Constitution, nor prohibited by it to the States, are reserved to the States respectively, or to the people.

AMENDMENT XI [1798]

The Judicial power of the United States shall not be construed to extend to any suit in law or equity, commenced or prosecuted against one of the United States by Citizens of another State, or by Citizens or Subjects of any Foreign State.

AMENDMENT XII [1804]

The electors shall meet in their respective states and vote by ballot for President and Vice-President, one of whom, at least, shall not be an inhabitant of the same state with themselves; they shall name in their ballots the person voted for as President, and in distinct ballots the person voted for as Vice-President, and they shall make distinct lists of all persons voted for as President, and of all persons voted for as Vice-President, and of the number of votes for each, which lists they shall sign and certify, and transmit sealed to the seat of the government of the United States, directed to the President of the Senate;— The President of the Senate shall, in presence of the Senate and House of Representatives, open all the certificates and the votes shall then be counted;—The person having the greatest number of votes for President, shall be the President, if such number be a majority of the whole number of Electors appointed; and if no person have such majority, then from the persons having the highest numbers not exceeding three on the list of those voted for as President, the House of Representatives shall choose immediately, by ballot, the President. But in choosing the President, the votes shall be taken by states, the representation from each state having one vote; a quorum for this purpose shall consist of a member or members from two-thirds of the states, and a majority of all the states shall be necessary to a choice. And if the House of Representatives shall not choose a President whenever the right of choice shall devolve upon them, before the fourth day of March next following, then the Vice-President shall act as President, as in the case of the death or other constitutional disability of the President.—The person having the greatest number of votes as Vice-President, shall be the Vice-President, if such number be a majority of the whole number of Electors appointed, and if no person have a majority, then from the two highest numbers on the list, the Senate shall choose the Vice-President; a quorum for the purpose shall consist of two-thirds of the whole number of Senators, and a majority of the whole number shall be necessary to a choice. But no person constitutionally ineligible to the office of President shall be eligible to that of Vice-President of the United States.

AMENDMENT XIII [1865]

Section 1. Neither slavery nor involuntary servitude, except as a punishment for crime whereof the party shall have been duly convicted, shall exist within the United States, or any place subject to their jurisdiction.

Section 2. Congress shall have power to enforce this article by appropriate legislation.

AMENDMENT XIV [1868]

Section 1. All persons born or naturalized in the United States, and subject to the jurisdiction thereof, are citizens of the United States and of the State wherein they reside. No State shall make or enforce any law which shall abridge the privileges or immunities of citizens of the United States; nor shall any State deprive any person of life, liberty, or property, without due process of law; nor deny to any person within its jurisdiction the equal protection of the laws.

Section 2. Representatives shall be apportioned among the several States according to their respective numbers, counting the whole number of persons in each State, excluding Indians not taxed. But when the right to vote at any election for the choice of electors for President and Vice President of the United States, Representatives in Congress, the Executive and Judicial officers of a State, or the members of the Legislature thereof, is denied to any of the male inhabitants of such State, being twenty-one years of age, and citizens of the United States, or in any way abridged, except for participation in rebellion, or other crime, the basis of representation therein shall be reduced in the proportion which the number of such male citizens shall bear to the whole number of male citizens twenty-one years of age in such State.

Section 3. No person shall be a Senator or Representative in Congress, or elector of President and Vice President, or hold any office, civil or military, under the United States, or under any State, who, having previously taken an oath, as a member of Congress, or as an officer of the United States, or as a member of any State legislature, or as an executive or judicial officer of any State, to support the Constitution of the United States, shall have engaged in insurrection or rebellion against the same, or given aid or comfort to the enemies thereof. But Congress may by a vote of two-thirds of each House, remove such disability.

Section 4. The validity of the public debt of the United States, authorized by law, including debts incurred for payment of pensions and bounties for services in suppressing insurrection or rebellion, shall not be questioned. But neither the United States nor any State shall assume or pay any debt or obligation incurred in aid of insurrection or rebellion against the United States, or any claim for the loss or emancipation of any slave; but all such debts, obligations and claims shall be held illegal and void.

Section 5. The Congress shall have power to enforce, by appropriate legislation, the provisions of this article.

AMENDMENT XV [1870]

Section 1. The right of citizens of the United States to vote shall not be denied or abridged by the United States or by any State on account of race, color, or previous condition of servitude —

Section 2. The Congress shall have power to enforce this article by appropriate legislation.

AMENDMENT XVI [1913]

The Congress shall have power to lay and collect taxes on incomes, from whatever source derived, without apportionment among the several States, and without regard to any census or enumeration.

AMENDMENT XVII [1913]

The Senate of the United States shall be composed of two Senators from each State, elected by the people thereof, for six years; and each Senator shall have one vote. The electors in each State shall have the qualifications requisite for electors of the most numerous branch of the State legislatures.

When vacancies happen in the representation of any State in the Senate, the executive authority of such State shall issue writs of election to fill such vacancies: *Provided,* That the legislature of any State may empower the executive thereof to make temporary appointments until the people fill the vacancies by election as the legislature may direct.

This amendment shall not be so construed as to affect the election or term of any Senator chosen before it becomes valid as part of the Constitution.

AMENDMENT XVIII [1919]

Section 1. After one year from the ratification of this article the manufacture, sale, or transportation of intoxicating liquors within, the importation thereof into, or the exportation thereof from the United States and all territory subject to the jurisdiction thereof for beverage purposes is hereby prohibited.

Section 2. The Congress and the several States shall have concurrent power to enforce this article by appropriate legislation.

Section 3. This article shall be inoperative unless it shall have been ratified as an amendment to the Constitution by the legislatures of the several States, as provided in the Constitution, within seven years from the date of the submission hereof to the States by the Congress.

AMENDMENT XIX [1920]

The right of citizens of the United States to vote shall not be denied or abridged by the United States or by any State on account of sex.

Congress shall have power to enforce this article by appropriate legislation.

AMENDMENT XX [1933]

Section 1. The terms of the President and Vice President shall end at noon on the 20th day of January, and the terms of Senators and Representatives at noon on the 3d day of January, of the years in which such terms would have ended if this article had not been ratified; and the terms of their successors shall then begin.

Section 2. The Congress shall assemble at least once in every year, and such meeting shall begin at noon on the 3d day of January, unless they shall by law appoint a different day.

Section 3. If, at the time fixed for the beginning of the term of the President, the President elect shall have died, the Vice President elect shall become President. If a President shall not have been chosen before the time fixed for the beginning of his term, or if the President elect shall have failed to qualify, then the Vice President elect shall act as President until a President shall have qualified; and the Congress may by law provide for the case wherein neither a President elect nor a Vice President elect shall have qualified, declaring who shall then act as President, or the manner in which one who is to act shall be selected, and such person shall act accordingly until a President or Vice President shall have qualified.

Section 4. The Congress may by law provide for the case of the death of any of the persons from whom the House of Representatives may choose a President whenever the right of choice shall have devolved upon them, and for the case of the death of any of the persons from whom the Senate may choose a Vice President whenever the right of choice shall have devolved upon them.

Section 5. Sections 1 and 2 shall take effect on the 15th day of October following the ratification of this article.

Section 6. This article shall be inoperative unless it shall have been ratified as an amendment to the Constitution by the legislatures of three-fourths of the several States within seven years from the date of its submission.

AMENDMENT XXI [1933]

Section 1. The eighteenth article of amendment to the Constitution of the United States is hereby repealed.

Section 2. The transportation or importation into any State, Territory, or possession of the United States for delivery or use therein of intoxicating liquors, in violation of the laws thereof, is hereby prohibited.

Section 3. This article shall be inoperative unless it shall have been ratified as an amendment to the Constitution by conventions in the several States, as provided in the Constitution, within seven years from the date of the submission hereof to the States by the Congress.

AMENDMENT XXII [1951]

Section 1. No person shall be elected to the office of the President more than twice, and no person who has held the office of President, or acted as President, for more than two years of a term to which some other person was elected President shall be elected to the office of the President more than once. But this Article shall not apply to any person holding the office of President when this Article was proposed by the Congress, and shall not prevent any person who may be holding the office of President, or acting as President, during the term within which this Article becomes operative from holding the office of President or acting as President during the remainder of such term.

Section 2. This article shall be inoperative unless it shall have been ratified as an amendment to the Constitution by the legislatures of three-fourths of the several States within seven years from the date of its submission to the States by the Congress.

AMENDMENT XXIII [1961]

Section 1. The District constituting the seat of Government of the United States shall appoint in such manner as the Congress may direct:

A number of electors of President and Vice President equal to the whole number of Senators and Representatives in Congress to which the District would be entitled if it were a State, but in no event more than the least populous State; they shall be in addition to those appointed by the States, but they shall be considered, for the purposes of the election of President and Vice President, to be electors appointed by a State; and they shall meet in the District and perform such duties as provided by the twelfth article of amendment.

Section 2. The Congress shall have power to enforce this article by appropriate legislation.

AMENDMENT XXIV [1963]

Section 1. The right of citizens of the United States to vote in any primary or other election for President or Vice President, for electors for President or Vice President, or for Senator or Representative in Congress, shall not be denied or abridged by the United States or any State by reason of failure to pay any poll tax or other tax.

Section 2. The Congress shall have power to enforce this article by appropriate legislation.[121]

[121] Clearly the text of the Constitution of the United States belongs in a book on Constitutionalism in America, and the document appropriately occurs in collocation with the adoption of the Constitution and the first ten amendments, sometimes called the Bill of Rights. However, as the plan of this book is generally chronological, perhaps some apology is due for including at this point the fourteen other amendments, adopted at different times during the following 172 years. Amendments XI to XXIV might have been severally inserted at the points where each is relevant in time; but somewhere the whole text should be available in one place. Chronology thus yielding to convenience, the text of all the amendments is here included.

The spelling and capitalization of the seven Articles of the Constitution are here given as they occur in the original hand-written document.

10. THE FIRST TEN YEARS OF
THE NEW CONSTITUTION[1]

THREE CHIEF JUSTICES, Jay, Rutledge, and Ellsworth, presided in
turn over the Court's first ten years. On October 5, 1789, Washington
appointed as the first Chief Justice of the Supreme Court of the
United States[2] John Jay of New York. Jay had been Chief Justice of
his State, Minister Plenipotentiary to Spain, a Commissioner to negotiate peace with Great Britain, and what amounted to Minister of
Foreign Affairs during the last weeks of the Continental Congress. He
presided from the Court's first session on February 1, 1790, until he
resigned on June 29, 1795. Congress then being in recess, President
Washington gave a recess appointment to John Rutledge of South
Carolina, who had previously been an Associate Justice, but had resigned from the Supreme Court to become Chief Justice of his State.
Rutledge took his new seat on August 12, 1795, but he was destined
never to have Senatorial confirmation. Shortly before his appointment,
in an ill-considered speech at Charleston, he had attacked the treaty
with Great Britain, negotiated by John Jay in 1794. His speech aroused
much federalist resentment. Rumors arose that he was mentally de-

---

[1] See generally Charles Warren, *The Supreme Court in United States History*
(3 vols.; Boston: Little, Brown and Co., 1922) I, Chapters 1–3.

[2] Jay was commissioned by this title, as were Rutledge, Ellsworth, Marshall,
Taney, Chase, and Waite. Fuller was commissioned "Chief Justice of the United
States." An Act of Congress on July 13, 1866, uses the term "Chief Justice of the
United States." Subsequent legislation has varied. See I Warren, *ubi supra*, foot-
note on pages 11 and 12. But the occasional practice of referring to the "Chief
Justice of the United States" began much earlier. In the Convention with France
of 1800, which Oliver Ellsworth and his two associates signed, Ellsworth is
described in French as "Chef de la Justice des Etats-Unis" and in English as
"Chief Justice of the United States." Usage, and well-earned respect for duty
done, have accustomed us to the shorter and more inclusive title.

bilitated, and indeed at times his intellect apparently was disturbed. Rutledge sat as Chief Justice only during the busy term of August 1795; the Senate when it convened rejected him. President Washington thereupon selected as the third of the Chief Justices, Oliver Ellsworth of Connecticut. Among other distinctions Ellsworth had been a principal draftsman of the Judiciary Act of 1789. He took his seat on March 4, 1796.

Custom of the eighteenth century, like that of the twentieth century, permitted what it did not prudently justify—occasional use of the Justices for governmental duties off the bench. Then, as now, this brought accompanying disadvantages.[3] Chief Justice Jay had been entrusted with negotiation of a new treaty with England in 1794; in 1799 Chief Justice Ellsworth was sent as an Ambassador to France. Ellsworth was not in strong health, and while still in France in 1800, he resigned his post as Chief Justice. President Adams, to fill the vacancy so created, nominated John Jay, who declined to resume the Chief Justiceship. Rutledge's instability, Ellsworth's illness, Jay's reluctance, all finally produced a great benefit for the United States. Adams, on January 20, 1801, appointed as Chief Justice his then Secretary of State, John Marshall of Virginia. Marshall's appointment begins a new era in American constitutionalism; with it end the first experimental ten years.

The reports and reporters of the Supreme Court of the United States deserve a word. The earliest reports were published as a private venture in a series of four volumes edited by Alexander James Dallas of the Philadelphia Bar. Dallas (1759–1817) was born in Jamaica, son of a Scots physician. After education at Edinburgh University, young Dallas practiced law for a short time in Jamaica. In 1773, he emigrated to Philadelphia, became a citizen, and from 1801 to 1814 was United States District Attorney. President Madison then appointed him Secretary of the Treasury; for a time he was Acting Secretary of War. He resigned in 1816, and died the next year.

Of the four volumes of Dallas' Reports, only the last three contain opinions of the Supreme Court of the United States. (See 2 Dallas 399–480; 3 Dallas 1–466; and 4 Dallas 1–46.) The first volume of Dallas' Reports contains opinions of Pennsylvania courts before and after the Revolution. The second volume contains reports of Pennsylvania courts, of the pre-1789 Federal Court of Appeals; of the Circuit

[3] President Roosevelt appointed Justice Roberts to investigate the Pearl Harbor debacle of December 7, 1941; Justice Jackson in 1945 served as prosecuting counsel in the principal War Crimes trial in Germany; the Supreme Court gained from neither assignment. At President Johnson's request Chief Justice Warren headed the Commission to investigate President Kennedy's assassination.

Court, Pennsylvania District, from 1792 on; and of the Supreme Court of the United States from the February, 1790, term. The third volume contains reports of Pennsylvania courts, of the federal Circuit Court for Pennsylvania, and of the Supreme Court of the United States through 1799. The fourth volume, besides similar reports, adds a Delaware opinion of 1788, and a Privy Council appeal from New Hampshire in 1760. Following Dallas' reports come nine volumes edited by William Cranch covering the Supreme Court's opinions from 1801 to 1815. Then come twelve volumes covering the years 1816 to 1827 edited by Henry Wheaton; these are often cited "Wheat." From 1828 to 1842 come sixteen volumes edited by Richard Peters, whom the Supreme Court formally appointed its Reporter. From 1843 to 1860 the official Court Reporter was Benjamin Howard, who published twenty-four volumes. There are two volumes of Jeremiah S. Black's reports that cover the years 1861 to 1862. John William Wallace in twenty-three volumes reported the Court's opinions through 1875; the volumes are often cited as "Wall." Wallace's twenty-third volume is sometimes designated as 90 U.S. Beginning with volume 91 U.S., the volumes are cited by number and not by the name of the official reporter. The reports since October, 1921, have been printed by the United States Government Printing Office, and they now appear at the rate of about three volumes per year. Two widely used commercially reprinted editions of the Court's reports are The Supreme Court Reporter published by West Publishing Company of St. Paul, Minnesota, and the Supreme Court Reports Lawyers' Edition, published by The Lawyers Co-operative Publishing Company of Rochester, New York.

About sixty opinions, handed down during the sixteen terms of the Supreme Court's first decade, appear in Dallas' second, third and fourth volumes.[4] The Court also decided a few other matters which Dallas omits. Charles Warren assembled miscellaneous references to this missing material in his *Supreme Court in United States History*.[5]

The Court first sat in New York, in the Royal Exchange, a building at the foot of Broad Street. In February 1791, it moved with the rest of the federal government to Philadelphia; there it sat in the new City Hall, east of Independence Hall, until the end of the term held in August 1800. On the nineteenth day of that month the Court rose, and next met at the Capitol in Washington.[6]

At the first meeting of the Court, which convened in New York for

[4] See 2 Dallas 399–480; 3 Dallas 1–466; and 4 Dallas 1–46.
[5] Warren, *Supreme Court in United States History*, I, p. 158, fn. 2.
[6] The Capitol was unfinished; the Court met in a room intended for the Senate Clerk. I Warren, 171.

the February 1790 term, there were present Chief Justice Jay, Associate Justices William Cushing of Massachusetts, James Wilson of Pennsylvania, John Blair of Virginia, and Attorney General Edmund Randolph of Virginia. The Court made rules prescribing the seal of the Supreme Court of the United States and of the Circuit Courts, and rules concerning the qualifications and oath of admission of Attorneys and Counsellors. It directed that until otherwise provided all process of the Court be in the name of the President of the United States. There being no litigated business ready, the Court then adjourned until the August term, again held in New York. In August 1790, the only business was reading James Iredell's commission as an Associate Justice. He had been appointed on February 10th, after adjournment of the Court's first term. At the third term, held in Philadelphia in February 1791, the only transaction was admission of a number of Counsellors and Attorneys.

At length, in the August 1791 term, the Supreme Court had some judicial business. The question in the Court's first case, *West* v. *Barnes*,[7] was one of procedure, and the merits were never reached. West, when seeking review, had got his writ of error from the Clerk of the Rhode Island Circuit Court; the Supreme Court held that only its own Clerk could issue such writs.[8]

States Summoned to Judgment

The second case mentioned in the reports of the August term, 1791[9] was, with a group of like cases, to raise another question which, in its essence, remains as acute in the late twentieth century as it was in the eighteenth. The question is the right of an individual, conceiving himself aggrieved by one of the States in the Union, to summon that State, against its will, to submit to the judgment of a Federal Court.[10]

[7] 2 Dallas 401 (1791). In due respect to the memory of the Justices, one should remind readers that circuit duties had kept the members of the Supreme Court amply occupied in the meantime.

[8] Similarly, refusal of review on the merits disposes of most matters which present-day litigants attempt to bring before the Supreme Court. See, e.g., "The Supreme Court, 1961 Term," 76 *Harvard Law Review* 75 *et seq.*, (1962). At the October 1961 term, which adjourned in June 1962, the Court disposed of 2,142 matters in all. 260 cases were decided on the merits. In 1,745 cases the Court denied certiorari thereby disclaiming any adjudication on merits; it disposed of another 137 matters other than cases decided on the merits.

[9] *Van Stophorst* v. *Maryland*, 2 Dallas 401. This first mention concerns only a motion for commissioners to take testimony in Holland.

[10] A comparable underlying emotional reaction has aroused State hostility to present-day suits in federal courts seeking to compel State public-school authorities to comply with the rule of *Brown* v. *Board of Education*, 347 U.S. 483 (1954).

The States had indebted themselves heavily to pay for the War of Independence. Now they faced the possibility that out-of-state holders of war-bonds might hale the debtor States before a federal court to compel payment. Article III of the Constitution extended the "judicial Power . . . to Controversies . . . between a State and citizens of another State." The terms of this grant of power did not limit it to cases where a State was plaintiff. Article I, Section 10 forbade the States to repudiate their debts.[11] Liability to creditors' suits in the new federal courts posed some threat to the States' financial defenses; it certainly hurt the States' touchy pride, and hurt badly. Other forms of liability, as well, threatened States. In some States the patriots, following a classic revolutionary pattern, had turned savagely against loyalists, confiscating tory lands, and arranging for payment of patriot debts to patriot sequestrators in place of tory creditors.[12] The prospect of suits brought against States in federal courts by tories seeking to right what they considered wrongs was not a merely imaginary horror; the Treaty of Paris that ended the War of Independence in 1783 contained threatening clauses about such claims. The fourth article of the treaty[13] provided—

> It is agreed that creditors on either side, shall meet with no lawful impediment to the recovery of the full value in sterling money, of all *bona fide* debts heretofore contracted.

There was another undertaking in more inclusive terms—

> And it is agreed, that all persons who have any interest in confiscated lands, either by debts, marriage settlements, or otherwise, shall meet with no lawful impediments in the prosecution of their rights.

Other provisions were less imperative. Congress was to . . . "earnestly recommend" to the several State legislatures to provide for the restitution of all confiscated properties belonging to British subjects, and also the estates, rights and properties of persons resident in districts in the possession of the royal forces, who had not borne arms against the United States.

[11] "No State shall . . . make any Thing but gold and silver Coin a Tender in Payment of Debts; pass any . . . Law impairing the Obligation of Contracts. . . ."
[12] For examples of confiscation see "An Act for the Forfeiture and Sale of the Estates of Persons who have adhered to the Enemies of this state . . .," Laws of New York, Third Session, October 22, 1779; and *Fairfax's Devisee* v. *Hunter's Lessee*, 7 Cranch 603 (U.S. 1813); *Martin* v. *Hunter's Lessee*, 1 Wheat. 304 (1816). For sequestration of indebtedness see *Ware* v. *Hylton*, 3 Dallas 199 (U.S. 1796).
[13] 8 Statutes at Large 82.

A clause guaranteed that persons with such claims could go to any part of the thirteen States and remain unmolested for a year while trying to get restitution. The aggregate meaning of these peace treaty provisions was somewhat uncertain. Implicitly negative was the clause calling on Congress to recommend, but not compel, State restitution to loyalists; likewise one suggestion that States require loyalists seeking to redeem forfeitures to refund to purchasers the price they had paid for confiscated lands. One purpose of the Jay Treaty of 1794 was to attempt clarification of loyalist rights.[14]

As early as the August 1791 term of the Supreme Court, preliminary stages of lawsuits against States begin to appear in the Reports. A Dutch banker named Van Stophorst and his associates were suing Maryland.[15] One Oswald was suing New York.[16] "The Indiana Company" started a suit against Virginia and evoked protests from that State's legislature.[17] The States were indignantly refusing to appear in court. At the February 1792 term, the Supreme Court ordered that Oswald should have judgment by default against New York unless the defendant State should appear in Oswald's suit by the first day of the next term, or show cause for not appearing.[18]

On July 11, 1792 the Marshal for the District of Georgia served on the Governor and the Attorney General of that State a writ in a suit brought in the United States Supreme Court against Georgia by one Chisholm and a co-plaintiff, both citizens of South Carolina, executors of a deceased British creditor. Counsel for the plaintiffs was Edmund Randolph, Attorney General of the United States.[19] On August 11, 1792 Randolph moved in the Supreme Court that unless Georgia should enter an appearance at the next term, the Chisholm plaintiffs should take judgment by default. The Court deferred consideration of the matter; but at the February 1793 term allowed Randolph to argue his motion. Georgia, though still not entering any formal appearance, filed a written protest against the Court's power to subject a State to adjudication. On February 18, 1793 the Court handed down a decision sustaining its jurisdiction. The Chisholm case, it held, was a controversy ". . . between a State and Citizens of another State,"

[14] See Articles VI, IX, and X of the Jay Treaty. 8 Stat. at Large 119–122.

[15] 2 Dallas 401.

[16] 2 Dallas 401; 2 Dallas 402.

[17] The "Indiana Company" case is not reported in Dallas. Warren tells of it in his *Supreme Court in United States History*, I, p. 92.

[18] 2 Dallas 415.

[19] At that time the Attorney General was permitted to appear for private clients where no conflict of interest arose. An account of the Chisholm case appears in Warren, *Supreme Court in United States History*, I, p. 93 *et seq.*

under Article III, Section 2 of the Constitution; that clause conferred jurisdiction where a State was a defendant as well as where it was a plaintiff.[20] The Justices all delivered opinions in turn. Only Iredell held against the jurisdiction; and his dissent was based on absence of explicit congressional authorization for such a suit.

There was still no judgment against Georgia, merely a holding that unless the State should appear, or show cause to the contrary, by the first day of the next term of court, the plaintiffs should have a default judgment. But even this preliminary jurisdictional decision produced immediate repercussions. More suits were started against States. A man named Huger sued South Carolina.[21] One of the loyalist Vassals of Massachusetts sued out a Supreme Court writ against that Commonwealth, and had it served on Governor John Hancock. The Governor forthwith called the legislature into session. The *Massachusetts Mercury* fulminated on July 23, 1793—

> The precept now served on the Governor and Attorney General is for monies arising from the sequestered property of a refugee. . . If he should obtain what he has sued for, what a wide extended door will it open for every dirty Tory traitor to his country's liberties to enter.[22]

On November 21, 1793 the lower House of the Georgia legislature passed a measure declaring that any federal marshal or other person who should attempt to enforce any process issued by any federal court to collect a judgment in the Chisholm case thereby should become guilty of felony and should "suffer death without benefit of clergy, by being hanged."[23] This emphatic piece of legislation never became law; but it demonstrates the intensity of feeling aroused by the Supreme Court's infringement of State "retained sovereignty."

Meantime the Congress was taking steps to undo the unwelcome decision. On February 20, 1793, two days after the Court had sustained its jurisdiction over Georgia in the Chisholm suit, a motion was made in the Senate[24] for a constitutional amendment, in terms almost exactly those of the present Eleventh Amendment, withdrawing from the judicial power of the United States suits against a State by citi-

[20] *Chisholm v. Georgia,* 2 Dallas 419 (1793).

[21] *Huger v. South Carolina,* 3 Dallas 339 (1797).

[22] The story of the Vassal suit is told and the newspaper quoted by Warren, *Supreme Court in United States History,* I, p. 99, fn. 3.

[23] Herman V. Ames, *State Documents on Federal Relations* (1911) pp. 9–11.

[24] The *Annals of Congress* do not give the name of the moving Senator. See 3 *Annals of Congress* 651. Warren, *Supreme Court in United States History,* I, p. 101, tells of a similar amendment introduced in the House on the 19th of February, 1793. It is not mentioned in the House *Annals* for that day.

zens of another State or by citizens or subjects of any foreign State. The measure delayed; on February 25, 1793 "the further consideration thereof was postponed."

On January 2, 1794 the resolution was re-introduced in the Senate, this time in the exact language of the present Eleventh Amendment.[25] On January 14, 1794 Senator Albert Gallatin of Pennsylvania, despite pending proceedings to unseat him because, his adversaries charged, he had not been an American citizen for the constitutional nine years, courageously proposed a change which would permit suits against States, "in cases arising under treaties made under the authority of the United States." This modification was beaten, though its effect would have honorably carried out national agreements with Great Britain; also beaten was a quite different proposal under which the amendment would have forbidden only suits on causes of action which arose before the amendment was ratified. The Senate, on the same day, then passed the Eleventh Amendment in its present form by 23 yeas to 2 nays. Senator Gallatin was one of the two dissenters.[26] On the fourth of March, 1794, the House, after decisively rejecting a proposal that the federal courts be closed to such suits only where State courts were open to them, approved the Eleventh Amendment by a vote of 81 to 9.[27] Artemas Ward of Massachusetts, one-time Major General in the Army of the Revolution, voted against the proposal. Eight others did the same; two Representatives from New Jersey, John Beatty and Elias Boudinot; two from Pennsylvania, Thomas Fitzsimmons and Thomas Scott; George Hancock of Virginia; William Hindman of Maryland; Andrew Pickens of South Carolina; and Silas Talbot of New York. It must have required a good deal of courage and a high sense of justice to vote against this amendment, when the popular pressures of State sovereignty and rancor against tories were all on the other side.

Ratification by the States was not immediate. On February 1, 1797, nearly three years after Congress proposed the amendment, the Senate and House requested the President to ascertain from Connecticut, New Jersey, Pennsylvania, Maryland, Virginia, Kentucky, Tennessee,

[25] 4 Annals of Congress, 25.

[26] 4 Annals of Congress 30, 31. John Rutherford of New Jersey cast the other negative vote. On February 28, 1794 the Senate by a vote of 14 to 12 resolved that Albert Gallatin's election as Senator was void as he had not been a citizen for the required period. He was elected to the House of Representatives later the same year. See 4 Annals of Congress 58. Gallatin became President Jefferson's Secretary of the Treasury, continued in that office in Madison's administration until 1813, and went on to a noted career in diplomacy.

[27] 4 Annals of Congress 478.

and South Carolina whether they had ratified what is now the Eleventh Amendment; and if they had, requested him to obtain the proper evidence thereof.[28]

When the amendment was finally ratified by the required three-quarters of the States, executive announcement was somewhat casual. On January 8, 1798, President Adams transmitted to Congress a report of the Secretary of State containing a certified copy of the ratification by Kentucky of what the President inaccurately described as "the Amendment of the Constitution of the United States proposed by Congress in their resolution of the 2nd day of December, 1793, relative to the suability of the States." The President then added that "the Amendment, having been adopted by three-fourths of the several States, may now be declared to be a part of the Constitution of the United States."[29] The Eleventh Amendment had not been proposed on December 2, 1793 but a month later; and the President's message did not specify the ratifying States nor the dates of ratification.[30] Nevertheless there has never been any substantial doubt that by January 1798 the amendment had become part of the Constitution.

The Supreme Court gave effect to it less than a month later. A number of actions against States were then pending; in the celebrated *Chisholm* v. *Georgia* a "writ of enquiry," (the then procedure for determining the plaintiff's damages where the defendant had defaulted) had been awarded but not yet "sued out and executed."[31] At the February term in 1798, Charles Lee, Attorney General of the United States appearing for the defendant State in another of the pending cases, *Hollingsworth et al* v. *Virginia*,[32] argued before the Supreme Court that the Eleventh Amendment had superseded all suits against any one of the United States by citizens of another State. Tilghman and Rawle, appearing for the plaintiffs, opposed, contending that an *ex post facto* amendment would work great hardship, and that the new amendment should be construed to apply only to future cases. They further objected that the amendment itself was inoperative, for it had never been submitted to the President for his approbation. Associate Justice Chase observed with respect to the argument against the validity of the amendment—

[28] 6 *Annals of Congress* 1538, 1560, 2223–2248, 2281–2284, 2296.

[29] 7 *Annals of Congress* 483.

[30] See Allen Caperton Braxton, "The Eleventh Amendment," 20 *Reports of Virginia State Bar Association* 172 (1907) pp. 192–193.

[31] 3 Dallas 480, fn. 1. Exactly what constituted "suing out and executing" a writ of enquiry under the practice current in 1798 is not clear, at least to me. Anyhow the procedure was still incomplete.

[32] See Warren, *Supreme Court in United States History*, I, p. 148; 3 Dallas 378 (1798).

The negative of the President applies only to the ordinary cases of legislation. He has nothing to do with the proposition or adoption of amendments to the Constitution.

On February 4, the day succeeding the argument, the Court deliv-livered a unanimous opinion in *Hollingsworth*—

> . . . that the amendment being constitutionally adopted there could not be exercised any jurisdiction, in any case, past or future, in which a state was sued by the citizens of another state, or by citizens, or subjects, of any foreign state.

The Eleventh Amendment has had a curious career. Almost a century after Chisholm, by a sort of judicial momentum, its principle was extended in 1890 to deny federal jurisdiction of a suit brought by a State's citizen against his own State.[33] Meantime the Fourteenth Amendment, which took effect in 1868, and which provides that no State shall "deprive any person of life, liberty or property without due process of law; nor deny to any person within its jurisdiction the equal protection of the laws," presented an unexpected question. Did the Eleventh Amendment, despite the later Fourteenth, prevent any affirmative legal action for redress against a State for violating the Fourteenth Amendment? The Fourteenth Amendment was clearly available as a shield, in case a State should attempt to exercise its judicial powers against the individual. If, for example, a State's court system should wrong such a person, he could seek reversal in the Supreme Court of the United States. But an individual seeking affirmative redress in the Federal Courts against a State official found himself in a dilemma; if the wrongdoing State official was not acting on behalf of the State, the Fourteenth Amendment had no effect because the State was then not the wrongdoer. If, on the other hand, the official was acting on behalf of the State, the Eleventh Amendment, or its principle as applied in *Hans* v. *Louisiana*, might arguably bar any federal court action by the one wronged, for that Amendment forbade suit against a State. In 1908 the Supreme Court of the United States, in *Ex parte Young*,[34] eliminated the dilemma by holding that, despite the Eleventh Amendment, an action would lie in the Federal Courts at the suit of a citizen of Iowa and of a citizen of Minnesota, against Edward T. Young, Attorney General of Minnesota and others,

---

[33] *Hans* v. *Louisiana* 134 U.S. 1 (1890).

[34] 209 U.S. 123. The proceeding then before the Supreme Court was *habeas corpus* by which Attorney General Young sought release from a federal court commitment for contempt. Attorney General Young argued that he was guilty of no contempt for disobeying an injunction against him as a Minnesota officer. See Kenneth Culp Davis, "Suing the Government by Falsely Pretending to Sue an Officer," 29 *Chicago Law Review* 435 (1962).

to enjoin the enforcement of a Minnesota statute establishing allegedly unreasonable maximum railroad passenger and freight rates. The Court rejected an Eleventh Amendment defense, relying on a Statement of Mr. Justice Harlan in *Smyth* v. *Ames*,[35] ten years earlier:

> It is the settled doctrine of this court that a suit against individuals for the purpose of preventing them, as officers of a state, from enforcing an unconstitutional enactment, to the injury of the rights of the plaintiff, is not a suit against the state within the meaning of that Amendment.

One who sympathizes with Harlan's desire to make the post-Civil War amendment practicably enforceable can still find difficulty distinguishing a State from the officers who constitute its government. Harlan's uncomfortable syllogism could have been avoided by reasoning that the Fourteenth Amendment had necessarily impaired the full force of the Eleventh. The Fourteenth Amendment was ratified about 70 years after the Eleventh Amendment had taken effect. During that period the relative positions of the nation and the States had been fundamentally changed; and if the Amendments of 1865–1870 were to have their full intended effect, the States must be amenable to justice at the suit of wronged citizens. A construction of the Fourteenth Amendment recognizing this change would have been well justified. But the Supreme Court was at first hesitant to acknowledge the extent of the effect produced by the war and by the Amendments which followed it.[36] However, by permitting a federal-court suit against a State officer in *Ex parte Young*,[37] and in many similar cases, the Supreme Court has in effect made some modifications of the Eleventh Amendment. Loyalist claims and debts incurred to finance the War of Independence are now only matter for history books. The loyalist, no longer a "dirty Tory traitor to his country's liberties," has at length won the sympathetic judgment of historians and the nostalgic praise of novelists.[38] Governmental immunity from suit is becoming unpopular, and modern statutes provide for actions against the States in their own courts, and against the United States in the Dis-

[35] 169 U.S. 466, 518 (1898).

[36] See the Slaughterhouse Cases, 16 Wall. 36 (1873) and Civil Rights Cases, 109 U.S. 3 (1883).

[37] 209 U.S. 123 (1908).

[38] A bibliography of historical writing is collected under the caption "The Loyalists" in Handlin and others, *Harvard Guide to American History* (Cambridge, Mass.: Harvard University Press, 1954) p. 301. Claude Halstead Van Tyne's *The Loyalists in the American Revolution* (New York: Peter Smith, 1929) is a scholar's survey. Kenneth L. Roberts' novel *Oliver Wiswell* (New York: Doubleday, Doran and Co., 1940) paints a vivid panorama of the loyalists in various parts of revolutionary America.

trict Courts and in the Court of Claims.[39] But the Eleventh Amendment still causes worry from time to time in situations which were not imagined by the indignant patriots who cried out against *Chisholm* v. *Georgia*.[40]

Treaties Conflicting with State Laws

From the time it attained independence, the United States felt the need for certain essentials of national existence which we still need nearly two centuries later. The new nation required alliances to strengthen its military resources. To live in peace, it needed reconciliation with its enemies. And as is true today, its people resented and feared foreign tampering within their boundaries. In 1787 Americans resented claims of foreigners to American lands. The people who had just won independence by armed force resented the prospect that subjects of their late enemy, George the Third, might hold claims for debts owed by Americans which American courts would enforce. In the 1780's, as in the 1960's, localism was stronger in State governments than in that of the United States. State laws often disabled aliens to inherit land.[41] A Virginia statute of 1777 provided that Virginians could discharge debts they owed to enemy aliens by paying Virginia officials.[42]

On February 6, 1778[43] the United States signed three treaties with France. These gave us a badly needed military ally. They changed much of our land law by giving to the nationals of each party-nation the right to inherit "goods moveable and immoveable" within each other's domains. The effect of this provision on contrary State laws

[39] See for the liability of the United States the Tucker Act, 28 U.S.C. 1346(a); the Tort Claims Act of 1948, 28 U.S.C. 1346(b), 2671 *et seq.* For State liability see, e.g. New York Court of Claims Act, § 8. A number of references are collected in Freund, Sutherland, Howe and Brown, *Constitutional Law; Cases and Other Problems*, (2nd ed.; Boston: Little, Brown and Co., 1961) p. 109 *et seq.* Cf. *Benz* v. *New York State Thruway Authority*, 369 U.S. 147 (1962).

[40] See *Worcester County Trust Co.* v. *Riley*, 302 U.S. 292 (1937); and see generally the annotations of the 11th Amendment in the U.S. Code Annotated,—e.g. *Stamey et al.* v. *State Highway Commission of Kansas*, 76 F. Supp. 946 (DC Kans. 1948).

[41] For the situation in New York, see Pratt, "Present Disabilities under New York State Law in Real Property," 12 *Brooklyn Law Review*, 1, 15 (1942); for Pennsylvania, *Lessee of Jackson* v. *Burns*, 3 Binn. 75 (Pa. 1810); the situation in Virginia is explained in *Martin* v. *Hunter's Lessee*, 1 Wheat, 304 (U.S. 1816).

[42] See *Ware* v. *Hylton*, 3 Dallas 199 (U.S. 1796).

[43] 8 Stat. 6, 12 (1778); 17 Stat. 795 (1778); D. H. Miller, ed., *Treaties and Other International Acts of the United States* (Washington: Government Printing Office, 1931) II, pp. 3, 35, 45, hereinafter cited as Miller, *Treaties*.

must have been a little uncertain. On May 4, 1778 the Congress ratified the three treaties, but Virginia separately ratified the first two
during the next year.[44] Thus in the inception of its foreign relations
the new United States faced a question still troublesome—the power
of the federal government to affect State law by treaties.

In 1782 a treaty between the Netherlands and the United States[45]
gave liberty of worship to Hollanders in America and to Americans in
Holland, and guaranteed reciprocal rights of inheritance: in both
respects State law might be thus impaired.

The British-American Treaty of 1783, which ended the War of
Independence,[46] attempted to provide satisfactorily for the debts
owed to British creditors, and for the British claims to lands in the
United States. For debts a laconic clause read: "It is agreed that
Creditors on either side, shall meet with no lawful Impediment to the
Recovery of the full value in Sterling Money of all bona fide Debts
heretofore contracted."[47] The Treaty forbade future confiscation of
loyalist lands.[48] Where lands had already been confiscated more difficult questions appeared, as the claims of subsequent purchasers had
now intervened. Instead of declaring invalid any titles created by
confiscation, one treaty term only required the Congress to recommend to the several American States that they make restitution.

Exhortation to justice was ineffective. During the Constitutional
Convention delegates repeatedly said that experience had demonstrated State tendencies to violate national treaties.[49] Madison's Preface to the Convention debates speaks of State disregard of the
Confederation's authority by violations of treaties with France and

---

[44] Miller, *Treaties and Other International Acts of the United States*, II, p. 30.
On June 17, 1799, Gerard, the French Minister, wrote from Philadelphia to the
Count de Vergennes that the Virginia action had somewhat offended the Congress,
as that body thought it contrary to its own prerogatives. See Henri Doniol,
*Histoire de la Participation de la France a l'Establissement des Etats-Unis
d'Amerique* (5 vols.; Paris: Imprimerie Nationale, 1886–92, IV.

[45] 8 Stat. 32 (1782); Miller, *Treaties and Other International Acts of the United
States*, II, p. 59. The guarantee of freedom of worship was notable at a time when
a number of states still retained established churches. See Sutherland, "Due
Process and Disestablishment," 62 *Harv. L. Rev.* 1306, 1323 (1949). The Treaty
with Sweden of 1783, 8 Stat. 60, Miller, *Treaties and Other International Acts of
the United States*, II, p. 123, and that with Prussia of 1785, 8 Stat. 84, Miller,
Treaties and Other International Acts of the United States, II, p. 162, also contain
reciprocal guarantees of inheritance and of freedom of worship.

[46] 8 Stat. 54 (1782); Miller, *Treaties and Other International Acts of the United
States*, II, p. 96. See page 224, above.

[47] Art. 4.

[48] Art. 6.

[49] Farrand, *Records of the Federal Convention of 1787* (New Haven: Yale University Press, 1911) I, pp. 164, 316; *Ibid.*, III, p. 113.

Holland, and of the Treaty of Peace of 1783 with England;[50] and when the Supremacy Clause in Article VI of the Constitution was being formulated, Madison secured the addition of phraseology ensuring that existing as well as future treaties be law in the several States and their courts.[51] The constitutional requirement that a treaty be ratified by "two thirds of the Senators present" was adopted to give some degree of protection to minorities of States, to quiet fears of New England lest a treaty hamper her fisheries, and fears of the West lest a treaty close the Mississippi.[52]

Litigation soon tested the relative competence of State statutes and contrary federal treaties. Before the War of Independence Daniel Hylton[53] and Company and Francis Eppes, Virginians, became indebted to Farrel and Jones, British subjects. In the midst of the war, in 1777, the Virginia legislature passed an act permitting Virginia debtors who owed money to British subjects to obtain discharges by paying the sums in question to a State Commissioner, an officer much like a modern alien property custodian but a State, not a national, functionary. In 1780, Hylton and Company thus "paid" part of their debt to the Virginia Commissioner. After the treaty of peace with its provisions for protecting British claims, and after the adoption of the Constitution with its provisions in Article VI for supremacy of treaties, the surviving British creditor sued Hylton in the United States Circuit Court for the District of Virginia. Hylton, as a partial defense, pleaded the partial payment made to the Virginia Commissioner.

---

[50] Farrand, *Records of the Federal Convention of 1787*, III, p. 548.

[51] Farrand, *Records of the Federal Convention of 1787*, II, p. 417.

[52] A House of Representatives Committee Report, made in 1944 and reissued in 1945, H.R. Rep. No. 139, 79th Cong., 1st Sess. (1945), stated that the two-thirds rule had been adopted in the eighteenth century to protect sectional interests against discriminatory treaties, not because of any fundamental theory of government. The same might be said for the Supremacy Clause of Article VI, which was intended to meet the problems of British claims and land titles—problems which have long since disappeared. But those who today fear the power of the executive to impair local prerogative by treaty would not abandon the two-thirds rule merely because New England no longer fears for her fish nor the river country for New Orleans; both the supremacy Clause and the two-thirds rule thus serve modern purposes. For a discussion of sectional influence in the 1787 Conventions, see Warren, "The Mississippi River and the Treaty Clause of the Constitution," 2 *George Washington Law Review* 271 (1934). The mid-twentieth century significance of this eighteenth century history is discussed generally in A. E. Sutherland, "Restricting the Treaty Power," 65 *Harv. L. Rev.* 1305 (1952). See also *Hearings*, before Subcommittee No. 3 of the House Committee on the Judiciary on H. Jt. Res. 6, etc., 78th Cong., 2nd Sess. (1944).

[53] "Daniel Hylton" was also the name of the plaintiff in the Carriage Tax case, *Hylton* v. *U.S.* 3 Dallas 171 (1796), discussed at page 237, *infra*. The Dictionary of American Biography does not refer to a Daniel Hylton; I do not know whether the same Hylton was a party in *Ware* v. *Hylton*, 3 Dallas 199 (1796) and *Hylton* v. *U.S.*, 3 Dallas 171 (1796).

The executor of the original plaintiff, in reply, relied on the Fourth Article of the treaty of peace of 1783—

> . . . that the creditors of either side shall meet with no lawful impediment to the recovery of the full value in sterling money of all *bona fide* debts, theretofore contracted;

and on the Supremacy Clause in Article 6 of the Constitution under which treaties prevail over State law. The Circuit Court nevertheless gave judgment in favor of the Virginia debtor defendants for so much of the debt as they had already paid under the Virginia statute. The disappointed English plaintiff brought error in the Supreme Court of the United States.[54] John Marshall of Virginia, in his only argument as counsel before that Court, contended on behalf of the defendant American debtors that the Circuit Court had properly credited them with what they had paid to the Virginia Commissioner. In words which have often been echoed in later years, in quite different causes, Marshall referred to ". . . those who wish to impair the sovereignty of Virginia . . ." He doubted ". . . whether Congress had a power to make a treaty that could operate to annul a legislative act of any of the States, and to destroy rights acquired by or vested in individuals in virtue of such acts."[55] But on March 7, 1796,[56] the Supreme Court handed down a judgment of reversal; the Virginians, it held, must pay again, this time to the British creditors whatever sum was unpaid to them. The treaty provision concerning creditors superseded action taken under the previous and inconsistent Virginia statutes and, the Court held, British creditors did not lose their treaty rights by reason of their own nation's violations in maintaining British garrisons in the United States at Niagara and Detroit, and in arming Indians who were raiding our people.[57]

---

[54] *Ware, Administrator of Jones* v. *Hylton,* 3 Dallas 199 (1796).

[55] *Ware, Administrator of Jones* v. *Hylton,* 3 Dallas 199 (1796) at 210 and 235.

[56] See Warren, *Supreme Court in United States History,* I, pp. 146, 149.

[57] The Court's disposition of the case appears at page 285 of 3 Dallas. The British creditors were to have $596, the sum originally awarded to them in the Circuit Court of Virginia, and in addition whatever sum should be found due them on a writ of enquiry to be issued by the Circuit Court. The new Chief Justice, Oliver Ellsworth, was not sworn-in until February 8, the day after the Court decided *Ware* v. *Hylton.* Iredell, who had sat below, did not participate. The other four Justices, Chase, Paterson, Wilson and Cushing, all upheld the treaty over the Virginia statute. The Supreme Court, as provided in the Judiciary Act of 1789, consisted of a Chief Justice and five Associate Justices.

Thomas Jefferson is said to have paid such a debt twice; once to the Virginia sequestrator, and then, compelled by the principle established in *Ware* v. *Hylton,* again to British creditors. See Dumas Malone, *Jefferson the Virginian* (Boston: Little, Brown and Co., 1948) p. 260.

Mr. Justice Iredell, who had been one of the judges deciding the case below, forbore taking any part in the decision; but read his Circuit Court opinion in favor of the debtors. Among other things he wrote, "I cannot therefore bring myself to say, that the present Defendants having once lawfully paid the money, shall pay it over again."

Jay's Treaty of 1794 was not influential in *Ware* v. *Hylton,* if indeed its provisions bore on the contentions of either side. The Treaty was concluded on November 19, 1794; ratifications were exchanged at London on October 28, 1795; and it was finally proclaimed on February 29, 1796,[58] only a week before the *Ware* case was decided. The Jay Treaty contained two Articles concerning debts to British creditors,[59] though neither counsel nor Court cited the treaty on the argument or in the opinions of *Ware* v. *Hylton.* Under the treaty the two nations set up Commissions to adjust claims of British creditors, and American claims for ships and goods which the British had seized during the naval operations between Great Britain and France. After some years of wrangling the two countries settled the debt claims in 1802, by a Convention under which the United States paid $2,664,000. The London Commission, which was concerned with seizures during

[58] 8 U.S. Stat. at Large 116.

[59] "*Article VI.* Whereas it is alleged by divers British merchants and others His Majesty's subjects, that debts, to a considerable amount, which were bona fide contracted before the peace, still remain owing to them by citizens or inhabitants of the United States, and that by the operation of various lawful impediments since the peace, not only the full recovery of the said debts has been delayed, but also the value and security thereof have been, in several instances, impaired and lessened, so that, by the ordinary course of judicial proceedings, the British creditors cannot now obtain, and actually have and receive full and adequate compensation for the losses and damages which they have thereby sustained; It is agreed, that in all such cases, where full compensation for such losses and damages cannot, for whatever reason, be actually obtained, had and received by the said creditors in the ordinary course of justice, the United States will make full and complete compensation for the same to the said creditors. But it is distinctly understood, that this provision is to extend to such losses only as have been occasioned by the lawful impediments aforesaid, and is not to extend to losses occasioned by such insolvency of the debtors or other causes as would equally have operated to produce such loss, if the said impediments had not existed; nor to such losses or damages as have been occasioned by the manifest delay or negligence, or wilful omission of the claimant. . . ."

"*Article X.* Neither the Debts due from Individuals of the one Nation, to Individuals of the other, nor shares nor monies, which they may have in the public Funds, or in the public or private Banks shall ever, in any Event of war or national differences, be sequestered, or confiscated, it being unjust and impolitick that Debts and Engagements contracted and made by Individuals having confidence in each other, and in their respective Governments, should ever be destroyed or impaired by national authority, on account of national Differences and Discontents."

the naval operations against France, found that British unlawful seizures amounted to \$5,849,082, offset by American seizures valued at \$143,428. The settlement of the two classes of claims left a balance in favor of the United States amounting to \$3,041,654.[60]

The *Ware* v. *Hylton*[61] treaty doctrine now seems obvious. The Court has ever since consistently held that the treaty power, like the war power, is not limited to those enumerated powers otherwise delegated to the Congress by the Constitution in Article I, Section 8 or elsewhere, and that treaties, executive agreements, or legislation enacted pursuant to them, can change the internal law of a State;[62] though (again like the war power) the treaty power is limited by the Bill of Rights, Amendments 1 to 8 inclusive.[63]

But *Ware* v. *Hylton,* decided in March 1796, forecast constitutional doctrine far beyond the law of treaties. Four Justices wrote opinions in favor of the Court's ruling. Justice Chase's opinion forecast a series of decisions during the next century and a half holding any provision of the federal Constitution, as interpreted by the Supreme Court, predominant over any inconsistent State law. Chase wrote—[64]

> If doubts could exist before the establishment of the present national government, they must be entirely removed by the 6th article of the Constitution which provides 'That all treaties made, or which shall be made, under the authority of the United States, shall be the supreme law of the land; and the judges in every State shall be bound thereby, anything in the Constitution, or laws, of any State to the contrary notwithstanding.' There can be no limitation on the power of the people of the United States. By . . . their authority the Constitution of the United States was established; . . . it is the declared duty of the State judges, to determine any Constitution, or laws of any State, contrary to that treaty (or any other) made under the authority of the United

---

[60] See Samuel Flagg Bemis, *Jay's Treaty* (New York: Macmillan, 1923) pp. 318–320.

[61] 3 Dallas 199 (1796).

[62] *Fairfax's Devisee* v. *Hunter's Lessee,* 7 Cranch 603 (U.S. 1813); *Martin* v. *Hunter's Lesee* 1 *Wheaton* 304 (U.S. 1816); *Hauenstein* v. *Lynham* 100 U.S. 483 (1880); *Missouri* v. *Holland* 252 U.S. 416 (1920). This principle has been extended to executive agreements in which the Senate has played no part. See *U.S.* v. *Belmont* 301 U.S. 324 (1937); *U.S.* v. *Pink* 315 U.S. 213 (1942). Persistent efforts to obtain the enactment of a constitutional amendment to change this feature of constitutional law have thus far been unsuccessful. See A. E. Sutherland, "Restricting the Treaty Power," 65 *Harvard Law Review* 1305 (1952).

[63] *Reid* v. *Covert* 354 U.S. 1. (1951); *Kinsella* v. *U.S. ex rel. Singleton* 361 U.S. 234 (1960); *McElroy* v. *Guagliardo; Wilson* v. *Bohlender* 361 U.S. 281 (1960). And see *Grisham* v. *Hagan* 361 U.S. 278 (1960). For Bill of Rights limitations on the war powers see *Trop* v. *Dulles* 356 U.S. 86 (1958).

[64] 3 Dallas at page 236–237.

States, null and void. National or Federal Judges are bound by duty and oath to the same conduct.

Justice Cushing's *Ware* opinion said the same in fewer words. Justice Wilson simply gave supremacy to the treaty without mention of the Supremacy Clause of the Constitution in its Article VI. Justice Paterson did the same as Wilson, adding an expression of general distaste for governmental confiscation of private debts. All four prevailing justices agreed in their conclusions: that the treaty was a senior law emanating from the national government; that it was supreme over any inconsistent State law, of any rank; that federal judges were bound to obey the predominant national law and to disregard inconsistent State enactments.

This conclusion flowed inevitably from the Supremacy Clause; and latent in it was much more. If the States were powerless to override the Constitution, was the Congress or the federal executive any less bound by its provisions? Article VI made supreme, as Law of the Land, the Constitution and those "Laws of the United States which shall be made in pursuance thereof . . ." What of laws of the United States not made in pursuance of the Constitution? As to such non-pursuant laws, could the Constitution be subordinate? The conclusion is not tenable.

Direct Taxes

In a conflict between the Constitution and an Act of Congress, the Supreme Court must follow the Constitution and disregard the conflicting statute—this was an unspoken premise of opinions of the three justices who participated in a decision on the day after *Ware* v. *Hylton.* This was *Hylton* v. *United States,*[65] decided on March 8, 1796. While the decision upheld the constitutionality of the challenged Act of Congress, the opinions assumed the judicial power and duty to decide the opposite where a conflict might appear.

Hylton v. *United States* was the first of a series of cases, continuing to the present day, construing or passing on the constitutionality of federal tax legislation. Under a statute of June 5, 1794, the Congress

[65] 3 Dallas 171. Warren, *Supreme Court in United States History,* I, p. 146, points out that *Hylton* v. *U.S.* was decided on the day after *Ware* v. *Hylton.* Evidently Dallas did not publish his reports of cases in the order of their decision. The Court then consisted of six justices. Chief Justice Ellsworth was only sworn in on March 8, 1796 and did not participate, nor did Cushing who had been ill when the case was argued, nor did Wilson, who had participated before.

had imposed a tax upon "carriages for the conveyance of persons." Article I, of the Constitution, in Section 9, Clause 4, requires that "No Capitation, or other direct, Tax shall be laid, unless in Proportion to the Census or Enumeration herein before directed to be taken." Article I, Section 2, Clause 3 provides that "Representatives and direct Taxes shall be apportioned among the several States which may be included within this Union, according to their respective Numbers, which shall be determined by adding to the whole Number of free Persons . . ." and so on. In contrast, Article I, Section 8, Clause 1 provides that all "Duties, Imposts and Excises shall be uniform throughout the United States." The Supreme Court held the carriage tax not "direct" and hence valid without apportionment among the States according to their population.[66] Associate Justice Chase cautiously remarked that determination of the Supreme Court's power to declare an act of Congress void on the ground that it conflicts with the Constitution was here unnecessary; he added ". . . but if the Court have such power, I am free to declare, that I will never exercise it, *but in a very clear case.*"[67]

The phrase "direct tax" is not defined in the Constitution. As the number of carriages in the United States was (and probably still is) not necessarily proportionate to population, apportionment of the sum to be raised among the several States according to their respective numbers would be impracticable. As Chase pointed out, apportionment as a "direct tax" in such a circumstance could tax carriages much higher in one State than in another—not necessarily a violation of the letter of the uniformity clause of Article 1, Section 8, Clause 1, if the

[66] As examples of direct taxes apportioned among the States see the acts of July 14, 1798, 1 Stat. at Large 597; and of August 5, 1861, 12 Stat. at Large 292. In such a tax the Congress levies a total sum to be raised, and specifies the parts of that sum to be raised by each of the States. Almost a hundred years after the *Hylton* case, there arose *Pollock* v. *Farmers Loan and Trust Company,* 157 U.S. 429 (1895), 158 U.S. 601 (1895) in which the Supreme Court held by a vote of 5 to 4 that a tax on the income from property was a direct tax within the meaning of the Constitution, and hence was void as not apportioned according to the census. But the *Pollock* case was put out of the way by amendment. The 16th Amendment which took effect February 25, 1913, in effect overruled the *Pollock* case. It provides "The Congress shall have power to lay and collect taxes on incomes, from whatever source derived, without apportionment among the several States, and without regard to any census or enumeration." The 16th Amendment left troublesome questions as to the nature of "incomes." See e.g. *Eisner* v. *Macomber* 252 U.S. 189 (1920). In *New York Trust Company* v. *Eisner,* 256 U.S. 345 (1921), Mr. Justice Holmes, writing for a unanimous court, commented that "a page of history is worth a volume of logic," and sustained an estate tax as an excise. See Corwin, ed., *Constitution of the United States of America* (Washington: Government Printing Office, 1952) pp. 317–349.

[67] *Hylton* v. *United States,* 3 Dallas 171 at 175 (1796). Chase's opinions bristle with italic. Like Queen Victoria, Mr. Justice Chase was a man of firm conclusions, which he similarly expressed by emphatic underlinings, printed as italic.

tax was not a duty, impost or excise, but a queer way to raise the national revenue. The Supreme Court, by holding the carriage tax not "direct," made unnecessary a holding that the Act of Congress was invalid. But the future *Marbury* v. *Madison*[68] was implicit in the opinions. *Hylton* v. *United States* was one of a number of constitutional developments during the Supreme Court's first decade which explain the absence of surprise in 1803 at John Marshall's *Marbury* decision.

Chase's resolve never to declare an Act of Congress unconstitutional unless *"in a very clear case"* forecast, like other constitutional utterances of the eighteenth-century Justices, difficulty which still abides among us. The language of the Constitution is more precise in some clauses than in others; the Seventh Amendment prescription of a jury for twenty-dollar lawsuits requires less judicial interpretation than the due process clause of the Fifth, or the elusive adjective "direct" which describes those taxes which must be apportioned. Ever since Chase's day, men prompted by inarticulate and probably unconscious distrust of judicial discretion, have tried to demonstrate in words the difference between declaring unconstitutional a statute which, say, should attempt to legislate a man guilty of treason,[69] and a statute which, as judges may come to decide, violates the due-process clause. The reaction against judicial improvisation is, of course, a very old one. Some time toward the middle of the seventeenth century Selden said in his *Table Talk*—[70]

> 1. Equity in Law is ye same yt ye spirit is in Religion, what ever one pleases to make it. Some times they Goe according to conscience some time according to Law some time according to ye Rule of ye Court.
>
> 2. Equity is A roguish thing, for Law wee have a measure know what to trust too. Equity is according to ye conscience of him yt is Chancellor, and as yt is larger or narrower soe is equity Tis all one as if they should make ye Standard for ye measure wee call A foot, to be ye Chancellors foot; what an uncertain measure would this be; One Chancellor ha's a long foot another A short foot a third an indifferent foot; tis ye same thing in ye Chancellors Conscience.

[68] 1 Cranch 137 (1803).

[69] Article I, Section 9, Clause 3. "No Bill of Attainder . . . shall be passed." Even this clause, with overtones of centuries-old parliamentary experience, has not been easy to construe. See e.g. *U.S.* v. *Lovett* 328 U.S. 303 (1946). One may compare with *Lovett* Chief Justice Warren's opinion written several years later in *Bolling* v. *Sharpe*, 347 U.S. 497 (1954) which, written for a unanimous Court, found denial of due process in Acts of Congress providing for racial segregation in the District of Columbia public schools.

[70] Sir Frederick Pollock, ed., *Table Talk of John Selden* (London: Quaritch, 1927) p. 43.

The early resistance to the introduction of equity[71] in the United States is a reflection of the same feeling. Men like to think of the law as a reasonable, definite system, complete and adequate for all needs of human governance, written down in constitutions, statutes and decisions—or else inferable from these by a syllogistic process, in which unimpeachable conclusions flow irresistibly from premises, if only human reason can function correctly. Considerations of equity or justice or social policy sometimes seem alien to this brooding omnipresent Law. Our perennial aspiration to a government of laws and not of men reflects the same feeling. Distrust of executive discretion has been continually notable in our constitutional tradition. Because John Locke wrote at approximately the time of the final overthrow of the Stuart dynasty in 1788, he was undoubtedly thinking of the antithesis between the powers of the Crown and the powers of the Parliament when he composed the eleventh chapter of his Second Treatise. Much of our American constitutional doctrine is related to the thought that Locke there exemplified when he wrote—[72]

> Absolute arbitrary power, or governing without settled standing laws, can neither of them consist with the ends of society and government, . . .

This fear of the governor's whim carries over, in our tradition, to a fear of the judge's whim. We tell ourselves that when we want a government of laws, not men, this goes for men who govern from the bench as well as men who govern in the Executive office.

As in so many governmental relations, there is, of course, an exactly contrary tendency. All men being different, there is a strong human desire to fit the law suitably to each. We have a feeling that because men are various, and variously situated, the law may operate "unjustly" when applied; and that there ought to be some way to correct the rigors of its unjustly strict application. This, of course, is the basis of the Chancellor's jurisdiction which became English equity. The jury, where we still use it; the elaborate processes of sentencing and parole in criminal cases; some of the virtues of flexibility ascribed to the administrative process; all exemplify a desire to have a government adjusted to the individual differences between men. Swung between these opposing pulls of certainty and of justice our law moves on its way, like some satellite held in its orbit by the counterbalance of gravity and the centrifugal urge to fly into remote space.

[71] See Roscoe Pound, *The Spirit of the Common Law* (Boston: Marshall Jones Co., 1921) p. 53.
[72] John Locke, *Second Treatise of Civil Government*, C. L. Sherman, ed., (New York: Appleton-Century Co., 1937) §137, p. 91.

In the 1950's and 1960's there have been somewhat fretful criticisms of the Supreme Court of the United States on the ground that it is deciding constitutional cases, not on the law, but on ill-defined considerations of policy related to social and economic conditions. On May 26, 1955, Senator Eastland of Mississippi told his colleagues—

> Mr. President, yesterday I submitted a resolution asking the Senate to endorse an investigation of the alleged scientific authorities upon which the Supreme Court relied to sustain its decision in the school integration cases of last year. . .
>
> Mr. President, in the long legal history of this country, there has never before been a time when an Appellate Court or Supreme Court of the United States relied solely and alone on scientific authority to sustain a legal decision. I am informed that in the long history of British jurisprudence, there has never been a time when the high courts of England have resorted to such dubious authority, but that their decisions have been based on the law. Mr. President, my information is that the one time when the high appellate court of any major western nation has resorted to textbooks and the works of agitators to sustain its decision was when the high court of Germany sustained Hitler's racist laws. . . .[73]

In this matter of clear and unclear judgments of unconstitutionality, as in other early emergences of abiding constitutional problems, the difficulty appeared immediately because it inhered in the nature of the constitutional compromises of power, negotiated in the Constitution of 1787. A written constitution must be general in its terms. We have learned from the twenty-dollar jury, guaranteed in the Seventh Amendment, that the most specific guarantees, leaving the least scope for application of judicial wisdom to new and unforeseen human conflicts, are probably not the most useful. "We must never forget that it is a *constitution* we are expounding."[74]

Chase, if willing to call an Act of Congress unconstitutional in "*a very clear case*" did not suggest, perhaps did not for the moment perceive, that there would always be borderline questions; that whether or not a given case was clear, but not very clear, would always be debatable. Mr. Justice Stone was struggling with the same difficulty in 1938, when he contrasted "specific" provisions with others in the Constitution, and called for a stronger "presumption of constitutionality" when the constitutional limitation was less specific.[75]

[73] 101 *Cong. Rec.* 7119–7120.

[74] John Marshall underlined "constitution" when he wrote these words in *McCulloch* v. *Maryland,* 4 Wheaton 316 (1819).

[75] *U.S.* v. *Carolene Products Co.* 304 U.S. 144, 152 (1938) fn. 4.

Ex Post Facto Laws and "Natural Rights"

At the August term in 1798, the Supreme Court handed down another decision forecasting its later course; it upheld as constitutional an Act of the Connecticut legislature despite a challenge under the clause of Article I, Section 10 which forbids any State to pass an *ex post facto* law.[76] But the opinions suggested no doubt of the Court's power to declare ineffective the State act if it had offended the *ex post facto* clause.

In March 1793, a probate court in Connecticut had disapproved the will of a Normand Morrison, under which a man named Bull was a beneficiary. In May 1795, after the time to appeal from this decree had expired, the Connecticut legislature passed a resolution or law which set aside the decree refusing probate, and granted a new hearing by the probate court. In July 1795, the probate court arrived at a conclusion opposite to its preceding decision and approved the will, ordering it recorded; this second decree had the effect of awarding the property to Bull. A man named Calder, who would have taken the property if the earlier decision had stood and the will had been denied probate, now unsuccessfully attempted in the higher Connecticut courts to set aside the new decree, and ultimately brought a writ of error in the Supreme Court of the United States. Calder argued that the action of the Connecticut legislature was an *ex post facto* law beyond the power of the State legislature under Article I, Section 10 of the Constitution.

At the August 1798 term, the Supreme Court of the United States affirmed the Connecticut judgment[77] upholding the legislation which had authorized the new trial. Justices Chase, Paterson and Iredell wrote opinions and Justice Cushing wrote a brief memorandum. All agreed that the *ex post facto* clause gave no protection to Calder. Justices Chase, Paterson, and Iredell stated that it applied only to criminal cases; but Mr. Justice Chase went beyond to make a statement of "natural rights" political theory. He wrote—

> I cannot subscribe to the omnipotence of a State Legislature, or that it is absolute and without controul; although its authority should not be expressly restrained by the Constitution or fundamental law of the

[76] Article I, Section 10 of the Constitution forbids any State to ". . . pass any Bill of Attainder, ex post facto Law, or Law impairing the Obligation of Contracts . . ."

[77] *Calder* v. *Bull*, 3 Dallas 386.

States. . . . The purposes for which men enter into society will determine the nature and terms of the social compact; and as they are the foundation of the legislative power, they will decide what are the proper objects of it. . . . There are certain vital principles in our free Republican governments, which will determine and overrule an apparent and flagrant abuse of legislative power; as to authorize manifest injustice by positive law; or to take away that security for personal liberty, or private property, for the protection whereof the government was established. An act of the Legislature, (for I cannot call it a law) contrary to the great first principles of the social compact cannot be considered a rightful exercise of legislative authority. . . . The genius, the nature, and the spirit of our State Governments, amount to the prohibition of such acts of legislation; and the general principles of law and reason forbid them.[78]

Chase ends his reasoning with a repetition of his *Hylton* v. *U.S.* dictum:

> . . . If I ever exercise the jurisdiction I will not decide *any law to be void, but in a very clear case.*[79]

Mr. Justice Iredell added to his opinion a caution against declaring statutes invalid on principles of natural justice,

> If . . . the Legislature of the Union, or the Legislature of any member of the Union, shall pass a law, within the general scope of their constitutional power, the Court cannot pronounce it to be void, merely because it is, in their judgment, contrary to the principles of natural justice. The ideas of natural justice are regulated by no fixed standard: the ablest and the purest men have differed upon the subject; and all that the court could properly say, in such an event, would be, that the legislature (possessed of an equal right of opinion) had passed an act which, in the opinion of the judges, was inconsistent with the abstract principles of natural justice.[80]

[78] Chase's italic in the quoted passage is not here indicated. It was profuse.

[79] 3 Dallas 171, p. 175 (1796). See pages 238–241 *supra*.

[80] 3 Dallas 386 at 399. A third of a century later Mr. Justice William Johnson wrote a note on the *ex post facto* clause and *Calder* v. *Bull*, published with the opinions of 1829, as an appendix to Volume II of Peters' Reports. He pointed out that Connecticut had no written constitution when its legislature granted Bull a new trial; thus its action could be considered judicial rather than legislative,—the legislature for this purpose being a judicial organ of the State government. Hence, argued Mr. Justice Johnson, no "law" in the sense of the *ex post facto* clause was passed by the Connecticut legislature. In light of this conclusion he criticizes the limitation of the *ex post facto* clause to criminal matters when this construction of the Constitution was not necessary to the decision.

> . . . This court has had more than once to toil uphill in order to bring within the restriction on the states to pass laws violating the obligation of contracts, the most obvious cases to which the Constitution was intended to

The student of political and constitutional theory studying *Calder* v. *Bull* in the mid-twentieth century may be principally interested in the disagreement between Chase and Iredell on "natural rights," on their being a part of American constitutional law so that the Supreme Court will hold legislation of Congress or of the States unconstitutional if it runs counter to such aspirations to a just order of things. He may question whether Iredell's renunciatory statements in *Calder* v. *Bull* have turned out to be sound predictions. Some limitations on government expressed in the Constitution—notably the due process clauses—are not sufficiently definite to spell out clear limitations on State or federal legislation. The Supreme Court has had to find principles which it considers of general validity to give content to such clauses in determining the constitutionality of legislation. Roscoe Pound wrote in 1921—

> . . . the American variant of natural law grew out of an attempt at philosophical statement of the power of our courts with respect to unconstitutional legislation. The constitution was declaratory of principles of natural constitutional law which were to be deduced from the nature of free government. Hence constitutional questions were always only in terms questions of constitutional interpretation. They were questions of the meaning of the document, as such, only in form. In substance they were questions of a general constitutional law which transcended the text; of whether the enactment before the court conformed to principles of natural law 'running back of all constitutions' and inherent in the very idea of a government of limited powers set up by a free people.[81]

Forty years after Dean Pound wrote these words, the subject of his discussion was still causing concern to the Justices of the Supreme

---

extend its protection; a difficulty, which it is obvious might often be avoided by giving to the phrase ex post facto its original and natural application. 2 Peters 686.

Professor W. W. Crosskey, writing in 1953, expressed the opinion that the draftsmen of the Constitution intended these words to apply to civil as well as criminal retrospective statutes. See his *Politics and the Constitution* (Chicago: University of Chicago Press, 1953) Chapter XI, especially pp. 330–331. He ascribes the limited application of that clause in *Calder* v. *Bull* to a judicial nervousness lest the federal power to pass bankruptcy acts be held not to include discharges of debtors. Mr. Crosskey pointed out that in 1796, Robert Morris, financier of the Revolution, was in a debtors' prison in Philadelphia where the Court was sitting, and that James Wilson of Pennsylvania, a signer of the Declaration and a member of the Constitutional Convention, had been caught with "illiquid assets" in the general financial debacle of 1796 and was in danger of arrest for imprisonment for debt. One can respect Professor Crosskey's long study of late eighteenth century events and still be a little skeptical about devious undisclosed reasons for judicial decisions.

[81] Pound, *Introduction to the Philosophy of Law* (New Haven: Yale University Press, 1922) pp. 50–51.

Court and to those who studied their work. Passage of the Fourteenth Amendment in 1868 had accentuated the theoretical difficulties of constitutional decision by prohibiting the State from denial of "due process" or "equal protection of the laws"—in the latter case with a latent proviso that of course the laws need not treat persons equally when there appears a justifiable reason for treating them unequally. And determination of what is justifiable presents the ancient question of the nature of justice, a question no constitution has ever answered.

In 1947 Mr. Justice Frankfurter wrote in *Adamson v. California*—[82]

> . . . As judges charged with the delicate task of subjecting the government of a continent to the Rule of Law we must be particularly mindful that it is 'a *constitution* we are expounding', so that it should not be imprisoned in what are merely legal forms even though they have the sanction of the Eighteenth Century.

Dissenting in the same case, Mr. Justice Black answered—[83]

> This decision reasserts a constitutional theory . . . that this Court is endowed by the Constitution with boundless power under 'natural law' periodically to expand and contract constitutional standards to conform to the Court's conception of what at a particular time constitutes 'civilized decency' and 'fundamental liberty and justice' . . . I think that . . . the 'natural law' theory of the Constitution . . . degrade[s] the constitutional safeguards of the Bill of Rights and simultaneously appropriate[s] for this Court a broad power which we are not authorized by the Constitution to exercise.

In the first decade of the Supreme Court, its Justices thus faced the same puzzling questions concerning the ultimate criteria of their judgments, which trouble the Justices and theoretical writers a century and two-thirds later.

International Law and Revolutionary France

The first ten years under the Federal Constitution coincided with the first ten years of the French Revolution—a coincidence which introduced Americans to the difficulties of standing aloof from Europe.[84]

[82] 332 U.S. 46 (1947) p. 66.
[83] *Ibid.*, p. 69. See also *Rochin v. California*, 342 U.S. 165 (1955), and *Irvine v. California*, 347 U.S. 128 (1954).
[84] See "Foreign and Indian Relations, 1789–1798," in Handlin *et al.*, *Harvard Guide to American History*, pp. 321–323, for a bibliography concerning our difficulties with Revolutionary France. A convenient account appears in T. A. Bailey, *A Diplomatic History of the American People* (3rd ed.; New York: Crofts and Co., 1947) Chapter VI.

At first, while France was still changing her government with some self-restraint, her revolution was widely admired in the United States, even by comparatively conservative people, who saw in it something like recent American political changes. French help in the War of Independence was still fresh in American minds. The French Declaration of Rights of Man and the Citizen, adopted by the National Assembly in 1789,[85] suggested to Americans their own Declaration of Independence. The French constitution of 1791,[86] drafted by the National Assembly and accepted by the now overmastered King, suggested the American Constitution; it provided for separation of powers between legislative, executive and judicial departments; it was predicated on the idea that the will of the people should ultimately govern. The good impression of this first revolutionary phase on the United States was not unlike that produced in America by the 1917 Kerensky revolution in Russia. The rise of the terror, however, began to alarm and disgust some original admirers. On January 21, 1793 the revolutionists guillotined Louis XVI. On February 1, 1793, France declared war on England and the United Provinces. Executioners were busy in Paris. Opinion in the United States became sharply divided between those on the one hand who remembered our war with England which had ended less than ten years before, who remembered the help France had given us in that struggle, and who sympathized with French egalitarian ideals; and those on the other hand who were profoundly shocked and alienated by the revolutionary excesses in France.[87] On April 22, 1793 Washington proclaimed our neutrality in the European war.[88] For our maritime nation, we found neutrality a complicated policy.

Citizen Edmond Genêt, the young first minister to the United States from the new French Republic, provided a good many of our American embarrassments. With the rash zeal of his twenty-eight years, and perhaps misled by the warm greeting of French sympathizers,

---

[85] See for the text of the French Declaration, Eugène Blum, *La Déclaration des Droits de l'Homme et du Citoyen; Texte avec Commentaire Suivi* (Paris: Firmin et Montane, 1902).

[86] For the text see *The French Constitution as Revised and Amended by the National Assembly and Presented to the King on the Third of September, 1791— To Which are Added, Its being Presented to the King; a Copy of the King's Letter . . . announcing his Acceptance; and the King's taking the Oath in Presence of the Assembly* (London: Debrett, 1811).

[87] Compare A. E. Sutherland, Jr., "British Trials for Disloyal Association during the French Revolution," 34 *Cornell Law Quarterly* 303 (1949).

[88] 4 *Annals of Congress* 1285; J. D. Richardson, *Messages and Papers of the Presidents* (10 vols.; Washington: Government Printing Office, 1896-99) I, p. 156; H. S. Commager, *Documents of American History* (7th ed.; New York: Appleton-Century-Crofts, 1963) p. 162.

he was instrumental in fitting out fourteen privateers in American ports, which then cruised under French colors and brought back to our harbors more than eighty British prizes, part taken in American waters. Some adventurous Americans, enrolling as officers on these privateers, created problems in our courts when they were later prosecuted on criminal charges.[89]

Citizen Genêt not only fitted out privateers in our ports; he also set up prize courts in the United States, manned by French consuls who purported to condemn vessels these privateers had captured. In 1793 when French privateers brought the *William* and the *Fanny,* American ships, into American ports as "prizes" captured in American waters, the American owners libeled the vessels in the Pennsylvania federal District Court. Pierre DuPonceau and Jared Ingersoll, eminent counsel for the French captors, contended that United States courts had no jurisdiction over French prizes. Under our treaty with France, they argued, the captors had a right to bring prizes into our ports, and if the owners had any grievances, the United States must seek redress by diplomatic negotiation.[90] District Judge Richard Peters held, with the French, that the District Court had no jurisdiction to pass on the legality of the prizes. President Washington, distressed by this result, directed the Governor of Pennsylvania to post guards over the *William*[91] and ordered that prizes taken by privateers in violation of our neutral rights be turned over to their owners if brought into our ports.[92]

The questions of international law presented by these complications were not entirely simple. At President Washington's direction, Jef-

[89] For Washington's unsuccessful request for advice from the Supreme Court on some of these difficult problems see Warren, *Supreme Court in United States History,* I, pp. 105 ff., and p. 248, *infra.*

[90] Warren, *Supreme Court in United States History,* I, p. 106 *et seq.*

[91] Warren's account leaves the reader wondering what became of the unfortunate *Fanny.* The index to "Federal Cases" lists a number of admiralty proceedings by that name, but they were all much later than the controversies here discussed.

[92] Warren, *Supreme Court in United States History,* I, p. 108. Washington finally became outraged when Genêt talked of "appealing to the people" from our government's decision to seize "The Little Sarah," which was outfitting as a French privateer. Genêt promised the government that the "Sarah" would not sail without notice; ten days later she slipped out of port, violating this agreement. The President convened his cabinet, which demanded Genêt's recall to France, But Genêt had meantime become embroiled with his own government which appointed one Fauchet his successor and instructed Fauchet to send Genêt home for trial on French charges. Paris was unwholesome for Frenchmen out of favor and on trial; Genêt preferred to remain in the United States. He was in some danger of deportation, but George Washington magnanimously intervened in his favor. Genêt settled in New York where he married Governor George Clinton's daughter and lived until 1834. See J. S. Bassett, *Short History of the United States* (New York: Macmillan, 1923) pp. 266–267.

ferson, his Secretary of State, on July 18, 1793 wrote to Chief Justice Jay asking whether the President might seek the legal advice of the justices of the Supreme Court. With the letter were transmitted twenty-nine questions relating to international law, neutrality, and the construction of our treaties with France and Britain.[93] On August 8, 1793, the justices of the United States Supreme Court replied to the President's questions in a letter which in substance stated the doctrine that under Article III of the Constitution, the Court could pass only on a "case or controversy." The Supreme Court has always, pursuant to this view, declined to entertain jurisdiction of a matter not truly adversary in its nature. They wrote to Washington:

> We have considered the previous question stated in a letter written by your direction to us by the Secretary of State, on the 18th of last month regarding the lines of separation, drawn by the Constitution between the three departments of the government. These being in certain respects checks upon each other, and our being judges of a court in the last resort, are considerations which afford strong arguments against the propriety of our extrajudicially deciding the questions alluded to, especially as the power given by the Constitution to the President, of calling on the heads of departments for opinions, seems to have been *purposely* as well as expressly united to the *Executive* departments.
>
> We exceedingly regret every event that may cause embarrassment to your administration, but we derive consolation from the reflection that your judgment will discern what is right, and that your usual prudence, decision and firmness will surmount every obstacle to the preservation of the rights, peace, and dignity of the United States.[94]

The determination of the Supreme Court not to be put in the position of a unilateral advisor to the Executive has been a rule of guidance ever since. In 1911, for example, that Court declined to pass on

---

[93] See Warren, *Supreme Court in United States History*, I, p. 109, and Henry P. Johnston, ed., *Correspondence and Public Papers of John Jay* (4 vols.; New York: G. P. Putnam's Sons, 1890–1893) III, p. 486, *et seq.*

[94] Johnston, *Correspondence and Public Papers of John Jay*, III, p. 488. Chief Justice Jay and Associate Justice Cushing, sitting in the New York Circuit Court, had previously declined, as a Court, to follow a statutory mandate to pass on pension claims when they considered the questions administrative rather than judicial. They consented to perform the duty "in the capacity of commissioners." Justices Wilson and Blair, with District Judge Peters, at the Pennsylvania Circuit; and Justice Iredell, with District Judge Sitgreaves at the North Carolina Circuit, had expressed opinions that the duties in question were non-judicial, in letters written to the Presdent of the United States. See the notes to *Hayburn's Case*, 2 Dallas 409 (1792). Attorney-General Randolph then moved the Supreme Court for a mandamus, requiring the Circuit Court in Pennsylvania to proceed in Hayburn's Case; while the matter was under advisement the Congress amended the statute, providing otherwise for such cases.

a question of constitutionality in what it found to be a non-adversary situation even when an Act of Congress specifically authorized the jurisdiction.[95]

Other questions arising from privateering activity occurred when American citizens who took part in French privateering were prosecuted on common-law criminal charges in American federal courts. On July 27, 1793, one Gideon Henfield was indicted in Philadelphia for acting as prizemaster of the celebrated French privateer *Citizen Genêt*, and for attacking and seizing ships of a nation with which the United States was at peace, in violation of the law of nations and treaties and laws of the United States. Henfield was brought to trial on this non-statutory charge before the United States Circuit Court in Philadelphia but the jury acquitted him.[96]

At this troubled moment, President Washington's policy was disturbed by a decision of the United States District Court for Maryland in *Glass* v. *The Sloop Betsey*.[97] The case arose when Captain de Johannene, commanding the Citizen Genêt, captured the sloop *Betsey* and sent the vessel into Baltimore as prize of war. Glass, with the other owners of the *Betsey* and her cargo, then filed a libel in the Maryland District Court, claiming restitution on the ground that the vessel belonged to neutrals, subjects of the King of Sweden, and that the cargo was owned by other neutrals, Swedes and Americans. The captors as in the earlier cases of the *William* and the *Fanny*[98] pleaded that the District Court had no jurisdiction; only in diplomatic proceedings, said the privateersmen, could the legality of the capture be questioned. The District Court, to the President's distress, agreed with the Frenchmen; if its judgment were to be generally followed, American shipping was at the mercy of French privateers unless we were willing to risk war at sea. The administration's concern increased when the Circuit Court affirmed the District Court's judgment. The

---

[95] *Muskrat* v. *United States*, 219 U.S. 354 (1911). See *U.S.* v. *Johnson*, 319 U.S. 302 (1943).

[96] See John Marshall, *Life of Washington* (5 vols.; Philadelphia: C. P. Wayne, 1804–1807) II, p. 273. For several years under the Constitution of 1789, courts were uncertain as to the legality of prosecution for non-statutory crimes against the United States. The question persisted at least until 1812 when the Supreme Court decided against the existence of non-statutory federal crimes, in *U.S.* v. *Hudson and Goodwin*, 7 Cranch 32 (1812). See *U.S.* v. *Coolidge*, 1 Wheaton 415 (1816). The matter is discussed and authorities are suggested in Hart and Wechsler, *The Federal Courts and the Federal System* (Brooklyn: Foundation Press, 1953) pp. 1086 *et seq.* But in 1942, crimes against the "law of War" were prosecuted before a Military Commission in the United States; the Supreme Court upheld the Commission's jurisdiction in *Ex parte Quirin.* 317 U.S. (1942).

[97] See 3 Dallas 6, February, 1794 Term.

[98] See p. 247 and following, above.

Betsey's owners appealed to the Supreme Court of the United States, where eminent counsel argued for five days, from February 8 to February 12, 1794. At the close of their presentation, the appellants somewhat summarily mentioned the attempt of French consuls to set up prize courts in American ports. The Supreme Court kept the case under advisement for six days, and then informed counsel that besides the question of judicial or diplomatic procedures which had been argued in the District Court, the record raised another question as to whether, in the absence of positive treaty stipulation, any foreign nation had a right to establish an admiralty tribunal in the United States. The Court asked to hear this question discussed. DuPonceau, for the captor, observed that "the parties to the appeal" (did he, one wonders, speak for the appellants as well as respondents?) did not consider themselves interested in the point, and that the French Minister had given no instructions for arguing it. Chief Justice Jay forthwith delivered the unanimous opinion of the Court[99] rejecting Captain de Johannene's argument that the District Court had no legal competence to consider whether the capture was lawful. The Supreme Court reversed the decree of the District Court of Maryland, and remanded the case to the lower federal courts, to pass on the merits of the claim of Glass and the other owners that the capture of the *Betsey* was unlawful. The Supreme Court's opinion added an observation that the admiralty jurisdiction which had been exercised in the United States by French consuls, not being warranted by any express treaty, was not sustainable.

Glass v. *The Betsey* was Chief Justice John Jay's last reported opinion. President Washington, shortly after the February, 1794 term ended, appointed him Special Ambassador to Great Britain, to negotiate a treaty intended to settle the still-troublesome unresolved questions of loyalist claims and unsurrendered frontier posts. The agreement which he negotiated, "Jay's Treaty" of 1794, contemplating an amicable adjustment of our remaining differences with Great Britain, aroused much French resentment against the United States, and much enmity among French sympathizers in this country.[100] France and England, at war with one another, sought to cripple each other's commerce, including commerce with nationals of the United States. The French continued to seize American ships and to mishandle American crews, arousing the anger of Federalist shipowners, but not much resentment among pro-French Jeffersonian farmers. At this troublesome moment, on March 4, 1797, John Adams succeeded

[99] *Glass* v. *The Sloop Betsey* 3 Dallas 6 (1794).
[100] See Samuel Flagg Bemis, *Jay's Treaty.*

Washington as President. On June 21, 1797, Secretary of State Pickering reported to President Adams, and the President next day sent to the Congress, a painful account of numerous vessels flying American colors which French cruisers had captured since July, 1796.[101] Adams, hoping to avert war and to patch matters up, sent to France a commission of three men—Charles Pinckney, Elbridge Gerry, and John Marshall. The American envoys arrived in Paris on October 4, 1797; three mysterious men shortly sought them out. Obviously these emissaries came from Talleyrand, the French Minister of Foreign Relations. They requested a large loan for France, and, to boot, a bribe for officials, to induce favorable attitudes toward the United States. The three American envoys reported these démarches to the United States Government, referring to the French emissaries as X., Y., and Z. in order to avoid complications in case the letters became public. Tradition ascribes these dispatches to John Marshall.[102]

President Adams laid the X.Y.Z. papers before Congress; 10,000 copies, distributed at public expense, were eagerly read by the anti-French Federalist partisans. Pinckney and Marshall, angered by the treatment the French had given them, came home to be received with applause in the United States. At the urging of Talleyrand, Elbridge Gerry stayed on in France until his Government recalled him. On May 28, 1798 the Congress authorized American naval vessels to capture French armed ships, and to recapture American merchant vessels which the French had taken.[103] On June 13, 1798 the Congress suspended commercial intercourse with France and with French dependencies.[104] On June 25, 1798 Congress authorized American merchant vessels to capture French armed vessels which attacked them, and to bring such French vessels into American ports to be sold, the proceeds to be divided equally between the captor ship's company and her owners[105]—a sort of limited license for privateering. On July 7, 1798 the Congress declared our treaties with France void on the ground that the French Government had repeatedly violated them.[106] So authorized by the Congress, the small American navy, aided by privately owned vessels, began an undeclared naval war which lasted over two years. American vessels captured more than

[101] See 9 *Annals of Congress*, Appendix, 3115 and following.

[102] A. J. Beveridge, *Life of John Marshall* (4 vols.; Boston: Houghton Mifflin and Co., 1916–19) II, p. 256.

[103] 1 Stat. at Large 561; see also Act of June 28, 1798, 1 Stat. at Large 574; and Act of July 9, 1798, 1 Stat. at Large 578.

[104] 1 Stat. at Large 565.

[105] 1 Stat. at Large 572.

[106] 1 Stat. at Large 578.

eighty armed French ships, principally privateers operating in West Indian waters.[107] Congress summoned Washington from retirement to command an augmented American army; Hamilton was appointed second in command. Talleyrand, not anxious for all-out war with America, let it be known to William Vans Murray, United States representative at the Hague, that an American diplomat would have a correct and respectful reception in France. Thereupon President Adams, despite considerable popular anger against France, sent to the Senate on February 18, 1799 the nomination of Murray as Minister to France. The Federalist party was annoyed at this conciliatory move, which tended to diminish its popularity. Adams, a week later, made a concession to the Federalists by expanding the nomination of Murray alone, to include the nomination of a commission of three; with Murray, President Adams named William R. Davie, late Governor of North Carolina, and Oliver Ellsworth, the Chief Justice of the Supreme Court. Opinion in the United States came to agree with Adams in this move, and the three envoys finally on September 30, 1800 arranged a convention by which the United States and France adjusted a number of issues concerning spoliations of commerce and neutral navigation.[108] Adams was defeated for re-election in the election of 1800; but his courageous peaceful adjustment of our differences with France in 1800 may have made practicable the Louisiana purchase three years later.[109]

---

[107] J. S. Bassett, in his *Short History of the United States*, p. 281, gives the number as 84.

[108] See 8 U.S. Stat. at Large 178 *et seq.*

[109] This account has obviously not undertaken an inclusive description of all prize litigation and other cases with international flavor in the Supreme Court during its first decade. Cases originating in the War of Independence were still pending as late as 1795. See *Penhallow* v. *Doane's Administrators* 3 Dallas 54 (1795). The defector furnished problems in 1795 as in 1963; Captain Barré, of the French frigate *Le Perdrix*, abandoned his ship and became a New York resident; the French Consul sought from District Judge Lawrence of New York a warrant for Captain Barré's arrest; the Consul asserted as authority a consular convention with France concerning return of "deserters." Judge Lawrence decided that the Consul's proof was inadequate. Bradford, Attorney-General of the United States, moved in the Supreme Court for a writ of mandamus commanding Judge Lawrence to issue the warrant; the Supreme Court refused to review Judge Lawrence's discretionary action. *U.S.* v. *Lawrence,* 3 Dallas 42 (1795). In John Rutledge's only term as Chief Justice,—that of August 1795—the Supreme Court, essentially on a basis of sovereign immunity, issued a writ of prohibition against District Judge Peters of Philadelphia, forbidding him to proceed on behalf of the owner of a captured schooner against the French naval vessel *The Cassius*. See *U.S.* v. *Peters,* 3 Dallas 121 (1795). At the same term the Supreme Court decided a bewilderingly complicated case, brought by Joost Janson, late master of the brigantine *Magdalena*, against Edward Ballard, captain of the armed schooner *L'Ami de la Liberté*, who with William Talbot, captain of another armed schooner *L'Ami de la Point a Pétre*, two purported French privateers, had brought the *Magdalena* into Charleston as

Aliens and Sedition

Revolution in France divided sympathies in the United States and produced violent stress between the nascent political parties. In 1798 the Federalist President John Adams and the working majority of congressional Federalists saw French revolutionary excesses with dismay, and resented such activities within our borders as those engaged in several years earlier by Citizen Genêt, the then Minister from France, who had used our ports as bases for privateering and had set up prize courts with French consuls as judges. Some Americans, distrustful of "the people," saw them as easy prey to Jacobin seducers. The Jeffersonian party, then called Republican, tended to view the developments in France with more sympathy. Jefferson thought that some bloodletting inevitably accompanied the destruction of outworn tyranny, and saw no reason why the United States should not be reasonably cooperative with the renovated nation which had b ꞓn our ally in the recent war against Britain. Each faction had its journalistic backers, who berated their adversaries with more zeal than reason.

---

prize. Both captors, and both their vessels seemed to have curiously American origins, despite the recently acquired French citizenship of the privateersmen and the French names and colors of their ships. One may wonder whether opportunities for doubtfully legitimated piracy, or political devotion to the liberties of the French, had more powerfully motivated the captors. The federal District, Circuit, and Supreme Courts all in turn decided in favor of the Netherlands owners of the *Magdalena*. *Talbot* v. *Janson*, 3 Dallas 133 (1795).

Decisions in other privateering cases, arising in various ways, went sometimes in favor of captors, sometimes of captives. *McDonough* v. *Dannery and the Ship Mary Ford*, 3 Dallas 188 (1796); *Geyer et al.* v. *Michel et al. and the Ship Den Onzekeren*, 3 Dallas 285 (1796); *United States* v. *La Vengeance*, 3 Dallas 297 (1796); *Moodie* v. *The Ship Phoebe Anne*, 3 Dallas 319 (1796); *Hills* v. *Ross*, 3 Dallas 184, 331 (1796); *Del Col* v. *Arnold*, 3 Dallas 336 (1797). At the February 1800 term of the Supreme Court an American naval recapture of an American merchant vessel which the French had taken, resulted in a salvage award under an Act of Congress of March 2, 1799, I Stat. at Large 709, 716, on the ground that the vessel thus retaken from the French had been retaken from "the enemy." This decision disgusted the Anti-Federalists who inclined to favor the French and who disliked the hostile term thus applied to that nation. *Bas* v. *Tingy*, 4 Dallas 37 (1800). The Anti-Federalist paper "Aurora" of Philadelphia urged that the justices who so voted should be impeached! See Warren, *Supreme Court in United States History*, I, p. 157. For a description of the "Aurora" and Benjamin Bache, its editor, see Miller, *Crisis in Freedom* (Boston: Little, Brown and Co., 1951) p. 26ff. In the first stage of another salvage case appears the name of a captor vessel famous in American naval annals. Silas Talbot, of *Talbot* v. *The Ship Amelia*, 4 Dallas 34 (1800) was the commander of the frigate *Constitution*. Officers and crew were awarded salvage in 1801; 1 Cranch 1; the Supreme Court's opinion was the first delivered by a new Chief Justice, appointed the preceding February; his name was John Marshall.

The Federalist Congress in June and July 1798, reacted to the French business by passing four drastic statutes. The Naturalization Act[110] required fourteen years' residence in the United States and five years' declaration of intention before naturalization. The Alien Act[111] provided that during the two year life of the statute, the President might order to be deported "all such aliens as he shall judge dangerous to the peace and safety of the United States or shall have grounds to suspect are concerned in any treasonable or secret machinations against the government thereof." The Alien Enemy Act[112] gave to the President a wide discretionary power to deport alien enemies. With a few minor changes it has remained in force ever since. The Sedition Act was the most rigorous of all.[113] The first of its two penal sections punished, with a fine not exceeding $5,000 or imprisonment from six months to five years, any conspiracy to oppose measures of the government if the persons combining advised or attempted to procure insurrection, riot, or unlawful assembly. The second section provided a fine not exceeding $2,000 or imprisonment not exceeding two years for any person who should write or publish any "false, scandalous and malicious writing or writings against the government of the United States, . . . or the President of the United States with intent to defame the said government . . . or to stir up sedition within the United States." The Sedition Act, by its own terms, was to continue effective only until March 3, 1801.

Despite the ominous restrictions of the Sedition Act, it gave to the accused certain substantive and procedural protections much more advantageous than those then generally obtaining in the law of criminal libel. The third section of the statute provided—

> That if any person shall be prosecuted under this act, for the writing or publishing any libel aforesaid, it shall be lawful for the defendant, upon the trial of the cause, to give in evidence in his defence, the truth of the matter contained in the publication charged as a libel. And the jury who shall try the cause, shall have a right to determine the law and the fact, under the direction of the court as in other cases.

[110] June 18, 1798, 1 Stat. at Large 566. Aliens who had been residents before January 29, 1795, were excepted. The statute was repealed in 1802.

[111] June 25, 1798, 1 Stat. at Large 570.

[112] July 6, 1798, 1 Stat. at Large 577. In its present form it is 50 U.S.C. § 21 (1946). It was construed and applied in *Ludecke* v. *Watkins,* 335 U.S. 160 (1948); and see *Jaegeler* v. *Carusi* 342 U.S. 347 (1952).

[113] July 14, 1798, 1 Stat. at Large 596. For a discussion of the constitutionality of this statute see Chafee, *Freedom of Speech* (New York: Harcourt, Brace and Howe, 1920) III, p. 30. And see generally Leonard W. Levy, *Freedom of Speech and Press in Early American History: Legacy of Suppression* (New York: Harper and Row, 1963).

Much history lay behind this language. "Down to the beginning of the eighteenth century . . . the essence of a libel was the intentional publication of a document bearing the seditious or defamatory meaning alleged by the prosecution. It followed that all the jury had to do was to find the fact of publication of a document bearing the meaning alleged by the prosecution; and that it was for the court to say, as a matter of law, whether what was published was seditious, defamatory, or otherwise malicious, and so a libel. This state of the law harmonized admirably with the current views as to the relations of rulers to their subjects. But, when those views changed, it gradually came to be wholly out of touch with current public opinion."[114] At the trial of John Peter Zenger for seditious libel, held in New York in 1735, Chief Justice Delancey of the Provincial Supreme Court charged the jury

> . . . as the facts or words in the information are confessed, the only thing that can come in question before you is whether the words as set forth in the information make a libel. And that is a matter of law, no doubt, and which you may leave to the Court.[115]

The Chief Justice had previously excluded evidence, offered by Zenger's counsel, that Zenger's statements were true, on the ground that "the greater appearance of truth in any malicious invective, so much the more provoking it is."[116] As the saying went, "The greater the truth, the greater the libel!"

In 1792 the Parliament passed Fox's Libel Act, "An act to remove doubts respecting the function of juries in cases of libel." This statute directed that the jury—

> . . . give a general verdict of guilty or not guilty upon the whole matter put in issue upon such indictment or information; and shall not be required or directed by the court or judge before whom such indictment or information shall be tried, to find the defendant or defendants guilty, merely on the proof of the publication . . . of the paper charged to be a libel and of the sense ascribed to the same in such indictment or information.[117]

Fox's Libel Act did not, however, change the long-established English rule that on a charge of criminal libel, truth of the facts was no de-

[114] Holdsworth, *History of English Law* (Boston: Little, Brown and Co., 1927) VIII, p. 345.
[115] See Buranelli, *The Trial of Peter Zenger* (New York: New York University Press, 1907) p. 132. See p. 119 above.
[116] Buranelli, *The Trial of Peter Zenger*, p. 111; see also Rutherford, *John Peter Zenger* (New York: Dodd, Mead and Co., 1904) p. 81 *et seq.*; James Alexander, *A Brief Narrative of the Case and Trial of John Peter Zenger*, Stanley Katz, ed., (Cambridge, Mass.: Harvard University Press, 1963).
[117] 32 Geo. III c. 60 (1792).

fense. This English rule was to remain law in New York, as it had been in Zenger's day, until 1805 when a celebrated prosecution in the State courts, brought against Harry Croswell, editor of the Hudson *Wasp*, for libeling President Thomas Jefferson, aroused the New York legislature to make truth a defense.[118] Truth did not become so provable in England until Lord Campbell's Libel Act of 1843.[119] Thus the Sedition Act, though entirely too sweeping in its condemnation of—

> . . . false, scandalous and malicious . . . writings against the government of the United States, or either house of the Congress of the United States, or the President of the United States, with intent to defame the said government, or either house of the said Congress, or the said President, or to bring them, or either of them, into contempt or disrepute;

—still in its provision of truth as a defense, and its commission of the general question of guilt to the jury, was more liberal than the generally prevailing law of its time.

While this alien and sedition legislation was being debated in Congress, Jeffersonian members denounced it as unconstitutional. They particularly condemned the Sedition Act; on July 10, 1798 Nathanial Macon of North Carolina told the House that the law, if passed, would not only violate the constitutional provision protecting freedom of speech and of the press, but would exceed the enumerated powers delegated to the Congress. ". . . [If] there be a majority determined to pass it, he could only hope that the Judges would exercise the power placed in them of determining the law an unconstitutional law, if, upon scrutiny, they find it to be so."[120]

Strong Republican States reacted vigorously against the Alien and Sedition Acts. On November 16, 1798 the Kentucky legislature passed a resolution, drafted by Thomas Jefferson, declaring the Sedition Act unconstitutional and void as exceeding the delegated powers of the national government, and as violating the First Amendment. On December 24, 1798 the Virginia legislature passed a similar resolution, drafted by James Madison, declaring the Alien and Sedition Acts unconstitutional on the same grounds, and adding

> that, in case of a deliberate, palpable, and dangerous exercise of . . . powers not granted by the said compact, the States who are parties

[118] See *People* v. *Croswell*, 3 Johnson's Cases 337 Appendix; 3 Wheeler's Criminal Cases 330 (1804) discussed at page 258, *infra*. Professor Levy points out in the preface to his *Freedom of Speech and Press in Early American History* that by 1792 Pennsylvania, Delaware, and Kentucky had empowered juries to decide law and fact in criminal libel, and had made truth a defense.

[119] 6 and 7 Vict. c. 97, August 24, 1843.

[120] 8 *Annals of Congress* 2152.

thereto, have the right and are in duty bound to interpose for arresting the progress of the evil, and for maintaining within their respective limits the authorities, rights, and liberties appertaining to them.[121]

"Interposition"—the doctrine suggested by the Virginia Resolution of 1798—was the same theory which Senator Calhoun popularized in South Carolina in 1832 under the banner of "nullification." Essentially it is a doctrine that any State which decides that an Act of Congress is unconstitutional can simply disregard it. The idea was revived in some States during the 1950's as a theory of resistance to the United States Supreme Court's 1954 decision on segregated schools.[122]

A constitutional license for any State to declare inoperative any Act of Congress which its State legislature may deem unconstitutional, would be a pattern of national anarchy. Some national agency must have the ultimate power to pass on the constitutional validity of national legislation, and this function the Supreme Court performs. "Interposition" asserted in the Kentucky-Virginia resolutions of 1798, has no basis in constitutional law; it is important only as showing a widespread understanding, already established in the early years of the Constitution, that national legislation which conflicted with that senior law was ineffective,—a doctrine which John Marshall was to proclaim five years later in *Marbury* v. *Madison*.[123]

As soon as prosecutions began under the Sedition Act, those accused set up its unconstitutionality as a defense. The Supreme Court never passed on the question, but some Supreme Court justices, sitting in Circuit Courts, upheld the statute. A Vermont grand jury in 1798 indicted Matthew Lyon, a Congressman from that State. Lyon was a rough-and-tumble Irish-born Republican, a voluble and vitriolic floor debater who had, by a narrow vote, missed expulsion from Congress after a fight in the House with a Connecticut Federalist named Griswold, in which Griswold's weapon was a cane and Lyon's a pair of fire tongs! The indictment against Lyon charged that he had published in the Vermont *Journal* an article declaring that under President Adams, "every consideration of the public welfare was swallowed up in a continual grasp for power, in an unbounded thirst for ridiculous pomp, foolish adulation, and selfish avarice." Honest men, wrote Lyon, were turned out of office, religion was prostituted for party purposes and the people were crushed beneath enormous taxes—mild enough

[121] The Kentucky-Virginia Resolutions of 1798 are printed, among other places, in H. S. Commager's *Documents of American History*, 7th ed., pp. 178 ff. See also Elliot, ed., *Debates in the Several State Conventions* (2nd ed.; 5 vols.; Washington: Elliot, 1836–1845) IV, pp. 540, 546.
[122] *Brown* v. *Board of Education* 347 U.S. 438.
[123] 1 Cranch 137 (1803).

charges, considering the tone of political writing in that day. Brought to trial in the federal Circuit Court before Mr. Justice Paterson of the Supreme Court, Lyon unsuccessfully argued the unconstitutionality of the statute. He was nevertheless convicted; but neither prosecution nor defense suggested that the Court lacked power to declare an Act of Congress unconstitutional. In April, 1800 Charles Holt, editor of the New Haven *Bee*, was similarly brought to trial before Mr. Justice Bushrod Washington in the Connecticut Circuit Court. Holt likewise urged the Court to hold the Act unconstitutional, but Washington, like Paterson, upheld the statute. The jury found Holt guilty, and he was sentenced to six months in prison with a fine of two hundred dollars.[124] In all ten persons were brought to trial under the Sedition Act, though a larger number were indicted;[125] but opposition to the legislation was much more heated than this comparatively small number of federal prosecutions might explain. To many anti-Federalists the Sedition Act seemed a mere device for silencing a political opposition. Then too, there were additional prosecutions for criminal libels, brought in State courts under State laws, which added to popular opposition. The Jeffersonian press cried out in fury against this suppression of republican liberties, while the Federalist journals denounced Jacobinism in equally violent terms.

The Alien and Sedition Acts may well have contributed to the election of Jefferson as President, and to the Republican victory in the Congressional elections of 1800. And the Jeffersonians soon taught the Federalists that prosecution for criminal libel could be used by more than one faction. In December 1800 a Pennsylvania State court imposed a fine of $2500 on John Ward Fenno, Jr., pugnacious editor of the Federalist "Gazette of the United States," for libeling a Republican.[126] In 1803 a jury in Columbia County, New York, convicted a Federalist editor named Croswell for printing "a scandalous, malicious and seditious libel upon Thomas Jefferson, the President of the United States"; the libel charged was a statement that Jefferson had paid one Callander to print libelous denunciations of John Adams and George Washington. Morgan Lewis, Chief Justice of the New York Supreme Court, presiding at the trial, refused to admit Croswell's offered proof that the story was true! Chief Justice Lewis's theory was the old English doctrine—"The greater the truth, the greater the libel." Croswell

---

[124] For the *Lyon* and *Holt* cases, see J. C. Miller, *Crisis in Freedom*, pp. 102–130. And see J. F. McLaughlin, *Matthew Lyon: The Hampden of Congress* (New York: W. H. Crawford Co., 1900).

[125] See J. S. Bassett, *Short History of the United States*, (3rd ed.; New York: Macmillan, 1939) p. 290.

[126] See Miller, *Crisis in Freedom*, p. 229, for an account of some of the State court proceedings against Federalists.

moved in the New York Supreme Court for a new trial. Alexander Hamilton argued his case in the spring of 1804, but the court was equally divided; Croswell's conviction stood, though the prosecution deferred a motion for his sentencing. Impressed by the injustice of the New York law of criminal libel, the State legislature at its 1805 session passed a statute making truth a valid defense[127] if the publication was made "with good motives and for justifiable ends," and providing that the trial jury

> . . . shall have a right to determine the law and the fact, under the direction of the court, in like manner as in other criminal cases, and shall not be directed or required by the court or judge, before whom such indictment or information shall be tried, to find the defendant guilty, merely on the proof of the publication by the defendant, of the matter charged to be libellous, and of the sense ascribed thereto, in such indictment or information;

At its next term, the New York Supreme Court granted Croswell, still at liberty, a new trial on the basis of this statute.[128]

Popular excitement over the Alien and Sedition laws disappeared in the swift flow of events, as the Jeffersonian victory of 1800, the Louisiana purchase, the rapid western expansion, and the rising trou-

[127] Hamilton, Croswell's counsel, had been killed in his duel with Burr in July 1804; the New York amendment was then carried through the legislature by Croswell's junior counsel, Assemblyman William W. Van Ness.

[128] See *People* v. *Croswell*, 3 Johnson's Cases 337, Appendix at page 412. The substance of the provision thus enacted in New York was made part of that State's Constitution in the revision of 1821. It is now Article I, § 8 of the New York Constitution. A provision like that of New York now appears in at least 24 State constitutions. In 1952 Mr. Justice Jackson called this principle "common sense of American criminal libel law." See his dissent in *Beauharnais* v. *Illinois*, 343 U.S. 250 at page 297. In that decision the Supreme Court of the United States affirmed, by 5 to 4, a criminal conviction under an Illinois group-libel act, which penalized any publication which "portrays depravity, criminality, unchastity, or lack of virtue of a class of citizens, of any race, color, creed or religion which said publication or exhibition exposes the citizens of any race, color, creed or religion to contempt, derision or obloquy . . ." Beauharnais' publication had imputed criminal tendencies to Chicago Negroes, and had called on the Mayor and City Council for restrictive action, which would undoubtedly have been unconstitutional. The Illinois trial court had refused an offer by the accused to prove truth; and had charged the jury ". . . if you find . . . that the defendant Joseph Beauharnais did . . . publish . . . in any public place the lithograph . . . then you are to find the defendant guilty . . . ," a curious resurgence of Chief Justice Delancey's 1735 ruling in Zenger's Case. At the end of their dissent from the Supreme Court's affirmance, Justices Black and Douglas referred to the remark of Pyrrhus, King of Epirus, who when congratulated on a costly victory over a Roman army, said, "Yes, but if we have another such victory we are undone." On March 9, 1964, the Supreme Court of the United States held that even untrue political criticism is protected, from legal attack, by the Fourteenth Amendment, if it is not malicious. See *New York Times* v. *Sullivan*, 376 U.S. 254.

ble with Britain which was to bring war twelve years later, all came to displace the alarums of Adams' administration. Perhaps, curiously, the most abiding effect of the once heated controversy over the Alien and Sedition laws was wider dissemination of the doctrine that courts should hold federal statutes void when they conflict with the Constitution. When, passing on a very different Act of Congress, the Marshall court so decided in 1803,[129] that aspect of its decision aroused little criticism.[130]

Trends in Constitutional Theory from 1789 to 1800

This book undertakes a survey of the development of five aspirations in the theory of American constitutionalism—self-government by the majority; justice in government regardless of majority will to the contrary; equality of men under government; diffusion of governmental power to assure man's freedom from government; and statement, in a fundamental writing, of governmental powers and of man's liberties, safeguarded against the facile changes of ordinary legislation. How did these five aspirations stand after a decade under the Constitution of 1789?

The first ten years produced less formal progress toward popular government than progress in the facts of American experience. One cardinal fact was the frontier. The end of the War of Independence in 1783 and the settlement of some remaining irritations by Jay's Treaty of 1794 made westward movement easier. Great land grants in what was then the West—the Phelps and Gorham purchase in western New York is only one example[131]—helped open up to pioneer population the territories ceded by Great Britain to the new United States. The people who went west to settle in new farms, villages, trading-posts and river-ports were not submissive and docile. Such men were predisposed to govern themselves. Perhaps allied to this fact was the development of political parties. While Washington was deploring ". . . the baneful effects of the spirit of party generally," with its "alternate domination of one faction over another, sharpened by the spirit of revenge natural

[129] In *Marbury* v. *Madison*, 1 Cranch 137 (1803).

[130] Charles Warren, in *Supreme Court in United States History*, I, pp. 248 ff., surveys the discussion of the *Marbury* case in the Republican press. The principal criticisms did not then attack judicial review of Acts of Congress, but assailed Marshall's effrontery in assuming that Madison, Jefferson's Secretary of State, was subject to a judicial order of mandamus.

[131] See for a brief description the opinion of Mr. Justice Stone in *Massachusetts* v. *New York*, 271 U.S. 65 (1926).

to party dissention"[132] there was coming into being the two-party system of government which, with all its defects, still operates today as a fairly effective means of organizing popular protest against a State or national governmental regime, to the end that another may displace it. Perhaps the First Amendment had the party system latent in its guarantees of free speech, press, assembly and petition. The American press at the close of the eighteenth century was a collection of vitriolic party organs. Papers such as the Baches' Philadelphia "Aurora" gave shrill testimony that parties had become effective devices of operative politics.[133] In our practice the political party system now performs an essential constitutional function. Its origins were old; it had become a well-evolved arrangement by the time the Federalists and the Democratic-Republicans fought out the election of 1800, and the Republicans elected Thomas Jefferson President of the United States. By 1800 the Electoral College, set up in Article II of the Constitution, had already become an obsolete form, replaced in substance by a system which had become essential to our constitutional life, though unmentioned by name in the Constitution itself—the party system.[134]

The first decade laid the foundations of the federal judicial system, which in the United States operates as an effective counterbalance to those elements of government which must be popular if they are to acquire and exercise any power whatever. Judicial review was not an ingenious political move, thought up by John Marshall to checkmate Thomas Jefferson. It was immanent in the structure of the written constitution; it was evident in the Federalist debates; it was discussed and never rejected in opinions of the Supreme Court in the 1790's. The doctrine of Marbury v. Madison[135] was not nearly the surprise that its opposite would have been.

Equality was strong on the frontier—if equality means the least possible impediment by government in the way of the naturally strong,

[132] Farewell Address, September 17, 1796, Richardson, Messages and Papers of the Presidents, I, pp. 213, 218–219. See generally Joseph Charles, The Origins of the American Party System (New York: Harper and Row, 1961).

[133] By the middle of the twentieth century the Supreme Court of the United States had acknowledged the constitutional status of political parties. See, e.g., Terry v. Adams, 345 U.S. 461 (1953) and the other cases cited therein; and see Sweezy v. New Hampshire, 345 U.S. 234 (1957).

[134] Walter Bagehot in his English Constitution (London: Chapman and Hall, 1867) made the classic study of an actual constitution, accepted and familiarly used, long unmentioned in constitutional documents.

[135] 1 Cranch 137 (1803), generally cited as the first case in which the Supreme Court held an Act of Congress invalid because it conflicted with the Constitution. See however U.S. v. Yale Todd, decided 1794 but unreported until 1851, 13 How. 52. See pages 327 and 331, below. See also Itayburn's Case, 2 Dall. 409 (1792).

gifted, and acquisitive getting ahead. There remained, of course, the great unequal institution of Negro slavery, recognized in the First and Fourth Articles of the Constitution. But the humanitarian impulses which were to become so strong in the United States during the next six decades were already stirring. William Wilberforce in England was working for the abolition of the slave trade, and an Act of Congress of March 22, 1794[136] had forbidden that commerce by citizens of the United States insofar as such legislation was possible within the limits of Article I, Section 9 of the Constitution.[137] Religious inequality was fast disappearing from State governments and was forbidden, in federal matters, by the First Amendment.[138] The popular movement that elected Thomas Jefferson in 1800, though it put in office a Virginia landowner with slaves and a gracious hilltop manor-house, made its appeal to men of egalitarian impulse. The next generation of voters who took their lead from the 1800 Jeffersonians, were the men who elected Andrew Jackson in 1828. By 1800 a far-sighted man might well have seen that neither Virginian aristocracy nor the political force of New England congregationalism had much future. Birth in a log cabin was to be a political asset for a long time.

Diffusion of governmental power was showing additional signs of its weaknesses and its advantages. Events had demonstrated the necessity of the Constitution of 1789, with its increased central powers. Once the new national government was erected, conflicts with State governments became inevitable. The subjection of the States to national direction in the federal courts aroused State resentment sufficiently strong to produce the Eleventh Amendment. The States began a long and unhappy education in an obvious and perennially distasteful truth—that man cannot eat his cake and have it, that the American people cannot have the advantages of national strength and well-being without considerable sacrifices of State sovereignty, that an economy national in its nature requires national direction, a truth which became most dramatically evident in 1935 and 1936. Washington's hesitation in 1791 over the bill creating the first Bank of the United States was as significant as his final signature of that measure. National leaders were looking to the past, but were wise enough finally to turn forward.

Faith in constitutional documents continued high; but the years' experience showed that national direction could not all be prescribed

[136] 1 Stat. at Large 347.
[137] "The Migration or Importation of Such Persons as any of the States now existing shall think proper to admit, shall not be prohibited by the Congress prior to the Year one thousand eight hundred and eight, but a Tax or duty may be imposed on such Importation, not exceeding ten dollars for each Person."
[138] See Chapter XI, "Church and State," hereafter.

in a writing. The Supreme Court and the Presidents had found that general propositions formulated in a constitutional instrument did not always decide specific instances; and that some of the most important choices still had to be made under the guidance of general theories of political philosophy and just order. Justice Chase's somewhat pathetic hope that in a very clear case the unconstitutional would appear separate from the constitutional, and except in such cases, unconstitutionality could be disregarded[139] was to be disappointed. Wherever the border might be, there would always be borderline cases. A sufficiently farsighted and wise man might have foreseen most of the coming history of the United States Supreme Court if he thoughtfully read the opinions of its first ten years.

[139] *Hylton* v. U.S. 3 Dallas 171 at 175 (1796).

11. CHURCH AND STATE
BEFORE 1800

IN THE SCHEME OF constitutionalism considered in this book, where is the principle of separation of church and state? The first admonition of the First Amendment is—"Congress shall make no law respecting an establishment of religion or prohibiting the free exercise thereof . . ." In 1948 four Justices of the Supreme Court, concurring with the Court that the Constitution forbids a State to provide religious education in a public school, referred to

> . . . what the Constitution sought to keep strictly apart. 'The great American principle of eternal separation'—Elihu Root's phrase bears repetition—is one of the vital reliances of our Constitutional system for assuring unities among our people stronger than our diversities. We renew our conviction that 'we have staked the very existence of our country on the faith that complete separation between the state and religion is best for the state and best for religion.'[1]

Why then should not separation of church and state, as a sixth constitutional premise, be added to majoritarianism, justice regardless of majorities, equality of men, diffusion of governmental power, and statement of constitutional essentials in a great charter? It might appropriately be so included in 1964, and probably many men would so choose. The Supreme Court has found this principle included in the sweeping generalities of due process and equal protection; it is closely related to the five aspirations heretofore considered. Its origins

[1] Mr. Justice Frankfurter, with whom Justices Jackson, Rutledge and Burton joined, in *Illinois ex rel. McCollum* v. *Board of Education*, 333 U.S. 203, at pages 231 and 232. In accord are *Engel* v. *Vitale*, 370 U.S. 421 (1962) and *School District of Abington Township, Pennsylvania* v. *Schempp; Murray* v. *Curlett, President, Board of School Commissioners of Baltimore City*, 374 U.S. 203 (1963).

and development rightly pertain to an essay on constitutionalism in America.

The idea that in a popularly-controlled polity, religious orthodoxy should be entirely dissociated from governmental authority, did not gain substantial lodgment in American law until late in the development of the thirteen colonies. Lay government is an idea comparatively new in man's thought. When the governors and the great mass of governed believed in supernatural governance, rulers quite reasonably identified themselves with religious observance and discipline. Religious tolerance—sufferance of dissent from an officially established religion—is apt to suggest some uncertainty as to premises, a difficult concession. Most men, by a compelling urge, are driven to correct the mistaken opinions of their misguided fellows.

Submission to such correction was unacceptable to many independent-minded immigrants attracted to America, and to pioneers who live in new country as they pleased.[2] They were apt to resent church government by strangers, much as they resented any rule but their own in any other matter. *Cuius regio eius religio* was true for the New Hampshire Grants and the Ohio country; where a pioneer made the law for his own clearing, he was disposed to decide what his own generation after generation went west from the American seaboard to church would be, or to decide for himself to have no church at all. He was not apt to support any religion reminding him of aristocrats overseas in England. Perhaps he developed some new Protestantism of his own. He cared very little what folk did or believed across the next range of hills.

In the larger settlements where society was more complex, toleration was a difficult enough development; but toleration was easier to conceive than complete abstention from any governmental support for a chosen religion. Occasionally the many tolerated the differing few. Tolerance can derive either from adequate confidence or from sophisticated indifference, both phenomena rare but not entirely unknown. Where a people believe some doctrine with enough assured certainty, make it an accepted part of their daily lives, integrate it in their governing, they may conceivably regard the odd dissenter as a harmless crank, an obviously silly man who can convince no one. By the confidently confirmed he could be suffered as the harmless village idiot was suffered; he could be thought a poor devil whose patent

---

[2] See generally the volumes of F. N. Thorpe, *Federal and State Constitutions, Colonial Charters and other Organic Laws* (7 vols.; Washington: Government Printing Office, 1909). A standard text is Sanford H. Cobb, *Rise of Religious Liberty in the United States* (New York: Macmillan, 1902). See also Anson Phelps Stokes, *Church and State in the United States* (New York: Harper and Brothers, 1950).

error was even faintly amusing but so ridiculous as not to be dangerous. Or, by the bored urbane, an eccentric but tiresome zealot might
be turned away with placating assurance that he almost persuaded his
wearied listener. Either sort of condescending tolerance, rare as it
was, differed *toto caelo* from any idea that government should not
support a religion accepted by everybody but the odd crank. Herbert
Spencer's argument against taxation of the childless to support State
education[3] is tolerated because it persuades no one. We continue to
support public schools. Two centuries ago public support for religion
was at least as obviously desirable.

These two different and relatively novel ideas—religious liberty, and
non-establishment; the injustice of prohibiting the free exercise of one
man's chosen religion, and the impropriety of governmentally encouraging the majority's religion even where dissenting minorities are left
free to worship as they will—these two ideas have had separate histories. Before independence from England they developed at different
rates, in different colonies. Their survivals after the revolution have
developed differently in different States. The literature of controversy
often sweeps them indifferently together; but non-establishment and
free exercise of religion are guaranteed separately in the First Amendment to the Constitution of the United States.

Official toleration of Protestant doctrinal differences was not unknown even in some tidewater areas of English America. Promoters of
new plantations were shrewd enough to see that Quakers, Presbyterians, Hugenots, Dutch, and German reformed Protestants, and
other hardworking, hard-headed men, harassed in Europe for religious
reasons, were highly desirable settlers who could be attracted to
America by promises of land and assurance of religious tolerance.
Still, Protestantism was one thing; "Papistry" another. In times of
trouble with France, lawmakers tended to classify Roman Catholicism
with the enemy, and to attempt to suppress that religion as a species
of sedition. Intermingling of politics and Church in England, with
resulting concomitant variations in governmental and religious policies, had faithful reflections in America. Catholicism achieved alternate toleration and condemnation in some colonies, depending on the
ruling power at home. The story of Church and State is different in
each of the thirteen colonies; facile generalization is tempting but
unwise. One has to look at the American plantations one after another.

Choice of the period between 1789 and 1800 as marking notable
changes in the relations between Church and State, may require some
justification. Perhaps the years between independence and 1800 would
be a more significant span to observe. Before the Fourteenth Amend-

[3] Spencer, *Social Statics* (New York: D. Appleton and Co., 1872) pp. 304 ff.

ment of 1868, Church-State relations were left to State Constitutions and statutes, with the First Amendment coming in 1791 only as a pledge of the federal government's abstention from laws respecting establishment, and as a guarantee against federal limitations of religious freedom. Independence, which occasioned new Constitutions for most of the thirteen late colonies, served to register in the fundamental laws of many of the new States a change in popular attitudes which had already become observable in the last years of the colonies. Some residue of religious establishment continued in certain States of the Union for years after the passage of the First Amendment; a little of it lasted well into the nineteenth century. But independence was a great moment of reappraisal; and while men do not change their attitudes toward government in sudden starts, they sometimes suddenly come to realize changes that have long been occurring, gradually and unobserved.

Massachusetts

Massachusetts in the beginning had the strongest religious establishment in British America.[4] The elemental cell of government was the town. Town meetings regulated church affairs and civil affairs alike, with none of the sense of change men feel today when they turn from political club to parish-house. Town meetings fixed the minister's salary, built him a parsonage, allotted seats in the meeting-house. In theory the congregation and the town may have been different entities, but the same men controlled both, and corporate separation made little difference.[5]

[4] The sources of information on Massachusetts in the mid-seventeenth century are numerous. Here I rely principally on *Records of the Governor and Company of the Massachusetts Bay in New England* edited by Nathaniel B. Shurtleff and printed by the Commonwealth Printer in 1853. These *Records* are chronologically arranged; they offer a vivid account of early governmental institutions, procedures and problems. They are here cited as *Records. The Colonial Laws of Massachusetts*, reprinted from the edition of 1672, with the supplements through 1686 containing also a bibliographical preface and introduction treating of all the printed laws from 1649 to 1686; together with the Body of Liberties of 1641 and the Records of the Court of Assistants, 1641–1644, edited by W. H. Whitmore, Record Commissioner, were published by order of the City Council of Boston in 1890. They are here cited as *Colonial Laws. The Laws and Liberties of Massachusetts*, Reprinted from the Copy of the 1648 Edition in the Henry E. Huntington Library, with an Introduction by Professor Max Farrand" was published by the Harvard University Press in 1929. It contains a photocopied facsimile of *The Book of The General Lauues and Libertyes Concerning the Inhabitants of the Massachusets*, dated 1647 and printed by order of the General Court in 1648. I cite it hereafter as Farrand, *Laws and Liberties*.

[5] Shurtleff, *Records*, p. 172, 3 March, 1635/6; and see Wertenbaker, *The Puritan Oligarchy* (New York: Charles Scribner's Sons, 1947) p. 44.

The royal Charter of 1629 vested the general government of Massachusetts in the Governor, Deputy Governor, a body of eighteen Assistants, and all "freemen" of the colony.[6] These were to meet four times each year in a General Court. To be a freeman, a man had to be a church member. On May 18, 1631, a General Court resolved

> . . . to the end the body of the comõns may be p̃served of honest & good men, it was . . . ordered and agreed that for time to come noe man shalbe admitted to the freedom of this body polliticke, but such as are members of some of the churches within the lymitts of the same[7]

Church membership was not lightly granted. The candidate had to satisfy the minister and elders of the congregation, in a series of interrogations, that his belief, his understanding of doctrine, and his conduct were all suitable, and that he was truly willing to enter the covenant of membership. And he might finally be questioned by the congregation on the floor of the meeting-house.[8] The early statutes of the colony showed the interlacing of ecclesiastical and civil authority. During the later 1630's, successive committees of the General Court undertook drafts of general laws "for the well ordering of this plantation." The one which finally gained approval was the work of Nathaniel Ward of Ipswich, sometime pastor of the church in that Town, who had had training both in divinity and in law. On the record of the General Court for December 10, 1641 Governor Winthrop wrote in his own hand—

> At this Court the bodye of lawes formerly sent forth among the ffreemen, etc, was voted to stand in force.[9]

This compilation is known as the "Body of Liberties." Its preamble is eloquent of the fusion of church and state in early Massachusetts.

> The free fruition of such liberties Immunities and priviledges as humanitie, Civilitie, and Christianitie call for as due to every man in his place and proportion without impeachment and Infringement hath ever bene and ever will be the tranquillitie and Stabilitie of Churches and Commonwealths. And the deniall or deprivall thereof, the disturbance if not the ruine of both.
> We hould it therefore our dutie and safetie whilst we are about the further establishing of this Government to collect and expresse all

[6] Shurtleff, *Records*, pp. 11, 12.

[7] Shurtleff, *Records*, p. 87.

[8] See Wertenbaker, *The Puritan Oligarchy*, pp. 66, 67.

[9] Shurtleff, *Records*, p. 346. Scholars have questioned whether the Body of Liberties of 1641 ever formally became law. See Farrand, *Laws and Liberties*, p. vi.

such freedomes as for present we foresee may concerne us, and our posteritie after us, And to ratify them with our sollemne consent.

We doe therefore this day religiously and unanimously decree and confirme these following Rites, liberties and priviledges concerneing our Churches, and Civill State to be respectively impartiallie and inviolably enjoyed and observed throughout our Jurisdiction for ever.[10]

A General Court held on January 14, 1647 at Boston "published" a revised version of the 1641 Body of Liberties called *The Book of the General Lauues and Libertyes Concerning the Inhabitants of the Massachusets*.[11] Its introductory Epistle was eloquent—

TO OUR BELOVED BRETHREN AND NEIGHBOURS
the Inhabitants of the Massachusets, the
Governour, Assistants and Deputies assembled
in the Generall Court of that Jurisdiction
with grace and peace in our Lord Jesus Christ.

So soon as God had set up Politicall Government among his people Israel hee gave them a body of lawes for judgement both in civil and criminal causes. These were breif and fundamental principles, yet withall so full and comprehensive as out of them clear deductions were to be drawne to all particular cases in future times. For a Common-wealth without lawes is like a Ship without rigging and steeradge. Nor is it sufficient to have principles or fundamentalls, but these are to be drawn out into so many of their deductions as the time and condition of that people may have use of. And it is very unsafe & injurious to the body of the people to put them to learn their duty and libertie from generall rules, nor is it enough to have lawes except they be also just. Therefore among other priviledges which the Lord bestowed upon his peculiar people, these he calls them specially to consider of, that God was neerer to them and their lawes were more righteous then other nations. . . .

For this end about nine years since wee used the help of some of the Elders of our Churches to compose a modell of the Judiciall lawes of Moses with such other cases as might be referred to them, with

[10] Whitmore, ed., *Colonial Laws*, p. 33.

[11] The Records contain no reference to a General Court held between November 1646 and "the 3ᵈ Month," 1647. Farrand, at page xii of the Introduction to his *Laws and Liberties*, states "No record exists of the formal adoption or approval of the new body of laws," but cites a number of Record references in 1648 to the Lawes as having been passed. For many years men of learning in the field of early colonial publications doubted that the Lawes were ever printed. But in 1906 when the library of the Mayor of Rye, England, was sold, a copy of the Lawes was discovered. This is now the Huntington Library copy, used by Professor Farrand. The title page recites that *The Book of the General Lauues and Libertyes* was "published in the General Court held at Boston the fourteenth of the first month Anno 1647."

intent to make use of them in composing our lawes, but not to have them published as the lawes of this Jurisdiction: nor were they voted in Court. For that book intitled *The Liberties &c*: published about seven years since (which conteines also many lawes and orders both for civil & criminal causes, and is commonly (though without ground) reported to be our Fundamentalls that wee owne as established by Authoritie of this Court, and that after three years experience & generall approbation: and accordingly we have inserted them into this volume under the severall heads to which they belong yet not as fundamentalls, for divers of them have since been repealed, or altered, and more may justly be (at least) amended heerafter as further experience shall discover defects or inconveniences for Nihil simul natum et perfectum. . . .

If any of you meet with some law that seemes not to tend to your particular benefit, you must consider that lawes are made with respect to the whole people, and not to each particular person: and obedience to them must be yeilded with respect to the common welfare, not to thy private advantage, and as thou yeildest obedience to the law for common good, but to thy disadvantage; so another must observe some other law for thy good, though to his own damage; thus must we be content to bear ōanothers burden and so fulfill the law of Christ.

That distinction which is put between the Lawes of God and the lawes of men, becomes a snare to many as it is mis-applied in the ordering of their obedience to civil Authoritie; for when the Authoritie is of God and that in way of an Ordinance Rom. 13. 1. and when the administration of it is according to deductions, and rules gathered from the word of God, and the clear light of nature in civil nations, surely there is no humane law that tendeth to common good (according to those principles) but the same is mediately a law of God, and that in way of an Ordinance which all are to submit unto and that for conscience sake. Rom. 13.5.

By order of the Generall Court
INCREASE NOWEL
SECR.

The Lawes and Libertyes were drawn up under alphabetical headings like a modern digest. After "Abilitie" (concerning legal disabilities of persons under twenty-one), "Actions" (having to do with power to make wills and other alienations of lands, and procedure in Court), "Age" (again treating of legal infancy), comes "Ana-Baptists."

Forasmuch as experience hath plentifully & often proved that since the first arising of the Anabaptists about a hundred years past they have been the Incendiaries of Common-wealths & the Infectors of persons in main matters of Religiō, & the Troublers of Churches in most places where they have been, & that they who have held the baptizing of Infants ûlawful, have usually held other errors or heresies together therewith (though as hereticks use to doe they have concealed the same untill they espied a fit advantage and opportunity to vent them by way of question or scruple) and wheras divers of this kinde have since our coming into New-England appeared amongst our selvs, some wherof as others before them have denied the Ordinance of Magistracy, and the lawfulnes of making warre, others the lawfulnes of Magistrates, and their Inspection into any breach of the first Table: which opinions if coñived at by us are like to be increased among us & so necessarily bring guilt upō us, infection, & trouble to the Churches & hazzard to the whole Common-wealth:

It is therefore ordered by this Court and Authorities thereof, that if any person or persons within this Jurisdiction shall either openly condemn or oppose the baptizing of Infants, or goe about secretly to seduce others from the approbation or use thereof, or shal purposely depart the Congregation at the administration of that Ordinance; or shal deny the Ordinance of Magistracy, or their lawfull right or author-itie to make war, or to punish the outward breaches of the first Table, and shal appear to the Court wilfully and obstinately to continue therin, after due meanes of conviction, everie such person or persons shall be sentenced to Banishment.

Under "Capital Lawes" are listed fifteen crimes. The first three are thus defined[12]—

If any man after legal conviction shall HAVE OR WORSHIP any other God, but the LORD GOD: he shall be put to death. *Exod. 22. 20. Deut. 13. 6. & 10. Deut. 17. 2. 6.*

2. If any man or woman be a WITCH, that is, hath or consulteth with a familiar spirit, they shall be put to death. *Exod. 22. 18. Levit. 20. 27. Deut. 18. 10. 11.*

3. If any person within this Jurisdiction whether Christian or Pagan shall wittingly and willingly presume to BLASPHEME the holy Name of God, Father, Son or Holy-Ghost, with direct, express, pre-sumptuous, or high-handed blasphemy, either by wilfull or obstinate denying the true God, or his Creation, or Government of the world: or shall curse God in like manner, or reproach the holy Religion of God as if it were but a politick device to keep ignorant men in awe; or shal utter any other kinde of Blasphemy of the like nature & degree they shall be put to death. *Levit. 24. 15. 16.*

13. Forasmuch as the open contempt of Gods word and Messengers thereof is the desolating sinne of civil States and Churches and that the preaching of the word by those whom God doth send, is the chief ordinary means ordained of God for the converting, edifying and saving the soules of the Elect through the preference and power of the Holy-Ghost, therunto promised: and that the ministry of the word,

---

[12] Farrand, *Laws and Liberties,* p. 5.

is set up by God in his Churches, for those holy ends: and according to the respect or contempt of the same and of those whom God hath set apart for his own work & imployment, the weal or woe of all Christian States is much furthered and promoted; it is therefore ordered and decreed,

That if any christian (so called) within this Jurisdiction shall contemptuously behave himselfe toward the Word preached or the Messengers therof called to dispense the same in any Congregation; when he doth faithfully execute his Service and Office therin, according to the will and word of God, either by interrupting him in his preaching, or by charging him falsely with any errour which he hath not taught in the open face of the Church; or like a son of *Korah* cast upon his true doctrine of himselfe any reproach, to the dishonour of the Lord Jesus who hath sent him to the disparagement of that his holy Ordinance, and making Gods wayes contemptible and ridiculous: that everie such person or persons (whatsoever censure the Church may passe) shall for the first scandall be convented and reproved openly by the Magistrate at some Lecture, and bound to their good behaviour. And if a second time they break forth into the like contemptuous carriages, they shall either pay five pounds to the publick Treasurie; or stand two hours openly upon a block or stool, four foot high on a lecture day with a paper fixed on his breast, written in Capital letters [AN OPEN AND OBSTINATE CONTEMNER OF GODS HOLY ORDINANCES] that others may fear and be ashamed of breaking out into the like wickednes.

A number of provisions were headed "Ecclesiasticall"—

14. It is ordered and decreed by this Court and Authoritie therof; That wheresoeve the ministry of the word is established according to the order of the Gospell throughout this Jurisdiction every person shall duly resort and attend therunto respectively upon the Lords days & upon such publick Fast dayes, & dayes of Thanksgiving as are to be generally kept by the appointmet of Authoritie: & if any person within this Jurisdiction shall without just and necessarie cause withdraw himselfe frō hearing the publick ministry of the word after due meanes of conviction used, he shall forfeit for his absence from everie such publick meeting five shillings. All such offences to be heard and determined by any one Magistrate or more from time to time.

The head "Gaming," although perhaps not germane to church-state relations, is impossible to omit—

Upon complaint of great disorder by the use of the game called Shuffle-board, in houses of common entertainment, wherby much pretious time is spent unfruitfully and much wast of wine and beer occasioned, it is therfore ordered and enacted by the Authoritie of this Court; That no person shall henceforth use the said game of Shuffle-board, in any such house, nor in any other house used as common for such purpose, upon payn for every Keeper of such house to forfeit for every such offence twenty shillings: and for every person playing at the said game in any such house, to forfeit for everie such offence five shillings: Nor shall any person at any time play or game for any monie, or moneyworth upon penalty of forfeiting treble the value therof: one half to the partie informing, the other half to the Treasury. And any Magistrate may hear and determin any offence against this Law . . .

"Heresie" is more relevant—

Although no humane power be Lord over the Faith & Consciences of men, and therfore may not constrein them to believe or profess against their Consciences: yet because such as bring in damnable heresies, tending to the subversion of the Christian Faith, and destruction of the soules of men, ought duly to be restreined from such notorious impiety, it is therfore ordered and decreed by this Court;

That if any Christian within this Jurisdiction shall go about to subvert and destroy the christian Faith and Religion, by broaching or mainteining any damnable heresie; as denying the immortalitie of the Soul, or the resurrection of the body, or any sin to be repented of in the Regenerate, or any evil done by the outward man to be accounted sin: or denying that Christ gave himself a Ransom for our sins, or shal affirm that wee are not justified by his Death and Righteousnes, but by the perfection of our own works; or shall deny the moralitie of the fourth commandment, or shall indeavour to seduce others to any the heresies aforementioned, everie such person continuing obstinate therein after due means of conviction shall be sentenced to Banishment.

To the dismay of the Puritan stock, the New England theocracy's flowering was brief. The very certitude of its righteousness foretold its decline. Its magistrates' conviction that they knew God's judgments and must enforce them on earth can not have convinced the mass of people: ordinary men must have sensed that the ineluctable logic of the Saints was flawed by its premises. In the records of a Quarter-Court held at Boston on January 5, 1643/4, among the usual fines for "being distempered with wine" is a terse and somber entry—

James Brittaine being found guilty of adultery with Mary Latham, he was condemned to death. Mary Latham being found guilty of adultery with James Brittaine, she was condemned to death.[13]

One finds difficulty in believing that such unyielding, righteous sternness seemed just or tolerable to men conscious of their own fallibility. Surely even in 1660 most people must have felt uneasy doubts

[13] Whitmore, ed., *Colonial Laws*, Preface, xlii.

when Mary Dyer and her Quaker brethren were hanged for their stubborn heresy; they must have been relieved when the skeptical and urbane Charles, remarking "Lo, these are my good subjects of New England," sent peremptory word to stiff-necked Governor Endicott that punishment of Quakers was to stop.[14]

The witchcraft trials and executions of 1692, if their tragedy had not obscured their other aspects, would in today's perspective seem most memorable as a reduction of theocratic certainty to the completely logical absurd. Premises no longer went unchallenged in the days of Newton, Locke, and the Royal Society; and while the old belief was proclaimed longer in America than in England,[15] the collapse of witchcraft prosecutions, the contrite confession of error made by Judge Samuel Sewall, all eroded theocratic prestige. The elders of Zion still cried out against sinners while the workers of iniquity boasted themselves. But a generation arose that knew not Joseph, and children born of the Pilgrims forsook their laws and walked not in their judgments. As the eighteenth century replaced the seventeenth the power went out of the Saints.[16] By 1800 there remained only a few remnants of what had been the seventeenth-century government of Puritans. Under the Third Article of the Declaration of Rights of the Massachusetts 1780 Constitution, towns were still authorized to maintain "public Protestant teachers of piety, religion, and morality, in all cases where such provision shall not be made voluntarily"; this provision was not repealed until 1833. Observance of the Lord's Day was nominally compulsory. But another clause of the Constitution of 1780 was an invitation to sad heresy; it declared that ". . . every denomination of Christians demeaning themselves peaceably and as good subjects of the commonwealth, shall be equally under the protection of the law and no subordination of any one sect or denomination to another shall ever be established by law." By the turn of the century the Puritan establishment was a shadow of what it had once been.

New Hampshire

New Hampshire's history has little religious non-freedom. But hers is the last State Constitution to provide for public support of ministers

---

[14] The story is well told in Wertenbaker's *Puritan Oligarchy*, pp. 229–241.

[15] See on this intellectual décalage W. E. H. Lecky, *History of the Rise and Influence of the Spirit of Rationalism in Europe* (2 vols.; rev. ed.; New York: D. Appleton and Co., 1886) I, p. 137 *et seq.*

[16] See Wertenbaker, *The Puritan Oligarchy*, p. 289. Vernon L. Parrington writes of this at the end of the second chapter of the first of his volumes, *Main Currents of American Thought* (New York: Harcourt, Brace and Co., 1930).

of religion. From 1784 to the present time her Constitutions have purported to empower the legislature to authorize—

> . . . the several towns, parishes, bodies-corporatè, or religious societies within this state to make adequate provision at their own expence for the support and maintenance of public protestant teachers of piety, religion and morality; . . .

and have during all that time guaranteed freedom of worship.

Connecticut

Connecticut stems from Massachusetts, but was never as drastically theocratic as her parent. She is principally indebted for her foundation to the Reverend Thomas Hooker, pastor of the Congregational Church in New Towne, later Cambridge, Massachusetts who, in May 1636, seeking a polity more according to his own ideas, a more generous franchise than that in Massachusetts, and better lands for his congregation, led a large group from Cambridge to what is now Hartford, where the newcomers by mutual agreement organized a new Puritan state. In 1662 Charles II granted Connecticut a charter which made her virtually self-governing. The Charter states as "the only and principal End of this Plantation" that "Our said People Inhabitants there may be so religiously, peaceably and civilly governed, as their good Life and orderly Conversation may win and invite the Natives of the Country to the Knowledge and Obedience of the only true God and the Saviour of Mankind, and the Christian Faith . . ."

Charles gave abundant power of self-rule to Connecticut in 1662. Under Charles' charter, during one hundred fifty-six years,[17] the parts of three centuries while it was Connecticut's fundamental law, the colony and State by its internal processes changed from Hooker's godly democracy to a modern State with "equal rights, power and privileges to Christians of every denomination. . . ."

The "General Laws and Liberties of Connecticut Colonie Revised and Published by Order of the General Court Held at Hartford in October 1672," under the topical heading "Ecclesiastical" expressly approved Congregational churches and forbade any "Ministry or Church Administration entertained or attended by the inhabitants of any Plantation" who might dissent from the regime observed by the "approved Minister of the place, except it be by approbation of this Court and Neighbor Churches . . ."

Under the title "Hereticks" the General Court in the same compila-

---

[17] A State Constitution replaced Charles' charter in 1818.

tion first recited, "This Court being sensible of the danger persons are in of being poysoned in their judgments and Principles by Hereticks, whether Quakers, Ranters, Adamites, or such like"; then prescribed fines for the offense of providing "any unnecessary entertainment" for such persons; authorized their imprisonment or deportation; fined "unnecessary discourse" with them or possession of their doctrinal books; and commanded masters of vessels who might bring such Hereticks to Connecticut to take them away again.

Under "Ministers Maintenance" the General Court in 1672 provided for "an Honourable allowance" to every minister, paid by rates "Collected and Levied as other Town Rates."

During the later colonial period the "General Court of Assembly" of Connecticut passed a series of Acts providing for support of ministers and churches; regulating meetings and other affairs of "Societies," (the statutory term for organized local churches); arranging for construction of new churches at taxpayers' expense. Revising the view of dissenters expressed in the legislation of 1672, the General Court passed toleration acts naming non-Congregational sects such as Quakers, Baptists, and members of the Church of England.[18]

Independence did not bring immediate disestablishment. The "Acts and Laws of the State of Connecticut" published in 1784 contains, under "Conscience" a guarantee of freedom of worship to dissenting Christian sects; an exemption from payment of taxes to support the Congregational establishments, apparently extended to ". . . all such Protestant Churches and Congregations as dissent from the Worship and Ministry established as aforesaid"—provided they paid rates to support their own churches. In 1795 the legislature provided a means by which proceeds of the sale of Connecticut lands lying west of Pennsylvania might be devoted to "the support of the Christian ministry or the public worship of God."[19] As late as 1816 the General Court hopefully appropriated whatever sums might be repaid to Connecticut

[18] See e.g. for various enactments concerning Churches "An Act for Preventing and Punishing Prophanations of the Sabbath or Lord's Day," 1721, *Acts and Laws of Connecticut, 1716 to 1749* (reissued in facsimile, 1919) p. 261; "An Act for preventing Disorders in the Worship of God" (1723) *ibid.*, p. 290; "An Act for providing how the Taxes levied on Professors of the Church of England for the Support of the Gospel, shall be disposed of; and for Exempting said Professors, from paying any Taxes, for the Building Meeting-Houses, for the present Established Churches of this Government" (1726) *ibid.*, p. 340. Other statutes concerning religion passed at various times during the second quarter of the century appear, *ibid.*, pp. 366, 372, 381, 433, and 568. Cobb gives a lively narrative with bibliographical footnotes in his *Rise of Religious Liberty in the United States*, pp. 238–290.

[19] Public Statute Laws of the State of Connecticut, Book 1, Title X, Chapter 1, "Appropriation," May 1795.

by the United States for her expenses during the "late war," to be "for the support of Religion and Literature." One-third was to go to "the Presbyterian or Congregational denomination of Christians, to be by them applied for the support of the Gospel in their respective societies, ..."; one-seventh was allotted to the Episcopalians; one-eighth to the Baptists; one-twelfth to the Methodists; one-seventh to Yale; the rest was to remain in the State Treasury.[20] In 1817, by "An Act securing equal rights, powers and privileges to Christians of every denomination in this State"[21] the Connecticut legislature allowed any person wishing to change his denomination of Christians to do so, thereby shifting to his new Church the power to tax him!

The end of the old order in Connecticut came with the new State Constitution of 1818. The third and fourth sections of its Declaration of Rights reads

> The exercise and enjoyment of religious profession and worship, without discrimination, shall forever be free to all persons in this State, provided that the right hereby declared and established shall not be so construed as to excuse acts of licentiousness, or to justify practices inconsistent with the peace and safety of the State.
>
> No preference shall be given by law to any Christian sect or mode of worship.

The Seventh Article of the 1818 Constitution is headed "Of Religion." It provides—

> *Section 1.* It being the duty of all men to worship the Supreme Being, the Great Creator and Preserver of the Universe, and their right to render that worship in the mode most consistent with the dictates of their consciences, no person shall by law be compelled to join or support, nor be classed with, or associated to, any congregation, church, or religious association. But every person now belonging to such congregation, church, or religious association, shall remain a member thereof until he shall have separated himself therefrom in the manner hereinafter provided. And each and every society or denomination of Christians in this State shall have and enjoy the same and equal powers, rights, and privileges; and shall have power and authority to support and maintain the ministers or teachers of their respective denominations, and to build and repair houses for public worship by a tax on members of any such society only, to be laid by a major vote of the legal voters assembled at any society meeting, warned and held according to law, or in any other manner.

[20] Ch. XIII, October Session 1816.
[21] Ch. I, May Session, 1817.

Section 2. If any person shall choose to separate himself from the society or denomination of Christians to which he may belong, and shall leave a written notice thereof with the clerk of such society, he shall thereupon be no longer liable for any future expenses which may be incurred by said society.[22]

Rhode Island

Of all the Anglo-American colonies, Rhode Island, by the work of its founder Roger Williams, achieved the most complete tolerance of religious dissent, the nearest to absolute dissociation of civil power from religious regulation. Williams was born in 1604, probably in London. As a youth he attracted the attention of Sir Edward Coke who helped him get an education at Sutton's Hospital, now Charterhouse School. He went on to Pembroke College, Cambridge, and appears to have taken orders in the Church of England; but Puritanism attracted him and in 1631 he emigrated to Massachusetts. During four troubled years he moved from Boston to Salem, from Salem to Plymouth, and back again to Salem, always in difficulties with the theocracy because of his outspoken insistence that religion was no concern of civil government. In 1635 the General Court of Massachusetts Bay banished him, and to avoid deportation to England he made a hazardous winter journey to what is now Rehoboth, thinking that he had gone outside the boundaries of Plymouth. Warned again by Governor Winslow of that plantation, he moved on south to the shores of Narragansett Bay where in 1636 a few followers joined him in founding Providence. Williams went to England in 1643 and obtained a charter which Parliament confirmed the next year. The 1643 charter made no provision for religion. Perhaps this was a significantly permissive omission, for the first legislative assembly under that charter enacted a code of civil laws which included this clause—

> And otherwise than this (what is herein forbidden) all men may walk as their consciences persuade them, every one in the name of his God.

The statute for its time was extraordinarily tolerant. Its assumption that everyone believed in some God was probably true of most men, and there was no compulsion for the non-believer. This religious freedom in Rhode Island drew strictures from its neighbors, who tended

---

[22] F. N. Thorpe, *Federal and State Constitutions, Colonial Charters and other Organic Laws*, I, pp. 537, 544.

to regard that plantation as a place of refuge for rogues. Williams persisted in his course, however, and in 1662 after the Restoration, presented to Charles II a petition for a new charter. The petition contained a famous clause—

> It is much in our hearts to hold forth a lively experiment, that a most flourishing civil State may stand, and best be maintained, with a full liberty of religious concernments.

Charles, who had his own reasons for favoring tolerance, granted what Williams sought. In his long and detailed charter occurs this clause—

> *And whereas,* in theire humble addresse, they have ffreely declared, that it is much on their hearts (if they may be permitted), to hold forth a livlie experiment, that a most flourishing civill state may stand and best bee maintained, and that among our English subject, with a full libertie in religious concernments; and that pure pietye rightly grounded upon gospell principles, will give the best and greatest security to sovereignetye, and will lay in the hearts of men the strongest obligations to true loyaltye: *Now know yee,* that wee beinge willinge to encourage the hopefull undertakeinge of oure sayd loyall and loveinge subjects, and to secure them in the free exercise and enjoyment of all theire civill and religious rights, appertaining to them, as our loveing subjects; and to preserve unto them that libertye, in the true Christian ffaith and worshipp of God, which they have sought with soe much travaill, and with peaceable myndes, and loyall subjectione to our royall progenitors and ourselves, to enjoye; and because some of the people and inhabitants of the same colonie cannot, in theire private opinions, conform to the publique exercise of religion, according to the litturgy, formes and ceremonyes of the Church of England, or take or subscribe the oaths and articles made and established in that behalfe; and for that the same, by reason of the remote distances of those places, will (as wee hope) bee noe breach of the unitie and unifformitie established in this nation: Have therefore thought ffit, and doe hereby publish, graunt, ordeyne and declare, That our royall will and pleasure is, that noe person within the sayd colonye, at any tyme hereafter, shall bee any wise molested, punished, disquieted, or called in question, for any differences in opinione in matters of religion, and doe not actually disturb the civill peace of our sayd colony; but that all and everye person and persons may, from tyme to tyme, and at all tymes hereafter, freelye and fullye have and enjoye his and theire owne judgments and consciences, in matters of religious concernments, throughout the tract of lande hereafter mentioned; they behaving themselves peaceablie and quietlie, and not useing this libertie to lycentiousnesse and profanenesse, nor to the civill injurye or outward disturbeance of others; any lawe,

statute, or clause, therein contayned, or to bee contayned, usage or custome of this realme, to the contrary hereof, in any wise, notwithstanding.[23]

The charter of 1663 constituted the frame of government of Rhode Island until 1842.[24]

New York

After Charles II had granted to his "dearest brother James, Duke of York" the varied and fortunate principality that still bears James' name, the "Duke's Laws" were promulgated for New York by Governor Nichols and the "Hempstede Convention" made up of delegates from Long Island and Westchester towns.[25] The Duke of York was probably a Roman Catholic. While the Duke's Laws established Protestantism as a State church,[26] they contained this clause, remarkable in its time for inclusive tolerance of all Christians:

> That no Congregation shall be disturbed in their private meetings in the time of prayer preaching or other divine Service. Nor shall any person be molested fined or Imprisoned for differing in Judgment in matters of Religion who profess Christianity.[27]

When James left the throne and William of Orange accepted the English crown[28] (thus for a third time putting New York under a Dutch king) William appointed Henry Sloughter Captain-General and Commander-in-Chief of that Province, and gave him power to make laws "with the consent of our said Councill and Assembly." As might be expected, his laws showed evidences of the political and religious changes in England. On May 13, 1691, the "Governor and Councill and the Representatives mett in general assembly" passed "An Act declaring what are the Rights and Privileges of their Majesties Subjects inhabiting within their Province of New York:" the enactment

[23] Thorpe, *Federal and State Constitutions*, VI, pp. 3212–13.

[24] For the circumstances of change in 1842, see *Luther* v. *Borden*, 7 Howard (U.S.) 1, (1849).

[25] Lincoln, *Constitutional History of New York* (Rochester, N.Y.: Lawyers Cooperative Publishing Co., 1906) I, p. 423. The text of the Duke's Laws appears in *Colonial Laws of New York* (5 vols.; Albany: James B. Lyon, State Printer, 1894) I, p. 6.

[26] *Colonial Laws of New York*, I, p. 24. The Duke's Laws recognized the Dutch antecedents of New York by a provision that no minister should officiate unless ". . . he hath Received Ordination either from some Protestant Bishop, or Minister within some part of his Majesties Dominions or the Dominions of any foreign Prince of the Reformed Religion . . ."

[27] *Colonial Laws of New York*, I, pp. 25–26.

[28] On Feb. 13, 1689.

guaranteed freedom of worship to all Christians, with an exception
relevant to James' unpopular faith and to William's militant Protestantism,

> Always provided that noething herein mentioned or Contained
> shall extend to give Liberty for any persons of the Romish Religion to
> exercise their manor of worshipp Contrary to the Laws and Statutes
> of their Majesties Kingdom of England.[29]

England and her American colonies engaged in war with France most
of the time between 1689 and 1713. In February 1690, a force of
French and Indians sacked and burned Schenectady on the northern
frontier. Jesuit missionaries were preaching and baptizing in the Indian villages of upper New York. Catholicism was French, and the
danger of tolerating a religion politically associated with an enemy
must have grown on the provincial Assembly. On August 9, 1700, that
legislature passed "An Act against Jesuits & popish preists" which
recited

> WHEREAS divers Jesuits preists and popish missionaries have of
> late, come and for Some time have had their residence in the remote
> parts of this Province and other his ma'tys adjacent Colonies, who by
> their wicked and Subtle Insinuations Industriously Labour to Debauch
> Seduce and w'thdraw the Indians from their due obed:ence unto his
> most Sacred ma'ty and to Excite and Stir them up to Sedition Rebellion
> and open Hostility against his ma'tys Goverm't . . .[30]

and ordered every Catholic clergyman to leave the province of New
York on or before November 1, 1700. The Act added that any such
clergyman

> . . . who shall Continue abide remaine or come into this province or
> any part thereof after ye first day of November aforesaid shall be
> deemed and Accounted an incendiary and disturber of the publick
> peace and Safety and an Enemy to the true Christian Religion and
> shal be adjudged to Suffer perpetuall Imprisonm't and if any person
> being So Sentenced and actually Imprisoned shall break prison and
> make his Escape and be afterwards retaken he shall Suffer such paines
> of Death penalties and forfeitures as in Cases of ffelony.[31]

This statute continued in force until the adoption of the first State
Constitution in 1777.

[29] *Colonial Laws of New York*, I, pp. 244–248.

[30] *Colonial Laws of New York*, I, p. 428. One who harbored such an offender was
liable to a fine of two hundred pounds (payable half to an informer) and was
to be set in the pillory "on three severall dayes."

[31] There was an exception in favor of Catholic clergy shipwrecked on the shores
of New York. *Colonial Laws of New York*, I, p. 430.

Meanwhile New York supported the Church of England by rates. Like the other Episcopal churches in the thirteen colonies it was under the jurisdiction of the Bishop of London.[32] This link may have held some colonial members of that Church faithful to the royal side during the differences with England that arose as the eighteenth century advanced, and may well have tended to generate corresponding hostility among American Whigs. The New York Assembly had a Calvinist flavor of religion, which accentuated quarrels with governors identified with the Church of England.

The Reverend Samuel Seabury, in 1774 Rector of St. Peter's in Westchester, was among the ablest and most respected of the Tory controversialists. His pamphlets, published over the pseudonym "A Westchester Farmer," were homely and shrewd, and Seabury's political loyalty brought down on him a hot persecution at the hands of his Whig adversaries. In November 1775, a group of patriots seized him in his schoolroom. Imprisoned in Connecticut for six weeks, he somehow made his way to New York City, and became chaplain of a Loyalist regiment.[33]

When the New York Convention adopted a Constitution, in April 1777, it probably had the political activity of the Loyalist clergy in mind: it included these sections:

> XXXVIII *And Whereas,* We are required, by the benevolent principles of rational liberty, not only to expel civil tyranny, but also to

[32] W. H. Hutton, *The English Church* (New York: Macmillan, 1903) p. 308. If the recitals in statutes may be believed, there was need of some pious encouragement to godliness. On November 3, 1685, the New York Assembly passed three bills (Second General Assembly, First Session, Chapters I, II, and III, *Colonial Laws of New York,* I, pp. 173–5. Chapter I, "against Sabbath Breaking," recites that "The Lord's day is a principall part of the true Service of God which in very many places of this province hath been and now is p'fained and neglected . . . by shooting horsehunting and horseracing rideing on steeds unnecessary hunting and tipling in Alehouses taverns & other publick houses and other unlawful Exercises and pastimes . . ." The second condemns "all prophane swearing and Cursing." The third, perhaps more fundamental than the others, is entitled "A Bill against Drunkennesse." After reciting that "Whereas the Lothsome and Odious Sinne of Drunkennesse is growne into Comon use within this province being the root and foundation of many other Enormous Sinnes as bloodshed stabbing murther swearing fornication Adultery and such like to the Great Dishonour of God and of this province," it imposes a fine of five shillings, or in default of payment, six hours in the stocks.

The effectiveness of this salutary legislation is difficult to measure. Since its enactment horsehunting and riding on steeds have perceptibly diminished in New York.

[33] G. O. Trevelyan, *The American Revolution* (London: Longmans, Green and Co., 1915) II, p. 339. Seabury later became the first Episcopal bishop in the United States.

guard against that spiritual oppression and intolerance wherewith the bigotry and ambition of weak and wicked priests and princes have scourged mankind: this convention doth further, in the name and by the authority of the good people of this state, *Ordain, Determine* and *Declare,* That the free exercise and enjoyment of religious profession and worship without discrimination or preference, shall forever hereafter be allowed within this state to all mankind. *Provided,* That the liberty of conscience hereby granted shall not be so construed as to excuse acts of licentiousness or justify practices inconsistent with the peace or safety of this state.

XXXIX *And Whereas,* the ministers of the gospel are, by their profession, dedicated to the service of God and the cure of souls, and ought not to be diverted from the great duties of their function; therefore, no minister of the gospel, or priest of any denomination whatsoever, shall, at any time hereafter, under any pretence or description whatever, be eligible to or capable of holding, any civil or military office or place within this state.[34]

A New York naturalization statute of April 9, 1782 required the two persons naturalized to have "abjured and renounced all allegiance and subjection to all and every foreign king prince potentate and State in all matters ecclesiastical as well as civil."[35]

On April 20, 1784, the New York legislature passed a law reciting that the pre-revolutionary statutes compelling payment of taxes for the support of the Episcopal church in New York were "contrary to every principle of justice and sound policy," and "the spirit of the said laws are [sic] repugnant to the constitution of this state as tending to establish and maintain a particular denomination of Christians and the ministers thereof . . ."; the statute expressly repealed all colonial laws levying rates for the support of churches, and with them expressly repealed the savage "Act against Jesuits & popish preists" of 1700,[36] already ineffective under the State constitution.

Pennsylvania and Delaware

Pennsylvania and Delaware, at first one entity, became separate only in 1704, and ever thereafter continued much alike in matters of Church and State. Both owe a great debt to William Penn, his Quaker principles, and his friends. Charles II, in 1681, gave Penn letters patent

[34] The disqualification was eliminated in 1846.
[35] N.Y. Laws 5th Sess. 1782, c. 32.
[36] N.Y. Laws 7th Sess. 1784, c. 38.

for this great tract, bounded with the magnificently indefinite generosity of the time.[37] Charles' grant made Penn "the true and absolute
Proprietarie of the Countrey aforesaid, and of all other the premisses . . ."; it left him comparatively free to establish what religious
governance he would. His choice was to make Pennsylvania and Delaware almost as unrestricted in religion as Rhode Island. From 1682
on, the only religious qualification for electors and public officers was
that they be "such as possess faith in Jesus Christ"; toleration was
accorded to "all persons who confess and acknowledge the one Almighty and eternal God to be the Creator, Upholder and Ruler of the
World."[38] Similar provisions as to qualifications of electors appear in
the Pennsylvania State Constitution of 1776.[39] In the Constitutions of
1790 and 1838 the religious qualifications were somewhat diminished—
"that no person who acknowledges the being of a God and a future
state of rewards and punishments, shall, on account of his religious
sentiments, be disqualified to hold any office or place of trust or profit
under this commonwealth."[40]

Delaware, like all the Middle Colonies, had some tendencies toward
the Reformed Church: her leaning can, at least in part, be ascribed to
the early Swedish settlements. Delaware's charter, after her separation
from Pennsylvania in 1704, continued throughout the colonial period
to guarantee freedom of religion and nonestablishment, save for a requirement that officeholders "profess to believe in Jesus Christ the
Saviour of the World." The first State Constitution, adopted in 1776,
required every legislator and every person "appointed to any office or
place of trust" to sign a declaration—

> I, AB, do profess faith in God the Father and in Jesus Christ His only
> Son, and in the Holy Ghost, one God, blessed for evermore; and I do
> acknowledge the holy scriptures of the Old and New Testament to
> be given by divine inspiration.

In 1792 a new Delaware Constitution provided—

> No religious test shall be required as a qualification to any office, or
> public trust, under this State.

[37] William Penn, whose then woodland bears his name, owed his grant to combined royal piety, ambition and gratitude. Charles in his Charter of 1681 recited
as his motives conversion of the Indians, enlargement of the Empire, and reward
to the son of Admiral Penn for the father's "Signall Battell and Victorie fought
and obteyned against the Dutch Fleete, commanded by the Heer Van Opdam,
in the yeare One thousand six hundred and sixty-five."

[38] See Laws Agreed Upon in England &c., 1682, XXXIV and XXXV, Thorpe,
Federal and State Constitutions, V, pp. 3059–3063.

[39] See Thorpe, *ibid.*, 3085.

[40] Thorpe, *Federal and State Constitutions*, V, pp. 3100–3113.

New Jersey

New Jersey, lying between nominally Anglican New York and Quaker-dominated Pennsylvania, showed points of resemblance to both. New Jersey had been first governed—insofar as any wild lands were then governed—by the Dutch of New Amsterdam. After the final English conquest the present State had a somewhat complex colonial career; it was divided into two proprietaries, East and West Jersey, the former settled mainly by English and Scottish Calvinists, the latter by Quakers. In 1702 both proprietors surrendered their rights to the Crown, and save for a brief union with New York, New Jersey has been one polity ever since.

The General Free Assembly of West New Jersey in November 1681 declared that they did "make and constitute these agreements to be as fundamentals to us and our posterity, to be held inviolable . . ."; and included among them unqualified freedom of worship.[41]

The Fundamental Constitutions for the Province of East New Jersey, proclaimed by its "four and twenty Proprietors" in 1683, gave freedom of worship to all "who confess and acknowledge the one Almighty and Eternal God," but also directed that—

> no man shall be admitted a member of the great or common Council, or any other place of publick trust, who shall not profaith [profess faith?] in Christ Jesus . . .[42]

In 1702 Queen Anne received the surrenders of the charters of both Jerseys, and entrusted the governorship of the area, with New York, to Queen Anne's cousin Edward Hyde, Lord Cornbury. His instructions were to permit liberty of conscience to all persons "except papists." Cornbury during his brief and incompetent governorship from 1702 to 1708 had wrangles with Quakers, Presbyterians, and other dissenters in a futile effort to prefer the Church of England. After Cornbury's day the Jerseys had more sporadic religious disputes, until independence ended most of them. The Constitution of 1776 forbade "establishment of any one religious sect in this Province, in preference to another"; but added, with curious unconsciousness of what today appears inconsistent, "that no Protestant inhabitant of this Colony shall be denied the enjoyment of any civil right, merely on account of his religious principles; but that all persons, professing a belief in any Protestant sect, who shall demean themselves peaceably

[41] Thorpe, *Federal and State Constitutions*, V, pp. 2565–2567.
[42] Thorpe, *Federal and State Constitutions*, V, pp. 2579–2580.

under the government, as hereby established, shall be capable of being elected into any office of profit or trust, or being a member of either branch of the Legislature, . . ."[43] This constitutional preference for Protestants remained the law of New Jersey until that State adopted a new Constitution in 1844.

Maryland

Southernmost of the Middle Colonies was Maryland, set up in 1632 under a patent issued by Charles I to Cecil Calvert, the second Lord Baltimore. The new Province was named for Henrietta Maria, Charles' Catholic queen. The Calverts, devout Roman Catholics, hoped that Maryland might become a refuge for their persecuted co-religionists. The 1632 charter was written in Latin; it granted to Lord Baltimore the advowson[44] of all churches to be built, and a license to erect churches, chapels, and oratories and for—

> . . . eaque dedicari et sacrari juxta leges ecclesiasticas Regni nostri Angliae . . .[45]

ambiguous language which anti-Catholic folk in other colonies might well take to mean a requirement for Church of England conformity. Lord Baltimore made clear, however, in appeals for colonizers, that he intended a polity in which all religions would be tolerated. In his first shipload of colonists, less than half were Catholics. The new government, though under control of Catholic leaders, imposed no legal disabilities on Protestants. However, to silence murmurs at what seemed Catholic government, Lord Baltimore displaced a number of Catholic officeholders and appointed Protestants in their places; these measures included removal of Baltimore's brother Leonard Calvert from the governorship and his replacement by a Protestant named Stone. A Toleration Act of 1649 guaranteed freedom to all Christians.

Lord Baltimore's fairness did not placate Protestant extremists. In 1652 a Puritan party, led by two men named Clayborne and Bennett, took forcible possession of the government, and in 1654 passed a measure repealing the Toleration Act and declaring that "None who profess the exercise of the Popish Religion, commonly known by the name of the Roman Catholic Religion, can be protected in this Province." To the surprise of this group Cromwell disallowed the 1654 Act, thus

---

[43] Thorpe, *Federal and State Constitutions*, V, pp. 2597–2598.

[44] Advowson—the right of presentation to a benefice, the right to nominate to a Bishop a candidate for ordination.

[45] Thorpe, *Federal and State Constitutions*, III, p. 1670.

reinstating the previous Toleration Act. But sufferance of all sects drew more Protestant immigrants than Catholics, and Protestant influence continued to increase. In 1675 the government in England ordered that all Provincial offices be staffed with Protestants. William revoked the Calvert charter in 1690 and sent over a Church of England governor named Copley, who summoned an Assembly which promptly established the Church of England with a supporting tax of forty pounds of tobacco levied on every taxable person. The Catholic Baltimores unsuccessfully attempted to get their charter renewed until Benedict Calvert, fourth Lord Baltimore, turned Protestant in 1715 when he came into the title. George I then renewed the Baltimore patent. But zeal was dying out of anti-Catholicism. In 1763, despite a formidable array of anti-Catholic legislation still on the books, Catholics built a church in Baltimore.[46]

The Maryland Constitution of 1776 recited that the "inhabitants of Maryland" were entitled to the Calvert properties. It provided for inclusive tolerance of all Christian religions, and authorized the Legislature, in its discretion, to lay a tax intended for the support of the Christian religion, allowing each taxpayer to direct its disposition—but permitting him if he wished not to support a Church, to designate "the poor in general of any particular county."[47]

The Thirty-Fifth Article is worth quoting.

> That no other test or qualification ought to be required, on admission to any office of trust or profit, than such oath of support and fidelity to this State, and such oath of office, as shall be directed by this Convention, or the Legislature of this State, and a declaration of a belief in the Christian religion.

In the mid-twentieth century this provision in the Maryland Constitution still persisted in a modified form,

> [N]o religious test ought ever to be required as a qualification for any office of profit or trust in this State, other than a declaration of belief in the existence of God. . . .

In 1960 a Marylander named Torcaso wished to be a Notary Public but refused to make the required declaration. He sought a writ of mandamus in the Maryland courts, to require the appropriate official to deliver him his commission,[48] and in 1961 he finally obtained from the Supreme Court of the United States a judgment that—

[46] The Maryland story is vigorously told in Cobb, *Rise of Religious Liberty in the United States*, pp. 362–398.

[47] Thorpe, *Federal and State Constitutions*, III, pp. 1686–90.

[48] *Torcaso* v. *Watkins*, 223 Md. 49 (1960). Mandamus to require delivery of a commission has honorable ancestry. *Marbury* v. *Madison*, 1 Cranch 137 (1803).

. . . neither a State nor the Federal Government can constitutionally force a person 'to profess a belief or disbelief in any religion.' Neither can constitutionally pass laws or impose requirements which aid all religions as against non-believers, and neither can aid those religions based on a belief in the existence of God as against those religions founded on different beliefs.

Much colonial history, many controversies that were still heated when the United States came into being, thus quietly ended with *Torcaso* v. *Watkins*.[49]

Virginia

Virginia had a Church of England establishment from the beginning; maintenance of this State-supported church caused trouble with dissenting Protestants for generations in pioneer areas, where discipline was slight and men were restless. Protestant-Catholic differences added to these complications. Human limitations on religious tolerance were as conspicuous in Virginia as elsewhere, and the French and Indian War aroused Virginians against Catholics, as it aroused the people of other colonies. It produced a Virginia act of 1756 "for Disarming Papists."[50] Among other provisions this law forbade any Catholic to keep a horse worth more than five pounds; perhaps the measure was prompted by fear of a seditious cavalry; perhaps it was mere resentful harassment of men whose allegiance was doubted.[51]

Economics as well as politics influenced the relation of Church to State in Virginia. By act of 1748, a parish clergyman under the Virginia establishment had his annual salary fixed at sixteen thousand pounds of tobacco. At the then current price of sixpence per pound this made a parson passing rich on four hundred pounds a year. But during the next decade crop failures and the expenses of the French war pressed hard on colonial farmers, and in 1758 the Two-Penny Act permitted, during a ten-month period, payment of any tobacco debt at twopence per pound. This cut clerical income by two-thirds; the clergy's indignation was compounded when the tobacco market rose sharply, and vestries staffed by growers continued to tender parish

[49] 367 U.S. 488 (1961).

[50] W. W. Hening, *Statutes at Large; Being a Collection of All the Laws of Virginia* (13 vols.; Philadelphia: Thomas DeSilver, 1823) VII, p. 35.

[51] 1756 may be a significant date. Cromwell, in an earlier war, had won by turning country civilians into ironsided horse-soldiers. For the colonial period generally see Sanford H. Cobb, *The Rise of Religious Liberty in the United States,* an admirable study of early Church-State relations.

salaries at the cut price. A number of ministers sued for their pay at the old rate and one of these suits, brought in 1763 by the Reverend James Maury, came to fame as "The Parsons' Cause." In it the Virginia court held the Two-Penny Act of 1758 invalid because not approved by King George:[52] but when a jury was directed to assess the parson's damages, a country lawyer named Patrick Henry, hitherto unknown, harangued so boldly in favor of the Two-Penny Act, and against a King who would refuse to uphold his distressed subjects' law, that the jurors brought in a verdict of one penny only! The Parsons' Cause may have contributed to popular dislike of tax support for an élite Church; the nominal verdict, eloquent of popular sentiment, foretold disestablishment to come.

Meantime large numbers of Protestant dissenters—Presbyterians, Moravians, Mennonites and Baptists—came to settle in the Virginia frontier country of the Blue Ridge and the hilly west. In the closing 1760's and early 1770's the Baptists for some reason incurred local prosecutions, on such conveniently vague accusations as disturbing the peace,[53] or "preaching the gospel contrary to law,"—this latter a charge which Patrick Henry once rode fifty miles to defend.[54] As late as 1774 Madison wrote to a friend that in one Virginia County there were ". . . not less than five or six well-meaning men in close jail, for publishing their religious sentiments which on the main are very orthodox."[55] But the same forces pressing toward independence from England trended toward disestablishment of England's Church. The Virginia Convention of 1776 which severed political relations from the mother country and set up a State government, also adopted a Declaration of Rights[56] which owed to Madison a clause providing

> That religion, or the duty which we owe to our CREATOR, and the manner of discharging it, can be directed only by reason and conviction, not by force or violence, and therefore all men are equally entitled to the free exercise of religion, according to the dictates of conscience; and that it is the mutual duty of all to practise Christian forbearance, love, and charity, towards each other.

[52] II or III? The argument was equally good or bad as to either George. George III came to the throne in 1760.

[53] Similarly vague accusations of "disturbing the peace," brought against unpopular agitators of another sort, came before the Supreme Court of the United States in 1961 and 1962. See *Garner* v. *Louisiana*, 368 U.S. 157 (1961); *Taylor* v. *Louisiana*, 370 U.S. 154 (1962).

[54] Cobb, *Rise of Religious Liberty in the United States*, p. 113.

[55] William C. Rives, *Life and Times of James Madison* (3 vols.; Boston: Little, Brown and Co., 1859–68) I, p. 44.

[56] Hening, *Statutes at Large*, IX, p. 111; and see *Proceedings of the American Historical Association, 1886–1887*, p. 23.

In 1784 the State legislature repealed all laws favoring what had been the English church.[57] Since that time Virginia has had no chosen State church.

But the idea of general religious establishment dies hard—the theory that the State should impartially support Christian religion generally, without distinction among sects.[58] In 1784, simultaneously with the disestablishment of Episcopalianism, a committee of the Virginia legislature reported favorably a "Bill for Establishing a provision for Teachers of the Christian religion." It prescribed a tax for support of ministers; each ratepayer was to designate the Church which should receive his compulsory payment. Washington, Patrick Henry, R. H. Lee, John Marshall, all favored the bill. Madison and Jefferson opposed it. The bill was printed and widely distributed to test public response,[59] and at George Mason's request, Madison drew, in protest against the measure, his celebrated "Memorial and Remonstrance against Religious Assessments."[60] This document, circulated for signatures, came back to the Virginia legislature so overwhelmingly supported that the bill for tax-supported religious teachers was abandoned. Jefferson had some years before drawn, and Madison now ably advocated, "An Act Establishing Religious Freedom," which became law in October, 1785.[61] Its passage presaged Madison's support in June, 1789 for the First Amendment to the Constitution of the United States.

The Carolinas

The two Carolinas were originally one colony, first settled by emigrants from Virginia, some of them religious nonconformists coming south to escape what they felt were undue restrictions in that colony, and some of them enterprising pioneers who were simply looking for more and better land. The first Carolina charter, granted in 1663,

---

[57] Hening, *Statutes at Large*, XI, pp. 89, 536.

[58] This perennial aspiration has survived for 177 years, and is not yet moribund. See Sutherland, "Establishment According to Engel," 76 *Harv. L. Rev.* 25 (1962) and *School District of Abington* v. *Schempp*, 374 U.S. 203 (1963) at 286.

[59] It is reprinted (from the Washington Papers in the Library of Congress) as the Supplemental Appendix to Mr. Justice Rutledge's dissenting opinion in *Everson* v. *Board of Education*, 330 U.S. 1, at 28 (1947).

[60] Gaillard Hunt, ed., *The Writings of James Madison* (9 vols.; New York: G. P. Putnam's Sons, 1900–1910) II, p. 183. Few papers have had such long respect. It is reprinted as the Appendix to Mr. Justice Rutledge's *Everson* dissent.

[61] Hening, *Statutes at Large*, XII, p. 84. Jefferson had drawn the bill in 1777; it had been reported to the Assembly in 1779. Thus the measure had been pending during six years of controversy. See P. L. Ford, ed., *Writings of Thomas Jefferson* (New York: G. P. Putnam's Sons, 1893) II, pp. 237–239.

created a proprietary government with eight Lords Proprietors, to whom the grant entrusted powers as wide as Maryland's charter gave to Lord Baltimore. Carolina's charter gave to the Lords Proprietors, as Maryland's had given to Lord Baltimore, patronage and advowsons of all churches to be erected, and power to build churches and cause them to be dedicated and consecrated "according to the ecclesiastical laws of our kingdom of England . . ."[62] A subsequent provision gave the Proprietors power to grant religious dispensations to such as could "not in their private opinion, conform to the publick exercise of religion according to the liturgy form and ceremonies of the church of England . . ." Under this proviso the Proprietors at once issued a "Declaration and Proposals," inviting settlers to the new colony and promising religious freedom.[63] In 1665, Charles II issued a new and amended charter with religious provisions like those of the first.[64] In 1669 the Lords Proprietors undertook an extraordinary experiment in political theory by enacting "The Fundamental Constitutions of Carolina."[65] This instrument, they declared, was intended "for the better settlement of the government of the said place, and establishing the interests of the lords proprietors with equality and without confusion; and that the government of this province may be made most agreeable to the monarchy under which we live and of which this province is a part; and that we may avoid erecting a numerous democracy . . ."

The "Fundamental Constitutions" have often been ascribed to John Locke, with some amendments introduced by the Earl of Shaftesbury; other researchers suggest that the proportionate contributions were the opposite.[66] At any rate the Carolinas thus had propounded for their government the most extraordinary system that English America has seen; it reflects a curious political illusion that thousands of hardy men, sufficiently bold and resolute to cut out homesteads in an unsettled wilderness, would tamely submit to a feudal government already obsolete in England. The Proprietors were to suffer disillusion, as did similar magnates later in New York.[67]

[62] W. L. Saunders, ed., Colonial Records of North Carolina (10 vols.; Raleigh: P. M. Hale, State Printer, 1886) I, pp. 20–22. Thorpe, Federal and State Constitutions, V, pp. 2743–2744.

[63] Thorpe, Federal and State Constitutions, V, pp. 2753–55.

[64] Thorpe, Federal and State Constitutions, V, pp. 2761–2771.

[65] Thorpe, Federal and State Constitutions, V, p. 2772. The colonial Carolinas had the benefit of extraordinarily copious constitutional documents.

[66] Compare Thorpe, Federal and State Constitutions, V, p. 2772, fn. A, with Cobb, Rise of Religious Liberty in the United States, p. 119 et seq. Saunders, Colonial Records of North Carolina, I, p. 187, ascribes the Fundamental Constitutions to John Locke.

[67] See A. E. Sutherland, "The Tenantry on the New York Manors," 41 Cornell Law Quarterly 620 (1956).

The Fundamental Constitutions set up the eldest Proprietor as a sort of senior overlord called the "Palatine." The remaining seven Proprietors were to be the principal dignitaries of the Province of Carolina—the Admiral, the Chamberlain, the Chancellor, the Constable, the Chief Justice, the High Steward, and the Treasurer. These "great offices" were to be initially assigned by lot. Beside these grandees, Carolina was to have a hereditary nobility, twelve "landgraves" and twenty-four "caziques." To "the dignity" of each landgrave were "hereditarily and unalterably annexed and settled" four baronies; to that of each cazique, two. Baronies were to have manors, each consisting of not less than three thousand acres, nor more than twelve thousand.

Justice was to be administered in feudal style—

> Sixteen. In every signiory, barony, and manor, the respective lord shall have power, in his own name, to hold court-leet there, for trying of all causes, both civil and criminal; but where it shall concern any person being no inhabitant, vassal, or leet-man of the said signiory, barony, or manor, he upon paying down of forty shillings to the lords proprietors' use, shall have an appeal from the signiory of the barony court to the county court, and from the manor court to the precinct court.[68]

There were to be other courts, civil and criminal. Appeals were available at a price; a man sentenced to hang could have an appeal for a fee of fifty pounds, paid to the Lords Proprietors' use.[69] There were to be no professional lawyers; "It shall be a base and vile thing to plead for money or reward."[70]

The provisions for religious matters deserve quotation.[71]

> Ninety-five. No man shall be permitted to be a freeman of Carolina, or to have any estate or habitation within it, that doth not acknowledge a God; and that God is publicly and solemnly to be worshipped.
>
> Ninety-six. As the country comes to be sufficiently planted and distributed into fit divisions, it shall belong to the parliament to take care for the building of churches, and the public maintenance of divines, to be employed in the exercise of religion, according to the Church of England; which being the only true and orthodox, and the national religion of all the King's dominions, is so also of Carolina; and, there-

---

[68] Thorpe, *Federal and State Constitutions*, V, p. 2774.

[69] Thorpe, *Federal and State Constitutions*, V, p. 2780.

[70] Thorpe, *Federal and State Constitutions*, V, p. 2781. The sentiment is old. Jack Cade in *Henry VI, Pt. 2*, Act IV, Scene 2, proposes to his fellows in the Rising of 1450, "The first thing we do, let's kill all the lawyers."

[71] Thorpe, *Federal and State Constitutions*, V, p. 2783.

fore, it alone shall be allowed to receive public maintenance, by grant of parliament.[a]

[To this article, Thorpe appends the following footnote. "a. This article was not drawn up by Mr. Locke, but inserted by some of the chief of the proprietors, against his judgment; as Mr. Locke himself informed one of his friends, to whom he presented a copy of these constitutions."]

Ninety-seven. But since the natives of that place, who will be concerned in our plantation, are utterly strangers to Christianity, whose idolatry, ignorance, or mistake gives us no right to expel or use them ill; and those who remove from other parts to plant there will unavoidably be of different opinions concerning matters of religion, the liberty whereof they will expect to have allowed them, and it will not be reasonable for us, on this account, to keep them out, that civil peace may be maintained amidst diversity of opinion, and our agreement and compact with all men may be duly and faithfully observed; the violation whereof, upon what pretence soever, cannot be without great offence to Almighty God, and great scandal to the true religion which we profess; and also that Jews, heathens, and other dissenters from the purity of Christian religion may not be scared and kept at a distance from it, but, by having an opportunity of acquainting themselves with the truth and reasonableness of its doctrines, and the peaceableness and inoffensiveness of its professors, may, by good usage and persuasion, and all those convincing methods of gentleness and meekness, suitable to the rules and design of the gospel, be won ever to embrace and unfeignedly receive the truth; therefore, any seven or more persons agreeing in any religion, shall constitute a church or profession, to which they shall give some name, to distinguish it from others.

Ninety-eight. The terms of admittance and communion with any church or profession shall be written in a book, and therein be subscribed by all the members of the said church or profession; which book shall be kept by the public register of the precinct wherein they reside.

Ninety-nine. The time of every one's subscription and admittance shall be dated in the said book or religious record.

One hundred. In terms of communion of every church or profession, these following shall be three; without which no agreement or assembly of men, upon pretence of religion, shall be accounted a church or profession within these rules:

1st. 'That there is a God.'

II. 'That God is publicly to be worshipped.'

III. 'That it is lawful and the duty of every man, being thereunto called by those that govern, to bear witness to truth; and that every church or profession shall, in their terms of communion, set down the external way whereby they witness a truth as in the presence of God, whether it be by laying hands on or kissing the bible, as in the Church of England, or by holding up the hand, or any other sensible way.'

One hundred and one. No person above seventeen years of age shall have any benefit or protection of the law, or be capable of any place of profit or honor, who is not a member of some church or profession, having his name recorded in some one, and but one religious record at once.

One hundred and two. No person of any other church or profession shall disturb or molest any religious assembly.

One hundred and three. No person whatsoever shall speak anything in their religious assembly irreverently or seditiously of the government or governors, or of state matter.

One hundred and four. Any person subscribing the terms of communion, in the record of the said church or profession, before the precinct register, and any five members of the said church or profession, shall be thereby made a member of the said church or profession.

One hundred and five. Any person striking out his own name out of any religious record, or his name being struck out by any officer thereunto authorized by each church or profession respectively, shall cease to be a member of that church or profession.

One hundred and six. No man shall use any reproachful, reviling, or abusive language against any religion of any church or profession; that being the certain way of disturbing the peace, and of hindering the conversion of any to the truth, by engaging them in quarrels and animosities, to the hatred of the professors and that profession which otherwise they might be brought to assent to.

One hundred and seven. Since charity obliges us to wish well to the souls of all men, and religion ought to alter nothing in any man's civil estate or right, it shall be lawful for slaves, as well as others, to enter themselves, and be of what church or profession any of them shall think best, and, therefore, be as fully members as any freeman. But yet no slave shall hereby be exempted from that civil dominion his master hath over him, but be in all things in the same state and condition he was in before.

One hundred and eight. Assemblies, upon what pretence soever of religion, not observing and performing the above said rules, shall not be esteemed as churches, but unlawful meetings, and be punished as other riots.

One hundred and nine. No person whatsoever shall disturb, molest, or persecute another for his speculative opinions in religion, or his way of worship."

The draftsman did not propose to have his ideas distorted or diluted by impertinent glossators; hence his Eightieth Article—

Since multiplicity of comments, as well as of laws, have great inconveniencies, and serve only to obscure and perplex, all manner of comments and expositions on any part of these fundamental constitutions, or on any part of the common or statute laws of Carolina, are absolutely prohibited.

The learned constitutionalist felt, one gathers, that the last word had been said. Locke died in 1704. Probably by then he knew that the Constitutions were to be neither fundamental nor lasting.

The Fundamental Constitutions were, at least formally, put in effect in 1669, when George, Duke of Albemarle, became the first "pallatin" of Carolina and the other Lords Proprietors assumed the Great Offices.[72] But in 1670 when issuing instructions to the "Governor and Councill of Albemarle," the Proprietors recited of their new "forme of government"—

Wee . . . not being able-at present to putt it fully in practise by reason of the want of Landgraves and Cassiques and a sufficient number of people. However intending to come as nigh it as we cann in the present state of affairs in all the Collony of our said Province. . .[73]

Nine years later the Proprietors made the same recital.[74] Feudalism was languishing.

Quakers and other dissenters considerably outnumbered the Church of England party in Carolina, but for a time the adherents of Establishment controlled colonial legislation. In 1704 two Acts of the Carolina Assembly offended dissenters by respectively providing that all legislators must be Church of England communicants, and that an ecclesiastical court of twenty laymen be empowered to regulate all church affairs. On a protest of offended Carolinians, supported by an address of the English Parliament and an opinion of the Attorney General and the Solicitor General, Queen Anne on June 10, 1706 declared the two acts void.[75]

The remaining seventy years of colonial rule in the Carolinas were marked by not very successful efforts of the Established Church in the face of a growing population of dissenters. In 1710 the Proprietors ordered that separate Governors be appointed for North and South Carolina,[76] but the first South Carolina constitutional document in Thorpe's collection is the temporary State Constitution of 1776. North Carolina's State Constitution was adopted in the same year; it declares—

[72] See minutes of a Meeting of the Proprietors, 21st October, 1669, in Saunders, ed., *Colonial Records of North Carolina*, I, p. 179.

[73] Saunders, *Colonial Records of North Carolina*, I, p. 181.

[74] *Ibid.*, p. 235.

[75] Saunders, *Colonial Records of North Carolina*, I, p. 643; see Cobb, *Rise of Religious Liberty in the United States*, p. 125 et seq.

[76] Saunders, *Colonial Records of North Carolina*, I, p. 749.

> That all men have a natural and unalienable right to worship Almighty God according to the dictates of their own consciences.

It provides that "there shall be no establishment of any one religious church or denomination in this State in preference to any other," and forbids taxes for church maintenance; but its Twenty-third Article inconsistently directs—

> That no person, who shall deny the being of God or the truth of the Protestant religion, or the divine authority either of the Old or New Testaments, or who shall hold religious principles incompatible with the freedom and safety of the State, shall be capable of holding any office or place of trust or profit in the civil department within this State.[77]

In 1835 this last provision was amended to omit the Protestant qualification. The Constitution of 1868 disqualified only those "who shall deny the being of Almighty God," and the same provision was carried forward into the Constitution of 1876.

The South Carolina Constitution of 1778[78] was curiously old-fashioned in its religious provisions. Its long Thirty-eighth Article includes this—

> That all persons and religious societies who acknowledge that there is one God, and a future state of rewards and punishments, and that God is publicly to be worshipped, shall be freely tolerated. The Christian Protestant religion shall be deemed, and is hereby constituted and declared to be, the established religion of this State. That all denominations of Christian Protestants in this State, demeaning themselves peaceably and faithfully, shall enjoy equal religious and civil privileges. . .

To be incorporated as a Church declared to be thus established, the members of a Society petitioning for incorporation were required to subscribe to five articles of belief,

> 1st. That there is one eternal God, and a future state of rewards and punishments.
> 2d. That God is publicly to be worshipped.
> 3d. That the Christian religion is the true religion.
> 4th. That the holy scriptures of the Old and New Testaments are of divine inspiration, and are the rule of faith and practice.
> 5th. That it is lawful and the duty of every man being thereunto called by those that govern, to bear witness to the truth."[79]

[77] Thorpe, *Federal and State Constitutions*, V, p. 2793.
[78] Thorpe, *Federal and State Constitutions*, VI, p. 3255.
[79] Thorpe, *Federal and State Constitutions*, VI, p. 3256.

A new Constitution of 1790, however, dropped this provision, retaining only a general guarantee of free worship without discrimination or preference.[80]

Georgia

Of Georgia, last of the thirteen colonies, the story of religion before and after independence is briefly told. James Oglethorpe obtained her charter from George II in 1732, only forty-four years before independence, to encourage colonization, by "many of our poor subjects [who] are through misfortunes and want of employment, reduced to great necessity"—thereby relieving these people, and defending the southern flank of the colonies from Indian incursions. The charter guaranteed "liberty of conscience allowed in the Worship of God, to all persons . . . and that all such persons, except papists, shall have a free exercise of their religion . . ."[81] In 1750 the Crown took over the Colony, and in 1758 the Colonial legislature formally established the Church of England. It made little progress.

Georgia's first State Constitution, of February, 1777, provided that State representatives should possess a modest property qualification and should be Protestants. A new Constitution of 1789 dropped this religious qualifications; it did not reappear in another new Constitution of 1798.

The Territories

Independence brought within our control frontier territories to the north-west and west of the original areas of the thirteen Colonies. In 1787 the Continental Congress in the Ordinance for the Government of the Territory of the United States northwest of the river Ohio" guaranteed in "articles of compact, between the original States and the people and States in the said territory" that "no person . . . shall ever be molested on account of his mode of worship or religious sentiments, in the said territory," adding however that "Religion, morality, and knowledge being necessary to good government and the happiness of mankind, schools and the means of education shall forever be encouraged."[82] In 1790 the Congress extended these "privileges, bene-

[80] Article VII; Thorpe, *Federal and State Constitutions*, VI, p. 3264. The same general guarantees in different words have remained in her Constitution ever since.
[81] Thorpe, *Federal and State Constitutions*, II, pp. 765–773.
[82] Thorpe, *Federal and State Constitutions*, II, pp. 957 ff.

fits and advantages" to the "territory of the United States south of the river Ohio."[83]

Vermont, Kentucky, and Tennessee

In 1777 Vermont constituted herself an independent State, with a Constitution acknowledging the "natural rights, and the other blessings which the Author of existence has bestowed upon man"; adding, "That all men have a natural and unalienable right to worship *Almighty God,* according to the dictates of their own consciences and understanding, regulated by the word of *God*; and that no man ought, or of right can be compelled to attend any religious worship, or erect, or support any place of worship, or maintain any minister, contrary to the dictates of his conscience; nor can any man who professes the protestant religion, be justly deprived or abridged of any civil right, as a citizen, on account of his religious sentiment, or peculiar mode of religious worship, and that no authority can, or ought to be vested in, or assumed by, any power whatsoever, that shall, in any case, interfere with, or in any manner controul, the rights of conscience, in the free exercise of religious worship: nevertheless, every sect or denomination of people ought to observe the Sabbath, or the Lord's day, and keep up, and support, some sort of religious worship, which to them shall seem most agreeable to the revealed will of *God*." Vermont adhered to these rights in a new Constitution of 1786, and, after her admission to the Union in 1791, in a third Constitution of 1793.[84] Kentucky, admitted in 1792, provided in her first Constitution, adopted in that year—

> 3. That all men have a natural and indefeasible right to worship Almighty God according to the dictates of their own consciences; that no man of right can be compelled to attend, erect, or support any place of worship, or to maintain any ministry against his consent; that no human authority can in any case whatever control or interfere with the rights of conscience; and that no preference shall ever be given by law to any religious societies or modes of worship.
> 4. That the civil rights, privileges, or capacities of any citizen shall in no ways be diminished or enlarged on account of his religion.

Tennessee, admitted in 1796, last of the eighteenth century States, provided in her Constitution of that year that,

[83] 1 Stat. at L. 123.
[84] See Thorpe, *Federal and State Constitutions,* VI, pp. 3737–3781.

Section 1. Whereas the ministers of the gospel are, by their professions, dedicated to God and the care of souls, and ought not to be diverted from the great duties of their functions; therefore no minister of the gospel, or priest of any denomination whatever, shall be eligible to a seat in either house of the legislature.

Section 2. No person who denies the being of God, or a future state of rewards and punishments, shall hold any office in the civil department of this State.

adding,

Section 3. That all men have a natural and indefeasible right to worship Almighty God according to the dictates of their own consciences; that no man can of right be compelled to attend, erect, or support any place of worship, or to maintain any ministry against his consent; that no human authority can in any case whatever control or interfere with the rights of conscience; and that no preference shall ever be given by law to any religious establishments or modes of worship.

Section 4. That no religious test shall ever be required as a qualification to any office or public trust under this State.[85]

The ideas of governmentally imposed orthodoxy in religion, and of governmental support for some religious system, both declined notably between the days of James I and the Presidency of Thomas Jefferson, in all the thirteen commonwealths which made up the original United States, and in their early westward projections. Both ideas in various degrees of strength were observable during the seventeenth century in the Puritan colonies of the northeast; in the Middle colonies of Dutch and Quaker antecedents; in the Calverts' Maryland; and in the Anglican colonies from Virginia southward. Rhode Island stood out as a forerunner of today's attitudes of religious dissociation; Pennsylvania was not far behind her. By 1800 imposed orthodoxy and subvention were both reduced to feeble remnants. One seeks the reasons for this dramatic change.

One explanation is the frontier. No matter what theory of a new commonwealth dedicated to a true faith may have inspired this or that group of leaders to seek a charter and lead or send the faithful to American lands, they all found that pioneers are intractable. Here, fundamentally, is the cause of the Revolution and the origin of independence. And in matters of religion men and women who resented dictation in England or in continental Europe and who had the energy and boldness to seek a new home in America, were not likely to submit

[85] See Thorpe, *Federal and State Constitutions*, VI, pp. 3420–3422.

to any religious régime they disliked. The west was too accessible to those with a strong bent of their spirits for new scenes. When Hooker marched from New Towne to Hartford in 1636, he led the way for millions.

But the frontiersman's unwillingness to submit to any dogma he disliked leaves unexplained the underlying attenuation of his religious zeal. One asks why Islam spread so far, in such distant new lands, sustained by such fiery conviction, while Christianity in America divided into a multitude of sects, most becoming somewhat tepid. The frontier explains how people could have what religion they pleased; it does not account for what pleased them.

The historian of European rationalism[86] points, without explaining it, to a similar change in the European intellectual climate—

> During the fierce theological controversies that accompanied and followed the Reformation, while a judicial spirit was as yet unknown, while each party imagined itself the representative of absolute and necessary truth in opposition to absolute and fatal error, and while the fluctuations of belief were usually attributed to direct miraculous agency, it was natural that all the causes of theological changes should have been sought exclusively within the circle of theology. Each theologian imagined that the existence of the opinions he denounced was fully accounted for by the exertions of certain evil-minded men, who had triumphed by means of sophistical arguments, aided by a judicial blindness that had been cast upon the deluded. His own opinions on the other hand, had been sustained or revived by apostles raised for the purpose, illuminated by special inspiration, and triumphing by the force of theological arguments. As long as this point of view continued, the position of the theologian and of the ecclesiastical historian was nearly the same. Each was confined to a single province, and each, recognising a primitive faith as his idea, had to indicate the successive innovations upon its purity. But when towards the close of the eighteenth century the decline of theological passions enabled men to discuss these matters in a calmer spirit, and when increased knowledge produced more comprehensive views, the historical standing-point was materially altered. It was observed that every great change of belief had been preceded by a great change in the intellectual condition of Europe, that the success of any opinion depended much less upon the force of its arguments, or upon the ability of its advocates, than upon the predisposition of society to receive it, and that that predisposition resulted from the intellectual type of the age. As men advance from an imperfect to a higher civilization, they gradually sublimate and refine their creed.

[86] W. E. H. Lecky, *History of the Rise and Influence of the Spirit of Rationalism in Europe,* Introduction.

Whatever the explanation may be, the course of Church-State relations was evident. By the time the independent United States was twenty-four years old, little was left of the once close linkage between religion and government.[87]

[87] In the twentieth century the national government of the United States, speaking through its Supreme Court, has, on a number of occasions, used the Fourteenth Amendment to suppress occasional survivals or petty renewals of State religious activities. See Sutherland, "Due Process and Disestablishment," 62 *Harv. L. Rev.* 1306 (1949) and "Establishment According to Engel," 76 *Harv. L. Rev.* 25 (1962). See also *School District of Abington Township* v. *Schempp*, and *Murray* v. *Curlett*, 374 U.S. 203 (1963); also *Sherbert* v. *Verner*, 374 U.S. 398 (1963).

12. FORECAST THROUGH A CENTURY AND TWO-THIRDS

A SURVEY OF American constitutionalism can not practicably follow either a strict chronology, or a purely conceptual arrangement. A study of the separation of powers from 1789 to 1964 would be interesting, but would then require a new start, say, on the separation of Church and State, during the same span of time. On the other hand, history of constitutional doctrine pronounced in successive presidential administrations, or Chief Justiceships, could become as tantalizing as an adventure story published serially, in which the heroine remains in jeopardy until the next issue of the magazine. Marshall's 1803 opinion in *Marbury* v. *Madison*[1] merely documented the Court's judgment that a petty procedural clause in the Judiciary Act of 1789 was ineffective because it conflicted with the Constitution—a judgment which acquires full significance only with relation to the *Income Tax Case* of 1895[2] and the New Deal decisions in 1935 and 1936.[3] So the plan of this book is chronological but not consistently so. The story leaps forward and back in time, as meets convenience.

All historical eras are arbitrarily defined. They do not in life begin and end as they do in books. But for purposes of this present discussion, the story of constitutionalism in America after 1800 divides, after a fashion, into five periods. The first of these occupies roughly the first half of the nineteenth century, say until 1856. In the judicial history of that time Marshall dominates the scene from 1801 to 1835, but one can give a false perspective by concentrating exclusively on judicial opinions. The temptation to do so derives from the fact that

[1] 1 Cranch 137 (1803).
[2] *Pollock* v. *Farmers' Loan and Trust Co.*, 157 U.S. 429 (1895).
[3] See for one example *United States* v. *Butler*, 297 U.S. 1 (1936).

only Justices have as a continuing official duty the exposition of political theory; and in the instance of John Marshall this temptation is compounded by the intense interest aroused, among today's political philosophers, by his *Marbury* opinion of 1803. But the dominant theme of constitutional development during the first five decades of the last century was increasing growth in the power of the national government, at the expense of State autonomy. This in one form or another appears in many opinions of the Marshall and Taney[4] courts; it appears in the Act of Congress incorporating the second Bank of the United States in 1816;[5] it appears in Andrew Jackson's firm and effective reaction in 1832 against South Carolina's attempt to "nullify" a federal tariff.[6]

The Civil War period, for this book, is the nineteenth century's second conspicuous epoch of constitutional development. It can begin with *Dred Scott's Case* in 1857[7] and end with the adoption of the Fifteenth Amendment in 1870, though obviously the tensions which finally broke into cannonading in 1861 arose before Dred Scott was born, and the effects of the war are felt today.[8] Those thirteen years demonstrated that great issues, essentially moral in character, could prompt us to change our constitutional structure in such a way as to impose the will of the majority of States and people on the minority. Those years gave evidence that as to matters which enough men thought important enough to amend the Constitution, we had come to rely for protection of the individual more on the United States than on our several States. They demonstrated that modern warfare called for central power exercised by a resolute executive; and at the same time showed us that man's freedom is in danger when the nation is aroused to swift, unquestioning action.[9]

---

[4] Roger Brooke Taney, Chief Justice, 1835–1864. See, for examples of such opinions under Marshall and Taney, *Fletcher* v. *Peck*, 6 Cranch 87 (1810) and *Bronson* v. *Kinzie*, 1 Howard 311 (1843).

[5] Act of April 10, 1816, 3 Stat. at L. 266. President Washington had been much concerned about the constitutionality of the Act creating the first Bank; see Act of Feb. 25, 1791, 1 Stat. at L. 191. Mr. Justice Story gives an account of the episode in his *Commentaries on the Constitution* (3 vols.; Boston: Hillard, Gray and Co., 1833) Book III, Chapter XXV.

[6] See Jackson's ringing proclamation in Richardson, *Messages and Papers of the Presidents* (10 vols.; Washington: Government Printing Office, 1896–99) II, p. 640.

[7] *Dred Scott* v. *Sandford*, 19 Howard 393.

[8] Mr. Justice Jackson once wrote of another war ". . . the effects and consequences of war . . . —as permanent as the war debts." See his concurring opinion in *Woods* v. *Miller Co.*, 333 U.S. 138 (1948).

[9] E.g., *Ex parte Milligan*, 4 Wallace 2 (1866).

The six decades between 1870 and 1930 take their dominant constitutional character from the industrialization of what had been a nation of farmers. Of course by the time of the Civil War, Thomas Jefferson's ideal of a race of self-respecting yeomen, each tilling his own modest acreage, had long since given way to other influences. But the last third of the nineteenth century and the first third of the twentieth brought conditions demanding constitutional changes, mostly traceable, immediately or remotely, to the invention and manufacture of larger and larger masses of machines. These in turn made at once necessary and possible greater and greater cities,[10] and greater and greater aggregates of non-governmental power in industrial organizations, which came to acquire something approaching governmental powers of their own, which in turn provoked reaction from non-governmental aggregates of laboring and agricultural people. These latter two, giving a new turn to the old instinct for diffusion of whatever power too concentratedly rules men, united with other groups to procure national and State legislation intended to break up and to regulate the combinations and activities of industrial and transportative power. Despite a number of inhibitory holdings by the Supreme Court, predicated on the theory that the Constitution forbade State and nation unreasonably to restrict private activity, the mass of effective industrial and commercial regulatory legislation on the State and national statute books continued to increase throughout the sixty years beginning in 1870. Much of the constitutional history of that time turns on the felt need for federal rather than State control of the economy. Men saw that if a few States refused to regulate industry as stringently as did most States, the standards of the cheaper production in the few, by a sort of industrial Gresham's Law, would attract the business of the States where industry and commerce were more costly, because more extensively regulated.[11]

The fifteen-year period from 1930 to 1945 brought, at an accelerated rate, constitutional change by judicial action. The first ten of those years were marked by severe economic depression and a fair measure of recovery; the last five were filled with war—at first undeclared, and after December 7, 1941 open and violent. By the time the fifteen years were half over there were left few observable constitutional obstacles in the way of complete federal control of the economy; the distinction between that which was local and that which was

[10] See Arthur M. Schlesinger, *The Rise of the City* (New York: Macmillan, 1933).

[11] Mr. Justice Holmes wrote in 1918, "The national welfare as understood by Congress may require a different attitude within its sphere from that of some self-seeking state." Dissent in *Hammer* v. *Dagenhart* (the "Child Labor Case") 247 U.S. 251 at 281.

national had disappeared; all was within the congressional competence. And whatever limits the Supreme Court might once have imposed on "unreasonable" national and State economic regulation, when
that Court should so find it, and should therefore hold that the
regulation conflicted with the due-process clauses of the Fifth or
Fourteenth Amendments—these inhibitions had now ceased to trouble.
What Professor Corwin called the Constitutional Revolution, Ltd.[12]
was quite complete. During the last five of those years war concen-
trated the power of the Congress and the national executive still
farther. The Constitution entrusts plenary power over foreign affairs
to the central government. In matters of war and diplomacy we are a
unitary nation. By the end of the active war in 1945, only in senti-
mental retrospect and in certain unchanging aspirations did we resemble the thirteen little republics of 1789.

In the years since 1945 the most conspicuous single theme affecting
us constitutionally has been our international involvement. One way
to consider our development ever since the Albany Plan of Union is
to think of us as continually emerging farther and farther from the
localism of an eighteenth-century farm village. We made the Constitution "to form a more perfect union." The first half of the nineteenth
century demonstrated, in many different ways, that the States could
not live to themselves; the Civil War period proved this with the ultimate logic of arms. Then, through the next two generations from 1870
to 1930, we transformed our nation into a single, immense, intricate
mechanism, as interdependent in its essential parts as any other complex machine, requiring for its operation a human organization as intricate as the mechanical aggregate. The fifteen years following 1930
proved, to our satisfaction or pain, that no part of the United States
could get on tolerably while another part was in distress; that we could
neither organize the apparatus of peace nor supply that of war unless
the nation functioned as a reasonably organized whole.

Since 1945 we have found out something very like this respecting
the entire world. Many conspicuous problems of balance between
public power and individual immunities which have arisen in these
years have come from the realization of our people that our national
independence was no longer secure. The difference between wartime
and peacetime organization of the United States has tended to disappear. Alliances of wartime we cultivate in what passes for peace;
and our most conspicuous internal problem—the status of the people
whose ancestors were once slaves—we try to solve not only because a

[12] See Edward S. Corwin, *Constitutional Revolution, Ltd.* (Claremont, California:
Claremont Colleges, 1941).

national conscience has aroused us to do justice, but also because we live in a world most of whose people are not of our domestically most numerous race. We can no longer live to ourselves, without a decent respect to the opinions of mankind.

The rest of this book contemplates our constitutional development through these five eras of the last century and two-thirds.

13. NATIONAL GOVERNMENT AND DECLINE OF STATE INDEPENDENCE: 1800-1856

John Marshall and the Judicial Function

ON JANUARY 20, 1801, President John Adams nominated John Marshall of Virginia as Chief Justice of the United States. He, more than any other one judge, shaped American constitutionalism, and established the judicial branch of the federal government as the steadying influence in the American democratic system.

Marshall's heredity and experience were fortunate for the·judicial duty that later came to him. He was born in what is now Fauquier but was then Prince William County, Virginia, on September 24, 1755, eleven weeks after Braddock's defeat on the Monongahela.[1] Marshall's mother was related to Jeffersons, Lees, Randolphs and Ishams. His father, Thomas Marshall, a friend of Washington, was a land-surveyor who became a member of the Virginia House of Burgesses, and Sheriff of Fauquier County. But John Marshall was born in a log house in the woods; his boyhood was that of a pioneer. His basic education would be thought primitive today. A young Scots deacon, aspiring to appointment as minister at the local established church of which Marshall's father was a vestryman, gave the boy his first schooling. By the time Marshall was twelve he had copied out every word of Pope's "Essay on Man." In 1772 when he was seventeen, his father subscribed to an American edition of Blackstone's Commentaries, and put it in his son's hands. The young man was sent to study for a brief time

---

[1] Albert J. Beveridge's *Life of John Marshall* (4 vols.; Boston: Houghton Mifflin and Co., 1916–19) is the best biography of the Chief Justice.

in a school maintained by the Reverend Archibald Campbell in West-moreland County. This ended his formal education, except for a few months' study of law, in 1780, under George Wythe at William and Mary.

In 1775 Culpeper, Orange, and Fauquier Counties raised a regiment of Minute-Men, in which Thomas Marshall was Major and John Marshall a Lieutenant. At the age of 19 Marshall saw action at Great Bridge, Virginia. Father and son later transferred to a Virginia regiment in the Continental service. Lieutenant Marshall, promoted Captain-Lieutenant, was in the campaigning in Pennsylvania, spent the winter of 1777–78 at Valley Forge, and became "Deputy Judge-Advocate in the Army of the United States." He served at the battle of Monmouth, was promoted full Captain, was in Wayne's forces at the taking of Stony Point on the Hudson, and on August 18, 1779, was in an audacious and successful night raid on a British position at Powles Hook, west of the Hudson opposite New York. The number of enlisted men in State regiments had declined leaving many surplus officers, and John Marshall as one of those was relieved from active duty on December 9, 1779.[2] However he retained his commission until February 12, 1781, when he resigned. Meanwhile in 1780 he attended George Wythe's lectures in law at William and Mary College for about six weeks. On May 18, 1780 he was there elected a member of the parent chapter of Phi Beta Kappa.[3] He left college in June, 1780, and secured in Richmond a license to practice law. On August 28, 1780, he was admitted to the Bar in Fauquier County.

At once he went into politics. In 1782 he was elected a member of the Virginia House of Delegates, and only eleven days later, somewhat to the pique of his elders, he was, by joint ballot of the Senate and House, elected a "Member of the Privy Council or Council of State" (the Governor's cabinet).[4] He resigned from the Council shortly, according to Beveridge because of the jaundiced criticism of those who thought him an upstart.[5] Fauquier County re-elected him to the House of Delegates in 1784. He did not stand in 1785–86; but he returned to the State legislature in 1787.

In 1788 Marshall, then thirty-three years old, was elected a member of the Virginia convention to ratify or reject the new Constitution drafted in Philadelphia the preceding year.[6] Marshall spoke several

---

[2] Beveridge, *Life of John Marshall*, I, p. 143.
[3] In those early times that celebrated society was as much joyous as philosophic.
[4] Beveridge, *Life of John Marshall*, I, pp. 209–210.
[5] *Ibid.*, p. 213.
[6] Beveridge, *Life of John Marshall*, I, p. 364.

times for the Constitution on the floor of the Convention.[7] One argument which he made sounds a little curious in light of *Chisholm* v. *Georgia,* decided five years later;[8] as to

> disputes between a state and the citizens of another state [he hoped] that no gentleman will think that a state will be called at the bar of a Federal court. . . It is not rational to suppose that the Sovereign power should be dragged before a court. The intent is to enable states to recover claims of individuals residing in other states.

After a somewhat bitter struggle the Virginia constitutionalists won by a final majority of only ten votes out of 168 members present and voting.[9] The victory was essential. Virginia had a population over three-fourths of that of all New England, almost double that of Pennsylvania, almost three times that of New York. About three-eighths of the inhabitants were slaves. Virginia had over three-fourths of all the population of the southern States, and over a fifth of the population of the Union.[10] Rejection of the Constitution by Virginia would have been a disaster.

George Washington, elected President under the new Constitution, appointed John Marshall United States Attorney for the District of Virginia.[11] Marshall declined the office, however, as he preferred to keep his seat in the Virginia General Assembly, to which he was re-elected in 1789. He declined to run again in 1791, and only went back into the State legislature in 1795.

In 1793 Citizen Genêt, Minister from the French Republic, began the fostering of privateering based in our ports which so gravely concerned President Washington and later President Adams. In 1794 Marshall, now Brigadier General of the Virginia Militia, commanded a force which kept a pro-French group from taking out of the hands of the United States Marshal the ship *Unicorn,* fitting out as a French privateer at Smithfield near Norfolk.[12] He declined appointment as

[7] *Ibid.,* pp. 408, 409; the speeches are abstracted in Elliot, ed., *Debates in the Several State Conventions* (2nd ed.; 5 vols.; Washington: Elliot, 1836–45) III, pp. 222–36, 419–20, 551–62. Marshall told the Convention that federal judges would hold unconstitutional statutes void, *ibid.,* p. 553.

[8] 2 Dallas 419 (1793).

[9] Beveridge, *Life of John Marshall,* I, p. 403, n. 5.

[10] H. B. Grigsby, *History of the Virginia Federal Convention of 1788* (2 vols.; Richmond: Virginia Historical Society, 1890–91) I, p. 8; Beveridge, *Life of John Marshall,* I, p. 359. Grigsby's figures seem a bit exaggerated when compared with the Bureau of the Census figures for 1790, quoted in Carman and Syrett, *A History of the American People* (2 vols.; New York: Alfred A. Knopf, 1952) I, p. 670. But the fact remains that Virginia was far and away the largest state.

[11] Nov. 23, 1789; Beveridge, *Life of John Marshall,* II, p. 53.

[12] Beveridge, *Life of John Marshall,* II, pp. 104–106.

Attorney-General of the United States in 1795 because of professional duties in Richmond,[13] but accepted election to the Virginia legislature the same year.

At the February, 1796 term Marshall argued his only case in the Supreme Court of the United States—*Ware* v. *Hylton*[14]—in which he unsuccessfully opposed the claims of Ware, the British creditor.[15] His notable argument carried his already eminent Virginia reputation far beyond the boundaries of his own State.[16] At this time he and his brother became investors in some of the Fairfax lands in the "northern neck" of Virginia. For ten years payment of what he owed for the price was a heavy burden.

This debt may have helped induce Marshall in the summer of 1797 to accept from President John Adams appointment and a comparatively generous salary[17] as one of the three envoys sent to France to attempt a friendly settlement of the pending controversies. Marshall and his fellow representatives Pinckney and Gerry were badly received in Paris; go-betweens from Talleyrand suggested that only by a large loan, plus another sum for personal bribery, could the Americans accomplish their aims. Marshall wrote reports of these démarches to Washington; President Adams on April 3, 1798 transmitted them to the Congress, denominating the French intriguers as X, Y, and Z to soften the diplomatic impact.[18] The sturdiness of the American attitude still further increased Marshall's popularity at home, at least with the anti-French Federalist party. He arrived in New York in mid-June 1798, and was warmly received. In September 1798 the President offered him appintment as an Associate Justice of the United States Supreme Court in place of Mr. Justice Wilson who had died. Marshall declined.

In August 1798, George Washington invited Marshall to visit Mount Vernon, and persuaded him, much against his inclination, to stand for the House of Representatives. The Republican movement was strong and the election appeared close. An indorsement from Patrick Henry may have turned the tide in Marshall's favor; when the election was held in April 1799 Marshall was elected by a margin of 108 votes. In May 1800, President Adams offered Marshall appointment as Sec-

[13] *Ibid.*, pp. 122–3.
[14] 3 Dallas 199.
[15] See page 233 above.
[16] Beveridge, *Life of John Marshall*, II, p. 187.
[17] About $14,000 more than his expenses. Beveridge, *Life of John Marshall*, II, p. 372.
[18] Beveridge, *Life of John Marshall*, II, p. 256.

retary of War, which he declined. But he did accept appointment as Secretary of State a little later in the spring of 1800,[19] and was holding that office in the final winter of Adams' administration, when on January 20, 1801 Adams nominated him as Chief Justice of the United States. Seven days later the Senate confirmed the nomination, and on January 31, 1801, as Marshall was still Secretary of State, the President directed Samuel Dexter, Secretary of War, to affix the seal of the United States to Marshall's commission as Chief Justice. He nevertheless continued to do the work of Secretary of State during the remaining days of Adams' administration. On the evening of the third of March Marshall was still sealing commissions of "midnight judges," as the victorious Republicans called them, appointed under the new Judiciary Act of February 13, 1801.[20] But at Thomas Jefferson's request Marshall next day administered the oath of office to the new President of the United States.

Marshall was forty-five years old when he became Chief Justice of the United States.[21] When he died on July 6, 1835, at the age of seventy-nine, he had held that office for thirty-four years—during the last days of the administration of John Adams; during both administrations of Jefferson; during Madison's two terms; during the two terms of Monroe; during John Quincy Adams' one; during all the first term of President Jackson, and most of his second. The Marshall Court wrote all the opinions of the nine volumes of Cranch (1801–1815); of the twelve volumes of Wheaton (1816–1827); and the first nine volumes of Peters (1828–1835). On the Supreme Court when Marshall was appointed Chief sat five associate justices, William Cushing of Massachusetts (1789–1810); William Paterson of New Jersey (1793–1806); Samuel Chase of Maryland (1796–1811); Bushrod Washington of Virginia (1798–1829) and Alfred Moore of North Carolina (1799–1804). Nine associate justices were named during Marshall's term, to replace those who died or resigned. One was appointed to fill the additional seat provided by the statute of February 24, 1807, which raised the number of justices from six to seven. These ten were William Johnson of South Carolina (1804–1834); H. Brockholst Livingston of New York (1806–1823); Thomas Todd of Kentucky (1807–1826); Joseph Story of Massachusetts (1811–1845); Gabriel Duval of Maryland (1811–1835); Smith Thompson of New York (1823–1843); Robert Trimble of Kentucky (1826–1828); John McLean of Ohio

[19] *Ibid.*, p. 489.
[20] See 2 Stat. at L. 89; Beveridge, *Life of John Marshall,* II, p. 560.
[21] He was sworn in on February 4, 1801.

(1829–1861); Henry Baldwin of Pennsylvania (1830–1844); and James M. Wayne of Georgia (1835–1867). When Marshall died in 1835 he was the last remaining member of the 1801 Court.

The connotations of such expressions as the "Marshall Era" or the "Marshall Court" should not be over-extended. During his Chief Justiceship John Marshall was, surely, the most notable judge in the United States, eminent in his leadership of the Supreme Court. But during those years other energetic and determined justices sat with him. Story, Bushrod Washington, and Brockholst Livingston would have been outstanding in any day. Mr. Justice Johnson had "one of the strongest minds in the Court's history."[22] Today men remember Marshall for his governmental opinions, which shaped the first contours of the amorphous powers which the new Constitution granted. But during the first third of the nineteenth century constitutional interpretation occupied a comparatively small part of the Court's time. Most of its reported opinions treat of ordinary civil and criminal litigation; in various ways they reflect the life of a coastal nation, only beginning its penetration of a wide and rich continent. Controversies over the ocean shipping which handled America's heavy transport fill a great part of the law reports of Marshall's time. Salvage, then as now, was a source of litigation.[23] War at sea, embargoes and blockades gave rise to many prize cases. Marshall's first opinion, handed down in August 1801, allowed salvage to the Captain and crew of the U.S.S. *Constitution* for recapturing a French prize.[24] The Embargo Act of 1807 with its amendments[25] and the Non-Intercourse Act of 1809[26] gave rise to a series of cases in the Supreme Court; such litigation continued until that Court had begun to pass on maritime cases arising from the War of 1812.[27]

[22] These words are those of Mr. Justice Frankfurter. See his "Marshall and the Judicial Function," in *Government Under Law*, A. E. Sutherland, ed., (Cambridge, Mass.: Harvard University Press, 1956) p. 13; see also Donald G. Morgan, *Justice William Johnson, the First Dissenter* (Columbia: University of South Carolina Press, 1954).

[23] *Mason and Others* v. *Ship Blaireau*, 2 Cranch 240 (1804).

[24] *Talbot* v. *Seeman*, 1 Cranch 1 (1801).

[25] 2 Stat. at L. 451. Its amendments, and litigation under these statutes, are described in a note, on that and the following pages of Volume 2 of the Statutes at Large.

[26] 2 Stat. at L. 528. Litigation under the non-intercourse laws is described in a note on page 528, 2 Statutes at Large.

[27] See, e.g. The Edward Scott, Claimant, 1 Wheat. 261 (1816), a proceeding against a ship for violating the Non-Intercourse Act by sailing from Savannah for Liverpool on 12 February 1810. The next preceding opinion, in 1 Wheaton, at page 238, is "L'Invincible," a libel for prize of war. *L'Invincible* was a private armed French ship, commissioned as a cruiser. In March 1813, the British Brig of War *La Mutine* captured *L'Invincible*. Later in the same month the American

Privateering was brisk during that war. American armed vessels are said to have taken 1344 prizes.[28] Much litigation ensued,[29] in which curious practices came to light. The war was not popular with everyone in New England, and owners of vessels were sometimes eager to find ways to avoid wartime restrictions. A simple scheme for an American wishing to trade with British merchants was to give his ship the outward appearance of a neutral vessel, entitled by international law to trade where it pleased. Mr. Justice Johnson in the *St. Nicholas*[30] wrote a blistering opinion in 1816 denouncing such an attempt as "a bungling artifice that would not cheat a novice in the arts of commercial evasion." Another scheme for introducing British manufactures into the United States was collusive capture, agreed on by an American privateer and a British shipowner as a means of importation. The United States could frustrate the enterprise by condemning the entire "prize," leaving nothing to divide between the amiable captor and the willing captive.[31]

The unpopularity of the war had a strange manifestation in Massachusetts. Months after the war began, the British consul in Boston was issuing licenses for American ships to pass through the British blockade. When American armed vessels captured ships carrying such documents, and brought them in as prizes, the Supreme Court upheld the seizures.[32]

A curious episode in the War of 1812 concerned the area around Castine, Maine. It was occupied by British forces during the war and their military government collected duties on goods imported into Castine. After the peace, the Supreme Court held that the importers need not pay a second import-duty, this time to the United States.[33]

---

privateer *Alexander* recaptured *L'Invincible*. But on May 10, 1813, a British squadron, composed of *Shannon* and *Tenedos*, frigates, again took *L'Invincible*. Later in that May the American privateer *Young Teazer* recaptured *L'Invincible* and finally took her into Portland, Maine, for adjudication as Prize of War. The *Young Teazer* got half her value as salvage. The French owners got the rest of the value of their optimistically-named vessel.

[28] See J. S. Bassett, *Short History of the United States* (New York: Macmillan, 1923) p. 329.

[29] See, e.g., *The Rapid*, Perry, Master, 8 Cranch 155 (1814); and *The Alexander*, Picket, Master, 8 Cranch 169 (1814).

[30] 1 Wheat. 417. The scheme here was fictitious transfer of the ship to a Russian residing in St. Petersburg, now Petrograd. The cargo was carried in the ownership of a Scotsman-turned-Spaniard then living in Spanish Florida. The opinion is well worth reading.

[31] See *The George*, 1 Wheat. 408 (1816), 2 Wheat. 278 (1817); *Greely* v. *The United States*, 8 Wheat. 257 (1823); *The Experiment*, 8 Wheat. 271 (1823).

[32] See *The Julia*, Luce, Master, 8 Cranch 181 (1814) and *The Aurora*, Pike, Master, 8 Cranch 203 (1814).

[33] *United States* v *Rice*, 4 Wheat. 247 (1819).

The British magnanimously devoted their customs receipts to the foundation of Dalhousie University in Halifax, where the visitor may read the story on a bronze tablet at the foot of the campus flagpole.

The Treaty of Ghent, approved by the Senate on February 15, 1815, ended American privateering against the British; but another type of maritime capture began to appear in the Supreme Court reports. In Central and South America, colonies were revolting against their Spanish and Portuguese masters. Enterprising captains could get letters of marque from revolutionary governments and capture the shipping of the mother-country. Some of the masters of such privateers had oddly Anglo-Saxon names. The schooner *Mangoree,* commissioned by the Supreme Provisional Director of the United Provinces of Rio de la Plata, was commanded by a captain named James Barnes. The *Mangoree* captured a Spanish vessel called the *Divina Pastora* and put "Don Daniel Utley" aboard her as Prize Master. Don Daniel, so he later explained, originally intended to sail his prize to Buenos Aires, via Port-au-Prince, but instead was obliged by stress of weather to take her into New Bedford, Massachusetts. The Spanish Consul at Boston libeled the *Divina Pastora* as unlawfully seized, and obtained an order of restitution in the Massachusetts District Court; the Circuit Court affirmed. Marshall, for the Supreme Court, however, remanded the case for determination of the question of violation of United States neutrality by the captor.[34] On June 21, 1819, after a full hearing, the Circuit Court again restored the *Divina Pastora* and her cargo to her owner, Don Juan Stoughton.[35]

Privateering could be hazardous. A commission, issued by a purported Chief of State, unrecognized by the United States, who called himself "Brigadier of the Mexican Republic and Generalissimo of the Floridas," was not a defense to a charge of piracy in the United States courts.[36] For South American privateering, a ship of war need not be large. In 1827 "a Maryland pilot-boat of sixty or seventy tons" fitted in Baltimore with a gun-port, and a carriage for a single gun, went on a cruise "under the Buenos Aires flag," and was able to take a number of prizes, including one ship and cargo which produced $35,000 for

[34] The *Divina Pastora,* 4 Wheat. 52 (1819).

[35] For this information as to the decree on remand I am indebted to Mr. John A. Canavan, Clerk of the United States District Court of the District of Massachusetts, and to Mr. John H. Shanks, Chief of the Federal Records Center, National Archives and Records Service. More details concerning Captain Barnes of the *Mangoree* are related by Mr. Justice Johnson in the *Bello Corrunes,* 6 Wheat. 152 (1821).

[36] *United States* v. *Klintock,* 5 Wheat. 144 (1820); and see *United States* v. *Pirates,* 5 Wheat. 184 (1820).

the privateer's crew! There was, to be sure, the disadvantage of prose-cution in the United States courts when the ship came in.[37]

The slave trade gave rise to other maritime cases. A series of Acts of Congress, beginning with that of March 22, 1794[38] forbade partici-pation in overseas slave-trading by United States mariners. Successive amendments strengthened the original Act; importation of slaves by any person was forbidden after January 14, 1808;[39] in 1820 Congress declared the overseas slave trade a variety of piracy, and provided the penalty of death for those guilty of it.[40] These various enactments gave rise to much litigation which ultimately reached the Supreme Court.[41]

Domestic slavery furnished some business to that Court. Suits for freedom in State courts presented none of the jurisdictional problems that were to make trouble for Dred Scott; and the Supreme Court sometimes reviewed such cases.[42]

Marine insurance cases illustrate other aspects of maritime trade.[43] Another type of litigation arose out of the activities of commercial agents. Communication was necessarily slow, and the purchase and sale of cargoes required much discretionary authority in distant agents; litigation over their scope of authority was inevitable.[44] Financing of sea-borne commerce gave rise to controversies; difficulties could arise with the letters of credit of that day.[45] The Supreme Court had to study respondentia and bottomry bonds.[46]

All these problems arose in connection with deep-water shipping. River steamboating appears rarely in Marshall's court. Fulton's *Clermont* made its first round trip between Albany and New York

---

[37] See *United States* v. *Quincy*, 6 Peters 445 (1832). For captures in American waters under odd flags, see Gardner W. Allen, *Our Navy and the West Indian Pirates* (Salem, Mass.: The Essex Institute, 1929).

[38] 1 Stat. at L. 347.

[39] Act of March 2, 1807; 2 Stat. at L. 426.

[40] 3 Stat. at L. 701 (1820).

[41] See, e.g., *United States* v. *Schooner Sally of Norfolk*, 2 Cranch 406 (1804); *The Antelope*, 10 Wheat. 66 (1825); *The Josefa Segunda*, 10 Cranch 312 (1825).

[42] See, e.g., *Lagrange* v. *Chouteau*, 4 Peters 287 (1830); see also *Menard* v. *Aspasia*, 5 Peters 505 (1831); *Lee* v. *Lee*, 8 Peters 44 (1834); *M'Cutchen* v. *Marshall*, 8 Peters 220 (1834), *Fenwick* v. *Chapman*, 9 Peters 461 (1835); com-pare *Dred Scott* v. *Sandford*, 19 How. 393 (1857).

[43] See, e.g., *Graves and Barnewall* v. *Boston Marine Insurance Company*, 2 Cranch 419 (1804); *The General Interest Insurance Company*, 12 Wheat. 408 (1827).

[44] See *Lanusse* v. *Barker*, 3 Wheat. 101 (1818).

[45] *Edmondston* v. *Drake and Mitchel*, 4 Peters 724 (1831).

[46] *Conrad* v. *The Atlantic Insurance Company of New York*, 1 Peters 386 (1828); *Conard* v. *Nicoll*, 4 Peters 291 (1830).

City in 1807.[47] Eighteen years later the Steamboat Case[48] finally freed inland naviation from State-granted monopoly.[49] In 1825 the Supreme Court held that the admiralty jurisdiction covered only shipping on tidewater,[50] a position abandoned 26 years later in The Genesee Chief.[51] The American railroads, which fill so many pages of subsequent Supreme Court reports, had their humble beginnings in the 1830's, but never reached Marshall's court.

Despite all this shipping business, great numbers of people in the United States thought of land, rather than cargoes, contracts and credits, as the principal source of wealth. Land was a promising subject of large scale speculation. The Marshall court was much concerned with litigation over great tracts, as settlement spread westward. Conflicting titles to the same acreage, rights of British loyalists to lands claimed under wartime forfeitures, disputed awards for military service, imperfect "entries" of lands granted by the States, and like questions continually occupied the Supreme Court. Such cases occur in every volume of the reports during Marshall's Chief Justiceship.[52] Typically they had to do with lands then or earlier in wild,

[47] See for the development of inland navigation Carman and Syrett, *History of the American People*, I, pp. 469ff.; and Warren, *Supreme Court in United States History* (3 vols.; Boston: Little, Brown and Co., 1922) II, pp. 57ff. Throughout "Warren" here refers to the first edition of 1922 in those volumes.
[48] *Gibbons* v. *Ogden*, 6 Wheat. 448 (1821); 9 Wheat. 1 (1824).
[49] For the log of this litigation during its thirteen years in State and federal courts see Warren, *Supreme Court in United States History*, II, p. 59.
[50] The Steamboat *Thomas Jefferson*, 10 Wheaton 428 (1825).
[51] 12 Howard 443 (1851).
[52] E.g. *Wilson* v. *Mason*, 1 Cranch 45 (1801), Kentucky; *M'Ilvaine* v. *Coxe's Lessee*, 2 Cranch 280 (1804), New Jersey; *Huidekoper's Lessee* v. *Douglass*, 3 Cranch 1 (1805), Pennsylvania; *Shearman* v. *Irvine's Lessee*, 4 Cranch 367 (1808), Georgia; *Bodley* v. *Taylor*, 5 Cranch 191 (1809), Kentucky; *Fletcher* v. *Peck*, 6 Cranch 87 (1810), Georgia; *Fitzsimmons* v. *Ogden*, 7 Cranch 2 (1812), New York; *Fairfax* v. *Hunter's Lessee*, 7 Cranch 603 (1813), Virginia; *Green* v. *Liter*, 8 Cranch 229 (1814), Kentucky; *Meigs* v. *M'Clung's Lessee*, 9 Cranch 11 (1815), North Carolina; *Martin* v. *Hunter's Lessee*, 1 Wheat. 304 (1816), Virginia; *McIver* v. *Regan*, 2 Wheat. 25 (1817), North Carolina/Tennessee; *Jackson ex dem. People of N.Y.* v. *Clarke*, 3 Wheat. 1 (1818), New York; *Burr* v. *Gratz Heirs*, 4 Wheat. 214 (1819), Kentucky; *Stevenson's Heirs* v. *Sullivant*, 5 Wheat. 207 (1820), Virginia; *Prevost* v. *Grtz et al.*, 6 Wheat. 481 (1821), New York; *Miller* v. *Kerr*, 7 Wheat. 1 (1822), Virginia; *Green* v. *Biddle*, 8 Wheat. 1 (1823), Kentucky; *Kirk* v. *Smith ex dem. Penn.*, 9 Wheat. 241 (1824), Pennsylvania; *Elmendorf* v. *Taylor*, 10 Wheat. 152 (1825), Kentucky; *Littlepage* v. *Fowler*, 11 Wheat. 215 (1826), Kentucky; *Henderson* v. *Poindexter's Lessee*, 12 Wheat. 530 (1827), Mississippi Territory; *Ross* v. *Doe ex dem. Barland*, 1 Peters 655 (1828), Mississippi; *Patterson* v. *Jenks*, 2 Peters 216 (1829), Connecticut/Pennsylvania; *Chinoweth* v. *Lessee of Haskell*, 3 Peters 92 (1830), Virginia; *Carver* v. *Jackson ex dem. Astor*, 4 Peters 1 (1830), New York; *Lessee of Clarke* v. *Courtney*, 4 Peters 319 (1831), Virginia; *Lindsey* v. *Lessee of Miller*, 7 Peters 666 (1832), Virginia/Ohio; *Holmes* v. *Trout*, 7 Peters 171 (1833), Kentucky; *United States* v. *Levi*, 8 Peters 479 (1834).

unoccupied frontier districts, originally granted in tracts of vast size.

Marshall's last case confirmed title to the greater part of a tract of 1,200,000 acres of land in Florida, claimed under Creek and Seminole Indian grants, which had been ratified by Spain before she ceded Florida to the United States. In a short statement, the Chief Justice declined to continue the cause to the next term. Mr. Justice Baldwin then delivered the opinion of the Court, upholding the title of one Mitchel to the great tract except for a parcel "appurtenant to the fortress of St. Mark's."[53]

Many other early grants conveyed immense areas. Roger Morris and Mary Philipse his wife forfeited 50,000 acres to the State of New York when they were attainted on October 22, 1779, because of their loyalism during the Revolution.[54] The "Phelps and Gorham Purchase" in western New York covered over two million acres.[55] In *Fitzsimmons* v. *Ogden*, decided in 1812[56] Mr. Justice Washington in his opinion stated, among the material facts of the case, that Robert Morris had bought from Massachusetts four million acres of land in what was then Ontario County in New York; that he had conveyed three million acres of land to the Holland Land Company, and conveyed a half-million acres to trustees for his creditors. Real estate dealers were giants in those days. In 1795 Georgia made a legislative grant of thirty-five million acres[57] to James Gunn and others. The next legislature attempted to revoke this deed for fraud, and so gave rise to *Fletcher* v. *Peck*.[58] The grant of 25,000 North Carolina acres to Major-General Nathaniel Greene for his revolutionary services seems modest enough by the standards of the time.[59] The West and Southwest were disposed of at wholesale, not retail.

Bank litigation fills many pages of the Marshall Court's reports. The first and second Banks of the United States were the most conspicuous corporate litigants before 1835; and the cashier of the Baltimore branch of the second Bank, James W. McCulloch, by circulating unstamped notes of that Bank in defiance of a Maryland statute, gave rise to one of the half-dozen most significant adjudications in the

---

[53] *Mitchel* v. *United States*, 9 Peters 711 (1835).

[54] See Laws of New York, 3d Session, Act of October 22, 1779; Flick, "Loyalism in New York," *Fourteen Studies in History, Economics and Public Law* (New York: Columbia University Press, 1902) pp. 159–60, 216; and *Carver* v. *Jackson*, 4 Peters 1 (1830).

[55] See *Massachusetts* v. *New York*, 271 U.S. 65, 83, 87 (1927).

[56] 7 Cranch 2.

[57] The figure given by Charles Warren, *Supreme Court in United States History*, I, p. 392.

[58] 6 Cranch 87 (1810).

[59] See *Rutherford* v. *Greene's Heirs*, 2 Wheat. 196 (1817).

history of the United States, in which Marshall declared the broad sweep of powers of the national government, and established the immunity of federal instrumentalities from State harassment.[60] James Bradley Thayer and Felix Frankfurter thought that "the conception of the nation which Marshall derived from the Constitution and set forth in *McCulloch* v. *Maryland* is his greatest single judicial performance."[61] State and private banks, as well, were often in court.

Lawsuits over disputed negotiable paper, contracts, suits on surety-bonds of public officers, all sorts of ordinary litigation arising in the District of Columbia, occupied a substantial part of the time of Marshall's court. The reported opinions between 1801 and 1835 picture a growing restless, adventurous, and litigious people, ready to take to court their inevitable and diverse controversies. Construction of the Constitution, and invalidation of federal and State statutes, of which today's student reads so much, occupied a minor part of the time of the Marshall court.

Unconstitutionality of Federal Statutes: Marbury v. Madison

To attempt a description of all the "constitutional" cases of Marshall's era, or of any other period of the nation's history, would require difficult choices. A constitutional question underlies every exercise of national power, and every exercise of State power which may be limited by the powers constitutionally vested in the United States. The indexes to the volumes of reports of 1801–1835 list under the heading Constitutional Law a substantial number of opinions with titles unfamiliar to most constitutionalists in the 1960's. *Slocum* v. *Mayberry* in 1817[62] upheld State court replevin of a cargo from a federal customs officer. *Society for the Propagation of the Gospel in Foreign Parts* v. *New Haven*[63] in 1823 upheld, despite the Revolution, the original title to "gospel lots" in Vermont. *Jackson* v. *Lamphire*[64] in 1830 sustained, despite the Contract Clause,[65] a New York statute facilitating speedy clearing of titles to land. A writer on constitutional theory does well not to attempt to describe every suit with constitutional implications. Exhaustive digests are readily available for any man who may seek to pursue all the reported cases.

[60] *McCulloch* v. *Maryland*, 4 Wheat. 316 (1819).
[61] Frankfurter, "John Marshall and the Judicial Function," in *Government under Law*, A. E. Sutherland, ed., p. 8.
[62] 2 Wheat. 1.
[63] 8 Wheat. 464.
[64] 3 Peters 280.
[65] Art. 1, Section 10.

Of all constitutional opinions delivered since the Supreme Court was created, probably Marshall's *Marbury* v. *Madison*,[66] handed down on February 24, 1803, has aroused more discussion than any other. The court there held that where an Act of Congress is inconsistent with a provision of the Constitution of the United States, courts will give effect to the constitutional provision and disregard the inconsistent statute. The amount of literature concerning *Marbury* v. *Madison* is immense, although to most readers, one supposes, its conclusion seems inevitable. A contrary result should startle. Any judge should surely refuse to enforce a congressional bill of attainder, if one were passed despite the prohibition in Article I, Section 9, such as New York's legislature had passed on Oct. 22, 1779—[67]

AN ACT, for the forfeiture and sale of the estates of persons who have adhered to the enemies of this State, and for declaring the sovereignty of the people of this State in respect to all property within the same.

WHEREAS during the present unjust and cruel war waged by the king of Great Britain against this State, and the other United States of America, divers persons holding or claiming property within this State have voluntarily been adherent to the said king his fleets and armies, enemies to this State and the said other United States, with intent to subvert the government and liberties of this State and the said other United States, and to bring the same in subjection to the crown of Great Britain by reason whereof the said persons have severally justly forfeited all right to the protection of this State and to the benefit of the laws under which said property is held or claimed.

And whereas the public justice and safety of this State absolutely require that the most notorious offenders should be immediately hereby convicted and attainted of the offence aforesaid in order to work a forfeiture of their respective estates and vest the same in the people of this State. *And whereas* the Constitution of this State hath authorized the legislature to pass acts of attainder, for crimes committed before the termination of the present war.

I. Be it therefore enacted by the People of the State of New York represented in Senate and Assembly and it is hereby enacted by the authority of the same, That, John Murray earl of Dunmore formerly governor of the colony of New York; William Tryon, Esq. late governor of the said colony, John Watts, Oliver DeLancey, Hugh Wallace, Henry White, John Harris Cruger, William Axtell and Roger Morris Esquires late members of the council of the said colony; George Duncan Ludlow and Thomas Jones, late justices of the supreme court

[66] 1 Cranch 137, 2 L. Ed. 60 (1803).
[67] See Ch. XXV, *Laws of New York*, Third Session.

of the said colony, John Tabor Kempe, late attorney general of the said colony, William Bayard Robert Bayard and James DeLancey now or late of the city of New York Esquires David Matthews, late mayor of the said city, James Jauncey, George Foliot, Thomas White, William McAdam, Isaac Low, Miles Sherbrooke, Alexander Wallace and John Wetherhead, now or late of the said city merchants, Charles Inglis of the said city, clerk and Margaret his wife; Sir John Johnson late of the county of Tryon, knight and baronet, Guy Johnson, Daniel Claus and John Butler now or late of the said county, Esquires and John Joost Herkemer, now or late of the said county yeoman, Frederick Philipse and James DeLancey now or late of the county of Westchester Esquires, Frederick Philipse (son of Frederick) nor or late of the said county gentleman, David Colden Daniel Kissam the elder, and Gabriel Ludlow now or late of Queens county Esquires, Philip Skeene, now or late of the county of Charlotte Esquire; and Andrew P. Skeene son of the said Philip Skeene and late of Charlotte county Benjamin Seaman and Christopher Billop, now or late of the county of Richmond Esquires, Beverly Robinson, Beverly Robinson the younger and Malcom Morrison now or late of the county of Dutchess Esquires, John Kane now or late of the said county, gentleman, Abraham C. Cuyler now or late of the county of Albany Esquire, Robert Leake, Edward Jessup and Ebenezer Jessup now or late of the said county gentlemen, and Peter Dubois and Thomas H. Barclay now or late of the county of Ulster Esquires, Susannah Robinson, wife to the said Beverly Robinson and Mary Morris wife to the said Roger Morris, John Rapalje of Kings county Esquire; George Muirson, Richard Floyd and Parker Wickham of Suffolk county Esquires, Henry Lloyd the elder late of the State of Massachusetts Bay merchant and Sir Henry Clinton knight be and each of them are hereby severally declared to be *ipso facto* convicted and attainted of the offence aforesaid, and that all and singular the estate both real and personal held or claimed by them the said persons severally and respectively, whether in possession, reversion or remainder, within this State, on the day of the passing of this act, shall be and hereby is declared to be forfeited to, and vested in the people of this State.

II. *And be it further enacted by the authority aforesaid,* That the said several persons hereinbefore particularly named shall be and hereby are declared to be forever banished from this State, and each and every of them who shall at any time hereafter be found in any part of this State, shall be and are hereby adjudged and declared guilty of felony, and shall suffer death as in cases of felony without benefit of clergy. . . .

Surely no judge since the First Amendment took effect in 1791 would have been willing to enforce an act of Congress making it a criminal offense for a Roman Catholic priest to remain in the United States.[68] That Amendment, ratified by expressions of popular will in the States, guarantees free exercise of religion; it would obviously displace any such federal statute under the Supremacy Clause of Article VI.[69]

Perhaps much of the criticism which has been directed at judicial review of federal legislation has arisen because some clauses of the Constitution are not specific but are general statements of aspiration to governmental decency, on the definition of which men's minds are apt to differ. The Fifth Amendment Due Process clause and the Freedom of Speech clause in the First Amendment offer examples. Critics who dislike the outcome of some piece of constitutional litigation may extend to the whole function of judicial review their dislike of the particular judicial application of such an unspecific clause. As late as the 1920's, judicial declaration of unconstitutionality of Acts of Congress was still sometimes condemned as "usurpation." In 1922 the elder Senator LaFollette of Wisconsin told the American Federation of Labor—

> From what source, it may be asked, have the Federal judges derived the supreme power which they now so boldly assert? Not only was such power not given to the judiciary in any Constitution, State or Federal, but the records of the Constitutional Convention show that when it was proposed . . . that judges should have a veto upon acts of Congress, it was decisively defeated on four separate occasions, and at no time received the support of more than three States. . .
>
> There is, therefore, no sanction in the written Constitution of the United States for the power which the courts now assert. They have secured this power only by usurpation. . .[70]

As these present words are written, more than forty years later, the outcry against the institution of judicial review seems to have almost disappeared. It has been replaced by protests at particular court decisions, or lines of decision. Thus on May 26, 1955, Senator Eastland of Mississippi told the Senate—

> Mr. President, yesterday I submitted a resolution asking the Senate to endorse an investigation of the alleged scientific authorities upon which the Supreme Court relied to sustain its decision in the school integration cases of last year. . . .

[68] See for such a statute in colonial New York, the Act of August 9, 1700, *Colonial Laws of New York*, I, p. 428.

[69] "This Constitution and the Laws of the United States which shall be made in Pursuance thereof . . . shall be the supreme Law of the Land."

[70] Speech at Cincinnati, June 21, 1922, reprinted in *Congressional Record*, vol. 62, p. 9077.

Mr. President, in the long legal history of this country, there has never before been a time when an Appellate Court or Supreme Court of the United States relied solely and alone on scientific authority to sustain a legal decision. I am informed that in the long history of British jurisprudence, there has never been a time when the high courts of England have resorted to such dubious authority, but that their decisions have been based on the law.[71]

But even the sharpest critics of various lines of decisions do not often renew the old outcry about "judicial usurpation." Perhaps the long progress toward general acceptance of the judges' constitutional function has now reached its successful end. Some history of this function through the years before its exemplification in *Marbury* v. *Madison*[72] is worth examination.

Today the supremacy of any act of Parliament over adjudication by any British court is taken as established.[73] But see the suggestion of possible exception to this statement for an Act of Parliament which conflicts with the Act of Union between England and Scotland in 1707, put forward in an opinion of Lord Cooper, in MacCormick v. Lord Advocate.[74]

This was not always so. In mediaeval England today's sharp distinction between the legislative and the adjudicating function had not appeared. "Statutes" in feudal times were in the main declaratory of existing custom; they were, as Jenks said of the Leges Barbarorum, "not enactments but records."[75] For the mediaeval thinker the validity of the law had its roots in religion which no human parliament could affect. The notion of a "higher law," essentially religious in its origin, ran through much mediaeval thinking.[76] The "brooding omnipresence" whose existence Holmes denied in his *Jensen* dissent[77] was very real in an Age of Faith. When Coke decided Dr. Bonham's case[78] in

---

[71] *Congressional Record*, vol. 101, pp. 7119–7120.

[72] 1 Cranch 137 (1803).

[73] See Hood Phillips, *The Constitutional Law of Great Britain and the Commonwealth* (London: Sweet and Maxwell, 1952); Holt, C.J. in *City of London* v. *Wood*, 12 Mod. at 687 (1711); *Lee* v. *Bude and Torrington Railway Co.* L.R. 6 C.P. 576 (1871).

[74] 1953 Session Cases 369, 411. And see J. D. B. Mitchell, *Constitutional Law* (Edinburgh: Green and Son, Ltd., 1964).

[75] See Jenks, *Law and Politics in the Middle Ages* (2nd ed.; London: J. Murray and Co., 1913) p. 61 and C. H. McIlwain, *The High Court of Parliament and Its Supremacy* (New Haven: Yale University Press, 1910) *passim*.

[76] See Corwin "The Higher Law Background of American Constitutional Law," 42 *Harvard Law Review* 149, 365 (1928–29).

[77] "The common law is not a brooding omnipresence in the sky but the articulate voice of some sovereign that can be identified. . . ." See *Southern Pacific Co.* v. *Jensen*, 244 U.S. 205, 222 (1917).

[78] 8 Rep. 118a. See page 61 above.

1610 he was expressing a theory then already outdated but which had had much vitality in the past of English law. Predominance of "common right and reason," as understood by the judges, over an Act of Parliament lacking in these qualities, was easier for Coke's contemporaries to understand than for his present-day successors.

Bonham's case became a conspicuous theoretical source of the American notion of "judicial review."[79] The wide influence of Blackstone's Commentaries in America has often been mentioned.[80] Of the law of nature Blackstone wrote ". . . no human laws are of any validity, if contrary to this. . . ."[81] In 1761 reliance on the theory of Bonham's case as a precedent for actual decision would have been long outdated in England; but in that year James Otis made an immense impression by his famous argument in Massachusetts in the Writs of Assistance Case, in which he cited Coke's Bonham case of a century and a half before.[82]

Judicial review by the Supreme Court of the United States also found support in the practice of the Privy Council in reviewing Colonial legislation.[83] An Act of Parliament, as a senior statute, prevailed over junior enactments. An Englishman today finds no surprise in a judgment that a municipal by-law which conflicts with an Act of Parliament has no validity.[84] He should find little to wonder at in the theory of predominance of the Constitution of the United States. The Constitution is a composite enactment by what might be thought of as a Great Parliament, an aggregate legislature made up of the original Convention, of the Congress, of State ratifying conventions and, later, of ratifying State legislatures. Such a Great Parliament is much more widely representative than the Congress, and there appears no theoretical difficulty in holding its enactments senior to ordinary Congressional acts.

[79] See Corwin, op. cit.

[80] See, e.g., Burke's Speech on Conciliation with America, in Burke's Speeches and Letters on American Affairs, Ernest Rhys, ed. (London: J. M. Dent and Sons, 1908) pp. 76–141.

[81] Commentaries (Oxford: Clarendon Press, 1768) I, p. 41.

[82] See page 126, above.

[83] See page 127, above, and see Thayer, "Origin and Scope of the American Doctrine of Constitutional Law," 7 Harv. L. Rev. 129 (1893), reprinted in Thayer, Legal Essays (Boston: Boston Book Co., 1908) I, pp. 1–41; McGovney, "The British Origin of Judicial Review of Legislation," 93 U. Pa. L. Rev. 1 (1944); J. H. Smith, Appeals to the Privy Council from the American Plantations (New York: Columbia University Press, 1950).

[84] See the discussion "Parliament and Subordinate Law Making Bodies" in Hood Phillips' The Constitutional Law of Great Britain and the Commonwealth, p. 51. I hesitate here to venture into the complex matter of the relation of Acts of Parliament to other legislative bodies in the Commonwealth. Hood Phillips discusses the matter at the point cited.

State courts had held State statutes invalid as "unconstitutional" during the Confederation either under a State Constitution or a treaty having predominance under the foreign-affairs competence of the federal government under the Articles of Confederation. Such a case was *Trevett* v. *Weeden,* decided in 1786 by the Supreme Court of Judicature of Rhode Island, in which that court held that a Rhode Island statute requiring acceptance of State paper currency as the equivalent of silver and gold was "repugnant and unconstitutional," or, according to another version, "unjust and unconstitutional.[85] Another case was *Den d. Bayard and Wife* v. *Singleton,* decided in 1787 by the Court of Conference of North Carolina,[86] in which the then highest court of that State held unconstitutional a State statute cutting off a right to jury trial in cases involving Loyalists' confiscated estates. The North Carolina Court's opinion is not explicit as to what constitutional provision it had in mind: possibly it was relying on the inconsistency, under the Articles of Confederation, between the statute forfeiting Loyalist estates and the Treaty with Great Britain of 1783.[87]

Great constitutional cases are apt to arise from profound differences of policy or politics; *Marbury* v. *Madison*[88] exemplifies this. The Federalist party, although defeated in the 1800 election, remained in control of the Congress during the "lame duck" session of the winter of 1801. The Federalists regarded themselves as the wise defenders of sound government; and by an Act of 13 February, 1801,[89] they undertook, in order "to provide for the more convenient organization of the courts of the United States," to create sixteen circuit judgeships, to relieve the Justices of the Supreme Court of the burdens of circuit duty, and to reduce the Supreme Court from six to five Justices when the next seat should fall vacant. On its merits this was a useful statute, whose principal feature, creation of Circuit Judgeships, has long been accepted; but it struck the Jeffersonian party as a political device to harass the prevailing Republicans by appointment of constitutionally irremovable federalist judges. Jefferson felt, perhaps with some color of right, that the Federalists had retired into the judiciary

[85] See page 165, above; and see Thayer, *Cases on Constitutional Law* (Cambridge, Mass.: George H. Kent, 1895) I, p. 73. *Trevett* v. *Weeden* is also reported in a pamphlet by James M. Varnum, Providence, John Carter, 1787; an account of the case appears in 2 Chandler's Crim. Tr. 269.

[86] 1 Martin N.C. 42; cf. Thayer, *Cases on Constitutional Law,* I, p. 78.

[87] See generally James B. Thayer, "The Origin and Scope of the American Doctrine of Constitutional Law" 7 *Harv. L. Rev.* 129 (1893); Thayer, *Legal Essays,* I, pp. 1–41.

[88] 1 Cranch 137 (1803).

[89] 2 Stat. at L. 89.

as a stronghold and planned from that battery to fire on the works of republicanism.[90]

On February 27, 1801, five days before Thomas Jefferson was to become President, there became law an organic Act for the District of Columbia, which, among other things, authorized appointment of "such number of discreet persons to be justices of the peace, as the President of the United States shall from time to time think expedient, to continue in office five years . . ."[91] President Adams hastened to nominate forty-two justices of the peace; the Senate confirmed; Adams signed their commissions. John Marshall, acting as Secretary of State in addition to his Chief Justiceship, sealed the commissions; but in the rush of final business on the evening of March 3, at least four of the commissions were never delivered. Angry Republicans coined the name "midnight judges" for these eleventh-hour appointees. It was a catchy phrase, and perhaps gave rise to the apocryphal story that at midnight Jefferson's Attorney-General-to-be, Levi Lincoln, with the new President's watch in his hand, went to Marshall's room where Marshall was still hurriedly sealing commissions. Lincoln dramatically pointed to the hour, announcing that by the President's watch the fourth of March had come and Marshall was to stop affixing the seal. Marshall, so the story ran, left in humiliation.

At any rate, President Jefferson amicably gave new appointments to twenty-five of Adams' justices of the peace; but the commissions of Marbury and three others, though signed and sealed, were undelivered. Their status was thus debatable. They moved at the December, 1801, term of the Supreme Court of the United States, for a rule to require Secretary of State Madison to show cause why *mandamus* should not issue from that Court, requiring the Secretary of State to deliver the petitioners' commissions. The Court issued an order requiring Madison to answer at the next term.

The next term turned out to be that of February, 1803! During the first two months of 1802, repeal of the Judiciary Act of 1801 was vigorously debated in the Senate and House, now controlled by the Jeffersonian Republican party. During that debate there was much discussion of the pending *Marbury* v. *Madison* and the power of the courts to declare Acts of Congress unconstitutional.[92] A burning question was the propriety, or lack of it, of a *mandamus* order issued to a cabinet officer.[93] On March 8, 1802, the Judiciary Act of 1801 was

[90] See Warren, *Supreme Court in United States History,* I, p. 193.
[91] 2 Stat. at L. 103.
[92] Beveridge, *Life of John Marshall,* III, p. 82.
[93] Beveridge, *Life of John Marshall,* III, pp. 78, 90.

repealed;[94] on April 29, 1802 the President approved a new Judiciary Act.[95] The Act of 1801 had provided for terms of the Supreme Court to be held in December and June and under that act the Supreme Court's order to Madison issued in December 1801 would have been returnable at the next term of Court in June 1802. But the new Judiciary Act of April 29, 1802 provided that the Supreme Court should convene only once each year, on the first Monday in February. Under this new statute the earliest term of the Supreme Court after April, 1802 was held in February, 1803.[96]

When the case was then called for hearing Madison entirely ignored the Court's order of December 1801, probably to assert his independence of its process. Levi Lincoln, Jefferson's Attorney-General, appeared only as a subpoenaed witness. He objected that "He did not think himself bound to disclose his official transactions while acting as Secretary of State," which he was at the time of some of the transactions in question. Furthermore, Lincoln said he "ought not to be compelled to answer any thing which might tend to criminate himself." After a night's consideration Lincoln testified that "He had no hesitation in saying that he did not know that they [the commissions] ever came to the possession of Mr. Madison, nor did he know that they were in the office when Mr. Madison took possession of it."[97] The Court ruled immaterial in the case against Madison further testimony as to what became of the commissions.

If the Supreme Court should command Madison to deliver the commissions, and Madison should refuse (as was certainly possible) there would be no practicable way to commit the Secretary of State for contempt. The Supreme Court would be a laughing-stock of the Jeffersonians. On the other hand if the Supreme Court should dismiss the case, the Republican doctrines that federal courts could not direct the executive branch to obey laws, and that the judges could not properly declare laws invalid as unconstitutional, would stand as accepted—at least in popular esteem. But the unanimous Court,[98] in an opinion delivered by the Chief Justice, first found that Marbury had acquired a right to the commission and to the office for five years, regardless of executive nondelivery, as soon as his commission had been signed by the President and sealed by the Secretary of State. The Court then found that *mandamus* against the Secretary of State

---

[94] 2 Stat. at L., 1802, effective July 1, 1802.
[95] See Beveridge, *Life of John Marshall*, III, p. 97. 2 Stat. at L. 156.
[96] For the constitutionality of the statutes of March 8 and April 29, 1802 which had been debated in the Congress, see Beveridge, *Life of John Marshall*, III, p. 91, and *Stuart* v. *Laird*, 1 Cranch 299 (1803).
[97] 1 Cranch 144.
[98] Marshall, Paterson, Cushing, Chase, Moore, and Washington, J.J.

was the proper remedy in the present case, where that Secretary was not exercising a discretionary power on the President's behalf but, as in the case at bar, was carrying out a clear duty on which the right of Mr. Marbury depended. And the Judiciary Act of 1789 empowered the Supreme Court to issue writs of *mandamus:* if the Court were to follow the Statute it would be required to order Secretary Madison to deliver the commission to Marbury. Thus if the Act of Congress was effective, the order ought to issue. But, the Court went on, the provisions of Article III give the Supreme Court original jurisdiction only over cases affecting ambassadors, other public ministers, and consuls, and over cases in which a State was a party. A statute attempting to confer original jurisdiction here for a *mandamus* to the Secretary of State was in clear conflict with this provision, and so invalid as unconstitutional. Rejecting the theory that collision between a statute and the Constitution was not judicially examinable, Marshall pointed to the prohibition against a federal tax on articles exported from a State.[99] Should the Court nevertheless enforce such a tax? The Constitution forbids a federal bill of attainder or ex post facto law.[100] Should a court, under such a law, "condemn to death those victims whom the Constitution endeavors to preserve"? If the legislature should declare one witness to an overt act, or a confession out of court, sufficient for a conviction of treason,[101] "must the constitutional principle yield to the legislative act?" The judge takes an oath to support the Constitution: if he is to decide cases in disregard of the Constitution, why the oath? In the Supremacy Clause[102] the Constitution, and "the Laws of the United States which shall be made in Pursuance thereof"—not federal laws, generally—are made the supreme law of the land. So the rule was discharged—that is, Secretary Madison was excused from answering the *mandamus.* Marbury had no order for the delivery of his commission; but he had had a part in establishing the most discussed doctrine of American constitutional law.

The "Mandamus Case," as it was often called in its time, was not a constitutional novelty, even under the 1789 Constitution. *Marbury* v. *Madison* was apparently not the first case in which the Supreme Court of the United States held a statute unconstitutional. In *U.S.* v. *Todd,* decided in 1794, reported only in a note to *United States* v. *Ferreira,*[103]

---

[99] Art. I § 9 Cl. 5.
[100] Art. I § 9 Cl. 3.
[101] Art. III § 3 Cl. 1.
[102] Art. VI, Cl. 2.
[103] 13 How. 40 (1851). Early reporting of opinions was a bit haphazard. See, for *U.S.* v. *Yale Todd,* p. 261 above. Marshall, in the Marbury opinion, does not cite this case by name but clearly refers to it. See 1 Cranch 171, 172.

the Supreme Court had held invalid a federal statute of 1792 which purported to impose on the Circuit Courts a non-judicial duty to certify pension claims. Marshall, in his Marbury opinion, refers to the pension controversy as a precedent.

The *Federalist* had recognized the power of the federal courts to reject statutes when they were inconsistent with the Constitution. Hamilton wrote in No. 78, in 1788—

> The interpretation of the laws is the proper and peculiar province of the courts. A constitution is, in fact, and must be regarded by the judges, as a fundamental law. It therefore belongs to them to ascertain its meaning, as well as the meaning of any particular act proceeding from the legislative body. If there should happen to be an irreconcilable variance between the two, that which has the superior obligation and validity ought, of course, to be preferred; or, in other words, the Constitution ought to be preferred to the statute, the intention of the people to the intention of their agents.[104]

Anti-federalist leaders had wholeheartedly committed themselves in 1798 to the doctrine that federal statutes were inoperative if in conflict with the Constitution. The statutes were the Alien and Sedition Acts of that year. Thomas Jefferson drafted a resolution passed by the Kentucky legislature, protesting these Acts, and Madison drew a similar resolution adopted by the Virginia legislature. The Virginia resolution, after reciting that the several States were bound by the federal compact no further than its "plain sense and intention," went on to state—

> . . . that in case of a deliberate, palpable, and dangerous exercise of other powers, not granted by the said compact, the states, who are parties thereto, have the right, and are in duty bound, to interpose, for arresting the progress of the evil, and for maintaining, within their respective limits, the authorities, rights, and liberties, appertaining to them.[105]

That the States were to be free to disobey a federal statute when they thought it was unconstitutional was a doctrine going far beyond the proposition that a court, obliged to choose between giving effect to the Constitution or an inconsistent Act of Congress, should effectuate the Constitution.

---

[104] *The Federalist*, Ernest Rhys, ed. (London: Dent and Sons, 1934) p. 397. See also Patrick Henry and John Marshall in the Virginia Convention, and Luther Martin's address to the Maryland Legislature, Elliot, *Debates*, III, 57, 553; I 380.
[105] Elliot, ed., *Debates*, IV, p. 528.

The most conspicuous immediate reaction to the decision in the Mandamus Case was harsh comment from hostile newspapers, in the bitter tone of the early partisan press. What Charles Warren considered the ablest criticism[106] was directed, however, not against the Court's exercise of power to declare a statute unconstitutional, but rather against the declaration of Marbury's right to his commission, and his right to obtain a *mandamus* order, despite the ultimate decision that the Court had no constitutional jurisdiction to pass on the case. In the late 20th century that criticism seems ill founded. If one engages, for a moment, in the hazardous business of reading, between the lines of an 1803 opinion, today's canons of judicial conduct governing constitutional litigation, the propriety of Marshall's opinion becomes abundantly justified. The power to declare an Act of Congress unconstitutional should be exercised reluctantly. If a ground of decision exists which makes unnecessary a decision of the constitutional point, today's doctrine requires the Court to utilize the non-constitutional ground and forego decision as to constitutional validity of the statute.[107] Thus if Marbury had no right to his commission, or if Madison, as Secretary of State, was immune from *mandamus*, the case could have been decided without passing on the constitutional validity of the statutory provision permitting a *mandamus* proceeding to originate in the Supreme Court. Marshall had to demonstrate that there was no adequate non-constitutional ground which would dispose of the case. He quite appropriately discussed the other two points before coming to the constitutionality of original *mandamus*.

Marbury v. *Madison* did not end all *mandamus* originating in the Supreme Court. There still remains the constitutional possibility of a writ of *mandamus* original in that Court, provided it be issued in aid of the appellate power.[108] The point was made as early as 1807, with respect to a motion for a writ of *habeas corpus*, original in the Supreme Court. Chief Justice Marshall wrote for the majority of the Court—[109]

> In the Mandamus case it was decided that this Court would not exercise original jurisdiction except so far as that jurisdiction was given by the constitution. But so far as that case has distinguished between original and appellate jurisdiction, that which the court is now asked to exercise is clearly appellate. It is the revision of a decision of an inferior court, by which a citizen has been committed to gaol.

[106] Warren, *Supreme Court in United States History*, I, p. 249.

[107] See the concurring opinion of Mr. Justice Brandeis in *Ashwander* v. *Tennessee Valley Authority*, 297 U.S. 288 at 341 (1936).

[108] *Ex Parte Peru*, 318 U.S. 578 (1943).

[109] 4 Cranch 75, 100, 101 in *Ex Parte Bollman* and *Ex Parte Swartwout*.

Evaluation of Marbury v. Madison

Much paper and much ink has been consumed in debate over the propriety of judicial power to declare Acts of Congress unconstitutional and so inoperative.[110] One apposite comment is the academic character of this debate: the institution of judicial review is as old as the Constitution. When the Fifteenth Amendment containing its express negative on federal action was ratified in 1870, the *Marbury* case was 67 years old. Did those who ratified the amendment intend that despite it, courts should enforce any Act of Congress which might be passed depriving the Negro of his vote?

The United States could have existed without court review of national legislation. A Justice of rare detachment who, more than most public men, had seen the operation of national and state judicial process, wrote in 1913—

> I do not think the United States would come to an end if we lost our power to declare an Act of Congress void. I do think the Union would be imperiled if we could not make that declaration as to the laws of the several States. For one in my place sees how often a local policy prevails with those who are not trained to national views and how often action is taken that embodies what the Commerce Clause was meant to end.[111]

Clear judgment is difficult to pass as to the effect on the United States, for good or ill, of the *Marbury* doctrine. Tabulation of the instances is a laborious undertaking. In 1936 the Legislative Reference Service of the Library of Congress made such a survey, and decided that, of more than 24,000 Acts of Congress passed since the Constitution took effect, the Supreme Court had held seventy unconstitutional.[112] That list must now be somewhat lengthened: it omits *United*

---

[110] See for bibliography, Association of American Law Schools, *Selected Essays on Constitutional Law* (Chicago: The Foundation Press, 1938) I, p. 128.

[111] Mr. Justice Holmes, "The Law and the Court," *Collected Legal Papers* (New York: Peter Smith, 1952) pp. 291, 295.

[112] Representative Snyder of Pennsylvania introduced the tabulation into the *Congressional Record* for June 8, 1936; see Vol. 80, p. 9251 *et seq.* Mr. Snyder appended this note: "Aside from the few instances where an entire act, or a complete title, etc., have been expressly held unconstitutional, the question of the exact scope of the decisions is frequently one of considerable difficulty. It is not always a matter simply of striking out; often it is to introduce qualifications or limitations. The indications given in the above list are, therefore, suggestive only. Any such list must be used with the utmost care, bearing in mind the established rule, that a decision against the validity of an act of Congress goes no further than is absolutely required by the case at bar."

States v. *Yale Todd*, decided in 1794 and long overlooked.[113] Perhaps a few other holdings might have been added. And there have been several instances since the 1936 list was compiled; one is *Ashton* v. *Cameron County Water District*, decided May 25, 1936 after the Library of Congress list was made.[114] Ten other cases were decided between 1943 and 1964, inclusive, holding unconstitutional Acts of Congress, or parts thereof.

How many times during the last 175 years have litigants unsuccessfully challenged the constitutionality of federal statutes? Compilation of such statistics is an immense labor. Professor Benjamin F. Wright has found that from February 1790 to June 1941 the Supreme Court passed on the constitutionality of federal and State legislation in more than two thousand cases, finding Acts of Congress unconstitutional in 79, and State legislation in 658.[115] Estimate of the evil or benign effects of these holdings of unconstitutionality depends on the social and political attitudes of the critics.

The decisions holding Acts of Congress unconstitutional can be sorted, roughly, into classes; but the sorting is unscientific at best; a case can be classified in different ways. The same decision may appear as a holding that a federal tax exceeds the powers granted by Article I, Section 8, Clause 1, and also as a holding that the Congress is invading State powers reserved under the Tenth Amendment, *e.g.*, the *Child Labor Tax Case*, 259 U.S. 20 (1922). But risking such inaccuracies, one can say that during the past century and three-quarters, at least eight decisions have held unconstitutional various Acts of Congress purporting to confer jurisdiction on the Federal Courts beyond that authorized by Article III of the Constitution, or otherwise conflicting with the judicial Article.[116] In a series of cases the Supreme Court has held that portions of the Uniform Code of Military Justice extended military jurisdiction over civilians beyond congressional power, in subjecting a one-time serviceman to court-

---

[113] See pp. 261 and 327 above and Chief Justice Taney's description of the case in a note following *United States* v. *Ferreira*, 13 Howard 40, p. 52.

[114] 298 U.S. 513. *Ashton*, held invalid a municipal bankruptcy act; in 1937 the Congress amended this statute; in 1938 the Supreme Court upheld the new municipal bankruptcy provision in *United States* v. *Bekins*, 304 U.S. 27. See 50 Stat. at L. 751.

[115] Benjamin F. Wright, *The Growth of American Constitutional Law* (Boston: Houghton Mifflin and Co., 1942) p. 243.

[116] *U.S.* v. *Yale Todd*, 13 Howard 53 (1794) reported in a note to *United States* v. *Ferreira*, 13 Howard 40, at page 52; *Marbury* v. *Madison*, 1 Cranch 137 (1803); *Gordon* v. *U.S.*, 2 Wallace 561 (1865); *The Alicia*, 7 Wall. 571 (1869); *Justices* v. *Murray*, 9 Wall. 274 (1870); *U.S.* v. *Klein*, 13 Wall. 128 (1873); *Muskrat* v. *U.S.*, 219 U.S. 346 (1911); *Keller* v. *Potomac Electric Power Co.*, 261 U.S. 428 (1923).

martial after his discharge, and in asserting court-martial jurisdiction over civilian dependents and civilian employees of the armed forces overseas.[117] In ten instances the Court has held that federal statutes denied the procedural protections guaranteed by the Constitution to defendants on criminal charges.[118]

In three cases the Court has held a penal Act of Congress so vague in its terms that it denies due process of law.[119] In four cases the Court has found that the Congress, entrusted by Article I with "all legislative powers," has unconstitutionally attempted to delegate these powers to some other officer or body.[120]

In six instances the Court found the Congress attempting to regulate economic matters not covered by the Commerce Clause.[121] In seven additional cases the Court held that the Congress had attempted to use the federal tax power to penalize activities reserved to the States' control.[122] In three cases the Court has held that the Congress had attempted unduly to intrude in the conduct of State or municipal government.[123]

In twelve cases the Court has held federal taxes unconstitutional for reasons other than their use as a covert means of regulating mat-

[117] U.S. ex rel. *Toth* v. *Quarles,* 350 U.S. 11 (1955); *Reid* v. *Covert,* 354 U.S. 1 (1957); *McElroy* v. *U.S.* ex rel. *Guagliardo,* 361 U.S. 281 (1960), and cases therein cited.

[118] *Boyd* v. *U.S.,* 116 U.S. 616 (1886); *Callan* v. *Wilson,* 127 U.S. 540 (1888); *Counselman* v. *Hitchcock,* 142 U.S. 547 (1892); *Wong Wing* v. *United States,* 163 U.S. 228 (1896); *Kirby* v. *United States,* 174 U.S. 47 (1899); *Rasmussen* v. *United States,* 197 U.S. 516 (1905); *United States* v. *Evans,* 213 U.S. 297 (1909); *United States* v. *Moreland,* 258 U.S. 433 (1922); *Tot* v. *United States,* 319 U.S. 463 (1943); *Kennedy* v. *Mendoza-Martinez,* 372 U.S. 144 (1963).

[119] *United States* v. *Cohen Grocery Co.,* 255 U.S. 81 (1921); *Weeds, Inc.* v. *United States,* 255 U.S. 109 (1921); *United States* v. *Cardiff,* 344 U.S. 174 (1952).

[120] *Knickerbocker Ice Co.* v. *Stewart,* 253 U.S. 149 (1920); *Panama Refining Co.* v. *Ryan,* 293 U.S. 389 (1935); *Industrial Accident Commission of California* v. *Rolph,* and *Washington* v. *Dawson,* 264 U.S. 219 (1924). In a number of other cases, undue delegation was an alternative ground; see, e.g., *Schechter Poultry Corporation* v. *United States,* 295 U.S. 495 (1935).

[121] *United States* v. *DeWitt,* 9 Wallace 41 (1870); *Hammer* v. *Dagenhart,* 247 U.S. 251 (1918); *Adair* v. *United States,* 208 U.S. 161 (1908); *R.R. Retirement Board* v. *Alton R.R.,* 295 U.S. 330 (1935); *Schechter Poultry Co.* v. *United States,* 295 U.S. 495 (1935); *Carter* v. *Carter Coal Co.,* 298 U.S. 238 (1936).

[122] *Bailey* v. *Drexel Co.,* 259 U.S. 20 (1922) (the "Child Labor Tax Case"); *Hill* v. *Wallace,* 259 U.S. 44 (1922); *Lipke* v. *Lederer,* 259 U.S. 557 (1922); *Trusler* v. *Crooks,* 269 U.S. 475 (1926); *United States* v. *Constantine,* 296 U.S. 287 (1935); *United States* v. *Butler,* 297 U.S. 1 (1936); *Rickert Rice Mills* v. *Fontenot,* 297 U.S. 110 (1936).

[123] *Coyle* v. *Oklahoma,* 221 U.S. 559 (1911); *Hopkins Federal Savings & Loan* v. *Cleary,* 296 U.S. 315 (1935); *Ashton* v. *Cameron County Water District,* 298 U.S. 513 (1936).

ters reserved to the States. Of these the most notable was the *Pollock* case of 1895, which held unconstitutional a federal income tax as a "direct" tax, not apportioned among States as Article I, Section 2, Clause 3 requires. Federal income taxes thus remained impossible until 1913 when the Thirteenth Amendment took effect. Other federal taxes were held invalid as taxes on exports, forbidden by Article I, Section 9; as taxes on judicial salaries, irreducible under Article III; as taxes on States or their income; as retrospective taxes on transfers of property which had already occurred; as taxes on Indian lands which the United States has agreed to exempt; as a tax on purported income which was not "income."[124]

In a melancholy list of seven decisions the Court, between 1876 and 1913, held that the post-Civil War amendments had not given the Congress adequate power to prevent individual (as distinguished from State) injustices to the enfranchised Negroes or their descendants, or to another unfortunate racial group, immigrant Chinese laborers.[125]

Economic due process, the theory that under some vague canon of constitutional traditionalism Congress could not modify economic arrangements, even within the acknowledged scope of the Commerce Power, in such a way as unreasonably to readjust the economic status of various groups, resulted in the downfall of other Acts of Congress.[126]

One wearies of these categories, long in the telling, comprising comparatively few instances out of all the Acts of Congress passed in a century and three-quarters. There were assorted others, most of little importance.[127] All the important doctrines of economic uncon-

[124] *Pollock v. Farmers' Loan & Trust Co.*, 157 U.S. 429, 158 U.S. 601 (1895); *Fairbanks v. United States*, 181 U.S. 283 (1901); *Choate v. Trapp*, 224 U.S. 665 (1912); *United States v. Hvoslef*, 237 U.S. 1 (1915); *Thames & Mersey Ins. Co. v. United States*, 237 U.S. 19 (1915); *Eisner v. Macomber*, 252 U.S. 189 (1920); *Evans v. Gore*, 253 U.S. 245 (1920); *Miles v. Graham*, 268 U.S. 501 (1925); *Spalding Bros. v. Edwards*, 262 U.S. 66 (1923); *Nichols v. Coolidge*, 274 U.S. 531 (1927); *Untermeyer v. Anderson*, 276 U.S. 440 (1928); *Heiner v. Donnan*, 285 U.S. 312 (1932).

[125] *United States v. Reese*, 92 U.S. 214 (1876); *United States v. Harris*, 106 U.S. 629 (1883); *Civil Rights Cases*, 109 U.S. 3 (1883); *Baldwin v. Franks*, 120 U.S. 678 (1887); *James v. Bowman*, 190 U.S. 127 (1903); *Hodges v. United States*, 203 U.S. 1 (1906); *Butts v. Merchants Transportation Co.*, 230 U.S. 126 (1913).

[126] For examples, *Adkins v. Children's Hospital*, 261 U.S. 525 (1923); *Louisville Joint Stock Bank v. Radford*, 295 U.S. 555 (1935). In a number of other instances the Fifth Amendment was a second ground of unconstitutionality. An example is *R.R. Retirement Board v. Alton R.R.*, 295 U.S. 330 (1935).

[127] Invalid efforts to impair vested land titles: *Reichart v. Felps*, 6 Wallace 160 (1868); *Jones v. Meehan*, 175 U.S. 1 (1899); a "bill of attainder" for ex-Confederates, *Ex parte Garland*, 4 Wallace 333 (1867); invalid extension of federal patent power to cover all trademarks, *Trade Mark Cases*, 100 U.S. 82 (1879);

stitutionalism, particularly conspicuous in 1935 and 1936 as limitations of the Commerce power and overgrowth of economic due process during the New Deal, have now disappeared.[128] The type of federal legislation held invalid since 1936 has been quite different, and the criticism the Court has evoked has come from quite different directions. Between 1895 and 1937 the principal complaint against the Supreme Court's function was its interference with legislation regulating the national economy.[129] *Adair* v. *United States*, in 1908,[130] held an anti-yellow-dog statute outside the commerce power; the ruling seems curious today, as the federal statute in question forbade an interstate carrier to discharge employees purely because of union affiliation, and since 1937 this type of regulation has been held clearly within congressional competence.[131] *Adkins* v. *Children's Hospital*,[132] in 1923, holding invalid under the Fifth Amendment due-process clause a minimum wage statute applicable to the District of Columbia, raised doubt of the future of much federal social legislation. The *Marbury* doctrine sometimes seemed socially lopsided.

Here perhaps a cautionary reminder is wise. One of the exasperating aspects of *Marbury* as it was applied between 1890 and 1936 was an appearance of whimsy. Much more federal legislation was sustained than was struck down. The Interstate Commerce Act of 1887,[133] the Sherman Anti-Trust Act of 1890,[134] the Food and Drug Act of 1906,[135] the Federal Reserve Act of 1913,[136] the Federal Trade Commission

---

invalid extension of bankruptcy power, to render criminal, acts done before bankruptcy, *United States* v. *Fox*, 95 U.S. 670 (1878); invalid statute making a postmaster irremovable, *Myers* v. *United States*, 272 U.S. 52 (1926); inadequate provision for compensation in eminent domain cases, *Monongahela Nav. Co.* v. *United States*, 148 U.S. 312 (1893); effort to restrict sale of liquor to Indians after their affairs had been turned over to a State, *Matter of Heff*, 197 U.S. 588 (1905); *Employers' Liability Cases*, 207 U.S. 463 (1908); an effort to control primary elections, *Newberry* v. *United States*, 256 U.S. 232 (1921); an Act of Congress attempting to invalidate yearly renewable veterans' insurance, *Lynch* v. *United States*, 292 U.S. 571 (1934). See, generally, 80 *Congressional Record* 1951 and following for a tabulation of such cases made by the Library of Congress.
[128] For an account of the constitutional crisis of 1935–1936 see Chapter XVI below.
[129] See, for examples, Maurice Finkelstein, "Judicial Self-Limitation," 37 *Harv. L. Rev.* 338 (1924); Henry Hart, "Processing Taxes and Protective Tariffs," 49 *Harv. L. Rev.* 610 (1936).
[130] 208 U.S. 161.
[131] *National Labor Relations Board* v. *Jones & Laughlin Steel Co.*, 301 U.S. 1 (1937).
[132] 261 U.S. 525 (1923).
[133] 24 Stat. at L. 379.
[134] 26 Stat. at L. 209.
[135] 34 Stat. at L. 768.
[136] 38 Stat. at L. 251.

Act of 1914,[137] and a host of others were enacted, applied, and if challenged sustained. The supposititious man-in-the-street (and his legal advisor if he had one) found difficulty in telling the difference between what was constitutional and what was not, as President Roosevelt shrewdly pointed out in a famous press conference held on May 31, 1935 just after the Supreme Court had declared invalid some important national legislation;[138] and as he wrote a few weeks later to Congressman Hill of the Ways and Means Committee about proposed legislation to regulate the bituminous coal industry—

> Manifestly, no one is in a position to give assurance that the proposed act will withstand constitutional tests, for the simple fact that you can get not ten but a thousand differing legal opinions on the subject . . . I hope your committee will not permit doubts as to constitutionality, however reasonable, to block the suggested legislation.[139]

But doubt of unconstitutionality tends toward sustaining legislation; the presumption favors validity. By 1935 there was in effect a great mass of federal legislation, and the overwhelming majority of challenges to Acts of Congress had been unsuccessful. The climax of the Supreme Court's adjudications that various instances of federal economic regulation were unconstitutional came in the two years 1935 and 1936, when that Court found invalid seven different measures all intended to alleviate one or another aspect of the economic distress then afflicting the country. The grounds of unconstitutionality were various; in some instances there were more than one. Thus the Court held a Retirement Act for railwaymen invalid both on the ground that it denied due-process, and on the ground that it exceeded the commerce power.[140] The same two reasons brought about the holding that the Bituminous Coal Conservation Act of 1935 was invalid.[141] Two parts of the National Industrial Recovery Act,[142] a farm mortgage moratorium statute,[143] the Agricultural Adjustment Act of 1933[144] and a municipal bankruptcy act,[145] all were held unconstitutional on various grounds, of which the most serious threats to an inclusive national economic program were the Fifth Amendment due-process

[137] 38 Stat. at L. 717.
[138] *New York Times,* June 1, 1935, p. 1, col. 8. See Chapter XVI, hereafter.
[139] S. I. Rosenman, ed., *Public Papers and Addresses of Franklin Delano Roosevelt* (13 vols.; New York: Random House, 1938–1950) IV, pp. 297–298.
[140] *Railroad Retirement Board* v. *Alton R.R.,* 295 U.S. 330 (1935).
[141] *Carter* v. *Carter Coal Co.,* 298 U.S. 238 (1936).
[142] *Panama Refining Co.* v. *Ryan,* 293 U.S. 389 (1935); *Schechter Poultry Co.* v. *United States,* 295 U.S. 495 (1935).
[143] *Louisville Joint Stock Bank* v. *Radford,* 295 U.S. 555 (1935).
[144] *United States* v. *Butler,* 296 U.S. 1 (1936).
[145] *Ashton* v. *Cameron County District,* 298 U.S. 513 (1936).

clause and, more threatening still, the elimination from national control under the Commerce Clause of the processes of extraction, agricultural production, and manufacture, on the ground that these did not come within power to control "commerce among the several States." Since 1936 however the adverse commerce-clause and eco-nomic due-process judgments of 1935 and 1936 have been overruled and no federal tax statute and no federal regulation of the economy has since then been held invalid.[146]

An account of the Court's change of position on economic legisla-tion belongs in a discussion of the New Deal in a later part of this book.[147] What is here attempted is an appraisal of the *Marbury* principle as a governmental institution—not whether it was reasonably derived, but whether it has operated to the national benefit.

Of course the national executive branch comes under judicial scrutiny, as does the legislature. Perhaps the most conspicuous exam-ple in our history occurred in 1952, when first a District Judge and then the Supreme Court of the United States held invalid seizure of the nation's steel industry on the ground that the Constitution allotted no such power to the executive.[148]

The effect of judicial review on national legislation is not limited to those cases in which congressional enactments are declared invalid. The possibility of future judgments of unconstitutionality may have an inhibitory advance effect on legislators, either in producing oppo-sition on the floor, or so shaping legislation as to avoid constitutional difficulties.[149] And the Supreme Court sometimes gives as a reason for its construction of legislation a desire to avoid risk of a holding of unconstitutionality.[150]

The effect of judicial review of constitutionality may sometimes be overrated, in the minds of susceptible readers or hearers, because of

[146] *United States* v. *Cardiff*, 344 U.S. 174 (1952), if an exception to this state-ment, is a petty and specialized one; the trouble was hasty drafting of a statute, easily reparable.

[147] See Chapter XVI.

[148] *Youngstown Sheet & Tube Co.* v. *Sawyer*, 343 U.S. 579. See for another example *Joint Anti-Fascist Refugee Committee* v. *McGrath*, 341 U.S. 123 (1951).

[149] See for two examples the preamble to the Oleomargarine Act of 1950, 64 Stat. at L. 20, 21 U.S. Code § 347(A) which recites the effect on interstate commerce in butter and margarine of sales, for on-premise consumption, of locally produced colored margarine, clearly to bring the statute within the Commerce Clause. And see the precautionary insertion in the Internal Security Act of 1950—

> "Neither the holding of office nor membership in any Communist organiza-tion . . . shall constitute *per se* a violation of subsection (a) . . . or of any other criminal statute." 50 U.S. Code § 783(F)

[150] See for examples *Screws* v. *United States*, 325 U.S. 91 (1945) and *United States* v. *Five Gambling Devices*, 346 U.S. 441 (1953).

the American habit of verbal exuberance in political discussion. The Attorney-General of New Hampshire commenting on decisions of the Supreme Court at the 1956 term, told the National Association of Attorneys-General on June 24, 1957, that recent decisions of the Supreme Court had set the nation back twenty-five years in its war against subversives;[151] the Minority Leader of the House of Representatives said in a broadcast on June 30, 1957 that the same decisions of the Court had "crippled" investigating committees of the Congress;[152] a cartoon in the Fort Wayne *News-Sentinel* for June 19, 1957 pictured the justices digging a way out of prison for insolent communist prisoners.[153]

Cool appraisal finds no reasonable accuracy in any one of these outcries. A separated judicial power is essential to a truly constitutional régime—if such a régime in the United States be taken to consist of a government in which ordinary legislation is subordinate to legislation of a senior order in which the Congress and legislative organs in the States have all participated.

Another difficulty with judicial review is the impossibility of being specific in drafting a document as general as a Constitution must be. Most provisions of the group of senior enactments making up the Constitution of the United States are not, and can not be, specific as to many of the instances in which they are applied. Judicial construction is necessary, as it was in *Bolling* v. *Sharpe* which held invalid in 1954, federal statutes providing for segregated schools in the District of Columbia on the ground that they conflicted with the Fifth Amendment Due-Process clause,[154] and in 1952, when the President was held to have no power to take over the nation's steel industry, even when the purpose of seizure stated by the President was to keep up a continuous supply of munitions "indispensable" for the war in Korea.[155] But construction of senior legislation is a familiar process, and not alone in the United States. Courts in modern England are required to determine whether or not an Act of Parliament conflicts with legislation of lesser rank, such as a municipal ordinance. No matter where the question arises, the distinction between making a rule and construing an existing rule is not clear; and this is so whether constitutional or other legislation is in question.

Popular ideas about the function of the federal courts, in declaring

[151] *N.Y. Times*, June 25, 1957, p. 1, col. 7.

[152] *N.Y. Times*, July 1, 1957, p. 1, col. 3.

[153] June 19, 1957, p. 6, cols. 5, 6.

[154] 347 U.S. 497.

[155] See President Truman's Executive Order of April 8, 1952, printed as an Appendix to *Youngstown etc. Co.* v. *Sawyer*, 343 U.S. 579 (1952), at page 589.

federal statutes unconstitutional, are apt to be oversimplified. Courts function differently in different instances. Sometimes, in an obvious case, the duty of the judge may be as plain as Mr. Justice Roberts saw it in the *Butler* case of 1936.[156]

> . . . to lay the article of the Constitution which is invoked beside the statute which is challenged and to decide whether the latter squares with the former.

Such a case was *Wong Wing* v. *United States*,[157] decided in 1896, where a federal statute purporting to authorize imprisonment at hard labor of an alien unlawfully in the United States, on the finding of a United States Commissioner, without grand or petit jury proceedings, was held invalid in the face of the Fifth and Sixth Amendments.

At the opposite end of the spectrum of judicial function is a case like *Bolling* v. *Sharpe* construing the Due-Process clause of the Fifth Amendment.[158] In such instances of general language, much more frequent than those in which there is patent conflict between a federal statute and the words of the Constitution, the judicial process suggests that described by Roscoe Pound—[159]

> . . . the American variant of natural law grew out of an attempt at philosophical statement of the power of our courts with respect to unconstitutional legislation. The constitution was declaratory of principles of natural constitutional law which were to be deduced from the nature of free government. Hence constitutional questions were always only in terms of questions of constitutional interpretation. They were questions of the meaning of the document, as such, only in form. For substance they were questions of a general constitutional law which transcended the text; of whether the enactment before the court conformed to principles of natural law 'running back of all constitutions' and inherent in the very idea of a government of limited powers set up by a free people.

Chief Justice Warren's opinion in *Bolling* v. *Sharpe*[160] furnishes an example—

> Although the Court has not assumed to define 'liberty' with any great precision, that term is not confined to mere freedom from bodily restraint. Liberty under law extends to the full range of conduct which

[156] *United States* v. *Butler,* 297 U.S. 1.

[157] 163 U.S. 228.

[158] 347 U.S. 497 (1954).

[159] Pound, *Introduction to the Philosophy of Law* (New Haven: Yale University Press, 1922) p. 50.

[160] 347 U.S. 497 (1954).

the individual is free to pursue, and it cannot be restricted except for a proper governmental objective. Segregation in public education is not reasonably related to any proper governmental objective, and thus it imposes on Negro children of the District of Columbia a burden that constitutes an arbitrary deprivation of their liberty in violation of the Due-Process Clause.

Conflicting assertions of governing power by different organs of government are not surprising in the complex organization of the modern State. One returns to the question, not of theoretical justification for leaving the last word with the Justices, but of the observable effect, good or evil, on the United States.

The *Marbury* doctrine interfered somewhat, but not gravely, nor long, with national regulation essential to the wholesome economic development. When this has been said, however, still the Supreme Court's Marbury function is not thereby justified. And the *Dred Scott* case of 1857 was much worse than a tolerable blunder; it was a disaster. Granted that all governmental power is liable to blundering misuse, and that government is not bad merely because misgovernment is possible—still misuses of an institution can raise questions of the propriety of the institution's existence. If the justification for entrusting a negative on legislation to a body like the Supreme Court is the value of its detached, essentially moral attitude—that justification could not be found in a solemn judgment that a whole class of our people were incapable of our citizenship, incapable even when some of them had achieved freedom from the slavery that had brought them here. The Civil War would have been fought, regardless of how *Dred Scott's* case came out; but the disastrous effect of that judgment was moral, not merely practical. The first clause of the 14th Amendment corrected the case formally, but the Court has come slowly and late to recognize the profoundness of the change that Amendment brought.

Marbury must be judged for its value today, not in 1803 or 1857, or 1935. Governing is done nationally to an increasing extent; the United States Code fills more and more shelf-space, year by year, and the more we are governed, the more risk there is that government, national or State, will do individual injustice when moved by sudden popular emotion. Thoughtful and temperate comment on judicial review has taken a new direction since 1945; and men whose fundamental attitudes seem Jeffersonian have come to praise John Marshall's thesis in *Marbury*.[161]

[161] See e.g. Eugene V. Rostow, "The Democratic Character of Judicial Review," 66 *Harv. L. Rev.* 193 (1952).

Since 1936 the Supreme Court has held unconstitutional ten Acts of Congress.

A provision of the Federal Firearms Act of 1938, 52 Stat. 1250, 15 U.S.C. § 902(f), declared that possession of a firearm or ammunition by any person who has been convicted of a crime of violence or is a fugitive from justice shall be presumptive evidence that the possessor shipped, transported or received the article in violation of the act. The Supreme Court held this inconsistent with due-process because it found no rational connection between the facts proved and the ultimate fact presumed. *Tot* v. *United States*, 319 U.S. 463 (1943).

Section 304 of the Urgent Deficiency Appropriation Act of 1943, Act of July 12, 1943, 57 Stat. 431, prohibited payment of any federal compensation to three named persons after November 15, 1943, except for jury duty or military service or for federal employment with senatorial advice and consent. The Supreme Court found this statute unconstitutional as a "bill of attainder or ex post facto law." *United States* v. *Lovett*, 328 U.S. 303 (1946).

The Food, Drug and Cosmetic Act, § 301(f) prohibited a factory operator "to permit entry or inspection as authorized by sec. 704." § 704 authorized federal officers to enter and inspect "at reasonable times" and "after first making a request and obtaining permission" from the operator. 52 Stat. 1040, 21 U.S.C. § 331(f). The Supreme Court held this contradictory enactment invalid because too vague for fairness. *United States* v. *Cardiff*, 344 U.S. 174 (1952).

Acts of Congress governing the schools of the District of Columbia provided for separate schools for Negro and white children. These statutes, of which the earliest is dated 1862, are listed in *Carr* v. *Corning*, 182 F 2d 14 (C.A.D.C. 1950). The Supreme Court held this invalid as a denial of due-process of law under the Fifth Amendment. *Bolling* v. *Sharpe*, 347 U.S. 497 (1954).

Article 3a of the Uniform Code of Military Justice, 64 Stat. 109, 50 U.S.C. § 553, subjected to military trial a man whose military status had been terminated but who was charged with a serious crime, committed while a serviceman, for which he was not subject to trial in a civil court. The Supreme Court held that this statute deprived an ex-serviceman of procedural protection granted by the Fifth and Sixth Amendments. *United States ex rel. Toth* v. *Quarles*, 350 U.S. 11 (1955).

Article 2(11) of the Uniform Code of Military Justice subjected all persons accompanying the armed forces outside the United States to military trial if authorized by treaty or international agreement. 50 U.S.C. § 552(11) The Supreme Court held this provision inconsistent with the Fifth and Sixth Amendments. *Reid* v. *Covert*; *Kinsella* v.

Kreuger, 354 U.S. 1 (1957). This holding was later extended to cover dependents charged with noncapital offenses and civilian employees without regard to the degree of the offense. *Kinsella* v. *United States ex rel. Singleton*, 361 U.S. 234 (1960); and *Grisham* v. *Hagan*, 361 U.S. 278 (1960), *McElroy* v. *United States ex rel. Guagliardo*; *Wilson* v. *Bohlender*, 361 U.S. 281 (1960).

Desertion from United States military forces in wartime, followed by conviction and dismissal from the service resulted in forfeiture of United States nationality under 8 U.S.C. § 1481(a)(8), 54 Stat. 1168, 1169. The Supreme Court held this unconstitutional as a "cruel and unusual punishment" under the Eighth Amendment. *Trop* v. *Dulles*, 356 U.S. 86 (1958).

The Nationality Act of 1940, as amended in 1944, and its successor, the Immigration and Nationality Act of 1952, 58 Stat. 746 and 66 Stat. 163, 267–268, 8 U.S.C. § 1481(a)(10), both deprived of nationality a United States national who left the country to avoid the draft. The Supreme Court held these provisions unconstitutional under the Fifth and Sixth Amendments. *Kennedy* v. *Mendoza-Martinez*, 372 U.S. 144 (1963).

Section 352 (a) (1) of the Immigration and Nationality Act of 1952 provided that any naturalized citizen should lose United States nationality by continuous residence for three years in his country of origin or former nationality. The Court held the discrimination between native-born and naturalized American nationals to be violative of Fifth Amendment Due Process. *Schneider* v. *Rusk*, 377 U.S. 163 (1964).

Section 6 of the Subversive Activities Control Act of 1950 forbade the use of a United States passport by a member of a Communist organization subject to a final order to register. The Supreme Court held this provision invalid as abridging the liberty guaranteed by the Fifth Amendment. *Aptheker* v. *Secretary of State*, 378 U.S. 500 (1964).

The Commerce Clause

The Constitution of 1789 had two underlying purposes. Its makers intended it primarily to give to the central government constitutional power to control foreign relations in war and in peace, and constitutional power to control that part of the economy which was national as distinguished from that which was local. Of course to accomplish these things the Constitution had to create the necessary national apparatus; it made provision for a national legislature with increased powers, for a national executive, for a national judiciary. But the underlying purposes were the two great necessities which had become evident under the Confederation.

Several constitutional clauses give to the Congress power over the economy, particularly those in the eighth section of Article One. The power to tax and spend, lodged in the first clause of that section, furnishes an effective means for much regulation. Provisions for bankruptcy (clause four), for currency (clause five), for post offices and post roads (clause seven), for patents and copyrights (clause eight), all contribute to national control of the economy. Section nine of the first article restricts in some ways the use of these national powers, and section ten places complementary restrictions on the States. The power to provide and maintain armed forces includes extensive national authority in economic matters. But over the years the great source of federal power to regulate the economy of the nation has been the third clause of section eight, which grants to the Congress power

> To regulate Commerce with foreign Nations, and among the several States, and with the Indian Tribes; . . .[162]

Much constitutional history during the past century and two-thirds has concerned the extent of that grant. Only gradually did it become apparent that to regulate interstate commerce, the Congress must often regulate activities conducted entirely within one of the States concerned. A wholly local activity which impedes commerce involving more States than one, becomes subject to national regulation. The extent of federal power under the Commerce Clause depends much less on the dictionary meaning of the words than it does on legislative judgment as to what regulation is wholesome.

Congress, as soon as it convened in 1789, began to enact legislation using its new powers. It imposed import duties, it established lighthouses, provided for beacons and buoys, erected public piers. It regulated the coasting trade. It made provisional arrangements for postal service. But far more important to the national commerce than these statutes were experiments then in progress on the Delaware River, where John Fitch between 1787 and 1790 developed a steam-driven

---

[162] ". . . that commerce which concerns more states than one . . . The genius and character of the whole government seem to be, that its action is to be applied to all the external concerns of the nation, and to those internal concerns which affect the states generally; but not to those which are completely within a particular state, which do not affect other states, and with which it is not necessary to interfere, for the purpose of executing some of the general powers of the government. The completely internal commerce of a state, then, may be considered as reserved for the state itself." *Gibbons* v. *Ogden*, 9 Wheat. 1, 194–195 (1824); see Robert L. Stern, "The Commerce Clause and the National Economy, 1934–1936," 59 Harv. L. Rev. 645 at 676–678 (1946). See for federal rent-control under the war power in Cleveland in 1947, *Woods* v. *Miller Co.*, 333 U.S. 138 (1948).

boat that ultimately carried passengers. In 1787 Fitch had obtained from the New York legislature a temporary monopoly for steam navigation. Next year that legislature repealed Fitch's grant and in its place granted a monopoly to Robert R. Livingston of New York. Fitch grew discouraged, went to France, failed to obtain backing, and came home to die. Meantime Robert Fulton, a young American painter and inventor, working in England on canal navigation, had become interested in steam vessels. In 1803 Fulton was experimenting on the Seine at Paris. Livingston, then Minister to France, supported Fulton, who attained a partial success in a trial run on August 9, 1803. Fulton ordered a new engine from the English engineering firm of Boulton and Watt and had the machine shipped to New York, where in August 1807 the first commercially successful steam vessel, later named the *Clermont* for Livingston's Hudson River estate, began regular runs between New York and Albany. The following spring the New York legislature, which had renewed Livingston's monopoly from time to time, passed another statute granting Livingston and Fulton a monopoly for thirty years, and forbidding any other person to navigate New York water by steam without a Livingston-Fulton license, on penalty of forfeiture of the offending steamer. Nicholas J. Roosevelt, Livingston's and Fulton's energetic associate, went over to Pittsburgh and built to a design of Fulton's a steamer called the *New Orleans*. The Livingston associates obtained from the legislature of Orleans Territory a franchise like that of New York, which promised them exclusive steamboating in the lower Mississippi.[163] Other States began to grant monopolies. Georgia, Massachusetts, New Hampshire, and Vermont followed the example of New York and Louisiana. Some States became irritated; New Jersey passed a statute allowing the owner of any boat that might be seized under the New York law to capture in retaliation a New York steamboat. Connecticut forbade any Livingston-Fulton vessel to enter Connecticut waters. Ohio, fearing the effect of New York's monopoly on Ohio lake-steamers, forbade New York steamers to land or receive passengers at any point on the Ohio shore of Lake Erie and imposed on the offender a penalty of one hundred dollars for each passenger landed. The interstate rivalries were suggestive of those which had given rise to the Constitutional Convention of 1787.

Private citizens began to defy the provisions of the New York monopoly. One James Van Ingen began running steamboats on the Hudson without Livingston-Fulton consent. The New York Court of Errors, highest court of the State, upheld the steamboat monopoly,

---

[163] For an account of the rise of the steamboat monopoly, see Beveridge, *Life of John Marshall*, IV, Chapter VIII.

and enjoined Van Ingen.[164] New litigation sprang up, however, in a different situation. One Aaron Ogden, a licensee of the New York monopoly, went into partnership with Thomas Gibbons, who operated two steamboats between certain New Jersey landings. Ogden would bring passengers from New York as far as Elizabethtown Point in New Jersey; Gibbons would pick them up there and carry them to various New Jersey points. Ogden and Gibbons had a common traffic agent in New York who booked passengers for the through journey. Livingston and Fulton sued Ogden and Gibbons for an injunction. James Kent, Chancellor of the then separate equity court of New York, refused to issue an injunction against Ogden, who was navigating under authority from Livingston; but Kent did enjoin Gibbons from navigating New York waters in New York Bay or the Hudson River.[165] Gibbons, irritated by the New York judgment, began to run his boats directly between New Jersey and New York ports in competition with his late partner, Ogden.[166] Ogden obtained from Chancellor Kent an injunction against Gibbons.[167] Gibbons appealed to the New York Court of Errors, which affirmed the Chancellor's decree.[168] Gibbons appealed to the Supreme Court of the United States, retaining as his counsel Daniel Webster and William Wirt, Attorney General of the United States. Ogden's counsel, Messrs. Oakley and Emmett, were perhaps less famous, but were highly competent. Counsel were not ready to argue the case until February 1824. Then the Supreme Court heard oral argument for nine days. On March 2, 1824, John Marshall delivered the Supreme Court's opinion upholding Gibbons' rights and adjudging the New York steamboat monopoly invalid.[169]

[164] *Livingston and Fulton* v. *Van Ingen et al.,* 9 Johnson's Reports 507 (1812).

[165] *Livingston* v. *Ogden and Gibbons,* 4 Johnson's Chancery 48 (1819).

[166] One regrets to relate that differences between Col. Ogden and Mr. Gibbons, neighbors in Elizabethtown, New Jersey, had by 1816 become somewhat heated. Ogden had Gibbons arrested in a suit on a note, by mistake. Gibbons then accused Ogden of interfering in a quarrel between Gibbons and Mrs. Gibbons; Gibbons went to Ogden's house with a horsewhip, and finding Ogden gone, and thinking he saw Ogden discreetly climbing a fence in retreat, posted on Ogden's door a challenge to a duel. Ogden then sued Gibbons for trespass, in the New Jersey Supreme Court, and won a verdict and judgment for $5,000. See *Ogden* v. *Gibbons,* 5 New Jersey Law 612 (1819). The New Jersey Court of Appeals in 1820 reversed this judgment, however, six members voting for reversal, five for affirmance, and two not voting. 5 New Jersey Law, Appendix, page 1005. Unfortunately for our history, the report gives only the vote, not the reasons for Gibbons' final triumph. Those were stirring times.

[167] *Ogden* v. *Gibbons,* 4 Johnson's Chancery 150 (1819).

[168] 17 Johnson's Reports 488 (1820). "Johnson's reports" include N.Y. Court of Errors cases. His "Chancery Reports" describe lower court proceedings in equity.

[169] *Gibbons* v. *Ogden,* 9 Wheaton 1.

Marshall first discussed the scope of the Commerce Clause—

Congress shall have Power. . .

To regulate Commerce with foreign Nations, and among the several States, and with the Indian Tribes; . . .[170]

Today's reader, who has in mind nearly a century and a half of experience with that clause, finds much in Marshall's opinion that would be obvious today, but was by no means obvious at the time. "Commerce," Marshall held, includes navigation, and carriage of passengers. Commerce "among the several States" cannot "stop at the external boundary line of each State, but may be introduced into the interior." To be sure, Marshall continued, he did not intend to say that these words comprehend commerce

carried on between man and man in a State, or between different parts of the same State, and which did not extend to or affect other States. Such a power would be inconvenient, and is certainly unnecessary.

Commerce "among the several States" is "that commerce which concerns more States than one."

Was any power to regulate interstate commerce retained in the States, or was the mere grant to the Congress in the Constitution inconsistent with any State regulation whatever? Marshall wrote—[171]

In discussing the question, whether this power is still in the States, in the case under consideration, we may dismiss from it the inquiry, whether it is surrendered by the mere grant to Congress or is retained until Congress shall exercise the power. We may dismiss that inquiry, because it has been exercised, and the regulations which Congress deemed it proper to make, are now in full operation. The sole question is, can a State regulate commerce with foreign nations and among the States, while Congress is regulating it? . . .

. . . the framers of our Constitution foresaw this state of things, and provided for it, by declaring the supremacy not only of itself, but of the laws made in pursuance of it. The nullity of any act, inconsistent with the Constitution, is produced by the declaration that the Constitution is the supreme law. The appropriate application of that part of the clause which confers the same supremacy on laws and treaties, is to such acts of the State legislatures as do not transcend their powers, but, though enacted in the execution of acknowledged State powers, interfere with, or are contrary to the laws of Congress, made in pursuance of the Constitution, or some treaty made under the authority of the United States. In every such case, the act of Congress, or the

[170] Art. I, § 8, Cl. 3.
[171] 9 Wheat. page 200.

treaty, is supreme; and the law of the State, though enacted in the exercise of powers not controverted, must yield to it.[172]

Marshall went on to review the consequences of the federal grant of a coasting license to the *Bellona* and the *Stoudinger,* Gibbons' craft. The act of a State, he wrote, inhibiting navigation of a federally licensed vessel propelled either by sail or steam, comes in direct conflict with the Act of Congress which provides for the license.

Mr. Justice Johnson wrote a concurring opinion. The unanimous Court issued its formal decree—

> . . . that so much of the several laws of the State of New York, as prohibits vessels, licensed according to the laws of the United States, from navigating the waters of the State of New York, by means of fire or steam, is repugnant to the said constitution, and void.[173]

The Supreme Court's decision in *Gibbons* v. *Ogden* was popular. Steamboat fares went down and steamboat service increased as more boats went into service. Steamboat arrivals had a gala atmosphere for a while. When two boats from Charleston arrived at Augusta, Georgia about two weeks after the decision, the Augustans greeted their coming with

> a feu de joie, accompanied by a band of music, which was returned by one of the boats, amidst repeated huzzas and cries of 'down with all monopolies of commerce and manufactories—one is as great an evil as the other. Give us free trade and sailor's rights.'[174]

One gathers that in those days crews of river-steamers had a high political literacy even when they were stimulated by huzzas and feux de joie.

Amid this rejoicing, there were still some who read Marshall's and Johnson's opinions and shook heads a little sadly. The Court's language was sweeping; and whatever assurance it gave of broad congressional powers under the Commerce Clause, was a correlative warning of diminished State immunity from national interference.

Diffusion of power over men is one gauge of freedom, and the *Steamboat Case* is here relevant. Our underlying constitutional aspirations can gain achievement through constitutional clauses that sometimes seem surprising. In 1946 the Supreme Court of the United States, confronted with an Act of Congress which purported to disqualify three men named Lovett, Watson and Dodd for federal employment, found in the Bill of Attainder clause a device for declaring

---

[172] 9 Wheat. pages 210, 211.
[173] 9 Wheaton page 240.
[174] *Georgia Journal,* April 6, 1824, quoted in Warren, *Supreme Court in United States History,* II, p. 75.

the Act unconstitutional and ineffective.[175] The Commerce Clause and an Act of Congress licensing coastal vessels might seem unlikely means of assuring human liberty; and doubtless many men in many States found the federal nullification of a State law a trampling-down of State rights and an invasion of vested property, a violation of one sort of liberty of the Livingston associates. Doubtless for similar reasons many men felt that the liberty of a proprietor to run his restaurant as he saw fit was invaded when the Supreme Court of the United States in 1960 held that the Interstate Commerce Act had displaced a Virginia trespass statute. The Virginia authorities, under their statute, had convicted a Negro traveler who insisted on service in the "white" portion of an interstate bus terminal.[176] All declare for liberty; few define it as essentially stopping one man from doing what he wants in order that another can do as he pleases.[177] Freedom for Gibbons probably seemed federal tyranny to Ogden; the Georgia deckhands' huzzas for sailors' rights did not sound alike to all ears.

Formulation of a relevant constitutional principle is the beginning of the solution of a problem, not its answer,[178] and whoever in 1824 thought that thereafter no State authority could interfere with any vessel carrying a federal license, was shortly to find that government under law is a complex set of reconciliations. Black Bird Creek was a small tidal waterway in Delaware, capable of use by federally licensed craft. Delaware passed a statute authorizing Black Bird Creek Marsh Company to dam the creek and "bank" the adjacent marsh; but when the Company did so, the owners of the federally licensed sloop *Sally* (of "95%₉₅ tons") broke a passage through the dam in order to sail up the creek. The Company sued the owners of the *Sally* for trespass, and the Delaware courts awarded judgment to the Company. The *Sally's* owners obtained a writ of error[179] from the Supreme Court of

[175] *United States* v. *Lovett*, 328 U.S. 303 (1946), decided under Art. I, § 9, Clause 3. "No Bill of Attainder or ex post facto Law shall be passed."

[176] *Boynton* v. *Virginia*, 364 U.S. 454. For a similar situation, not related to an interstate journey and so arising under the Fourteenth Amendment instead of the Commerce Clause and the Interstate Commerce Act, see *Peterson* v. *Greenville*, 373 U.S. 244 (1963).

[177] See A. E. Sutherland, *The Law and One Man Among Many* (Madison: University of Wisconsin Press, 1956) p. 35 and following.

[178] The words are those of Mr. Justice Frankfurter, concurring in *Illinois* ex rel. *McCollum* v. *Board of Education*, 333 U.S. 203, at 212 (1948).

[179] At the time of the litigation in question, review of a State court judgment either at law or in equity was granted under Section 25 of the Judiciary Act of 1789 by a "writ of error," on a "citation," an order, issued by the State chief justice or chancellor, or by a justice of the United States Supreme Court, bringing the State court judgment up for review. The procedure for review of a decree in equity, as *Gibbons* v. *Ogden* illustrates, was often called "appeal," perhaps for traditional reasons, despite the terminology of Section 25.

the United States directed to the High Court of Errors and Appeals of Delaware, to bring the case before the Supreme Court in 1829. There counsel for the *Sally's* owners urged as a conclusive authority for reversal, the Supreme Court's decision in *Gibbons* v. *Ogden* five years before and indeed the precedent seemed apposite. New York by statute had purported to give Livingston and his licensees exclusive rights in New York waters, yet when Gibbons took his federally licensed vessels into these waters the Supreme Court had held Gibbons' rights superior to those granted by New York. Delaware, by statute, had purported to give to the Black Bird Creek Marsh Company the right to exclude, by a barrier, federally licensed vessels from a tidal waterway. The owners of the federally licensed *Sally* had opened up the waterway, as had Gibbons, by simply disregarding the State law.

Nevertheless the Supreme Court, in a short opinion by Chief Justice Marshall, held that the Delaware judgment upholding the Delaware dam had been correct.[180] He did not explain just how *Gibbons* v. *Ogden* differed from the *Black Bird Creek* case. Marshall mentions "those small navigable creeks into which the tide flows, and which abound throughout the lower country of the Middle and Southern States"; Congress had, he wrote, undoubted power to control State legislation over such waterways. "But" he continued somewhat cryptically, "congress has passed no such act."

One senses here the effort of a wise man to reach a correct result, in the face of considerable intellectual difficulty. He wished to make a federal coasting license a passport into the important deep-water harbor of New York even where New York opposed; he did not wish to give the same effect to the same federal license when applied to a small, sluggish backwater. Marshall reads this "construction" into the licensing act, without so many words. Twenty years later, in the "Passenger Cases,"[181] the Supreme Court held unconstitutional statutes of Massachusetts and of New York, each of which imposed a tax on the master of any vessel, of a sum for each alien passenger; the several justices composing the majority of the Court could not agree on the reasons for their judgment. Mr. Justice McLean, one of the majority, relied on *Gibbons* v. *Ogden* of 1824,[182] and found the *Black Bird Creek* case difficult to explain. McLean wrote of that case[183]—"It must be admitted that the language of the eminent Chief Justice who wrote

---

[180] *Willson* v. *Black Bird Creek Marsh Co.*, 2 Peters 245 (1829).
[181] 7 Howard 283 (1849).
[182] 9 Wheaton 187.
[183] at 7 Howard 397.

the opinion is less guarded than his opinions generally were on constitutional questions"; he went on to suggest the difference in degree between Black Bird Creek and the Hudson River.

The task of determining what degree of State interference with commerce on navigable waters was tolerable gave the Supreme Court much difficulty.[184] Ultimately the Congress mitigated the immediate Black Bird Creek problem by transferring the question of propriety of damming any "navigable water of the United States" to the executive branch for decision. By statute of 1890[185] authority to construct such works must have approval of the Chief of Engineers and the Secretary of the Army. But application of any general statute to specific situations seems inevitably to require construction by the judiciary, in much the same way as Marshall construed the federal statute authorizing a coasting license in the *Black Bird Creek* case; and after 1890 one begins to find the justices seeking to decide what waterways are "navigable waters of the United States."[186]

The Justices 1836–1856

The theme of this chapter is national government and the decline of State independence between 1800 and 1856. One might suppose, *a priori*, that when the long Chief Justiceship of John Marshall ended in 1835, and President Jackson appointed his Secretary of the Treasury, Roger Brooke Taney of Maryland as Chief Justice, there would be a drastic change in the history of the Supreme Court of the United States. But this view is predicated on an exaggerated estimate of the part that allegiance to a political party plays in the life of a lawyer and a politician after he becomes a judge. This view underrates the effect of a lifetime of discipline in professional detachment, of training in the estimate of the merits and demerits of a cause, of professional engagement in advocacy of a wide variety of controversies. That a party man completely ceases to be a party man once he ascends the federal bench is of course an overstatement. He retains some political attitudes, but the personal motives for political bias disappear when a man comes to the Supreme Court of the United States. And doctrinal attitudes, unassociated with the passionate fervor of party alliance, are subject to change under the influence of reason, which

[184] Compare for example *New York* v. *Miln,* 11 Peters 102 (1837) with the *License Cases,* 5 Howard 504 (1847) and with the Passenger Cases, 7 Howard 283 (1849).

[185] Now 33 U.S. Code § 401.

[186] *Economy Light & Power Co.* v. *United States,* 256 U.S. 113 (1921).

is at any rate the aspiration of those trained in the tradition of the common law.

So with the appointment of Roger Brooke Taney, the flavor of the Supreme Court of the United States was not abruptly changed. Until 1857, which brought the Dred Scott decision, the court under Taney's Chief Justiceship continued in a fairly uneventful prolongation of its character in Marshall's day. Between the inauguration of President Jackson and the end of President Pierce's administration, on March 4, 1857, twelve Justices were appointed. President Jackson appointed four: John McLean, who sat from 1829 to 1861; Henry Baldwin, who sat from 1830 to 1844; James M. Wayne, who sat from 1835 to 1867; and Phillip P. Barbour, 1836–1841. President Van Buren appointed three, John Catron, 1837–1865; John McKinley, 1837–1852; Peter V. Daniel, 1841–1860. President Tyler appointed one Justice, Samuel Nelson, 1845–1872. President Polk appointed two: Levi Woodbury, 1845–1851, and Robert C. Grier, who sat from 1846 to 1870. President Fillmore appointed Benjamin R. Curtis of Boston, who sat from 1851 until just after the decision of the *Dred Scott* case in 1857. President Pierce appointed John A. Campbell of Alabama, who sat from 1853 until 1861. Campbell opposed secession, but resigned his place on the bench to go with the Confederacy.

Of all these men, no one impressed his personality on the Supreme Court as deeply as had John Marshall. Mr. Justice Curtis might have done so, had he remained longer on the bench. His somewhat bitter difference with Chief Justice Taney over the Dred Scott decision caused him to resign as a Justice in 1857, and to resume a distinguished career as one of the leaders of the bar of Massachusetts and indeed of the United States. But a fair estimate of the record of the Court in the twenty years following Marshall's death is that it continued evenly in not-unexpected judicial behavior.

The Commerce Clause, Continued

The most notable Commerce Clause case which the Court decided in the Chief Justiceship of Taney was *Cooley* v. *The Board of Wardens of the Port of Philadelphia*.[187] This case, from a passage in the Court's opinion written by Mr. Justice Curtis, has given "The Cooley Doctrine" to the law of the Commerce Clause. The facts and the law were quite simple. One of the first statutes passed by the Congress in 1789[188] provided—

[187] 12 Howard 299 (1852).
[188] 1 Statutes at Large 53, § 4, Aug. 7, 1789.

That all pilots in the bays, inlets, rivers, harbors, and ports of the United States, shall continue to be regulated in conformity with the existing laws of the States, respectively, wherein such pilots may be, or with such laws as the States may respectively hereafter enact for the purpose, until further legislative provision shall be made by Congress.

In 1803 the legislature of Pennsylvania passed a statute to establish a Board of Wardens for the Port of Philadelphia and to regulate pilots and pilotages. That statute required that every ship or vessel coming from any foreign port and any vessel of seventy-five tons or more sailing outward to a port not within the River Delaware should be obliged to receive a pilot. A master who refused to take on a pilot as the statute required, must pay a penalty of half the pilotage fees, at the suit of the Board of Wardens. Under this provision the wardens brought an action against one Cooley in the Pennsylvania State courts to recover half pilotage fees. After the Supreme Court of Pennsylvania had affirmed a judgment in favor of the Wardens, Cooley brought the case to the Supreme Court of the United States on a writ of error, contending among other arguments that the law was invalid because it clashed with the Commerce Clause. The Supreme Court upheld Pennsylvania's Board of Wardens.[189] To succeed, Cooley would have had to persuade a majority of the Supreme Court that even where the Congress had expressly authorized the States to legislate in some matter affecting interstate commerce, the power of the Commerce Clause was such that State action would be invalid.

In the long history of attempted reconciliation of national and State power over the economy, at least three type-situations can be identified. In one of these the Congress has acted in a manner inconsistent with State action, as the Marshall Court found in the Steamboat Case of 1824.[190] In the face of federal legislation, contrary State action will always fall unless the Supreme Court finds that the Congress has acted entirely beyond its delegated power under the Commerce Clause. Whatever may once have been the danger of the Supreme Court's holding an Act of Congress *ultra vires* as beyond the commerce power, since 1936 that Court has held no legislation invalid as exceeding the powers delegated by Article 1, Section 8, Clause 3. A striking application of this doctrine of *Gibbons* v. *Ogden* occurred in 1957 when the Supreme Court held that although the National Labor Relations Board had expressly disclaimed its jurisdiction over a predominantly local labor dispute in Utah, nevertheless the National Labor

[189] *Cooley* v. *Board of Wardens,* 12 Howard 299 (1852). The Supreme Court has presented a kind attitude toward pilots. See *Kotch* v. *Board of River Port Pilot Commissioners,* 330 U.S. 552 (1947).

[190] *Gibbons* v. *Ogden,* 9 Wheaton 1.

Relations Act so completely displaced State jurisdiction affecting inter-state commerce that any intervention by the State Labor Relations Board was a nullity.[191]

At the opposite pole from the federal negation of State legislation is the situation in the *Cooley* case, where, on the contrary, the Congress has explicitly authorized the State to act. One would suppose that only a surprisingly strong instance of the need for national control of commerce among the several States would overcome an express delegation by the Congress of competence to the States to act accord-ing to their own policy. Perhaps something like such a holding occurred in *Panama Refining Co.* v. *Ryan,* the "Hot Oil Case" of 1935.[192] Here the Supreme Court held unconstitutional a Presidential executive order, expressly authorized by an Act of Congress; the President's order forbade interstate transportation of petroleum produced in ex-cess of a State regulation. A majority of the Supreme Court, in an opinion by Chief Justice Hughes, found this delegation to State legis-lators to be beyond the power of the Congress, though an alternative ground for invalidity was a lack in the executive order of any state-ment of the ground of the President's action.

A much more frequent type-situation is the third, where the Con-gress has neither acted in such a manner as to exclude the State, as was true in *Gibbons* v. *Ogden;* nor has expressly authorized the State to act, as was true in *Cooley* v. *The Port Wardens;* but where the Congress has left the field completely unoccupied by its legislation. A difficult feat of judicial construction is required, to find such entire absence of Congressional action in the seventh decade of the twentieth century when the mass of Congressional legislation is so great that Congress seems to have legislated something or other about practically everything. However, where the Supreme Court finds that Congress has not occupied the field, there becomes particularly relevant the "Cooley Doctrine" expressed thus by Mr. Justice Curtis,

> Now, the power to regulate commerce, embraces a vast field, contain-ing not only many, but exceedingly various subjects, quite unlike in their nature; some imperatively demanding a single uniform rule, oper-ating equally on the commerce of the United States in every port; and some, like the subject now in question, as imperatively demanding that diversity, which alone can meet the local necessities of navigation.
>
> Either absolutely to affirm, or deny, that the nature of this power requires exclusive legislation by Congress, is to lose sight of the nature of the subjects of this power, and to assert concerning all of them, what is really applicable but to a part. Whatever subjects of this

[191] *Guss* v. *Utah Labor Relations Board,* 353 U.S. 1 (1957).
[192] 293 U.S. 389.

power are in their nature national, or admit only of one uniform system, or plan of regulation, may justly be said to be of such a nature as to require exclusive legislation by Congress. That this cannot be affirmed of laws for the regulation of pilots and pilotage is plain. The Act of 1789 contains a clear and authoritative declaration by the first Congress, that the nature of this subject is such, that until Congress should find it necessary to exert its power, it should be left to the legislation of the States; that it is local and not national; that it is likely to be the best provided for, not by one system, or plan of regulations, but by as many as the legislative discretion of the several States should deem applicable to the local peculiarities of the ports within their limits.

. . . How, then, can we say, that by the mere grant of power to regulate commerce, the States are deprived of all the power to legislate on this subject, because from the nature of the power the legislation of Congress must be exclusive. . .

The Cooley Doctrine, then, is a statement of a duty, which the Supreme Court of the United States necessarily assumes, to determine which subjects are of such a nature that even in the absence of congressional negation, State regulation is invalid. It illustrates the policy function of that Court, often unrecognized and unacknowledged; but as Justice Holmes in 1881 wrote of the policy function on the first page of his "Common Law"—

To accomplish the task other tools are needed besides logic. It is something to show that the consistency of a system requires a particular result, but it is not all. The life of the law has not been logic: it has been experience. The felt necessities of the time, the prevalent moral and political theories, intuitions of public policy, avowed or unconscious, even the prejudices which judges share with their fellow-men, have had a good deal more to do than the syllogism in determining the rules by which men should be governed. The law embodies the story of a nation's development through many centuries, and it cannot be dealt with as if it contained only the axioms and corollaries of a book of mathematics. In order to know what it is, we must know what it has been, and what it tends to become. We must alternately consult history and existing theories of legislation. But the most difficult labor will be to understand the combination of the two into new products at every stage. The substance of the law at any given time pretty nearly corresponds, so far as it goes, with what is then understood to be convenient; but its form and machinery, and the degree to which it is able to work out desired results, depend very much upon its past.

The "Cooley Doctrine" prescribes for the Supreme Court that it take as the substance of the Commerce Clause at any given time pretty nearly what it then understands to be convenient for the United States of America. Of this operation a prime example occurred in 1945 in *Southern Pacific* v. *Arizona*.[193] The Arizona Train Limit Law of 1912 had made it unlawful for any railroad within the State to operate a train of more than fourteen passenger or seventy freight cars. The statute authorized the State to recover a money penalty for each violation of the Act just as the Act of 1803 authorized the Port Wardens of Philadelphia to recover a money penalty from the captain of a pilotless ship. In 1940 Arizona sued the Southern Pacific Company to recover the statutory penalty for operating such a passenger train and such a freight train, both of which were engaged in interstate journeys. The highest court of Arizona upheld the State statute and directed the payment of the penalty, but the Supreme Court of the United States, after considering the elaborate evidence introduced in a long trial in the Arizona court of first instance, concluded that the policy of the Commerce Clause was here inconsistent with the State regulation. Because of the distant location of marshalling yards west of Arizona, the Arizona statute made necessary the break-up of longer trains at points outside of Arizona, and at the far side of that State the Arizona law often controlled the flow of traffic as far east as El Paso, Texas. The Supreme Court discussed *Black Bird Creek Marsh*[194] and *Cooley* v. *The Port Wardens*,[195] but found that the policy underlying *Gibbons* v. *Ogden*[196] would here control, and held that the Arizona Train Limit Law was invalid in the presence of the Commerce Clause.

At the same term in which the Court decided the *Cooley* case, it again discussed *Willson* v. *Black Bird Creek Marsh* in the first opinions in which appears conflict between water transport and a new agency of commerce, the railroad. This case was *Pennsylvania* v. *Wheeling and Belmont Bridge Company*.[197] It was argued three times, the last argument on December 18 and 22, 1851. Virginia had authorized the construction of a bridge across the Ohio River at Wheeling, downstream from the western line of Pennsylvania. Pennsylvania had made extensive improvements by canals, railroads and turnpikes for transportation within her borders; she claimed that the Wheeling Bridge would obstruct the passage of the largest type of steamboats running up the river to Pittsburgh, Pennsylvania. On February 6, 1852, the Supreme Court of the United States, on Pennsylvania's original

193 325 U.S. 761.
194 2 Peters 245 (1829).
195 12 Howard 299 (1852).
196 9 Wheaton 1 (1824).
197 13 Howard 518 (1852).

Bill in Equity, enjoined the maintenance of what it found a nuisance and directed that the nuisance be abated by changing the construction of the bridge. Chief Justice Taney and Associate Justice Daniel dissented vigorously.

Daniel's dissent neatly turned the tables on *Gibbons* and the steamboats of a generation before. Then New York had been trying to preserve a monopoly in her waters for her novel steamboats. Daniel now saw Pennsylvania trying to keep her place in steamboating by judicial decree, when convenient bridges might facilitate a newer and more adequate means of transport.

> Thus, notwithstanding the high improvement in navigation by steam and by sails, which seems to have carried it to its greatest perfection, we see the railroad in situations where no deficiency of water and no artificial or natural obstruction to vessels exist, . . . The obvious superiority of the railroad, from its unequalled speed, its greater safety, its exemption from dependence upon wind or on depth of water, but above all, its power of linking together the distant and extended regions interposed between the rivers of the country, spaces which navigation can never approach, must give it a decided preference . . . unless arrested in its progress by the fiat of this court. . .[198]

The rest of the Wheeling Bridge story appears in the 18th volume of Howard's Reports.[199] The Bridge Company never did remodel their bridge to accord with the Supreme Court's 1852 decree. In August of 1852 the Congress passed a statute declaring the bridge lawful as it was. In 1854 a windstorm blew it down. The Bridge Company started to rebuild on the old level. Pennsylvania returned to the Supreme Court to protest. In 1856, over the dissents of Justices McLean, Grier and Wayne, that Court upheld the federal statute as a valid regulation of interstate commerce and as provision for a post road.[200] So, after all the argument, the bridge stayed as it was.

The second *Wheeling Bridge* case is a variant of *Cooley* and the *Port Wardens*. In *Cooley*, the Congress had authorized the State action in advance; in the *Belmont Bridge* case, the Congress authorized it after the Supreme Court had once held it invalid. In both situations the Congress proved dominant.

In the first half of the nineteenth century, the power of Congress to control the economy was thus well developed in cases which involved movement of goods or of agencies of commerce across State lines. There remained for later demonstration the doctrine that whatever

[198] 13 Howard 603.
[199] p. 421.
[200] 18 Howard 421 (1856).

occurred exclusively within the four corners of a State, but had repercussions upon that portion of the economy concerned with more States
than one, would though local fall within national control. This development first came after the Civil War, with the *Daniel Ball,* in
1871;[201] that case concerned a river steamboat running entirely within
the State of Michigan, but carrying goods and passengers on part of a
journey which by other means was destined to continue in other States.
The Supreme Court held that the *Daniel Ball* must comply with federal licensing laws. This doctrine was further developed in the *Shreveport Rate Case* in 1914,[202] in which the Supreme Court held that the
Congress and the Interstate Commerce Commission were competent,
under the Commerce Clause, to forbid Texas to so regulate intrastate
railroad rates as to favor Texas trade to the disparagement of competing trade originating in Louisiana. Whatever activity, though local,
still "affects" interstate commerce, falls within the Congressional competence under the Commerce Clause. The "effect" theory reached its
farthest extrapolation in *Wickard* v. *Filburn* in 1942[203] in which the
Supreme Court of the United States held that under an Act of Congress the Secretary of Agriculture could enforce a limit on the production of wheat on a farm, by a penalty for excess production, even
though the entire produce was consumed on the farm where it grew.
The argument which sustained this regulation was the "effect" of the
local production on potential commerce in grain which might flow
across State lines. But the story of this ultimate extension of the Commerce power belongs in an account of the United States under the
New Deal.

The Contract Clause

The effect of the Commerce Clause, as an inhibition on State legislation or executive action, depends on an unexpressed emanation from
that constitutional language, a judicially imposed negative, a finding
that the particular instance of State localism is inconsistent with the
national economic well-being; or else it depends upon Congressional
action, taken under the Commerce Clause which, whether so expressed
or not, is inconsistent with the State activity under examination. But
besides this doctrine there are other explicit constitutional limitations
on State activity dangerous to national economic unity prescribed in
the tenth section of Article One of the Constitution; the draftsmen

[201] 10 Wallace 557.
[202] 234 U.S. 342.
[203] 317 U.S. 111.

of 1787 inserted certain express negatives restricting the States in ways which seemed essential to the new frame of government. Just as the new Constitution was intended to vest in the national government power over foreign affairs and the national economy,[204] so Section Ten was designed to inhibit by its own terms, without the necessity for any Congressional action, certain State activities inconsistent with national well-being in these two respects. Thus the States, lest they interfere with the nation's international objectives in war and peace, were forbidden to enter into any "treaty, alliance, or confederation"; they were further forbidden, unless the Congress should consent, to enter into any arrangement with a foreign power, of undefined lesser order, called an "agreement or compact"; they were forbidden to create State privateers; they were forbidden to keep State troops or a State navy in peacetime save with Congressional consent; they were forbidden to engage in war unless invaded or in "imminent" danger.

The State parochialism, the destructive rivalries which had emerged under the Confederation, called forth a different set of constitutional provisions. Section Ten of the First Article limits the State powers to tax in a number of respects. Without the consent of Congress no State may lay "imposts or duties on imports or exports" save such as may defray the cost of inspections. Nor may any State lay a "duty of tonnage," unless Congress consents. And in no event may the States "coin money; emit bills of credit; make anything but gold and silver coin a tender in payment of debts; . . . pass any law . . . impairing the obligation of contracts . . ." Perhaps connected with the xenophobia remaining from wartime emotions, which might still be a fertile field for international discontents, were the prohibitions against "any bill of attainder" or "*ex post facto* law"; perhaps these provisions expressed a moral sense as well, a feeling of contrition at some of the things which had been done by the States under the Confederation. The command that no State shall grant any title of nobility seems a reaction of frontier democracy; like its counterpart in Section Nine, it is a suspicious exorcism of magnates bedecked with glittering Orders; it is a little aside from the other prohibitions of Section Ten.

In our constitutional history the Contract Clause, forbidding any "law impairing the obligation of contracts . . ." has been the most-discussed provision of that Section. That clause was probably intended to inhibit a sort of State legislation, well-known during the Confederation, which granted various forms of relief to debtors pressed by post-war hardships.[205] But the first Supreme Court opinion to construe

[204] See Marshall in *Gibbons* v. *Ogden*, 9 Wheat. 1, 194–195 (1824).
[205] See John Fiske *The Critical Period of American History* (Boston: Houghton Mifflin and Co., 1888) Chapter IV, for a vivid account now out of fashion.

it, *Fletcher* v. *Peck* in 1810,[206] dealt with a colossal Georgia land-jobbing scheme.

The Georgia legislature in 1795 had granted to General James Gunn and his associates, operating as four land companies, a tract originally supposed to contain twenty million acres, but (as in those days sometimes happened) subsequently found to contain thirty-five million.[207] For this grant Gunn and his friends agreed to pay Georgia five hundred thousand dollars. The price was thus a little under a cent and a half an acre. Even in those days of huge land sales of tracts with dubious titles, then almost entirely inaccessible, unsurveyed, partly occupied by hostile Indian tribes—still this purchase was quite a bargain. Gunn and his friends, so men generally thought, had bribed the great majority of the Georgia legislators; the people of Georgia were infuriated. Next year they turned the rascals out; a newly elected legislature, convened in 1796, repealed the Act of 1795 and publicly burned the offending statute by starting a fire with rays of sun focused by a burning glass, in order that Heaven itself might condemn the iniquitous deed![208] Unfortunately, perhaps, for Georgia, one of the four land companies had sold a large tract of the lands to a group of Boston capitalists, who in turn sold exclusively to investors, who lived in Pennsylvania, New Jersey, New York and New England. The buyers argued that any equity of rescission which Georgia might originally have had was cut off by bona fide purchase, and that they as buyers in good faith were not linked up with any Gunn fraud. They insisted the titles vested in them could not be divested by subsequent State legislation. Georgia ceded its claims to the United States in 1802 and for six years the claimants under the 1795 title made unavailing efforts to get Congress to pay for their lands. In 1803, a group of the claimants decided to try judicial remedies. Before the revocation by the 1796 Georgia legislature, the Gunn syndicate had granted part of a tract to one Greenleaf, and Greenleaf in turn had conveyed to a man named Prime. After the revocatory act of the Georgia legislature, further conveyances from Prime and his successors had brought to a man

[206] 6 Cranch 87.

[207] The acreage figures I take from Charles Warren, *Supreme Court in United States History*, I, p. 392.

[208] See for a justification of the propriety of the original sale of the Georgia lands, M. C. Klingelsmith, "James Wilson and the So-called Yazoo Fraud" 56 *Univ. of Pennsylvania Law Review* (Old Series) 1 (1908). Mr. Klingelsmith points out that Georgia's "Western lands" had uncertain boundaries and a still more uncertain title. England, Spain, Georgia, the United States, and scanty scattered settlers, all asserted various claims to the lands, and disputed these with the Indians. Georgia needed money badly. Mr. Klingelsmith argues with considerable persuasive force that for such a pig-in-a-poke, a half-million dollars was a fair enough price. Some of the buyers were thoroughly respectable citizens.

named John Peck a tract lying on the east side of the Mississippi River, a comparatively modest grant for those times, supposed to contain only fifteen thousand acres. In 1803 Peck had sold the fifteen thousand acres to Robert Fletcher, for three thousand dollars. Peck's deed to Fletcher contained an express covenant—

> . . . that the title to the premises so conveyed by the State of Georgia, and finally vested in the said Peck, has been in no way constitutionally or legally impaired by virtue of any subsequent act of any subsequent legislature of the said State of Georgia.[209]

Fletcher in 1803, immediately after buying the land brought an action against Peck, the seller, in the United States Circuit Court for the district of Massachusetts, alleging that Peck's warranty had been broken by the legislature which had revoked the grant. The case was "continued" by consent from term to term until October, 1806, when a jury, by special verdict,[210] found the history of the title, and the Circuit Court, on which Associate Justice William Cushing of the Supreme Court sat as Circuit Justice, rendered its judgment in favor of Peck, thus upholding the validity of the grant to Fletcher, and adjudging the invalidity of the revocatory act of 1796. Thereupon Fletcher sued out a writ of error, bringing the case to the Supreme Court of the United States at the 1809 term.

Counsel for both sides were eminent for professional ability and for conservative, respectable character. For Fletcher, Luther Martin of Maryland made the first argument and later a reargument ordered by the Court. For the defendant, Peck, as his counsel at the first argument appeared at the February term, 1809, John Quincy Adams and Robert Goodloe Harper. At the February, 1810, term of the Supreme Court of the United States, the defendant Peck appeared by Harper again and by Joseph Story, later to be a Justice of the Supreme Court, first Dane Professor at Harvard Law School, and author of *Commentaries on the Constitution*.

This was not the first litigation concerning the validity of the Georgia grant and the attempted revocation. In 1799 the Supreme Judicial Court of Massachusetts had passed on the question in the case of *Darby* v. *Blake*, reported many years later in 226 Massachusetts 618 from an account published in the Columbian Centinel, a Boston newspaper, of October 9, 1799. In that case a purchaser of part of the Georgia land, who had given a note for the price, resisted payment of the note on the ground that the consideration had failed because of

---

[209] See 6 Cranch 87, p. 88.
[210] A "special verdict" finds in some detail what the facts are, instead of finding simply for the defendant, or in favor of the plaintiff for so many dollars.

the revocatory act of the Georgia legislature. The Supreme Judicial Court of Massachusetts held that the Georgia revocatory act was

> a mere nullity—as a flagrant, outrageous violation of the first and fundamental principles of social compacts. . . . The Repealing Act of Georgia was moreover declared void, because it was considered directly repugnant to Article First, Section Ten of the United States Constitution, which provided that 'no State shall pass any *ex post facto* law, or law impairing the obligation of contracts.'

The Supreme Court of the United States in *Fletcher* v. *Peck* on March 16, 1810 unanimously upheld Fletcher's title and therefore found that Fletcher had no cause of action against Peck, and so found that Georgia's revocatory act was ineffective. John Marshall, who wrote the opinion of the Court, found that a grant of land was a contract which had been executed; the obligation of the grant still continued. A revocatory statute could not forfeit

> the estate of Fletcher for a crime not committed by himself, but by those from whom he purchased. This cannot be effected in the form of an *ex post facto* law or bill of attainder; why, then is it allowable in the form of a law annulling the original grant? . . .

> It is, then, the unanimous opinion of the court, that, in this case, the estate having passed into the hands of a purchaser for a valuable consideration, without notice, the state of Georgia was restrained, either by general principles, which are common to our free institutions, or by the particular provisions of the Constitution of the United States, from passing a law whereby the estate of the plaintiff in the premises so purchased could be constitutionally and legally impaired and rendered null and void.[211]

Mr. Justice Johnson, like others, had had some qualms lest the case be an amicable one, intended to document the validity of the title; but the eminence of counsel had stifled his doubts.[212] Johnson recited at the close of his opinion concurring in the Supreme Court's upholding of Fletcher's title—

> I have been very unwilling to proceed to the decision of this cause at all. It appears to me to bear strong evidence, upon the face of it, of being a mere feigned case. It is our duty to decide on the rights, but not on the speculations of parties. My confidence, however, in the respectable gentlemen who have been engaged for the parties, has

[211] See 6 Cranch 138, 139. Mr. Justice Johnson wrote a concurring opinion. An "opinion of the Court" is one in whose reasoning and language a majority agree. A "concurring opinion" may agree in the result, but not in the reasons; or it may add other reasons. A dissenting opinion explains a differing minority result.

[212] For a biography of Mr. Justice Johnson see Donald G. Morgan, *Justice William Johnson, the First Dissenter* (Columbia: Univ. of South Carolina Press, 1954).

induced me to abandon my scruples, in the belief that they would never consent to impose a mere feigned case upon this court.

Fletcher v. *Peck* was the first case in which the Supreme Court of the United States declared invalid a State statute on the ground of its conflict with the Constitution. Georgia representatives on the floor of the Congress cried out in fury at the iniquity of the Court's decision. On the other hand the buyers in Fletcher's situation sought recompense from Congress. After long debate the Congress on March 31, 1814, adopted an Act providing for the indemnification of claimants of public lands "in the Mississippi Territory" concerned in the grants described in *Fletcher* v. *Peck*. The statute required the claimants to surrender their claims to the United States of America, in return for which, when nine-tenths of the granted lands should have been surrendered, the Treasury of the United States was to issue "certificates of stock, not bearing interest, and expressing on their face, that the same are payable out of the first moneys in the Treasury of the United States, arising from the sale of public lands in the Mississippi Territory, after the money due to the State of Georgia and the expense of surveying such lands have been satisfied."[213] Persons claiming under the Upper Mississippi Company were to have three hundred and fifty thousand dollars; those claiming under the Tennessee Company, six hundred thousand dollars; those claiming under the Georgia-Mississippi Company, one million five hundred and fifty thousand dollars; and those claiming under the Georgia Company, two million two hundred and fifty thousand dollars; another category of claimants described as "claiming under citizens' rights" were to have two hundred and fifty thousand dollars. Thus at length not only the Supreme Court but the Congress gave recognition to the titles derived through the 1795 Act of the Georgia legislature.

In 1819 the Supreme Court decided another famous Contract Clause dispute, the *Dartmouth College* case, holding invalid a New Hampshire statute which, in place of Dartmouth's original royal charter, purported to substitute a more democratic charter which would make Dartmouth a sort of State university.[214] Daniel Webster presented the argument on behalf of the trustees claiming under the old charter. Dartmouth had been Webster's college, and his argument (tradition insists) came to a climax with this moving declaration, "It is a small college, but there are those who love it."[215]

---

[213] See 3 Statutes at Large, p. 116.

[214] *Dartmouth College* v. *Woodward*, 4 Wheaton 518.

[215] Webster's *Works* print his argument, which included many references to English decisions concerning colleges at English universities. However that text does not contain the famous sentence about Dartmouth.

A few days after the Dartmouth College decision, the Supreme Court handed down another Contract Clause judgment, *Sturges* v. *Crowninshield*,[216] which delivered still another blow to State autonomy. Directly involved was a New York insolvency statute which purported to discharge insolvents from their debts. The Court held the New York act unconstitutional. At the time of this decision the United States was in the midst of a financial depression which followed the war of 1812–1815. No national bankruptcy act was in effect, and *Sturges* v. *Crowninshield*, which made clear to the people of the country their dependency on national legislation, emphasized the increasing importance in daily life of the central government and the secondary position which the States were acquiring.

By 1819 then, the Supreme Court of the United States had by virtue of the Contract Clause held land titles, corporate charters, and promises to pay money, immune from State erosion. One might from these decisions have expected that the Contract Clause would remain a powerful force for maintaining the economic *status quo ante*. However, its effect was cut down by later decisions and by ingenious legislation. In 1827 the Supreme Court held that a contract made after a State insolvency law had become effective, was dischargeable by such a statute. The Contract Clause had no application; the law in effect when the parties made the contract became an implied condition of the obligation. This disposed of cases where debtor and creditor were both in the enacting State when the contract was made, and the suit was brought in that State's courts. But where Saunders, a Kentuckian, sued Ogden, on a contract Ogden had executed in New York when he lived there, the Supreme Court held by a vote of four justices to three that debtor Ogden got no defense from a discharge he had obtained under a New York insolvency statute. New York or other States could not thus "pass beyond their own limits, and the rights of their own citizens, and act upon the rights of citizens of other States . . ."[217] In the then absence of a federal bankruptcy statute the conflict of State laws thus made difficult a discharge from debt where the debtor was a large trader with commercial relations in several States. But for the local farmer or tradesman a State insolvency law, if antecedent to his debts, could do a great deal. States were not always prompt enough with

[216] 4 Wheaton 122 (1819). Though *Sturges* v. *Crowninshield* is reported earlier in the fourth volume of Wheaton than the *Dartmouth College* case, Warren points out that it was decided a week later. See 1 Warren p. 492. The early reporters did not print the opinions of the Supreme Court in the order of the decision of the cases, and the early reports are dated only by the term in which they were decided. Modern opinions give the day, month and year, which much facilitates chronology.

[217] *Ogden* v. *Saunders*, 12 Wheaton 213 (1827).

their legislation, however. A serious depression struck the United States at the end of the 1830's; Illinois enacted a supervening mortgage-relief statute, extending the period for redemption from foreclosure, and prohibiting foreclosure sales unless two-thirds of the value of the premises, as fixed by appraisal, were bid. The Supreme Court held that the legislation offended the Contract Clause.[218] Perhaps a difference in social attitudes, produced by nearly a century of time, accounts for the opposite result in 1934.[219]

One of the early decisions of the Taney court decided the important question whether the Contract Clause guaranteed a prior chartered corporation against competition from technologically improved devices operated by corporations set up by the same State. This was the *Charles River Bridge Case*, involving a chartered toll-bridge between Charlestown and Boston in Massachusetts. That State, by a charter granted subsequent to the charter of the old Bridge Company, provided for a new bridge which was to become free of toll after a fairly short time. Clearly this would much diminish the value of the earlier charter. This case was one of Webster's defeats.[220] He argued that the new charter unconstitutionally impaired the contract of the old. Chief Justice Taney, however, writing the prevailing opinion, rejected Webster's argument on behalf of the old proprietors, and held that as the old charter did not in terms create an exclusive privilege, the Court would not so construe it.

The *Charles River Bridge* case was important in at least two ways. For one thing, many States had chartered toll-bridges, toll-roads, and canals, but now newly invented steam railroads were arriving, which promised rapid development of the country unless the charters of the older means of transport invalidated corporations which would effectively destroy them by competition. The *Bridge Case* made clear that the Supreme Court recognized the importance of a considerable measure of State retained control over economic matters, and hence that the effect of the Contract Clause should not be expanded by implication.

The *Bridge Case* has another significant aspect. Chief Justice Taney's opinion, in a very modern fashion, took into account what might be called the "legislative" considerations which influenced his non-exclusive construction of the older charter. He pointed to the millions of dollars invested in railroads and canals on lines of travel hitherto occupied by turnpike corporations. He wrote

> Let it once be understood that such charters carry with them this unknown and undefined property in a line of travelling, and you will

[218] *Bronson* v. *Kinzie,* 1 Howard 311 (1843).
[219] *Home Building and Loan Ass'n* v. *Blaisdell,* 290 U.S. 398.
[220] *Charles River Bridge* v. *Warren Bridge,* 11 Peters 420 (1837).

soon find the old turnpike corporations awakening from their sleep, and calling upon this court to put down the improvements which have taken their place. . . . We shall be thrown back to the improvements of the last century, and obliged to stand still until the claims of the old corporations shall be satisfied, and they shall consent to permit these States to avail themselves of the lights of modern science. . . .[221]

Associate Justice Henry Baldwin, who did not dissent from the court's judgment, still felt dismay when counsel in the *Bridge Case* cited matter other than traditional legal precedents. He published a protesting pamphlet;[222] he wrote

> . . . we have been referred for the true interpretation of the Constitution to books, essays, arguments, opinions, speeches, debates in conventions and legislative bodies, by jurists and statesmen, and by some who were neither; which would not be suffered to be read in any court, as entitled to respect in construing an ordinary act of legislation, or a contract between individuals.

Men always hope, a little wistfully, that there can be found some definite and established discipline, "the law," which can be found written down in books of statutes, and which will eliminate the difficult search for policy and the choice between social objectives. Thus in April 1956 the then Attorney General of Georgia, with an associate, wrote in the American Bar Association Journal concerning the school segregation cases

> The doctrine of judicial notice extends only to those things of common knowledge that lie without the realm of science, or to that one science in which judges are presumed to be learned or experts themselves—the science of law. . . . The findings of social science are sometimes regarded as elaborate statements of what everybody knows in language that nobody understands.

> While little harm can come from such an undertaking, great harm will result when a social scientist takes his deductions and generalizations into the field of judicial interpretation and treats them as the equivalent of law.[223]

---

[221] Louis D. Brandeis was not engaged in rash innovation when in a 1908 brief he wrote to uphold an Oregon statute prescribing a ten-hour work day for women, he introduced a mass of medical and sociological data to demonstrate the reasonableness of the enactment. The Supreme Court found the statute valid despite a 14th Amendment attack. *Muller* v. *Oregon* 208 U.S. 412. Lawyers still call this sort of written argument a "Brandeis Brief."

[222] Printed in an appendix to 9 Lawyers' Edition, Supreme Court Reports, p. 869 *et seq.*

[223] Eugene Cook and William I. Potter "The School Segregation Cases: Opposing the Supreme Court" Am. Bar Ass'n Journal (1956) 313, 315, 317.

Other and later decisions of the Supreme Court still further diminished the importance of the Contract Clause. In 1880 the Supreme Court held that although Mississippi had chartered a lottery corporation, that State retained its power to protect "the public health or the public morals," and despite the Contract Clause could therefore impose a subsequent prohibition of all lotteries, which would make the charter of the lottery corporation valueless.[224] And State legislatures, soon after the *Dartmouth Case*[225] was decided, adopted as a precautionary device statutes which made all corporate charters thereafter granted subject, at the pleasure of the State legislature, to amendment, alteration or repeal; some States instituted similar constitutional provisions. In 1882 the Supreme Court upheld such a statute enacted in Massachusetts.[226] Since 1898 a national bankruptcy act has continuously been in effect and there appears to be no movement toward its repeal. As an effective guarantee of the economic *status quo* the Contract Clause had a fairly short life. For a half-century, however, from 1886 through 1936, the Due Process Clause of the Fourteenth Amendment operated somewhat similarly in limiting the more drastic innovations in State economic regulation. Only the "constitutional revolution" of 1937 caused "economic due process" to fade into the background with the Commerce Clause.

Banks, National and State[227]

In 1780 banks were, to most Americans, novel and bewildering creations. Parliament had created the Bank of England in 1694;[228] during the 18th century some American Colonies had organized loan offices to which men could mortgage their land in exchange for colonial notes of various denominations, which the borrower could use to pay debts or finance operations.[229] In 1780, to provide money to obtain needed supplies for Washington's army, ninety patriotic Philadelphians organized themselves as "The Pennsylvania Bank." They lent their own funds to the Bank, receiving in return its notes which bore six per cent interest. The Continental Congress passed a resolution to protect the

[224] *Stone* v. *Mississippi*, 101 U.S. 814.

[225] 4 Wheaton 518, 1819.

[226] *Greenwood* v. *Freight Co.*, 105 U.S. 13.

[227] See generally Bray Hammond, *Banks and Politics in America* (Princeton: Princeton University Press, 1957).

[228] 5 Wm. and Mary, c. 20.

[229] Mr. Justice Story reviews the history of such colonial note-issues, or "bills of credit" in his dissenting opinion in *Briscoe* v. *The Bank of the Commonwealth of Kentucky*, 11 Peters 257 (1837).

associates against loss,[230] and in due course did repay the subscribers, who liquidated the Bank in 1784.

Meantime in 1781 the Congress chartered "The President and Company of the Bank of North America," though congressional authority to incorporate a bank was doubtful. Under a charter obtained from the Pennsylvania legislature in 1782 the Bank of North America continued its business until 1929 when it was merged with another Philadelphia bank. In New York Alexander Hamilton organized the Bank of New York in 1784, without a public charter. In 1791 Aaron Burr obtained legislative authorization for a rival New York institution, the Bank of the Manhattan Company, by a clause inserted in the charter of a corporation with the purported primary purpose of bringing drinking-water to the people of New York. The Manhattan Company did indeed install a water system, and did start banking operations under its charter. It is now one of the component institutions of the Chase Manhattan Company. The Massachusetts legislature incorporated "The Massachusetts Bank" in 1784; it is now a component of the First National Bank of Boston. In 1790 Maryland chartered the Bank of Maryland. Thus by that year banks were operating in Philadelphia, New York, Boston, and Baltimore.

To the man in the street or on the farm, banks were remote, mysterious, and somewhat fearsome creations. Their power to create "money," simply by affixing signatures to pieces of paper, seemed a sort of necromancy, practiced by adepts who could thus dominate the lives of plain hard-working and honest folk. For uncomplex citizens banks symbolized all that went with cities, fine linen, and incomprehensible, shifty dealing; common men tended to suspect them.

In 1790 Hamilton, Secretary of the Treasury, proposed a federally chartered bank, and in 1791 the Congress incorporated the Bank of the United States.[231] The justificatory preamble of the statute recited that the institution—

> . . . will be very conducive to the successful conducting of the national finances; will tend to give facility to the obtaining loans, for the use of the government, in sudden emergencies; and will be productive of considerable advantages to trade and industry; . . . .

The Bank was to have capital stock of ten millions of dollars divided into twenty-five thousand shares, each of four hundred dollars. Subscription for shares were to be open to the public, including any "body politic." The corporation was to have as its official name "The Presi-

---

[230] *Journals of the Continental Congress* (34 vols.; Washington: Government Printing Office, 1904–37) XVII pp. 542, 548–49.
[231] 1 Stat. at L. 191.

dent, Directors and Company, of the Bank of the United States" and was to continue as a corporation until the fourth day of March 1811.

The laudatory preamble of the Act of incorporation was a wise provision, legally and politically. President Washington hesitated to approve the measure, in troubled doubt as to the constitutional power of the Congress to charter a Bank. Edmund Randolph, the Attorney General, and Thomas Jefferson, the Secretary of State, both found it unconstitutional. Jefferson submitted a memorandum in which he wrote that the Bank was perhaps "convenient but certainly not necessary"; and therefore was not within the last clause of Article I, Section 8 of the Constitution, which authorized the Congress—

> To make all Laws which shall be necessary and proper for carrying into Execution the foregoing Powers, and all other Powers vested by this Constitution in the Government of the United States, or in any Department or Officer thereof.

However Hamilton handed to President Washington a memorandum in which he argued that the "necessary and proper" clause entrusted to the Congress all the means requisite and fairly applicable to the attainment of the powers enumerated in the Constitution, not specifically precluded by restrictions and exceptions specified in its text, not immoral, and not contrary to the essential ends of political society.[232] Washington had asked Madison to prepare a veto message, but on February 25, 1791, convinced by Hamilton, he instead approved the Act creating the Bank of the United States. Between 1792 and 1805 the Bank opened branch offices in Boston, New York, Baltimore, Charleston, Norfolk, Washington, Savannah and New Orleans.

A good deal of local jealousy arose against this powerful federal instrumentality. States imposed taxes which became threatening burdens. A Georgia tax collector seized two thousand dollars in silver from the vaults of the Savannah branch of the Bank of the United States. The Bank sued the collector in the United States Circuit Court for the district of Georgia to recover the sum taken; the Circuit Court dismissed the action on the ground that mere federal incorporation was not a ground of jurisdiction in a federal court. The Supreme Court reversed the Circuit Court with an opinion by Chief Justice Marshall; if all the plaintiffs who composed the corporation as individuals were citizens of States other than Georgia, Marshall wrote, the United States courts would have jurisdiction based on diversity of citizenship, even though the corporation itself was not then regarded as a "citizen."[233] The law reports leave the reader in suspense, at a loss

---

[232] Hammond, *Banks and Politics in America*, pp. 116–118.
[233] See *Bank of the United States* v. *Deveaux*, 5 Cranch 61 (1809).

to know whether the Savannah branch of the Bank of the United States ever got back its two thousand dollars.

The charter of the first Bank of the United States by its terms was to expire in 1811.[234] The Senate divided evenly in voting on a statute of renewal, and Vice President George Clinton, a staunch anti-Federalist, cast the deciding vote against extending the Bank's life. Stephen Girard of Philadelphia, the Bank's largest stockholder, thereupon took over its Philadelphia operations; the Bank of the United States continued doing business in the same banking house with the same staff, though now unincorporated and wholly owned by Girard. In 1815 the Congress passed a bill creating a new Bank of the United States; President Madison vetoed the measure on the ground that it proposed a Bank too free from government control. However, in 1816 the Congress again passed a measure chartering a second Bank of the United States which President Madison this time approved.[235] The Bank flourished at first; by the end of 1817 it had eighteen branches. When a serious recession swept the country in 1818 the bank's efforts to collect outstanding loans made it extremely unpopular. And news got about that in Baltimore James W. McCulloch, the cashier of the Bank's local branch, was unscrupulously using the Bank's resources to promote the large speculations of a group of financiers.

Tennessee, Georgia, North Carolina, Kentucky, Ohio, and Maryland enacted vindictive tax legislation directed against the Bank of the United States. The Maryland statute required a tax stamp on each bank-note issued by any bank not operating under a Maryland charter, and imposed a penalty of five hundred dollars for each violation. The Baltimore branch of the Bank of the United States ignored the Maryland tax, whereupon Maryland sued McCulloch, a rising young Baltimore businessman and cashier of that branch, to recover the statutory penalty. The parties agreed that if Maryland was entitled to recover, it should have judgment for twenty-five hundred dollars. Maryland recovered in the County Court of Baltimore County; the Maryland Court of Appeals affirmed. Thereupon McCulloch by writ of error brought the case to the Supreme Court of the United States. The leaders of the American bar were briefed in the Bank case. Daniel Webster, William Pinkney and William Wirt, Attorney General of the United States, argued for McCulloch. Maryland was represented by Luther Martin, Attorney General of that State and by able associates

---

[234] Modern corporate charters ordinarily have no stated limit of existence; but in earlier times when corporations were eyed suspiciously, legislatures often gave them only a prescribed life.

[235] 3 Statutes at Large 266.

Joseph Hopkinson of Philadelphia and Walter Jones of Washington.[236] For nine days the Court heard these distinguished advocates. Only three days after the close of the arguments, John Marshall delivered the opinion of the unanimous Supreme Court, which ruled in favor of McCulloch, reversing the judgment of the Maryland courts.[237] He commented on the absence, among the powers specifically entrusted to Congress in the Constitution, of any mention of power to establish a bank or create a corporation. But, he said (and his words were wise), "in considering this question . . . we must never forget that it is a *constitution* we are expounding."[238]

The United States had the constitutional power to lay and collect taxes, to borrow money, to regulate commerce, to declare and conduct war, to raise and support armies and navies. To carry out these functions the Congress was authorized to make "all laws which shall be necessary and proper." Necessity did not mean absolutely physical necessity, an indispensable means of existence. The act to incorporate the Bank of the United States was sufficiently "necessary and proper" to be "a law made in pursuance of the Constitution" and a part of the "supreme law of the land." Might the State of Maryland, then, tax that "means employed by the government of the Union for the execution of its powers?" ". . . [T]he power to tax," Marshall wrote with enduring rhetoric, "involves the power to destroy . . ." Such a tax, Marshall thought, must be unconstitutional.[239]

[236] Marshall had owned seventeen shares of stock in the Bank; he sold them before the argument and never thereafter acquired any.

[237] *McCulloch* v. *Maryland*, 4 Wheaton 316 (1819).

[238] "I believe, the single most important utterance in the literature of constitutional law—most important because most comprehensive and comprehending." Mr. Justice Felix Frankfurter, in "Marshall and the Judicial Function," 69 *Harv. L. Rev.* 217 (1955).

[239] *McCulloch* v. *Maryland*, 4 Wheaton 316 (1819). In 1928 Justice Holmes dissented from the Supreme Court's judgment in *Panhandle Oil Company* v. *Mississippi*, 277 U.S. 218. A majority of the Court had there struck down, as an undue invasion of the federal government's powers, a Mississippi tax levied on one of its citizens for selling gasoline to the United States for the Coast Guard and a veterans' hospital; the tax had been upheld by the State Supreme Court. Holmes wrote

> It seems to me that the State court was right. I should say plainly right, but for the effect of certain dicta of Chief Justice Marshall which culminated in or rather were founded upon his often quoted proposition that the power to tax is the power to destroy. In those days it was not recognized as it is today that most of the distinctions of the law are distinctions of degree. If the States had any power it was assumed that they had all power, and that the necessary alternative was to deny it altogether. But this court which so often has defeated the attempt to tax in certain ways can defeat an attempt to discriminate or otherwise go too far without wholly abolishing the power to tax. The power to tax is not the power to destroy while this court sits.

McCulloch v. *Maryland* did not end all the difficulties of the Bank of the United States. In 1819, Osborn, State Auditor of Ohio, claiming not to be bound by the *McCulloch* case, sent a State officer, John L. Harper, to the Chilicothe Office of the Bank to collect one hundred thousand dollars which Ohio claimed as taxes due. Harper seized and took away from the Bank's vault the sum required, and after deducting a fee of two thousand dollars for his services, deposited the balance in another bank to the credit of the State of Ohio. Thereupon the Bank of the United States sued Osborn and Harper to get its money back. The charter of the second Bank of the United States had eliminated the jurisdictional difficulty of the *Deveaux* case[240] by expressly authorizing the Bank to sue in any circuit court of the United States. Ohio set up the Eleventh Amendment as a defense to the Bank's action.[241] The court overrode this defense and gave judgment for return of the money seized.[242]

McCulloch, one regrets to say, came to the end of his banking career under some suspicion in the courts. Maryland prosecuted him and two colleagues, Buchanan and Williams, for conspiracy to take a large sum of money from the Bank of the United States and convert it to their own use. After two trials and an intermediate appeal they were acquitted of this charge.[243]

McCulloch, though acquitted, still did not pay what he owed the Bank. He ultimately brought disaster on a number of his one-time colleagues. He was a young man, with no assets, with a salary of four thousand dollars a year as cashier of the Baltimore branch of the Bank. Yet McCulloch with two associates, the President of the Baltimore branch, and a director of the parent Bank, to finance their own commercial operations had borrowed from that institution three million four hundred and ninety-seven thousand, seven hundred dollars. When the parent Bank of the United States finally investigated the matter, McCulloch offered to procure sixteen merchants of Baltimore, each to become bound for twelve thousand five hundred dollars as surety for McCulloch's debts; he did produce a substantial number who signed. The Bank appropriately dismissed McCulloch from its service, and years later, at the 1826 term, the Supreme Court upheld a judgment

---

[240] See page 367 for *Bank of United States* v. *Deveaux*, 5 Cranch 61 (1809).

[241] See for the history of suits against States page 223 and following, above.

[242] *Osborn* v. *Bank of the United States*, 9 Wheaton 738 (1824).

[243] See *State* v. *Buchanan*, 5 Harris and Johnson (Md.) 317 (1823), and Hammond, *Banks and Politics in America*, p, 271. The proceedings came to be called the "Baltimore Conspiracy Cases."

against one of the sixteen merchants for the sum he had agreed to pay on McCulloch's debts.[244]

In the decade of the 1820's the Bank suffered in general esteem from two adverse influences. What people called the "Baltimore Conspiracy" in which McCulloch and his associates engaged, the manipulation, by insiders, of the Bank's power to issue paper that passed as money, and thus to make large loans to themselves,—this had shaken the confidence of honorable and scrupulous men. In 1819 the Bank installed as a new President Langdon Cheves[245] of South Carolina, who began the painful tasks that all banks must undertake in times of depression. But a large segment of the optimistic promoters of an expanding America then resented the Bank's efforts to conduct its affairs in a restrained and conservative manner. Cheves kept the Bank in better order, but resigned at the end of 1822. Nicholas Biddle of Philadelphia succeeded him as President. Both men aroused the anger of the State banks because the Bank of the United States insisted that State banks pay notes promptly. The Planters' Bank of Georgia, for example, made large loans to Georgians, issuing to them notes of the Planters' Bank which the borrowers could use as money. A good many Georgians owed large debts to the Bank of the United States, and promptly paid their debts to the United States Bank with the notes issued by the Georgia bank. When the United States Bank required the Planters' Bank of Georgia to pay its notes, the Georgia financiers were genuinely pained. Cheves and Biddle, they felt, were unprogressive, out of harmony with a flourishing young Republic. Why not recognize that bank-notes were money; the more money around, the richer and more progressive the nation? The Bank of the United States unkindly sued the Planters' Bank of Georgia on its notes in the United States Circuit Court in Georgia; the Planters' Bank, among other defenses, pointed out that the State of Georgia was part-owner of the Planters' Bank, and asserted that under the Eleventh Amendment Georgia was immune from suit. In due course the litigation reached the Supreme Court of the United States which unanimously held that the Planters' Bank had asserted no valid defense.[246]

[244] See *Etting* v. *The Bank of the United States,* 11 Wheaton 59 (1826).

[245] Hammond explains (p. 262) that Cheves pronounced his name Chivis. He was an able and honorable man, who undertook harassing and thankless work: he deserves to have his name spoken as he wished.

[246] *Bank of the United States* v. *Planters' Bank of Georgia,* 9 Wheaton 904 (1824). In 1941 the Reconstruction Finance Corporation, a lending institution owned by the United States, set up its government ownership as a defense to liability for court-costs. Counsel for its opponent, Menihan Corporation, cited *Bank of United States* v. *Planters' Bank of Georgia,* in which Marshall had

The political journals of the time were violent and abusive. Biddle was a Philadelphian, urbane, traveled, cultivated. Newspapers in the more rural and frontier areas pictured him not only supercilious but presumably knavish, a devious financier of the McCulloch type, misusing the congressional charter of the Bank to make money at the expense of worthy and less sophisticated men. Andrew Jackson, a frontiersman himself, was the hero for the growing west. A cartoon, evidently dated about 1833, pictures Jackson as a severe, grave, towering figure, destroying the Bank with lightning while a crowd of little terror-stricken men, including Daniel Webster and Henry Clay, are trying to escape the thunderbolts. Last of the fleeing wretches is Biddle; he has hoofs instead of feet; horns grow from his head, and a spear-pointed tail springs from under his elegant tail-coat![247]

In early July 1832 the Congress passed a bill to extend the 1816 charter of the Bank of the United States for a further term of fifteen years, but on July 10, 1832 Jackson vetoed the measure with a long denunciatory message. He pointed out among other things that, of the twenty-eight million dollars of the stock of the bank, more than eight millions were held by foreign stockholders "mostly of Great Britain"; and over thirteen and a half millions were held in the Middle and Eastern States. Renewal of the charter would add 20 or 30 per cent to the value of the Bank's stock. As Jackson put it, "for these gratuities to foreigners and to some of our own opulent citizens the act secures no equivalent whatever."[248] In this message President Jackson asserted that the Supreme Court's earlier judgment of the Bank's constitutionality did not bind him; he was under a duty to decide for himself whether the Bank's charter had been beyond the powers of Congress.

---

written, "It is, we think a sound principle that when a government becomes a partner in any trading company, it divests itself, so far as concerns the transactions of that company, of its sovereign character, and takes that of a private citizen." Commenting on this effort of the Reconstruction Finance Corporation to cloak itself in the immunity of its governmental owner, counsel for Menihan cited in their brief two lines from King John, Act III, Scene 1—

> Thou wear a lion's hide! Doff it for shame
> And hang a calfskin on those recreant limbs.

The Supreme Court, as it had in Planters' Bank, held the corporation liable despite governmental ownership. *Reconstruction Finance Corporation* v. *J. G. Menihan Corp.*, 312 U.S. 81 (1941). The Court's opinion, written by Chief Justice Hughes, does not disclose whether it was more influenced by Marshall or by Shakespeare.

[247] The cartoon is reproduced from the Bettmann Archive, in Carman and Syrett, *History of the American People* (2 vols.; New York: Alfred A. Knopf, 1952) I, opposite p. 390.

[248] See Richardson, *Messages and Papers of the Presidents* (10 vols.; Washington: Government Printing Office, 1896–99) III, pp. 1139–1142.

If the opinion of the Supreme Court covered the whole ground of this act, it ought not to control the coordinate authorities of this Government. The Congress, the Executive, and the Court, must each for itself be guided by its own opinion of the Constitution. Each public officer who takes an oath to support the Constitution swears that he will support it as he understands it, and not as it is understood by others.

Meantime the Bank of the United States had three years more to operate, and was fortified by deposits of federal funds. On September 20, 1833, President Jackson announced his intention to withdraw these United States deposits. The Secretary of the Treasury, William J. Duane, refused to do so. The President dismissed him, and appointed in his place the Attorney General, Roger Brooke Taney. On September 26, Taney announced that, beginning on the first of October, he would cease to make deposits to the credit of the United States in the Bank of the United States, and would instead make government deposits in seven State-chartered banks.

Not every public man agreed with the move. On March 28, 1834 the Senate resolved, by a vote of 26 out of 46 senators present and voting,

. . . that the President in the late Executive proceedings in relation to the public revenue, has assumed upon himself authority and power not conferred by the Constitution and law, but in derogation of both.

The President on April 15, 1834 sent to the Senate a "Protest" justifying the removal of the deposits and his dismissal of Secretary Duane.[249] The Senate ordered that Jackson's "Protest" be not entered on its journal.

The federal charter of the Bank of the United States expired in 1836. Only two weeks before the Bank's life would have ended, the Pennsylvania legislature gave it a new State charter, under which it continued a somewhat hectic existence until it finally failed in 1841.

Not all constitutional problems affected the federal Bank. Hard times prompted a number of States to charter their own Banks as public institutions. When farmers needed money, and the Bank of the United States or stiff-necked private banks would not lend, what was a more logical course for a State's farmers than to turn to their legislature, get it to charter a bank authorized to take a farmer's notes, secured by a mortgage on his farm or by the endorsement of his friends, and issue to him notes of the State bank, in various denominations which would circulate as currency, and which the farmer could then use to pay his bills, to support his family, and to conduct

[249] See Richardson, *Messages and Papers of the Presidents,* III, p. 1288.

his farming operations? There was, however, a little constitutional problem here. The tenth section of Article I of the federal Constitution includes among its prohibitions—

No State shall . . . emit Bills of Credit; . . .

In June 1821, the Missouri legislature passed an act establishing institutions called "loan offices," through which the State treasury was directed to issue to borrowers "certificates" in denominations of fifty cents to ten dollars, receivable for all Missouri taxes or other debts to the State, not exceeding two hundred thousand dollars in all. In 1822 one Craig, with two associates named Moore, borrowed one hundred ninety-nine dollars and ninety-nine cents[250] at one of the State loan offices, giving their promissory note for the certificates borrowed. In 1823, Missouri sued Craig and the two Moores on their note; the borrowers defended on the ground that Missouri's operations violated the Bills of Credit Clause in Article I, section 10; a note given for void Missouri notes was itself void, they argued. The Missouri State courts gave judgment in favor of the State, requiring the borrowers to pay their note; but on a writ of error the United States Supreme Court reversed this judgment. Chief Justice Marshall wrote the Court's opinion from which Justices Thompson, Johnson and McLean dissented. The Missouri certificates were issued in violation of the constitutional provision; therefore the note signed by Craig and his associates was void because Missouri gave no valid consideration for it.[251] Marshall wrote with full understanding of the States' sensitivity.

> In the argument we have been reminded by one side of the dignity of a sovereign State; of the humiliation of her submitting herself to this tribunal; of the dangers which may result from inflicting a wound on that dignity: by the other, of the still superior dignity of the people of the United States, who have spoken their will in terms which we cannot misunderstand.
>
> To these admonitions we can only answer, that if the exercise of that jurisdiction which has been imposed upon us by the Constitution and laws of the United States shall be calculated to bring on those dangers which have been indicated, or if it shall be indispensable to the preservation of the Union, and consequently, of the independence and liberty of these States, these are considerations which address them-

[250] This odd figure probably is explained by a section of the Missouri statute which authorized loans of "less than two hundred dollars" on personal security alone; that is, on the promise of individuals to pay the debt if the principal did not, without any mortgage of property.

[251] *Craig, et al.*, v. *The State of Missouri*, 4 Peters 409 (1830).

selves to those departments which may with perfect propriety be influenced by them. This department can listen only to the mandates of law, and can tread only that path which is marked out by duty.[252]

In 1820, Kentucky had established a system of loans like that of Missouri, but, a little more prudently, set up a corporation, the Bank of the Commonwealth of Kentucky, which was to issue its own bank notes rather than notes of the State of Kentucky. The Commonwealth of Kentucky owned all the stock in the bank, the president and twelve directors were chosen by joint ballot of both houses of the general Assembly of the State. The president was required to report to the legislature annually, and the notes issued by the bank were receivable in payment of taxes and all debts to the State. Supplementary Acts authorized the president and directors to issue three millions of dollars of bank notes and instructed the treasurer of the State to receive any dividends the bank might earn.

In 1831, the Bank of the Commonwealth of Kentucky sued George Briscoe and others, in the Kentucky State courts, on a note for two thousand forty-eight dollars and thirty-seven cents, which Briscoe and his associates had given to the bank in return for its bank notes. Like Craig, Briscoe defended on the ground that the Bank of the Commonwealth of Kentucky was issuing State bills of credit in violation of the tenth section of Article I of the Constitution. The State courts gave judgment for the bank requiring Briscoe and the others to repay their loans; in 1837 a majority of the Supreme Court of the United States in an opinion by Mr. Justice McLean upheld the State Court judgment. His opinion found determinative difference between the *Craig* and *Briscoe* cases in the fact that the Craig notes were issued directly by the State of Missouri, while Briscoe's notes were issued by a corporation Kentucky had chartered. One finds it a little difficult to see why the Bank of the United States, federally incorporated but in large part privately owned, was so much an agency of the federal government that it was held immune from State taxation in *McCulloch* v. *Maryland*[253] but the Bank of the Commonwealth of Kentucky was sufficiently detached from that State so that its note issues were not State bills of credit within the prohibition of Section 10, Article I. Mr. Justice Story wrote a dissenting opinion in Briscoe reviewing the history of colonial bills of credit, and setting forth his view that *Craig* v. *Missouri* should control in the *Briscoe* case.[254] Story by 1837 was an

---

[252] *Craig, et al.,* v. *The State of Missouri,* 4 Peters 437, 438 (1830).

[253] 4 Wheaton 382 (1819).

[254] *Briscoe et al.* v. *Bank of the Commonwealth of Kentucky,* 11 Peters 257 (1837).

aging, lonely man, missing Marshall and the past. *Briscoe*, he noted, had been argued twice, the first time during Marshall's life; at the conclusion of the first argument Marshall and a majority of the Court had favored deciding the case as *Craig* had been decided. Story felt that he owed this mention to his dead Chief.

Two years later, in 1839, *Bank of Augusta* v. *Earle*,[255] with an opinion for the majority of the Supreme Court written by Chief Justice Taney, upheld the national economy in despite of what was argued as contrary State law. Two banks with State charters, the Bank of Augusta, Georgia, and the Bank of the United States under its new Pennsylvania charter, and the New Orleans and Carrollton Railroad, all brought actions in the Circuit Court of the United States for the southern district of Alabama against Alabama defendants who had executed written promises to pay money, bills of exchange, which the banks and railroad had bought in Alabama. The debtors sought to defend on the ground that the plaintiff corporations were all chartered outside Alabama and hence were limited in their activities to their own States, or at any rate could do no business in Alabama, so counsel for the defense argued, for Alabama's law limited banking in Alabama to Alabama State institutions. Therefore the intruders from outside the State were in no position to sue in Alabama, even in the federal Court, to collect debts from Alabama citizens on commercial paper bought in Alabama by agents of out-of-state plaintiffs. The United States Circuit Court in Alabama upheld this ringing proclamation of economic parochialism as a valid defense. Mr. Justice McKinley of the United States Supreme Court presided at the trial, and the Circuit Court's judgment caused a good deal of alarm in the business community. What if the Supreme Court were to affirm this judgment and thus establish a rule of law that a corporation could engage in business only within the State that chartered it, or that a State, if it wished, could bar all outside corporations? More and more citizens were using the corporate form for the conduct of their business affairs. If a jealous State could ban the transactions of all but her own corporate creatures, what had become of the policy of the Constitution's Fourth Article, whose second section guarantees that "The Citizens of each State shall be entitled to all Privileges and Immunities of Citizens in the several States"? The Supreme Court reversed the judgment of the Circuit Court, and enforced the bills against the Alabama debtors. Chief Justice Taney wrote for the majority of the Court that he could find no definite statement in the law of Alabama intending to exclude out-of-State corporations from purchasing negotiable paper in Alabama.

[255] 13 Peters 519.

And it will be remembered that it is not the State of Alabama which appears here to complain of an infraction of its policy. Neither the State, nor any of its constituted authorities have interfered in this controversy. The objection is taken by persons who were parties to those contracts, and who participated in the transactions which are now alleged to have been in violation of the laws of the State.[256]

Bank of Augusta v. *Earle* was extremely useful to the economy of a growing country. At the time that the case was decided there was still much wilderness to be overcome; there were dams to be built, railroads and bridges waiting to be constructed; the United States needed the whole complex apparatus by which the products of its farms and forests were transported to places where they might be converted into useful form, and further carried and sold to men who needed them for existence. This whole process, absolutely essential to modern America, would have been retarded for a time if the Supreme Court had encouraged the States to engage in a sort of short-sighted autarchy.[257]

The scope of Taney's opinion was not so broad as the American public at first supposed. The Supreme Court did hold, to be sure, that nothing in the nature of a corporation kept it from making a contract within a State where it was not chartered; Taney wrote

> . . . we can perceive no sufficient reason for excluding them, when they are not contrary to the known policy of the State, or injurious to its interests.[258]

The Chief Justice disclaimed any intention to base the Court's judgment on any right of an out-of-State corporation to the privileges and immunities of citizens of the non-chartering State.[259] He wrote only,

> There is no law of the State [of Alabama] which attempts to define the rights of foreign corporations.[260]

To this day[261] the matter of corporate business done outside the State of charter remains one of the difficult problems in reconciliation of opposites inevitable under our federal structure. That federal system,

---

[256] *Bank of Augusta* v. *Earle*, 13 Peters 519 at 597 (1839).

[257] See Sutherland and Vinciguerra, "The Octroi and the Airplane," 32 *Cornell Law Quarterly* (1946) and A. E. Sutherland, "The Nation's Economy and State Frontiers" 8 *Stanford Law Review*, 26 (1955).

[258] 13 Peters at 589.

[259] *Ibid.*, pages 586, 587.

[260] *Ibid.*, page 597. Of course the Chief Justice was here using "foreign corporation" to mean one chartered outside the State in which it was acting—in a different State of the United States, not necessarily in a foreign country.

[261] These words are written in September 1964. They are probably not the last to be concerned with this subject.

unitary as to some matters such as interstate commerce, discrete in the States as to others such as State incorporation—necessarily presents for settlement, and for settlement not once but recurrently, in new situations as the national economy changes and develops, the choice of policies in *Bank of Augusta* v. *Earle*. To allow for an increasing population and a new social organization, more and more urban, less and less organized according to the political boundaries between States, the central government seeks to impose its norms on the economy of the nation which takes little note of internal frontiers. States, in theory at least, retain the capacity of deciding what wholly intrastate business may be carried on within their borders by men acting in the corporate form. Justice Holmes took this as a premise when he wrote in 1910[262]

> I . . . assume that it is not intended to deny or overrule what has been regarded as unquestionable since *Bank of Augusta* v. *Earle*, 13 Pet. 539, that, as to foreign corporations seeking to do business wholly within a State, that State is the master, and may prohibit or tax such business at will. . .

Difficulties arise when the Privileges and Immunities Clause of Article IV is proposed as a vehicle to carry the out-of-State corporation into a non-charter State to do business in every way as though it were locally incorporated. Does Article IV authorize Maine to charter corporations for business local to California? But there is another clause of the Constitution which applies as soon as commerce concerns more States than one. The Supreme Court has long held that a State may not unreasonably[263] impede the national commerce by regulation or tax.[264] And from time to time that Court has applied the Fourteenth Amendment to achieve the same result.[265] Justices of the Supreme Court have on several occasions suggested the desirability that the underlying problem in *Bank of Augusta* v. *Earle* requires congressional study and legislation,[266] and under Acts of Congress of 1959 and 1961 such a study is in progress in 1964.[267]

[262] Dissenting in *Western Union Telegraph Co.* v. *Kansas*, 216 U.S. 1.

[263] This word covers a multitude of considerations; behind it lies a great mass of decisional material. See for example Freund, Sutherland, Howe, and Brown, *Constitutional Law: Cases and Other Problems* (2nd ed.; Boston: Little, Brown and Co., 1961) I, Chapter IX.

[264] See e.g. *Northwestern States Portland Cement Co.* v. *Minnesota*, 358 U.S. 450 (1959).

[265] See e.g. *Miller Bros. Co.* v. *Maryland*, 347 U.S. 340 (1954).

[266] See e.g. the dissent of Justices Black, Frankfurter and Douglas in *McCarroll* v. *Dixie Greyhound Lines*, 309 U.S. 176 (1940).

[267] See Title II of 73 Stat. at L. 555, 15 U.S. Code § 381, note.

Cherokees and Georgia

Litigation in the Supreme Court, during Jackson's administration, concerning the status of the Cherokee Indians in Georgia, deserves mention here. It represents a momentary set-back for the assertion of federal power in competition with that of the States. The Cherokee nation had signed a number of agreements, designated "treaties," with the United States of America defining the status and the rights of the Cherokees. But to the white settlers of the State of Georgia the Cherokees appeared a savage people, an impediment to occupation, clearing, and cultivation of wild westward woodland. Within her borders Georgia felt that she should control matters, including the treatment of Indians, without interference by "outsiders."

In the autumn of 1830 Georgia authorities arrested a Cherokee named Corn Tassel, who had killed another Indian in tribal territory; Georgia tried him under State law, and sentenced him to hang. Counsel for Corn Tassel on December 22, 1830 obtained from the United States Supreme Court a writ of error directed to the State trial court, to test the legality of Georgia's laws in the face of the federal treaty. Governor Gilmer of Georgia treated the Supreme Court writ with disdain. Georgia's officers hanged Corn Tassel on December 24, 1830.[268]

Three days after Corn Tassel's execution the Cherokee nation caused to be served on the Governor of Georgia a writ in an action, original in the Supreme Court of the United States, to enjoin the enforcement of Georgia statutes, contrary to Indian treaties with the United Sates of America. Jackson's first annual message of December 8, 1829, had spoken sympathetically of the situation of Indian tribes within the limits of Georgia and Alabama, but had stated that it would be impossible for these people to erect an independent government within the boundaries of States. On March 18, 1831, the Supreme Court, in an opinion by Chief Justice Marshall, declined to entertain jurisdiction of the motion for an injunction brought by the Cherokees to prevent the enforcement of acts of the Georgia legislature.[269] The opinion suggests the "political question" doctrine, which the Taney court discussed in 1849 in a dispute over which of two rival organizations was the legitimate government of the State of Rhode Island.[270]

[268] See Warren, *The Supreme Court in United States History*, II, p. 193.
[269] See Richardson, *Messages and Papers of the Presidents*, III, p. 1020, and *Cherokee Nation* v. *Georgia*, 5 Peters 1 (1831).
[270] *Luther* v. *Borden*, 7 Howard 1 (1849). The doctrine asserts that the Supreme Court will disclaim jurisdiction over matters essentially "political" rather than judicial. The definition of such "political questions" has never been clear. See e.g. *Baker* v. *Carr*, 369 U.S. 186 (1962).

The following year, 1832, saw an even more serious difference between the Supreme Court and the State of Georgia. In the excitement attending on the first *Cherokee* case, the Georgia legislature had passed a statute forbidding white men to live within the limits of the lands allotted to the Cherokee nation in Georgia without a license from the governor of that State or from his agents. Two missionaries, Samuel A. Worcester and Elizur Butler, refused to obtain the required license or to leave the Cherokee area; they were convicted in a Georgia court, and sentenced to four years' imprisonment at hard labor. The United States Supreme Court issued a writ of error to the Georgia Superior Court, which was duly served on the governor and on the State attorney-general but which the Georgia authorities disregarded. On February 20, 1832, William Wirt and John Sergeant argued the *Missionaries'* case on behalf of the plaintiffs in error; no counsel appeared for Georgia. Several Cherokees, delegated by their nation, listened to the argument. When it was over Story wrote in a private letter (a little indiscreetly, for a judge) that he blushed for the country when he perceived that such legislation was suffered to pass with the silent approbation of the government of the United States.[271] On March 3, 1832, Chief Justice Marshall gave the opinion of the Supreme Court, reversing the convictions of Worcester and Butler on the ground that the treaties of the United States with the Cherokees had superseded any conflicting Georgia legislation, and hence that Georgia had no right to punish the two missionaries who were doing only what the Cherokee treaty authorized. The Supreme Court's decree reversed and annulled the Georgia court's judgment and directed that Worcester and Butler be released from custody.[272]

A statement, if repeated often enough, can come to be accepted as established; tradition has it that Andrew Jackson, on hearing of the Worcester opinion, remarked, "Well, John Marshall has made his decision. Now let him enforce it." The words probably are apocryphal.[273] But the sentiment is not incredible. In a letter Jackson wrote to the American Board of Missionaries in September 1832 he stated that he would be abusing his constitutional powers if he were to interpose his authority in the case of the missionaries.[274] However, on November

[271] Warren, *The Supreme Court in United States History*, II, p. 215.

[272] *Worcester* v. *Georgia*, 6 Peters 515.

[273] The first reference Charles Warren was able to find to Jackson's alleged remark was written thirty-two years later by Horace Greeley in his book, *The American Conflict*, I, 106. Greeley ascribed it to the then deceased Governor George N. Briggs of Massachusetts, who had been in Washington as a member of Congress when the *Worcester* case was handed down. Whether Governor Briggs had heard Jackson, or Briggs was quoting someone else, does not appear. See Warren, *The Supreme Court in United States History*, II, p. 219n.

[274] See Warren, *The Supreme Court in United States History*, II, p. 229, fn. 1.

24, 1832 the South Carolina legislature enacted its nullification ordinance. This measure, passed to contest an import tariff, contained a serious attack on the jurisdiction of the Supreme Court in a provision that in no case in law or equity decided in South Carolina courts should any appeal be taken or allowed to the Supreme Court of the United States, and the State courts should enforce their judgments without reference to any such appeal, and the person attempting such an appeal would be treated as in contempt of the South Carolina courts.[275]

On December 10, 1832 Jackson issued a proclamation denouncing the nullification measure. His premises and reasoning were clearly applicable to the Georgia situation, and Georgia saw the wisdom of some retreat in the *Missionary* case. So did the missionaries. Worcester and Butler notified Governor Lumpkin that they were instructing counsel to discontinue prosecution of their case, though, they added, they continued to think that they were in the right. The Governor of Georgia, though somewhat disgruntled by this last clause, was mollified by a second letter from the missionaries, and pardoned their offenses. This compromise eliminated an embarrassing predicament of the Jackson administration; the President, an old military campaigner in the then Southwest, did not wish to offend Georgia in a controversy over a lot of Indians, but could not consistently suppress nullification in South Carolina and tolerate it in Georgia.

Nation and State: 1800–1856

This is a good place to stop and view the ground. Of course the lawyer tends to exaggerate Supreme Court decisions as indicia of constitutional development; but still in those judgments from 1800 through 1856 becomes apparent a significant fact—that during a period of vigorous national development and of abundant national legislation, when State loyalties were still primary in the minds of many men, and when national and State power came into frequent conflict, in no case involving federal-State relations was there a decision that any federal statute was constitutionally invalid because it exceeded the delegated powers.

During this half century the Court, in judgments upholding treaties painful to some States,[276] in a series of cases involving Acts of Congress which restricted State control of the economy when it conflicted with

[275] See for the attitude of the Supreme Court of South Carolina toward this legislation *State* v. *McCready,* 2 Hill 1 (1834).

[276] See pp. 231ff. above.

federal control,[277] in a bitterly criticized opinion upholding the jurisdiction of the Supreme Court to review State criminal adjudications
which the accused claimed conflicted with federal right,[278] in all these
the Supreme Court sustained national power, sometimes over violent
protests of offended States.

This was a period when the Executive's influence in the nation was
growing. Treaties are primarily executive moves; the Senatorial function does not initiate any international transaction; it only confirms or
rejects what the President does. The Court upheld treaties when
obliged to choose between them and State law. The Louisiana Purchase in 1803, acquisition of that immense tract of land governed
by the nation, not then the States, stemmed from executive action.
The Twelfth Amendment to the federal Constitution in 1804 made
changes in the mode of electing the President and Vice President,
retaining in essence arrangements which had originally been intended to detach selection of the President from factional influence,
but which, from the election of Jefferson onward, served to designate
the President a party leader. The Jeffersonians' failure in 1803 to remove Mr. Justice Chase from the United States Supreme Court—the
only attempt at such an impeachment in our national history—seemed
to Jefferson a personal defeat at the time; but if the national legislature had then developed a custom of turning Supreme Court Justices
out of office by the impeaching process, the status of the Executive
too would have been far less secure during moments of political unpopularity.

Jackson's veto of the bill to renew the charter of the Bank of the
United States, his discontinuation of federal deposits in that Bank,
with the distribution of new deposits among State banks, was a form
of promotion of State policy; but this was an assertion of national
presidential power. Jackson wrote his "protest" to the Senate on April
15, 1834 in response to a rebuke from that body asserting that the
President had "assumed upon himself authority and power not conferred by the Constitution and laws, but in derogation of both."
Jackson's resounding proclamation on the tenth day of December,
1832 concerning nullification efforts by South Carolina was a powerful
exertion not only of Presidential, but of national will against State
activity.

One constitutional fact concerning the pre-Civil War United States
is difficult to keep in mind a century later—the absence of the Thirteenth, Fourteenth, and Fifteenth Amendments. Some of the then
unhampered State powers are startling today. In 1833 the Supreme

[277] See the discussion of the Commerce Clause, pp. 341, 350, and following, above.
[278] *Cohens* v. *Virginia*, 6 Wheaton 264 (1821).

Court held in *Barron* v. *Baltimore*[279] that nothing in the federal Constitution prevented a State from taking a man's property for public use without compensation—a seizure expressly forbidden to the national government by the Fifth Amendment. In *Permoli* v. *First Municipality of New Orleans,* decided in 1845,[280] the Supreme Court held that no provision of the Constitution prevented an agency of the State of Louisiana from restricting church services in a manner that would be clearly unconstitutional in the mid-twentieth century. But of all the differences in the constitutional system before and after the war of 1861–1865, the most tragic in its consequences, for the States of the North and the South alike, was the constitutional tolerance of Negro slavery. The Supreme Court's 1857 decision in favor of continued slavery when a slaveholder took his slave into free territory and then back into a slave State, was one of the most dramatic episodes which aroused public opinion in the North and touched off the war four years later.[281]

But perhaps the most important constitutional development of the nineteenth century's first half was the acquisition, and in part the peopling, of a continent. In 1800 five and a third millions of people inhabited the United States, two-thirds of them within fifty miles of tide-water, their center of population eighteen miles from Baltimore.[282] These men lived in sixteen States, not created from territory originally federal; all sixteen States had a strong sense of local loyalties; all but three[283] had been separate colonial entities. In 1803 we acquired Louisiana from France; in 1819 Florida from Spain. In 1845 the Republic of Texas joined the United States by treaty; in 1846 Great Britain ceded to us her claims to Oregon; during the same year the Mexican War, and the treaty of Guadalupe Hidalgo of two years later which settled that conflict, resulted in Mexico's cession of New Mexico and California—more than a half million square miles of territory—and her recognition of our acquisition of Texas. In 1853 James Gadsden of South Carolina, as our envoy, negotiated the purchase of more than 45,000 square miles south of the Guadalupe Hidalgo line, giving us the only available railway route from the southern United States to the Pacific coast.

Thus in the half-century 1803–1853, by war and by treaty, we

[279] 7 Peters 243.

[280] 3 Howard 589.

[281] *Dred Scott* v. *Sandford,* 19 Howard 393 (1857).

[282] See the panoramic first chapter of Henry Adams' *History of the United States during the Administration of Thomas Jefferson* (4 vols.; New York: Charles Scribner's Sons, 1889) I.

[283] Vermont, admitted as a State in 1791; Kentucky, admitted 1792; Tennessee, admitted 1796.

acquired by far the greatest part of what is now the continental United States.[284] This immense territory, already peopled in mid-century by many times more inhabitants than in 1800, was obviously going to contain a vastly greater population, and was to be divided into many States. Even while these were still thinly populated, their two Senators apiece would have a powerful influence in the federal government. The prospective division of this territory between slave-holding and free States was a prominent cause of the war of 1861–1865. Much of this land was to be settled by vigorous pioneers, suspicious of the East, of cities, of financiers; its people were ready to demand federal legislation for the protection of their interests as farmers, lumbermen, cattlemen and miners.

Five million or so of immigrants came to the United States between 1820 and 1860; nearly two million were Irish, a million and a half were German, while only three-quarters of a million came from Great Britain.[285] Most of these Irish and Germans came in the decade 1845–1855, urged by hunger and by political discontent in Europe. The Irish newcomers tended to settle in eastern cities where they soon developed a talent for political affairs which has permanently affected the government of the northern Atlantic seaboard. Germans somewhat more readily went westerly and more readily took to farming.[286] But very few immigrants went South to settle in the slavery States.

Between 1800 and 1856, then, the United States had expanded from the Atlantic seaboard to govern all the way to the Pacific, between the present Canadian and Mexican borders. Its North and South had different characters; the latter had a smaller population, dependent on slavery for plantation agriculture; the other was more populous, made up of free States and territories, which in the northeast and mid-Atlantic areas had already developed the beginnings of an industrial-urban society, and in the mid-west and west was peopled by hardy and independent pioneers, who neither needed nor wanted slaves. In this cleavage lay the causes of the Civil War, and the explanation for its outcome.

[284] Not including, of course, Alaska, which came to us from Russia in 1867.

[285] Convenient sources for these statistics, giving references to other sources, are J. S. Bassett, *Short History of the United States* (New York: Macmillan, 1923) Chapter XXII; and Carman and Syrett, *History of the American People*, I, Chapter XVII.

[286] One should beware of generalization: any informed student of American westward movements can point to notable exceptions to this statement of distribution of newcomers. For discussion see Bassett, *Short History of the United States*, p. 461; Carman and Syrett, *History of the American People*, I, pp. 450–51.

14. CIVIL WAR

Dred Scott

THE WAR OF 1861–1865 was the gravest constitutional disturbance in
the history of the country, resulting in a deep change in the relative
position of nation and States. Since the beginning of national life
under the Constitution a series of other emergencies, never reaching
open warfare between the States, had demonstrated the difficulty of
keeping together as one nation a federally organized union in which
the component States retained their chosen structures of government,
separate each from the other, maintained their own armed forces, and
cultivated their own local loyalties. The resistance of New England
States, led by Massachusetts, to vigorous prosecution of the war of
1812, the nullification movement of 1832 in South Carolina, both
demonstrated that the continued existence of the United States could
not be taken for granted. And during the thirty years which succeeded the South Carolina demonstration, the racial and economic
organization in the South; the dependence of the South on slavery for
the maintenance of its system; the moral fervor of the abolitionist
movement in the North; the hardening of southern resolution which
that movement produced; all made clear the possibility of attempted
secession, and, if it should come, the necessity of active warfare to
prevent it. This explosive emotional and political situation gave the
Dred Scott Case its ominous meaning. The opinions of the Supreme
Court of the United States on great constitutional issues are far more
than judgments in lawsuits between man and man; they are state
papers undertaking to define the fundamental nature of our constitutional system. The American people rightly so understand them.

  Dred Scott's Case of 1857 involved bitter and long-standing disputes
over the establishment or prohibition of slavery in the States to be

385

formed from western territories. Missouri was originally part of Louisiana Territory; most of Missouri lies north of thirty six degrees thirty minutes of latitude. When admission of Missouri as a State was under consideration and its slavery status was debated, the "Missouri Compromise" of 1820 provided, by Acts of Congress of March 3 and 6, 1820, for the admission of Maine and Missouri as States, each free to decide on slavery or not within her own borders. As a practical matter this made Missouri a slavery State, Maine a free State. The Missouri Act went on, however, to express the celebrated Compromise by a provision that except for Missouri, in the rest of the Louisiana Purchase north of thirty six degrees, thirty minutes—

> . . . slavery and involuntary servitude, otherwise than in the punishment of crimes, whereof the parties shall have been duly convicted, shall be and is hereby, forever prohibited: . . .[1]

Dred Scott was born a slave. Prior to 1846, his owner took him north into the State of Illinois, where the State Constitution proscribed slavery; and also took him into that part of the Louisiana Purchase where the "Missouri Compromise" had forever prohibited involuntary servitude. Scott's owner later took Scott back to Missouri, a slavery State.

Dred Scott began his course of litigation in 1846. In that year he sued for his freedom in the Missouri Circuit Court, which held that his residence with his master in free territory had automatically made him a free man. However, Scott's master appealed to the Missouri Supreme Court which in 1852 reversed the trial court's judgment.

Meanwhile, legislation enacted by the Congress had been dividing the western parts of the United States into free and slavery territory by a sort of bargaining process. The story is complex. Texas was admitted to the Union as a slavery State in 1845.[2] The Congress in 1848 closed the Oregon Country to slavery.[3] In 1850 the Congress com-

---

[1] For Maine, see the Act of March 3, 1820, 3 Stat. at L. 544. For Missouri see the Act of March 6, 1820, 3 Stat. at L. 545. The Missouri Act contained a fugitive slave clause covering the free portion of Louisiana Territory—"*Provided always*, that any person escaping into the same, from whom labour or service is lawfully claimed, in any state or territory of the United States, such fugitive may be lawfully reclaimed and conveyed to the person claiming his or her labour or service as aforesaid." This clause applied only to a *fugitive*; it left indeterminate the status of a slave whose master took him into free territory. The Missouri Compromise is discussed in Carman and Syrett, *History of the American People*, I, p. 355 and following.

[2] 5 Stat. at L. 797.

[3] 9 Stat. at L. 323, 329. Section 14 of this Act extends to the inhabitants of Oregon the "rights, privileges and advantages" of the "articles of compact" in the Northwest Ordinance of July 13, 1787, enacted by the Continental Congress

promised the bitter dispute over slavery or free territory in the areas which became part of the United States under the treaty of Guadalupe Hidalgo at the conclusion of the war with Mexico. By statutes of that year Congress opened what are now New Mexico and Utah to slavery if their Constitutions should so provide on admission to Statehood, admitting California[4] to Statehood with a no-slavery Constitution. This compromise of 1850 left in effect the Missouri Compromise legislation of 1820 which had "forever" forbidden slavery in the Louisiana Territory north of latitude 36 degrees 30 minutes, except for the slavery State of Missouri.

The Compromise of 1850 did not satisfy all conflicting assertions, however. In 1854 the Congress passed a new statute concerning the territory to the west and northwest of Missouri, which had been made "forever" free by the statute of 1820. This 1854[5] Act of Congress altered the Missouri Compromise of 1820, by dividing what was left of Louisiana Territory into Kansas Territory and Nebraska Territory, which that statute allowed to decide by "popular sovereignty" their future slave or free status.[6] Believers in free territory settled Nebraska, which became safe for the North; but Kansas Territory was disputed ground in which slavery advocates and anti-slavery men like John Brown fought a minor but bitter civil war for control of the Territory. The fight cost two hundred lives, including that of a son of John Brown. And amid this killing appears a fact ironically tragic— there were very few slaves in Kansas Territory; the 1860 census showed only two. But the division of the West into free and slave areas, regardless of details, was a cause for which men were ready to kill one another.

---

for the government of the Territories of the United States northwest of the Ohio River. Article VI of that document provides—

> There shall be neither slavery nor involuntary servitude in the said territory, otherwise than in the punishment of crimes, whereof the party shall have been duly convicted: *Provided always,* That any person escaping into the same, from whom labor or service is lawfully claimed in any one of the original States, such fugitive may be lawfully reclaimed, and conveyed to the person claiming his or her labor or service as aforesaid. . . .

The Northwest Ordinance is available in many places, see e.g. I Burns Indiana Statutes 372; Pages Ohio Revised Code App'x, p. 329. A recent commentary, with the text, is in Perry and Cooper, *Sources of Our Liberties* (Chicago: American Bar Foundation, 1959) pp. 387–398. The Ordinance is a deeply significant constitutional document.

[4] New Mexico, 9 Stat. at L. 446, 447; California, 9 Stat. at L. 452; Utah, 9 Stat. at L. 453.

[5] New litigation, brought by Dred Scott in federal court, was then pending.

[6] 10 Stat. at L. 277.

Violence appeared in the Capitol in Washington. On May 19, 1856, Senator Sumner of Massachusetts delivered a denunciatory abolitionist speech including harsh criticism of Senator Andrew P. Butler of South Carolina. Three days later Senator Butler's nephew, Congressman Preston Brooks of South Carolina, came into the Senate Chamber; as Sumner sat at his desk Brooks beat him unconscious with a cane.

In this state of national emotion Dred Scott had, in November 1853 begun a new case in the United States Circuit Court in St. Louis.[7] The prospect of a few judges purporting to decide on freedom or slavery in the north and west aroused added excitement. Scott's lawyers were notable anti-slavery advocates in Missouri; to obtain federal diversity-of-citizenship jurisdiction Scott's owner, his former owner's widow, now wife of an anti-slavery enthusiast, transferred title to Scott to her brother John F. A. Sandford of New York. On May 15, 1854 the federal Circuit Court ruled against Scott's suit as a matter of law; his lawyers sued out a writ of error in the Supreme Court of the United States. On May 30, 1854 the Kansas-Nebraska Act repealed the Missouri Compromise Act. This repeal left Scott's argument unaffected, however, as his master had taken him into Illinois, which was admittedly free territory, and had taken him into the Louisiana Territory while that was free under the Missouri Compromise, before the new legislation of 1854. Scott's case was reached for argument in the Supreme Court on Monday, February 11, 1856. On May 12, 1856, ten days before Congressman Brooks assaulted Sumner in the Senate, the Supreme Court ordered Dred Scott's case reargued; the matter largely disappeared from the newspapers for six months while the presidential election campaign was in progress. In November 1856 John Buchanan was elected President. Dred Scott's case was reargued December 15, 16, 17, and 18, 1856. One unfortunate feature of the reargument, from today's point of view, was the fact that among Scott's counsel there now appeared the brother of Mr. Justice Curtis, George Ticknor Curtis of Massachusetts, who argued in favor of Scott's constitutional rights.

Another unhappy aspect of the *Dred Scott Case* was the currency, in advance of the decision, of rumors concerning the attitudes of various Justices. Self-discipline of the Justices seems to have been less

---

[7] In this federal-court action, counsel stipulated: "It is agreed that Dred Scott brought suit for his freedom in the Circuit Court of St. Louis County; that there was a verdict and judgment in his favor; that on a writ of error to the Supreme Court, the judgment below was reversed, and the cause remanded to the Circuit Court, where it has been continued to await the decision of this case. Field for plaintiff. Garland for defendant." This stipulation is printed in Mr. Justice Daniel's opinion in the Dred Scott case, 19 Howard at pages 471, 472. Scott's earlier State court litigation was thus not yet finally ended, and was not *res adjudicata* preventing the federal suit.

tight a century ago than it now is; Mr. Justice Catron even wrote a confidential letter on February 19, 1857 to John Buchanan, President-elect, suggesting that Buchanan write Mr. Justice Grier to urge that Grier take a position on the constitutionality of the Act of Congress which had prohibited slavery in the Louisiana Territory, the Missouri Compromise of 1820. Rumors were afloat in Washington, which turned out to be well-founded, that the Court had under consideration at least two questions: one, whether Dred Scott, as a slave and descendant of slaves, could be a "citizen" and hence have access to a federal court under the diversity jurisdiction of Article 3. The other question was the constitutionality of the Missouri Compromise. On Friday, March 6, two days after the inauguration of President Buchanan, Chief Justice Taney delivered the opinion of the Court.[8] His opinion occupies fifty-four pages of the nineteenth volume of Howard's reports. A state paper of this gravity requires some quotation.

> . . . [I]t becomes . . . our duty to decide whether the facts stated in the plea are or are not sufficient to show that the plaintiff is not entitled to sue as a citizen in a court of the United States.
>
> This is certainly a very serious question, and one that now for the first time has been brought for decision before this court. But it is brought here by those who have a right to bring it, and it is our duty to meet it and decide it.
>
> The question is simply this: Can a negro, whose ancestors were imported into this country, and sold as slaves, become a member of the political community formed and brought into existence by the Constitution of the United States, and as such become entitled to all the rights, and privileges, and immunities, guaranteed by that instrument to the citizen? One of which rights is the privilege of suing in a court of the United States in the cases specified in the Constitution.
>
> It will be observed, that the plea applies to that class of persons only whose ancestors were negroes of the African race, and imported into this country, and sold and held as slaves. The only matter in issue before the court, therefore, is, whether the descendants of such slaves, when they shall be emancipated, or who are born of parents who had become free before their birth, are citizens of a State, in the sense in which the word citizen is used in the Constitution of the United States. And this being the only matter in dispute on the pleadings, the court must be understood as speaking in this opinion of that class only, that is, of those persons who are the descendants of Africans who were imported into this country, and sold as slaves.
>
> The situation of this population was altogether unlike that of the Indian race. The latter, it is true, formed no part of the colonial communities, and never amalgamated with them in social connections or in government. But although they were uncivilized, they were yet a

[8] *Dred Scott* v. *Sandford*, 19 Howard 393 (1857).

free and independent people, associated together in nations or tribes, and governed by their own laws. . . .

In discussing this question, we must not confound the rights of citizenship which a State may confer within its own limits, and the rights of citizenship as a member of the Union. It does not by any means follow, because he has all the rights and privileges of a citizen of a State, that he must be a citizen of the United States. He may have all of the rights and privileges of the citizen of a State, and yet not be entitled to the rights and privileges of a citizen in any other State. For, previous to the adoption of the Constitution of the United States, every State had the undoubted right to confer on whomsoever it pleased the character of citizen, and to endow him with all its rights. But this character of course was confined to the boundaries of the State, and gave him no rights or privileges in other States beyond those secured to him by the laws of nations and the comity of States. Nor have the several States surrendered the power of conferring these rights and privileges by adopting the Constitution of the United States. Each State may still confer them upon an alien, or any one it thinks proper, or upon any class or description of persons; yet he would not be a citizen in the sense in which that word is used in the Constitution of the United States, nor entitled to sue as such in one of its courts, nor to the privileges and immunities of a citizen in the other States. The rights which he would acquire would be restricted to the State which gave them. The Constitution has conferred on Congress the right to establish an uniform rule of naturalization, and this right is evidently exclusive, and has always been held by this court to be so. Consequently, no State, since the adoption of the Constitution, can by naturalizing an alien invest him with the rights and privileges secured to a citizen of a State under the Federal Government, . . .

It becomes necessary . . . to determine who were citizens of the several States when the Constitution was adopted. And in order to do this, we must recur to the Governments and institutions of the thirteen colonies, when they separated from Great Britain and formed new sovereignties, and took their places in the family of independent nations. We must inquire who, at that time, were recognised as the people or citizens of a State, whose rights and liberties had been outraged by the English Government; and who declared their independence, and assumed the powers of Government to defend their rights by force of arms.

In the opinion of the court, the legislation and histories of the times, and the language used in the Declaration of Independence, show, that neither the class of persons who had been imported as slaves, nor their descendants, whether they had become free or not, were then acknowledged as a part of the people, nor intended to be included in the general words used in that memorable instrument.

It is difficult at this day to realize the state of public opinion in relation to that unfortunate race, which prevailed in the civilized and enlightened portions of the world at the time of the Declaration of Independence, and when the Constitution of the United States was framed and adopted. But the public history of every European nation displays it in a manner too plain to be mistaken.

They had for more than a century before been regarded as being of an inferior order, and altogether unfit to associate with the white race, either in social or political relations; and so far inferior, that they had no rights which the white man was bound to respect; and that the negro might justly and lawfully be reduced to slavery for his benefit. He was bought and sold, and treated as an ordinary article of merchandise and traffic, whenever a profit could be made by it. This opinion was at that time fixed and universal in the civilized portion of the white race. It was regarded as an axiom in morals as well as in politics, which no one thought of disputing, or supposed to be open to dispute; and men in every grade and position in society daily and habitually acted upon it in their private pursuits, as well as in matters of public concern, without doubting for a moment the correctness of this opinion.

And in no nation was this opinion more firmly fixed or more uniformly acted upon than by the English Government and English people. They not only seized them on the coast of Africa, and sold them or held them in slavery for their own use; but they took them as ordinary articles of merchandise to every country where they could make a profit on them, and were far more extensively engaged in this commerce than any other nation in the world.

The opinion thus entertained and acted upon in England was naturally impressed upon the colonies they founded on this side of the Atlantic. And, accordingly, a negro of the African race was regarded by them as an article of property, and held, and bought and sold as such, in every one of the thirteen Colonies which united in the Declaration of Independence, and afterwards formed the Constitution of the United States. The slaves were more or less numerous in the different Colonies, as slave labor was found more or less profitable. But no one seems to have doubted the correctness of the prevailing opinion of the time.

The legislation of the different Colonies furnishes positive and indisputable proof of this fact.

It would be tedious, in this opinion, to enumerate the various laws they passed upon this subject. It will be sufficient, as a sample of the legislation which then generally prevailed throughout the British Colonies, to give the laws of two of them; one being still a large slaveholding State, and the other the first State in which slavery ceased to exist.

The Province of Maryland, in 1717 (ch. 13, sec. 5), passed a law declaring 'that if any free negro or mulatto intermarry with any white woman, or if any white man shall intermarry with any negro or mulatto woman, such negro or mulatto shall become a slave during life, excepting mulattoes born of white women, who, for such intermarriage, shall only become servants for seven years, to be disposed of as the Justices of the County Court, where such marriage so happens, shall think fit; to be applied by them towards the support of a public school within the said county. And any white man or white woman who shall intermarry as aforesaid, with any negro or mulatto, such white man or white woman shall become servants during the term of seven years, and shall be disposed of by the justices as aforesaid, and be applied to the uses aforesaid.'

The other colonial law to which we refer was passed by Massachusetts in 1705 (chap. 6). It is entitled 'An Act for the better preventing of a spurious and mixed issue,' etc.; and it provides, that 'if any negro or mulatto shall presume to smite or strike any person of the English or other Christian nation, such negro or mulatto shall be severely whipped, at the discretion of the justices before whom the offender shall be convicted.'

And 'that none of Her Majesty's English or Scottish subjects, nor of any other Christian nation, within this province, shall contract matrimony with any negro or mulatto; nor shall any person, duly authorized to solemnize marriage, presume to join any such in marriage, on pain of forfeiting the sum of fifty pounds; one moiety thereof to Her Majesty, for and towards the support of the government within this province, and the other moiety to him or them that shall inform and sue for the same, in any of Her Majesty's courts of record within the Province, by bill, plaint, or information.'

We give both of these laws in the words used by the respective legislative bodies, because the language in which they are framed, as well as the provisions contained in them, show, too plainly to be misunderstood, the degraded condition of this unhappy race. They were still in force when the Revolution began, and are a faithful index to the state of feeling towards the class of persons of whom they speak, and of the position they occupied throughout the thirteen colonies, in the eyes and thoughts of the men who framed the Declaration of Independence and established the State constitutions and governments. They show that a perpetual and impassable barrier was intended to be erected between the white race and the one which they had reduced to slavery, and governed as subjects with absolute and despotic power, and which they then looked upon as so far below them in the scale of created beings, that intermarriages between white persons and negroes or mulattoes were regarded as unnatural and immoral, and punished as crimes, not only in the parties, but in the person who joined them in marriage. And no distinction in this respect was made between the free negro or mulatto and the slave, but this stigma, of the deepest degradation, was fixed upon the whole race.

We refer to these historical facts for the purpose of showing the fixed opinions concerning that race, upon which the statesmen of that day spoke and acted. It is necessary to do this, in order to determine whether the general terms used in the Constitution of the United States, as to the rights of man and the rights of the people, was intended to include them, or to give to them or their posterity the benefit of any of its provisions.

The language of the Declaration of Independence is equally conclusive.

It begins by declaring that, 'when in the course of human events it becomes necessary for one people to dissolve the political bands which have connected them with another, and to assume among the powers of the earth the separate and equal station to which the laws of nature and nature's God entitle them, a decent respect for the opinions of mankind requires that they should declare the causes which impel them to the separation.'

It then proceeds to say: 'We hold these truths to be self-evident: that all men are created equal; that they are endowed by their Creator with certain inalienable rights; that among them is life, liberty, and pursuit of happiness; that to secure these rights, governments are instituted, deriving their just powers from the consent of the governed.'

The general words above quoted would seem to embrace the whole human family, and if they were used in a similar instrument at this day, would be so understood. But it is too clear for dispute, that the enslaved African race were not intended to be included, and formed no part of the people who framed and adopted this Declaration; for if the language, as understood in that day, would embrace them, the conduct of the distinguished men who framed the Declaration of Independence would have been utterly and flagrantly inconsistent with the principles they asserted; and instead of the sympathy of mankind, to which they so confidently appealed, they would have deserved and received universal rebuke and reprobation.

Yet the men who framed this Declaration were great men—high in literary acquirements—high in their sense of honor, and incapable of asserting principles inconsistent with those on which they were acting. They perfectly understood the meaning of the language they used, and how it would be understood by others; and they knew that it would not, in any part of the civilized world, be supposed to embrace the negro race, which, by common consent, had been excluded from civilized governments and the family of nations, and doomed to slavery. They spoke and acted according to the then established doctrines and principles, and in the ordinary language of the day, and no one misunderstood them. The unhappy black race were separated from the white by indelible marks, and laws long before established, and were never thought of or spoken of except as property, and when the claims of the owner or the profit of the trader were supposed to need protection.

This state of public opinion had undergone no change when the Constitution was adopted, as is equally evident from its provisions and language.

The brief preamble sets forth by whom it was formed, for what purposes, and for whose benefit and protection. It declares that it is formed by the people of the United States; that is to say, by those who were members of the different political communities in the several States; and its great object is declared to be to secure the blessings of liberty to themselves and their posterity. It speaks in general terms of the people of the United States, and of citizens of the several States, when it is providing for the exercise of the powers granted or the privileges secured to the citizen. It does not define what description of persons are intended to be included under these terms, or who shall be regarded as a citizen and one of the people. It uses them as terms so well understood that no further description or definition was necessary.

But there are two clauses in the Constitution which point directly and specifically to the negro race as a separate class of persons, and show clearly that they were not regarded as a portion of the people or citizens of the government then formed.

One of these clauses reserves to each of the thirteen States the right to import slaves until the year 1808, if it thinks proper. And the importation which it thus sanctions was unquestionably of persons of the race of which we are speaking, as the traffic in slaves in the United States had always been confined to them. And by the other provision the States pledge themselves to each other to maintain the right of property of the master, by delivering up to him any slave who may have escaped from his service, and be found within their respective territories. By the first above-mentioned clause, therefore, the right to purchase and hold this property is directly sanctioned and authorized for twenty years by the people who framed the Constitution. And by the second, they pledge themselves to maintain and uphold the right of the master in the manner specified, as long as the government they then formed should endure. And these two provisions show, conclusively, that neither the description of persons therein referred to, nor their descendants, were embraced in any of the other provisions of the Constitution; for certainly these two clauses were not intended to confer on them or their posterity the blessings of liberty, or any of the personal rights so carefully provided for the citizen. . .

No one, we presume, supposes that any change in public opinion or feeling, in relation to this unfortunate race, in the civilized nations of Europe or in this country, should induce the court to give to the words of the Constitution a more liberal construction in their favor than they were intended to bear when the instrument was framed and adopted. Such an argument would be altogether inadmissible in any tribunal called on to interpret it. If any of its provisions are deemed unjust, there is a mode prescribed in the instrument itself by which it may be amended; but while it remains unaltered, it must be construed now as it was understood at the time of its adoption. . . Any other rule of construction would abrogate the judicial character of this court, and make it the mere reflex of the popular opinion or passion of the day. This court was not created by the Constitution for such purposes. . . .

And upon a full and careful consideration of the subject, the court is of opinion that . . . Dred Scott was not a citizen of Missouri within the meaning of the Constitution of the United States, and not entitled as such to sue in its courts; and, consequently, that the Circuit Court had no jurisdiction of the case. . .

Taney had thus far written enough to outrage the northern abolition-ists. He went on, despite his disclaimer of jurisdiction—

We proceed . . . to inquire whether the facts relied on by the plaintiff entitled him to his freedom. . . .

In considering this part of the controversy, two questions arise: 1. Was he, together with his family, free in Missouri by reason of the stay in the territory of the United States hereinbefore mentioned [Upper Louisiana north of latitude 36° 30′ north, and north of the State of Missouri]? And 2. If they were not, is Scott himself free by reason of his removal to Rock Island, in the State of Illinois . . .?

We proceed to examine the first question.

The act of Congress, upon which the plaintiff relies, declares that slavery and involuntary servitude, except as a punishment for crime, shall be forever prohibited in all that part of that territory ceded by France, under the name of Louisiana, which lies north of thirty-six degrees thirty minutes north latitude, and not included within the limits of Missouri. And the difficulty which meets us at the threshold of this part of the inquiry is, whether Congress was authorized to pass this law under any of the powers granted to it by the Constitution; for if the authority is not given by that instrument, it is the duty of this court to declare it void and inoperative, and incapable of con-ferring freedom upon one who is held as a slave under the laws of any one of the States.

The counsel for the plaintiff has laid much stress upon that article in the Constitution which confers on Congress the power 'to dispose of and make all needful rules and regulations respecting the territory or other property belonging to the United States;' but, in the judgment of the court, that provision has no bearing on the present controversy, and the power there given, whatever it may be, is confined, and was intended to be confined, to the territory which at that time belonged to, or was claimed by, the United States, and was within their boun-daries as settled by the Treaty with Great Britain, and can have no influence upon a territory afterwards acquired from a foreign govern-ment. It was a special provision for a known and particular Territory, and to meet a present emergency, and nothing more. . . .

The Territory being a part of the United States, the Government and the citizen both enter it under the authority of the Constitution, with their respective rights defined and marked out; and the Federal Government can exercise no power over his person or property, beyond what that instrument confers, nor lawfully deny any right which it has reserved.

A reference to a few of the provisions of the Constitution will illustrate this proposition.

For example, no one, we presume, will contend that Congress can make any law in a territory respecting the establishment of religion or the free exercise thereof, or abridging the freedom of speech or of the press, or the right of the people of the territory peaceably to assemble and to petition the government for the redress of grievances.

Nor can Congress deny to the people the right to keep and bear arms, nor the right to trial by jury, nor compel anyone to be a witness against himself in a criminal proceeding.

These powers, and others in relation to rights of person, which it is not necessary here to enumerate, are, in express and positive terms, denied to the general government; and the rights of private property have been guarded with equal care. Thus the rights of property are united with the rights of person, and placed on the same ground by the fifth amendment to the Constitution, which provides that no person shall be deprived of life, liberty and property, without due process of law. And an Act of Congress which deprives a citizen of the United States of his liberty or property, merely because he came himself or brought his property into a particular Territory of the United States, and who committed no offense against the laws, could hardly be dignified with the name of due process of law.

So, too, it will hardly be contended that Congress could by law quarter a soldier in a house in a territory without the consent of the owner, in time of peace; nor in time of war, but in a manner prescribed by law. Nor could they by law forfeit the property of a citizen in a territory who was convicted of treason, for a longer period than the life of the person convicted; nor take private property for public use without just compensation.

The powers over person and property of which we speak are not only not granted to Congress, but are in express terms denied, and they are forbidden to exercise them. And this prohibition is not confined to the States, but the words are general, and extend to the whole territory over which the Constitution gives it power to legislate, including those portions of it remaining under Territorial Government, as well as that covered by States. . . .

But there is another point in the case which depends on state power and state law. And it is contended, on the part of the plaintiff, that he is made free by being taken to Rock Island, in the State of Illinois, independently of his residence in the territory of the United States; and being so made free, he was not again reduced to a state of slavery by being brought back to Missouri.

Our notice of this part of the case will be very brief; for the principle on which it depends was decided in this court upon much consideration, in the case of *Strader et al.* v. *Graham*, reported in 10th

Howard, 82. In that case, the slaves had been taken from Kentucky to Ohio, with the consent of the owner, and afterwards brought back to Kentucky. And this court held that their *status* or condition, as free or slave, depended upon the laws of Kentucky, when they were brought back into that State, and not of Ohio; and that this court had no jurisdiction to revise the judgment of a state court upon its own laws. This was the point directly before the court, and the decision that this court had not jurisdiction, turned upon it, as will be seen by the report of the case.

So in this case: as Scott was a slave when taken into the State of Illinois by his owner, and was there held as such, and brought back in that character, his *status*, as free or slave, depended on the laws of Missouri, and not of Illinois.

It has, however, been urged in the argument, that by the laws of Missouri he was free on his return, and that this case, therefore, cannot be governed by the case of *Strader et al.* v. *Graham*, where it appeared, by the laws of Kentucky, that the plaintiffs continued to be slaves on their return from Ohio. But whatever doubts or opinions may, at one time, have been entertained upon this subject, we are satisfied, upon a careful examination of all the cases decided in the State courts of Missouri referred to, that it is now firmly settled by the decisions of the highest court in the State, that Scott and his family upon their return were not free, but were, by the laws of Missouri, the property of the defendant. . . .

When the Chief Justice had read his opinion, Justices Nelson and Catron read theirs. This consumed the rest of the day's session. On the following day Justices Daniel, Grier, Campbell and Wayne read their respective concurring opinions, and McLean and Curtis read their dissents.[9] The judgments[10] for affirmance, against Scott, were long and full of technicalities. There was much discussion of the propriety of the Court's decision on the merits of Scott's claim, after holding that the Circuit Court had no jurisdiction because Scott lacked citizenship. At any rate six of the Judges, Taney, writing for the Court, and Wayne, Catron, Daniel, Grier, and Campbell, all concurred in holding first, that a Negro, descendant of slaves, could not be a citizen of the United States.[11] The same Justices also held, apparently *obiter*, that the Congress, under the Fifth Amendment, could not exclude slavery from the territories. Mr. Justice Nelson expressed

[9] Warren gives the order of the opinions differently from Howard.

[10] The word "judgment," in strict American usage, means the brief and precise dispositive provision by a court, awarding damages in an action at law, or denying recovery. In England "judgment" may serve for "opinion"; with us "opinion," in strict usage, is a judicial statement of the reasoning on which the decision is made. One needs occasional synonyms.

[11] This opinion had not been held by everyone. See page 438, hereafter for arguably contrary instances.

only the opinion that the Court must follow the law already laid down by the Missouri Supreme Court that Dred Scott was a slave. Justices McLean and Curtis, both dissenting from the Court's judgment, delivered elaborately reasoned opinions in which they differed from the majority of the Court as to Scott's citizenship and standing to sue, as to the constitutionality of the Missouri Compromise, and as to the binding quality of the Missouri Supreme Court adjudication.

During the century and more which has succeeded the Dred Scott decision, criticism of the Court for deciding as it did has never ceased, though the sound and fury has largely died away. The opinions were reported by the newspapers of the day, of course, and violent denunciation immediately came from anti-slavery men. The Supreme Court was in no enviable position in any event; in the spirit of the times any decision would have subjected it to bitter denunciation. In no good way could the Court have avoided passing on the case. Rewriting history is a profitless venture; but today, for the honor of our federal courts, one might wish that the judgment had been that once Dred Scott went into free Illinois, he became a free man. Lord Mansfield so decided in 1771 when he held that Somersett's slavery ended when he set foot on English soil.[12] The Supreme Court might better then have held that, once a free man, Scott was a citizen of the United States like any other Illinoisian; that he did not forfeit his vested citizenship by returning to Missouri: that Missouri had no standing to remove his citizenship by any process; and that like any other citizen, Scott had access to the federal courts to establish a citizen's rights. This would have disposed of the entire controversy; the Court might better have said nothing about the constitutionality of the Missouri Compromise of 1820 which had been superseded by a new statute in 1854.[13] But no judgment, in favor of Dred Scott or against him, would have stilled the controversies which ended in the war of 1861.

Chief Justice Taney was a kindly man. He had voluntarily freed his own slaves many years before, and watched over their interests after their manumission.[14] In the course of his Dred Scott opinion in which he undertook to demonstrate that a Negro could not be a citizen, Chief Justice Taney described what he took, quite accurately, to be the general attitude toward Negroes in 1787 when the Constitution was drafted. But men being as they are, one is not surprised to find

[12] *Somersett's Case*, 20 Howell's State Trials 1.

[13] See An Act to Organize the Territories of Nebraska and Kansas 10 Stat. at Large. 277.

[14] See Carl Brent Swisher, *Roger Brooke Taney* (Hamden, Conn.: Archon Books, 1961) p. 94. Taney retained a few disabled slaves to protect them.

that abolitionists read Taney's passages concerning the negro's status in 1787 as though they expressed the philosophy of the Chief Justice and those who concurred in his judgment in 1857. Anti-slavery men ascribed to Taney a simple formula—the negro has no rights that the white man is bound to respect. The ascription was unjust, but it was effective; it helped make Dred Scott's name a rallying symbol.[15]

In 1854 another noted slavery case arose in Wisconsin, when an anti-slavery editor named Sherman Booth was prosecuted under the federal Fugitive Slave Law.[16] That statute made it a federal crime to help a fugitive slave to escape. It was widely violated; the "underground railroad" was a loose organization of anti-slavery men and women who passed escaping slaves north to Canada and freedom; to its members and their sympathizers the Fugitive Slave Law seemed so cruel as to be unconstitutional. In 1854 in Boston, when proceedings were pending before United States Commissioner Loring for the return of a slave named Anthony Burns to his Virginia master, the authorities felt it necessary to call out a large force of State militia and some regular artillery troops from the harbor garrison, to be sure that sympathizers would not rescue Burns.[17]

There was little or no doubt of the constitutional power of the Congress to enact a properly drawn Fugitive Slave Law; the second section of Article IV of the Constitution is explicit—

> No person held to Service or Labour in one State, under the Laws thereof, escaping into another, shall, in Consequence of any Law or Regulation therein, be discharged from such Service or Labour, but shall be delivered up on Claim of the Party to whom such Service or Labour may be due.

This section of the Constitution had no application to Dred Scott's case; Scott was not a runaway in Illinois or in the Louisiana Territory; his master had voluntarily taken him to both places for considerable stays. But in 1854 Booth helped a fugitive slave escape from a deputy-marshal in Wisconsin; the federal authorities arrested Booth on a

[15] Dramatic unity would call for Scott to suffer some sorry end to symbolize the tragedy of civil war; but human affairs are not arranged as in a Racine play. Scott's owner manumitted Scott and his family two months after Taney's decision. By that time nationally famous, Dred Scott became porter in a St. Louis hotel. See Vincent C. Hopkins, *Dred Scott's Case* (New York: Fordham University Press, 1951).

[16] Act of Feb. 12, 1793, 1 Stat. at L. 302 as amended Sept. 18, 1850, 9 Stat. at L. 462. "Fugitive Slave Law" was a popular term, not the actual title of the Statute.

[17] See the pamphlet *The Boston Slave Riot and Trial of Anthony Burns* (Boston: Fetridge & Co., 1854).

charge of violating the Act of 1850, indicted him in January 1855, and
a federal jury found him guilty. Both before and after his trial, Booth
brought habeas corpus proceedings in the Wisconsin State courts
against United States Marshal Ableman, who had Booth in custody.
The Supreme Court of Wisconsin held that Ableman's detention of
Booth was illegal; the Fugitive Slave Act was unconstitutional because
it provided no jury trial to determine the status of the fugitive slave.[18]
The Supreme Court of the United States reversed the Wisconsin
judgment, however, in March 1859, almost exactly two years after
Dred Scott's Case.[19]

Action by the Congress pursuant to its constitutional powers, as
adjudicated by the Supreme Court of the United States, was para-
mount to any inconsistent State policy; this was obvious, and in the
abstract was accepted doctrine in the North. But the case concerned
help to a man escaping from slavery, and this aroused still more the
anti-slavery North. Wisconsin stirred with something like North
Carolina's nullification. People are not often detached about judgments
of courts on public questions. For most men the result is what counts;
and the result of *Ableman* v. *Booth* was to hammer home the outrage
of *Dred Scott's Case*. The Supreme Court had approved punishment
of an anti-slavery man in free Wisconsin for helping a slave to attempt
the freedom which his rescuer thought he read in the Declaration of
Independence. Something had gone wrong with the idea of the United
States. Plain men were getting ready to lose their lives about it, in
Kansas, at Harper's Ferry, at Ball's Bluff, and at Gettysburg.

Commander-in-Chief

The presidential election of 1860 aligned the forces for four years
of tragic warfare. The Democratic national convention met at Charleston, South Carolina on April 23, 1860; when the northern delegates
would not accept a southern proposal to guarantee slave property in
the Territories, the Alabama chairman announced that his party had
instructed its delegation in this event to withdraw from the Convention. With them went the delegates of South Carolina, Mississippi,
Louisiana, Florida, Texas, Arkansas and Georgia. What was left of
the convention, representing the northern border Democrats, nomi-

---

[18] In Re Booth, 3 Wisc. 1, at 70 (1854); at 157 (1855).
[19] 21 Howard 506; see also 18 Howard 470, and 476, for earlier stages in the
review of the Wisconsin decision. The litigation is described by Warren, in *The
Supreme Court in U.S. History*, (3 vols.; Boston: Little, Brown and Co., 1922)
II, pp. 532 ff.; see also III, pp. 42 ff.

nated Stephen A. Douglas of Illinois, late successful opponent of Abraham Lincoln in the Illinois senatorial election.[20]

The Republican convention nominated Lincoln, and in the November election, though he became President by a heavy collegial majority, his popular vote showed much less general support. Lincoln's opponents received, in all, over nine hundred thousand votes more than Lincoln. The Republican party returned a minority to the Senate and to the House. When the news that Lincoln was to be President reached South Carolina, that State called a convention which declared that the Union was dissolved. By February 4, secession had been declared in five more States: Georgia, Alabama, Mississippi, Louisiana and Florida. On that day a convention at Montgomery, Alabama established a Constitution for "The Confederate States of America," and chose Jefferson Davis as its President and Alexander H. Stephens as Vice President. On February 23, the people of Texas voted for secession.

Of eight federal forts in the southern States, six had no garrisons and could easily be occupied by secessionists. President Buchanan's only move to reinforce the federal forts in the seceding States had been on January 5 when he dispatched from New York a merchant vessel, *Star of the West*, with two hundred troops, to strengthen Major Anderson's garrison of eighty-four at Fort Sumter, Charleston, South Carolina. Fire from Confederate batteries at the harbor entrance turned her back to New York.[21] Fort Pickens at Pensacola, Florida had a garrison of forty-eight men, whom Buchanan left to shift for themselves. They held out until reinforced; Fort Pickens never fell to the Confederacy.

Lincoln was inaugurated on March 4, 1861, while three agents of the Confederate government were in Washington trying to negotiate for the recognition of independence. On April 8 relief ships started south from New York for Fort Sumter, but on April 12 General Beauregard's forces on shore opposite Fort Sumter began the Civil War with a mortar shot. At the end of thirty-four hours' bombardment Major Anderson surrendered. The Confederates let him and his troops go north by sea.

The outbreak of hostilities at Charleston called for a number of difficult decisions which had to be made at once, and Lincoln did not hesitate to make them. In Article 2 of the Constitution, the first section describes the manner of choosing the President; the second section

[20] Occasion of the Lincoln-Douglas debates.
[21] Why are not these shots, rather than those fired on Fort Sumter on April 12, properly called the first of the Civil War?

assigns his duties, and the first duty assigned is to be Commander in Chief of the Army and the Navy of the United States. As Commander in Chief, how was Lincoln to treat the seceding States? As enemies? As parts of the United States filled with criminal individuals? Would Lincoln blockade the South with naval forces, as though it were a foreign enemy? If our navy captured Southern vessels, would they be prizes of war? Acts of Congress prescribed the size of national forces; would Lincoln wait until Congress had assembled and deliberated before he recruited soldiers and sailors and provided armament for them? In some of the border States seditious men were active in the Confederate cause. Were these men exercising "political" rights guaranteed by the First Amendment? Or were they traitors?

Lincoln, on April 15, 1865, summoned the Congress to assemble on July 4. Without waiting for the Congress he called for volunteer soldiers to increase the army by more than a hundred thousand, and ordered, in addition, the enlistment of twenty-three thousand regular troops. He increased the navy by eighteen thousand men. On April 19, 1861, he declared a blockade of southern ports. Under Buchanan the navy had become widely scattered during the immediate pre-secession period. Lincoln at once directed the purchase and arming of ships to make the blockade effective. Between May 4 and June 24 Arkansas, Virginia, North Carolina and Tennessee seceded. Maryland, Kentucky and Missouri hung in the balance for a long time. Missouri was the most critical. The Governor was a secessionist. General Nathaniel Lyon, commanding the federal forces in that State, seized the city of St. Louis and called a State convention, which declared against secession and deposed the Missouri Governor.[22]

Active sedition in wartime is apt to raise questions about power to suspend the writ of habeas corpus. Unless the draftsmen of a constituent charter wish to leave a convenient vagueness (as may sometimes

[22] J. G. Randall, in 1926 wrote a detailed and scholarly analysis of the matters discussed in this chapter in his *Constitutional Problems under Lincoln* (rev. ed.; Urbana: University of Illinois Press, 1951). Professor Clinton Rossiter of Cornell, in his *Supreme Court and Commander in Chief* (Ithaca, N. Y.: Cornell University Press, 1951) restudies Randall's thesis, and brings down through the war of 1941–45 the questions Randall discusses. Professor Rossiter's *Constitutional Dictatorship: Crisis Government in the Modern Democracies* (Princeton: Princeton University Press, 1948) treats some of the same matters appraising comparative constitutionalism. Volumes V and VI of James D. Richardson's *Messages and Papers of the Presidents* (10 vols.; Washington: Government Printing Office, 1896–99) present a particularly useful collection of documents. Many scholars have written histories of the United States during the period of the Civil War. A convenient study, with maps showing the congressional compromises concerning free or slave territories in the American West is Harry J. Carman and Harold C. Syrett, *History of the American People* (2 vols.; New York: Alfred A. Knopf, 1952) I, Chapter XXI.

seem expedient), they do well to avoid use of the passive voice; the Constitution suggests that when the public safety so requires in cases of rebellion, the writ may "be suspended"; the clause leaves unspecified the organ of government which is to suspend it—

> The Privilege of the Writ of Habeas Corpus shall not be suspended, unless when in Cases of Rebellion or Invasion the Public Safety may require it.[23]

Since 1787 men have wondered whether this contemplates that only the Congress may suspend the writ of habeas corpus; or whether the President may do so by executive order; or whether perchance either the Congress or the President may exercise this function. But whichever suspends the writ, elimination of judicial protection poses a grave issue, at least as old as the *Five Knights Case* during the controversy between Parliament and Charles the First.[24] The issue is the character, the characteristic habit of thought, of the man who is to pass on the physical liberty of the subject or the citizen. Will this be the executive, charged with the direction of affairs, informed of the national crises, but subject to the impatient zeal of men seeking a great objective with their whole hearts? Or shall the question of human liberty be decided by the Judge, traditionally aloof from the urgencies of politics, chargeable not with origination and direction of policy, but with reflective and reasoned choice between imposition of governmental sanctions on the individual, and fulfillment of an objective of human liberty? This is not a choice easily or wisely made; just considerations may be brought forward on both sides.

In the second month of his presidency, this choice presented itself to President Lincoln. On the twenty-fifth of April, 1861 he wrote to Lieutenant-General Winfield Scott, commanding the Army of the United States—[25]

EXECUTIVE ORDERS

Washington, April 25, 1861

Lieutenant-General Scott.

My Dear Sir: The Maryland legislature assembles to-morrow at Annapolis, and not improbably will take action to arm the people of that State against the United States. The question has been submitted

---

[23] Article I, Sec. 9.

[24] See *Darnel's Case* (1627), 3 Howell's State Trials 1; Gardiner, *Constitutional Documents of the Puritan Revolution, 1625–1660*, (3rd ed.; Oxford: Oxford University Press, 1906) pp. 57ff.; see also Catherine Drinker Bowen, *The Lion and the Throne* (Boston: Little, Brown and Co., 1957) pp. 478ff.; and see earlier in this book, pp. 66, 67.

[25] Richardson, *Messages and Papers of the Presidents*, VI, p. 17.

to and considered by me whether it would not be justifiable, upon the ground of necessary defense, for you, as General in Chief of the United States Army, to arrest or disperse the members of that body. I think it would not be justifiable nor efficient for the desired object.

First. They have a clearly legal right to assemble, and we can not know in advance that their action will not be lawful and peaceful, and if we wait until they shall have acted their arrest or dispersion will not lessen the effect of their action.

Secondly. We can not permanently prevent their action. If we arrest them, we can not long hold them as prisoners, and when liberated they will immediately reassemble and take their action; and precisely the same if we simply disperse them—they will immediately reassemble in some other place.

I therefore conclude that it is only left to the Commanding General to watch and await their action, which, if it shall be to arm their people against the United States, he is to adopt the most prompt and efficient means to counteract, even, if necessary, to the bombardment of their cities and, in the extremest necessity, the suspension of the writ of *habeas corpus*.

Your obedient servant,
ABRAHAM LINCOLN

Lincoln followed with a formal directive two days later—[26]

The COMMANDING GENERAL OF THE ARMY OF THE UNITED STATES:

You are engaged in suppressing an insurrection against the laws of the United States. If at any point on or in the vicinity of any military line which is now or which shall be used between the city of Philadelphia and the city of Washington you find resistance which renders it necessary to suspend the writ of *habeas corpus* for the public safety, you personally, or through the officer in command at the point where resistance occurs, are authorized to suspend that writ.

Given under my hand and the seal of the United States, at the city of Washington, this 27th day of April, 1861, and of [Seal]   the Independence of the United States the eighty-fifth.

ABRAHAM LINCOLN

By the President of the United States:
WILLIAM H. SEWARD,
Secretary of State

Baltimore was debated ground in May of 1861. Word came to Major General Keim commanding federal forces near Baltimore, that secessionists had formed a military company in Baltimore, had ob-

[26] Richardson, *Messages and Papers of the Presidents,* VI, p. 18.

tained arms belonging to the United States, and were preparing to join the Confederate forces. John Merryman of Baltimore, so General Keim learned, was a lieutenant in that company. Keim ordered Merryman arrested.

At two o'clock in the morning of May 25, 1861, the military took Merryman from his house and confined him in Fort McHenry, commanded by Major General Cadwalader. General Cadwalader, however, allowed Merryman's brother-in-law and his counsel to visit the prisoner, and later, on the twenty-sixth day of May, Merryman's counsel presented to Chief Justice Taney a petition, signed on the twenty-fifth by Merryman and his counsel, George H. Williams, praying for a writ of *habea corpus* requiring the production of Merryman before Chief Justice Taney to inquire into the cause of his detention. Taney immediately directed the Clerk of Court to issue the writ, returnable before the Chief Justice on May 27th in the courtroom of the United States Circuit Court in Baltimore. The marshal served the papers on General Cadwalader on the twenty-sixth. The following day in response to the writ, Colonel Lee, an officer of General Cadwalader's command, appeared before Chief Justice Taney with the General's return.[27] General Cadwalader respectfully notified the Chief Justice that Merryman had been arrested by a Colonel Yohe, under the orders of Major General Keim, then on duty in Pennsylvania, both in the military service of the United States, not with the knowledge or direction of General Cadwalader; nevertheless General Cadwalader was holding the prisoner. He informed the Chief Justice that the President had authorized him to suspend the writ of *habeas corpus*

> This is a high and delicate trust, and it has been enjoined upon him that it should be executed with judgment and discretion, but he is nevertheless also instructed that in times of civil strife, error should be on the side of the safety of the country.

General Cadwalader's return requested the Chief Justice to postpone further action upon the case until the General should receive instructions from the President.

Thereupon Chief Justice Taney ordered that an attachment[28] be issued to General Cadwalader. The United States Marshal for the District of Maryland was Washington Bonifant. Bearing the writ of the Chief Justice of the United States, Marshal Bonifant went to Fort McHenry on the twenty-eighth day of May and sent in his card from the outer gate. The messenger returned with the reply as reported by

[27] Tradition has it that Colonel Lee appeared complete with sash. War had not yet become an affair of dungarees.

[28] Order for arrest.

Bonifant "that there was no answer to my card"; the marshal thereupon certified to Chief Justice Taney that he could not serve the writ as he was not permitted to enter the gate of Fort McHenry.

The Chief Justice then observed that the marshal had the power to summon the *posse comitatus*[29] to aid him to seize and to bring before the Court the party named in the attachment, who would be liable to punishment by a fine and imprisonment. Taney observed, however, that the power here opposing obedience was so notoriously superior to any the marshal could command that the marshal was excused. The Chief Justice stated that he proposed to deliver an opinion in writing on the case, setting forth his conclusions that the President cannot suspend the writ of *habeas corpus,* nor authorize a military officer to do so; that a military officer has no right to arrest and detain a person not subject to the Articles of War for an offense against the laws of the United States; that it is the duty of the military officer to deliver such a person immediately to the civil authority; that Merryman was entitled to be discharged immediately. The Chief Justice stated that he should cause his opinion when filed, and all the proceedings to be laid before the President, that the President might perform his constitutional duty to enforce the laws by securing obedience to the process of the United States.

Chief Justice Taney's opinion reviews the history of *habeas corpus* in England, of the arbitrary imprisonments by Charles the First, of the Petition of Right and of *habeas corpus* in the United States. The Chief Justice concluded—

> Chief Justice Marshall, in delivering the opinion of the supreme court in the case of Ex parte Bollman and Swartwout, uses this decisive language, in 4 Cranch [8 U.S.] 95: "It may be worthy of remark, that this act (speaking of the one under which I am proceeding) was passed by the first congress of the United States, sitting under a constitution which had declared 'that the privilege of the writ of habeas corpus should not be suspended, unless when, in cases of rebellion or invasion, the public safety may require it.' Acting under the immediate influence of this injunction, they must have felt, with peculiar force, the obligation of providing efficient means, by which this great constitutional privilege should receive life and activity; for if the means be not in existence, the privilege itself would be lost, although no law for its suspension should be enacted. Under the impression of this obligation, they give to all the courts the power of awarding writs of habeas corpus." And again on page 101: "If at any time, the public safety should require the suspension of the powers vested by this act in the courts of the United States, it is for the legislature to say so. That

---

[29] "Power of the County"—citizens whom a peace-officer may choose to call to overcome resistance to lawful process.

question depends on political considerations, on which the legislature is to decide; until the legislative will be expressed, this court can only see its duty, and must obey the laws." I can add nothing to these clear and emphatic words of my great predecessor.

But the documents before me show, that the military authority in this case has gone far beyond the mere suspension of the privilege of the writ of habeas corpus. It has, by force of arms, thrust aside the judicial authorities and officers to whom the constitution has confided the power and duty of interpreting and administering the laws, and substituted a military government in its place, to be administered and executed by military officers. For, at the time these proceedings were had against John Merryman, the district judge of Maryland, the commissioner appointed under the act of congress, the district attorney and the marshal, all resided in the city of Baltimore, a few miles only from the home of the prisoner. Up to that time, there had never been the slightest resistance or obstruction to the process of any court or judicial officer of the United States, in Maryland, except by the military authority. And if a military officer, or any other person, had reason to believe that the prisoner had committed any offence against the laws of the United States, it was his duty to give information of the fact and the evidence to support it, to the district attorney; it would then have become the duty of that officer to bring the matter before the district judge or commissioner, and if there was sufficient legal evidence to justify his arrest, the judge or commissioner would have issued his warrant to the marshal to arrest him; and upon the hearing of the case, would have held him to bail, or committed him for trial, according to the character of the offence, as it appeared in the testimony, or would have discharged him immediately, if there was not sufficient evidence to support the accusation. There was no danger of any obstruction or resistance to the action of the civil authorities, and therefore no reason whatever for the interposition of the military.

Yet, under these circumstances, a military officer, stationed in Pennsylvania, without giving any information to the district attorney, and without any application to the judicial authorities, assumes to himself the judicial power in the district of Maryland; undertakes to decide what constitutes the crime of treason or rebellion; what evidence (if indeed he required any) is sufficient to support the accusation and justify the commitment; and commits the party, without a hearing, even before himself, to close custody, in a strongly garrisoned fort, to be there held, it would seem, during the pleasure of those who committed him.

The constitution provides, as I have before said, that "no person shall be deprived of life, liberty or property, without due process of law." It declares that "the right of the people to be secure in their persons, houses, papers and effects, against unreasonable searches and seizures, shall not be violated; and no warrant shall issue, but upon probable cause, supported by oath or affirmation, and particularly describing the place to be searched, and the persons or things to be seized." It provides that the party accused shall be entitled to a speedy trial in a court of justice.

These great and fundamental laws, which congress itself could not suspend, have been disregarded and suspended, like the writ of habeas corpus, by a military order, supported by force of arms. Such is the case now before me, and I can only say that if the authority which the constitution has confided to the judiciary department and judicial officers, may thus, upon any pretext or under any circumstances, be usurped by the military power, at its discretion, the people of the United States are no longer living under a government of laws, but every citizen holds life, liberty and property at the will and pleasure of the army officer in whose military district he may happen to be found.[3]

In such a case, my duty was too plain to be mistaken. I have exercised all the power which the constitution and laws confer upon me, but that power has been resisted by a force too strong for me to overcome. It is possible that the officer who has incurred this grave responsibility may have misunderstood his instructions, and exceeded the authority intended to be given him; I shall, therefore, order all the proceedings in this case, with my opinion, to be filed and recorded in the circuit court of the United States for the district of Maryland, and direct the clerk to transmit a copy, under seal, to the president of the United States. It will then remain for that high officer, in fulfilment of his constitutional obligation to "take care that the laws be faithfully executed," to determine what measures he will take to cause the civil process of the United States to be respected and enforced"[30]

3 The constitution of the United States is founded upon the principles of government set forth and maintained in the Declaration of Independence. In that memorable instrument the people of the several colonies declared, that one of the causes which "impelled" them to "dissolve the political bands" which connected them with the British nation, and justified them in withdrawing their allegiance from the British sovereign, was that "he (the king) had affected to render the military independent of, and superior to, the civil power." [Footnote from 17 Federal Cases 152]

Lincoln never answered Taney's inquiry, but after the Chief Justice filed his opinion the military authorities released Merryman from Fort McHenry; the federal marshal took him into civil custody; and a grand jury indicted him for treason, in the United States District Court of Baltimore. Merryman filed a bail bond for twenty thousand dollars to secure his appearance in the United States Circuit Court; the Court continued[31] his case from time to time, and finally dropped it without further action.[32]

30 17 Federal Cases 144, at 152, 153.
31 I.e., postponed.
32 See J. G. Randall, *Constitutional Problems under Lincoln*, p. 162.

On April 15, 1861, President Lincoln called a special session of the Congress to meet on July 4, 1861.[33] A century later one wonders a little about the delay of more than two months and a half, during which Lincoln did many things by Executive Orders. Did the President think it not the moment for debate? When Congress assembled the President sent a special message[34] in which he reviewed the situation arising out of the insurrection which had broken out, and among other things discussed the matter of suspending the writ of habeas corpus. The President's proclamation of suspension had not been issued lightly or unadvisedly, and he set forth the considerations eloquently in his presidential message—

> . . . [The Virginia forces have] seized the United States armory at Harpers Ferry and the navy-yard at Gosport, near Norfolk. They received—perhaps invited—into their State large bodies of troops, with their warlike appointments, from the so-called seceded States. They formally entered into a treaty of temporary alliance and cooperation with the so-called "Confederate States," and sent members to their congress at Montgomery; and, finally, they permitted the insurrectionary government to be transferred to their capital at Richmond.
>
> The people of Virginia have thus allowed this giant insurrection to make its nest within her borders, and this Government has no choice left but to deal with it *where* it finds it; and it has the less regret, as the loyal citizens have in due form claimed its protection. Those loyal citizens this Government is bound to recognize and protect, as being Virginia.
>
> In the border States, so called—in fact, the Middle States—there are those who favor a policy which they call "armed neutrality;" that is, an arming of those States to prevent the Union forces passing one way or the disunion the other over their soil. This would be disunion completed. Figuratively speaking, it would be the building of an impassable wall along the line of separation, and yet not quite an impassable one, for, under the guise of neutrality, it would tie the hands of the Union men and freely pass supplies from among them to the insurrectionists, which it could not do as an open enemy. At a stroke it would take all the trouble off the hands of secession, except only what proceeds from the external blockade. It would do for the disunionists that which of all things they most desire—feed them well and give them disunion without a struggle of their own. It recognizes no fidelity to the Constitution, no obligation to maintain the Union; and while very many who have favored it are doubtless loyal citizens, it is, nevertheless, very injurious in effect.
>
> Recurring to the action of the Government, it may be stated that at first a call was made for 75,000 militia, and rapidly following this

---

[33] See 12 U.S. Statutes at Large 1258.
[34] See Richardson, *Messages and Papers of the Presidents,* VI, pp. 20ff.

a proclamation was issued for closing the ports of the insurrectionary districts by proceedings in the nature of blockade. So far all was believed to be strictly legal. At this point the insurrectionists announced their purpose to enter upon the practice of privateering.

Other calls were made for volunteers to serve three years unless sooner discharged, and also for large additions to the Regular Army and Navy. These measures, whether strictly legal or not, were ventured upon under what appeared to be a popular demand and a public necessity, trusting then, as now, that Congress would readily ratify them. It is believed that nothing has been done beyond the constitutional competency of Congress.

Soon after the first call for militia it was considered a duty to authorize the Commanding General in proper cases, according to his discretion, to suspend the privilege of the writ of *habeas corpus,* or, in other words, to arrest and detain without resort to the ordinary processes and forms of law such individuals as he might deem dangerous to the public safety. This authority has purposely been exercised but very sparingly. Nevertheless, the legality and propriety of what has been done under it are questioned, and the attention of the country has been called to the proposition that one who is sworn to "take care that the laws be faithfully executed" should not himself violate them. Of course some consideration was given to the questions of power and propriety before this matter was acted upon. The whole of the laws which were required to be faithfully executed were being resisted and failing of execution in nearly one-third of the States. Must they be allowed to finally fail of execution, even had it been perfectly clear that by the use of the means necessary to their execution some single law, made in such extreme tenderness of the citizen's liberty that practically it relieves more of the guilty than of the innocent, should to a very limited extent be violated? To state the question more directly, Are all the laws *but one* to go unexecuted, and the Government itself go to pieces lest that one be violated? Even in such a case, would not the official oath be broken if the Government should be overthrown when it was believed that disregarding the single law would tend to preserve it? But it was not believed that this question was presented. It was not believed that any law was violated. The provision of the Constitution that "the privilege of the writ of *habeas corpus* shall not be suspended unless when, in cases of rebellion or invasion, the public safety may require it" is equivalent to a provision— is a provision—that such privilege may be suspended when, in cases of rebellion or invasion, the public safety *does* require it. It was decided that we have a case of rebellion and that the public safety does require the qualified suspension of the privilege of the writ which was authorized to be made. Now it is insisted that Congress, and not the Executive, is vested with this power; but the Constitution itself is silent as to which or who is to exercise the power; and as the provision was plainly made for a dangerous emergency, it can not be believed the framers of the instrument intended that in every case the danger should run its course until Congress could be called together, the very assembling of which might be prevented, as was intended in this case, by the rebellion.

No more extended argument is now offered, as an opinion at some length will probably be presented by the Attorney-General. Whether there shall be any legislation upon the subject, and, if any, what, is submitted entirely to the better judgment of Congress.

Attorney General Bates, in an opinion delivered on the fifth of July, 1861,[35] upheld the presidential power. During the hurried special session beginning July 4, 1861, the Congress took no explicit action on the *habeas corpus* question. To a short "Act to Increase the Pay of the Privates in the Regular Army and in the Volunteers in the Service of the United States and for other Purposes" approved August 6, 1861,[36] the Congress added these words—

. . . [A]ll the acts, proclamations, and orders of the President of the United States after the fourth of March, eighteen hundred and sixty-one, respecting the army and navy of the United States, and calling out or relating to the militia or volunteers from the States, are hereby approved and in all respects legalized and made valid, to the same intent and with the same effect as if they had been issued and done under the previous express authority and direction of the Congress of the United States.

In its terms this was wide enough by a strained construction to justify the President's suspension of the writ. The suspension was to help soldiers keep people like Merryman in military custody. But the President's message had pointedly called the matter to congressional attention and one would have expected some more specific statute. The act of August 6 at most granted a retrospective absolution to the President; it gave no authorization for future orders of suspension, save as it may have served as a precedent.

On September 24, 1862, President Lincoln issued a proclamation—[37]

BY THE PRESIDENT OF THE UNITED STATES OF AMERICA:

A PROCLAMATION

WHEREAS, it has become necessary to call into service not only volunteers but also portions of the militia of the states by draft in order to suppress the insurrection existing in the United States, and disloyal

---

[35] 10 Opinions of the Attorney General 74; see Randall, *Constitutional Problems under Lincoln*, pp. 123, 124.
[36] 12 Statutes at Large 755.
[37] See 13 Statutes at Large 730.

persons are not adequately restrained by the ordinary processes of law from hindering this measure and from giving aid and comfort in various ways to the insurrection:

Now, therefore, be it ordered, First.—That during the existing insurrection and as a necessary measure for suppressing the same, all rebels and insurgents, their aiders and abettors within the United States, and all persons discouraging volunteer enlistments, resisting militia drafts, or guilty of any disloyal practice, affording aid and comfort to rebels against the authority of the United States, shall be subject to martial law and liable to trial and punishment by courts-martial or military commissions:

Second.—That the writ of habeas corpus is suspended in respect to all persons arrested, or who are now, or hereafter during the rebellion shall be, imprisoned in any fort, camp, arsenal, military prison, or other place of confinement by any military authority or by the sentence of any court-martial or military commission.

In witness whereof, I have hereunto set my hand, and caused the seal of the United States to be affixed.

Done at the city of Washington, this twenty-fourth day of [L.S.]   September, in the year of our Lord one thousand eight hundred and sixty-two, and of the Independence of the United States the eighty-seventh.

ABRAHAM LINCOLN.

By the President:

WILLIAM H. SEWARD, *Secretary of State.*

Not until March 3, 1863, did the Congress finally pass a statute[38] providing—

That, during the present rebellion, the President of the United States, whenever, in his judgment, the public safety may require it, is authorized to suspend the privilege of the writ of habeas corpus in any case throughout the United States or any part thereof.

The fourth section of the same statute provided that an order of the President or an order made under presidential authority at any time "during the existence of the present rebellion" should be a defense in all courts to any civil or criminal action for any search, seizure, arrest, or imprisonment made "by virtue of any such order, or under color of any law of Congress . . ."

On the thirteenth of April, 1863, Major General Burnside, commanding the Military Department of Ohio, issued his General Orders No. 38—[39]

[38] 12 Stat. at Large 755.
[39] See *Ex parte Vallandigham*, Federal Cases No. 16816, Circuit Court, S.D. Ohio, May 16, 1863.

Headquarters Dept. of the Ohio. Cincinnati, O., April 13, 1863. General Orders No. 38.

. . . [Hereafter all persons] . . . found within our lines, who commit acts for the benefit of the enemies of our country, will be tried as spies or traitors, and, if convicted, will suffer death. This order includes the following class of persons: Carriers of secret mails. Secret recruiting officers within the lines. Persons who have entered into an agreement to pass our lines for the purpose of joining the enemy. Persons found concealed within our lines, belonging to the service of the enemy, and, in fact, all persons found improperly within our lines, who could give private information to the enemy. All persons within our lines who harbor, protect, conceal, feed, clothe, or in any way aid the enemies of our country. The habit of declaring sympathies for the enemy will not be allowed in this department. Persons committing such offences will be at once arrested, with a view to being tried as above stated, or sent beyond our lines into the lines of their friends. It must be distinctly understood that treason, expressed or implied, will not be tolerated in this department. All officers and soldiers are strictly charged with the execution of this order.

By command of Major General Burnside.

LEWIS RICHMOND,
Asst. Adjutant General.

Official: D. R. Larned,
Captain and Assistant Adjutant General.

Eight days later General Burnside issued a special order setting up a Military Commission for the trial of such persons as might be brought before it, detailing officers to constitute it, and appointing a Judge-Advocate. On the fifth of May, 1863, soldiers arrested one Clement Vallandigham at his house in Ohio and took him before the Military Commission where he was charged with—

publicly expressing in violation of General Orders No. 38 . . . . sympathy for those in arms against the government of the United States, and declaring disloyal sentiments and opinions with the object and purpose of weakening the power of the government in its efforts to suppress an unlawful rebellion.

Expressions charged against Vallandigham were these: that on the first day of May at Mount Vernon in Knox County, Ohio, he uttered sentiments in words or to the effect,[40]

. . . [T]hat the present war was a wicked, cruel and unnecessary war, one not waged for the preservation of the Union, but for the purpose of crushing out liberty, and to erect a despotism; a war for the freedom of the blacks, and the enslavement of the whites, and that if the

[40] 1 Wallace 243, at pp. 244–245.

administration had not wished otherwise, that the war could have been honorably terminated long ago; that peace might have been honorably made by listening to the proposed intermediation of France; that propositions by which the Southern States could be won back and the South guaranteed their rights under the Constitution, had been rejected the day before the late battle of Fredericksburg, by Lincoln and his minions, meaning the President of the United States and those under him in authority. Also charging that the Government of the United States was about to appoint military marshals in every district to restrain the people of their liberties, and to deprive them of their rights and privileges, characterizing General Order No. 38 from Headquarters of the Department of the Ohio, as a base usurpation of arbitrary authority, inviting his hearers to resist the same by saying, "the sooner the people inform the minions of usurped power that they will not submit to such restrictions upon their liberties, the better;" and adding that he was at all times and upon all occasions resolved to do what he could to defeat the attempts now being made to build up a monarchy, upon the ruins of our free government; and asserting that he firmly believed, as he had said six months ago, that the men in power are attempting to establish a despotism in this country, more cruel and oppressive than ever existed before.

The Commission found Vallandigham guilty of the offense charged, though not of all the expressions in question; the Commission sentenced Vallandigham to close confinement in some fortress of the United States, to be kept there during the war. On May 16, 1863, District Judge Humphrey H. Leavitt of Ohio refused to issue a writ of *habeas corpus* for Vallandigham.[41] On May 19, 1863, the President commuted the sentence, directing Major General Burnside to send Vallandigham to the headquarters of General Rosecrans, by him to be put beyond the federal military lines. This order General Rosecrans carried out by releasing Vallandigham south of the Union outposts at Murfreesboro, Tennessee. Vallandigham chose not to spend the rest of the war among the Confederates; he made his way to Bermuda, thence to Halifax, and for a time settled down in Canada where he was separated from the city of Detroit only by the width of a river. From this point he attended to the news of his case and conducted an absentee campaign as a Peace Democrat for the office of Governor of Ohio.

In June 1864, Vallandigham made his way back into Ohio. Until the war was over he continued his Copperhead activities,[42] ignored

[41] See Federal Case No. 16816, 28 Fed. Cas. 874.
[42] Confederate sympathizers in the mid-West used to cut the head of the Goddess of Liberty out of a copper cent and wear it as a badge.

by the federal authorities. In the meantime his lawyers instead of attempting to appeal from District Judge Leavitt's order, had applied to the Supreme Court of the United States for an original writ of certiorari to be directed to the Judge Advocate General of the Army, to send up the proceedings of the Military Commission to the Supreme Court of the United States for review. The Supreme Court denied certiorari on the ground that it had no power to entertain proceedings in their nature appellate from a military commission.[43] The Supreme Court's original jurisdiction was barred by the principle of *Marbury* v. *Madison.*[44]

The intense opposition of some politicians to Lincoln and the war is difficult to understand a century later. Vallandigham wrote to Horatio Seymour, Democratic Governor of New York, "Your voice— the voice of New York, to the Administration, will break my bonds." The Ohio State Convention of the Democratic party nominated Vallandigham for Governor. The Resolutions Committee of the Democratic State Convention at Albany, New York, deplored Lincoln's unconstitutional action. On June 12, 1863, Lincoln gave to the newspapers a letter addressed to "Hon. Erastus Corning and Others," constituting the Resolutions Committee at Albany. Lincoln wrote— and his words must have appealed to the parents of thousands of Union soldiers—

. . . [H]e who dissuades one man from volunteering, or induces one soldier to desert, weakens the Union cause as much as he who kills a Union soldier in battle. Yet this dissuasion or inducement may be so conducted as to be no defined crime of which any civil court would take cognizance. . . . Must I shoot a simple-minded soldier boy who deserts, while I must not touch a hair of a wily agitator who induces him to desert? This is none the less injurious when effected by getting a father, or brother, or friend into a public meeting, and there working upon his feelings till he is persuaded to write the soldier boy that he is fighting in a bad cause, for a wicked administration of a contemptible government, too weak to arrest and punish him if he shall desert. I think that, in such a case, to silence the agitator and save the boy is not only constitutional, but withal a great mercy.[45]

[43] *Ex parte Vallandigham*, 1 Wallace 243 (1864).

[44] 1 Cranch 137 (1903). See page 318ff., above.

[45] See Sandburg, *Abraham Lincoln: The War Years* (4 vols.; New York: Harcourt, Brace and Co., 1939) II, pp. 167–168. And see Justice Holmes, writing of another war in *Schenck* v. *United States*, 249 U.S. 47, p. 52 (1919). "When a nation is at war many things that might be said in time of peace are such a hindrance to its effort that their utterance will not be endured so long as men fight, and that no Court could regard them as protected by any constitutional right."

Another case, that of Lambdin P. Milligan, involved graver matters than Clement Vallandigham's harangue. In October 1864, by order of General Hovey, commanding the military district of Indiana, Milligan and some of his associates were arrested, held in military custody, and tried by a military commission on charges of "affording aid and comfort to the rebellion, inciting insurrection, disloyal practices, and violation of the laws of war." The specifications of these charges set forth that Milligan, with others, formed a secret military force of which Milligan was an officer. This force was intended to capture a United States arsenal in Indiana, release prisoners of war confined in a military prison, arm the prisoners, join them with the secret, newly-armed forces, march into Kentucky and Missouri and there cooperate with the rebel forces. The specifications charged Milligan and his associates with communicating with the Confederate forces in order to urge invasion of Kentucky, Indiana and Ilinois.

The military commission convened on October 21, 1864, tried Milligan, and sentenced him to be hanged on Friday, May 19, 1865. The war ended and the President was assassinated, both in the middle of April, 1865. On the tenth of the following May, Milligan presented a petition to the United States Circuit Court for the district of Indiana seeking discharge from his allegedly unlawful imprisonment. He contended that on January 2, 1865, after the proceedings before the military commission were at an end, a grand jury had been convened by the United States Circuit Court for Indiana at Indianapolis and had made no presentment against Milligan; he insisted that he was entitled to be tried by a civil tribunal, before a jury. The judges of the Circuit Court were divided in their opinion; they certified to the Supreme Court questions whether on the facts stated in the petition and exhibits a writ of *habeas corpus* ought to be issued, and whether on those facts Lambdin Milligan ought to be discharged from custody, and whether on those facts the military commission had jurisdiction legally to try Milligan.

On the 19th of May Milligan was not hanged. President Johnson commuted his death sentence to life imprisonment. Nearly a year after the end of the war, distinguished counsel for Milligan and for the government presented to the Supreme Court argument lasting from March 5 to March 13, 1866. Both sides cited precedents from English and American history. The Attorney General of the United States referred to the *Vallandigham* case,[46] the case of Major André during the American Revolution and to *Luther* v. *Borden*,[47] which had concerned a contest between two purported governments of the State of

[46] 1 Wallace 243 (1864).
[47] 7 Howard 43 (1849).

Rhode Island. David Dudley Field, on Milligan's behalf, cited the instance of the Earl of Lancaster who commanded insurgent forces against Edward the Second of England. Lancaster was defeated and beheaded; but the first Parliament of Edward the Third declared, so Field informed the Supreme Court, "that in the time of peace no man ought to be adjudged to death for treason or any other offense, without being arraigned and held to answer. That regularly when the Kings courts are opened it is a time of peace in judgment of law." Field also cited Sir Thomas Darnel's case in 1627[48], and Magna Carta.

On April 3, 1866, Chief Justice Chase announced the Supreme Court's judgment. Milligan was to be discharged from custody, according to the statute of March 3, 1863, "An Act Relating to Habeas Corpus, and Regulating Judicial Proceedings in Certain Cases"; that the military commission had no jurisdiction to try, and to sentence him.[49] The court's opinion was not delivered until December 17, 1866. Mr. Justice Davis then read the majority opinion, finding that the statute of March 3, 1863, had conferred jurisdiction on the Circuit Court of Indiana to issue a writ of habeas corpus, once the Grand Jury had assembled and failed to indict Milligan. On the substantive question the Court proclaimed the "open court rule," that so long as the ordinary civil courts are open and conducting judicial business, court-martial of a civilian is not authorized by the Constitution.

Mr. Justice Davis referred to the procedural provisions of the Bill of Rights in criminal cases, the guarantee of indictment by grand jury and trial by petit jury, and stated—

> These securities for personal liberty thus embodied, were such as wisdom and experience had demonstrated to be necessary for the protection of those accused of crime. And so strong was the sense of the country of their importance, and so jealous were the people, that these rights, highly prized, might be denied them by implication that when the original Constitution was proposed for adoption it encountered severe opposition; and, but for the belief that it would be so amended as to embrace them, it would never have been ratified.
>
> Time has proven the discernment of our ancestors; for even these provisions, expressed in such plain English words, that it would seem the ingenuity of man could not evade them, are now, after the lapse of more than seventy years, sought to be avoided. Those great and good men foresaw that troublous times would arise, when rulers and people would become restive under restraint, and seek by sharp and decisive measures to accomplish ends deemed just and proper; and that the principles of constitutional liberty would be in peril, unless established by irrepealable law. The history of the world had taught

[48] 3 Howell's State Trials 1; also called the *Five Knights' Case.*
[49] *Ex parte Milligan*, 4. Wall. 2 (1866).

them that what was done in the past might be attempted in the future. The Constitution of the United States is a law for rulers and people, equally in war and in peace, and covers with the shield of its protection all classes of men, at all times, and under all circumstances. No doctrine, involving more pernicious consequences, was ever invented by the wit of man than that any of its provisions can be suspended during any of the great exigencies of government. Such a doctrine leads directly to anarchy or despotism, but the theory of necessity on which it is based is false; for the government, within the Constitution, has all the powers granted to it which are necessary to preserve its existence, as has been happily proved by the result of the great effort to throw off its just authority.

Four of the Justices, with an opinion delivered by Chief Justice Chase, would have rested the discharge of Milligan solely upon the statute of 1863. All agreed in the result.

Milligan, released from military custody on April 10, 1866, on March 13, 1868 brought an action against General Hovey in the Illinois courts, for damages because of his arrest. Under the federal statute of March 3, 1863, General Hovey removed the suit to the federal Circuit Court. The jury rendered a verdict in favor of Milligan, but only for nominal damages, as a two-year statute of limitations was in effect, and Milligan's delay in bringing his action left recoverable only whatever damages he suffered by confinement between March 13 and April 10, 1866.[50]

The war of 1941–1945 between the United States and Italy, Germany and Japan again raised some of the Milligan questions. In June 1942 two groups of men landed by German submarines came ashore in Florida and Long Island, New York, dressed in German uniforms, planning sabotage. They buried their uniforms, dressed in civilian clothes, and within two weeks of their landing, before they could accomplish anything, they were arrested by federal authorities. President Roosevelt, by an order of July 2, 1942, appointed a military commission of seven Generals, directing it to try the persons in question for offenses against "the law of war" and the Articles of War. The President also directed by proclamation of the same day that persons attempting to enter the United States through coastal or boundary defenses to commit hostile or warlike acts should be subject to the jurisdiction of military tribunals and denied access to courts. Military counsel was appointed to defend the accused saboteurs, and the Commission began the military trial on July 8.

As promptly as possible the prisoners' officer lawyers sought writs of

[50] The story is told in Warren, *Supreme Court in United States History* (3 vols.; Boston: Little, Brown and Co., 1922) III, p. 149.

habeas corpus in the lower federal courts of the District of Columbia and in the Supreme Court of the United States. One of the accused, Hans Haupt, claimed to be a citizen of the United States; his contention raised questions under the Treason Clause of the Constitution, Article 3, Section 3. The District Court of the District of Columbia denied leave to file a petition for *habeas corpus;* the United States Court of Appeals affirmed. The assigned military counsel for the accused then petitioned for certiorari and for leave to file an original petition for *habeas corpus* in the Supreme Court. The Supreme Court of the United States granted certiorari, heard argument on July 29 and 30, 1942, and on July 31, 1942 announced its decision affirming the order of the District Court and denying leave to file the original petition for *habeas corpus* in the Supreme Court of the United States.

The Military Commission had interrupted its sessions during the judicial proceedings. It resumed immediately after the Supreme Court decision of July 31. On August 3, the Commission sent its decision with the record to the President. On August 8, 1942 the President announced that six of the prisoners had been electrocuted, one sentenced for life, one for thirty years. Haupt, the man who claimed citizenship, was among those executed.

The Supreme Court's opinion, by Chief Justice Stone, was filed later—on October 29, 1942. The Chief Justice found it unnecessary to determined the contention of the accused, Haupt, that he was a citizen of the United States, deciding his case on the same basis of those who were admittedly German nationals. He turned aside the Milligan precedent stating that "the Court concluded that Milligan, not being a part of or associated with the armed forces of the enemy, was a non-belligerent, not subject to the law of war save as—in circumstances found not there to be present and not involved here—martial law might be constitutionally established." The Chief Justice went on to say that it was not necessary to define with meticulous care the ultimate boundaries of the jurisdiction of military tribunals, but it was enough that the accused in the case then under consideration, were within those boundaries.[51]

The *Milligan* and *Vallandigham* cases again played a part in the Supreme Court in 1946, in a case which arose in the Hawaiian Islands.[52] Section 67 of the Hawaiian Organic Act authorized the Territorial Governor to place the Territory under "Martial Law . . .

---

[51] *Ex Parte Quirin,* 317 U.S. 1 (1942). See Robert E. Cushman "Ex parte Quirin *et al.*—The Nazi Saboteur Case," 28 *Cornell Law Quarterly* 54 (1942); Alpheus Thomas Mason, "Inter Arma Silent Leges: Chief Justice Stone's Views," 69 *Harvard Law Review* 806 (1956). See also Willard Hurst, "Treason in the United States," 58 *Harv. L. Rev.* 226, 395, 806 (1944, 1945).

[52] *Duncan v. Kahanamoku,* 327 U.S. 304.

in case of rebellion or invasion, or imminent danger thereof, when the public safety requires it." The Governor's action was to remain effective only "until communication can be had with the President and his decision thereon made known." The Japanese air force attacked Pearl Harbor on December 7, 1941; the Governor immediately suspended *habeas corpus* and put the Territory under martial law. On December 9, 1941, the President approved the Governor's action.

The Governor's proclamation requested the Commanding General to exercise all the powers "normally exercised" by the Governor and by "the judicial officers and employees of this Territory." The Commanding General immediately proclaimed himself Military Governor and established military tribunals to take the place of the civilian courts. Assurance of uninterrupted military control was further guaranteed by an order of August 25, 1943, prohibiting the acceptance of a petition for a writ of *habeas corpus* by a judge or judicial employee, or the filing of such a petition by a prisoner or by his attorney.

In 1942 the military arrested white, a stock-broker, and brought charges of embezzlement against him. He was, over his protest at military jurisdiction, brought before a military tribunal, a Provost Court, and three days after his arraignment, was tried and convicted. The Provost Court sentenced him to five years' imprisonment, later reduced to four years.

In 1944 a civilian shipfitter named Duncan, employed at Honolulu at the Navy Yard, engaged in a brawl there with two armed marine sentries. By this time the civilian courts had been authorized to "exercise their normal jurisdiction" except that only military tribunals were to try "criminal prosecutions for violations of military orders." Duncan was tried before a military court for violation of a military order which prohibited assault on military and naval personnel with attempt to resist or hinder them in the discharge of their duty. Duncan, though he appropriately protested the military jurisdiction, was convicted and sentenced to six months' imprisonment.

Duncan and White filed petitions for *habeas corpus* in the United States District Court for Hawaii in March and April 1944. Kahanamoku, Sheriff of Honolulu, and Colonel Steer, Provost Marshal of the Central Pacific Area, made returns that *habeas corpus* had been suspended and that the District Court had no jurisdiction to issue it. The District Court held in each case that the courts were able to function, that there was no military necessity to close them, that the military trials were void; the Court ordered the prisoners released. The United States Court of Appeals for the Ninth Circuit reversed this judgment, holding that the military trials were authorized. On February 25, 1946 the Supreme Court of the United States reversed the Court of

Appeals and upheld the District Court, ruling that the military tribunals were without jurisdiction. This was done as a matter of statutory construction of the Organic Act, not constitutional law; Mr. Justice Black wrote, for the Supreme Court—

> We believe that when Congress passed the Hawaiian Organic Act and authorized the establishment of "martial law" it had in mind and did not wish to exceed the boundaries between military and civilian power, in which our people have always believed, which responsible military and executive officers had heeded, and which had become part of our political philosophy and institutions prior to the time Congress passed the Organic Act. The phrase "martial law" as employed in that Act, therefore, while intended to authorize the military to act vigorously for the maintenance of an orderly civil government and for the defense of the Islands against actual or threatened rebellion or invasion, was not intended to authorize the supplanting of courts by military tribunals. Yet the government seeks to justify the punishment of both White and Duncan on the ground of such supposed Congressional authorization. We hold that both petitioners are now entitled to be released from custody.[53]

The Court repeatedly cited *Ex parte Milligan* to justify its conclusion. Mr. Justice Black pointed out that under *Vallandigham* there was no direct appellate court review, as military tribunals are not part of the judicial system.[54]

In 1957 and 1960 the Supreme Court of the United States decided that the provisions of the Bill of Rights concerning procedure in criminal cases applied to American civilians accompanying the armed forces overseas either as dependent members of families of military men, or as civilian employees of the armed forces. Hence such civilians were not subject to the jurisdiction of military tribunals overseas.[55]

By proclamations of April 19 and April 27, 1861,[56] President Lincoln ordered a blockade of the Confederate seaports, and provided that vessels attempting to run the blockade should be forfeit as prize with their cargoes. President Buchanan had not assembled the navy; Lincoln at once directed that federal naval vessels be despatched as soon as possible to carry out the blockade and in the meantime undertook to equip the navy with additional armed ships. Federal naval vessels

[53] *Duncan v. Kahanamoku*, 327 U.S. 304, at 324 (1946).
[54] 4 Wallace 2. See Charles Fairman, "The Law of Martial Rule and the National Emergency" 55 *Harvard Law Review* 1253 (1942); and also Professor Fairman's "The Supreme Court on Military Jurisdiction: Martial Rule in Hawaii and the Yamashita Case" 59 *Harvard Law Review* 834 (1946).
[55] *Reid v. Covert*; *Kinsella v. Kreuger*, 354 U.S. 1 (1957); *McElroy v. U.S. ex rel Guagliardo*, 361 U.S. 281 (1960).
[56] Richardson, *Messages and Papers of the Presidents*, VI, pp. 14–15.

captured a number of blockade runners, some domestic, some of foreign registry. The captors brought the captured ships into ports of the United States and there petitioned District and Circuit Courts to condemn them as prizes. The owners resisted on various grounds— one of which was that the President had no power as Commander in Chief to order a blockade. A statute of July 13, 1861[57] purported to authorize future blockading, but, so the counsel for the blockade runners argued, it had no retrospective effect to validate prizes taken before that statute was enacted. The captured ships involved in the litigation had all been taken in May, June, and in July prior to the federal blockade law.

The lower federal courts held that with certain exceptions the blockade runners and their cargoes were lawful "prize of war," and were forfeited because of their blockade-running activities. The owners appealed to the Supreme Court of the United States, still challenging the President's constitutional power to blockade. The cases were argued for twelve days in February, 1863 and the Supreme Court, though with various dissents by Chief Justice Taney and Justices Catron, Nelson and Clifford, upheld the validity of the blockade and declared the vessels forfeit.[58]

Financing and "Legal Tender"[59]

War requires money. By Act of July 17, 1861[60] the Congress authorized the Secretary of the Treasury to borrow two hundred and fifty million dollars on an interest-bearing bond issue; but permitted him to issue instead as part of that loan treasury demand notes, not bearing interest, usable "to pay for salaries or other dues from the United States" not exceeding fifty millions of dollars in denominations of not less than ten dollars. On February 25, 1862 the Congress[61] authorized the Secretary of the Treasury to issue one hundred and fifty millions of dollars of United States notes, bearing no interest, payable to bearer

[57] 12 Statutes at Large 255.

[58] The *Prize Cases*, 2 Black 635 (1863).

[59] "Tender" is a word of art among lawyers. It is an offer to pay. If made in lawful money, and if the money is kept formally available to the creditor, the tender stops the accrual of interest and may end the creditor's right to take property the debtor has mortgaged as security; to "repossess the car" for example. See Braucher and Sutherland, *Commercial Transactions—Text, Cases and Problems* (3rd ed.; Brooklyn: The Foundation Press, 1964) pp. 308, 309; and see a U.S. Silver Certificate (dollar bill) or Federal Reserve Note (five-dollar bill).

[60] 12 Stat. at L. 259.

[61] 12 Stat. at L. 345.

in denominations of not less than five dollars. Fifty millions of these were to take up the fifty million of treasury demand notes authorized on the preceding July 17. The Act of February 25, 1862 further directed that the notes issued under its authorization were to be "lawful money and a legal tender in payment of all debts, public and private, within the United States, except duties on imports and interest as aforesaid."[62]

The first of these "greenback" notes were issued in March 1862 and for a time they did not depreciate in general value far below gold. However, two years later, by July 1864, a dollar in gold would buy two dollars and eighty-five cents worth of greenbacks. By 1870 the greenbacks were remarkably reestablished and a gold dollar would then buy only a dollar and twenty cents worth of paper money.

The statute of February 25, 1862, was retrospective in its effect on legal tender; that is to say, it required a creditor who had contracted before the date of the Act, when the federal statutes made coin the only legal tender, nevertheless to accept paper, dollar for dollar, in discharge of his claims. On June 11, 1862 one Lewis H. Meyer of New York tendered in greenbacks issued under the Act of February 25, 1862, to his creditor James J. Roosevelt, eight thousand one hundred and seventy-one dollars, as the full amount of an 1854 mortgage bond which Mr. Meyer owed to Mr. Roosevelt. Roosevelt refused to receive the paper money as legal tender, claiming that he was entitled to be paid in United States gold coin. The New York Court of Appeals held that the federal statute of February 25, 1862 was valid; and that Meyer was entitled to discharge his debt by paying Roosevelt in greenbacks. Roosevelt thereupon sued out a writ of error in the Supreme Court of the United States. On December 21, 1863 the Supreme Court, with only one dissent (by Mr. Justice Nelson) held that it had no jurisdiction of the case as the federal statute had been upheld, not held invalid, by the State court; the Supreme Court paid no attention to Roosevelt's claim that the Legal Tender Act invaded his rights under the federal Constitution, which would have supported the Supreme Court's appellate jurisdiction.[63]

In 1865 a man named Rodes owed one Bronson $1507.00, the prin-

[62] I.e., interest on United States bonds and notes. This legal tender clause was repeated in subsequent Acts of Congress, as the war called for more and more spending. See, e.g., Acts of July 11, 1862, 12 Stat. at L. 583; Act of March 3, 1863, 12 Stat. at L. 709.

[63] *Roosevelt* v. *Meyer*, 1 Wallace, 512. The Supreme Court expressly overruled *Roosevelt* v. *Meyer* in 1872, finding that jurisdiction was lodged in the Supreme Court to consider a contention that a State court had wrongly upheld an Act of Congress which conflicted with the Constitution. *Trebilcock* v. *Wilson*, 12 Wallace 687.

cipal and interest of a bond secured by a mortgage[64] on New York land. The loan had been made in 1851, and the borrower had agreed in so many words to pay principal and interest in gold or silver coin. In 1865 Rodes tendered to Bronson United States notes, "greenbacks," for the principal and interest due on the bond and mortgage. At this time a dollar in coin would buy two dollars and twenty-five cents in United States notes. Bronson refused the tendered payment; Rodes deposited greenbacks in a New York bank to the credit of Bronson, and brought an action in the New York courts for a declaration that the mortgaged premises were relieved from the lien of the mortgage, and for a decree that Bronson be compelled to deliver to Rodes a receipt in full for the mortgage debt. The New York Court of Appeals in 1866 upheld the right of Rodes to pay in greenbacks.[65] Bronson brought the case to the Supreme Court of the United States, and on February 15, 1869, in an opinion by Chief Justice Chase, that Court reversed the judgment of the New York Court of Appeals.[66] Chase's opinion rested upon a construction of the statute; he wrote that the Congress could not be supposed to have intended to make payment of paper serve to carry out an express contract to pay coin. Justice Miller dissented; Congress, he said, had intended to make United States notes legal tender for all debts; the only legal tender in existence at the time the mortgage had been executed was United States metallic currency; the explicit promise to pay in coin, recited in the bond, merely stated what the law would require in any event.[67] A few days later the Court reached the same result concerning a lease, executed long before the Legal Tender Acts, with rent payable in gold English guineas. Paper tender was no good. Again Miller dissented.[68]

In December 1869 the Supreme Court sustained an Act of Congress imposing a tax of ten per cent on the amount of circulating notes of any State bank.[69] The Court rested its decision on the congressional powers to tax and to "coin money, regulate the value thereof." The statute would inevitably and immediately end the issuance, by State-chartered banks, of their own notes for use as currency, and make

[64] A bond is a written promise to pay money. A mortgage is a conveyance of a security interest in something—often real estate—for recourse by the creditor if the debtor fails to pay the bond. The two may be put on one paper but generally occur in two documents. In common speech the two are called "a mortgage."

[65] 34 New York 649.

[66] Bronson v. Rodes, 7 Wallace 229 (1869).

[67] An account of the pre-Civil War legislation as to legal tender in coin appears in Chief Justice Chase's opinion in Bronson v. Rodes, op. cit.

[68] Butler v. Horowitz, 7 Wallace 258 (1869).

[69] 14 Stat. at Large 146.

federal currency the only sort in use.[70] So three years after the end of the war the Legal Tender Acts stood and the national currency served well enough—thanks partly to concessions in cases of antecedent contracts to pay in metal coins; thanks partly to a dubious procedural barrier in the way of Supreme Court review; thanks partly to driving out of circulation notes of State banks; but thanks most of all to victory in the war.

In June 1865 the Kentucky Court of Appeals, unlike a number of courts in other States, had held the Legal Tender Acts unconstitutional. In the Kentucky case a creditor named Griswold sued Susan and Henry Hepburn to enforce a note the Hepburns had signed in 1860, payable in 1862. When Griswold sued, the Hepburns deposited with the Kentucky court a sum in greenbacks equalling principal and interest of the note, and court-costs, contending that they thus made a legal tender of all they owed. The Kentucky Court of Appeals held tender of paper money ineffectual to discharge a contract made prior to the Legal Tender Acts when the only legal tender had been metal coin. The debtors, who were thus required to pay in "hard money" or its inflated equivalent in more dollars of depreciated paper if the creditor should choose to accept it, brought the case to the Supreme Court of the United States. On February 7, 1870 a majority of the Supreme Court, in an opinion by Chief Justice Chase, held that the judgment of the Court of Appeals of Kentucky must be affirmed. The Legal Tender Acts when retrospectively applied were unconstitutional.[71] Chief Justice Chase and the majority found no authorization given by the Constitution to the Congress to make a Legal Tender Act applicable to antecedent debts. Chase, one-time Secretary of the Treasury, could find authority neither in the fifth clause of Article I, Section 8, which authorized Congress—

. . . to coin money, regulate the value thereof, and of foreign coin . . .

nor in the power to make war and support armies, even taken together with the "necessary and proper" clause. While the Contract Clause operated as a prohibition only against the States, Chase found that a federal statute impairing the obligation of contract would be "inconsistent with the spirit of the Constitution." So it was, too, with the

[70] *Veazie Bank* v. *Fenno*, 8 Wallace 533. Thus the Congress successfully and constitutionally used against State bank-notes the identical weapon which a half-century earlier the Marshall court had forbidden Maryland's legislature to use against the Bank of the United States. *McCulloch* v. *Maryland*, 4 Wheaton 316 (1819).
[71] *Hepburn* v. *Griswold*, 8 Wallace 603.

Fifth Amendment Eminent Domain Clause and with its Due Process Clause.

> We are obliged to conclude that an Act making mere promises to pay dollars a legal tender in payment of debts previously contracted, is not a means appropriate, plainly adapted, really calculated to carry into effect any express power vested in Congress: that such an Act is inconsistent with the spirit of the Constitution; and that it is prohibited by the Constitution.

Chase added at the end of his opinion a few words concerning the views of Justice Grier. Grier had retired during the week preceding the announcement of the judgment; but he had been a member of the Court when the case was decided in conference on November 27, 1869; on January 29, 1870, when a majority had directed that Chase's opinion be read, Grier had stated his view that the Legal Tender Clause, properly construed, had no application to antecedent debts; but upon the construction given to the Act by the other judges that it did so apply, Grier thought it unconstitutional. Justices Miller, Swayne and Davis dissented from the judgment of the Court.

When the decision in *Hepburn* v. *Griswold* was handed down, the Court consisted of only seven members. Here an explanation of the number and character of the Justices making up the Supreme Court during the Civil War period becomes desirable.

The Supreme Court had consisted of six Justices from 1789 to 1807; Congress increased it to seven in 1807,[72] and to nine in 1837.[73] By Act of March 3, 1863[74] a tenth Justice was added. In the autumn of 1864 Chief Justice Roger Brooke Taney had nine Associate Justices— Samuel Nelson of New York, Nathan Clifford of Maine, James M. Wayne of Georgia, Robert E. Grier of Pennsylvania, Samuel F. Miller of Iowa, Noah H. Swayne of Ohio, John Catron of Tennessee, David Davis of Illinois, and Stephen J. Field of California. Taney, after serving as Chief Justice for twenty-eight years, died on October 12, 1864. In place of Chief Justice Taney, President Lincoln appointed Salmon P. Chase of Ohio who had been Secretary of the Treasury until he had resigned that office in June of 1864. Justice Catron died in 1865, reducing the Court to nine. After Johnson became President, and his differences with the Congress became acute, that body by Act of July 23, 1866[75] directed that the membership of the Supreme Court be reduced to seven, as losses should occur—a move to diminish Johnson's

[72] 2 Stat. at Large 420.
[73] 5 Stat. at Large 176.
[74] 12 Stat. at Large 794.
[75] 14 Stat. at Large 209.

powers to appoint. Justice Wayne died in 1867, reducing the Court to eight members, its number on November 27, 1869, when the Court, in conference, voted in *Hepburn* v. *Griswold* by five to three, to hold the Legal Tender Acts unconstitutional. Chief Justice Chase (who had been Secretary of the Treasury when the Legal Tender Act was passed) and Justices Nelson, Clifford, Field and Grier voted for unconstitutionality. Justices Swayne, Miller and Davis, all appointed by Lincoln in 1862, voted at the November conference to uphold the Act.[76]

Meantime the Congress on April 10, 1869 again revised the number of Supreme Court Justices, by an Act to take effect on the first Monday in December, 1869.[77] General Grant had been elected President in November 1868; the Congress was willing to trust his appointments when it would not trust Andrew Johnson's; the new statute raised the Court's membership to nine Justices. Grier was aging and uncertain. In December 1869 a committee of the Justices told the unhappy old man he should resign.[78] He sent in his resignation December 15, effective February 1. At the conference on his last day as a Justice he approved Chase's opinion for unconstitutionality of the Legal Tender Acts of 1862. Grier then departed, and thus a seven-man Court on February 7, 1870, by a vote of four to three, adjudged the Legal Tender Acts unconstitutional as to antecedent debts.[79]

On that day the Court was thus short two Justices of the nine authorized the preceding April. At about the hour when the Court was announcing the four-to-three decision in *Hepburn* v. *Griswold,* President Grant sent to the Senate for confirmation the nominations of two new Justices, William Strong of Pennsylvania and Joseph P. Bradley of New Jersey. On April 30, 1870 the Court ordered a reargument of *Knox* v. *Lee,* which had been argued in November 1869, and in which the validity of the Legal Tender Acts was concerned. On February 23, 1871 counsel for both sides, rearguing *Knox* v. *Lee,* conceded the va-

---

[76] Field had been appointed by Lincoln in 1863; Lincoln had appointed Chase as Chief Justice in 1864. Of eight Justices who voted at conference on *Hepburn* v. *Griswold,* five were Lincoln's appointees. The figures on the vote can easily be deduced from Chief Justice Chase's note on Grier's vote, at the end of Chase's opinion. And see Fairman, *Mr. Justice Miller and the Supreme Court, 1862–1890* (Cambridge, Mass.: Harvard University Press, 1939) pp. 160ff.

[77] 16 Statutes at Large 44.

[78] See Justice Miller's "A Statement of Facts," subscribed by Justices Miller, Swayne, Davis, Strong, and Bradley on April 30, 1870, published in 1901 in the *Miscellaneous Writings of the Late Hon. Joseph P. Bradley,* Charles Bradley, ed., (Newark, N. J.: L. J. Hardman, 1901). And see Fairman, *Mr. Justice Miller and the Supreme Court,* p. 171; and Warren, *Supreme Court in United States History,* III, p. 245, fn. 1.

[79] *Hepburn* v. *Griswold,* 8 Wallace 603.

lidity of the Legal Tender Acts which supposedly had been laid to rest in *Hepburn* v. *Griswold*. But Clarkson N. Potter, who had argued in *Hepburn* v. *Griswold* on the side of invalidity of the Act, now asked a second reargument of *Knox* v. *Lee,* that he might assert the correctness of the 1870 decision. The Supreme Court consented, and on April 18 and 19, 1871 heard *Knox* v. *Lee* argued a third time, with Mr. Potter contending that the Legal Tender Acts were unconstitutional. The Attorney General of the United States, Amos T. Akerman, argued for constitutionality. On May 1, 1871, the Supreme Court overruled *Hepburn* v. *Griswold,* and held that the majority of four had been wrong in that case. The new majority of five consisted of the old minority of three and the two new Justices, Bradley and Strong: they held that the Legal Tender Acts were constitutional for antecedent as well as future contracts.[80] The old majority of four, now a minority, all dissenting, were of the same opinion still.

The new majority was a cautious one. In 1872 the Court followed its 1869 decision that the Congress had not intended to apply the Legal Tender Acts to contracts where the debtor had explicitly promised to pay in "hard money."[81] But men were heated about the law and the morals of paying debts in cheap paper. There was talk that "Grant had packed the Court"—a phrase with undertones of corrupt scheming, with a suggestion that the President, forewarned of *Hepburn's Case,* had arranged with Bradley and Strong to trade appointments for votes. Such a bargain was completely out of character for either of the new Justices, and no one has ever found any evidence of such a prearrangement.[82] The legal question, as is so often true in the law of the Constitution, presented a difficult choice between two excellent aspirations—the stability of contracted arrangements on which men may plan their course of action, and a government empowered to manage the economy. When Bradley and Strong voted for this latter they only anticipated what Chief Justice Hughes and four colleagues were to do more emphatically in the *Gold Clause Cases* of 1935.[83] But that story is part of the New Deal, not part of the Civil War.

[80] *Knox* v. *Lee,* 12 Wallace 457 (1871).
[81] *Trebilcock* v. *Wilson,* 12 Wallace 687 (1872). Here the debtor had agreed, before the enactment of the Legal Tender Act of 1862, to pay "in specie." As in *Bronson* v. *Rodes,* 7 Wallace 229 (1869) the majority here did not purport to decide what the powers of Congress might have been as to antecedent specie contracts. Miller and Bradley dissented in *Trebilcock* v. *Wilson.* In 1884 the Supreme Court found that the Congress had power to make paper legal tender in peace as well as in war—*Juilliard* v. *Greenman,* 110 U.S. 421—but still left open the question of agreements to pay in hard money.
[82] See Warren, *Supreme Court in U.S. History,* III, pp. 247ff.
[83] *Norman* v. *Baltimore & Ohio R.R.,* 294 U.S. 240.

Emancipation and Reconstruction

As the war drew to its close, other difficult and complex constitutional problems became apparent. No written charter can provide a pattern for returning, to amicable coexistence in a federal union, a group of semi-sovereign States ruled by a class of men who have been engaged in conducting war against the Union. As proximate victory began to appear probable, the federal government had to improvise a plan for that reunion. Some means had to be arranged to permit a reasonable measure of democracy in the South, and still to prevent government there by the group of men, most familiar with the process of governing, who had managed the Confederate insurrection. This meant a political overhaul, by which a new class of white men would succeed the late Confederate leaders; and by which the Negroes would come to take an equal part in self-governing. But this latter process meant a social revolution calling for much ingenuity and persistent patience, an entirely new relation between the five and one-half million whites and the three and one-half million Negroes in the eleven Confederate States; a change with which some whites in the North, and most in the South, were unsympathetic. The history of the post-war years can be read as a contest between the men who tried to hasten this process and those who tried to slow it, or bring it to a stop. To some extent this contest continues a century later.

Freeing the slaves was the first undertaking, and even this was not universally desired even in the North. There was much talk of the war being fought to save the Union, not to free the slaves. Opinion in favor of emancipation grew as the war went on, and with that change in opinion came a series of steps in its direction. The constitutional power of Congress to end all slavery was then doubtful to say the least, but slaves were Confederate assets; they worked on fortifications, drove wagons carrying military supplies, and as field-hands released white men who could serve as soldiers. When Virginia seceded on May 23, 1861, General Benjamin F. Butler was commanding at Fortress Monroe; in civil life Butler had been a Massachusetts lawyer fertile in resource, and when slaves came into his military lines he refused to return them to their owners, stating that they were "contraband of war."[84] In the Union armies "contraband" came to be a

---

[84] Supplies recognized in international law as subject to confiscation when seized by a belligerent from a neutral who is attempting to deliver them to the captor's enemy.

common term for a refugee slave. A Confiscation Act passed by Congress on August 6, 1861[85] provided that property used for insurrectionary purposes was subect to confiscation—and a slave's services if so used, were forfeited. On April 16, 1862 an Act of Congress provided compensated liberation for all slaves in the District of Columbia.[86] On June 19, 1862, with Roger Brooke Taney still Chief Justice and *Dred Scott's Case* still on the books, the Republican majority in Congress abolished slavery in all Territories.[87] On July 17, 1862 the Second Confiscation Act freed slaves, owned by persons engaged in rebellion, who came within the Union lines; and provided for freeing slaves as a punishment of those convicted of the crimes of treason, or of engaging in the rebellion.[88]

In the early part of 1862 Lincoln was impressed with the general increase of sentiment in the North for freeing the slaves, and with the desirability of executive steps to achieve emancipation. On September 22, 1862, less than a week after Lee had been turned back at Antietam, Lincoln issued the preliminary Emancipation Proclamation declaring that on January 1, 1863, all slaves in any part of the Confederacy then in rebellion should be forever free.[89] On January 1, 1863 the President issued a new Emancipation Proclamation, confirming the first and announcing that former slaves would be recruited into the Union forces.[90] Border and occupied States began to act. Missouri, Tennessee, Maryland, and parts of Louisiana, Arkansas and Virginia, abolished slavery between 1863 and 1865.[91]

On February 1, 1865, before the close of the war, Congress proposed the Thirteenth Amendment.[92] Lincoln had been assassinated and Andrew Johnson was President when the Amendment was ratified on December 18, 1865.[93] Its brief terms formulated the principal result of the Civil War—

> Neither slavery nor involuntary servitude, except as a punishment for crime whereof the party shall have been duly convicted, shall exist within the United States, or any place subject to their jurisdiction.

[85] 12 Stat. at Large 319.
[86] 12 Stat. at Large 376.
[87] 12 Stat. at Large 432.
[88] 12 Stat. at Large 589.
[89] 12 Stat. at Large 1267.
[90] 12 Stat. at Large 1268.
[91] An account of the progress of emancipation and the reaction to it at home and abroad, appears in Carman and Syrett's *History of the American People*, I, pp. 645ff.
[92] 13 Stat. at Large 567.
[93] 13 Stat. at Large 774.

Congress shall have power to enforce this article by appropriate legislation.

Lee surrendered at Appomattox on April 9, 1865. President Lincoln died on the morning of April 15, 1865, of the gunshot wound given him at Ford's Theatre on the evening before, and Vice President Andrew Johnson of Tennessee thus became President. Johnson's presidency was marked by bitter conflicts between executive and legislature, inherent possibilities of a Constitution of separated powers. Johnson, in general, favored restoration of Southern States to something like their pre-war status as soon as reasonably possible, which inevitably meant some continuation of the subordinate position of the Negro in the reconstructed States. Opposed to Johnson was the "radical" element, in control of the Republican Congress, dedicated to a thoroughgoing social and political reform of the recently Confederate States, with electoral enfranchisement of the Negro. Mixed, in the Radicals, with a genuine idealistic impulse, was a vengeful feeling toward the late Confederacy; possibly, too, there was a measure of political ambition, which could be served by Republican control of States in which the balance of political power would be held by voting Negroes, grateful to their liberators.

In early 1865 Congress passed an Act, which President Lincoln approved on March 3, creating the Freedmen's Bureau, an agency intended to aid the recent slaves, to take that group out of the control of their late masters and put them under the guidance of Northern officials. Johnson vetoed a new Freedmen's Bureau Bill, passed in February 1866.[94] Congress on July 16, 1866 passed another Freedmen's Bureau Act over Johnson's veto.[95] A lengthening series of federal statutes intended to effectuate drastic social and political change in the South, of veto messages condemning these measures, and of prompt passage over Johnson's vetoes, began to show what would be the issue between Congress and President in Johnson's term.

The constitutional status of those who had been active in the Confederate cause raised a number of questions which, in one way or another, came before the Supreme Court of the United States. An Act of Congress of January 24, 1865[96] provided that after March 4 of that year no person should practice in any court of the United States unless he should have first taken an oath that he had not voluntarily given aid to persons engaged in armed hostility to the United States, or held

[94] Richardson, *Messages and Papers of the Presidents,* VI, p. 394.
[95] Richardson, *Messages and Papers of the Presidents,* VI, p. 422; 14 Stat. at Large 173.
[96] 13 Stat. at Large 424.

any office under any pretended authority in hostility to the United States, or given voluntary support to any hostile pretended government within the United States. This statute, if enforced, would take out of the practice of law many of the ablest public men in the South, even when they had in the first instance opposed secession, and had reluctantly gone with their States at a time when the relative obligations of national and of State allegiance were not as clear as they are to us now, a century later.

One of these men was Augustus Hill Garland of Arkansas. He was a prominent lawyer, and had become a member of the United States Supreme Court Bar in 1860. He opposed secession in 1861, but during the Civil War became a member of the Confederate Congress, first of the lower House, then of the Senate. Andrew Johnson in July 1865 pardoned him for taking part "in the late Rebellion"; and in 1866 Garland moved for leave to practice at the Bar of the Supreme Court without taking the specified oath. The Court on January 14, 1867 held the statute unconstitutional as a violation of the federal Bill of Attainder and Ex Post Facto Clauses (Article I, Section 9); and as an alternative ground the Court held that Presidential clemency had eliminated the penalty for Garland's activity with the Confederacy.[97] On the same day the Supreme Court held invalid on similar grounds (Art. I, § 10) Missouri legislation forbidding a number of public and professional activities, including those of a minister of religion, to all who would not take a prescribed oath of non-participation in the late Confederate cause. The case in question involved Father John A. Cummings, a Roman Catholic priest, who had been fined by a Missouri court for continuing his religious duties without taking the prescribed oath.[98] Mr. Justice Miller wrote a dissenting opinion in the *Garland* case in which Chief Justice Chase and Justices Swayne and Davis joined. The same four Justices dissented in *Cummings* v. *Missouri*.

The Civil Rights Act of 1866 and the Genesis of the Fourteenth Amendment

The story of the Fourteenth Amendment could well begin with Dred Scott's case in 1857,[99] which gave to many men a conscientious urge to change the judgment in that case, to change any rule there

[97] *Ex parte Garland*, 4 Wallace 333. In 1877 Garland became a United States Senator from Arkansas. In 1885 President Cleveland appointed him Attorney General of the United States.

[98] *Cummings* v. *Missouri*, 4 Wallace 277 (1867).

[99] 19 Howard 393.

might be that a Negro slave or his descendant was incapable of citizenship in the United States. In that sense the origins of the Fourteenth Amendment are the origins of the Civil War. The Amendment's more immediate history begins in the early months of 1866, with passage, over the veto of President Johnson, of "An Act to protect all Persons in the United States in their Civil Rights and furnish the Means of their Vindication."[100] The text of the statute deserves quotation—

An Act to protect all Persons in the United States in their Civil Rights, and furnish the Means of their Vindication.

Be it enacted by the Senate and House of Representatives of the United States of America in Congress assembled, That all persons born in the United States and not subject to any foreign power, excluding Indians not taxed, are hereby declared to be citizens of the United States; and such citizens, of every race and color, without regard to any previous condition of slavery or involuntary servitude, except as a punishment for crime whereof the party shall have been duly convicted, shall have the same right, in every State and Territory in the United States, to make and enforce contracts, to sue, be parties, and give evidence, to inherit, purchase, lease, sell, hold, and convey real and personal property, and to full and equal benefit of all laws and proceedings for the security of person and property, as is enjoyed by white citizens, and shall be subject to like punishment, pains, and penalties, and to none other, any law, statute, ordinance, regulation, or custom, to the contrary notwithstanding.

Sec. 2. And be it further enacted, That any person who, under color of any law, statute, ordinance, regulation, or custom, shall subject, or cause to be subjected, any inhabitant of any State or Territory to the deprivation of any right secured or protected by this act, or to different punishment, pains, or penalties on account of such person having at any time been held in a condition of slavery or involuntary servitude, except as a punishment for crime whereof the party shall have been duly convicted, or by reason of his color or race, than is prescribed for the punishment of white persons, shall be deemed guilty of a misdemeanor, and, on conviction, shall be punished by fine not exceeding one thousand dollars, or imprisonment not exceeding one year, or both, in the discretion of the court.

Sec. 3. And be it further enacted, That the district courts of the United States, within their respective districts, shall have, exclusively of the courts of the several States, cognizance of all crimes and offences committed against the provisions of this act, and also, concurrently with the circuit courts of the United States, of all causes, civil and criminal, affecting persons who are denied or cannot enforce in the courts or judicial tribunals of the State or locality where they may be any of the rights secured to them by the first section of this

[100] 14 Stat. at L. 27.

act; and if any suit or prosecution, civil or criminal, has been or shall be commenced in any State court, against any such person, for any cause whatsoever, or against any officer, civil or military, or other person, for any arrest or imprisonment, trespasses, or wrongs done or committed by virtue or under color of authority derived from this act or the act establishing a Bureau for the relief of Freedmen and Refugees, and all acts amendatory thereof, or for refusing to do any act upon the ground that it would be inconsistent with this act, such defendant shall have the right to remove such cause for trial to the proper district or circuit court in the manner prescribed by the "Act relating to habeas corpus and regulating judicial proceedings in certain cases," approved March three, eighteen hundred and sixty-three, and all acts amendatory thereof. The jurisdiction in civil and criminal matters hereby conferred on the district and circuit courts of the United States shall be exercised and enforced in conformity with the laws of the United States, so far as such laws are suitable to carry the same into effect; but in all cases where such laws are not adapted to the object, or are deficient in the provisions necessary to furnish suitable remedies and punish offences against law, the common law, as modified and changed by the constitution and statutes of the State wherein the court having jurisdiction of the cause, civil or criminal, is held, so far as the same is not inconsistent with the Constitution and laws of the United States, shall be extended to and govern said courts in the trial and disposition of such cause, and, if of a criminal nature, in the infliction of punishment on the party found guilty.

Sec. 4. And be it further enacted, That the district attorneys, marshals, and deputy marshals of the United States, the commissioners appointed by the circuit and territorial courts of the United States, with powers of arresting, imprisoning, or bailing offenders against the laws of the United States, the officers and agents of the Freedmen's Bureau, and every other officer who may be specially empowered by the President of the United States, shall be, and they are hereby, specially authorized and required, at the expense of the United States, to institute proceedings against all and every person who shall violate the provisions of this act, and cause him or them to be arrested and imprisoned, or bailed, as the case may be, for trial before such court of the United States or territorial court as by this act has cognizance of the offence. And with a view to affording reasonable protection to all persons in their constitutional rights of equality before the law, without distinction of race or color, or previous condition of slavery or involuntary servitude, except as a punishment for crime, whereof the party shall have been duly convicted, and to the prompt discharge of the duties of this act, it shall be the duty of the circuit courts of the United States and the superior courts of the Territories of the United States, from time to time, to increase the number of commissioners, so as to afford a speedy and convenient means for the arrest and examination of persons charged with a violation of this act; and such commissioners are hereby authorized and required to exercise and discharge all the powers and duties conferred on them by this act, and the same duties with regard to offences created by this act, as they are authorized by law to exercise with regard to other offences against the laws of the United States.

Sec. 5. And be it further enacted, That it shall be the duty of all marshals and deputy marshals to obey and execute all warrants and precepts issued under the provisions of this act, when to them directed; and should any marshal or deputy marshal refuse to receive such warrant or other process when tendered, or to use all proper means diligently to execute the same, he shall, on conviction thereof, be fined in the sum of one thousand dollars, to the use of the person upon whom the accused is alleged to have committed the offence. And the better to enable the said commissioners to execute their duties faithfully and efficiently, in conformity with the Constitution of the United States and the requirements of this act, they are hereby authorized and empowered, within their counties respectively, to appoint, in writing, under their hands, any one or more suitable persons, from time to time, to execute all such warrants and other process as may be issued by them in the lawful performance of their respective duties; and the persons so appointed to execute any warrant or process as aforesaid shall have authority to summon and call to their aid the bystanders or posse comitatus of the proper county, or such portion of the land or naval forces of the United States, or of the militia, as may be necessary to the performance of the duty with which they are charged, and to insure a faithful observance of the clause of the Constitution which prohibits slavery, in conformity with the provisions of this act; and said warrants shall run and be executed by said officers anywhere in the State or Territory within which they are issued.

Sec. 6. And be it further enacted, That any person who shall knowingly and wilfully obstruct, hinder, or prevent any officer, or other person charged with the execution of any warrant or process issued under the provisions of this act, or any person or persons lawfully assisting him or them, from arresting any person for whose apprehension such warrant or process may have been issued, or shall rescue or attempt to rescue such person from the custody of the officer, other person or persons, or those lawfully assisting as aforesaid, when so arrested pursuant to the authority herein given and declared, or shall aid, abet, or assist any person so arrested as aforesaid, directly or indirectly, to escape from the custody of the officer or other person legally authorized as aforesaid, or shall harbor or conceal any person for whose arrest a warrant or process shall have been issued as aforesaid, so as to prevent his discovery and arrest after notice or knowledge of the fact that a warrant has been issued for the apprehension of such person, shall, for either of said offences, be subject to a fine not exceeding one thousand dollars, and imprisonment not exceeding six months, by indictment and conviction before the district court of the United States for the district in which said offence may have been committed, or before the proper court of criminal jurisdiction, if committed within any one of the organized Territories of the United States.

Sec. 7. And be it further enacted, That the district attorneys, the marshals, their deputies, and the clerks of the said district and territorial courts shall be paid for their services the like fees as may be allowed to them for similar services in other cases; and in all cases where the proceedings are before a commissioner, he shall be entitled to a fee of ten dollars in full for his services in each case, inclusive of all services incident to such arrest and examination. The person or persons authorized to execute the process to be issued by such commissioners for the arrest of offenders against the provisions of this act shall be entitled to a fee of five dollars for each person he or they may arrest and take before any such commissioner as aforesaid, with such other fees as may be deemed reasonable by such commissioner for such other additional services as may be necessarily performed by him or them, such as attending at the examination, keeping the prisoner in custody, and providing him with food and lodging during his detention, and until the final determination of such commissioner, and in general for performing such other duties as may be required in the premises; such fees to be made up in conformity with the fees usually charged by the officers of the courts of justice within the proper district or county, as near as may be practicable, and paid out of the Treasury of the United States on the certificate of the judge of the district within which the arrest is made, and to be recoverable from the defendant as part of the judgment in case of conviction.

Sec. 8. And be it further enacted, That whenever the President of the United States shall have reason to believe that offences have been or are likely to be committed against the provisions of this act within any judicial district, it shall be lawful for him, in his discretion, to direct the judge, marshal, and district attorney of such district to attend at such place within the district, and for such time as he may designate, for the purpose of the more speedy arrest and trial of persons charged with a violation of this act; and it shall be the duty of every judge or other officer, when any such requisition shall be received by him, to attend at the place and for the time therein designated.

Sec. 9. And be it further enacted, That it shall be lawful for the President of the United States, or such person as he may empower for that purpose, to employ such part of the land or naval forces of the United States, or of the militia, as shall be necessary to prevent the violation and enforce the due execution of this act.

Sec. 10. And be it further enacted, That upon all questions of law arising in any cause under the provisions of this act a final appeal may be taken to the Supreme Court of the United States.

SCHUYLER COLFAX,
Speaker of the
House of Representatives

LA FAYETTE S. FOSTER,
President of the Senate,
pro tempore.

In the Senate of the United States, April 6, 1866.

The President of the United States having returned to the Senate, in which it originated, the bill entitled "An act to protect all persons in the United States in their civil rights, and furnish the means of their vindication," with his objections thereto, the Senate proceeded, in pursuance of the Constitution, to reconsider the same; and,

Resolved, That the said bill do pass, two-thirds of the Senate agreeing to pass the same.

Attest:

J. W. FORNEY,
Secretary of the Senate.

In the House of Representatives U.S., April 9th, 1866.

The House of Representatives having proceeded, in pursuance of the Constitution, to reconsider the bill entitled "An act to protect all persons in the United States in their civil rights, and furnish the means of their vindication," returned to the Senate by the President of the United States, with his objections, and sent by the Senate to the House of Representatives, with the message of the President returning the bill:

Resolved, That the bill do pass, two-thirds of the House of Representatives agreeing to pass the same.

Attest: EDWARD MC PHERSON, Clerk,
by CLINTON LLOYD, Chief Clerk.

Had the Congress constitutional power to enact the Civil Rights Bill of 1866? The question had been much debated while the Act was pending in Congress. The first section, declaring our native-born to be citizens regardless of race, found support in early legislation and administrative rulings. An Act of Congress of February 28, 1803 forbade the master of any vessel to import into the United States any Negro "not being a native, a citizen, or registered seaman of the United States . . ."[101] Clearly Congress thought in 1803 that some Negroes were

[101] 2 Stat. at Large 205. The Act prohibited importation only into States which barred importing Negroes.

citizens. A statute of September 4, 1841, had granted citizens homesteads on public lands to which the Indian title had been extin-
guished. In 1843 Attorney General Legare gave a written opinion, in
response to an inquiry from Secretary of the Treasury Spencer, to the
effect that a "free man of color, a native of this country," could home-
stead land under this section.[102] In 1862 Secretary of the Treasury
Salmon P. Chase asked Attorney General Bates whether a "colored
man" could be a master of an American ship, in light of an Act of
Congress requiring that such a commander be a citizen.[103] Attorney
General Bates rendered to the Secretary his opinion that a free colored
native of the United States was a citizen and, if otherwise qualified,
was competent to be master of a vessel in the coasting trade.[104]

Congressman Wilson of Iowa, speaking in favor of the Civil Rights
Act in the House on March 1, 1866 supported the first clause of the
bill by these references. The second section of the Civil Rights Act,
Mr. Wilson supported by the Thirteenth Amendment. He argued—[105]

> Mr. Speaker, if all our citizens were of one race and one color we
> would be relieved of most of the difficulties which surround us. This
> bill would be almost, if not entirely, unnecessary, and if the States,
> seeing that we have citizens of different races and colors, would but
> shut their eyes to these differences and legislate, so far at least as
> regards civil rights and immunities, as though all citizens were of one
> race and color, our troubles as a nation would be well-nigh over. But
> such is not the case, and we must do as best we can to protect our
> citizens, from the highest to the lowest, from the whitest to the
> blackest, in the enjoyment of the great fundamental rights which
> belong to all men.
>
> It will be observed that the entire structure of this bill rests on the
> discrimination relative to civil rights and immunities made by the
> States on "account of race, color, or previous condition of slavery."
> That these things should not be is no answer to the fact of their
> existence. That the result of the recent war, and the enactment of the
> measures to which the events of the war naturally led us, have inten-
> sified the hate of the controlling class in the insurgent States toward
> our colored citizens is a fact against which we can neither shut our
> ears nor close our eyes. Laws barbaric and treatment inhuman are the
> rewards meted out by our white enemies to our colored friends. We
> should put a stop to this at once and forever. And yet I would not
> do this in a way which would deprive a white man of a single right

[102] 4 Opinions of Attorney General 147.

[103] Act of December 31, 1792, 1 Stat. at L. 287.

[104] 10 Opinions of Attorney General 382. But see an opinion given by Attorney
General Wirt in 1821 as to "free persons of color" in Virginia. 1 Ops. Atty. Gen.
506, 507.

[105] See *Congressional Globe*, 39th Congress, 1st Session, (1866) p. 1118.

to which he is entitled. I would merely enforce justice for all men; and this is lawful, it is right, and it is our bounden duty.

In order to accomplish this end it is necessary to fortify the declaratory portions of this bill with such sanctions as will render it effective. The first of these is found in the second section, and in these words:

Sec. 2. And be it further enacted, That any person who, under color of any law, statute, ordinance, regulation, or custom, shall subject, or cause to be subjected, any inhabitant of any State or Territory to the deprivation of any right secured or protected by this act, or to different punishment, pains, or penalties on account of such person having at any time been held in a condition of slavery or involuntary servitude, except as a punishment for crime whereof the party shall have been duly convicted, or by reason of his color or race, than is prescribed for the punishment of white persons, shall be deemed guilty of a misdemeanor, and on conviction shall be punished by a fine not exceeding $1,000, or imprisonment not exceeding one year, or both, in the discretion of the court.

Now, sir, unless I am mistaken in all that I have said up to this point, our power to enact this section cannot be questioned. If citizens of the United States, as such, are entitled to possess and enjoy the great fundamental civil rights which it is the true office of Government to protect, and to equality in the exemptions of the law, we must of necessity be clothed with the power to insure to each and every citizen these things which belong to him as a constituent member of the great national family. But it may be urged that we can exercise only such powers as are delegated by express provision of the Constitution or arise by implication from its express provisions. And following this may come the demand for the express or implied powers to support this and the subsequent sections of this bill.

Well, sir, as to those citizens who may be in danger of being subjected to slavery or involuntary servitude, I answer that the express power supporting this measure may be found in the following provision of the Constitution:

"Sec. 1. Neither slavery nor involuntary servitude, except as punishment of crime whereof the party shall have been duly convicted, shall exist in the United States, or in any place subject to their jurisdiction."

"Sec. 2. Congress shall have power to enforce this article by appropriate legislation."

Here, certainly, is an express delegation of power. How shall it be exercised? Who shall select the means through which the office of this power shall effect the end designed by the people when they placed this provision in the Constitution? Happily, sir, we are not without light on these questions from the Supreme Court. In the celebrated case of *McCulloch* vs. *The State of Maryland*, Chief Justice Marshall, in delivering the opinion of the court, says:

"We admit, as all must admit, that the powers of the Government are limited, and that its limits are not to be transcended. But we think the sound construction of the Constitution must allow to the national Legislature that discretion with respect to the means by which the powers it confers are to be carried into execution, which will enable that body to perform the high duties assigned to it in the manner most beneficial to the people. Let the end be legitimate, let it be within the scope of the Constitution, and all means which are appropriate, which are plainly adapted to that end, which are not prohibited, but consist with the letter and spirit of the Constitution, are constitutional." —4 *Wheaton's Reports,* p. 420.

Who will say that the means provided by this second section of the bill are not appropriate for the enforcement of the power delegated to Congress by the second section of the amendment abolishing slavery, which I have quoted? The end is legitimate, because it is defined by the Constitution itself. The end is the maintenance of freedom to the citizen. What means more appropriate could be selected than that which punishes a man by commonly inflicted punishments through the ordinary channels of the law and the courts for depriving the citizen of those rights which, while he enjoys them, are his sure defense against efforts to reduce him to slavery? A man who enjoys the civil rights mentioned in this bill cannot be reduced to slavery. Anything which protects him in the possession of these rights insures him against reduction to slavery. This settles the appropriateness of this measure, and that settles its constitutionality.

Of the necessity of the measure Congress is the sole judge. This is clearly announced in the case just cited, and in this language:

"Where the law is not prohibited, and is really calculated to effect any of the objects intrusted to the Government, to undertake here to inquire into the degree of its necessity would be to pass the line which circumscribes the judicial department and to tread on legislative ground."—*Page* 423.[106]

Despite the ultimate passage of the Civil Rights Bill there neverthe-less remained in the minds of many Congressmen considerable doubt of the power of the Congress to enact it, and a feeling that its guaran-tees should appear in the Constitution. On February 13 and 26, 1866, before the passage of the Civil Rights Bill, Congressman John A. Bing-ham of Ohio had introduced on behalf of the Joint Committee on Reconstruction a proposed amendment to the Constitution—

The Congress shall have power to make all laws which shall be neces-sary and proper to secure to the citizens of each State all privileges and immunities of citizens in the several States, and to all persons in

[106] The Thirteenth Amendment is directed against action by individuals as well as by States. It was urged as a source of federal power by Justice Harlan, dis-senting in the *Civil Rights Cases,* 109 U.S. 3 (1883) and in *Plessy* v. *Ferguson,* 163 U.S. 537 (1896). Advocates of additional civil rights legislation urged that Amendment as a constitutional basis during the 1963 session of Congress.

the several States equal protection in the rights of life, liberty, and property.[107]

On April 30, 1866, the Joint Committee proposed a new amendment, containing the essence of what are now the Privileges and Immunities, the Due Process and the Equal Protection Clauses, together with a grant of legislative power to the Congress to enforce these measures.[108] The Senate added the Citizenship Clause on May 30, 1866 when the Amendment took its final shape. Its Due Process and Equal Protection Clauses protect "persons"; they are not in terms limited to former slaves, to any one race, or indeed to men doing business in unincorporated form. The suggestion has sometimes been made that this protection for all "persons," including corporate entities, was slyly introduced into the Amendment by the drafting committee, who took a sort of conspiratorial advantage of sympathy for the freedmen to provide shelter for the undeserving. The demonstration of the validity of this "conspiracy theory" is somewhat scanty.[109] A joint resolution of both Houses of Congress on June 16, 1866 submitted the present Fourteenth Amendment to the several States for ratification.[110] It was at length ratified in July 1868.

Reconstruction

Since his inauguration Johnson's policy had been one of presidential pardon for all but important Confederate leaders, leaving thus to a class of men much like those who had controlled the pre-war South the reconstitution of State governments. The late Confederate States had elected legislatures which had proceeded to pass "black codes," restricting Negroes to a status as similar as was possible to that before emancipation. Of these eleven States, Tennessee was the first to ratify the Fourteenth Amendment—in July, 1866, the month after the Congress submitted it. Tennessee, Johnson's State, was the first accepted by Congress as "reconstructed"; and she was not included in the Military Districts set up by the Reconstruction Acts of 1867. But in the

---

[107] *Congressional Globe*, 39th Cong., 1st Sess. 813, 1034. As finally adopted, the 14th Amendment forbids only State action. Purely private wrong—as many now consider is done to a Negro when a private restaurateur refuses him service—therefore is outside Congressional power derived solely from that Amendment. See the *Civil Rights Cases* 109 U.S. 3 (1883). Congressman Bingham's form might have helped solve some modern problems. See e.g. *Lombard* v. *Louisiana*, 373 U.S. 267 (1963). Cf. Title II, Civil Rights Act of 1964, 78 Stat. 241.

[108] *Congressional Globe*, 39th Cong., 1st Sess. 2286.

[109] *Congressional Globe*, 39th Cong., 1st Sess. 2897. See H. J. Graham, "The Conspiracy Theory of the Fourteenth Amendment" 47 *Yale L. J.* p. 371 (1938).

[110] 14 Stat. at L. 358.

autumn of 1866 six of the southern States, through their old-style legislatures, rejected the Fourteenth Amendment—Texas, Georgia, Florida, North Carolina, Arkansas, and South Carolina. In January 1867 three of the remaining four rejected it—Kentucky, Virginia, and Mississippi. Louisiana took no action.[111]

Not only State legislatures but privately organized groups undertook to "keep the negro in his place." Loosely organized terrorist circles with many different names—Knights of the White Camelia, Constitutional Union Guards, Pale Faces, White Brotherhood, Council of Safety, Association of '76, or Ku Klux—all commonly known as the Ku Klux Klan, expanded their aspirations from keeping down "saucy" Negroes to keeping down whites who sided with Negroes, or to intimidating anybody who was known to vote "wrong."

Two years of this had exasperated the congressional Radicals; their response was passage of the Reconstruction Acts, largely reflecting the ideas of Thaddeus Stevens of Pennsylvania, Chairman of the House Committee on Reconstruction. First was that of March 2, 1867,[112] entitled "An Act to provide for the more efficient Government of the Rebel States"; the second, enacted three weeks later, supplemented the first, adding to its title ". . . and to facilitate Restoration."[113] In part these statutes undoubtedly were exasperated countermeasures in the quarrel between President Johnson and the congressional Radicals allied with Secretary of War Stanton; but in part they recognized the deplorable situation that had become widespread in the late Confederacy, and in good faith undertook to bring about an orderly correction of conditions which had brought on the Civil War.

The preamble of the first Reconstruction Act was significant—

> Whereas no legal State governments or adequate protection for life or property now exists in the rebel States of Virginia, North Carolina, South Carolina, Georgia, Mississippi, Alabama, Louisiana, Florida, Texas and Arkansas; and whereas it is necessary that peace and good order should be enforced in said States until loyal and republican State governments can be legally established: Therefore, . . .

The Act of March 2, 1867 went on to divide the ten named States into five Military Districts: the First consisted of Virginia (less, of course, West Virginia, which had become a Union State in 1863); the Second, of the Carolinas; the Third, of Georgia, Florida, and Alabama; the Fourth, of Mississippi and Arkansas; and the Fifth, of Texas and Louisiana. The statute directed the President, with consent of the

---

[111] See Professor Fairman's table of ratifications and rejections in 2 *Stanford Law Review*, opposite page 134.

[112] 14 Stat. at Large 428.

[113] March 23, 1867; 15 Stat. at Large 2.

Senate, to appoint a general officer as commander of each District. Each such officer was to keep order, using for that purpose civil tribunals or, when in his judgment necessary, military commissions.

When the people of any one of the named States should have formed a Constitution conforming with that of the United States, framed by a convention of delegates elected by male citizens, residents for at least a year before the election, regardless of race or previous servitude, (except for those disfranchised for felony or participation in the rebellion); and when a majority, so qualified, voting on ratification, should have ratified the new Constitution; and when Congress should have approved the new Constitution; and when the State's legislature elected under the new Constitution should have adopted the Fourteenth Amendment; and when that Amendment should have become part of the Constitution of the United States—then the State should be entitled to representation in the Congress, and the provisions for military government should be inoperative in that State. But, the statute added, no one excluded from office by the Fourteenth Amendment[114]

> shall be eligible to election as a member of the convention to frame a constitution for any of said rebel States, nor shall any such person vote for members of such convention.
>
> Sec. 6. And be it further enacted, That, until the people of said rebel States shall be by law admitted to representation in the Congress of the United States, any civil governments which may exist therein shall be deemed provisional only, and in all respects subject to the paramount authority of the United States at any time to abolish, modify, control, or supersede the same; and in all elections to any office under such provisional governments all persons shall be entitled to vote, and none others, who are entitled to vote, under the provisions of the fifth section of this act; and no person shall be eligible to any office under any such provisional governments who would be disqualified from holding office under the provisions of the third article of said constitutional amendment.

The President vetoed this Act; Congress promptly passed it over his veto.[115] On March 11, 1867 Johnson assigned able generals who had distinguished themselves during the war, to the five commands.[116]

---

[114] "Sec. 3. No person shall be a senator or representative in Congress, or elector of President and Vice President, or hold any office, civil or military, under the United States, or under any State, who having previously taken an oath, as a member of Congress, or as an officer of the United States, or as a member of any State legislature, or as an executive or judicial officer of any State, to support the Constitution of the United States, shall have engaged in insurrection or rebellion against the same, or given aid or comfort to the enemies thereof. But Congress may by a vote of two thirds of each House, remove such disability."

[115] 14 Stat. at Large 429.

[116] Richardson, *Messages and Papers of the Presidents*, VI, p. 551.

Military government turned out to need a lot of legislation. The supplemental Reconstruction Act of March 23, 1867 set up machinery for carrying out the Act of March 2, including military supervision of the elections there provided. The President vetoed this measure also; Congress at once passed it over his veto.[117] By July additional clarification was necessary. Were the powers of the military to dismiss State officers and supervise elections subject to any civilian control? On July 19 the Congress by statute made the judgment of the army conclusive. Johnson disapproved the measure, writing to the House in his veto message

> Now by this declaratory act it appears that Congress did not by the original act intend to limit the military authority to any particulars or subjects therein 'prescribed,' but meant to make it universal. Thus over all these ten States this military government is now declared to have unlimited authority. It is no longer confined to the preservation of the public peace, the administration of criminal law, the registration of voters, and the superintendence of elections, but 'in all respects' is asserted to be paramount to the existing civil governments. . . .[118]

When the House had heard the message read on July 19, Thaddeus Stevens of Pennsylvania addressed the Speaker—

> Mr. Speaker, I suppose that we may as well proceed at once to take the vote upon this question. . . . It has been so often discussed that I presume we all understand the argument of the President and the argument against him. . . . I prefer myself that the previous question should be called,[119] and the bill passed and sent to the other branch of Congress, that they may decide upon it and be enabled to tell us when we can go home, so that the committee of this House, so diligently engaged in providing for the impeachment of the President, may complete their work in the shortest possible time. . . .[120]

On that day the Congress overrode the President's veto, and enacted the third Reconstruction Act.[121]

Johnson's presidency, a series of wrangles with the Republican "Radicals" from the start, grew more and more deadlocked as the four sorry years went on. Edwin M. Stanton, Secretary of War, was one of the most inveterate of the Radicals. He had held the same office

---

[117] 15 Stat. at Large 2.

[118] July 19, 1867; Richardson, *Messages and Papers of the Presidents,* VI, pp. 536–537.

[119] Motion for the "previous question"—in U.S. parliamentary procedure, a motion to cut off debate and bring the main question to an immediate vote.

[120] *Congressional Globe,* 40th Cong. 1st Sess., 1867, p. 743.

[121] 15 Stat. at Large 14.

under Lincoln during the war, had resigned when Lincoln died, and Johnson had reappointed him. Stanton, like Thaddeus Stevens and others of the same view who constituted the majority in Congress, favored a military control of reconstruction. When the Congress enacted the first Reconstruction Act, it also passed, on the same day, again over Johnson's veto, the Tenure of Office Act of March 2, 1867[122] which among other limits on the President's power of removal, forbade him to dismiss Cabinet officers without consent of the Senate. A constitutional issue appeared, the respective delimitations of presidential and congressional power, on which the Constitution is not explicit, and on which it can not well be, unless it is to be a detailed code of laws. President Johnson, who had made up his mind that the Act was unconstitutional, on August 12, 1867, dismissed Secretary of War Stanton and directed General Grant to perform the duties of Secretary.[123] Stanton refused to say he was lawfully out of office: he wrote to the President, "I have no alternative but to submit, under protest, to superior force."[124] Stanton's dismissal was the last straw for the Congress; the House of Representatives determined to carry out its plan to get rid of Johnson by the drastic process of impeachment.

Impeachment has two stages: accusation of wrongdoing, and trial of these charges. The constitutional provisions occur in the second and third sections of Article I.

> The House of Representatives . . . shall have the sole Power of Impeachment.

> The Senate shall have the sole Power to try all Impeachments. When sitting for that Purpose, they shall be on Oath or Affirmation. When the President of the United States is tried, the Chief Justice shall preside: And no Person shall be convicted without the Concurrence of two thirds of the Members present.

> Judgment in Cases of Impeachment shall not extend further than to removal from Office, and disqualification to hold and enjoy any Office of honor, Trust, or Profit under the United States: but the Party convicted shall nevertheless be liable and subject to Indictment, Trial, Judgment, and Punishment, according to law.

---

[122] 14 Stat. at Large 430.

[123] The President's powers of dismissal finally reached the Supreme Court for adjudication in 1926, in *Myers* v. *U.S.*, 272 U.S. 173, in which Chief Justice Taft, former President, upheld President Wilson's power to dismiss a Postmaster without Senatorial consent. This opinion was somewhat weakened in 1935 however by a decision reaching the opposite result in the case of a Federal Trade Commissioner, *Humphrey's Ex'r* v. *United States*, 295 U.S. 602.

[124] The correspondence is printed in Richardson, *Messages and Papers of the Presidents,* VI, pp. 583 ff.

In February 1868 the House brought against Johnson its principal charges—his dismissal of Stanton, his declarations that certain laws were unconstitutional, certain speeches he had made in the Congressional campaign of 1866, and his opposition to Congressional reconstruction. For his trial before the Senate, Johnson obtained as his Chief Counsel Benjamin R. Curtis of Boston, former Justice of the Supreme Court, who had resigned after his differences with Chief Justice Taney concerning the Dred Scott opinion. Attorney General Stanbery resigned his office to appear as one of associate counsel for Johnson. A substantial majority of the Senate favored President Johnson's conviction; but of fifty-four Senators who finally voted in the matter, thirty-six would have to vote for conviction if the impeachment were to succeed. When on a vote taken on May 26, 1868, only thirty-five Senators voted for conviction, and nineteen voted for acquittal, some remaining Articles were dropped, as the necessary two-thirds were clearly unobtainable. The impeachment had failed. Johnson continued his contentious relations with the Congress and so finished out his term.

General Grant was elected in November 1868 as Johnson's successor. Johnson returned to Greenville, Tennessee, and after he had passed some hard years that State elected him United States Senator in 1875. He died in office the following July. Time has shown him a better man than the Radicals said.

Of the only two conspicuous attempts at impeachment of federal officers, both the case of Associate Justice Chase of the Supreme Court in 1803 and of President Johnson in 1868 thus resulted in acquittals. Reluctance to use the impeaching process has become part of our Constitution in the English sense, part of our custom of governing ourselves. That reluctance has been essential to the maintenance of constitutional separation of powers in the government of the United States. Had we developed the habit of dismissing Presidents or other executive officers by impeachment when the Congress became dissatisfied with them, we should have had a national government more like that of Great Britain, in which the legislature wields the ultimate power; and in which the Executive, more closely than with us, necessarily reflects the will of legislative majorities.

Jurisdictional obstacles defeated three efforts to obtain from the Supreme Court a judgment on the constitutionality of the Reconstruction Acts. Mississippi attempted the first such case against "Andrew Johnson, President of the United States."[125] Attorney General Stanbery opposed Mississippi's motion for leave to file an original bill of com-

[125] 14 Wallace 475.

plaint in the Supreme Court of the United States, and Chief Justice Chase on April 15, 1867 delivered an opinion in which the Court held that the statutes imposed on the President, duties not ministerial but "purely executive and political," demanding the exercise of executive discretion. The Court, Chase wrote, had no jurisdiction of such an application. Mississippi had also joined as a defendant General E. O. C. Ord, commanding the Fourth Military District of Mississippi and Arkansas; without discussing the difference between the President and his military officer, the Court, by dismissing the bill, prevented Mississippi's attempt to restrain the President's military representative.

In May 1867 the Supreme Court decided together two other cases in which Georgia and Mississippi made a similar try, but this time against Secretary of War Stanton, General U. S. Grant, and, in Georgia's case, Major General Pope, commanding the military district consisting of Georgia, Florida, and Alabama and, in the second case, General E. O. C. Ord. The States, as in *Mississippi* v. *Johnson*, attempted to utilize the original jurisdiction of the Supreme Court of the United States. The Supreme Court, as in the suit against President Johnson, dismissed the bills for want of jurisdiction on the ground that the questions presented were primarily political and not judicial.[126]

The third case involved William H. McCardle, editor of a Mississippi newspaper, who had published material critical of the military government in that State. By authority of Major General Gillem, commanding the Sub-District of Mississippi, part of General Ord's District of Mississippi and Arkansas, McCardle was arrested and held for trial by a Military Commission under the authority of the Reconstruction Acts. The charges against McCardle were disturbing the public peace; inciting to insurrection, disorder, and violence; libel; and impeding reconstruction. McCardle sued out a writ of *habeas corpus* in the United States Circuit Court for the district of Mississippi. That Court issued its writ to Generals Ord and Gillem, directing them to produce McCardle in Court and show the cause of the imprisonment. General Gillem surrendered McCardle to the Court and the Court admitted him to bail. The Circuit Court adjudged that McCardle be remanded to General Gillem's custody; McCardle then appealed to the Supreme Court of the United States.

The situation was familiar: the *Milligan* case[127] was two years old. The civil courts were open. The First Amendment was binding on Radicals as well as anybody else. McCardle was hard to hush-down. Counsel for the respondent generals moved in the Supreme Court to

[126] 6 Wallace 50.
[127] See page 416, above.

dismiss the appeal on the ground that the Supreme Court had no authority to entertain it. The law was clearly against the Generals on
this and Chief Justice Chase, in an opinion for the Court, upheld its
jurisdiction on February 17, 1868.[128] Thereupon counsel for both parties argued the merits of McCardle's case. Rumors ran 'round that the
Supreme Court was about to hold the Reconstruction Acts unconstitutional. While the decision was awaited with interest and anxiety,
the Congress undertook to pass legislation to take away the Supreme
Court's jurisdiction to decide it. Article III of the Constitution gives
the Supreme Court appellate jurisdiction "with such Exceptions . . . as
the Congress shall make." The Habeas Corpus Act of March 5, 1867,[129]
had provided an appeal to the Supreme Court from a Circuit Court
judgment refusing a release on that writ. That appeal had been intended to protect federal officers engaged in reconstruction, but appeals are sometimes surprising. On March 27, 1868, the surprised
Congress passed, as a second section, tacked to an otherwise innocuous
statute concerning judgments against a revenue officer, a provision
depriving the Supreme Court of appellate jurisdiction "on appeals
which have been or may hereafter be taken" under the 1867 statute.
Be it remembered to President Johnson's lasting credit that despite his
impeachment trial then in progress, he vetoed the bill, and the Congress had to pass it over his veto.[130]

The Supreme Court, faced with this new question, deferred the
matter until the next term. On April 12, 1869, the unanimous Supreme
Court, with an opinion by Chief Justice Chase, announced that the
Supreme Court no longer had jurisdiction of the appeal; hence it must
be dismissed.[131]

The *McCardle* case was the last attempt to end the Reconstruction
Acts by judicial decree.

Ratification of the Fourteenth Amendment was a long and complicated process.[132] When Nebraska was received as the 37th State of the
Union on March 1, 1867, the constitutional requirement of ratification
by three-quarters of the States made necessary ratification by a total
of twenty-eight. In 1866 occurred six ratifications; sixteen more States

[128] *Ex parte McCardle*, 6 Wallace 318.
[129] 14 Stat. at Large 385.
[130] 15 Stat. at Large 44.
[131] *Ex parte McCardle*, 7 Wallace 505 (1869).
[132] Horace Edgar Flack wrote a pioneer study in 1908, *The Adoption of the
Fourteenth Amendment* (Baltimore: Johns Hopkins University Press, 1908). The
most scrupulous recent study is that of 1949, by Charles Fairman, "Does the
Fourteenth Amendment Incorporate the Bill of Rights?—The Original Understanding," 2 *Stanford Law Review* 5.

ratified in 1867. Six more were still necessary. Iowa ratified in April 1868. By this time the recently Confederate States had perceived that under the Reconstruction Acts they must ratify or continue subject to military government. In April 1868 came Arkansas. In June Florida ratified. In July 1868 came North Carolina, Louisiana, South Carolina, and Alabama, the twenty-ninth State. But in January 1868 Ohio, and in April 1868 New Jersey, had purported to withdraw their ratifications. On July 20, Secretary of State Seward issued a conditional proclamation: the Amendment was in effect "if" Ohio's and New Jersey's withdrawals were ineffective![133] On July 21, the Governor-elect of Georgia telegraphed the Speaker of the House that Georgia had ratified. This would make twenty-eight States even without counting Ohio and New Jersey. After some discussion of the authenticity of telegraphic notice, the House declared the Amendment ratified.[134] The Senate had declared the same, without waiting for Georgia.[135] The Secretary of State proclaimed the Amendment without any "if" on July 28, 1868.[136] Oregon purported to withdraw in October 1868, but Virginia ratified in 1869 and Mississippi and Texas in 1870. The Fourteenth Amendment had a clear three-quarters of the States before the Supreme Court first considered its effect.

By the end of 1870 Congress had declared all ex-Confederate States back in the Union in all respects; their own elected State governments were functioning after a fashion, and their Representatives and Senators had taken seats in the national legislature. Under the terms of the Reconstruction Acts, the Army had therefore ceased to govern these States directly; Army officers no longer had power to unseat State officers and take over their duties. Nevertheless some Army units remained in Southern posts and from time to time local officials called on them to aid in local affairs. Particularly difficult were controversies between two factions in this State or that, each claiming to be lawfully entitled to govern, and calling on the Army for aid. The Army became to some extent thus involved in a disputed election in South Carolina in 1876,[137] which evoked resentment in the Congress and re-

---

[133] 15 Stat. at Large, Appendix, p. x.

[134] *Congressional Globe*, July 21, 1868, p. 4296.

[135] *Ibid.*, p. 4266.

[136] 15 Stat. at L. Appendix, p. xii.

[137] For a detailed account of the use of troops in such matters see Senate Document 263, 67th Congress, 2d Session. The book is mistakenly entitled *Federal Aid in Domestic Disturbances, 1903–1922* (Washington: Government Printing Office, 1922). Actually it also includes a previous publication which covered the same subject from 1787 to 1903.

sulted in a failure of the 44th Congress, which adjourned in March, 1877, to adopt any pay for the Army for the next fiscal year.[138] President Hayes took steps shortly after he was inaugurated[139] to restrict the use of troops in the South. He wrote in his First Annual Message of December 3, 1877[140]

> The discontinuance of the use of the Army for the purpose of upholding local governments in two States of the Union was no less a constitutional duty and requirement, under the circumstances existing at the time, than it was a much-needed measure for the restoration of local self-government and the promotion of national harmony. The withdrawal of the troops from such employment was effected deliberately, and with solicitous care for the peace and good order of society and the protection of the property and persons and every right of all classes of citizens.

The congressional debates over the use of troops culminated in the "Posse Comitatus Act" of June 18, 1878, which is still in force. It forbids the use of federal troops, at the behest of local officials, to engage in ordinary police duties.[141]

Hayes' "withdrawal of the troops" did not mean marching every federal soldier out of the late Confederate States. A statute of 1877 directed the Army to keep a force on the Mexican border of Texas[142] and provided for the cost of Army transports in the Gulf of Mexico. The President's words were "withdrawal . . . from such employment." Furthermore neither Hayes' orders nor the Posse Comitatus Act eliminated the use, under certain circumstances, of federal aid for State authorities under legislation first enacted in 1795 and remaining effective, with amendments, at the present time.[143] A statute enacted in 1871 directs the President to use "the militia or the armed forces, or both" with which he "shall take such measures as he considers

---

[138] See a Proclamation of President Hayes, May 5, 1877, calling a Special Session for October 15, 1877, in Richardson, *Messages and Papers of the Presidents*, X, p. 4399 and the debate in the House of November 8, 1877, in 6 *Congressional Record* 285ff., and in the Senate on June 7, 1878, in 7 *Congressional Record* 4241ff.

[139] A bitter dispute over the legitimacy of competing presidential electors from Oregon, Louisiana, South Carolina and Florida was decided by an Electoral Commission, set up by Congress, consisting of five Senators, five Representatives, and five Justices of the Supreme Court. The Commission by an 8—7 vote seated the Hayes electors. Hayes won over Tilden by one electoral vote!

[140] See Richardson, *Messages and Papers of the Presidents*, VII, 458.

[141] 20 Stat. at L. 152, now 18 U.S. Code § 1385.

[142] 20 Stat. at L. 2. Hayes approved the Act Nov. 21, 1877.

[143] See 10 U.S. Code, Sections 331–334.

necessary to suppress, in a State, any . . . domestic violence" which hinders the execution of State or federal law and so denies any constitutional right—where the State authorities "are unable, fail, or refuse to protect that right . . ."[144] Under this and its companion sections President Eisenhower in 1957 ordered troops to intervene in disorders barring Negroes from a public high school in Little Rock, Arkansas, and in 1962 President Kennedy ordered troops to carry out a federal court order admitting a Negro to the University of Mississippi.[145]

The Fifteenth Amendment, of 1870, seems an anti-climax after the Fourteenth. But when the Fourteenth Amendment was finally ratified, in the summer of 1868, a good many people questioned whether the right of the freedom to vote could be supported by its due process and equal protection clauses. On February 27, 1869, the Congress proposed the Fifteenth Amendment which, in a few lines, guaranteed the right of citizens of the United States to vote against abridgment or denial either by the United States or by any State on account of race, color or previous condition of servitude. The Fifteenth Amendment, like the Fourteenth and the Thirteenth, gave Congress the power to enforce the article by appropriate legislation. Probably the Supreme Court could have found all the protection of the Fifteenth Amendment in the Fourteenth as years passed.

Much of the constitutional history of the United States since the Civil War has been written in judicial interpretation of the Fourteenth, and in a lesser degree the Fifteenth, Amendments. The history of nations has few sudden entrances and exits, and all divisions in time are arbitrary. But there is a certain symmetry in starting the story of the Civil War with Dred Scott's case in which the Supreme Court held that a Negro, descended of slaves, could not be a citizen; and in ending it thirteen years later with the adoption of the Fifteenth Amendment. Schoolboys at the turn of the twentieth century were told that the Thirteenth Amendment made the Negro a free man; the Fourteenth Amendment made him a citizen; and the Fifteenth Amendment made him a voter. If this were all so, the Fifteenth Amendment would be an even neater point of division in our history. Unfortunately, changes in constitutional institutions are never so sudden as this, no matter how badly needed they may be. They depend on men's habits, which are conservative by definition. What these three amendments at once did was to express an aspiration which has only gradually been worked out, through succeeding generations, by the decisions of courts, by political pressures, by the insistent demands of a once-suppressed peo-

[144] See 17 Stat. at L. 14, which in its present form is 10 U.S. Code § 333.
[145] See 10 U.S. Code Annotated § 332 et seq., with annotations.

ple, and by the conscience of earnest men.[146] To underrate this last impulse in reconstruction—the conscience of earnest men—is an easy mistake, particularly when those men were contending in the dust and clamor of political struggles. Old Thaddeus Stevens of Pennsylvania, born in Washington's first presidential term, had been the House leader in reconstruction legislation. He died three weeks after the Fourteenth Amendment took effect; he directed that his grave be in an obscure Lancaster burying-ground, and that his stone bear this inscription:

> I repose in this quiet and secluded spot, not from any natural preference for solitude, but, finding other cemeteries limited as to race by charter rules, I have chosen this, that I might illustrate in my death the principles which I advocated through a long life, Equality of Man before his Creator.

[146] *Gomillion* v. *Lightfoot,* 364 U.S. 339 (1960); see also the Civil Rights Acts of 1957, 71 Stat. 637, 42 U.S. Code, Section 1971, construed in *United States* v. *Raines,* 662 U.S. 17 (1960), and the Civil Rights Act of July 2, 1964. See also for an application of the Fourteenth Amendment to ensure equal representation in State legislatures, *Reynolds* v. *Sims,* 377 U.S. 533 (1964).

15. INDUSTRIALIZATION; AND CONTROL BY NATION AND STATE: 1870-1930

Information of the State of the Union

THE LIVES of nations and their people are not packaged in standard-size containers called centuries. Effective relation between the course of human events and the numbers ascribed to calendar years is slight if it exists at all. Passage from 1899 to 1900 presents no good reason for a break in constitutional history. To be sure, the brief war with Spain in 1898, our acquisition of Puerto Rico and the Philippine Islands, and the incorporation of the Hawaiian Islands as part of the United States in 1898 do mark a turning point in one respect. The United States then for the first time found itself administering large areas far removed from the American continent, a process for which the Constitution did not provide. In the *Insular Cases* the Supreme Court had to explore the incidents of new relationship with these territories, and with some areas temporarily occupied. *Neely* v. *Henkel* in 1901[1] concerned Cuba; *Downes* v. *Bidwell*,[2] in the same year, concerned Puerto Rico; the subject of *Hawaii* v. *Mankichi*,[3] decided in 1903, is obvious; *Dorr* v. *United States*,[4] decided in 1904, had to do with the Philippine Islands. But constitutional problems concerning the acquisition of overseas islands arose as early as the

[1] 180 U.S. 109.
[2] 182 U.S. 244.
[3] 190 U.S. 197.
[4] 195 U.S. 138.

1850's and were still arising in 1947.[5] The nation's new concerns come gradually rather than suddenly; from 1898 down to the present time we have steadily increased our involvement with matters overseas. The war in Europe in which the United States took part from 1917 to 1918, and President Wilson's participation in the ensuing Peace Conference, were indications of the change in our national preoccupations which became inevitable with steel ships, efficiently propelled, and with instantaneous communication all over the world.

Samuel F. B. Morse's successful telegraph line between Washington and Baltimore in 1844; Cyrus West Field's New York, Newfoundland and London Telegraph Company, organized in 1854, and his first successful undersea message from Queen Victoria to President Buchanan in 1858; Field's permanent success in establishing a cable from Ireland to Newfoundland in 1866; Guglielmo Marconi's establishment of trans-Atlantic wireless communication in 1902 and its steady development from then on; these were a few instances of the swift, multiple, expanding technology which fundamentally gives character to the period between 1870 and 1930. The results of these many inventions, which in the course of about sixty years were to make interdependent a large proportion of the nations of the earth, were at first most conspicuous at home. They produced a shift in social status, in which the few, manufacturing desirable marvels for the many, came to be controlled by the many, who, paying the price, could call the tune. In the United States the Civil War had immensely stimulated manufacture. From the 1870's on there began to appear new legal devices for merchandising, which were destined to stimulate mass consumption, and so mass production, and so bring about the great industrial aggregates and the large-scale politico-economic controls of sixty years later. A decade after the close of the Civil War there begin to occur, in American law reports, opinions dealing with time-payment purchases of cottage organs and of sewing machines. While this system of financing consumer purchasing had been used in buying livestock as early as the 1820's, it only began in volume about 1870. Here was a legal apparatus which would facilitate the distribution of American inventions,[6] and thus the attainment of our affluent society.

---

[5] See *Jones v. United States,* 137 U.S. 202 (1890) which concerned the Guano Islands Act of August 18, 1856, and the occupation of Navassa, near Jamaica, in 1857; and see *United States v. Fullard-Leo,* 331 U.S. 256 (1947), which passed on the status of Palmyra Island in the Pacific.

[6] The Federal Reserve Bulletin of July 1963 shows outstanding sixty-four billions of consumer credit, including thirty-three billions of installment-credit for automobiles and other consumer goods, among our, say, 190 million people—a significant index of the American Way of Life. Here, by and large, the lender is servant to the borrower.

The pages of the reports of the United States Supreme Court after the sixties contain a surprising number of pictures of machines, concerning the patents for which inventors were litigating. Railroads transported the munitions to support the Civil War; by 1880 railroads had become powerful far-flung enterprises, controlling the outlets from farms and cattle ranches, eyed suspiciously by shippers dependent upon them for economic existence. Coal and steel being necessary for machines, "coal barons" arose. Great industrial combines came to control large parts of the nation's petroleum and other fuels, and metals, sugar, tobacco. These "trusts"[7] brought inevitable reaction, as farmers, ranchers and consumers demanded State, and in due course national, regulation.

The Patrons of Husbandry was a secret fraternal society founded in 1867. Each local chapter was called a "Grange"; delegate bodies constituted State Granges and the National Grange. During the 1870's an agricultural depression beset the United States and farmers joined "the Grange" in large numbers. By the autumn of 1874 there were more than twenty thousand Granges, most of them in the Middle West and in the South. The Granges undertook to be non-political; but "Grange Halls" did provide places for farmers to come together and talk, and so paved the way for the rise of "anti-monopoly" or farmers' parties in western States. The farmers' upsurge met resistance by men who did not want their affairs regulated by State legislatures or the Congress. The term "Granger Movement" started in derision. But Grangers had votes and legislators wanted these votes.

Labor Unions began to rise at the same time. The union movement, gaining strength in the 1880's and 1890's, survived such episodes as the ending of the Pullman strike[8] by federal troops under orders of President Cleveland in 1894 and became a political force demanding national regulation of industry. Consumers, recognizing their inability to deal at arms' length with mass manufacture, demanded and got

[7] A curious term for any large industrial aggregate. It probably derives from the form used in 1882 for the Standard Oil Trust, arranged by transfer of the shares of component corporations to a group of trustees who then concerted the activities of all.

[8] Which gave rise to a famous decision of the Supreme Court—*In re Debs*, 158 U.S. 564 (1895). Mr. Justice Brewer wrote for the Court—"The case . . . is this: The United States, finding that interstate transportation of persons and property, as well as the carriage of the mails, is forcibly obstructed, and that a combination and conspiracy exists to subject the control of such transportation to the will of the conspirators, applied to one of their courts, sitting as a court of equity, for an injunction to restrain such obstruction and prevent carrying into effect such conspiracy." Debs, a well-known Socialist writer and labor enthusiast, violated an injunction granted by a lower federal court. Imprisoned for contempt, he sought *habeas corpus* on the ground that Congress had nowhere specifically authorized such an injunction. The Supreme Court found no ground for *habeas corpus*.

State and national regulation of foods and drugs. The first such national statute was the Food and Drug Act of 1906[9]

This self-assertion by many men, their rise in social and political stature, is as important in the constitutional panorama of the late nineteenth and early twentieth century as was the rise in value of English farm-labor in the mid-fourteenth century, with consequent end of villeinage, and with reactions in the Statutes of Labourers.[10] "People of small Substance, and of no Value—every one of them pretended a voice equivalent as to such Elections to be made, with the most Worthy Knights and Esquires," just as they had in 1430.[11] Justice Holmes in 1913 told the Harvard Law School Association of New York about a time, twenty years before then, when "a vague terror went over the earth and the word 'socialism' began to be heard." People of substance and value wondered what the familiar world was coming to. In 1902 there was a question of governmental intervention to bring about achievement of the miners' wishes in a pending coal strike. One of the coal barons of the day felt that this would be an impious move. He wrote

> The rights and interests of the laboring man will be protected and cared for—not by the labor agitator, but by the Christian men to whom God in his infinite wisdom has given control of the property interests of the country.[12]

The Courts and the untested range of the due process clauses, national and State, seemed to offer possible remedy to men who saw their businesses regulated, who sensed that their individual freedoms were being taken away. The Courts might reestablish a diffusion of governing power, taking back some from the nation and the several States, and returning the retaken power to the proprietors of businesses to whom God, in his infinite wisdom, had given a control now shaken by infidels. Much of the constitutional history of the sixty years between 1870 and 1930 thus concerns the pulling and hauling between many and few. The contest was waged in State legislatures and in the Congress; to a smaller degree it was waged in the courts of the nation. Judicial invalidation of legislation is so dramatic, it is so clearly documented by the judges' opinions that it presents a tableau of the contest

[9] Now the Food, Drug and Cosmetic Act of 1938, as amended, 21 U.S. Code 301 and following.

[10] See page 44 and following above.

[11] See a discussion of the Forty-Shilling Freehold Act of 1430, page 38 and following, above. The Knights are dust; their swords are rust; and every one of the people has a voice equivalent as to our present elections. See *Reynolds* v. *Sims*, 377 U.S. 533, (1964); *Lucas* v. *Colorado*, 377 U.S. 713, (1964).

[12] Mr. George F. Baer, quoted by Frederick Lewis Allen in *The Big Change* (New York: Harper and Brothers, 1952) p. 83.

more striking than the unashamed compromises of legislation. Constitutional litigation has moral overtones. Hindsight is proverbially better than foresight: nearly a century after the Fourteenth Amendment one can see that it never could have controlled the division of American assets. For one thing, the heavier battalions were so very much heavier. As the aggregate vote increases the position of the *status quo* gets more parlous. In 1860 the population of the United States stood at about thirty-one and one-half millions. By 1900 it was just under seventy-six millions. During that period about fourteen million immigrants had come to the United States. By 1930 the population of the United States was nearly 123 million people. Of this increase of about forty-seven million between 1900 and 1930, immigration contributed a little more than eighteen million. Immigrants or others, the new millions were town-dwellers. Farm boys moved to town and had their children there. Politically self-conscious, influenced by mass circulation of newspapers and, more recently, by the radio, this vast population inevitably got its will from legislatures, from attentive State and national executives. Ultimately some of these urges were reflected in constitutional amendment and in constitutional adjudication. And the few did not really suffer in the economic upgrading of the many: fantastically efficient machines for farms and factories filled our American world with an extraordinary number of things.

The six decades summarized in this chapter saw not only a steady increase in the national control of the economy through the political process, but also saw the growing mass of both State and national legislation directed more and more toward political and economic egalitarianism. During most of that sixty years the "levelling" came to white men, however. Only slowly, through the last decades of the nineteenth century, increasing bit by bit in the twentieth, the status of the Negro was improved.

More steeply graduated income taxation of individuals and of corporations; heavy taxation of inheritances, both by the nation and by the States, moved in the direction of equalization of economic status, delayed only for a time by the Supreme Court decision handed down in 1895 that a federal income tax was unconstitutional.[13]

This chapter deals with several aspects of this six-decade change.

Federal Regulation and Its Constitutional Limitations: 1870–1930

Development of constitutional doctrine in the United States in any period of time cannot well be studied by concentrating attention on

[13] *Pollock v. Farmers' Loan and Trust Co.*, 157 U.S. 429; 158 U.S. 601.

some one clause or another, and forgetting the rest of the Constitution. But surely a significant factor in the later decades of the nineteenth century was the unexpressed negative on State legislation, emanating from the Commerce Clause, which played a great part in judicial contests between shippers and railroads. The Supreme Court's judgments called forth congressional legislation to regulate this application of the Commerce Clause.

In 1886 there came before the Supreme Court one of the grievances which affected midwestern shippers of agricultural produce—favoritism on the part of the railroads for one shipper over another. This grievance had elicited a statute of Illinois which provided a penalty of five thousand dollars and three times the damage sustained by an aggrieved party, with costs and attorney's fees, where any railroad should charge or receive the same or greater compensation for a short haul of passengers or freight than for a long haul. The Wabash, St. Louis and Pacific Railway charged a shipper 15 cents per hundred pounds for a carload of goods shipped from Peoria, Illinois to New York City; on the same day, from Gilman, Illinois, eighty-six miles closer to New York City than Peoria, the railroad charged another shipper twenty-five cents per hundred pounds. In 1882, the Supreme Court of Illinois held that the Illinois statute applied. Part of the journey had occurred with the State of Illinois.[14]

The feeling of the times emerges from a concurring opinion of Mr. Justice Pinkney H. Walker of the Illinois Supreme Court—

> If the doctrines contended for were allowed, it would be to release and entirely exempt all corporate bodies in the State from the governing or sovereign power of the State to prevent wrong and oppression of the people by such bodies. It would be to hold that the State, by creating and endowing railroads with the simple and necessary power to fix charges for carrying persons and property, had, through the legislature, without intending it, sold or surrendered the governing power of the State, and that such bodies are empowered to extort from the masses annually, for all time to come, sums greater than the revenues of the Federal government, beyond fair compensation for such carriage. If such bodies can not be controlled, to the same extent and under the same necessities for the general welfare, by the State, as natural persons, then the powers of government have been subverted and the States virtually destroyed, and they have become useless and expensive appendages to our governmental system. . . .

Nevertheless the Supreme Court of the United States reversed this judgment with an opinion by Mr. Justice Miller, which held the Illi-

[14] *Wabash, etc. Ry. Co.* v. *The People,* 104 Ill. 476 (1882); 105 Ill. 236 (1883).

nois regulation void as applied to an interstate haul.[15] Miller referred to the Cooley Doctrine;[16] he wrote

> That this species of regulation is one which must be, if established at all, of a general and national character, and cannot be safely and wisely remitted to local rules and local regulations, we think is clear from what has already been said. And if it be a regulation of commerce, as we think we have demonstrated it is, and as the Illinois Court concedes it to be, it must be of that national character, and the regulation can only appropriately exist by general rules and principles, which demand that it should be done by the Congress of the United States under the commerce clause of the Constitution.

On February 4, 1887, in prompt response to the challenge of the Wabash case, the Congress passed the Interstate Commerce Act, sometimes known as the Cullom Act.[17] Today, much expanded, it regulates a large share of the American carriage of goods by railroad, water and highway motor-carriers.[18] As originally passed, the Interstate Commerce Act directed that all railroad rates in interstate commerce, whether for passengers or property, be "reasonable and just" and declared any other rate unlawful. The statute created a regulatory body, the Interstate Commerce Commission, with wide authority to investigate railroad rates and practices, to hear the complaints of any person or municipality concerning violations of the Act, to order the carrier in question to cease and desist from such violation, or make reparation, or both. The statute also authorized the United States Circuit Courts to issue injunctions directing the railway in question to obey the Commission's orders. Such orders were to run not only against the corporate respondent but against its individual officers concerned.

The Interstate Commerce Commission was the forerunner of many other similar independent regulatory commissions;[19] it set the pattern for much succeeding federal regulation. These bodies combine judicial functions, interstitial legislation, and executive functions—a departure from the theory of separation of powers, a deviation which in earlier times used to awaken much protest from the regulated entities. The

[15] *Wabash, St. Louis and Pacific Railway Co.* v. *Illinois*, 118 U.S. 557 (1886). Three Justices dissented.

[16] See page 350 supra.

[17] 24 Stat. at L. 379; now, much amended, title 49 U.S. Code, Section I and following.

[18] Carriers by air are regulated by a separate administrative body, the Civil Aeronautics Board (49 U.S. Code § 401 and ff).

[19] See Robert E. Cushman "The Independent Regulatory Commissions" 24 *Cornell Law Quarterly* 13, 163 (1938–1939).

Federal Reserve Act of 1913 gave the Federal Reserve Board a wide supervision over the nation's banking system.[20] The Federal Trade Commission Act of 1914[21] declared "unfair methods of competition" in interstate commerce to be unlawful, and in 1938 this statute was amended to extend that prohibition to cover "unfair or deceptive acts or practices" regardless of their competitive quality.[22] This statute entrusted a wide discretionary power to the Federal Trade Commission by that language. Such administrative bodies now govern a great part of the national economy—the Federal Communications Commission;[23] the Federal Power Commission;[24] the National Labor Relations Board, set up in 1935.[25] And much federal regulation is handled by Departments—Agriculture, for example.

The federal structure of the United States has left much need for adjustment of economic regulation between State and national powers. State regulatory commissions had preceded the federal,[26] and the regulated industries sometimes sought to avoid State regulation by contending that national legislation had so preempted the area as to exclude that of the States. In 1913 the Supreme Court, in the *Minnesota Rate Cases*[27] found that the Interstate Commerce Act had left the States free to regulate exclusively intrâ-state rates; but in 1914 the Court held that the Interstate Commerce Commission could prohibit low intrâ-state rates where these adversely competed with higher interstate rates which the federal Commission had found reasonable.

The intrâ-state rates thus favored trade between points in the same State, hurt trade across the State line, and constituted a sort of State protective tariff.[28]

During the sixty years here discussed, federal economic legislation ran two main constitutional risks—the risk of being held *ultra-vires*, beyond the powers of the national government delegated in the Constitution, and the risk of the Due Process Clause in the Fifth Amendment.[29] Both are now interesting only to students of constitutional

[20] 38 Stat. at L. 251, 12 U.S. Code § 221 ff.

[21] 38 Stat. at L. 717, now 15 U.S. Code, § 41 ff.

[22] 52 Stat. at L. 111.

[23] 47 U.S. Code § 151 ff.

[24] 16 U.S. Code § 792 ff.

[25] 49 Stat. at L. 449, 29 U.S. Code § 151 ff.

[26] New York set up a Railroad Commission in 1855. See the introduction to Vol. 47, McKinney's Consolidated Laws of New York (the Public Service Law), by Kent H. Brown, Counsel to the N. Y. Public Service Commission (1955).

[27] *Simpson* v. *Shepard*, 230 U.S. 352 Not *Minnesota Rate Case* of 1890, p. 463, hereafter.

[28] *Shreveport Rate Cases*, 234 U.S. 342 (1914).

[29] At page 331, earlier in this book, appears an analysis of federal statutes held unconstitutional, and references to the cases which so held them.

history: the Supreme Court adjudications of this sort came to a halt more than a quarter-century ago. And a man who turns over the pages of the many volumes of the United States Code will be much more impressed by the mass of effectuated legislation, than by the occasional Acts that were struck down.

The Fourteenth Amendment and Social Statics: 1870–1930

Striking phrases have often played a part in constitutional law, and of these Justice Holmes made his full share. In *Lochner* v. *New York* a majority of five of the Supreme Court held in 1905 that the Fourteenth Amendment invalidated a New York law prescribing a sixty-hour work week in bakeries. Justices Harlan, White, Day and Holmes all dissented. Holmes wrote—

> The 14th Amendment does not enact Mr. Herbert Spencer's Social Statics.[30]

Spencer's "curious book," as Holmes once called it, was naïve in its negative attitude toward the whole business of what is now called "welfare legislation." Nevertheless sometimes men impatient with economic inequalities, past and present, have assumed that Holmes' ironic reduction to the absurd was a considered description of something the Supreme Court had imposed on the American people by misuse of the Fourteenth Amendment. That is hardly accurate either as a reading of constitutional history or of Holmes' opinion. Some recapitulation of the Supreme Court's judgments predicated on that amendment and affecting economic regulation in the States, is here appropriate.

One should remember that this is an account of the past. The Fourteenth Amendment Due Process Clause, as a limit on State economic regulation, dwindled in 1934 with the case of *Nebbia* v. *New York*[31] when the Supreme Court, by a majority of five to four, upheld the power of the New York legislature to fix minimum retail prices to be charged by vendors to retail purchasers of milk in bottles. The story of how this came about has a retrospective interest.

[30] 198 U.S. 45, 74. Spencer wrote his *Social Statics* in 1851, eight years before the publication of Darwin's *Origin of Species*. But Spencer's ideas are associated with "social Darwinism." Spencer was a shy man, not much exposed to the roughness of the world, which may account for the bookish brutality of *Social Statics*. He there expounds the theory that political intervention in favor of the weak, the poor, the unfortunate, is dysgenic; nature's way is to let these ill-adapted mercifully die, making way for the able. His views have not proved popular.
[31] 291 U.S. 502.

In 1873, five years after the Fourteenth Amendment took effect, the Supreme Court declined to set aside a Louisiana statute granting to a favored corporation a monopoly of the slaughterhouse business in New Orleans.[32] Disgruntled butchers had attacked the statute under the Thirteenth and Fourteenth Amendments. Mr. Justice Miller, who wrote the Court's opinion, had no trouble denying any contention that the slaughterhouse monopoly imposed a "servitude" in Thirteenth Amendment terms. As to the "Privileges and Immunities Clause"[33] of the Fourteenth, the Justice easily found that engaging in the slaughterhouse business was not a privilege of national citizenship; but so effectively did he narrow the definition of the latter that little was left of it. He brushed off any argument based on due process and equal protection. Of the latter he wrote—

> We doubt very much whether any action of a state not directed by way of discrimination against the negroes as a class, or on account of their race, will ever be held to come within the purview of this provision.

And the butchers, he wrote, were not deprived of any "property" within the meaning of the Due Process Clause, which thus had no effect. The result in the *Slaughterhouse Cases* was undoubtedly correct: to make New Orleans' meat supplies easily inspectable was a reasonable enough measure. But Miller's opinion dealt a blow to the "privileges and immunities" clause from which it has never recovered.

Four years later in 1877 another attempt to use the Fourteenth Amendment to eliminate State regulatory measures came to nothing in *Munn* v. *Illinois*[34] and seven other "Granger Cases."[35] *Munn* upheld an Illinois statute fixing rates for grain elevators. On the same day the Court upheld legislative rate-fixing for railroads by the legislatures of Wisconsin, Iowa and Minnesota.[36]

Chief Justice Waite's opinion in *Munn* v. *Illinois* is not entirely clear, but it stresses the fact that a grain elevator is "clothed with a public interest"; and reasons that the owner therefore subjects himself to whatever regulation a legislature may choose to impose on him. Clearly the argument can be extrapolated to an extreme conclusion,

[32] *Slaughterhouse Cases,* 16 Wallace 36 (1873).

[33] "No State shall make or enforce any law which shall abridge the privileges or immunities of citizens of the United States. . ."

[34] 94 U.S. 113 (1877).

[35] This name, commonly given to these cases, indicates the attribution of the legislation, at the time, to the Granger movement. This was probably not correct. See Fairman, "The So-called Granger Cases" 5 *Stanford Law Review* 587 (1953).

[36] The railroad cases, seven in number, are reported in comparatively brief opinions or memoranda immediately after *Munn* in 94 U.S.

which, in effect, would justify confiscation of the owner's property by eliminating its capability for any earning; the judgment might be read to leave the legislators under no restraint but their own discretion. From this Justices Field and Strong dissented.

Probably few thoughtful lawyers were surprised when the Supreme Court in 1890 held that the reasonableness of a railroad rate was judicially examinable, despite a State statute purporting to make final the rate fixed by a Commission.[37] This conclusion has sometimes been ascribed to a sort of conspiracy among the draftsmen of the Fourteenth Amendment,[38] supplemented by a reactionary regard, among the Justices, for the vested rights of corporations.[39] But property, along with life and liberty, had been included in the Fifth Amendment Due Process Clause since 1791; the words of the Fourteenth Amendment are the same. And today a multitude of people of small substance conduct their filling stations and variety stores under the corporate limitation of liability—"persons" under the Fourteenth Amendment. Owners of a public utility get little commercial benefit from their property if it is unable to earn a fair return. If a State can abolish this possibility, it abolishes the value of the property. The Supreme Court was not in a happy position when asked to hold such a measure consonant with the Fourteenth Amendment; and, not surprisingly, it found that regulation would thus become confiscation.

But the *Minnesota Rate Case* of 1890 left the Court with a number of problems, all centering around the fact that, in plain terms, the decision sets the Supreme Court to re-deciding questions concerning the reasonableness of governmental measures, instead of leaving the legislatures to decide these questions with finality.[40] In the *Minnesota* question of rate-fixing, for example, how will a Court fix a standard for determining the fair value of a public-utility system? No satisfactory answer has emerged in the seventy-four years since the *Minnesota Rate Case*.[41]

---

[37] The *Minnesota Rate Case* (*Chi. M. & St. P. Ry. Co.* v. *Minn.*), 134 U.S. 418 (1890). Justice Bradley wrote in dissent, "I cannot agree to the decision . . . It practically overrules *Munn* v. *Illinois*. . ."

[38] See, for a fair-minded examination into the substance of this idea, Graham, "The 'Conspiracy Theory' of the Fourteenth Amendment," 47 *Yale Law Journal* 371 (1938).

[39] For comment on the theory that the Fourteenth Amendment should not protect property held by a corporation, see Justice Jackson's opinion in *Wheeling Steel Corp.* v. *Glander*, 337 U.S. 562, at 574 (1949).

[40] See Judge Charles Merrill Hough's witty and wise 1918 Irvine Lecture at Cornell, "Due Process of Law Today" 32 *Harvard Law Review* 218 (1919) in which he examined *Munn* and *Minnesota Rate Case* and their sequelae.

[41] Compare *Smyth* v. *Ames*, 169 U.S. 466 (1898), prescribing a fair return on "fair present value"; *McCardle* v. *Indianapolis Water Co.*, 272 U.S. 400 (1926),

Has the Due Process Clause any proper part to play in preventing a State from trying to do things within its borders which "reasonably" concern only its neighbor States? To penalize, for example, a Louisianan who mails a letter from New Orleans to New York, there effecting marine insurance in a company not authorized to do business in Louisiana?[42] To seize a truck coming into Maryland from a neighbor State, and hold the truck to ransom because its owner had not paid to Maryland "use taxes" on goods shipped from Delaware into Maryland?[43] What if Kentucky taxes a corporation she has chartered, calculating the amount of the tax on the total value of a fleet of refrigerator cars the corporation owned, although at any one time most of the fleet was outside the State?[44] In each of these instances the Supreme Court found that the State's action had violated the Due Process Clause; but in the Kentucky case Holmes wrote a dissent worth quoting in full—

> It seems to me that the result reached by the court probably is a desirable one, but I hardly understand how it can be deduced from the 14th Amendment; and as the Chief Justice feels the same difficulty, I think it proper to say that my doubt has not been removed.

If "unreasonable" State-imposed rates are equivalent to State confiscation and so a deprivation of property without due process, why is not any State statute equally unconstitutional when it interferes unreasonably with a man's use of his property? The question is not easy to answer. Perception of reasonableness is often unilateral; the one who protests at some readjustment in property relations, does not readily see that one man's poison is another man's meat. Whoever contends for legislative finality in such redistributive choices may not be sensitive to the lack of disinterest in legislators whose tenure of office can depend on the redistribution. Some such idea, half-formulated, emerges from the 1905 opinion of Justice Peckham, writing for the majority of five in *Lochner* v. *New York* that a sixty-hour week law for bakers was unconstitutional—

> There must be more than the mere fact of the possible existence of some small amount of unhealthiness to warrant legislative interference with liberty. It is unfortunately true that labor, even in any depart-

---

defining fair value as replacement cost less depreciation; and *Federal Power Commission* v. *Hope Natural Gas Co.*, 320 U.S. 591 (1944) deploring *Smyth* v. *Ames* but not presenting a better rule. See Rose, "The Hope Case and Public Utility Valuation in the States," 54 Colum. L. Rev. 188 (1954).

[42] *Allgeyer* v. *Louisiana*, 165 U.S. 578 (1897).

[43] *Miller Bros.* v. *Maryland*, 347 U.S. 340 (1954).

[44] *Union Refrigerator Transit Co.* v. *Kentucky*, 199 U.S. 194 (1905).

ment, may possibly carry with it the seeds of unhealthiness. But are we all, on that account, at the mercy of legislative majorities?[45]

This was the case that evoked Holmes' remark about Mr. Herbert Spencer's "Social Statics"; and as Holmes pointed out in that dissent, the Supreme Court had upheld much State regulation despite challenges under the vague inhibitions of the Due Process Clause. The Court in 1898 had upheld a Utah eight-hour-day law for miners and smelter-workers and men engaged in ore reduction.[46] In 1903 the Court had upheld a provision in the California State Constitution forbidding sales of stock on margin or for future delivery.[47] In 1908 the Court upheld, despite due process challenge, an Oregon ten-hour day law limited to women.[48] In its difficult divinations of the reasonable, the Court wavered during the first three decades of the present century between upholding much and invalidating some. A Kansas anti-yellow-dog contract law was held unconstitutional in 1915[49] but in 1917 the Court upheld another Oregon ten-hour day law for men and women alike,[50] (with time-and-a-half for a limited overtime). The objecting employer urged *Lochner* in vain; the Court silently laid it to rest.

Another Fourteenth Amendment problem began to trouble the Supreme Court during this sixty years—the use of the "reasonable" definition of due process and equal protection in fields other than property and contract, in matters of free political activity and racial discrimination. Reasonableness is a concept latent in the Equal Protection Clause, less obvious, even, than in due process, but still persistently present. For men are not equal and no one contends that government should treat all alike. *Muller* v. *Oregon*[51] was a liberal triumph in 1908; the Oregon law was upheld not because it gave all Oregonians equal protection but precisely because Louis D. Brandeis of Boston, retained as counsel for Oregon, demonstrated that women were different, and reasonably required compulsory working hours that differed from those of men. Children and adults, veterans and non-veterans, sick and well, criminals and upright—State laws treat them all differently, the Equal Protection Clause raising only the question

[45] 198 U.S. 45 (1905).
[46] *Holden* v. *Hardy,* 169 U.S. 366.
[47] *Otis* v. *Parker,* 187 U.S. 606.
[48] *Muller* v. *Oregon,* 208 U.S. 412.
[49] *Coppage* v. *Kansas,* 236 U.S. 1. The "yellow-dog contract" was one in which an employer, as a condition of employment, proscribed union membership: under it the employee agreed to forfeit his employment if he joined a union.
[50] *Bunting* v. *Oregon,* 243 U.S. 426 (1917).
[51] 208 U.S. 412.

of the reasonableness of the difference. In 1886 the Court found race and nationality no justification for differentiation in State awards of laundry licenses, permitted itself to see through the specious equality in the words of a San Francisco ordinance, and to perceive beneath it the actual practices of licensing officials, who found white men worthy and Chinese not.[52]

A more difficult equal-protection question received an unfortunate answer in 1896. States differed in their legal attitudes toward the matter of race. In 1895 New York provided—[53]

> That all persons within the jurisdiction of this State shall be entitled to the full and equal accommodations, advantages, facilities and privileges of inns, restaurants, hotels, eating-houses, bath-houses, barbershops, theatres, music-halls, public conveyances on land and water, and all other places of public accommodation or amusement, subject only to the conditions and limitations established by law and applicable alike to all citizens.

However a Louisiana statute of 1890[54] required railways to provide

> equal but separate accommodations for the white and colored races, by providing two or more passenger coaches for each passenger train, or by dividing the passenger coaches by a partition so as to secure separate accommodations: . . . No person or persons shall be permitted to occupy seats in coaches other than the ones assigned to them, on account of the race they belong to . . .

In 1896 the Supreme Court found that this Louisiana statute violated neither the Thirteenth nor the Fourteenth Amendment.[55] The rule of "equal but separate" was applied as late as 1927 in a public school case arising in Mississippi.[56] The rule had a difficult time thereafter, as the Courts began to scrutinize public accommodations furnished, and find them different in fact,[57] until in 1954 the Supreme Court, overruling *Plessy*, found "equal but separate" a denial of equal protection when prescribed by State law,[58] and a denial of due process when prescribed by Act of Congress.[59] The Court in 1917 struck down

[52] *Yick Wo* v. *Hopkins*, 118 U.S. 356 (1886).
[53] By chapter 1042 of the Laws of 1895. In a much-expanded form this is now § 40 of the New York Civil Rights Law.
[54] Acts 1890, No. 111, p. 152.
[55] *Plessy* v. *Ferguson*, 163 U.S. 537 (1896).
[56] *Gong Lum* v. *Rice*, 275 U.S. 78 (1927).
[57] E.g., *Sweatt* v. *Painter*, 339 U.S. 629 (1950).
[58] *Brown* v. *Board of Education*, 347 U.S. 438.
[59] *Bolling* v. *Sharpe*, 347 U.S. 497. The Constitution does not expressly require the national government to grant "equal protection"; the requirement is latent in the Fifth Amendment Due Process Clause. In *Bolling* the unanimous Court

an ordinance of Louisville, Kentucky, restricting residence of Negroes and white men respectively to predominantly Negro- and white-occupied blocks.[60] In 1927 it held unconstitutional a Texas statute providing

> in no event shall a negro be eligible to participate in a Democratic party primary election held in the State of Texas.[61]

Nebraska in 1919 enacted a statute forbidding instruction in any language but English to any child who had not passed the eighth grade. When an instructor in a Lutheran parochial school was convicted of violating this Act, the Supreme Court found that the statute was invalid under the Fourteenth Amendment Due Process Clause;[62] as it lacked any "reasonable relation to any end within the competency of the State." In 1925 the Court held invalid at the suit of a Catholic Order and of a private military academy an Oregon law which obliged all children to attend public schools.[63] The investments in the schools would, the Court wrote, be impaired by this State action.[64]

One required to pass judgment on the rôle of the Fourteenth Amendment in American government, during the Amendment's first six decades, would find difficulty in putting its performance in a neat phrase. The full effect of the Amendment was, at first, hard for judges to implement. They found difficulty in accepting the profound difference it had brought about in the relative powers of the national government and the States. Its net effect on economic regulation was not great: State legislatures went on passing laws concerning the economy, and few of these came to grief. The equal-but-separate doctrine of the nineties delayed for two generations many of the benefits the Amendment had intended for the Negroes. But the promise was there; and a judicial function of passing on the reasonableness of legislation could, in time, protect a range of human values far wider than had been evident in 1868.

---

held that, "Segregation in public education is not reasonably related to any proper governmental objective, and thus it imposes on Negro children of the District of Columbia a burden that constitutes an arbitrary deprivation of their liberty in violation of the Due Process Clause."

[60] *Buchanan* v. *Warley*, 245 U.S. 60.

[61] *Nixon* v. *Herndon*, 273 U.S. 536.

[62] *Meyer* v. *Nebraska*, 262 U.S. 390 (1923).

[63] *Pierce* v. *Society of Sisters; Pierce* v. *Hill Military Academy*, 266 U.S. 510.

[64] It has been pointed out that not only can the devil quote scripture, but that sauce for the goose will sometimes serve for the gander.

16. THE SUPREME COURT AND THE GENERAL WILL[1]

Foreword to the Constitutional Crisis of the 1930's

> . . . la volonté générale est toujours droite et tend toujours à l'utilité publique; mais il ne s'ensuit pas que les délibérations du peuple aient toujours la même rectitude. On veut toujours son bien, mais on ne le voit pas toujours; . . .
>
> Il y a souvent bien de la différence entre la volonté de tous et la volonté générale: . . .[2]

THE PRINCIPAL difficulty in government by majority is that the majority is sometimes wrong. Few men will always accept as a criterion of truth "the majority vote of that nation that could lick all others."[3] Instead, with comforting reliance on the power of reason, one postulates rightness, discoverable by taking thought; and deplores the occasional and, one hopes temporary, divergences therefrom by the multitude. The difficulty arises in distinguishing the occasions when the majority is wrong, from those instances in which the minority itself falls into error despite the superior discernment it is apt to sense in its members. Truth is exasperatingly elusive.

A nation devoted to the majoritarian principle but conscious of its proneness to occasional error, and hopeful that the swings of politi-

[1] To the American Academy of Arts and Sciences I am most grateful for permitting me to use in this chapter and the next a large part of a communication which that Academy invited me to present at one of its meetings held in 1953. The original appears in Volume 82 of the Proceedings of the Academy, at page 169 and following.

[2] Rousseau, *Du Contrat Social*, Book II, Chapter 3.

[3] A wry definition of Holmes'; see "Natural Law," *Collected Legal Papers* (New York: Peter Smith, 1952) p. 310.

cal power may, after a while, correct its mistakes, does well to look for some governmental device to define and correct majority error during the intervals of aberration. The requirement is an institution of unusual intelligence, detached from the politics of organized pressure, and so respected that, at least for a while, a majority will follow it against the majority's own current of desires. The men who staff it need not, can not, detach themselves from the "felt necessities of the time, the prevalent moral and political theories, intuitions of public policy, avowed or unconscious. . . ." But to succeed they must be primarily rational rather than ambitious.

In the United States we have found such an institution in the Supreme Court. We have given it a limited mandate to correct mistakes made by State or national majorities, describing that mandate in conveniently general terms which permit the Court to adapt its judgments to unforeseen needs as they arise—defining its objectives by such phrases as "due process of law," and "freedom of speech or of the press," which express aspirations rather than rules. This duty the Court performs with some deference to legislative wisdom, conventionally stated in terms of a "presumption of constitutionality."

With a mission described in such inclusive terms, with a duty to choose the good law and reject the bad, but with no convenient way of determining by objective test which is which, the Court is sure from time to time to arouse substantial resentment. Of course, soon or late, by constitutional amendment or by judicial interpretation, the majority will have its way. That law will be a good law which a majority desires with enough persistence. The role of the Supreme Court will, in the long run, be what the people want it to be. It is therefore important to see what the people of the United States from time to time expect of their Court.

Here can be only a cursory examination of one small segment of opinion during a limited time, recollection of what certain liberals thought of the Supreme Court's function a generation ago, and some thought of what has happened to that opinion since that day. And, lest I be thought too naïf in using the term "liberals," I make haste to acknowledge its unsatisfactory character. It means many things to many men; it varies in usage from generation to generation. One can only be confident in a negative—that it has not, in the time of men now in middle life, been generally taken to describe people who believed that government should keep hands off the economic processes of society.[4] There are terms that are obscured rather than clari-

---

[4] See Guido de Ruggiero, "Liberalism," *Encyclopedia of Social Sciences*, E. R. A. Seligman and Alvin Johnson, eds. (15 vols.; New York: Macmillan, 1930–34) V, pp. 435–440.

fied by attempts at definition. For the purposes of this discussion only, I take a "liberal" to mean the sort of man who enjoyed the *New Republic* about 1923.

At least one human trait is so common as to approach universality. It is a sort of intellectual myopia, tending to limit the view of each observer to that part of a problem directly under his eyes. So those who have undertaken to appraise the part played by our federal judiciary have sometimes been misled by undue attention to problems of the immediate moment. Forty years ago, liberal opinion tended to think of the Supreme Court only as an obstacle in the way of desirable social and economic reforms. In those simpler times, critics needed fewer doubts. Earnest young writers knew, then, that the general will expressed itself through freely elected legislatures; and that when the Supreme Court interfered with the work of the legislators, the Supreme Court was almost always wrong.

Some zealous critics knew that it was always wrong. Comments of the practicing politician are apt to be less guarded than those of the scholar, and the elder Senator LaFollette felt no need to mince words when he denounced the judicial power to find statutes unconstitutional. In 1922 he told the American Federation of Labor:

> From what source, it may be asked, have the Federal judges derived the supreme power which they now so boldly assert? Not only was such power not given to the judiciary in any Constitution, State or Federal, but the records of the Constitutional Convention show that when it was proposed . . . that judges should have a veto upon acts of Congress, it was decisively defeated on four separate occasions, and at no time received the support of more than three States . . .
>
> There is, therefore, no sanction in the written Constitution of the United States for the power which the courts now assert. They have secured this power only by usurpation . . .[5]

Academic commentators, somewhat more restrained, still tended to view the Supreme Court with alarm. Francis B. Sayre, then a professor at the Harvard Law School, wrote in the May 1, 1923, *Survey:*

> If the Fifth and Fourteenth Amendments are to be so interpreted that henceforth legislation is to be declared unconstitutional whenever it is out of accord with the economic and social theories of five members of the Supreme Court, a blow is struck at one of the most fundamental principles of our government. The legislature then becomes not an independent and supreme body framing policies into law; it becomes subordinate to the Supreme Court which becomes virtually a

[5] Speech before the American Federation of Labor at Cincinnati, June 21, 1922, reprinted in *Congressional Record*, vol. 62, p. 9077.

House of Lords, exercising an actual veto power of such laws as fail to accord with the social theories of five of its members.

Writing in the *Harvard Law Review* in 1924, Maurice Finkelstein, an eminent and philosophical member of the New York Bar, urged that the Supreme Court renounce its jurisdiction of cases challenging social and industrial legislative policy for the same reasons which sometimes move it to forgo jurisdiction in cases where "political controversies" are involved.

> . . . [A] great deal of the so-called unconstitutional social and industrial legislation might have fared better at the hands of the court had it been treated from the point of view of a political question. This would involve the surrender on the part of the court of the prerogative of passing upon the policy of an act as enunciated by the legislature . . . For, in truth, in cases involving the industrial policy of a state or nation the measure of due process approaches very closely to the measure of political wisdom. The function of determining the political policy of the government belongs to the legislature. . . . No matter in what terms the opinions of jurists have been couched, it is apparent that it is the fear of consequences or the lack of adequate data that has impelled the courts to refrain from entering upon the discussion of the merits of prickly issues. It seems to us that these very considerations should have compelled the refusal by the courts to take jurisdiction of cases raising the question of the constitutionality of social and industrial legislation. It is difficult for the courts, dependent as they are upon counsel for their facts, to have before them the material considerations that have caused state legislatures to pass a limited-hour day for laborers, or a minimum wage law for women and children. The legislative industrial policy of a state or nation can hardly even be stated in classical legal terminology. It would therefore seem the better statesmanship to have included all of these questions in the general category of "political questions". . . .

The most interesting common feature of these and like comments of a generation ago is the concentration of attention on what was described as social and economic legislation, and the feeling that, left to themselves without court interference, legislators would do well for the people. From occasional malfunction of the judicial negative on majorities we tended to conclude, not that any human institution is subject to sporadic aberration, but that judicial review of majoritarian decision was in its nature a Bad Thing.[6] To suggest that this attitude was anywhere near unanimous in the United States would,

---

[6] See, generally for Good Things and Bad Things, a work of those eminent historians W. C. Sellar and R. J. Yeatman, *1066 and All That* (London: Methuen and Co., 1931).

of course, be a distortion. But it could fairly be said to represent the "liberal" point of view. Mr. Finkelstein seemed untroubled by any possibility that a day might come when the Supreme Court's inaction in controversies which it called "political" would produce liberal protest. He did not foresee the Court's refusal to require a correction of gross inequality of congressional districting in Illinois,[7] or of the comparable "county unit rule" in Georgia.[8] His recognition of the political importance of much industrial and social legislation was fully justified. But he apparently foresaw no possible application of this doctrine of judicial abstention to suits brought before the federal judiciary seeking to correct State injustice to the Negro—a political issue of some warmth. That "human rights" are not always easy to distinguish from "property rights"; that judicial restraint in cases of the latter sort, but not in the former, would be difficult to achieve—this seemed to cause little worry in the mid-twenties.

American liberal opinion in the 1920s tended to approve of the Congress and to regard assertion of constitutional rights as legalistic and insincere. Witness the reaction to a presidential reminder in 1924.

On April 11, of that year, Mr. Coolidge sent a message to the Senate protesting at the manner in which a Senate Committee had investigated the official conduct of a Cabinet officer—the Secretary of the Treasury, Andrew Mellon. The President wrote:

> Under a procedure of this kind, the constitutional guarantees against unwarranted search and seizure break down, the prohibition against what amounts to a Government charge of criminal action without the formal presentment of a Grand Jury is evaded, the rules of evidence which have been adopted for the protection of the innocent are ignored, the department becomes the victim of vague, unformulated and indefinite charges, and instead of a Government of law we have a Government of lawlessness.[9]

With editorial scorn the *New Republic* of April 23rd took the President to task:

> . . . Mr. Coolidge accuses the Senate of lawlessness [in] the evasion by committees of that body of "the prohibition of what amounts to a government charge of criminal action without the formal presentment of a Grand Jury," and the ignoring of "the rules of evidence which have been adopted for the protection of the innocent." . . . It is based on the preposterous assumption that an investigation into the conduct

---

[7] *Colegrove* v. *Green*, 328 U.S. 549 (1946).

[8] *South* v. *Peters*, 339 U.S. 276 (1950). The "political question" is no longer an obstacle in reapportionment cases. See *Baker* v. *Carr*, 369 U.S. 186 (1962); and *Wesberry* v. *Sanders*, 376 U.S. 1 (1964).

[9] *New York Times*, April 12, 1924, p. 1.

of public officials who are suspected of wrong doing should be conducted under all the limitations of a criminal trial. If the Walsh and Wheeler committees had not acted in the way which the President denounces as lawless, they would never have obtained the information which the government is now using in order to prosecute ex-Secretary Fall or which justified the President in dismissing Harry Daugherty.[10] Mr. Coolidge demands the placing of restrictions on congressional investigations into the conduct of executive officers which would fatally hamper the investigators in obtaining testimony from unwilling witnesses. If Congress yielded to his demands, the record of administrative officials would thereafter be immune from effective inquiry unless the accused official admitted sufficient evidence of crime to warrant an indictment. . . .

The President's final decision to attack the investigators and disparage the practice of investigations is particularly deplorable for one reason. It is always undesirable that select congressional committees should have to conduct investigations for the purpose of exposing corruption in office rather than for the purpose of seeking methods of improving the administration of the laws. Investigations of this kind would not be necessary, if administrative officials could be trusted to report indications of corruption on the part of their fellow officials; and when they are necessary it is only because a certain number of public employes and private citizens enter into a tacit or overt conspiracy to allow the corruption to continue. When the exposure finally takes place, popular opinion justifiably suspects the existence of such a conspiracy, and its suspicions are bound to increase and to become reckless in so far as any indication exists of a successful plan to suppress the facts and to force the investigators to quit.[11]

Here again there is no evidence of a gift of foresight. That a day might come when investigations by a Senate committee would suggest that a certain number of public employees and private citizens had entered into a different sort of conspiracy; that in such an event constitutional protection of those accused might appear in a different light—none of this seems to have been thought of by the stern and righteous editorialist.

Aesop's frogs disliked their activist stork king, and wished for his inert predecessor. The problem facing a constitutional philosopher in the United States involves a similar alternation in governmental policy. The constitutionalist must construct a theory by which the Supreme Court will keep hands off the other branches of the Federal govern-

[10] These episodes concerned the "Teapot Dome" oil reserve matters. See *McGrain* v. *Daugherty*, 273 U.S. 135 (1927); and *Sinclair* v. *U.S.*, 279 U.S. 263 (1929).

[11] I am indebted to Dr. Albert Mavrinac, now Professor of Government at Colby College, for reference to this *New Republic* editorial, and for much wise and helpful counsel through many years.

ment, and hands off the States, when aloofness is proper; and yet will act against each at proper times. We must have King Log and King Stork, turn and turn about, as each role is proper. This is not simple, for opinions on questions of propriety are rarely unanimous.

Liberal impatience with the United States Supreme Court in the twenties was mainly based on four of its lines of decision. The most exasperating was the limitation the Court found in the powers of the federal Congress to control the nation's economy. Economic activity in the nation was unitary, making little question of interstate and intrâ-state. Procession of necessities of life, from the sea and the mine and the forest and the farm to the men who used or consumed them, went on without much relation to State boundaries. And activity within the borders of one State had repercussions elsewhere. Comprehensive and costly factory legislation in New York, in the New England States, and in many others, made it difficult for these to compete in manufacturing with States having a minimum program of social legislation. Yet the Supreme Court, clinging to the undeniable historic fact that the Congress had been entrusted with power to regulate only commerce with foreign nations and among the several States,[12] continued to hold that production of goods was outside the power of the national legislature. Commerce began when goods were ready for trade. Naturally, those who did not wish to be bothered by federal regulation were gratified by this declaration of federal impotence. Conversely, the struggling cause of liberalism called for an expanded power in the national government which could oblige the dissenting minority of States to comply with the ideas of the more progressive majority. But the Supreme Court, by no means unreasonably, persisted in the idea that the grant to the Congress of power over commerce between the States meant that power over other commerce was not granted; that the expression of the one excluded the other; and that there must have been some economic activity not entrusted to the national government. Accordingly the Court was vigilant to block evasive devices by the Congress. In 1918 it held that a congressional attempt to forbid movement of the products of child labor from State to State was an indirect effort to control conditions of production in factories; commerce only began when manufacture ended; accordingly manufacture was beyond the power of the federal Congress.[13] When the Congress promptly retaliated by imposing a prohibitive tax on the

[12] U.S. Constitution, Article I., Section 8, Clause 3, "The Congress shall have Power . . . To regulate Commerce with foreign Nations, and among the several States. . . ." Commerce with "the Indian Tribes" no longer troubles us.
[13] *Hammer v. Dagenhart*, 247 U.S. 251 (1918), the "Child Labor Case."

manufacturer who utilized child labor, the Supreme Court saw through this device as well, and in 1922 struck it down.[14]

A second grievance of liberals arose because, even where legislation was clearly within the scope of the powers delegated to the Congress (when it sought to regulate interstate railroads, or to govern the District of Columbia, for example), the Court occasionally held that the due-process clause of the Fifth Amendment[15] invalidated federal statutes. Thus regulation of anti-union discrimination by railroads,[16] and minimum wage legislation affecting the District of Columbia hospitals[17] were both held invalid, for, said the Court, these statutes deprived those affected of their liberty and property without due process of law.

The Supreme Court aroused a third complaint by its restriction of State legislation. Not only did the Court sometimes declare that Congress had no power to correct local economic injustice, but the Court had from time to time used the clause of the Fourteenth Amendment which forbids any State to "deprive any person or life, liberty, or property, without due process of law," to take from the States, as well, reasonable power to correct economic and social inequities. The "yellow dog" contract is almost forgotten now; the term described an agreement, required of a man seeking employment, that he would forfeit his job if he joined a union. The Kansas State legislature forbade this restrictive practice; the Supreme Court declared the Kansas law invalid under the Fourteenth Amendment;[18] liberal men were pained. When Kansas attempted to regulate labor matters by establishing a system of compulsory arbitration with a Court of Industrial Relations similar to that in Australia, the Supreme Court likewise declared that this deprived the affected parties of liberty and property without due process of law.[19] When Tennessee in 1929 attempted to fix the retail price of gasoline, the Supreme Court held that this move, too, was invalid under the Fourteenth Amendment.[20] New Jersey was similarly forbidden to fix the fees of employment agencies,[21] New York to fix the charges of theater ticket brokers.[22] Oklahoma was

[14] *Bailey* v. *Drexel Furniture Co.*, 259 U.S. 20 (1922), the "Child Labor Tax Case."

[15] "No person shall . . . be deprived of life, liberty, or property, without due process of law. . . ."

[16] *Adair* v. *U.S.* 208 U.S. 161 (1908).

[17] *Adkins* v. *Children's Hospital*, 261 U.S. 525 (1923).

[18] *Coppage* v. *Kansas*, 236 U.S. 1 (1915).

[19] *Wolff Pkg. Co.* v. *Court of Industrial Relations*, 262 U.S. 522 (1923).

[20] *Williams* v. *Standard Oil*, 278 U.S. 235 (1929).

[21] *Ribnik* v. *McBride*, 277 U.S. 350 (1928).

[22] *Tyson* v. *Banton*, 273 U.S. 418 (1927).

forbidden to limit competition in the ice business.[23] The Fourteenth Amendment thus guaranteed in the States a measure of laissez-faire sufficient to annoy those urging reform legislation.

The Court aroused a fourth grievance by construing the Commerce Clause[24] as a self-executing limitation of State power. That grant of competence to Congress was not in terms a restriction on the States; but the Court found in it an unexpressed negative, prohibiting various State commercial regulations which affected more States than one, and limiting power of States to tax multi-State economic operations. The Court felt a danger that economic parochialism, expressed by creation of what amounted to disguised State protective tariffs, could tend to divide the nation into a multitude of protectionist segments, to the danger of the United States as an economic whole. The Court found in the Commerce Clause a not-implausible basis for declaring ineffectual State regulation, and State taxation, which tended to such unreasonable fragmentation of the national economy. But this invalidation of State laws had the effect of freeing certain large commercial operations from some State legislative jurisdiction—at least until the Congress should give its consent to State action; and this consent was not always forthcoming. Here was another occasion for complaints against the federal judiciary.

The opinions of the Supreme Court were not always unanimous, of course. The detachment with which Holmes viewed the human comedy led him to much more tolerance of legislation[25] than was shown by the majority of his brethren. In 1916 Brandeis came to join the Court; Stone succeeded McKenna in 1925; the three, Holmes, Brandeis, Stone, saw much alike. But throughout the twenties the majority of the Court continued to hold unconstitutional some State legislation and occasional federal statutes, and thereby to draw down the criticisms of liberal men.

Depression

In the mid-1920's some skeptical pessimists thought they saw signs of deceleration in the American economic whirl. Agriculture was in a slump. Nevertheless a somewhat hectic optimism persisted in most of American business. When Herbert Hoover was elected President in

[23] New State Ice Co. v. Liebman, 285 U.S. 262 (1932).

[24] See footnote 12, page 474, above, and Baldwin v. Seelig, 294 U.S. 511 (1935).

[25] Exemplified by Holmes' famous remark about Spencer's Social Statics in his Lochner dissent. See page 461, supra and Lochner v. New York, 198 U.S. 45, 75 (1905).

November 1928, prices on the New York Stock Exchange rose sharply. People went on buying stocks on margin, and buying merchandise on the installment plan, though farmers found themselves producing more wheat, milk, corn and tobacco than they could conveniently market, and prices of agricultural products continued to decline. Oil fields produced more petroleum than we could use. We were embarrassed by our plenty; somehow we were unable to distribute the great total of all we produced.

Then, suddenly in October 1929, the New York Stock Exchange demonstrated a belated and naïvely suddenly loss of confidence in the American economy. Prices of stocks dropped abruptly, and doubts of the future spread more widely than the securities market. People stopped buying new merchandise; many defaulted on installment payments due for what they had already bought. Homeowners fell behind in mortgage payments they owed to banks; the banks had little choice but to foreclose on many such defaulted loans, only to find that there were few buyers for the foreclosed houses. Bank failures increased, and no institution like today's Federal Deposit Insurance protected the depositors. Numbers of business houses dismally closed doors. People lost their jobs. In some places sad families, the father out of work and with no lodging, built ramshackle shelters in shantytowns called, bitterly, "Hoovervilles." We were in the Great Depression.

Congress attempted various relief measures. On January 22, 1932, it chartered the Reconstruction Finance Corporation,[26] a great federal bank, authorized to make loans to other banks, insurance companies, credit unions and the like; if we could shore up credit, we might shore up the whole faltering economy. On May 19, 1932, the Congress liberalized the Federal Farm Loan Act of 1916.[27] On July 22, 1932, the Congress established a system of Federal Home Loan Banks, intended to take over, from financial institutions, mortgages which the owners could not keep up.[28] But none of these measures started moving the economy out of the doldrums. A disastrously large percentage of the normal work force was unemployed; production of goods stayed slack; banks attempting to foreclose farm mortgages found farmers organizing to resist foreclosure sales. Dairy farmers, resentful at seeing their own milk sold for a pittance, sometimes dumped their neighbors' full milk cans in the road. The country became rather despondent.

The 1932 Democratic nominee for President was Franklin Delano Roosevelt, Governor of the State of New York; he had been Assistant

[26] 47 Stat. at Large 5.
[27] 47 Stat. at Large 159, amending 39 Stat. at Large 360.
[28] 47 Stat. at Large 725.

Secretary of the Navy in World War I. Mr. Roosevelt had suffered a severe attack of poliomyelitis in 1921, which for the rest of his life forced him to stand with braces; but he had courageously continued his public career and had made a notable impression by his governorship. He waged a free-swinging presidential campaign in 1932; his buoyant, optimistic voice brought hope to a great many downcast Americans, discouraged about the state of the nation; he promised the people a New Deal.

President Hoover, nominated by the Republican Party, had had an outstandingly able and useful career as director of Belgian Relief in the early stages of World War I, and as director of Russian Relief at the close of that War. He had then fed millions of distressed people. As Secretary of Commerce he had become familiar with the operation of the American economy at large. Nevertheless, he failed to inspire the American people with a sense that he was ready to mobilize all the resources of the national government to reestablish prosperity. In November 1932, Franklin D. Roosevelt was triumphantly elected.

This victory could not immediately stop the economy's downward drift, which continued during the winter of 1932–33. When President Roosevelt was sworn in on March 4, 1933, banks were closing all over the country. The new President at once announced and pushed forward a confident program that inspired millions of Americans. His voice was resilient, heartening; the new device of nation-wide radio broadcasting enabled him to talk to the entire American people in a series of what he called Fireside Chats. He began each with the salutation, "My friends and neighbors . . . ." Men were anxious to hope that now, at last, the national government was going to do something drastic about the Depression. The new President summoned to Washington a corps of bright young intellectuals to make up a "brain trust" to advise him on the recovery program. Five days after his inauguration he called the Congress in a special session. That body, happy to follow the President's lead, in a little over three months passed a series of sweeping measures intended to restore prosperity.

On May 12, 1933, President Roosevelt approved the Agricultural Adjustment Act.[29] Congress there declared as its policy the establishment and maintenance of a balance between production and consumption of agricultural commodities, to reestablish crop prices at a level giving the farmers' products a purchasing power relative to articles which farmers had to buy, equivalent to the purchasing power the farmer enjoyed between 1909 and 1914.[30] The Congress devised an ingenious plan to make farm crops thus increase in exchange value.

[29] 48 Stat. at Large 310.
[30] For tobacco the Act set a different "base period"—1919–1929.

The statute provided for a "processing tax" on the first domestic processing of the agricultural commodities in question. The rate of this tax was to vary from time to time so as to equal the difference between the current average price paid to the farmer and the "fair exchange value" of the farmer's crop—the value which would give his crop the same purchasing power, for articles he had to buy, as the same crop used to have in the "base period" of happy memory between 1909 and 1914.

The Secretary of Agriculture was then directed to make agreements with farmers to reduce the acreage which they planted; the Secretary was to recompense the farmers for their diminution of salable crops by giving them "benefit payments." The government would obtain the necessary increased revenues from the processing taxes, of which the burden would ultimately rest on consumers. Thus the consumers, who had been getting farm products too cheaply, would pay the cost of reestablishing the farmers. Assuming the soundness of the premises, the success of the plan was certain. As planted acreage diminished, total production would grow less; scarcity would increase the price of the commodity in question; as prices approached parity the rate of the processing tax would proportionately decline. When farm crops reached parity, the processing tax would be eliminated, and the object of the statute would have been accomplished.

On June 13, 1933, the President approved the Home Owners' Loan Act of 1933[31] which improved and strengthened the operation of the Federal Home Loan Bank Act of July 22, 1932. On June 16, 1933, the President approved the "Banking Act of 1933" intended to restore to health the disastrous condition of American banks. Section 12B of that statute[32] created the Federal Deposit Insurance Corporation which insured depositors in participating banks up to $10,000 for the full amount of their bank deposits, and insured a proportion of larger deposits. On June 5, 1933, the President approved a joint resolution authorizing the payment of every obligation of the United States and of every other public or private debtor, in any currency authorized by law even though the bond or other contract stated that the debt was payable in gold.[33] Something like the "greenback" currency of Civil War times thus became the sole legal tender (except for silver dollars and minor coinage) for all debts, public and private; a man who had bought a government bond or a railroad bond relying on a gold clause now had to take his pay in paper. Indeed, people had long since grown used to paper money; gold had been only a possible alternative,

[31] 48 Stat. at Large 128.
[32] 48 Stat. at Large 162, 168.
[33] 48 Stat. at Large 112.

thought by its availability to give steadiness to the exchange value of paper currency. But now the use of gold became illegal.

On June 16, 1933, President Roosevelt approved the National Industrial Recovery Act.[34] Under its provisions any trade or industrial association or group could apply to the President for approval of a "code of fair competition" covering the trade or industry in question. Section 3B of the statute provided that after the President should have approved any such code, its provisions should be governing standards for that trade or industry. Any violation in any transaction "in or affecting interstate or foreign commerce" should be treated as a violation of the Federal Trade Commission Act, and should also be a misdemeanor, punishable by a fine of $500 for each offense. Each day during which the disobedience continued would be a separate offense. Codes might specify hours and wages. In case of destructive wage or price cutting, the President could "license" the business in question, and enforce the code of fair competition by revocation of the license. The theory of the statute was that "unfair" conditions had resulted in a downward economic spiral; purchasing power of the employees would be restored by the codes; unfair price cutting would end; and industrial recovery would be stimulated.

The President appointed as administrator of the National Industrial Recovery Act a former Brigadier General of cavalry named Hugh Johnson. The General struck the public imagination at once. He had a confident swagger, a rasping voice, a flair for the dramatic. He devised the Blue Eagle, symbol of compliance with code standards, which a business man was entitled to display in his window to show his cooperative spirit. Blue Eagles appeared by the thousand in shop windows from Maine to California. In the summer of 1933 the General organized Recovery parades in towns and cities across the continent; delegations of butchers, bakers, and candlestick makers, escorted by soldiers and sailors, inspired by brass bands, marched through the evening streets, all in honor of Recovery. This activity did not greatly improve the nation's economy, perhaps, but it certainly improved men's feelings. The marchers, swinging along in the streets, felt that at last something was stirring.

The first congressional session of Franklin D. Roosevelt's presidency, which gave rise to all these measures and more, began on the ninth of March and ended on the sixteenth day of June, 1933. Surely few sessions of any Congress have ever enacted so many significant statutes in such a short space of time. The pattern of them all was vigorous intervention by the national government in the economy, an intention to aid the common man, a resolve to start the stalled economic life of

[34] 48 Stat. at Large 195.

the United States on a new upward spiral. In all this, national hope and attention centered on President Franklin D. Roosevelt. The national executive was to save the nation.

The Supreme Court and the New Deal

The story of the New Deal in the Supreme Court is one of the conspicuous chronicles of constitutional history. It deserves telling in some detail. The mass of New Deal legislation aroused substantial constitutional doubts. The Supreme Court had long before found that the commerce power was not unlimited; and there remained as additional threats the "vague contours of the Fifth Amendment" as Holmes had once called them.[35] Curiously enough, the first significant step toward what ultimately was the constitutional establishment of the New Deal came not in federal but in State legislation. Like all the other farmers in the United States, New York dairymen found themselves distressed in the late 1920's and early 1930's. The immediate cause was over-production of milk which producers could barely sell at a rate sufficient to pay their costs. The New York Legislature, after a thorough review of milk production and marketing, passed in 1933 a statute[36] which created a Milk Control Board empowered, among other things, to fix minimum retail prices which customers must pay. A sale lower than the price thus established was a criminal offense, for which the storekeeper was punishable. The theory of the Milk Control Act was that, ultimately, the price paid by the customers, maintained by law at a level higher than that to which it would sink under uncontrolled competition, would ultimately percolate downward and alleviate the distress of the dairy farmer.[37]

[35] In *Adkins* v. *The Children's Hospital*, 261 U.S. 525 (1923).

[36] Chapter 158 of the Laws of 1933.

[37] Time can produce curious changes. One doubts that the following editorial, which appeared in the *New York Times* of April 2, 1964, would have expressed that journal's opinion in 1933 —

CONTROLS OVER MILK

The New York Legislature's sorry record was not improved by passage in its closing hours of a milk-licensing bill that would in effect give the State Agricultural Commissioner power to control the retail price of milk. This disguised form of price-fixing meets the demands of the milk lobby, the distributors and the processors, who have long campaigned for higher milk prices.

But it does not serve the interests of either the dairy farmer or the consumer. This is a shocking attempt to price-fix milk via the backdoor. If it becomes law, it will be harmful to both the pocketbook and the health of the public. . . .

This newspaper has expressed strong opposition to price-fixing or other

This legislation faced constitutional hazards. The Supreme Court of the United States, ever since *Munn* v. *Illinois* in 1877,[38] had followed the theory that some callings were "affected with a public interest"— those of warehousemen, common carriers, public utilities, and the like. For these a price fixed by law was constitutional; for others, for "common callings," governmentally fixed prices deprived the affected parties of due process of law. Chief Justice Taft in 1923 had written in an opinion of the Supreme Court which held unconstitutional wage fixing in the meat packing industry, imposed by the Kansas Court of Industrial Relations—[39]

> It has never been supposed, since the adoption of the Constitution, that the business of the butcher, or the baker, the tailor, the wood chopper, the mining operator, or the miner was clothed with such a public interest that the price of his product or his wages could be fixed by State regulation. It is true that in the days of the early common law an omnipotent Parliament did regulate prices and wages as it chose, and occasionally a Colonial legislature sought to exercise the same power; but nowadays one does not devote one's property or business to the public use or clothe it with a public interest merely because one makes commodities for, and sells to, the public in the common callings of which those above mentioned are instances.

The New York Milk Control Act raised a question whether this long-established difference between businesses still held good; whether in 1933 any part of the economy was not "affected with the public interest." If the Constitution entrusted control of the price of a bottle of milk to the political process, the future of the American economy was evidently destined to differ from its past.

In the spring of 1933 the New York Milk Control Board fixed nine cents as the minimum retail price for a quart of milk. Leo Nebbia, proprietor of a small grocery store in Rochester, sold two quarts of milk and a five cent loaf of bread for eighteen cents, an evident violation of the New York price regulation. He was tried in the Criminal Branch of the City Court of Rochester for this disobedience of the Board's order and, despite his assertion that such price control de-

---

controls over the sale of liquor. But a law that involved any form of price-fixing for milk would be intolerable. . . . It would positively harm lower income groups, for whom milk at as low a price as possible is an absolute necessity.

Senate Minority Leader Joseph Zaretzki has done a service in exposing the milk lobby's devious effort to eliminate competition and raise prices of milk. In view of Governor Rockefeller's determined stand against liquor price fixing, it is inconceivable that he would bow to the milk lobby and to the Legislature by agreeing to anything that might lead to fixing prices for milk. A veto is called for. [The bill was vetoed. N.Y. Times, Apr. 26, '64, p. 46]

[38] 94 U.S. 113.

[39] *Wolff Pkg. Co.* v. *Court of Industrial Relations*, 262 U.S. 522.

prived him of due process and equal protection guaranteed by the Fourteenth Amendment, the Court found him guilty and imposed a five dollar fine. As in most cases of constitutional litigation, the underlying controversy was much wider than appeared in the immediate facts of the case. Large milk dealers tended to favor retail price regulation more than small independent marginal dealers like Nebbia. The large dealers supported the prosecution of Nebbia as a test case; a group of smaller dealers came to his aid. Nebbia appealed unsuccessfully to the Monroe County Court, then to the New York Court of Appeals. Defeated in these efforts, he ultimately appealed to the Supreme Court of the United States.

On the fifth of March, 1934, that Court, with an opinion by Mr. Justice Owen J. Roberts, affirmed the judgment against Nebbia and thus upheld the constitutionality of New York price-fixing, and ended the constitutional distinction between rate-making in businesses "affected with a public interest" and in the "common callings." Concurring with Justice Roberts were Chief Justice Charles Evans Hughes, and Associate Justices Brandeis, Cardozo, and Stone. Dissenting, and so indicating that in their opinion price fixing in such a "common calling" as selling milk was a denial of due process, were Justices McReynolds, Van Devanter, Butler, and Sutherland. From March 14, 1932 when Associate Justice Cardozo was sworn in to replace Mr. Justice Holmes, until June 1, 1937 when Mr. Justice Van Devanter retired, the Supreme Court was made up of the same nine Justices who sat in the *Nebbia* case. Constitutional evolution during the crisis of the New Deal thus continued without any change in that Court's personnel. The balance between the Justices of the one attitude and those of the other, which had been evident in *Nebbia's Case*, remained as close, on some issues, during the next three tense years.

Constitutional litigation is not carried out in a few days or weeks, and the first challenge to a New Deal statute was heard in the Supreme Court in late 1934. On December 10 and 11 of that year counsel for two petroleum companies asserted before the Court the unconstitutionality of Section 9 (c) of the National Industrial Recovery Act, and an executive order issued under it. Section 9 (c) authorized the President to prohibit transportation, in interstate or foreign commerce, of petroleum produced or drawn from storage in violation of any State regulation, then commonly called "hot oil." On January 7, 1935 the Court, with an opinion by Chief Justice Hughes, held that the section in question was invalid because the Congress, entrusted with the legislative function under Article I of the Constitution, had attempted to delegate this constitutional duty to the President, with no standards prescribed to control his executive action. Furthermore the Court held the President's action invalid on another ground; the executive order making the regulation contained ". . . no finding, no statement of the grounds of the President's action in enacting the prohibition." Only Mr. Justice Cardozo dissented from this judgment.[40]

The *Hot Oil Case* was a blow to the President—not because of its practical effect, which was comparatively slight, but because of its overtones. For two years the overwhelming majority of the Congress and the American people had united in praising the President and his program. Criticism of President Roosevelt had been ascribed to economic royalists, to selfish rich men in luxurious clubs. Now eight of the nine Justices of the Supreme Court, including the great liberal Justice Brandeis, including Justice Stone, late Dean of the Columbia Law School, and including the Chief Justice of the United States, had found a part of the Recovery program unconstitutional because the Presidential element in it was too unlimited. The President was not fond of criticism, nor accustomed to hearing it from sources within the government.

On February 18, 1935, the Supreme Court in practical effect upheld the statute which required payment in paper money, of "Gold Clause" bonds. As to obligations of private organizations—in this instance the Baltimore and Ohio Railroad Company—a majority of five Justices sustained the statute in an opinion by Chief Justice Hughes. The Chief Justice reviewed the *Legal Tender Cases* of 1871; the present statute could stand, he wrote on the constitutional grant of power

> 'To coin money, regulate the value thereof, and of foreign coin.' Article I, Section 8, Para. 5. But the Court in the legal tender cases did not derive from that express grant alone the full authority of the Congress in relation to the currency. The Court found the source of that authority in all the related powers conferred upon the Congress and appropriate to achieve 'the great objects for which the government was framed,'—'a national government, with sovereign powers.' . . . . The broad and comprehensive national authority over the subjects of revenue, finance and currency is derived from the aggregate of the powers granted to the Congress, embracing the powers to lay and collect taxes, to borrow money, to regulate commerce with foreign nations and among the several States, to coin money, regulate the value thereof, and of foreign coin, and fix the standards of weights and measures, and the added express power 'to make all laws which shall be necessary and proper for carrying into execution' the other enumerated powers.[41]

[40] *Panama Refining Company* v. *Ryan*, 293 U.S. 388 (1935). Compare, however, *United States* v. *Sharpnack*, 355 U.S. 286 (1958).

[41] *Norman* v. *Baltimore & Ohio Railroad Co.*, 294 U.S. 240. See page 422 ff., above, for a discussion of the *Legal Tender Cases* of 1871.

Justices McReynolds, Van Devanter, Sutherland, and Butler dissented.

On the same day, however, the Court's opinion in a case involving the "Gold Clause" in bonds of the United States, written by Chief Justice Hughes, was quite different in tone. The majority of the Court concluded that the Constitution had conferred on the Congress no power "to alter or destroy those obligations" which it had undertaken. "We conclude that the Joint Resolution of June 5, 1933, insofar as it attempted to override the obligation created by the bond in suit, went beyond the Congressional power."[42] However the Court went on to find that the plaintiff had not proved his damages; he had not demonstrated that the gold dollar had a larger purchasing power than the paper dollar. Therefore the plaintiff in the action against the United States obtained no judgment in his favor. Mr. Justice Stone, while concurring in the position that the government had no power to repudiate its obligation, added

> As much as I deplore this refusal to fulfill the solemn promise of bonds of the United States, I cannot escape the conclusion, announced for the Court, that in the situation now presented, the Government, through the exercise of its sovereign power to regulate the value of money has rendered itself immune from liability for its actions . . . . In this posture of the case it is unnecessary, and I think undesirable, for the Court to undertake to say that the obligation of the Gold Clause in Government bonds is greater than in the bonds of private individuals. . . .

Mr. Justice McReynolds delivered a dissenting opinion in which Justices Van Devanter, Sutherland, and Butler concurred; they wrote "Loss of reputation for honorable dealing will bring us unending humiliation; . . ." Thus while the substance of the Gold Clause cases was a success for the administration, the language of the Court was not flattering, and again, the presence in the government of nine men, exempt from the pressures of the political process, who from this detached position criticized a measure essential to the New Deal, was a fact somewhat irritating to the administration's supporters.

On Monday, May 6, 1935, the Supreme Court held that a retirement pension plan, required by Act of Congress for interstate carriers, was beyond the Commerce Power, and deprived the carriers of property without due process.[43] On June 27, 1934, President Roosevelt had approved the Railroad Retirement Act.[44] This statute required a retirement and pension system for employees of all carriers subject to the Interstate Commerce Commission. The retirement fund was to

[42] *Perry* v. *United States*, 294 U.S. 330.
[43] *Railroad Retirement Board* v. *Alton Railroad Co.*, 295 U.S. 330.
[44] 48 Stat. at Large 1283.

arise from compulsory contributions made by present and future employees and by the carriers. Mr. Justice Roberts delivered the Court's opinion holding the Act unconstitutional; Justices McReynolds, Van Devanter, Butler, and Sutherland concurred; Chief Justice Hughes wrote a dissenting opinion; Justices Brandeis, Cardozo, and Stone agreed with the Chief Justice. Mr. Justice Roberts and the majority found that the Retirement Act not only violated the Fifth Amendment due process clause, but purported to apply to matters entirely outside the proper scope of the Commerce Clause. Work beginning thirty years before the statute, and compensated in full according to the agreement between the parties, could now be the basis of pension payments provided only the relation of employer and employee should continue for any period, however brief, after the passage of the Act. "This clearly arbitrary imposition of liability to pay again for services long since rendered and fully compensated is not permissible legislation . . . The Court below held the provision deprived the railroads of their property without due process, and we agree with that conclusion." Some railroads were solvent and some not and the Retirement Board conceded that the plan would result in solvent railroads being obliged to furnish the money necessary to meet the demands of the system upon insolvent carriers. Many carriers subject to the Interstate Commerce Act had gone out of existence; and employees, part of whose careers had been spent with carriers now defunct, were treated on the same basis as employees of continuously existing carriers; past service for a carrier no longer existing was to be added to service thereafter rendered to an operating carrier, to compute a pension whose whole burden would fall on carriers still functioning.

Furthermore the majority held that even if those unconstitutional features just stated were out of the Act, still the statute was not a regulation of interstate commerce within the meaning of the Constitution. The majority questioned the theory that a man who had "an assurance against future dependency will do his work more cheerfully, and therefore more efficiently. The question at once presents itself whether the fostering of a contented mind on the part of an employee by legislation of this type, is in any just sense a regulation of interstate transportation." The pension system would not affect "fulfillment of the railroad's duty to serve the public in interstate transportation."

Chief Justice Hughes wrote in a dissenting opinion that the gravest aspect of the majority's decision was its denial to the Congress of power to pass any compulsory pension act whatever for railroad employees. With the Chief Justice concurred Justices Brandeis, Stone, and Cardozo.

The New Deal's blackest day in the Supreme Court was May 27, 1935. On that Monday, the Court handed down three decisions, all decidedly unwelcome to the Roosevelt administration. One of these held that President Roosevelt had no power to dismiss a Federal Trade Commissioner during the term for which President Hoover had appointed him.[45] The Federal Trade Commission Act provided that a Commissioner should hold office for seven years, but might be removed by the President for "inefficiency, neglect of duty, or malfeasance in office." President Hoover on December 10, 1931 had appointed Commissioner William E. Humphrey for the seven-year term. On July 25, 1933 President Roosevelt wrote Commissioner Humphrey asking for his resignation, disclaiming any reflection on Mr. Humphrey personally or upon his services, but asserting that the work of the Commission could be carried out better with personnel of President Roosevelt's own selection. Mr. Humphrey declined to resign and on October 7, 1933 the President wrote him a letter notifying him that he was removed. By the spring of 1935 Mr. Humphrey had died, and his executor had brought suit in the United States Court of Claims for salary during the last period of Commissioner Humphrey's life. The Supreme Court unanimously held that the Federal Trade Commission Act permitted the President to remove a Commissioner only for the specific causes enumerated in that Act; and further held that this limitation of the President's power was valid under the Constitution of the United States.[46] In 1927, the Supreme Court had held that a President had unrestrictable power to remove a postmaster, a "purely executive officer," but Congress had created the Federal Trade Commission in order to carry out legislative and judicial powers and "as an agency of the legislative and judicial departments"; a Trade Commissioner was different in character from a postmaster. The Humphrey case, again, had little practical effect on the New Deal. Humphrey was dead, and by the time it was decided, the President was free to appoint in Humphrey's place any Trade Commissioner he saw fit. The Humphrey case was a blow to his pride and independence rather than any practical threat.

Another Black Monday case, decided by the unanimous Supreme Court with an opinion by Mr. Justice Brandeis, held unconstitutional an amendment of June 28, 1934 to the federal Bankruptcy Act.[47] The statute was intended to aid farmers who had mortgaged their farms for amounts now disproportionately large compared to their value. It gave the farmer five years' delay in paying his principal debt, and

[45] *Humphrey's Executor* v. *United States*, 295 U.S. 602.
[46] *Humphrey's Executor* v. *United States*, 295 U.S. 602 (1935).
[47] 48 Stat. at Large 1289.

permitted him then to discharge it by paying what should appear a fair value on an independent appraisal. Mr. Justice Brandeis wrote that only in the legislation here in question had any instance been found of "either a statute or decision compelling the mortgagee to relinquish the property to the mortgagor free of the lien unless the debt was paid in full."[48] This decision was somewhat more painful to the New Deal than the Humphrey case. The farmer is a perennial favorite of legislative attention; mortgagees are rarely popular. The idea was unwelcome that legislation intended to relieve necessitous farmers from unreasonably large land-debts they owed to banks was a violation of the Fifth Amendment. The Court's opinion added that if the public interest required that the property of mortgagees be taken to relieve the necessities of individual mortgage debtors, resort must be had to eminent domain "so that through taxation, the burden of the relief afforded in the public interest must be borne by the public."

The most ominous of the three Black Monday decisions held unconstitutional the National Industrial Recovery Act insofar as it attempted to justify a "code of fair competition" applied to a poultry slaughterhouse and market in Brooklyn, New York.[49] The Act by its terms was to expire on June 16, 1935, two years after its original enactment, so that on May 27, 1935, the statute had less than three weeks of remaining life. Its operation had not been entirely smooth, and perhaps the codes of fair competition had passed their peak of usefulness. But the grounds of the decision were serious for the future of such measures; the death of the Recovery Act threatened the validity of other similar national legislation.

The case involved the Schechter Poultry Corporation and its individual members, who were indicted for violating the Live Poultry Code promulgated under Section 3 of the NIRA. The Code regulated weekly days and hours of work, fixed minimum pay of 50¢ an hour, and forbade employment of workers under 16 years of age. It also regulated merchandising; it required that in selling poultry, buyers purchasing for resale must accept "the run of any half coop, or coops as purchased by slaughterhouse operators, except for culls." The indictment charged the Schechters with eighteen violations of the Live Poultry Code, including infraction of the wage and hour restrictions, and of the requirement that wholesalers not allow retail dealers and butchers any selection of individual chickens taken from particular coops or half coops. Another count charged sale to a butcher of an

[48] *Louisville Joint Stock Land Bank v. Radford*, 295 U.S. 555.
[49] *Schechter Poultry Corporation* and others v. *United States*, 295 U.S. 495 (1935).

unfit chicken; the Schechter prosecution attracted much newspaper attention as "the Sick Chicken case."

The unanimous Supreme Court of the United States held the National Industrial Recovery Act unconstitutional as applied to the Schechters. Chief Justice Hughes delivered the Court's opinion; he found that the Congress, in authorizing the President to promulgate the Code had attempted undue delegation of its legislative power. Furthermore resale of the chickens by the Schechters to their customers in Brooklyn was a local transaction, having only "indirect effect on commerce among the several States," and was beyond the Congress' legislative competence under the Commerce Clause. Mr. Justice Cardozo wrote a concurring opinion stating substantially the same reasoning; Mr. Justice Stone joined with him.

The downfall of the National Industrial Recovery Act was a hard blow to the New Deal. The Blue Eagle and all that it symbolized had provided a colorful diversion in the long drabness of the depression. The letdown was shocking when nine elderly Justices declared that the whole business had been unconstitutional all along, simply because the President had been entrusted with too much discretion, and because merchandising was local, not interstate commerce.

On May 31, four days after the decision came down, President Roosevelt held a press conference at the White House. Two hundred newspapermen were present, with Mrs. Roosevelt, Senator Robinson, the Democratic leader, and Charles Michaelson, publicity agent for the Democratic National Committee. The President went over the NIRA opinion in detail. He said that the decision was more important than any other in the lifetime of anyone present. The Commerce Clause of the Constitution had been written in the horse and buggy days of the eighteenth century when commercial problems were far simpler than those of 1935 and communities were largely self-supporting. Conditions were different now. He said that the issue was whether the country was going to go one way or the other, whether it was going to recognize the right of the federal government to control economic conditions which needed control, or was going to turn back to the State functions of horse and buggy days.[50] His review of the opinion was able but caustic. A President is not apt to enjoy an authoritative statement that he has been exercising unconstitutional power.

Despite this reverse the President continued the battle for federal power over the national economy. The bituminous coal industry of the country was in a sad state, and federal legislation was pending before the Congress designed to bring some order into soft-coal pro-

[50] *New York Times*, June 1, 1935, p. 1, col. 8.

duction, marketing and labor relations. On July 6, 1935, Mr. Roosevelt wrote of this bill to Congressman Hill of the Ways and Means Committee:

> Manifestly, no one is in a position to give assurance that the proposed act will withstand constitutional tests, for the simple fact that you can get not ten but a thousand differing legal opinions on the subject. . . I hope your committee will not permit doubts as to constitutionality, however reasonable, to block the suggested legislation. . .[51]

The Congress stilled any qualms it may have had and passed the Act.[52]

The procession of adverse judgments continued. On December 9, 1935 the Court struck down a part of the Home Owners Loan Act of 1933 as amended in 1934 and 1935.[53] The statute purported to permit a State-chartered banking institution to convert itself into a Federal Savings and Loan Association on a vote of a majority of the shareholders, without regard to opposition by the State banking authorities. Mr. Justice Cardozo, in an opinion for the unanimous Court wrote "In this there is an invasion of the sovereignty or quasi-sovereignty of Wisconsin and an impairment of its public policy, which the state is privileged to redress as a suitor in the courts so long as the Tenth Amendment preserves a field of autonomy against federal encroachment . . . [We] are constrained to the holding that there has been an illegitimate encroachment by the government of the nation upon a domain of activity set apart by the Constitution as the province of the states . . . [We] hold that the conversion of petitioners from state into federal associations is of no effect when voted against the protest of Wisconsin."[54] As was true of several other Supreme Court decisions in 1935 and 1936, the Wisconsin Savings and Loan case was more important as a symbol than as a dispositive judgment. Transmutation of State Savings and Loan Associations into federal associations of the same character was scarcely a key provision of the New Deal program; but on the other hand, the unanimous ruling by the Supreme Court, predicated on the Tenth Amendment, was adversely relevant to the New Deal's general reliance on federal and not State action. The *Hopkins* case had unpleasant echoes of the *Child Labor* and *Child Labor Tax* cases of 1918 and 1922.

[51] S. I. Rosenman, ed., *The Public Papers and Addresses of Franklin Delano Roosevelt* (13 vols.; New York: Random House, 1938–50) IV, pp. 297–298.

[52] Bituminous Coal Conservation Act of 1935, August 30, 1935, 49 Statutes at Large 991.

[53] 48 Stat. at Large 128; 48 Stat. at Large 643; 49 Stat. at L. 297.

[54] *Hopkins Federal Savings and Loan Assn.* v. *Cleary et al.*, 296 U.S. 315, 337, 338, 343.

The second year of the New Deal's judicial disasters began on the sixth of January, 1936 when the Supreme Court held unconstitutional the Agricultural Adjustment Act of 1933.[55] The Court, in an opinion by Mr. Justice Roberts, cast aside the elaborate structure of the statute intended to restore parity of purchasing power to the farmer, and held that the whole arrangement was "a statutory plan to regulate and control agricultural production, a matter beyond the powers delegated to the federal government. The tax, the appropriation of the funds raised, and the direction for their disbursement, are but parts of the plan. They are but means to an unconstitutional end." In this opinion Mr. Justice Roberts caused some wonderment among constitutional students by writing for the Court:

> When an act of Congress is appropriately challenged in the courts as not conforming to the constitutional mandate the judicial branch of the Government has only one duty,—to lay the article of the Constitution which is invoked beside the statute which is challenged and to decide whether the latter squares with the former. All the court does, or can do, is to announce its considered judgment upon the question.

No clause of the Constitution forbade in so many words any of the provisions contained in the Agricultural Adjustment Act. The Court rested its judgment entirely upon the theory that the combination of a tax on processors and benefits to farmers amounted in the aggregate to a control of the amount of crops produced, and that this was beyond the interstate commerce power. It was difficult to apply Mr. Justice Roberts' parallel-column jurisprudence to the Agricultural Adjustment Act. Mr. Justice Stone handed down a dissenting opinion, joined by Justices Brandeis and Cardozo. He wrote that the Congress clearly had power to levy an excise tax upon the processing of agricultural products; he differed with the view of the six prevailing justices that the levy should be held invalid, not because of any want of power in the Congress to lay such a tax, but because of the use of its proceeds to purchase compliance with a plan to restrict agricultural production.[56]

Even this was not the last of the sad procession of cases. On May 18, 1936 the Bituminous Coal Conservation Act, passed in August 1935 at the President's urging, was declared invalid under the federal Due Process and Commerce Clauses.[57]

A majority of the Court in an opinion written by Mr. Justice Sutherland found that the statute, insofar as it attempted to regulate hours

[55] *United States* v. *Butler*, 297 U.S. 62, 68. But see *Wickard* v. *Filburn*, 317 U.S. 111 (1942).

[56] *U.S.* v. *Butler*, 297, U.S. 1, at p. 79.

[57] *Carter* v. *Carter Coal Co.*, 298 U.S. 238 (1936).

and wages in the mining of coal was an attempted federal control of a purely intrâ-state activity, and so was beyond the power entrusted to the Congress.

Furthermore the statute, so Mr. Justice Sutherland and those who concurred with him found, delegated the power to fix the whole industry's maximum hours of labor to only a part of the producers and miners, to producers of more than two thirds of the annual national tonnage for the preceding calendar year, and to a majority of the employed mine workers; by two similar majorities the statute delegated power to fix minimum wages throughout the industry. This, Justice Sutherland found, was legislative delegation of an obnoxious type, which deprived those adversely affected of rights safeguarded by the Fifth Amendment due-process clause. The Bituminous Coal Act also provided price-fixing for the coal when marketed. Mr. Justice Sutherland and the majority of five overrode a "separability clause" in the statute providing that if part of it should be found unconstitutional the rest should not be affected. The majority of the Justices held that despite the "separability clause," the labor provisions found unconstitutional were such a central part of the Act that the price-fixing of coal must also fall. Chief Justice Hughes wrote a separate opinion in which he agreed that mining was not interstate commerce and that the federal government lacked power to regulate the extraction of coal. He also agreed that the attempted congressional delegation of regulatory power was unconstitutionally broad. However, he found that the provisions for fixing coal prices in interstate commerce were within the national power, and that the coal marketing arrangements should be separately upheld. Mr. Justice Cardozo, with whom Justices Brandeis and Stone joined, wrote that the statute's price fixing provisions should be upheld, and that the provisions concerning labor relations were not properly before the Court.[58]

Still the adverse judgments were not finished. On May 25, 1936, a week after the *Carter* decision a statute designed to make available a modified form of bankruptcy to insolvent municipalities was adjudged unconstitutional on the ground that the United States was unduly interfering with State matters.[59] And on June 1, 1936, although the Court had two years before upheld price fixing in the milk industry in New York,[60] it now turned about and held that a New York statute fixing minimum wages for women was a violation of the Fourteenth

[58] See *Carter* v. *Carter Coal Co.*, 298 U.S. 317 for Chief Justice Hughes' opinion, and page 324 for that of Mr. Justice Cardozo.
[59] *Ashton* v. *Cameron County Water Imp. Dist.*, 298 U.S. 513 (1936).
[60] *Nebbia* v. *New York*, 291 U.S. 502 (1934).

Amendment Due Process Clause.[61] Mr. Justice Roberts, who had written the opinion upholding New York milk price-fixing, now without explanation voted with the majority against New York minimum wages. Hughes, Stone, Brandeis, and Cardozo dissented.

This parade of decisions, made while the depression was still severe, raised criticism of the Supreme Court to a high point. People came to feel that the Court, or at least part of it, was intellectually and emotionally sclerotic. Drew Pearson and Robert S. Allen in 1936 published a book entitled *The Nine Old Men* criticizing the Court and its decisions. The book was neither temperate, nor scholarly, nor just to the Justices who struggled with difficult questions; but it was exciting, and above all had a catchy title. A comment of the authors on the Bituminous Coal decision was:

> Right may have been on the side of the miners, but might was on the side of the operators. Five reactionary justices bent on legislative murder count for more than three liberals, regardless how righteous their cause and how irrefutable their logic.[62]

Messrs. Pearson and Allen, however, were not as drastic as a Mr. Louis Goldberg and Miss Eleanore Levenson, who in a book called *Lawless Judges* published in 1935 by the Rand School Press in New York, after a critique of the *National Industrial Recovery Act Case,* wrote (pages 241, 242):

> . . . The recall of judges and judicial decisions must be generally established. People must be aroused to the point of using the recall as one means of protecting themselves against judicial tyranny.
>
> Until the recall of judges and judicial decisions shall become effective, we advocate the impeachment of any judge who deliberately misinterprets a statute or law, and that the process of impeachment be made simpler. . .
>
> We know that it is difficult to strip the ermine from judicial shoulders, but the worshipful attitude of the people towards the courts must be changed through education. . .

The most effective criticism of the Supreme Court was the election of 1936, when an overwhelming majority returned President Roosevelt to the presidency. Three months after this popular vindication, he sent to the Congress a message[63] proposing legislation which, if enacted, would work an immediate change in the complexion of the

---

[61] *Morehead* v. *New York ex rel. Tipaldo,* 298 U.S. 587 (1936).

[62] Drew Pearson and Robert S. Allen, *The Nine Old Men* (Garden City, N. Y.: Doubleday, Doran and Co., 1937) p. 313.

[63] *Congressional Record,* Feb. 5, 1937, vol. 81, p. 877.

Supreme Court, and of the lower federal courts. He mentioned the age of federal judges as a disadvantage in their work and pointed to conflicting constitutional decisions in lower federal courts and delay in getting cases to the Supreme Court as hampering the federal government. He wrote:

> Life tenure of judges, assured by the Constitution, was designed to place the courts beyond temptations or influences which might impair their judgments; it was not intended to create a static judiciary. A constant and systematic addition of younger blood will vitalize the courts and better equip them to recognize and apply the essential concepts of justice in the light of the needs and the facts of an ever-changing world.

With his message the President sent a draft of a bill[64] providing that when any federal judge on life tenure reached the age of seventy, had been in office ten years, and within six months had neither resigned nor retired, the President should appoint an additional judge to the same court. Various limiting clauses were written in the draft, including a provision that the members of the Supreme Court should not exceed fifteen.

This proposal produced a surprisingly hostile reaction, both in and out of Congress. Opponents of the measure called it the "court-packing bill," borrowing a term from the trial bar where "jury-packing" is the intentional introduction of prejudiced jurors into the jury-box. Despite its opinions in the constitutional cases concerning the New Deal, the Supreme Court turned out to be widely revered, and the "packing" proposal appeared to debase it. The American Bar Association Journal for 1937 was largely taken up with articles discussing the plan, and, while some authorities supported it (Professor Thurman Arnold of Yale Law School, to mention only one prominent example), the preponderance of opinion was hostile.

The "court-packing" part of the President's program was never enacted. However, the 1937 Congress did adopt some other useful judicial reforms. Retirement privileges for Supreme Court Justices were provided on March 1st of that year.[65] Another statute, which became a law on August 24, 1937, authorized the Attorney General to intervene in any case involving the constitutionality of an Act of Congress affecting the public interest; authorized a direct appeal to the Supreme Court from any decision of a United States District Court holding an Act of Congress unconstitutional; and required a three-judge District Court in any case where an injunction was sought against enforcement of a federal statute on constitutional grounds;

[64] *Congressional Record*, vol. 81, p. 880; U.S. Law Week Supp. 9 Feb. 1937.
[65] 50 Stat. at Large 24.

the Act, here as well, provided a direct appeal to the Supreme Court.[66] The August 1937, provisions helped ensure that federal legislation would have speedy and thorough judicial consideration.

Some literature on judicial history suggests that although the "court-packing" proposal itself came to nothing legislative, Mr. Justice Roberts, alarmed at the President's message, and concerned for the future of the Court, prudently determined to throw in his judicial lot with Chief Justice Hughes and Associate Justices Brandeis, Stone, and Cardozo, thus converting a four-man minority favorable to the program to a prevailing majority of five, salvaging the New Deal, and leaving as a stubborn rearguard of reaction Justices Butler, Reynolds, Sutherland, and Van Devanter. This legendary version of a "switch in time that saved nine"[67] somewhat oversimplifies a matter that was not really very simple.

For one thing, the division in the Court was not as consistently neat as that theory suggests. The opinions of the Supreme Court in the various cases which had gone counter to the New Deal in 1935 and 1936 had principally rested on two different constitutional theories, both limiting action by the national government; on the Fifth Amendment Due Process Clause, construed to impose on the federal government a vague canon of economic traditionalism; and, much more troublesome, on the limited congressional power to control the nation's economy, constitutionally, restricted to matters which concerned more States than one. The Commerce Clause gave the Congress power to control only "Commerce with foreign Nations, and among the several States, and with the Indian Tribes"; specification of some "commerce" would, on normal canons of construction exclude that commerce not specified. The Agricultural Adjustment Act had been held unconstitutional in January, 1936,[68] by a majority of six, on the ground that production of crops was a local, not an interstate activity. Chief Justice Hughes and Justice Roberts had then joined Justices Butler, McReynolds, Van Devanter, and Sutherland in thus adhering to a view that (one can only guess) to Marshall also would have seemed proper. In the *Carter* bituminous coal mining case[69] decided in May 1936, Chief Justice Hughes had again found the Commerce Clause inadequate to empower Congress to regulate the conditions of mining coal. If the majority of the Supreme Court was to turn about and hold congressional commerce power adequate to regulate such local activi-

---

[66] Judiciary Act of 1937, 50 Stat. 751. The "three-judge Court" rule had obtained for U.S. District Court injunctions against State action since 1913. See 27 Stat. 938; see 28 U.S. Code Sections 2281–2284 inclusive; see also Sec. 2403.

[67] The phrase was a widespread jest of the day.

[68] *United States* v. *Butler*, 297 U.S. 1 (1936).

[69] *Carter* v. *Carter Coal Co.*, 298 U.S. 238 (1936).

ties, two more justices were needed to support Brandeis, Stone and Cardozo; perhaps even these latter three needed persuasive reassurance that making real property into personal property with a pickaxe fell within the constitutional grant of power to regulate commerce among the several States.

What of the idea that the Court-packing bill converted Roberts? The Due Process obstacle in the path of the New Deal had been predictably put out of the way by Roberts' own *Nebbia* opinion in 1934, though doubt was cast on this by the *Morehead case* in 1936 in which Roberts had joined in holding a New York minimum wage law unconstitutional. Before President Roosevelt's overwhelming re-election in the November 1936 elections, Roberts had been one of the Justices who at the conference of the Court in October 1936 had voted in *West Coast Hotel* v. *Parrish*[70] to hear argument on the constitutionality of a Washington statute regulating women's wages. The *Parrish* case had been argued before the Court in December 1936. After the argument, still in December 1936, six weeks before President Roosevelt's court reform message, Roberts and three other Justices had voted at conference to uphold that Washington State legislation despite a due-process challenge. Four Justices voted to hold the State statute unconstitutional. Stone was ill; he returned to duty on February 1, 1937 and in conference of the Court on February 6, voted to uphold the Washington minimum wage act, making a majority of five.

Why did Roberts thus vote to overrule *Morehead* v. *New York* ex. rel. *Tipaldo*,[71] decided such a short time earlier in 1936? Nineteen years later, after Roberts' death, when the constitutional crisis of the New Deal was long over and secrecy of the Court's 1936 conference no longer mattered, Justice Frankfurter in a Law Review article in his honor[72] made public a memorandum Roberts had written, and had delivered to Justice Frankfurter in 1945. Roberts explained that he had considered the constitutional question of wage and hour legislation not properly raised in *Morehead* and for that reason had not voted to uphold the New York statute. Sometimes many years spent as a professor of law—Owen Roberts' early career—make a man sensitive to procedural niceties. At any rate on March 29, 1937, Roberts made one of a majority of five which joined in the judgment publicly announced on that day, sustaining the Washington minimum-wage legislation involved in *West Coast Hotel* v. *Parrish*. Roberts thus adhered to his *Nebbia* position of 1934.[73] His conference votes of October and

[70] 300 U.S. 374 (1937). For *Nebbia* and *Morehead*, see pages 482, 493 above.
[71] 298 U.S. 587 (1936).
[72] Frankfurter, "Mr. Justice Roberts," 104 *U. of Pa. Law Review* 311 (1955).
[73] 291 U.S. 502.

December 1936 in *West Coast Hotel* v. *Parrish*, can not be ascribed to fear engendered by a Presidential message not delivered until February 1937.

Of course *West Coast Hotel* arose under the Fourteenth Amendment due process clause, while the New Deal involved federal legislation challenged under the due process clause of the Fifth Amendment. But surely due process in minimum wage legislation is the same under both due process clauses; when Roberts cast his vote in December 1936, *Adkins* v. *Children's Hospital* of 1923 was as good as overruled.

A more serious problem remained for decision—the extent of power over the economy delegated to the federal government. Granted the elimination of "due process" as a norm of compulsory economic traditionalism, was the national government empowered to prescribe uniform economic revision for the entire nation, or must improvement in the national economy await discrete legislation in the several States? The Supreme Court did not conclusively answer this question in the spring of 1937, though it then gave strong advance prediction of its final answer. Explanation requires a little historical review.

Nearly a third of a century before, in 1905, Holmes had written the Court's opinion sustaining a bill for a Sherman Act injunction, against a group of meat dealers who had combined to raise prices.[74] Beef cattle originated on western cattle ranches; then traveled by rail to great stockyards in Chicago; were there sold; were slaughtered; and as steak went on to consumers' tables in New York or Boston. In this 1905 case, *Swift* v. *United States*, Holmes wrote of "a current of commerce among the States," not interrupted by the incident of a sale from one dealer to another in Chicago, midway on the journey from producer to consumer. In 1921 the Congress passed the Packers and Stockyards Act putting the practices of stockyards and their patrons under control of the Secretary of Agriculture. In 1922 the Supreme Court upheld this statute with an opinion by Chief Justice Taft;[75] he cited the *Swift* case of 1905, and wrote of

> the great central fact that such streams of commerce from one part of the country to another which are ever flowing are in their very essence, the commerce among the States . . .

The Supreme Court would not, Taft wrote, take such a stream out of complete national regulation

> by a nice and technical inquiry into the non-interstate character of some of its necessary incidents and facilities when considered alone and without reference to their association with the movement of which they were an essential but subordinate part.

[74] 196 U.S. 375 (1905). A "Bill" is a formal complaint in an equity suit.
[75] *Stafford* v. *Wallace*, 258 U.S. 495 (1922).

A pause in the Chicago stockyards, sale and purchase there, slaughter and processing, did not divert any part of this current outside of interstate commerce. In 1930 the Congress had used the phrase "current of commerce" to define the scope of its Perishable Agricultural Commodities Act.[76] The concept was well established.

On April 12, 1937, the Supreme Court decided *National Labor Relations Board* v. *Jones & Laughlin Steel Corp.*,[77] upholding national regulation of labor relations in a steel plant in Aliquippa, Pennsylvania. The evidence showed that Jones & Laughlin Corporation owned or controlled mines in Michigan and Minnesota, ore steamships on the Great Lakes, river barges and towboats, and a railroad. By such means of interstate transport, iron ore, limestone and coal flowed to Jones & Laughlin's Pennsylvania plant. Its manufactured products moved on to its warehouses in Chicago, Detroit, Cincinnati, and Memphis. Jones & Laughlin sent semi-finished materials to Long Island City, New York and to New Orleans, Louisiana. Chief Justice Hughes, who had found coal mining, farming and chicken-selling too local for the commerce clause, now wrote the Court's opinion holding that the Jones & Laughlin operation "affected" interstate commerce so directly that labor relations in its Pennsylvania mills came within congressional control. He cited *Stafford* v. *Wallace*,[78] the Packers and Stockyards case of 1922, which had relied on the "current of commerce" concept. None of the previous New Deal statutes had presented a state of facts so closely resembling that in the Stockyards cases. Roberts, Brandeis, Cardozo, and Stone joined Chief Justice Hughes to make a majority of five in favor of the constitutionality of the National Labor Relations Act as applied to the current of ore, limestone and coal which flowed from several States into the Jones & Laughlin plant in Pennsylvania, and which flowed out again to many other States as manufactured steel. The decision purported to follow precedent, not to overturn it. Justices Butler, McReynolds, Sutherland, and Van Devanter dissented.

Justice Van Devanter was 78 years old when the Jones & Laughlin case was decided. He had sat as a Justice since 1911. Not the simple threat of the court reform bill, but perhaps still more effectively passage of years and the President's power to appoint new Justices, seem to account for the evolution of the commerce power between 1937 and 1942. In June 1937, Justice Van Devanter announced his retirement. President Roosevelt appointed in his place Senator Hugo L. Black of Alabama; the new Justice had been a strong supporter of New Deal legislation in the Senate. In January 1938, Justice Sutherland retired

[76] 46 Stat. at Large 531.
[77] 301 U.S. 1.
[78] 258 U.S. 495 (1922).

at the age of 75; the President then appointed Solicitor General Stanley Reed. Here were two reasonably predictable supporters of an expanded commerce power, who with Brandeis, Cardozo, and Stone would make a majority of the Court.

But recruitment is not the whole story; Chief Justice Hughes and Justice Roberts do appear to have modified their views about the commerce power between 1936 and 1939. The Congress in 1938, undeterred by the *Butler* case, passed a new Agricultural Adjustment Act,[79] this time setting up a system of marketing quotas for cotton, wheat, corn, tobacco and rice, subject to approval by referendum of two-thirds of the growers of each. Any farmer who should market more than the Secretary of Agriculture had allotted to his farm, was to pay a heavy penalty. The law put no "direct" restriction on growing crops; the farmer could grow as much as he pleased; he was merely forbidden to sell a surplus when he had grown it! In *Mulford* v. *Smith*,[80] decided in 1939 with an opinion written by Justice Roberts, in which Chief Justice Hughes and five other Justices concurred, the Court upheld this 1938 Agricultural Act, and substantially overruled, *sub silentio, United States* v. *Butler* of two years before, in which Roberts had written the Court's opinion holding the AAA unconstitutional, in which Hughes had concurred.[81] Roberts made no mention in *Mulford* of his 1936 *Butler* opinion or of its underlying theme, the Tenth Amendment. Only Justices Butler and McReynolds were left dissenting. This commerce-clause conversion of Hughes and Roberts need not be ascribed to personal or institutional panic. Persuasion sometimes comes, after a while, from the logic of events. In 1939 few products began and ended their careers within the borders of a single State; and at least as early as 1914[82] the Supreme Court laid down the doctrine that even purely intrastate events come within federal control when they have repercussions on commerce moving between one State and another. Quite evidently a purely local dynamiter who blows up the Interstate Express may incur a federal penalty; and purely local economic interference, by strikes or price cutting or competition by child labor, may also affect commerce among the several States. When the Fathers drafted Article I, Section 8, Clause 3, they provided no good place to stop.

In 1940 the Supreme Court deeply undercut its *Carter* decision of 1936 by *Sunshine Anthracite Coal Co.* v. *Adkins*,[83] in which it upheld

[79] 52 Stat. 31 (1938); and see 7 U.S.C. sec. 1281 (1940).
[80] 307 U.S. 38 (1939).
[81] 297 U.S. 1 (1936).
[82] In the *Shreveport Rate Case*, 234 U.S. 342.
[83] 310 U.S. 381 (1940).

the new Bituminous Coal Act of 1937. To be sure, the new Coal Act covered only prices, not labor conditions, while the Act of 1935 had covered both; but for labor matters the National Labor Relations Act was available for application wider than the precise facts of the *Jones & Laughlin* case;[84] and the Fair Labor Standards Act of 1938 was awaiting constitutional test. By the time of the *Sunshine Coal* decision Mr. Justice Butler had died, and of the old guard only Justice McReynolds still remained to dissent.

On February 3, 1941, the Supreme Court in *United States* v. *Darby Lumber Co.*[85] upheld the Fair Labor Standards Act of 1938, holding constitutional an Act of Congress which regulated hours and wages in the production of goods "for interstate commerce." Of the Child Labor Case of 1918,[86] *Hammer* v. *Dagenhart,* the Court said, ". . . such vitality, as a precedent, as it then had has long since been exhausted. It should be and now is overruled." Mr. Justice McReynolds had retired two days before *Darby* was announced. No one was left to dissent: the eight justices were unanimous.

The Court was rapidly changing its makeup; on June 2, 1941, Chief Justice Hughes also retired; on the following October 6 Associate Justice Stone became Chief Justice in his place; Attorney-General Robert Jackson, who had argued *Sunshine Coal* the year before, was appointed to Stone's old seat, and James F. Byrnes succeeded Justice McReynolds. Of the pre-Roosevelt Court, only Justice Roberts now remained.

The ultimate stage of progress toward complete federal constitutional power over the national economy came on November 9, 1942, when the unanimous Supreme Court, in an opinion by Mr. Justice Jackson, held constitutional the Agricultural Adjustment Act of 1938 as amended in 1941.[87] It imposed a federal penalty on a farmer for producing more wheat on his farm than he was permitted under an acreage allotment prescribed by the Secretary of Agriculture. The Court rejected the farmer's argument that as to wheat grown and consumed on his own farm, the Statute certainly deprived him of constitutional rights. His due-process argument was without merit the Court held; and the Commerce Power covered the production of home-consumed wheat because production, even on a farm where the wheat is consumed, affects interstate commerce in wheat. The more of his needs a farmer produces, the less he has to buy, and, ultimately, the less comes into the State.

[84] 301 U.S. 1 (1937).

[85] 312 U.S. 100.

[86] 247 U.S. 251, discussed at pages 474, 475 above.

[87] 52 Stat. at Large 32; 55 Stat. at L. 203; *Wickard* v. *Filburn,* 317 U.S. 111 (1942).

We believe that a review of the course of decision under the Commerce Clause will make plain, however, that questions of the power of Congress are not to be decided by reference to any formula which would give controlling force to nomenclature such as "production" and "indirect" and foreclose consideration of the actual effects of the activity in question upon interstate commerce.[88]

Not since 1936 has the Supreme Court held any Act of Congress regulating the economy invalid as beyond the Commerce Power, or invalid as denying "economic due process" because it rearranged economic relationships in a non-traditional manner. That Court has ceased to serve as an impediment to economic change. Its present function in protecting "First Amendment rights" is no less striking than that it performed in the mid-1930's. But its intervention affects other interests, held by social groups different from those who, for a while, waged their law over the New Deal.

War

Foreign affairs, in peace and during hostilities, have preoccupied the United States to an increasing extent since 1898; and this complex of national concerns always tends to increase the part played in our federal structure by the central government; and to increase the part in that government played by the President. International negotiation; preparation for war when it is threatening; the conduct of military operations—no one of these is well suited to the publicity of parliamentary debate or the compromises of party management. The presidential role was conspicuous in 1933 when, by an executive agreement made by interchange of notes between President Roosevelt and Maxim Litvinoff, People's Commissar for Foreign Affairs of the U.S.S.R., the United States recognized the Soviet régime in Russia, and Russia transferred to the United States whatever claims she had to the assets in the United States of certain insurance corporations chartered by the pre-1917 Imperial Russian Government. In 1942 the Supreme Court held that this presidential transaction had effectively altered legal rights otherwise within the sole control of the courts of the State of New York.[89]

As the last part of the 1930's passed, the probability became clearer that the United States would become involved in war against Germany. By 1940 we had begun to mobilize our forces, and to give aid, in various ways short of declared war, to England and the other coun-

[88] *Wickard*, p. 120.
[89] *United States* v. *Pink*, 315 U.S. 203 (1942).

tries associated with her. We labored under certain disadvantages
derived from a theory which had earlier been convincing to many men
—a theory that wars were caused by traffickers in arms. To avoid war,
a nation need only prevent trade in weapons. This theme had appeared in various pieces of congressional legislation, and in 1936
emerged in the Supreme Court's opinion in *United States* v. *Curtiss-
Wright Export Corporation.*[90] There the Court upheld an indictment
for conspiracy to sell arms to Bolivia. The Congress by a Joint Resolution[91] approved by President Roosevelt on May 28, 1934, had authorized the President to forbid by proclamation any sale of arms to
countries then engaged in armed conflict in the Chaco area, whenever
he might find that this prohibition would "contribute to the reestab-
lishment of peace. . . ." The Resolution penalized any violator by fine
and imprisonment. The President issued such a proclamation, and
Curtiss-Wright Export and others were indicted thereafter for a violation. The District Court for the Southern District of New York found
the indictment insufficient because the Congress had attempted what
that court found an undue delegation of its powers to the executive
branch. But the Supreme Court reversed this judgment, upheld the
indictment, and the effectiveness of the Presidential proclamation. The
opinion, by Justice Sutherland, stressed the sweeping powers of the
President in foreign affairs, which justified a discretionary delegation
more extensive than might otherwise be allowable.

Attorney-General Robert Jackson used *Curtiss-Wright* in the summer of 1940 to justify, in an opinion given to President Roosevelt, the
exchange with the British Government, made by executive agreement
in which the Senate had no part, of a number of United States Navy
destroyers for naval and air bases in Newfoundland, Bermuda, and in
the Caribbean area. The Attorney-General had another difficulty; he
was faced with a statute of 1917 which made it "unlawful to send out
of" the United States any vessel "built . . . as a vessel of war . . . with
any intent or under any agreement or contract . . . that such vessel
shall be delivered to a belligerent nation," when the United States was
a neutral. Jackson ruled that the clause "with any intent" related to
"built," not to "send out."[92]

In December 1941 the United States ceased to be a neutral, and
the Congress recognized the need for great areas of executive discretion by passage of a series of statutes imposing wide economic controls, administered by the executive branch, and having no relation to
the enumerated powers of Article I, Section 8. The Emergency Price

[90] 299 U.S. 304.
[91] 48 Stat. at Large 811.
[92] 39 Opinions of the Attorney-General 484.

Control Act of 1942 authorized a Price Administrator to fix maximum prices of commodities and maximum rentals for realty, regardless of any interstate-intrâ-state character. The Supreme Court upheld both provisions,[93] and went on to uphold federal rent-control in States, imposed by Act of Congress in 1947, after the shooting had, for a time, ceased.[94] The control was imposed because of the aftermath of the war of 1941–45—not because of the imminent "Cold War" of which the Korean hostilities became a related and decidedly hot phase. In foreign relations, peaceful or hostile, we are a unitary nation.[95]

By the end of the fifteen-year period beginning in 1930 and closing with the armistice of 1945, two imperatives of existence had, then, deeply affected our constitutional ideas. Underlying the detail of the Constitution of 1789 appear the necessity of national unity in foreign relations; and national competence to control the national economy. These same two imperatives were demonstrated anew between 1930 and 1945. Ill-defined fears of too much national power had evoked the Bill of Rights of 1791; vague fears had, perhaps, broadened the Fourteenth Amendment to protect all persons against undefined State tyranny. But those fifteen years demonstrated that the whole economy of the nation was interrelated; and that the American people could not and should not look to the federal judges to protect them against change in the law affecting their property, regulating its use in ways the Congress thought reasonable, and equalizing its acquisition by taxation and distribution. Legislative innovation by States was similarly unleashed.

Granted the withdrawal of the federal judiciary from most restraint on economic change, a gravely troubling question remains. The deeply felt emotions aroused by economic trouble, social readjustment, or international peril, can produce governmental action which affects a set of interests vaguely felt as "human rights" rather than "property rights." Is it possible to devise a constitutional system in which readiness for war is a continuing necessity; in which government controls an incomprehensibly complex economic and social apparatus which houses, clothes, feeds and services nearly two hundred million people; and still, doing all this, is it possible to entrust ultimate decisions to the will of these people or a majority of them; to insure that their decisions will be just, and will protect human values, tolerate individual differences; that this system will produce equality where equal-

[93] *Yakus* v. *United States*, 321 U.S. 414 (1944); *Bowles* v. *Willingham*, 321 U.S. 503 (1944).
[94] *Woods* v. *Miller Co.*, 333 U.S. 138 (1948).
[95] Even as to migratory wild fowl. See e.g. *Missouri* v. *Holland*, 252 U.S. 416 (1920).

ity is just; that government will not be so impersonally monolithic that it crushes; that somehow all this will be defined in a Great Charter enforced by wise guardians of the State, servants of the many but not dominated by the many when the many are cruel? What are the prospects for constitutionalism in America as the twenty-first century approaches?

17. GOVERNMENT FROM REFLECTION AND CHOICE

> . . . the important question, whether societies of men are really capable or not of establishing good government from reflection and choice, or whether they are forever destined to depend for their political constitutions on accident and force.[1]

THIS BOOK undertook a survey of five ideas conspicuous in the history of American constitutionalism—men's freedom, acting through organized majorities, to control their own political and economic fate; aspiration to just government, regardless of majority; equality of men before government despite their inequality of strength and talent; diffusion of governmental power, lest it be too strong for man's individual liberty; and a written compact, stating the essentials of our constitutional system, amendable only by wide consensus, so that hasty and intemperate swings of opinion, by our rulers for the time, may not change the underlying ideals of our polity. Some survey of the state of these matters in our day is meet and right for a summing up.

Majoritarianism in Our Time

Constitutionalism in America, or anywhere else, is complicated by its inherent contradictions. If the concert of most voices is to get what those voices ask, how be sure that what they ask will be just? Just to whom? On what standard of justice? And passing these questions for the moment, one asks what majority? We began our career under the Constitution of 1789, and in many respects we still continue it,

---

[1] 'Publius,' in the New York Independent Journal, October 27, 1787. This first of the *Federalist* papers is generally ascribed to Hamilton.

with a difficult complex of majorities. As to some matters we govern ourselves by discrete majorities in each of the several States; as to other matters we govern the aggregate of States by the majority of voices in the nation, save as the will of this majority may be affected by the equal vote in the national Senate of every State, no matter how small. The matter has been complicated, for many years, by a steady increase in the proportion of our total government conducted from the national capital. Transmission of national majority will to the centers of national power may be more difficult than transmission to local centers. Then, too, not everyone votes, either in national or State elections, even when he might.

Even if everyone were zealous to vote for local, State, and federal officers, our States and national government have for a long time offered no opportunity of equal representation. In this the national Senate, of course, gives the most conspicuous example; by the constitutional compromise of 1787 Rhode Island or Vermont get as many Senators as New York or California. But no similar provision of the national constitution gives any State the constitutional power to allot a greater electoral power to some of her residents than to others. Yet in most of the States residents of some areas have had a substantially greater representation in the national House of Representatives, or in one or the other House of the State legislatures, than have the inhabitants of other parts of the same States. Characteristically in the rural areas, a smaller number of electors could choose a Congressman or a State legislator than was true of urban electors.

In 1946 the Supreme Court considered an appeal from an Illinois federal District Court, in which qualified voters in Illinois Congressional districts had sought to enjoin the appropriate Illinois officials from conducting an election for Congressman from districts laid out by Illinois law, as authorized by Article I, Section 4 of the federal Constitution. Congress had in force no Statute requiring equality of population in congressional districts. The plaintiffs pointed out that in Illinois some rural votes counted nine times as much as urban votes in electing Congressmen; they contended that Illinois denied them, as urban residents, the equal protection of the laws guaranteed by the Fourteenth Amendment. The District Court refused to pass on the matter. It was, that Court held, a non-justiciable controversy, a "political question." The Supreme Court affirmed, though no five Justices agreed in an opinion.[2] Despite this lack of consensus, the Illinois case, *Colgrove* v. *Green,* was generally taken, for sixteen years, to establish the principle that federal courts would not adjudicate questions of

[2] *Colgrove* v. *Green,* 328 U.S. 549 (1946).

federal or State electoral districting. Nor did Congress or many State legislatures intervene. Then in 1962 the Supreme Court created a sensation by deciding in *Baker* v. *Carr*[3] that inequality of representation in Tennessee's General Assembly presented a justiciable issue after all. A large number of such actions immediately arose, in at least 34 States of the Union. In 1963 the Court held that the Georgia "county unit system" as applied to primary elections for U.S. Senator and State-wide State officers, denied under-represented voters equal protection guaranteed by the Fourteenth Amendment.[4] In February 1964 the Supreme Court decided in *Wesberry* v. *Sanders*[5] that Article I § 2 of the federal Constitution, which provides that Representatives in Congress be chosen "by the People of the several States," meant choice as nearly as practicable by giving each man's vote a weight equal another's.

There remained a final unresolved question. In a State with a bicameral legislature, if the lower House was elected by "one man one vote," was it still permissible despite the Equal Protection Clause of the Fourteenth Amendment, to elect the State Senate from territorial areas regardless of equality of population. On June 15, 1964, in *Reynolds* v. *Sims*[6] and a group of companion cases, the Court held that both houses in a State legislature must, under the Fourteenth Amendment, be chosen on an equal population basis. The "federal analogy," the Supreme Court found "inapposite and irrelevant to state legislative districting schemes." Equal representation of States in the national Senate was "conceived out of compromise and concession indispensable to the establishment of our federal republic." That compromise of 1787 was limited to the national Senate; it proclaimed no "pattern or model for . . . seats in state legislatures"; the Northwest Ordinance, adopted in 1787 apportioned seats in the territorial legislature on a guarantee that "The inhabitants of the said territory shall always be entitled to the benefits . . . of a proportionate representation of the people in the legislature."

The Redistricting Cases are numerous; the Supreme Court has only decided a few, thus far, but it has proclaimed the governing principles and shows no signs of retreating from the principle of one-man-one-vote, of election on an equal population basis. A State-wide electoral approval in Colorado of unequal popular representation in the State Senate did not deprive that individual voter of his right under the Equal Protection Clause to cast an equally weighted vote. Here as in

[3] *Baker* v. *Carr*, 369 U.S. 186.
[4] *Gray* v. *Sanders*, 372 U.S. 368.
[5] 376 U.S. 1.
[6] 377 U.S. 533. The case concerned the Alabama Senate.

other great constitutional issues, the principle underlies the Constitutional text. In *Wesberry* v. *Sanders*[7] the Court found the imperative of equal representation in the words of Article I, § 2; in *Reynolds* v. *Sims*[8] the Court found it in the Equal Protection Clause. In all the cases emerges the basic proposition that a majority of the human beings concerned will determine their political and economic fate. "Again, people, not land or trees or pastures, vote."[9]

The results of this profound constitutional change are not as yet clearly perceivable. It probably will transfer more of the governing power, State and national, to the growing urban populations. There will undoubtedly be as much argument over the good or bad features of this change as there were over the extensions of the franchise in England in 1832. The desirability, or the opposite, of the extension depends on the observer's point of view. There will still be those who echo Chancellor Kent's words, spoken to the New York Constitutional Convention of 1821 in protest at eliminating the freehold qualification for electors to the State Senate—

> There is a constant tendency in human society, and the history of every age proves it,—there is a tendency in the poor to covet and share the plunder of the rich; in the debtor to relax or avoid the obligation of contracts; in the majority to tyrannize over the minority and trample down their rights; in the indolent and the profligate, to cast the whole burthens of society upon the industrious and virtuous; and there is a tendency in ambitious and wicked men to inflame these combustible materials. . . .
>
> We are no longer to remain plain and simple republics of farmers, like the New England colonists, or the Dutch settlements on the Hudson. We are fast becoming a great nation, with great commerce, manufactures, population, wealth, luxuries, and with the vices and miseries that they engender.
>
> The growth of the city of New York is enough to startle and awaken those who are pursuing the *ignis fatuus* of universal suffrage. In 1773 it had 21,000 souls; in 1801 it had 60,000 souls; in 1806 it had 76,000 souls; in 1820 it had 123,000 souls.
>
> It is rapidly swelling into the unwieldy population, and with the burdensome pauperism, of a European metropolis. New York is destined to become the future London of America; and in less than a century, that city, with the operation of universal suffrage, and under skilful direction, will govern this state.[10]

[7] 376 U.S. 1 (1964).

[8] 377 U.S. 533 (1964). The Colorado case is *Lucas* v. *Forty-Fourth General Assembly of Colorado*, 377 U.S. 713 (1964).

[9] *Reynolds* v. *Sims*, 377 U.S. 533 at 581. (1964).

[10] Carter and Strong, *Reports of the Proceedings and Debates in the Convention of 1821* (Albany, N.Y.: E. and E. Hosford, 1821) p. 221.

In September 1964, as these words are written, the Congress is debating measures intended to curb or to delay the federal courts' action in political redistricting. Proposals are discussed to amend the Constitution in order to assure to any State the right to have one of its Houses represent territorial units rather than equal groups of voters.

But still, with all these complications, by and large the people of the United States come as close to expressing and achieving their choices in great matters of government as is possible in a complex world. The President, the members of Congress, probably some State officers, maintain secretarial staffs who anxiously tabulate correspondence from constituents on stirring questions. Newspapers, even scurrilous ones, enjoy a considerable immunity from punishment for criticisms of government; and where that government is engaged in the judicial process, criticism, especially when it concerns pending decisions may sometimes tend to destroy the peculiar values of adjudication.[11]

In recent years the Supreme Court under the Fourteenth Amendment due process clause has granted new immunities to organs of collective political protest, and at the same time has thereby demonstrated the increase of federal control over State policies. In some of the once Confederate States, there remain in considerable force two of the same conditions which made national government difficult in reconstruction days—State governing classes who resent federal interference and who are prepared to make ingenious use of constitutional complications to resist federal control; and large numbers of Negroes, descendants of the 1865 freedmen, who are still encumbered by their inheritance of stigmatized centuries. The former have shown remarkable inventive talent in devising plans to obstruct practical enfranchisement of the latter.

Effective political influence requires that men associate themselves in organized groups, a fact which the First Amendment recognizes in "the right of the people peaceably to assemble, and to petition the Government for a redress of grievances." Where a white political organization effectively controls the government of a State or one of its subordinate public entities, how can Negroes make their voices heard in that organization despite the efforts of whites to exclude them? Here there is involved the difference between that which is "public" and that which is "private." Where the State, or one of its officers, is admittedly acting to bar the Negro, the Fourteenth and

---

[11] *Near v. Minnesota*, 283 U.S. 697 (1931); *Times-Mirror Co. v. Superior Court*, 314 U.S. 252 (1941); *Pennekamp v. Florida*, 328 U.S. 3 (1946); *Craig v. Harvey*, 331 U.S. 367 (1947). Cf. *New York Times v. Sullivan*, 376 U.S. 254 (1964), which did not concern criticism of the judicial process.

Fifteenth Amendments come into play,[12] but here, as elsewhere in the American constitutional system, ". . . mere formulation of a relevant Constitutional principle is the beginning of the solution of a problem, not its answer."[13] Some States have persisted in attempting evasion of the Fourteenth and Fifteenth Amendments by statute or other admittedly public action. The Supreme Court had to strike down in 1939, on the ground that it discriminated unfairly under the Fifteenth Amendment, a State statute allowing to Negroes, previously disfranchised, only a twelve-day period in which to apply for registration to vote. Mr. Justice Frankfurter wrote for the Court—

> The Amendment nullifies sophisticated as well as simple-minded modes of discrimination. It hits onerous procedural requirements which effectively handicap exercise of the franchise by the colored race although the abstract right to vote may remain unrestricted as to race.[14]

Other "sophisticated" but unsuccessful plans to exclude Negroes from politics rested on the fact that the Fourteenth and Fifteenth Amendments bar only public action, inhibit only governmental wrongdoing. Neither Amendment forbids purely private discrimination against anybody. If victory in the primaries in a given State meant automatic success in the final election, and if private "political clubs," for whites only, could control selection in the primaries, such private clubs offered a tempting means of evading the Fourteenth and Fifteenth Amendments. The United States Court of Appeals for the Fourth Circuit held in 1949, however, that Negroes were entitled to enrollment in the Democratic Clubs in South Carolina.[15] In Texas a county political association called the Jaybird Democratic Association, or Jaybird Party, was organized in 1889; its members were whites only; it conducted "private" polls of its members; from 1889 to the 1950's, endorsement by a Jaybird pre-primary "private" election turned out almost always to mean victory in the Democratic public primaries, and so in the final election. The Supreme Court of the United States in 1953 held that the Jaybird arrangement denied to Negroes, excluded from membership in the Jaybirds, the political rights secured by the Fifteenth Amendment. The "State action" point proved so

[12] Even if tedious, a reminder may be useful. The Fourteenth Amendment bars only "State" action, which includes action of any State officer, or any officer of any State subordinate governmental entity, a village, or a school district, or any other. The Fifteenth Amendment forbids any abridgement of the right to vote "by the United States or by any State on account of race, color, or previous condition of servitude."

[13] The words quoted are those of Mr. Justice Frankfurter in *Illinois* ex rel. *McCollum* v. *Board of Education*, 333 U.S. 203 (1948) at p. 212.

[14] *Lane* v. *Wilson*, 307 U.S. 268.

[15] *Baskin* v. *Brown*, 174 F.2d 391 (CA 4C).

troublesome that no majority of justices expressed the Court's conclusion in any one opinion,[16] and Justice Minton found that he had to
dissent.

What of a group, clearly non-governmental, which welcomes Negroes and their friends in its ranks, and undertakes to aid them in
asserting their constitutional rights? Such a political mechanism inevitably wakes resentment and arouses resistance of groups in control of certain State governments. If these latter can find at hand
traditional governmental procedures, not overtly related to racial suppression, but applicable in such a way as to break up the pro-Negro
organization, the Supreme Court may find difficulty in formulating its
expressed reasons for intervening in favor of the organization under
attack. The ideal of "neutral principles of constitutional law"[17] is one
aspect of aspiration to equality of men under government. Save as the
three post-Civil War Amendments may have otherwise prescribed, the
same governmental procedures apply, under the Constitution, to organizations favoring the Negro's effective enfranchisement and to those
opposing his political equality.

This dilemma has appeared in a series of cases in the Supreme Court
in which States have attempted to apply against the National Association for the Advancement of Colored People, laws requiring registration of out-of-State corporations, tax-procedures, and laws forbidding
"champerty and maintenance"—forbidding one man to stir up and
support litigation brought by another. An analogous situation arose
when Alabama utilized her laws against libel, ancient laws familiar in
one form or another throughout the civilized world, effectively to end
newspaper criticism of State procedures which Negro people resent.
The legal situation is not unlike that in California in the 1880's when
laws racially neutral in text, in form intended to safeguard the pre-
vention of fires in dangerous buildings, were applied to keep only
Chinamen out of the laundry business.[18]

For many years States have from time to time put in effect a policy

---

[16] *Terry* v. *Adams,* 345 U.S. 461. I again remind any reader who may be unfamiliar with judicial customs that a difference exists between the decision of a case—
a decision in favor of one litigant, against another—and the essay in which one or
more judges express the reasons which led them to vote for this result, or against
that one. Many decisions of the Supreme Court are made without any opinion.
See, e.g., *Ahoyian* v. *Massachusetts Turnpike Authority,* 371 U.S. 286 (1962).

[17] The phrase is Professor Herbert Wechsler's; see his Oliver Wendell Holmes
lecture at Harvard in 1959, 73 *Harv. L. Rev.* 1 (1959) and Wechsler, *Principles,
Politics and Fundamental Law* (Cambridge, Mass.: Harvard University Press,
1961).

[18] See *Yick Wo* v. *Hopkins,* 118 U.S. 356 (1886) in which the Supreme Court
found a violation of the Fourteenth Amendment in this discriminatory application of a textually neutral law, and forbade the discrimination.

that corporations organized elsewhere may not engage in local business, without registering themselves and submitting in various ways to supervision of the State into which they come to operate. On its face such a regulation is eminently reasonable; "foreign" incorporation[19] should not give an outside organization immunity from the regulation applied to local business.

[20] Alabama has a statute similar to those of many other States which requires a foreign corporation, except as exempted, to qualify before doing business by filing its corporate charter with the Secretary of State and designating a place of business and an agent to receive service of process. The statute imposes a fine on a corporation transacting intrastate business before qualifying and provides for criminal prosecution of officers of such a corporation. Ala. Code, 1940, Tit. 10, §§192–198. The National Association for the Advancement of Colored People is a nonprofit membership corporation organized under the laws of New York. Its purposes, fostered on a nationwide basis, are those indicated by its name, and it operates through chartered affiliates which are independent unincorporated associations, with membership therein equivalent to membership in petitioner. The first Alabama affiliates were chartered in 1918. Since that time the aims of the Associations have been advanced through activities of its affiliates, and in 1951 the Association itself opened a regional office in Alabama, at which it employed two supervisory persons and one clerical worker. The Association has never complied with the qualifications statute, from which it considered itself exempt.

In 1956 the Attorney General of Alabama brought an equity suit in the State Circuit Court, Montgomery County, to enjoin the Association from conducting further activities within, and to oust it from, the State. Among other things the bill in equity alleged that the Association had opened a regional office and had organized various affiliates in Alabama; had recruited members and solicited contributions within the State; had given financial support and furnished legal assistance to Negro students seeking admission to the state university; and had supported a Negro boycott of the bus lines in Montgomery to compel the seating of passengers without regard to race. The bill recited that the Association, by continuing to do business in Alabama without complying with the qualification statute, was '. . . causing irreparable injury to the property and civil rights of the residents and citizens of the State of Alabama for which criminal prosecution and civil actions at law afford no adequate relief. . .' On the day the complaint was

[19] In this field the word "foreign" is equivalent to "out-of-State"; it is not limited in its usage to corporations chartered in foreign countries.

[20] This narrative is quoted from the opinion of Mr. Justice Harlan, delivered for the Supreme Court, in *National Association for the Advancement of Colored People* v. *Alabama*, 357 U.S. 449 (1958). For clarity I substitute "The Association" for the expression "petitioner."

filed, the Circuit Court issued *ex parte* an order restraining the Association, *pendente lite*, from engaging in further activities within the State and forbidding it to take any steps to qualify itself to do business therein.

[The Association] . . . moved to dissolve the restraining order. It contended that its activities did not subject it to the qualification requirements of the statute and that in any event what the State sought to accomplish by its suit would violate rights to freedom of speech and assembly guaranteed under the Fourteenth Amendment to the Constitution of the United States. Before the date set for a hearing of this motion, the State moved for the production of a large number of the Association's records and papers, including bank statements, leases, deeds, and records containing the names and addresses of all Alabama 'members' and 'agents' of the Association. It alleged that all such documents were necessary for adequate preparation for the hearing, in view of [the Association's] denial of the conduct of intrastate business within the meaning of the qualification statute. Over [the Association's] objections, the court ordered the production of a substantial part of the requested records, including the membership lists, and postponed the hearing on the restraining order to a date later than the time ordered for production.

Thereafter [the Association] filed its answer to the bill in equity. It admitted its Alabama activities substantially as alleged in the complaint and that it had not qualified to do business in the State. Although still disclaiming the statute's application to it, [the Association] offered to qualify if the bar from qualification made part of the restraining order were lifted, and it submitted with the answer and executed set of the forms required by the statute. However [the Association] did not comply with the production order, and for this failure was adjudged in civil contempt and fined $10,000. The contempt judgment provided that the fine would be subject to reduction or remission if compliance were forthcoming within five days but otherwise would be increased to $100,000.

At the end of the five-day period [the Association] produced substantially all the data called for by the production order except its membership lists, as to which it contended that Alabama could not constitutionally compel disclosure, and moved to modify or vacate the contempt judgment, or stay its execution pending appellate review. This motion was denied. While a similar stay application, which was later denied, was pending before the Supreme Court of Alabama, the Circuit Court made a further order adjudging [the Association] in continuing contempt and increasing the fine already imposed to $100,000. Under Alabama law, . . . the effect of the contempt adjudication was to foreclose [the Association] from obtaining a hearing on the merits of the underlying ouster action, or from taking any steps to dissolve the temporary restraining order which had been issued *ex parte*, until it purged itself of contempt. . .

The State Supreme Court thereafter twice dismissed petitions for certiorari to review this final contempt judgment, the first time, 91 So. 2d 221, for insufficiency of the petition's allegations and the second time on procedural grounds. 265 Ala. 349 . . . [The Supreme Court of the United States] granted certiorari because of the importance of the constitutional questions presented. 353 U.S. 972.

The Supreme Court of the United States held that Alabama had

> . . . fallen short of showing a controlling justification for the deterrent effect on the free enjoyment of the right to associate which disclosure of membership lists is likely to have. Accordingly, the judgment of civil contempt and the $100,000 fine which resulted from [the Association's] refusal to comply with the production order in this respect must fall.[21]

Six years later the Association was still litigating with Alabama. On March 24, 1963, the NAACP was back in the Supreme Court a third time,[22] still contending with Alabama's arguments that the Association's procedural errors in the Alabama State courts precluded those courts from examining the merits of the NAACP's right to associational liberty.[23] At the argument on that day the Chief Justice of the United States announced from the bench that the Supreme Court itself would now pass on those merits.

The questions involved are not entirely simple. In 1928 the Supreme Court upheld a New York law requiring the Ku Klux Klan of that State to disclose its membership;[24] in its 1958 opinion in *NAACP* v. *Alabama*, the Supreme Court distinguished the Ku Klux case from that of the NAACP on the reasonable-enough ground of the demonstrated difference between the two associations. Neutrality of principle does not necessarily require blindness to fact. On June 1, 1964, the unanimous Supreme Court, with a somewhat stern opinion by Mr. Justice Harlan, reversed the Alabama court's judgment and directed it to vacate its decree and to permit the NAACP to qualify to function in Alabama.[25]

[21] *NAACP* v. *Alabama*, 357 U.S. 449 at page 466 (1958).
[22] For the third appearance see the *New York Times* of March 25, 1964, page 21, column 1. The second episode resulted in a *per curiam* reversal of a State judgment. 360 U.S. 240 (1959).
[23] Exhaustion of the Supreme Court's patience with labyrinthine procedures is not limited to the South, nor to racial cases. In 1947 Mr. Justice Rutledge wrote, in a concurring opinion, of the remedies Illinois afforded for a man who contended that he had been unjustly convicted of crime ". . . the Illinois procedural labyrinth is made up entirely of blind alleys, each of which is useful only as a means of convincing the federal courts that the state road which the petitioner has taken was the wrong one." *Marino* v. *Ragen*, 332 U.S. 561 (1947).
[24] *New York ex rel. Bryant* v. *Zimmerman*, 278 U.S. 63.
[25] 377 U.S. 288 (1964).

Taxation is of course the inevitable price paid for civilization;[26] and men who associate themselves together for good causes are not necessarily excused from bearing the municipal burdens of Little Rock and North Little Rock, Arkansas. These two municipalities levied annual license taxes on various businesses, but exempted charities. In 1957 both municipalities adopted ordinances requiring organizations operating in the two communities to disclose certain facts about themselves. Under this authorization each municipality demanded a list of the members of the local NAACP.

[27] [Mrs. Daisy] Bates was the custodian of the records of the local branch of the National Association for the Advancement of Colored People in Little Rock, and [Mrs. Birdie] Williams was the custodian of the records of the North Little Rock branch. These local organizations supplied the two municipalities with all the information required by the ordinances, except that demanded under §2E of each ordinance which would have required disclosure of the names of the organizations' members and contributors. Instead of furnishing the detailed breakdown required by this section of the North Little Rock ordinance [Mrs.] Williams wrote to the City Clerk as follows: . . .

'I am attaching my affidavit as president indicating that we are a Branch of the National Association for the Advancement of Colored People, a New York Corporation.'

'We cannot give you any information with respect to the names and addresses of our members and contributors or any information which may lead to the ascertainment of such information. We base this refusal on the anti-NAACP climate in this state. It is our good faith and belief that the public disclosure of the names of our members and contributors might lead to their harassment, economic reprisals, and even bodily harm. Moreover, even aside from that possibility, we have been advised by our counsel, and we do so believe that the city has no right under the Constitution and laws of the United States, and under the Constitution and laws of the State of Arkansas to demand the names and addresses of our members and contributors. We assert on behalf of the organization and its members the right to contribute to the NAACP and to seek under its aegis to accomplish the aims and purposes herein described free from any restraints or interference from city or state officials. In addition we assert the right of our members and contributors to participate in the activities of the NAACP anonymously, a right which has been recognized as the basic right of every American citizen since the founding of this country. . .'

A substantially identical written statement was submitted on behalf of the Little Rock branch of the Association to the Clerk of that city.

26 The idea was a favorite of Holmes.
27 The narrative is excerpted from the opinion of Stewart, J., written for the Court in *Bates* v. *Little Rock*, 361 U.S. 516 (1960).

In Arkansas State courts, Mrs. Bates and Mrs. Williams were convicted of violating the tax ordinance, and fined $25 each. The Supreme Court of the United States, reversing this conviction in 1960, wrote—

> We conclude that the municipalities have failed to demonstrate a controlling justification for the deterrence of free association which compulsory disclosure of the membership lists would cause. The petitioners cannot be punished for refusing to produce information which the municipalities could not constitutionally require. The judgments cannot stand.[28]

One who stirs up or solicits or promotes other men's lawsuits has for centuries been the object of suppression by law, and since 1849 Virginia has by statute outlawed the solicitation of legal business by "runners" or "cappers," men paid to discover and bring in clients. The National Association for the Advancement of Colored People, and its incorporated Defense Fund, had for some years prior to 1956 been furnishing legal aid to Virginia Negroes seeking by litigation to assert their constitutional rights. In 1956 the Virginia legislature broadened the 1849 statute to cover any agent for an individual or organization which retains a lawyer in an action to which the individual or organization is not a party, and in which it has no money interest. In 1963 the Supreme Court of the United States found that this statute, when applied to the NAACP, deprived it of First Amendment freedoms which the Fourteenth Amendment similarly guarantees against State action.[29]

The recourse of a man who is unjustly defamed is traditionally a suit for libel or slander—an orderly and rational substitute for the challenge to a duel, or for an assault on the defamer. Recently a number of States have discovered, in the use of this time-honored procedure, temporarily effective means of silencing critics. In 1960 the *New York Times* published a paid full-page advertisement headed "Heed Their Rising Voices" setting forth certain grievances of Negroes against government officials in various States, and appealing for contributions to a "Committee to Defend Martin Luther King and the Struggle for Freedom in the South." The advertisement bore the names of sponsors from many parts of the United States, including those of four Alabama Negro clergymen.

The advertisement contained several misstatements of fact. Montgomery, Alabama police had not "ringed" the Alabama State College campus as the advertisement said, though they were, on three occasions, deployed near the campus in large numbers. Dr. King had been

[28] *Bates et al.,* v. *Little Rock,* 361 U.S. 516, 527 (1960).
[29] *NAACP* v. *Button,* 371 U.S. 415 (1963).

arrested not seven times as the published statement said, but four. Students were expelled from college, by the State Board of Education as the advertisement said, but not for singing patriotic songs on the State Capitol steps; they were, in fact, expelled for demanding service at a Montgomery, Alabama, lunch counter. There were other misstatements of similar degree. 394 copies of that issue of the Times reached Alabama; 35 of them came to Montgomery County. Mr. L. B. Sullivan, Commissioner of Public Affairs of Montgomery, and thereby head of the Montgomery police department, brought an action for libel in the Alabama courts, against the New York Times and the four Negro clergymen; he contended that the advertisement untruthfully charged him with dereliction in his police duties. Although Commissioner Sullivan proved no loss of income by reason of the libel, the jury returned a verdict of $500,000 in his favor. The Supreme Court of the United States reversed it.[30] Mr. Justice Brennan wrote in the Court's opinion—

> We hold that the rule of law applied by the Alabama courts is constitutionally deficient for failure to provide the safeguards for freedom of speech and of the press that are required by the First and Fourteenth Amendments in a libel action brought by a public official against critics of his official conduct. We further hold that under the proper safeguards the evidence presented in this case is constitutionally insufficient to support the judgment for respondent . . . [W]e consider this case against the background of a profound national commitment to the principle that debate on public issues should be uninhibited, robust, and wide-open, and that it may well include vehement, caustic, and sometimes unpleasantly sharp attacks on government and public officials. . . The present advertisement, as an expression of grievance and protest on one of the major public issues of our time, would seem clearly to qualify for the constitutional protection. The question is whether it forfeits that protection by the falsity of some of its factual statements and by its alleged defamation of respondent.
>
> Authoritative interpretations of the First Amendment guarantees have consistently refused to recognize an exception for any test of truth, whether administered by judges, juries, or administrative officials— and especially not one that puts the burden of proving truth on the speaker. . . . The constitutional protection does not turn upon "the truth, popularity, or social utility of the ideas and beliefs which are offered." NAACP v. Button, 371 U.S. 415, 344. . . As Madison said, "Some degree of abuse is inseparable from the proper use of every thing; and in no instance is this more true than in that of the press." 4 Elliot's Debates on the Federal Constitution (1876), p. 571. . .
>
> We hold today that the Constitution delimits a State's power to award damages for libel in actions brought by public officials against

[30] *New York Times Company* v. *Sullivan,* 376 U.S. 254 (1964).

critics of their official conduct. Since this is such an action, the rule requiring proof of actual malice is applicable. . .

Applying these standards, we consider that the proof presented to show actual malice lacks the convincing clarity which the constitutional standard demands, and hence that it would not constitutionally sustain the judgment for respondent under the proper rule of law.

During the two decades following the end of the Civil War the Congress enacted a series of Civil Rights Acts, directed to achieving for the Negro that equality before the law which the post-Civil War Amendments contemplated. After 1875 came a hiatus of more than eighty years until 1957, when the Civil Rights Act of the latter year[31] authorized the Attorney General of the United States to institute a civil action to enforce the citizen's right to vote. This measure took the burden of court proceedings from individuals and made available the litigating resources of the United States Department of Justice. In 1960 the Supreme Court upheld the constitutionality of this Act when applied against certain election officials of the State of Georgia.[32] And in 1960 the Congress passed the second Civil Rights Act since 1875, strengthening that of 1957.[33] Political participation by Negroes remains minimal in some areas; federal intervention is slowly tending to increase it.

On July 2, 1964, after a long Senate filibuster had finally been ended by a vote of cloture, the strongest Civil Rights Act since Reconstruction received President Johnson's signature. The Civil Rights Act of 1964 marshals the executive and judicial agencies of the United States to eliminate some of the most acute grievances felt by the American Negro, though the terms of the new statute extend to the benefit of any other group denied equal treatment by reason of race, color, religion, national origin, and also in the case of appropriate employment, by reason of sex. The statute is long; as finally passed, the bill occupied seventy-one printed pages. It contains eleven Titles. The First Title strengthens previous legislation protecting the right to vote, including a provision for a presumption of literacy for voting in a federal election, in favor of everyone with a sixth-grade schooling. The

---

[31] 71 Stat. at Large 637, 42 U.S. Code § 1971.

[32] *United States* v. *Raines*, 362 U.S. 17. The statute was, in its terms, broad enough to apply to non-public interference with voting in non-federal elections. The Supreme Court reversed a District Court (172 F. Supp. 552) which had held that as in such a hypothetical case the statute would exceed federal powers, the statute was unconstitutional even when applied against State action, a situation clearly covered by the Fifteenth Amendment. In so deciding the Supreme Court overruled the 1876 case of *United States* v. *Reese*, 92 U.S. 214.

[33] 74 Stat. at L. 86, 42 U.S. Code § 1974. See for a discussion of the whole political situation of the American Negro, "Voting," the 1st volume of the 1961 Report of the United States Commission on Civil Rights.

Second Title undertakes to reverse the result of the unfortunate Civil Rights Cases of 1883;[34] it gives to all persons equal access to all places of "public accommodation" which affect interstate commerce, or in which discrimination or segregation is supported by State action. This Title covers inns, restaurants, theaters, or other places of entertainment of every sort. Title III strengthens desegregation of public facilities; Title IV reenforces the Supreme Court's decisions desegregating public education. Title V supports the Commission on Civil Rights. Title VI authorizes the withdrawal of federal support from any program or activity which discriminates because of race, color, or national origin. Title VII, again relying on the commerce power, forbids discrimination respecting equal employment opportunity by reason of race, color, religion, sex, or national origin. The statute creates a Commission charged with promoting the policies of Title VII. Title VIII directs the Secretary of Commerce to compile relevant registration and voting statistics: in it is a latent hint at possible future utilization of the hitherto unused second section of the Fourteenth Amendment which reduces a State's representation in the Congress proportionately to the State's denial of federal electoral participation to qualified citizens. Title IX facilitates removal to federal courts of State court actions concerning civil rights. Title X establishes a Community Relations Service to assist "communities and persons therein" in resolving racial problems. Title XI contains various procedural details, particularly concerning contempt of court.

A conspicuous feature of the Civil Rights Act of 1964 is its recurrent provisions for intervention by the Attorney General of the United States in litigation seeking to effectuate civil rights. Hitherto the burden of such court proceedings has mainly rested on such organizations as the National Association for Advancement of Colored People. The United States of America will be an adversary difficult to dislodge.

Full effectuation of the new Act's objectives will take time. One minority group it will aid at once: the members of the federal judiciary, particularly the Justices of the Supreme Court. The Congress, passing this comprehensive measure by large majorities, has expressed popular approval of many judgments of federal courts, often handed down despite bitter and irrational criticism. The Civil Rights Act of

---

[34] 109 U.S. 3. These cases held the Civil Rights Act of 1875 unconstitutional as beyond any power entrusted to Congress by the Fourteenth Amendment, inasmuch as the 1875 statute attempted to forbid racial segregation in inns, theaters and public conveyances which were "privately" operated, and in which segregation was not required by "State action". The Supreme Court, in this 1883 decision found that Congress had not relied on the commerce power, even respecting common carriers; the Court refused any relevant effect to the Thirteenth Amendment.

1964 is a dramatic demonstration that under our Constitution, the judiciary can lead the way.

Aspiration to popular self-government, which at first glance appears a simple matter of allowing every man a vote of equal weight, becomes more complex on closer acquaintance. Limitation of political activity may be necessary to prevent some men getting undue political power—a delicate business for this is political limitation of certain minorities. In the early years of the present century the political influence of some business corporations appeared to be menacing the democratic process, and in 1907 Congress enacted legislation forbidding any national bank or any federally chartered corporation to contribute money to any election campaign, and forbidding any corporation whatever to contribute money to an election campaign for federal office.[35] By Act of June 23, 1947 Congress extended this prohibition to cover labor organizations as well,[36] and in 1957 the Supreme Court upheld an indictment under this Act against the International Union United Automobile, Aircraft and Agricultural Implement Workers of America.[37] As the case had not yet been tried, the majority of the justices found the constitutional question not ripe for adjudication, though Mr. Justice Frankfurter wrote in the Court's opinion—

> . . . what is involved here is the integrity of our electoral process, and not less, the responsibility of the individual citizen for the successful functioning of that process. This case then raises issues not less than basic to a democratic society.

Justice Douglas, with whom joined Chief Justice Warren and Justice Black, dissented from this disposition of the case. He wrote—

> What the Court does today greatly impairs those rights. It sustains an indictment charging no more than the use of union funds for broadcasting television programs that urge and endorse the selection of certain candidates for the Congress of the United States. The opinion of the Court places that advocacy in the setting of corrupt practices. The opinion generates an environment of evil-doing and points to the oppressions and misdeeds that have haunted elections in this country.
>
> Making a speech endorsing a candidate for office does not, however, deserve to be identified with antisocial conduct. Until today political speech has never been considered a crime. The making of a political speech up to now has always been one of the preferred rights protected by the First Amendment.[38]

[35] 34 Stat. at Large 864.
[36] 61 Stat. at Large 136, 159.
[37] *United States* v. *International Union* (UAW-CIO) 352 U.S. 567.
[38] *U.S.* v. *International Union* (UAW-CIO) 352 U.S. 507, at page 594.

An increasing proportion of the population of the United States works for the national, State or local governments. Civil Service legislation guarantees to a large part of the federal executive employees security against dismissal save for cause; the theory of the Civil Service is the development of a corps of able public servants working without partisan diversion of attention, who will serve with equal zeal and security a government whose political control is in the hands of one party or another. The Hatch Act of 1940[39] forbade any employee of the executive branch of the Federal government, with stated exceptions, ". . . to use his official authority or influence for the purpose of interfering with an election or affecting the result thereof" or to ". . . take any active part in political management or in political campaigns." Employees' rights to vote and "to express their opinions on all political subjects and candidates" were explicitly preserved. In 1947 the Supreme Court upheld this statute as it applied to a "roller" in the Philadelphia Mint who was a ward executive committeeman of a political party.[40] Mr. Justice Black, dissenting, pointed out that the Act applied to approximately three million federal employees, and also to all State employees who work for any State agency financed in whole or in part by federal grants or loans. He wrote—

> The right to vote and privately to express an opinion on political matters, important though they be, are but parts of the broad freedoms which our Constitution has provided as the bulwark of our free political institutions. Popular government, to be effective, must permit and encourage much wider political activity by all the people. . .
>
> Legislation which muzzles several million citizens threatens popular government, not only because it injures the individuals muzzled, but also because of its harmful effect on the body politic in depriving it of the political participation and interest of such a large segment of our citizens. Forcing public employees to contribute money and influence can well be proscribed in the interest of "clean politics" and public administration. But I think the Constitution prohibits legislation which prevents millions of citizens from contributing their arguments, complaints, and suggestions to the political debates which are the essence of our democracy; prevents them from engaging in organizational activity to urge others to vote and take an interest in political affairs; bars them from performing the interested citizen's duty of insuring that his and his fellow citizens' votes are counted. Such drastic limitations on the right of all the people to express political action would be inconsistent with the First Amendment's guaranty of freedom on speech, press, assembly, and petition.[41]

[39] 54 Stat. at Large 767.
[40] *United Public Workers of America* v. *Mitchell*, 330 U.S. 75 (1947).
[41] *United Public Workers of America* v. *Mitchell*, 330 U.S. 75 at p. 110.

In the 1950's and 1960's a more difficult problem of theory and practical application has faced the country. If one assumes that a group of citizens of the United States is active in promoting a change in the government of that nation in such a manner as to abolish its democratic values and its independent existence, do the guarantees of political freedom in the Constitution assure to such a group immunity from governmental restraint? This, fundamentally, was the problem before the Congress which passed the Internal Security Act of 1950.[42] This statute while not proscribing the Communist Party of America, did impose on it certain requirements of registration and publicity. In 1961 the Supreme Court, dividing five-to-four, upheld the requirement of registration,[43] though as Mr. Justice Frankfurter, writing for the majority, was careful to point out, the Court's judgment related only to the Party, leaving for decision, as cases may arise, the rights of individual members. These rights could be the privilege against self-incrimination of the Fifth Amendment, or perhaps First Amendment rights of political expression and association. Mr. Justice Black wrote in a dissenting opinion

> I do not believe that it can be too often repeated that the freedoms of speech, press, petition and assembly guaranteed by the First Amendment must be accorded to the ideas we hate or sooner or later they will be denied to the ideas we cherish. The first banning of an association because it advocates hated ideas—whether that association be called a political party or not—marks a fateful moment in the history of a free country. That moment seems to have arrived for this country.[44]

The Communist Party in the United States has posed a dilemma. Our constitutional theory takes for premises not only freedom of political advocacy, but with it majoritarianism, operating in an independent national unit, strong enough to retain the values of that independence in an envious world. What if among us arises an anti-majoritarian group, aspiring to seize power as revolutionaries have always seized power, and to end our independence in the interests of

[42] 64 Stat. at Large 987, 50 U.S. Code § 781 as amended.

[43] *Communist Party of the United States* v. *Subversive Activities Control Board*, 367 U.S. 1 (1961).

[44] Free advocacy of moral concepts widely disparaged is also a Fourteenth Amendment right. In 1959 the Supreme Court reversed a New York suppression of a film version of *Lady Chatterley's Lover*. Mr. Justice Stewart wrote in the Court's opinion, "What New York has done, therefore, is to prevent the exhibition of a motion picture because that picture advocates an idea—that adultery under certain circumstances may be proper behavior. . . . The State, quite simply, has thus struck at the very heart of constitutionally protected liberty. . . ." *Kingsley International Pictures Corp* v. *Regents*, 360 U.S. 684 (1959).

another, covertly hostile power? What if that revolutionary group dresses itself in the disguise of persuasive political activity?[45]

On the other hand suppose that among us a majority becomes persuaded that in today's world neither economic individualism nor our present independent nationalism is still possible. Is that majority not to have its way? And if the advocates of these ideas are now few, are they not entitled to attempt persuasion? Are not majorities always starting as minorities?

One line of cleavage we have devised is the distinction between "force and violence" on the one hand, and peaceful persuasion on the other. Violent revolution is unnecessary because of our constitutional provision for political and economic change: therefore we treat those who demonstrably plan violent revolution, not as politicians, but as those who conspire to commit any other crime of violence. The distinction is satisfyingly simple until one considers the actualities of proof.

In 1948 a Grand Jury in the Southern District of New York indicted twelve men for violating the Smith Act of 1940,[46] in that they wilfully and knowingly conspired to organize, as the Communist Party of the United States, a group of persons "who teach and advocate the overthrow and destruction of the Government of the United States by force and violence," and further conspired "knowingly and willfully to advocate and teach the duty and necessity of overthrowing the Government of the United States by force and violence." After a long trial a jury found eleven of the accused guilty.[47] The United States Court of Appeals for the Second Circuit and the Supreme Court in turn affirmed the conviction.[48]

This *Dennis* case presented the Supreme Court with one of many occasions to apply a formula, first phrased by Justice Holmes' *Schenck*

---

[45] Article 21 of the "Bonn Constitution" of the German Federal Republic provides,

    (1) The political parties participate in the forming of the political will of the people. They may be freely formed. Their internal organization must conform to democratic principles. They must publicly account for the sources of their funds.

    (2) Parties which, by reason of their aims or the behavior of their adherents, seek to impair or destroy the free democratic basic order or to endanger the existence of the Federal Republic of Germany are unconstitutional. The Federal Constitutional Court decides on the question of unconstitutionality.

    (3) Details will be regulated by Federal legislation.

Under this provision the Federal Constitutional Court on August 17, 1956, held the Communist Party unconstitutional. See KPD-Verbotsurteil, 5 Entscheidungen des Bundesverfassungsgerichts 85.

[46] 54 Stat. at Large 670.

[47] The twelfth, old and ill, was not physically fit to stand trial.

[48] *Dennis et al.* v. *United States*, 341 U.S. 494 (1951).

opinion of 1919,[49] for aid in the intellectual process of prescribing the boundary-line between the freedom of advocacy promised by the First Amendment, and the constitutional postulate that as revolution by political persuasion is open to us, its peaceful possibility eliminates the tolerability of incitement to a violent coup d'état. Holmes wrote in the 1919 *Schenck* case—

> The question in every case is whether the words used are used in such circumstances and are of such a nature as to create a clear and present danger that they will bring about the substantive evils that Congress has a right to prevent.

Holmes would have been unlikely to suggest that his "clear and present danger" phrase offered a mechanical device to compute the balance of constitutional values between free advocacy of governmental change, and freedom from conspiratorial revolutionary violence. Both are admirable aspirations of our constitutional régime. The "clear and present danger" formula, offered as a guide in thinking of the comparative evaluation of these two objectives, sometimes inconsistent, only puts the question, does not decide it. For one thing, "clear and present" is a pair of metaphors, and metaphor is a rhetorical device for avoiding precise expression. Clarity and presence are two terms drawn from the sciences of optics and spatial measurement. What is to be decided in a case like *Dennis* is the greater constitutional desirability, in the then circumstances, of applying the aspiration to tolerance of expression, or the aspiration to independent survival, under norms of orderly advocacy prescribed by the national legislature. This choice can not be made by any incantational utterance.

> The decision of a question of importance on grounds of policy is rarely easy. Exercise of judgment is apt to be painful where each alternative has some merit; and men find it natural to seek some clear and impersonal rule to eliminate the harsh necessity of self-reliance in choice. All men tend to look for a philosopher's stone of judgment, for an easier solution, for a resolving formula; and judges, being men, sometimes join in this search. Decorous convention leads us all to reassure ourselves, from time to time, by saying that we are governed by laws and not by men. A little wistfully we sometimes speak of "the law" as though it were a complete existing system, adequate to all human needs—as though it had been written ages ago on great hidden tablets by sages wiser because much older than we are; as though it were still existing somewhere; as though if only we could think aright, we could still find it out.[50]

[49] In *Schenck v. United States*, 249 U.S. 47.
[50] One cites, with appropriate apology, A. E. Sutherland, "Due Process and Disestablishment," 62 *Harv. L. Rev.* 1306, from which the quotation is borrowed.

The Supreme Court, affirming the conviction of the eleven accused in the *Dennis* case, could not muster any five justices to agree on the reasons for affirmance—on the rationale of the statement of account, in the case at Bar, between freedom of expression and freedom from violent revolution. Chief Justice Vinson wrote for himself and Justices Reed, Burton, and Minton—

> In this case we are squarely presented with the application of the "clear and present danger" test, and must decide what that phrase imports. We first note that many of the cases in which this Court has reversed convictions by use of this or similar tests have been based on the fact that the interest which the State was attempting to protect was itself too insubstantial to warrant restriction of speech. [Citations omitted.] Overthrow of the Government by force or violence is certainly a substantial enough interest for the Government to limit speech. Indeed, this is the ultimate value of any society, for if a society cannot protect its very structure from armed internal attack, it must follow that no subordinate value can be protected. If, then, this interest may be protected, the literal problem which is presented is what has been meant by the use of the phrase "clear and present danger" of the utterances bringing about the evil within the power of Congress to punish.
>
> Obviously, the words cannot mean that before the Government may act, it must wait until the *putsch* is about to be executed, the plans have been laid and the signal is awaited. If Government is aware that a group aiming at its overthrow is attempting to indoctrinate its members and to commit them to a course whereby they will strike when the leaders feel the circumstances permit, action by the Government is required. The argument that there is no need for Government to concern itself, for Government is strong, it possesses ample powers to put down a rebellion, it may defeat the revolution with ease needs no answer. For that is not the question. Certainly an attempt to overthrow the Government by force, even though doomed from the outset because of inadequate numbers or power of the revolutionists, is a sufficient evil for Congress to prevent. The damage which such attempts create both physically and politically to a nation makes it impossible to measure the validity in terms of the probability of success, or the immediacy of a successful attempt. In the instant case the trial judge charged the jury that they could not convict unless they found that petitioners intended to overthrow the Government "as speedily as circumstances would permit." This does not mean, and could not properly mean, that they would not strike until there was certainty of success. What was meant was that the revolutionists would strike when they thought the time was ripe. We must therefore reject the contention that success or probability of success is the criterion. . . .

Chief Judge Learned Hand, writing for the majority below, interpreted the phrase as follows: "In each case [courts] must ask whether the gravity of the 'evil', discounted by its improbability, justifies such invasion of free speech as is necessary to avoid the danger." 183 F. 2d at 212. We adopt this statement of the rule. As articulated by Chief Judge Hand, it is as succinct and inclusive as any other we might devise at this time. It takes into consideration those factors which we deem relevant, and relates their significances. More we cannot expect from words.

Likewise, we are in accord with the court below, which affirmed the trial court's finding that the requisite danger existed. The mere fact that from the period 1945 to 1948 petitioners' activities did not result in an attempt to overthrow the Government by force and violence is of course no answer to the fact that there was a group that was ready to make the attempt. The formation by petitioners of such a highly organized conspiracy, with rigidly disciplined members subject to call when the leaders, these petitioners, felt that the time had come for action, coupled with the inflammable nature of world conditions, similar uprisings in other countries, and the touch-and-go nature of our relations with countries with whom petitioners were in the very least ideologically attuned, convince us that their convictions were justified on this score. And this analysis disposes of the contention that a conspiracy to advocate, as distinguished from the advocacy itself, cannot be constitutionally restrained, because it comprises only the preparation. It is the existence of the conspiracy which creates the danger. Cf. Pinkerton v. United States, 328 U.S. 640; Goldman v. United States, 245 U.S. 474; United States v. Rabinowich, 238 U.S. 78. If the ingredients of the reaction are present, we cannot bind the Government to wait until the catalyst is added.

Justices Frankfurter and Jackson wrote separate concurring opinions. Justices Black and Douglas dissented, and Justice Clark took no part.

In 1957 the same difficult problem arose in a slightly different form. In the Southern District of California Oleta O'Connor Yates and others were convicted under the Smith Act for conspiracy similar to that charged in *Dennis*. After the Court of Appeals had affirmed the conviction, the Supreme Court, on the accused's petition for certiorari, agreed to hear the case argued, and reversed the convictions, because the trial judge had failed to instruct the jury (despite requests both by the accused and by the United States) that to convict the accused it must find—

> . . . that the proscribed advocacy was not of a mere abstract doctrine of forcible overthrow, but of action to that end, by the use of language reasonably and ordinarily calculated to incite persons to such action.[51]

[51] *Yates v. United States*, 354 U.S. 298 (1957).

Here, too, is a difficult line of distinction. In 1925 Holmes wrote, dissenting in *Gitlow* v. *New York*[52]

> Every idea is an incitement. It offers itself for belief and if believed it is acted on unless some other belief outweighs it or some failure of energy stifles the movement at its birth. The only difference between the expression of an opinion and an incitement in the narrower sense is the speaker's enthusiasm for the result. Eloquence may set fire to reason.

In the abundant American literature begot by the constitutional controversy over communism[53] one finds much criticism of what is sometimes called the Supreme Court's "balancing test"—much adverse comment, which overlooks the truth that government must always be a balance of interests, made by men entrusted with the power to govern.[54] Surely wisdom suggests that the most one can hope for is judgment arrived at by balancing interests, made by men detached from self-interest, by men conscious of the plural relevances of their choices. To detail all the intricacies of such plural choices by legislature, by executive, by judges, governing under nation and States, would mean no end to the making of many books; at some point this one book must come to its conclusion. To this end,—here one quotes Holmes quoting Lehuërou—"Nous faisons une théorie et non un *spicilège*."[55]

The Unjust Majority

The majority can, in general, have its way. Will anything stop it if that way is "wrong"? Not permanently; but the system of separated

[52] 268 U.S. 652 at p. 673.

[53] See, for much case-material and bibliography, Freund, Sutherland, Howe, and Brown, *Constitutional Law: Cases and other Problems* (2nd ed.; Boston: Little, Brown and Co., 1961) II, pp. 1377–1694. See also the publications of the Fund for the Republic, Inc., *Digest of the Public Record of Communism in the United States,* and *Bibliography on the Communist Problem in the United States,* both published in 1955.

[54] See, for one example among many, the contrast in balancing made in *Sweezy* v. *New Hampshire,* 354 U.S. 234 (1957) and *Uphaus* v. *Wyman,* 360 U.S. 72 (1959).

[55] The words are quoted from Julien Marie Lehuërou, *Histoire des Institutions Carolingiennes* (2 vols.; Paris: Joubert, 1843) I, p. 118. Holmes quotes the last phrase of this apology as a conclusion to the preface of his "Common Law." A commingling of gratitude and common honesty here calls for an acknowledgment. After an hour's leafing through Lehuërou's two volumes had failed to turn up Holmes' quotation, I thought of my omniscient colleague Mark Howe, who immediately told me the page!

powers of the federal government can stop it for a while. When is stopping the majority "just"? One returns to the perennial problem of defining justice.

We no longer define it as departure, by governmental action, from a long-standing inequality between haves and have-nots which becomes unwelcome to a majority. The Supreme Court, since 1936 has represented in the eyes of the American liberal something entirely different from the Supreme Court of the preceding eighteen years. All the justices of the 1932–1936 Court have left the bench. Of the four doctrines of the twenties which gave pain to political and academic critics, three have ceased from troubling. The scope of the commerce power now would satisfy the most enthusiastic Hamiltonian in the New Deal; the Court has upheld federal wage-fixing for elevator operators in an office building.[56] Interstate commerce is now vertical as well as horizontal. So inclusive have the powers of the National Labor Relations Board proved to be, that that body has perforce adopted a set of rules limiting its own undertakings, lest its calendars be littered with a mass of business concerning unionization of corner drugstores and the like.[57] The Supreme Court has held no congressional statute invalid as outside the commerce power since 1936.

Nor, with one possible exception, has the Due Process Clause of the Fifth Amendment restricted any federal economic legislation since 1936. On December 8, 1952, the Court held fatally vague a section of an Act of Congress making it a crime for a factory owner to refuse permission for an official of the Food, Drug, and Cosmetic Administration to enter his premises. And the ground of this decision is significant. Justice Douglas in his opinion compares the section under attack to the laws of Caligula—of whom it is written—

> . . . inasmuch as many offenses were committed through ignorance of the letter of the law, he at last, on the urgent demand of the people, had the law posted up, but in a very narrow place and in excessively small letters, to prevent the making of a copy.[58]

Here it is not easy to say whether the Court is protecting "property rights" or "human rights." Here, perhaps, a troublesome problem of today's Court is exemplified. It is not always easy to choose the liberal side of the case. In a mixture of resignation and frustration, I confess

[56] *Borden Company* v. *Borella*, 325 U.S. 679, 65 Sup. Ct. 1223 (1945). See Richard I. Fricke, "Interstate Commerce: Fair Labor Standards Act: Office Building Maintenance Employees," 31 Corn. L. Quarterly 376, (1946).

[57] See the 23rd Annual Report of NLRB for the fiscal year ending June 30, 1958, p. 8.

[58] Suetonius tells the story in *Lives of the Caesars*, translated by J. C. Rolfe, (Cambridge, Mass.: Harvard University Press, 1944) Book IV, p. 469.

inability to understand, and so inability to explain, the qualitative difference between "human rights" and "property rights." In a classic account of two men in one city, the one rich and the other poor, when the rich man took the poor man's ewe lamb, one senses the chronicler's feeling that a "human right" of the poor man was invaded.[59] In much of today's world the people of countries that lack subsistence would only be irritated by the distinction. When liberal literature expresses protest against judicial protection of "property rights," the protest is really against excess of property, a reaction born of an egalitarian spirit. Then, too, the protest is in part a resentment at misuse of power. One tends to overlook the common origin of governance and property.[60] In the Middle Ages men understood this better than most Americans understand it today; but a sense of it emerged in phrases like "the coal barons" that used to be heard in the days of Theodore Roosevelt, and "economic royalists" that we heard in the 1930's.

During the last quarter-century the Court has been much more severe on State legislation than on Acts of the Congress, but even in State cases it has declared invalid very little economic regulation. It has, instead, intervened to protect interests of personality. The constitutional clause it relies on is that part of the Fourteenth Amendment which forbids any State to deprive any person of life, liberty, or property without due process of law. The Supreme Court has forbidden States to provide prayers, religious instruction of children, or Bible-reading, in public school buildings during school hours,[61] because these conflict with the First Amendment "incorporated" in the Fourteenth. It has forbidden New York to penalize the publication of accounts of "bloodshed, lust, or crime" on the ground that the statute is too vague to enforce,[62] and has forbidden the same State to shut down exhibition of a motion picture film as "sacrilegious."[63] It has struck down restrictions imposed by States on the rights of the Negro to vote,[64] to attend a university,[65] a professional school, a grade school, or to ride on a public conveyance.[66] It has forbidden a State

[59] The story is told in the twelfth chapter of the second Book of Kings.

[60] See A. E. Sutherland "Private Government and Public Property," *The Yale Review*, Spring 1952.

[61] *McCollum* v. *Board of Education*, 333 U.S. 203 (1948); *Engel* v. *Vitale*, 370 U.S. 421 (1962); *Abington Township* v. *Schempp*, 374 U.S. 203 (1963).

[62] *Winters* v. *New York*, 333 U.S. 507 (1948).

[63] *Burstyn* v. *Wilson*, 343 U.S. 495 (1952).

[64] *Smith* v. *Allwright*, 321 U.S. 649 (1944).

[65] *McLaurin* v. *Oklahoma State Regents*, 339 U.S. 637 (1950).

[66] *Sweatt* v. *Painter*, 339 U.S. 629 (1950); *Brown* v. *Board of Education*, 347 U.S. 438 (1954); *Gayle* v. *Browder*, 352 U.S. 903 (1958).

to convict a defendant of serious crime without the advantage of advice of counsel,[67] to extract from a defendant testimony against his will or by use of drugs,[68] and to try a defendant in secret.[69] it has forbidden Illinois to penalize a speech solely because it "stirs the public to anger, invites dispute, brings about a condition of unrest, or creates a disturbance."[70] It has forbidden New York to require a license as a condition of preaching in the streets.[71] On November 24, 1952, it forbade New York to enforce a statute purporting to turn over the temporalities of one warring branch of a Russian church to another branch on the ground that it interfered with the free exercise of religion.[72]

The "human rights" here protected against the States—freedom of expression, freedom of religion, freedom from unreasonable rigor in criminal justice—are all included in the phrase "life, liberty, or property:" "due process of law" guarantees them all. A difficulty with this language is its vagueness. It says nothing about Russian churches, street preachers, or magazines full of bloodshed, lust or crime. The Justices have to find these things buried in "life, liberty, or property"; and they have to discover that whatever the State did, took away these rights without "due process." Some of today's Justices are troubled because their predecessors used these same words under the *ancien régime* to prevent legislatures from insisting that employers exact only reasonable hours of labor and pay reasonably adequate wages.

This ambiguous language of the Fourteenth Amendment has aroused one of the notable differences of theory in the recent Court. Mr. Justice Black remembers the bad old days, and sees them threatening still. He wishes for definition in the language of the Due Process Clause, so that it will not by those words, protect economic selfishness. In 1947 the Court had before it the case of a man named Admiral Dewey Adamson,[73] who was charged with murder in California. In that State, under certain circumstances, a judge and prosecutor was allowed comment on the failure of a defendant to take the

---

[67] *Gibbs* v. *Burke,* 337 U.S. 773 (1949); *Gideon* v. *Wainwright,* 372 U.S. 335 (1963); *Escobedo* v. *Illinois,* 378 U.S. 478 (1964).

[68] *Rochin* v. *California,* 342 U.S. 165 (1952); *Townsend* v. *Sain,* 372 U.S. 293 (1963). See *Escobedo,* footnote 67, for confessions *incommunicado.*

[69] *Re Oliver,* 333 U.S. 257 (1948).

[70] *Terminiello* v. *Chicago,* 337 U.S. 1 (1949).

[71] *Kunz* v. *New York,* 340 U.S. 290 (1951).

[72] *Kedroff* v. *St. Nicholas Cathedral,* 344 U.S. 94 (1952).

[73] *Adamson* v. *California,* 332 U.S. 46 (1947). The holding in the *Adamson* case was overruled on June 15, 1964, in *Malloy* v. *Hogan,* 378 U.S. 1; Mr. Justice Brennan, wrote for the Court, "We hold today that the Fifth Amendment's exception from compulsory self-incrimination is also protected by the Fourteenth Amendment against the States." And see *Escobedo,* 378 U.S. 478 (1964).

witness stand and explain the evidence against him; and Adamson was convicted after such proceedings. The Court upheld this statute; but in a dissent Mr. Justice Black protested against what he described as:

> a constitutional theory . . . that this Court is endowed by the Constitution with boundless power under "natural law" periodically to expand and contract constitutional standards, to conform to the Court's conception of what at a particular time constitutes "civilized decency" and "fundamental liberty and justice."

He went on to say that the Fourteenth Amendment had been intended to effect a sort of shorthand incorporation by reference of all the prohibitions against federal action contained in the Bill of Rights—no more and no less—including freedom from the sort of compulsory self-incrimination California used on Adamson. In this way, he thought, all the freedoms of the first eight amendments would be available against the States as well as the federal government, and yet the danger of economic vetoes would be eliminated.

There are two theoretical difficulties with this reasoning of Mr. Justice Black. One is the unclear historical evidence available to demonstrate the intention he ascribes to those who adopted the Fourteenth Amendment.[74] The other objection is that the language of much of the Bill of Rights is ill adapted to restrictions on the States; and as the Fifth Amendment itself contains a clause prohibiting deprivations of "life, liberty, or property without due process of law," Mr. Justice Black in getting rid of one ambiguity would incorporate by reference its identical twin.

On the other hand, the alternative is not simple.

On January 2, 1952, Mr. Justice Frankfurter expressed himself forcibly about the Black theory of incorporation by reference.[75] He said, among other things:

> . . . In dealing not with the machinery of government but with human rights, the absence of formal exactitude, or want of fixity of meaning, is not an unusual or even regrettable attribute of constitutional provisions. Words being symbols do not speak without a gloss. On the one hand the gloss may be the deposit of history, whereby a term gains technical content . . . On the other hand, the gloss of some of the verbal symbols of the Constitution does not give them a fixed technical content. It exacts a continuing process of application.
>
> When the gloss has thus not been fixed but is a function of the process of judgment, the judgment is bound to fall differently at different times and differently at the same time through different judges. . . .

[74] See Charles Fairman and Stanley Morrison, "Does the Fourteenth Amendment Incorporate the Bill of Rights?" 2. *Stan. L. Rev.* 5 (1949).

[75] *Rochin* v. *People of California,* 342 U.S. 165, 169 (1952).

The vague contours of the Due Process Clause do not leave judges at large. We may not draw on our merely personal and private notions and disregard the limits that bind judges in their judicial function. Even though the concept of due process of law is not final and fixed, these limits are derived from considerations that are fused in the whole nature of our judicial process. . . .

Due process of law thus conceived is not to be derided as a resort to a revival of "natural law." To believe that this judicial exercise of judgment could be avoided by freezing "due process of law" at some fixed stage of time or thought is to suggest that the most important aspect of constitutional adjudication is a function for inanimate machines and not for judges. . . .

Mr. Justice Black views this looseness with alarm. He answers Mr. Justice Frankfurter in a special concurring opinion in *Rochin*:

. . . There is, however, no express constitutional language granting judicial power to invalidate *every* state law or *every* kind deemed "unreasonable" or contrary to the Court's notion of civilized decencies; yet the constitutional philosophy used by the majority has, in the past, been used to deny a state the right to fix the price of gasoline, Williams v. Standard Oil Co., 278 U.S. 235; and even the right to prevent bakers from palming off smaller for larger loaves of bread, Jay Burns Baking Co. v. Bryan, 264 U.S. 504. These cases, and others, show the extent to which the evanescent standards of the majority's philosophy have been used to nullify state legislative programs passed to suppress evil economic practices. What paralyzing role this same philosophy will play in the future of economic affairs of this country is impossible to predict.

The Black-Frankfurter difference of theory goes to the heart of the problem facing one who contemplates constitutional government in the United States today. The majority is entitled to have its way. But what if the majority is wrong? By what criterion shall right be determined if not by fifty-one percent of the votes? By the Constitution? What words in it? In what narrow place is this Constitution posted up? In what small letters is it written?

The possibility of majority error poses a problem not limited to our own time nor to our own country, nor to constitutional law. For centuries men have tried to devise a form of words which will so describe error as to make it recognizable. Defined in religious terms, as a violation of the law of nature for which another name is the will of God, it becomes philosophically neat. Says John Locke:

Thus the law of nature stands as an eternal rule to all men, legislators as well as others. The rules that they make for other men's actions must, as well as their own, and other men's actions be conformable to the law of nature, i.e. to the will of God, of which that is a declaration, and the fundamental law of nature being the preservation of mankind, no human sanction can be good or valid against it.[76]

This satisfies the need of a pamphleteer who seeks to justify a glorious, and of course successful, revolution better than it does the need of a judge who is asked by a litigant to disregard a statute. Despite the respect which a beneficiary of the Declaration of Independence owes to the Laws of Nature and of Nature's God, he must concede that these have never been codified sufficiently to serve as practical criteria of constitutionality.

Can France of the Enlightenment offer any more definite guide? Rousseau, over two centuries ago, saw men joining in a social compact to form a nation governed by what he called the "general will," which by his definition is always right and tends always to the public benefit. Granted only a well-informed citizenry and no communication among citizens (says the displaced Genevese), what small errors might arise in this or that man would cancel themselves out; the result of popular deliberation would then always be good.[77] But the misguided people will persist in talking to one another; they are incurable joiners. Parties, associations grow up; by and by one group grows so powerful that it carries the day over all the others. The result, unhappily, is no longer the general will.[78] Dwellers in big cities are peculiarly subject to being thus led astray. An adroit rogue, a sly talker, can get his way with the people of Paris or London when the Bernese or Genevese, more rustic and therefore less gullible, would run him out of town.[79]

Majorities, that is to say, can err like monarchs. Fifty-one percent of the populace, expressing their will through fifty-one percent of the legislators, still may not achieve Rousseau's ideal volonté générale— this built-in correctness of mankind-if-it-doesn't-make-mistakes. Such an enviable posture of affairs is, one gathers, achieved only by a citizenry which, having first renounced life in great cities, then

[76] *An Essay Concerning the True Original, Extent, and End of Civil-Government,* Ch. XI, p. 135.

[77] *Contrat Social,* Book 2, Ch. 3, "Si, quand le peuple suffisamment informé délibère, les Citoyens n'avaient aucune communication entre eux, du grand nombre de petites différences résulterait toujours la volonté générale, et la délibération seroit toujours bonne."

[78] Book 2, Ch. 3, "Si la Volonté Générale Peut Errer." Madison in the Federalist No. 10 repeats this idea in terms suggestive of Rousseau's.

[79] Book IV, Ch. 1. Notwithstanding Rousseau, rural demagoguery can exist.

deliberates on public affairs with adequate information but without communication between citizens. Lacking these essential and somewhat infrequent conditions for automatic freedom from majoritarian error, the United States has turned to the Supreme Court and Due Process of Law.

Holmes in 1905[80] tried his hand (and a skilled one it was) at defining the sort of majority mistakes which are so bad as to make a State statute invalid. "I think," he wrote, "that the word liberty in the Fourteenth Amendment is perverted when it is held to prevent the natural outcome of a dominant opinion, unless it can be said that a rational and fair man necessarily would admit that the statute proposed would infringe fundamental principles as they have been understood by the traditions of our people and our law." Habit, then, has something to do with rightness. The "traditions of our people" must not too intemperately be offended by a transient majority. Rightness has some connotations of national history.

Justice Frankfurter has followed his great precursor in stating criteria of that which is rightful. It can be tested, he has said, by "that feeling of just treatment which has been evolved through centuries of Anglo-American constitutional history and civilization,"[81] and "the notions of justice of English-speaking peoples"[82] (though one Justice in 1952 expressed "doubt as to why we should consider only the notions of English-speaking peoples to determine what are immutable and fundamental principles of justice").[83] And traditions cannot of course become so fixed as to prevent change. Habit cannot deprive the States of opportunity for reforms in legal process. "Law must be stable and yet it cannot stand still."[84] Whoever has sympathetically followed the struggles of men to describe rightness in a phrase must have become convinced of the impossibility of the task. The jesting Pilate was wise not to stay for an answer. Before he found out what truth was, he would have had a long wait.

Still, whatever may be the theoretical difficulties of definition or of "incorporation," the Supreme Court is proceeding rapidly toward requiring the States to grant all the "human rights" enumerated in the First Amendment. This was a presupposition of the opinions an-

---

[80] Dissenting in *Lochner* v. *New York*, 198 U.S. 45, 76 (1905).

[81] Frankfurter, J., in *Joint Anti-Fascist Refugee Committee* v. *McGrath*, 341 U.S. 123, 162 (1951).

[82] Frankfurter, J., in *Malinski* v. *New York*, 324 U.S. 401, 417 (1945).

[83] Black, J., concurring in *Rochin* v. *California*, 342 U.S. 165, 176 (1952).

[84] Pound, *Interpretations of Legal History* (Cambridge: Cambridge University Press, 1923) p. 1.

nouncing judicial proscription of a "non-denominational" prayer in New York.[85] The search-and-seizure provision of the Fourth Amendment was applied to the States in two successive steps—in the *Wolf* case in 1949, and the *Mapp* case in 1961.[86] The guarantee against self-incrimination of the Fifth Amendment was *literatim* applied against the States on June 15, 1964.[87] The Fourteenth Amendment includes the substance of the Fifth Amendment's eminent domain clause.[88] The Sixth Amendment's right to counsel was established for defendants in State courts in 1963;[89] the present most acute question of right to counsel concerns the period of police interrogation. On June 22, 1964, the Supreme Court held that where Illinois police and a prosecuting attorney obtained from a suspect admissions incriminatory of murder, during interrogation from which the officials barred the suspect's retained counsel, and where the officials gave the suspect no explicit advice of his constitutional right to remain silent, the admissions so obtained could not constitutionally be used against the accused.[90] One may perhaps assume that the prohibition of cruel and unusual federal punishments, contained in the Eighth Amendment, would similarly apply to the States.[91] One sees no signs of an indiscriminate "incorporation" for the whole Bill of Rights; the Seventh Amendment's guarantee of a jury in any civil case where more than twenty dollars is at stake, is a customary *reductio ad absurdum* in discussion of the matter. But in any situation arousing a "sense of injustice"[92] the Supreme Court is moving State standards of justice toward those of the United States.

This is not occurring without stresses. The Supreme Court, in 1964 as in other years, has been the target of bitter criticism; it has been

---

[85] *Engel* v. *Vitale*, 370 U.S. 421 (1962), discussed in A. E. Sutherland, "Establishment According to Engel," 76 Harv. L. Rev. 25 (1962).

[86] *Wolf* v. *Colorado*, 338 U.S. 25; *Mapp* v. *Ohio*, 367 U.S. 643.

[87] *Malloy* v. *Hogan*, 378 U.S. 1.

[88] This is a presupposition of reexamination, under the federal constitution, of the reasonableness of State rate regulation. See *Chicago, M. & St. P. Ry. Co.* v. *Minnesota*, (the Minnesota Rate case) 134 U.S. 418 (1890); and see Hough, "Due Process of Law—Today," 32 Harv. L. Rev. 218 (1919).

[89] *Gideon* v. *Wainwright*, 372 U.S. 335 (1963).

[90] *Escobedo* v. *Illinois*, 378 U.S. 478.

[91] This was a presupposition of a dissenting opinion of Justice Goldberg, in which Justices Douglas and Brenner joined, delivered October 21, 1963, protesting against the Court's refusal to grant certiorari to reexamine the constitutionality of the State-imposed death penalty for rape. *Rudolph* v. *Alabama*, 375 U.S. 889.

[92] The phrase is Edmund Cahn's. See his book of that title, which makes an attempt to define the difference between the just and the unjust. And see A. E. Sutherland, *The Law and One Man Among Many* (Madison: University of Wisconsin Press, 1956).

charged with encouraging criminality by coddling criminals, thereby neglecting the public interest. The wisdom of judicial insulation by life tenure is apparent.

"... [C]reated equal"

In some respects most of the United States agrees on one point of rightness—that government is wrong when it discriminates against a man on the ground of his race. In our day the third of the underlying principles considered in this book is here most dramatically demonstrated.

The history of the American movement toward equality between negro and white would fill many books, and has.[93] The principal constitutional problems are two; how far do the three post-Civil War Amendments inhibit State action which tends to disparage the descendants of the freedom of 1865; and how far does the Constitution empower the national government to legislate in aid of the Negro against private action which also tends to disparage him. The most dramatic race-relations cases in the last decade were those involving segregation in public grade-schools. State public-school cases which arose in Kansas, Delaware, Virginia, and South Carolina, decided by the Supreme Court May 17, 1954, are known collectively as *Brown* v. *Board of Education.*[94] While that unanimous school opinion, was only then the latest of a series of decisions, reaching back to the 1930's, holding various State governmental moves invalid because unfair to Negroes[95] it shocked States which had taken segregated education for granted. It rejected the concept of "equal but separate" which the Court, in the 1896 case of *Plessy* v. *Ferguson,*[96] had made part of its constitutional doctrine—the doctrine that a State accorded the equal protection of the laws guaranteed by the Fourteenth Amendment if it provided equal facilities for Negro and white, even if it commanded that the two races stay separate. "Separate educational facilities are inherently unequal," the Court said, citing psychological experts who found that the Negro child did less well in a segregated school. In the State cases the Court found no

---

[93] A publication which currently collects and reduces to order the great mass of relevant material is the *Race Relations Law Reporter,* edited by Vanderbilt Law School, published quarterly by Southern Education Reporting Service. Gunnar Myrdal's *American Dilemma* (New York: Harper and Row, 1944) is now the classical reference for background.

[94] 347 U.S. 483 (1955).

[95] The *Brown* opinion summarizes the series.

[96] 163 U.S. 537.

need to examine the Fourteenth Amendment due process clause. A companion case, *Bolling* v. *Sharpe*,[97] held unconstitutional the Acts of Congress providing for segregated schools in the District of Columbia. There is no equal protection clause applicable to the federal government; the unanimous Court joined in Chief Justice Warren's opinion finding that segregation in public grade-schools denied the Negro child due process of law.

> Although the Court has not assumed to define "liberty" with any great precision, that term is not confined to mere freedom from bodily restraint. Liberty under law extends to the full range of conduct which the individual is free to pursue, and it cannot be restricted except for a proper governmental objective. Segregation in public education is not reasonably related to any proper governmental objective, and thus it imposes on Negro children of the District of Columbia a burden that constitutes an arbitrary deprivation of their liberty in violation of the Due Process Clause.

While the District of Columbia schools by direction of President Eisenhower at once obeyed the Court's decision, State compliance has come more slowly. On May 31, 1955 the Court handed down a supplemental opinion as to the decree to be entered.[98] It provided for remand to the lower federal and State courts in which the respective actions had been brought, in order that they might devise the appropriate decrees to procure admission to the affected schools; the Supreme Court used an ancient phrase in chancery matters, "with all deliberate speed."

Resistance to desegregation has continued in many areas; on March 4, 1964, a U.S. District Court in Mississippi entered the first school desegregation order in that State,[99] by September, 1964 at least "token desegregation" had taken place in every State of the Union. On March 30, 1964 the Supreme Court heard yet another appeal in one of the

[97] 347 U.S. 497 (1954).
[98] A word of explanation may be useful for the non-professional reader. One must distinguish three different actions of a court. It renders a *decision*; that is, it announces in a sentence or two the prevailing party in the litigation. "Judgment for the defendant"; or "the judgment of the lower court is reversed," or whatever it may be. A court sometimes explains that decision, sometimes does not, in an essay on the law of the case, called an *opinion*. The Reports of the Supreme and other courts consist of these opinions, which may run to a hundred or more pages in length and consist of elaborately documented historical or political-theoretical papers. Finally a court, often after considerable time issues a *decree* or *judgment*. This is a comparatively brief document, not citing authority or reasoning as does an opinion, but telling the affected party precisely what he is required to do—to pay so many dollars to so-and-so, or to perform a specified act, or refrain from doing a specific thing.
[99] See *Southern School News*, Vol. 10, No. 9, March 1964.

original cases reported under the title of *Brown* v. *Board of Education.* This one concerned Prince Edward County, Virginia, which had closed all its public schools to attempt to avoid the *Brown* decree. Counsel for Prince Edward County school children contended in the argument on March 30 that when that County abandoned public education, the State of Virginia, of which Prince Edward County is an organ, had denied to the school children of that County protection of its laws equal to that granted to children in Counties better favored educationally. On May 25, 1964, the Supreme Court decided in favor of the plaintiff school children.[99a]

The new Civil Rights Act[100] of July 2, 1964, by its Title IV authorizes the Attorney General of the United States to institute legal proceedings to achieve desegregation on behalf of parents of minor children who are barred from a public school because of its failure to desegregate. This provision, if vigorously enforced, can remove from individual litigants, or from such private supporting agencies as the NAACP, much of the present burden of conducting the long litigation required to attain a measure of that equality which the Fourteenth Amendment promised 96 years ago. And the passage of Title IV, after more than ten years, puts a Congressional stamp of approval on the Supreme Court's desegregation decisions of May 17, 1954.

Meantime the principle of the school segregation cases has been applied to other problems of racial segregation. The Court has required the States to afford equal access to all publicly maintained institutions—to schools, to parks, to public transportation, and to establishments leased by states to private tenants.[101] As in the case of public schools, the Congress has expressed its concurrence in the Supreme Court's action by passing Title III, "Desegregation of Public Facilities," as part of the Civil Rights Act of 1964.

Perhaps the most puzzling problems under the Equal Protection Clause arise in cases of restaurants and similar non-governmental institutions which refuse to serve Negroes. Where the public authority supports the private discrimination the Supreme Court has held that support unconstitutional.[102] The Court has, on this theory, recently reversed State court convictions for "trespass" by sit-in protesters—persons who insist on service in segregated restaurants despite racially

---

[99a] *Griffin* v. *County School Board of Prince Edward County,* 377 U.S. 218 (1964).

[100] Public Law 88–352, 78 Stat. at p. 241.

[101] See for examples *Gayle* v. *Browder,* 352 U.S. 903 (1956); *Burton* v. *Wilmington Parking Authority,* 365 U.S. 715 (1961) and *Turner* v. *Memphis,* 369 U.S. 350 (1962).

[102] *Shelley* v. *Kraemer,* 334 U.S. 1 (1948).

prompted objection by the proprietor, who then calls the local police. And the Congress, to the extent the Commerce Clause authorizes it, has given its support to the Supreme Court by the "Public Accommodations" provisions, Title II, of the Civil Rights Act of 1964.[103]

One can think of the Church-State question as one of equality. For centuries in Europe and in America one governmental regime or another sought to dominate the religion of its people; or this Church or that sought to control a government. The Protestant was in hazardous subordination in Mary's England; the Catholic ran risks in the England of Elizabeth. Congregational Massachusetts banished heretical Roger Williams to Narragansett Bay, and, for her persistent Quakerism, hanged Mary Dyer on Boston Common.

The first words of the First Amendment of 1791 forbade the Congress to make any ". . . law respecting an establishment of religion, or prohibiting the free exercise thereof. . . ." The newly established central government of the United States was not to force a favored federal religion on the various States which had vestigial establishments of their own. As the nineteenth century went on, men saw the impossibility of equal State favor to all religions. Inevitably one or another seemed, to rival sectaries, to get more than its share of public favor. Gradually, as we moved into the twentieth century, a theory gained more and more acceptance that while governmental facilities of a lay sort—justice, transport, schools, hospitals—must be available equally to all sects, on the other hand fairness to adherents of all sects, and to those who belonged to none, could only be achieved by complete abstention from any governmental participation in religious activity.

This doctrine has proved difficult to apply. Lay and religious matters have been intermingled for so many centuries that complete dissociation is now unworkable. We send armies of our young men to war; can we send no Chaplains with them? What of the teaching of history to students in public high schools? Do we maintain neutral silence about Henry the Eighth? The Council of Trent? Do we permit public transport to parochial schools? Inspectoral accreditation of parochial schools for compulsory education?

Before the adoption of the Fourteenth Amendment in 1868, there had been no federal limitation on a State's establishment of religion, or on hardship which might be imposed by a State on persons because

---

[103] See, for example, for sit-in cases *Peterson* v. *Greenville*, 373 U.S. 244 (1963); *Bell* v. *Maryland*, 378 U.S. 226 (1964). The Supreme Court on December 14, 1964, held Title II constitutional. *Heart of Atlanta Motel* v. *U.S.*, 85 Sup. Ct. 348; *Hamm* v. *Rock Hill*, 85 Sup. Ct. 384; *Katzenbach* v. *McClung*, 85 Sup. Ct. 377.

of religious affiliation.[104] Until 1833 Massachusetts still supported a Protestant religion by public taxation; absence from church was a Massachusetts crime until 1836.[105] In 1845 the Supreme Court of the United States held that the federal constitution was no bar to an ordinance of Municipality No. 1 of the City of New Orleans which penalized by fine any priest who should celebrate a funeral in any of the Catholic churches of that municipality. The ordinance confined such funeral activities to an obituary chapel on Rampart Street. Mr. Justice Catron wrote for the Court:

> The Constitution makes no provision for protecting the citizens of the respective states in their religious liberties; this is left to the state constitutions and laws: nor is there any inhibition imposed by the Constitution of the United States in this respect on the states.[106]

A man newly come from a far country, reading the words of the Fourteenth Amendment, without knowledge of its judicial history since adoption in 1868, might be surprised to learn of its effect on the constitutional law of church-state relations. He would find in it no mention of religion, no expressed intent to incorporate by reference the terms of the first amendment, would find only general prohibitions against a state's depriving citizens of unspecified federal privileges, and against depriving any person of life, liberty or property without due process, or denying equal protection of the laws.[107] The privileges and immunities clause of the Fourteenth Amendment, he would learn, has had but little effective force since the *Slaughter-House Cases* of 1873.[108] The only additions to the Constitution, in 1868, which might bear upon a religious "establishment" in a state school must be the due process and equal protection clauses; the new inquirer would perhaps be a bit puzzled to hear these provisions used for anything but protection of the individual against undue state oppression.

The judicial history of the Fourteenth Amendment, insofar as it concerns religion and public schools, begins only with *Cochran* v.

---

[104] To the Harvard Law Review I am greatly indebted for their generous permission here to use parts of my piece "Establishment According to Engel," 76 *Harv. L. Rev.* 25 (1962).

[105] Mass. Acts & Resolves 1782–83, ch. 23, at 65 (1782), as amended by Mass. Acts & Resolves 1790–91, ch. 58, at 353 (1791), repealed by Mass. Laws 1834–36, ch. VII, at 593 (1836).

[106] *Permoli* v. *Municipality No. 1*, 44 U.S. (3 How.) 589, 609 (1845).

[107] "No State shall make or enforce any law which shall abridge the privileges or immunities of citizens of the United States; nor shall any State deprive any person of life, liberty, or property, without due process of law; nor deny to any person within its jurisdiction the equal protection of the laws."

[108] 83 U.S. (16 Wall.) 36 (1873).

Louisiana State Board of Education in 1930.[109] This was a taxpayer's suit, brought to restrain any State official from expending any part of a "severance tax fund" to supply free schoolbooks to the schoolchildren of Louisiana. Cochran, a complaining taxpayer, contended that taxation to buy schoolbooks to aid private, religious, sectarian and other schools not in the public educational system, was a taking of public property for a private purpose which the Fourteenth Amendment forbade. The Supreme Court of Louisiana upheld the statute, construing it not to provide religious texts, but to furnish the nonreligious books supplied to pupils in public schools. The unanimous Supreme Court of the United States affirmed in an opinion by Chief Justice Hughes; that Court held that the taxing power of the State was exerted for a "public purpose." The opinion discusses neither establishment of religion nor interference with its free exercise.

Thirteen years after *Cochran,* the Supreme Court decided *West Virginia State Board of Education* v. *Barnette.*[110] West Virginia had ordered that the flag salute be a regular part of the program of all public schools; that all teachers and pupils be required to participate; and that refusal be regarded as a punishable act of insubordination. A child who refused was subject to expulsion; he thereupon became "unlawfully absent," might be treated as a delinquent; and his parents were liable to a fine of fifty dollars and thirty days in jail. Children of Jehovah's Witnesses, believing that the flag was an image within the prohibition of the fourth and fifth verses of *Exodus* 20, refused to give the salute. They were expelled from school, were threatened with confinement in reformatories for criminally inclined juveniles, and their parents were prosecuted for causing delinquency. On the complaint of a group of Witnesses, a three-judge federal district court held the statute unconstitutional, and the Supreme Court of the United States affirmed this holding.[111] The Court's opinion assumed that the test of unconstitutionality of the state requirement was its nonconformity with the Fourteenth Amendment, which the Court treated as including "the principles of the First."[112]

In 1947 came *Everson* v. *Board of Education.*[113] Here the Supreme Court of·the United States, affirming the Supreme Court of New Jersey in a taxpayer's suit, upheld, despite a Fourteenth Amendment challenge, repayment from public funds, to a school child's parents,

[109] 281 U.S. 370 (1930).
[110] 319 U.S. 624 (1943).
[111] *Minersville School Dist.* v. *Gobitis,* 310 U.S. 586 (1940), decided three years before, was thereby overruled.
[112] 319 U.S. at 639. "Congress shall make no law respecting an establishment of religion, or prohibiting the free exercise thereof . . . ."
[113] 330 U.S. 1 (1947).

of the cost of the child's bus transportation to a parochial school. Public school children were similarly transported. The taxpayer had challenged the New Jersey statute providing for this practice as a "law respecting an establishment of religion" on the ground that the Fourteenth Amendment made the First Amendment's establishment clause applicable to States. Mr. Justice Black wrote the Supreme Court's opinion; he included a statement, there *dictum*, which has become the most influential single announcement of the American law of church and state:

> The "establishment of religion" clause of the First Amendment means at least this: Neither a state nor the Federal Government can set up a church. Neither can pass laws which aid one religion, aid all religions, or prefer one religion over another. Neither can force nor influence a person to go or to remain away from church against his will or force him to profess a belief or disbelief in any religion. No person can be punished for entertaining or professing religious beliefs or disbeliefs, for church attendance or non-attendance. No tax in any amount, large or small, can be levied to support any religious activities or institutions, whatever they may be called, or whatever form they may adopt to teach or practice religion. Neither a state nor the Federal Government can, openly or secretly, participate in the affairs of any religious organizations or groups and *vice versa*. In the words of Jefferson, the clause against establishment of religion by law was intended to erect "a wall of separation between church and State."[114]

A year after *Everson* came *McCollum,* in which the Supreme Court declared unconstitutional an Illinois plan for religious education in the public schools,[115] given by volunteer outside teachers at no public expense. The complainant's minor son, Terry, had rendered himself noticeable to his classmates by requesting permission to leave the classroom while religious instruction was given. The permission was readily accorded. Mr. Justice Jackson, though agreeing with the majority judgment, set down in a special concurrence his doubts about the instant jurisdiction of the Court, and his ideas of the standing of litigants in such cases. He pointed out that a federal court could interfere with local school authorities only when they invaded either a personal liberty or a property right protected by the federal constitution. Ordinarily, Jackson wrote, this would come about in one of two ways. A person might be required to submit to some religious rite or instruction which interfered with his freedom. As a typical example he mentioned the flag salute case. If any comparable State oppression was imposed on the McCollum child, it lay in his being

[114] *Everson,* 330 U.S. 1 at 15, 16 (1947).
[115] *Illinois ex rel. McCollum* v. *Board of Education,* 333 U.S. 203 (1948).

obliged to seek exemption from the religious exercise in question; his nonparticipation then set him apart as an embarrassed dissenter. Jackson felt some doubt

> whether the Constitution which, of course, protects the right to dissent, can be construed also to protect one from the embarrassment that always attends nonconformity, whether in religion, politics, behavior or dress.[116]

A second ground of jurisdiction, he wrote, might be taxation by the State for such an unconstitutional purpose as support of a religious establishment. Jurisdiction for a court to hear the case argued on the merits was so sustained in the *Everson* schoolbus case, though ultimately the Supreme Court found that refund of busfares was not "an establishment of religion." But Jackson found no proof of any cost to taxpayers for the religious instruction in *McCollum,* and therefore, he also doubted jurisdiction on that ground. But doubting, he still voted with the majority of the Court for unconstitutionality. No Justice criticized Jackson's analysis of the type of wrongs protected by the fourteenth amendment.

In 1952 the Supreme Court, in *Doremus* v. *Board of Education,*[117] threw additional light on its *McCollum* holding. Doremus, a New Jersey taxpayer,[118] had unsuccessfully sought in the New Jersey state courts a declaratory judgment of the unconstitutionality of a State statute requiring the reading without comment of five verses of the Old Testament at the opening of each public school day. He contended that the Bible reading was a violation of the establishment clause of the first amendment, applicable, he argued, through the terms of the due process or equal protection clauses of the fourteenth. When defeated in the State courts, he appealed to the Supreme Court of the United States. Mr. Justice Jackson, there writing for the *Doremus* majority, found in the record no proof that reading the five verses cost any public money. In this respect the case differed from *Everson,* in which for busfares there was a demonstrated outlay of enumerated public funds. Doremus, the taxpayer, therefore had no sufficient interest to sustain his appeal to the Federal Supreme Court, which dismissed it without passing on the merits of the case. The *Doremus* decision thus was retrospectively informative about the

[116] 333 U.S. at 233.

[117] 342 U.S. 429 (1952).

[118] In the New Jersey courts the parent of a schoolchild who had been exposed to the reading in class had also been a plaintiff. Unfortunately for jurisdiction, the schoolchild had graduated before the case reached the Supreme Court of the United States, leaving as sole appellant the New Jersey taxpayer, who had no child in school.

standing of the plaintiff in *McCollum*. As in *Doremus*, so in *McCollum*, there had been no allegation or proof that the exercise added any sum whatsoever to the cost of conducting the school. In retrospect, therefore, the interest of the appellant in *McCollum* seemed only to have been the personal oppression of the school child, whose mother as plaintiff spoke for him. Illinois could be thought to have humiliated young Terry McCollum when singling him out as a classroom dissenter. If it were not for this, if the *McCollum* appeal had rested only on a taxpayer's contention of "establishment," it should, if the two holdings were consistent, have been dismissed like that in *Doremus*.

In another 1952 case, *Zorach* v. *Clauson*,[119] the Supreme Court wrote a further gloss on *McCollum*. Here the parents of children attending New York City public schools appealed to the Supreme Court of the United States from a decision of the New York Court of Appeals which had upheld a "released time" program. Students released from the public schools on the written request of their parents were permitted during specified periods of school time to go to private religious centers, off school premises, for religious instruction or for devotional exercises. Those not released stayed in public schoolrooms. Churches made reports to the schools, monitoring the attendance of the children released. The Supreme Court upheld the program with an opinion by Mr. Justice Douglas. He found no need to seek taxpayer standing by proof of public expenditure, lacking in *Doremus*. The *Zorach* appellants were parents of children in the affected public schools, which sufficed for jurisdiction. But Mr. Justice Douglas found that it would take "obtuse reasoning to inject any issue of the 'free exercise' of religion into the present case." He wrote, "The problem, like many problems in constitutional law, is one of degree." He cited *McCollum*, but found he could not expand it to cover the released time program in issue. Mr. Justice Douglas' prevailing opinion in *Zorach* contained these words:

> We are a religious people whose institutions presuppose a Supreme Being. We guarantee the freedom to worship as one chooses. We make room for as wide a variety of beliefs and creeds as the spiritual needs of men deem necessary. We sponsor an attitude on the part of government that shows no partiality . . . . When the state encourages religious instruction or cooperates with religious authorities by adjusting the schedule of public events to sectarian needs, it follows the best of our traditions. For it then respects the religious nature of our people and accommodates the public service to their spiritual needs. To hold that it may not would be to find in the Constitution a require-

[119] 343 U.S. 306 (1952).

ment that the government show a callous indifference to religious groups.

Justices Frankfurter, Jackson and Black dissented. Jackson wrote:

> The greater effectiveness of this system over voluntary attendance after school hours is due to the truant officer who, if the youngster fails to go to Church school, dogs him back to the public schoolroom. Here schooling is more or less suspended during the "released time" so that nonreligious attendants will not forge ahead of the church-going absentees. But it serves as a temporary jail for the pupil who will not go to Church. It takes more subtlety of mind than I possess to deny that this is governmental constraint in support of religion.[120]

Next came *Engel* v. *Vitale,* the New York Regents' Prayer case.[121] The Board of Regents, a body which has had the duty of supervising public education in New York since the late 18th century, felt in the 1950's that a "non-denominational" prayer would be desirable to start the schoolday, and composed, for optional use, as local school authorities might decide, this prayer—

> Almighty God, we acknowledge our dependence upon Thee, and we beg Thy blessings upon us, our parents, our teachers and our country.

The Regents' Prayer occurred daily in the New Hyde Park, New York, schools after the morning pledge of allegiance to the flag; its recital added substantially less than one minute to that patriotic ritual. The Board of Education adopted a regulation providing, "Neither teachers nor any school authority shall comment on participation or nonparticipation in the exercise nor suggest or request that any posture or language be used or dress be worn or be not used or not worn." Moreover, a child's parent could arrange for him to leave the room during the recital.[122] Here is a certain similarity to *McCollum,* in which the Court in 1948 held unconstitutional an Illinois arrangement for religious education in public schools.[123] In *McCollum,* as here, the plaintiff was parent of a schoolchild. In *McCollum,* as here, the public school exercise took place in school hours. In *McCollum,* as here, attendance at the exercise was not compulsory. In *McCollum,* as in *Engel,* one might find some possible embarrassment to a child required to choose between presence at an unwelcome religious exer-

---

[120] *Zorach* v. *Clauson,* 343 U.S. 306 (1952).

[121] 370 U.S. 421 (1962).

[122] Supplemental Record, New York Court of Appeals, pp. 152–53. See 370 U.S. at 438. The source of the board's regulations was the opinion of Justice Meyer in the trial court, 18 Misc. 2d 659, 696, 191 N.Y.S.2d 453, 492–93 (Sup. Ct. 1959).

[123] See Sutherland, "Due Process and Disestablishment," 62 *Harv. L. Rev.* 1306 (1949).

cise, and assertion that he was different from his fellows. On the other hand, in *McCollum* unpaid volunteer teachers of various religions carried on doctrinal instruction for their respective adherents in separate schoolrooms, for weekly periods of thirty to forty-five minutes duration. The New York practice differed from that of Illinois in the bland neutralism and brevity of the Regents' Prayer; in the leadership by public school teachers; and in the exposure of all unexcused children, regardless of religious affiliation, to the identical exercise.

The degree of likeness of the facts in any one case to the facts in another is insusceptible of scientific measurement. The authority of one decision for another depends upon undemonstrable factors; no optical device will tell whether precedent is in focus; no calipers can measure the divergence or proximateness of *Engel* and *McCollum*. The New York Court of Appeals, with two judges dissenting, upheld the constitutionality of the Regents' Prayer in public schools. But the Supreme Court felt obliged to take a different course, holding the Regents' Prayer unconstitutional as a state "establishment," without regard to whether any person was oppressed, or was taxed for an unconstitutional purpose.[124]

After *Engel* there could be little surprise in two decisions in June, 1963, holding unconstitutional repetition of the Lord's Prayer and readings from the Bible in Pennsylvania and Maryland public schools.[125]

There is, one might venture, another egalitarian movement well under way, so universal and so obvious that it sometimes passes unnoticed. Less apparent than the movement toward racial equality is a tide setting toward equality of possessions. We are so much in the midst of it that we are unconscious of it, as man, most of the time, takes little notice of the air around him. But the movement is nonetheless a pervasive part of our habit of government. Counsel who argued the *Income Tax Case* of 1895[126] felt it vaguely, and were troubled, and protested. The Income Tax Amendment of 1913 was an indication. Heavy inheritance taxation is another. Characteristic of our time is an increase of sympathy evident in many matters—the Belgian Relief of 1914; the Russian and Near East Relief efforts of the years immediately following World War I; the Social Security Cases of 1937 in which the Supreme Court upheld arrangements for

---

[124] *Engel v. Vitale,* 370 U.S. 421 (1962).
[125] *School District of Abington Township, Pennsylvania v. Schempp; Murray v. Curlett et al., School Commissioner of Baltimore,* 374 U.S. 203 (1963).
[126] *Pollock v. Farmers' Loan and Trust Co.,* 157 U.S. 429.

unemployment payment and old-age pensions;[127] the federal Fair Labor Standards Act of 1938;[128] the use of public powers of eminent domain and taxation to provide appropriate dwellings where slums have been.[129] The impulse that moved the Levellers of Freeborn John Lilburn's day is quick in us more than three centuries later. In the spring of 1964 the President of the United States announced that abolition of poverty would be a prominent objective of his administration.

One could multiply instances endlessly. Descendants of men who accumulated great fortunes turn to public service and devote themselves to the general welfare. Men, most men, feel uncomfortable enjoying abundance in the presence of poverty. And our productive devices are so overwhelmingly efficient that we must distribute all this abundance or be in trouble. To write of this great change is to invite misunderstanding, because to remark it may suggest indifference to crying inadequacies that persist. But this essay attempts to show great movements, not to point exceptions, even crying ones.

> Nous cherchons à remonter jusqu'aux principes et à ne négliger aucune des conséquences de quelque valeur; mais nous n'avons pas mission de descendre jusqu-aux moindres déviations, ou de relever de simples bizarreries. Ceci est une esquisse; ce n'est point un traité. Nous faisons une théorie et non un *spicilège*.[130]

Diffusion of Power

Felix Frankfurter wrote in his *Steel Seizure* opinion—

> A scheme of government like ours no doubt at times feels the lack of power to act with complete, all-embracing, swiftly moving authority. No doubt a government with distributed authority, subject to be challenged in the courts of law, at least long enough to consider and adjudicate the challenge, labors under restrictions from which other governments are free. It has not been our tradition to envy such goverments. In any event our government was designed to have such restrictions. The price was deemed not too high in view of the safeguards which these restrictions afford.[131]

[127] *Steward Machine Co.* v. *Davis,* 301 U.S. 548; *Helvering* v. *Davis,* 301 U.S. 619.

[128] 52 Stat. at Large 1060; sustained in *United States* v. *Darby Lumber Co.,* 312 U.S. 100 (1941).

[129] See for two examples, the *New York Public Housing Law,* Ch. 44A of the Consolidated Laws of New York; and *Berman* v. *Parker,* 348 U.S. 26 (1954).

[130] Lehuërou, *Histoire des Institutions Carolingiennes,* p. 118.

[131] *Youngstown Sheet & Tube Co.* v. *Sawyer,* 343 U.S. 579, at 613 (1952).

One wonders. Division of governing power between nation and States, and parceling the States' share in fifty fragments provide our most conspicuous examples of diffusion; and diffusion among the States is waning with the dwindling State autonomy.[132] The necessities of modern existence appear to permit less and less of the fragmented government to which our fathers aspired. The federal Fair Labor Standards Act was necessary to correct the local injustices Holmes decried in his *Child Labor* dissent; the Supreme Court had to intervene to end State injustice to the Negro in regions where Confederate memories were strongest. And the most insistent of our concerns involve international matters, and these bear little relation to State boundaries. Our large corporate organizations of production and distribution are not parceled by States; our greatest city is only in form limited to the State of New York; it has to arrange some of its concerns by a two-State governmental entity;[133] it plans others by a compact of three States[134] Within the national government the executive functions expand. War and diplomacy are alike unsuited to public debate, compromise by bargaining, domestic political maneuver.

Robert Jackson wrote in his *Steel Seizure* opinion—

> The actual art of governing under our Constitution does not and cannot conform to judicial definitions of the power of any of its branches based on isolated clauses or even single Articles torn from context. While the Constitution diffuses power the better to secure liberty, it also contemplates that practice will integrate the dispersed powers into a workable government.[135]

A Great Charter

So finally comes reflection on the value today of the idea of a great writing in which a society of men, by reflection and choice, undertake to establish the controlling and abiding premises of their government. Here again disclaimer is prudent; in our society between 1787 and 1789 not every member was asked for, or gave assent to the Consti-

---

[132] This observation is made neither in joy nor in sorrow. It is made most frequently and most emphatically by those who most deplore the phenomenon.

[133] See for the Port of New York Authority, New York Unconsolidated Laws of New York, § 6401 and following; see for the consent of Congress, Resolution of August 23, 1921, 42 Stat. at L. 174. The New Jersey legislation occurs in Chapter 151 of the New Jersey Laws of 1921.

[134] See the Tri-State Transportation Compact, contemplated for Connecticut, New Jersey and New York, N.Y. Laws of 1963, c. 617.

[135] 343 U.S. at page 625 (1952).

tution, and the draftsmen of 1787 were a much smaller group than the members of ratifying conventions, and neither the drafting convention nor those which ratified were unanimous. The reflection and choice of a society is somewhat limited when these functions are achieved through a representative process. And even if we comfort ourselves by assurances that continued general acceptance of the constituent charter has come to demonstrate the reflection and choice of our society, still that acceptance was given only to sweeping principles; general propositions do not automatically decide concrete cases, and their decision is apt to depend on a judgment or intuition more subtle than any articulate major premise; we must never forget that it is a *constitution* we are expounding.[136] While all declare for liberty, few losers will cheer a specific decision granting liberty to the other man, and him undeserving, at the cost of the man who thinks himself more worthy. But the nature of a constitution is, case by case, to extend its immunities to individuals; and in these selective judgments the society at large is not consulted. What we have done by our measure of reflection and choice is to establish a system of making decisions in the governing process, and to express aspirations as to the nature of these choices, between one man and many.

This might sound like little enough. But considering the countries of the world it is a very great deal. Written constitutions are multiplying as newly independent nations draft their own.[137] And groups of nations are forming unions, much as Benjamin Franklin hoped the Albany Congress would form a union in 1754.[138] The United Nations is, of course, the most notable and inclusive of such groups. In their formation the example of the Constitution of the United States has had a very great influence.

Within the United States we tend to be too ready to see flaws in operation, and to overlook the great successes. In an area comparable in size to Europe, with a population now approaching two hundred million, we have got on together for nearly two centuries with only one internal war. Within this great area there are no State trade barriers. Flow of population from any point to any other within the national boundaries is constitutionally forbidden to any State.[139]

And, not perfectly, not even satisfactorily, but still remarkably, we

---

[136] At the risk of belaboring the familiar, I remind the reader that these words derive from Holmes' dissent in Lochner, 198 U.S. 45 (1905), and John Marshall's opinion in *McCulloch* v. *Maryland*, 4 Wheaton 316 (1819).

[137] See Amos J. Peaslee, *Constitutions of Nations* (3 vols.; Concord, N. H.: Rumford Press, 1950), for a compilation of the texts up to that date, with commentary.

[138] See Peaslee's *International Governmental Organizations* (2 vols.; Hague: M. Nijhoff, 1956).

[139] *Edwards* v. *California*, 314 U.S. 160 (1941).

progress toward insistence on fairness to everyone in each State. The national machinery creaks but it runs. Who shall say that we have not steadily formed a more perfect Union, and provided for the common defense? To a surprising extent we achieve domestic tranquillity and establish justice. We try to promote the general welfare, not alone within our borders. And we still hope as did our fathers, to secure the Blessings of Liberty to ourselves and our Posterity.

TABLE OF CASES

BIBLIOGRAPHY

The numbers at the end of each reference
are the page numbers in this book
on which these sources are mentioned.

PREFACE

BURDICK, CHARLES K., and FRANCIS M. *The Law of the American Constitution. Its Origin and Development.* New York and London: G. P. Putnam's Sons, 1922.   v

COOLEY, THOMAS M. *A Treatise on the Constitutional Limitations Which Rest Upon the Legislative Power of the States of the American Union.* Boston: Little, Brown & Co., 1868.   v

CORWIN, EDWARD S. (ed.). *The Constitution of the United States of America* (82nd Cong., 2d Sess; Sen. Doc. 170). Washington: U.S. Government Printing Office, 1953.   vi

HORN, A. M. "Judicial Power over Policies under State Constitutions," VI *Public Policy* 47 (1955).   vi

ROTTSCHAEFER, HENRY. *Handbook of American Constitutional Law.* St. Paul: West Publishing Co., 1939.   v

STORY, JOSEPH. *Commentaries on the Constitution of the United States with a Preliminary Review of the Constitutional History of the Colonies and States, Before the Adoption of the Constitution.* Boston: Hilliard, Gray & Co., 1833.   v

WILLOUGHBY, WESTEL WOODBURY. *The Constitutional Law of the United States.* 2 vols. New York: Baker Voorhis & Co., 1910.   v

WILLOUGHBY, WESTEL WOODBURY. *The Constitutional Law of the United States.* 2nd ed. (1929) 2 vols. New York: Baker Voorhis & Co., 1910.   v

CHAPTER 1

BALDWIN, HENRY. "A General View of the Origin and Nature of the Constitution and Government," Philadelphia, 1837. Reprinted in 9 *Lawyers' Edition of the Supreme Court Reports* 869.   7

GARDINER, S. R. *Constitutional Documents of the Puritan Revolution.* 3rd ed. "Agreement of the People" (Cromwell's Army Council, January 15, 1649). Oxford: Oxford University Press, 1906.   4

HOLMES, O. W. "The Path of the Law," 10 *Harvard Law Review* 45 (1897); reprinted in *Collected Legal Papers*. New York: Peter Smith, 1952.   1

JONES, HOWARD MUMFORD. *The Pursuit of Happiness.* Cambridge: Harvard University Press, 1953.   2

LOCKE, JOHN. *Second Treatise of Government.* 4th ed. London: John Churchill, 1713.   3, 6

McILWAIN, C. H. *The High Court of Parliament and Its Supremacy.* New Haven: Yale University Press, 1910.   6

POUND, ROSCOE. *An Introduction to the Philosophy of Law.* New Haven: Yale University Press, 1922.   1, 4

SUTHERLAND, ARTHUR E. *The Law and One Man Among Many.* Madison: University of Wisconsin Press, 1956.   4

TUNC, ANDRÉ. "The Royal Will and the Rule of Law." *Government Under Law,* ed. Arthur E. Sutherland. Cambridge: Harvard University Press, 1956.   3

U.S. *Congressional Record.* Vol. 100, Part 5. Second Session of the 83rd Congress, May 18, 1954.   7

CHAPTER 2

BLACKSTONE, WILLIAM. *Magna Carta.* Oxford: Clarendon Press, 1759.   16, 17, 18

BURKE, EDMUND. *Speeches and Letters on American Affairs,* ed. Ernest Rhys. London: J. M. Dent and Sons, 1908.   13

CHAFEE, ZECHARIAH. *How Human Rights Got into the Constitution.* Boston: Boston University Press, 1952.   31

COKE, EDWARD. *Second Institute.* London: W. Clarke & Sons, 1817.   18, 21

CORWIN, EDWARD S. "Due Process of Law Before the Civil War," 24 *Harvard Law Review* 366 (1911).   32

GLADSTONE, WILLIAM E. "Kin Beyond the Sea," *North American Review,* (September, 1878), p. 179.   11

HALLAM, HENRY. *View of the State of Europe during the Middle Ages.* 8th ed. 2 vols. London: J. Murray, 1841.   25

LUNT, W. E. *History of England.* New York: Harper & Brothers, 1957.   15

MAITLAND, F. W. *Domesday Book and Beyond.* Cambridge: Cambridge University Press, 1897.   13

MARCHAM, F. G., and STEPHENSON, CARL. *Sources of English Constitutional History.* New York: Harper & Brothers, 1937.   18, 22

McILWAIN, C. H. "Due Process of Law in Magna Carta," 14 *Columbia Law Review* 27 (1914).   29, 31

McKECHNIE, W. S. *Magna Carta.* 2nd ed. Glasgow: J. Maclehose & Sons, 1914.   17

PARIS, MATTHEW. *Chronica Majora.* 7 vols. London: Longman and Co., 1872–83. 15

PERRY, RICHARD L., and COOPER, J. C. (eds.). *Sources of Our Liberties.* Chicago: American Bar Foundation, 1959. 18

POUND, ROSCOE. *Development of Constitutional Guarantees of Liberty.* New Haven: Yale University Press, 1957. 31

RALPH OF COGGESHALL. *Chronicon Anglicanum,* ed. Stevenson, 1875. 15, 17

ROGER OF WENDOVER. *Flowers of History.* Giles translation. 2 vols. (1849). 15, 30

STUBBS, WILLIAM. *Constitutional History of England.* 3 vols. Oxford: Clarendon Press, 1873. 15, 30

STUBBS, WILLIAM. *Select Charters.* 8th ed. Oxford: Clarendon Press, 1895. 18, 31

TASWELL-LANGMEAD, T. P. *English Constitutional History.* 9th ed. London: Sweet & Maxwell, 1929. 15

THOMPSON, FAITH. *Magna Carta, Its Role in the Making of the English Constitution.* Minneapolis: University of Minnesota Press, 1948. 31

THOMSON, RICHARD. *An Historical Essay on the Magna Carta of King John.* London: Printed for J. Major, 1829. 18

TREVELYAN, G. M. *A Shortened History of England.* London: Longmans, Green & Co., 1942. 31

CHAPTER 3

A Concise Abstract of All the Laws Relating to Parliamentary Elections, by a Gentleman of the Inner Temple. London: Printed for J. Walker, n.d. 46

BOWEN, CATHERINE DRINKER. *The Lion and the Throne: The Life and Times of Sir Edward Coke.* Boston: Little, Brown & Co., 1957. 35

BROUGHAM, HENRY. *Historical Sketches of Statesmen.* 3 vols. London: Richard Griffin & Co., 1855. 42

CLARK, G. N. *Later Stuarts, 1660–1714.* Oxford: Clarendon Press, 1934. 41

De Republica Anglorum. Printed by Henrie Midleton for Gregorie Seton, 1584. 35

HOBBES, THOMAS. *Leviathan.* London, 1651; New York: E. P. Dutton and Co., 1950. 42

HUTCHINSON, H. F. *The Hollow Crown.* New York: John Day Co., 1961. 47

KEIR, D. L. *The Constitutional History of Modern Britain.* 3rd ed. London: A. and C. Black, 1946. 38

LODGE, E. C., and THORNTON, G. A. *English Constitutional Documents, 1307–1485.* Cambridge: Cambridge University Press, 1935. 40

LUNT, W. E. *History of England.* New York: Harper & Brothers, 1957. 40

MAITLAND, F. W. *Constitutional History of England.* Cambridge: Cambridge University Press, 1909. 35, 36, 38

MAUDSLEY, R. H. "The House of Lords," 15 *University of Miami Law Review* 174 (1960). 37

McILWAIN, C. H. *The High Court of Parliament and Its Supremacy.* New Haven: Yale University Press, 1910. 42

McKINLEY, A. E. *Suffrage Franchise in the Thirteen English Colonies in America.* Boston: Ginn and Co., 1905. 38

PHILLIPS, HOOD. *Constitutional Law.* London: Sweet & Maxwell, 1952. 37, 40

POLLARD, A. F. *The Evolution of Parliament.* London: Longmans, Green & Co., 1920. 37

PORRITT, E., and A. PORRITT. *The Unreformed House of Commons.* Cambridge: Cambridge University Press, 1903. 34, 38, 39

PUTNAM, BERTHA H. "The Enforcement of the Statutes of Labourers During the first Decade after the Black Death, 1349–1359," *Columbia University Studies in History, Economics and Public Law,* XXXII (1908), Appendix 8. 44, 45

ROSSITER, CLINTON. *Seedtime of the Republic.* New York: Harcourt, Brace & Co., 1953. 50

STUBBS, WILLIAM. *The Constitutional History of England.* 3 vols. Oxford: Clarendon Press, 1880. 35

STUBBS, WILLIAM. *Select Charters.* 8th ed. Oxford: Clarendon Press, 1895. 35, 36, 38

TANNER, J. R. "Composition of Parliament," *Tudor Constitutional Documents.* Cambridge: Cambridge University Press, 1922. 41

TASWELL-LANGMEAD, T. P. *English Constitutional History.* 9th ed. London: Sweet & Maxwell, 1929. 36, 37, 48

TASWELL-LANGMEAD, T. P. *English Constitutional History,* ed. T. F. T. Plucknett. London: Sweet & Maxwell, 1960. 40

THACKERAY, W. M. *The Four Georges.* New York: Doubleday-Dolphin, n.d. 42

TREVELYAN, G. M. *History of England.* 3 vols. Garden City, N. Y.: Doubleday Anchor, 1953. 36, 47

TREVELYAN, G. M. *Illustrated English Social History.* 4 vols. London: Longmans, Green & Co., 1952. 41, 44, 47

TUNC, ANDRÉ. "The Royal Will and the Rule of Law." *Government Under Law,* ed. Arthur E. Sutherland. Cambridge: Harvard University Press, 1956. 43

VINOGRADOFF, PAUL. *Villainage in England.* Oxford: Clarendon Press, 1892. 44, 47

CHAPTER 4

Book of Common Prayer. Royal Declaration prefixed to the Articles of Religion. 73

BOWEN, CATHERINE DRINKER. *The Lion and the Throne.* Boston: Little, Brown & Co., 1957. 51, 58, 59, 63, 64, 65, 68

CAMPBELL, JOHN. *Lives of the Chief Justices.* London: J. Murray, 1849. 51, 60, 63, 64, 67

CHAFEE, ZECHARIAH. *Three Human Rights in the Constitution of 1787.* Lawrence: University of Kansas Press, 1956. 65

COBBETT, WILLIAM. *State Trials.* London: Hansard, 1809. 56

COKE, SIR EDWARD. *Second Institute.* London: W. Clarke & Sons, 1817. 56

CORWIN, EDWARD S. "The 'Higher Law' Background of American Constitutional Law," 42 *Harvard Law Review* 149 and 365 (1928–1929). Reprinted in *Selected Essays on Constitutional Law.* Chicago: Foundation Press, 1938. 61, 62

FRERE, W. H. *History of the English Church in the Reigns of Elizabeth and James I, 1558–1625.* London: Macmillan, 1904. 53

GARDINER, S. R. *Constitutional Documents of the Puritan Revolution, 1628–1660.* Oxford: Clarendon Press, 1889. 67, 68, 73, 74

GIBB, M. A. *John Lilburne the Leveller.* London: L. Drummond, 1947. 60

HOLDSWORTH, WILLIAM S. *History of English Law.* Boston: Little, Brown & Co., 1927. 51, 64

HUTTON, W. H. *A History of the Church of England from the Ascension of Charles to the Death of Anne.* London: Macmillan, 1903. 73

KEIR, D. L. *The Constitutional History of Modern Britain.* 3rd ed. London: A. and C. Black, 1946. 54

MAGUIRE, MARY HUME. "The Oath Ex Officio," *Essays in History and Political Theory in Honor of Charles H. McIlwain.* Cambridge: Harvard University Press, 1936. 56

McILWAIN, C. H. *The High Court of Parliament and Its Supremacy.* New Haven: Yale University Press, 1910. 61

MONTAGU, BASIL (ed.). *The Works of Francis Bacon.* London: J. Murray, 1825–1834. 62

PLUCKNETT, T. F. T. "Bonham's Case and Judicial Review," 40 *Harvard Law Review* 30 (1926). 61

SIDGWICK, HENRY. *The Elements of Politics.* 2d ed. London and New York: Macmillan Co., 1897. 61

STUBBS, WILLIAM. *Select Charters.* 8th ed. Oxford: Clarendon Press, 1895. 68

STUBBS, WILLIAM. *The Constitutional History of England.* 3 vols. Oxford: Clarendon Press, 1875. 68

TANNER, J. R. *English Constitutional Conflicts of the Seventeenth Century, 1603–1689.* Cambridge: Cambridge University Press, 1928. 74

TANNER, J. R. *Tudor Constitutional Documents, 1485–1603.* Cambridge: Cambridge University Press, 1922. 54, 55

TASWELL-LANGMEAD, T. P. *English Constitutional History.* 9th ed. London: Sweet & Maxwell, 1929. 73, 74

THORNE, SAMUEL E. "Dr. Bonham's Case," 54 *Law Quarterly Review* 543 (1938). 61

TREVELYAN, G. M. *History of England.* 3 vols. Garden City, N. Y.: Doubleday Anchor, 1953. 71

USHER, ROLAND G. *The Rise and Fall of the High Commission.* Oxford: Clarendon Press, 1913.   56

CHAPTER 5

FARRAND, MAX (ed.). *Records of the Federal Convention of 1787.* New Haven: Yale University Press, 1911.   75
FIRTH, C. H. *The Last Years of the Protectorate, 1656–1658.* London: Longmans, Green & Co., 1909.   87
GARDINER, SAMUEL R. *Constitutional Documents of the Puritan Revolution, 1628–1660.* Oxford: Clarendon Press, 1889–1906 (3 editions).
     75, 76, 78, 87
GARDINER, SAMUEL R. *History of the Commonwealth and Protectorate, 1649–1656.* 4 vols. London: Longmans, Green & Co., 1903.   87
GARDINER, SAMUEL R. *History of the Great Civil War.* 4 vols. 3rd ed. New York: Longmans, Green & Co., 1904–05.   76
KEIR, LINDSAY. *The Constitutional History of Modern Britain.* 3rd ed. London: A. and C. Black, 1946.   87
MAITLAND, F. W. *Constitutional History of England.* Cambridge: Cambridge University Press, 1909.   88
SHAW, W. A. *The Commonwealth and the Protectorate.* (*Cambridge Modern History,* Vol. IV.) New York: Macmillan, 1908.   88
TREVELYAN, G. M. *England Under the Stuarts.* 11th ed. New York: G. P. Putnam's Sons, 1924.   75

CHAPTER 6

HALLAM, HENRY. *Constitutional History of England.* London: J. Murray, 1827.   98
HANSARD, T. C. *Parliamentary History of England.* 36 vols. London: Hansard, 1809.   89
KEIR, D. L. *Constitutional History of Modern Britain.* 3rd ed. London: A. and C. Black, 1946.   89
MACAULAY, THOMAS B. *History of England.* London: Longmans, Green & Co., 1862.   90
MONTAGUE, F. C. *Elements of English Constitutional History.* London: Longmans, Green & Co., 1894.   89
PICKERING, DANBY (ed.). *Statutes at Large, 1 Will. & Mary to 8 Will. 3.* Vol. 9. Cambridge: Bentham, Printer to the University, 1764.   97
TEMPERLEY, H. W. V. "The Revolution and the Revolution Settlement in England," *Cambridge Modern History,* Vol. V. New York: Macmillan, 1908.   90

CHAPTER 7

BECKER, CARL L. *The Declaration of Independence: A Study in the History of Political Ideas.* New York: Alfred A. Knopf, 1941.   106
BROUGHAM, HENRY. *Works.* Edinburgh: A. and C. Black, 1872–73.   103
CLARK, G. N. *Later Stuarts, 1660–1714.* Oxford: Clarendon Press, 1934.
     104, 107

FRANK, JOSEPH. *The Levellers*. Cambridge: Harvard University Press, 1955.
107

GARDINER, S. R. *Constitutional Documents of the Puritan Revolution, 1625–1660*. 3rd ed. Oxford: Clarendon Press, 1906. 107

HALLAM, HENRY. *Constitutional History of England*. London: J. Murray, 1827. 109

LOCKE, JOHN. *Two Treatises of Government*, ed. Laslett, Peter. Cambridge: Cambridge University Press, 1960. 100

ROBERTSON, C. G. *Select Statutes, Cases and Documents to Illustrate English Constitutional History, 1660–1832*. 6th ed. London: Methuen and Co., 1935. 108

TASWELL-LANGMEAD, T. P. *English Constitutional History*. 9th ed. London: Sweet & Maxwell, 1929. 99

WEDGWOOD, C. V. *Cromwell*. London: Duckworth, 1939. 107

CHAPTER 8

ABBOTT, W. E. *New York in the American Revolution*. New York: Charles Scribner's Sons, 1929. 114

ALEXANDER, JAMES. *A Brief Narrative of the Case and Trial of John Peter Zenger*, ed. Katz, Stanley. Cambridge: Harvard University Press, 1903.
120

American Historical Documents. "Harvard Classics," Vol. 43. New York: Collier, 1910. 131

BECKER, CARL L. *Beginnings of the American People*. Boston and New York: Houghton Mifflin Co., 1915. 111

BLACKSTONE, SIR WILLIAM. *Commentaries*. 2nd ed. Oxford: Clarendon Press, 1766. 129

BROWN, ROBERT E. *Middle Class Democracy and the Revolution in Massachusetts, 1691–1780*. Ithaca: Cornell University Press, 1955. 114, 115

BURKE, EDMUND. *Speeches and Letters on American Affairs*, ed. Ernest Rhys. London: J. M. Dent Sons, 1908. 115, 129

CARMAN, H. J., and SYRETT, H. C. *History of the American People*. New York: Alfred A. Knopf, 1952. 129

CHANNING, EDWARD. *History of the United States*. 6 vols. New York: Macmillan, 1924. 129

COMMAGER, HENRY S. *Documents of American History*. 5th ed. New York: Appleton-Century-Crofts, 1949. 131

CORWIN, E. S., and KOENIG, L. W. *The Presidency Today*. New York: New York University Press, 1950. 116

HOLMES, OLIVER W. "The Law and the Court," *Collected Legal Papers*. New York: Peter Smith, 1952. 127

KEIR, D. L. *The Constitutional History of Modern Britain*. 3rd ed. London: A. and C. Black, 1946. 115

KEITH, A. B. *Constitutional History of the First British Empire*. Oxford: Clarendon Press, 1930. 115

KELLOGG, LOUISE. "The American Colonial Charter," *American Historical Association Annual Report for 1903*, pp. 185–341. 112

KENNEDY, JOHN F. *Profiles in Courage.* New York: Harper & Brothers, 1956. 116

LABAREE, LEONARD W. (ed.). *Royal Instructions to British Colonial Governors, 1670–1776.* New York: D. Appleton-Century Co., 1935. 119

MACDONALD, WILLIAM. *Documentary Source Book of American History, 1606–1926.* 3rd ed. New York: Macmillan, 1934. 112, 125, 126

MACDONALD, WILLIAM. *Select Charters and Other Documents Illustrative of American History, 1606–1775.* New York: Macmillan, 1899.
127, 131

MCKINLEY, ALBERT E. *Suffrage Franchise in the Thirteen English Colonies in America.* Boston: Ginn & Co., 1905. 115

MILLER, PERRY. *From Colony to Province.* Cambridge: Harvard University Press, 1953. 114

MONTESQUIEU. *De L'Esprit des Loix.* Translated by Nugent and Prichard. New York: Appleton & Co., 1900. 130

NETTELS, C. P. *The Roots of American Civilization.* New York: Crofts, 1938. 112

OSGOOD, H. L. *The American Colonies in the Eighteenth Century.* 4 vols. New York: Macmillan, 1924. 112

OSGOOD, H. L. *The American Colonies in the Seventeenth Century.* 3 vols. New York: Macmillan, 1904–07. 112

ROSSITER, C. L. *Seedtime of the Republic.* New York: Harcourt, Brace & Co., 1953. 110, 111, 112, 113, 119

RUTHERFORD, LIVINGSTON. *John Peter Zenger, His Press, His Trial, and a Bibliography of Zenger Imprints.* New York: Dodd, Mead & Co., 1904.
120

SMITH, J. H. *Appeals to the Privy Council from the American Plantations.* New York: Columbia University Press, 1950. 113, 128

STORY, JOSEPH. *History of the Colonies. (Commentaries on the Constitution of the United States,* 2nd ed., Vol. I.) Boston: Little, Brown & Co., 1851. 110, 112

SYDNOR, CHARLES S. *Gentlemen Freeholders.* Chapel Hill: University of North Carolina Press, 1952. 115

THAYER, FRANK. *Legal Control of the Press.* Chicago: The Foundation Press, 1944. 124

THAYER, JAMES B. *Cases on Constitutional Law.* 2 vols. Cambridge: George H. Kent, 1895. 127

WAMBAUGH, EUGENE. *Cases on Constitutional Law.* Cambridge: Harvard University Press, 1914. 127

WILLIAMSON, CHILTON. *American Suffrage from Property to Democracy.* Princeton: Princeton University Press, 1960. 114

CHAPTER 9

ALEXANDER, D. S. *Political History of the State of New York.* 4 vols. New York: H. Holt & Co., 1906. 184

BASSETT, J. S. *Short History of the United States.* New York: Macmillan, 1923. 165

BECKER, CARL L. *Declaration of Independence: A Study in the History of Political Ideas.* New York: Alfred A. Knopf, 1942. 143, 144

BURKE, EDMUND. *Speeches and Letters on American Affairs,* ed. Ernest Rhys. London: J. M. Dent Sons, 1908. 199

CARMAN, H. J., and SYRETT, H. C. *History of the American People.* New York: Alfred A. Knopf, 1952. 134, 137, 138, 143

CARSON, H. L. *The Supreme Court of the United States.* Philadelphia: J. Y. Huber Co., 1891. 160

CHINARD, GILBERT (ed.). *The Commonplace Book of Thomas Jefferson.* Baltimore: Johns Hopkins Press, 1926. 143

COMMAGER, HENRY S. *Documents of American History.* 7th ed. New York: Appleton-Century-Crofts, 1963. 134, 136, 161

CURTIS, GEORGE T. *History of the Origin, Formation, and Adoption of the Constitution.* 2 vols. New York: Harper & Brothers, 1860–61. 159

DAVIS, J. C. BANCROFT. "Federal Courts Prior to the Adoption of the Constitution," 131 U.S. Appendix xix (1889). 159

ELLIOT, JOHNATHAN (ed.). *Debates in the Several State Conventions.* 2nd ed. 5 vols. Washington: Elliot, 1836–1845. 180, 181, 183, 184

FARRAND, MAX. *Framing of the Constitution of the United States.* New Haven: Yale University Press, 1913. 170, 171, 173

FARRAND, MAX. *Records of the Federal Convention of 1787.* 4 vols. New Haven: Yale University Press, 1911–1937.
163, 169, 170, 171, 172, 173, 174, 178

"Federalist Papers," sub. nom. "Publius," published 1787–1788 in several New York newspapers; written by Hamilton, Madison, Jay. New York: Modern Library, 1937. 182

FISKE, JOHN. *The American Revolution.* Boston: Houghton Mifflin and Co., 1891. 143, 147

FISKE, JOHN. *The Critical Period of American History, 1783–1789.* Boston: Houghton Mifflin and Co., 1888. 148

GLADSTONE, WILLIAM E. "Kin Beyond Sea," *North American Review,* (September, 1878), p. 179. 132

HAMILTON, ALEXANDER, see "Federalist Papers."

HAMMOND, BRAY. *Banks and Politics in America.* Princeton: Princeton University Press, 1957. 202

HOLMES, OLIVER W. "The Law and the Court," *Collected Legal Papers.* New York: Peter Smith, 1952. 164

HUGHES, CHARLES EVANS. *Addresses and Papers.* New York: G. P. Putnam's Sons, 1908. 203

HUNT, GAILLARD, and SCOTT, JAMES BROWN (ed.). *Debates in the Federal Convention of 1787.* New York: Oxford University Press, 1920. 168

JAY, JOHN, see "Federalist Papers."

JENSEN, MERRILL. *The New Nation.* New York: Alfred A. Knopf, 1962.
148, 165

Journals of the Continental Congress. 34 vols. Washington: U.S. Government Printing Office, 1904–1937.
137, 138, 139, 140, 142, 143, 148, 149, 157

LABAREE, LEONARD W. (ed.). *The Papers of Benjamin Franklin*. New Haven: Yale University Press, 1962.   134

MACDONALD, WILLIAM. *Documentary Source Book of American History, 1606–1926*. 3rd ed. New York: Macmillan, 1934.   134

MACDONALD, WILLIAM. *Select Charters and Other Documents Illustrative of the History of the United States, 1606–1775*. 2nd ed. New York: Macmillan, 1904.   136, 137, 138, 161

MADISON, JAMES, see "Federalist Papers."

MCLAUGHLIN, ANDREW C. *The Confederation and the Constitution, 1783–1789*. New York: Harper and Brothers, 1905.   165

MINOT, GEORGE RICHARD. *History of the Insurrection in Massachusetts in the Year Seventeen Hundred and Eighty-Six and the Rebellion Consequent Thereon*. Worcester: Isaiah Thomas, 1788.   166

POWELL, T. R. "State Taxation of Imports," 58 *Harvard Law Review* 858 (1945).   162

RUTLAND, ROBERT ALLEN. *The Birth of the Bill of Rights*. Chapel Hill: University of North Carolina Press, 1955.   190

SMITH, T. B. *The United Kingdom*. London: Stevens and Sons, 1955.
                                                        183

SPARKS, JARED (ed.). *The Writings of George Washington*. 12 vols. Boston: Hilliard, Gray and Co., 1834–37.   159

STORY, JOSEPH. *Commentaries on the Constitution of the United States*. 2nd ed. 3 vols. Boston: Little, Brown and Co., 1851.   159, 160

SUTHERLAND, ARTHUR E. "Private Government and Public Policy," 41 *Yale Review* 405 (1952).   203

SUTHERLAND, ARTHUR E. "Restricting the Treaty Power," 65 *Harvard Law Review* 1305 (1952).   161

SUTHERLAND, ARTHUR E. "The Tenantry on the New York Manors," 41 *Cornell Law Quarterly* 620 (1956).   201

TANSILL, CHARLES C. (ed.). *Documents Illustrative of the Formation of the Union of American States*. Washington: Legislative Reference Service, 1927.   170, 184

THAYER, JAMES B. *Cases on Constitutional Law*. 2 vols. Cambridge: George H. Kent and Co., 1895.   162

WARREN, CHARLES. *Making of the Constitution*. Boston: Little, Brown and Co., 1928.   170, 182

WARREN, CHARLES. "New Light on the History of the Federal Judiciary Act of 1789," 37 *Harvard Law Review* 49 (1923).   186

United States Bureau of the Census. *Sixteenth Census of the United States: 1940. Population*, Vol. I.   132

U.S. *Annals of Congress*. Vol. I.   191

CHAPTER 10

ALEXANDER, JAMES. *A Brief Narrative of the Case and Trial of John Peter Zenger*. ed. Stanley Katz. Cambridge: Harvard University Press, 1963.
                                                        255, 256

BAGEHOT, WALTER. *English Constitution.* London: Chapman and Hall, 1867. 261

BAILEY, T. A. *A Diplomatic History of the American People.* 3rd ed. New York: Crofts and Co., 1947. 245

BASSETT, J. S. *Short History of the United States.* 3rd ed. New York: Macmillan, 1939. 247, 252, 258

BEMIS, SAMUEL FLAGG. *Jay's Treaty.* New York: Macmillan, 1923. 236, 250

BEVERIDGE, A. J. *Life of Marshall.* 4 vols. Boston: Houghton Mifflin and Co., 1916–1919. 251

BLUM, EUGÉNE. *La Déclaration des Droits de l'Homme et du Citoyen; Texte avec Commentaire Suivi.* Paris: Firmin et Montane, 1902. 246

BRAXTON, ALLEN CAPERTON. "The Eleventh Amendment," 20 *Reports of Virginia State Bar Association* 172 (1907). 228

BURANELLI, VINCENT. *The Trial of Peter Zenger.* New York: New York University Press, 1907. 255

CHAFEE, ZECHARIAH. *Freedom of Speech.* New York: Harcourt, Brace and Howe, 1920. 254

CHARLES, JOSEPH. *The Origins of the American Party System.* New York: Harper and Row, 1961. 261

COMMAGER, HENRY S. *Documents of American History.* 7th ed. New York: Appleton-Century-Crofts, 1963. 246

CORWIN, EDWARD S. (ed.). *Constitution of the United States of America.* Washington: U.S. Government Printing Office, 1953. 238

DAVIS, KENNETH CULP. "Suing the Government by Falsely Pretending to Sue an Officer," 29 *Chicago Law Review* 435 (1962). 229

ELLIOT, JOHNATHAN (ed.). *Debates in the Several State Conventions.* 2nd ed. 5 vols. Washington: Elliot, 1836–1845. 257

FARRAND, MAX (ed.). *Records of the Federal Convention of 1787.* 4 vols. New Haven: Yale University Press, 1911–1937. 232, 233

The French Constitution as Revised and Amended by the National Assembly and Presented to the King on the Third of September, 1791—To Which are Added, Its being Presented to the King; a Copy of the King's Letter . . . announcing his Acceptance; and the King's taking the Oath in Presence of the Assembly. London: Debrett, 1811. 246

FREUND, PAUL, SUTHERLAND, ARTHUR E., HOWE, MARK DEWOLFE, and BROWN, ERNEST J. *Constitutional Law; Cases and Other Problems.* 2nd ed. 2 vols. Boston: Little, Brown and Co., 1961. 231

DONIOL, HENRI. *Histoire de la Participation de la France a l'Establissement des Etats-Unis d'Amerique.* 5 vols. Paris: Imprimerie Nationale, 1886–1892. 232

HANDLIN, OSCAR, and others. *Harvard Guide to American History.* Cambridge: Harvard University Press, 1954. 232, 245

HART, HENRY M., and WECHSLER, HERBERT. *The Federal Courts and the Federal System.* Brooklyn: Foundation Press, 1953. 249

HOLDSWORTH, WILLIAM S. *History of English Law.* Boston: Little, Brown and Co., 1927. 255

JOHNSTON, HENRY P. (ed.). *Correspondence and Public Papers of John Jay* 4 vols. New York: G. P. Putnam's Sons, 1890–1893. 248

LEVY, LEONARD W. *Freedom of Speech and Press in Early American History: Legacy of Suppression.* New York: Harper and Row, 1963.
254, 256

LOCKE, JOHN. *Second Treatise of Civil Government,* ed. C. L. Sherman. New York: Appleton-Century Co., 1937. 240

MALONE, DUMAS. *Jefferson the Virginian.* Boston: Little, Brown and Co., 1948. 234

MARSHALL, JOHN. *Life of Washington.* 5 vols. Philadelphia: C. P. Wayne, 1804–1807. 249

McLAUGHLIN, J. F. *Matthew Lyon: The Hampden of Congress.* New York: W. H. Crawford Co., 1900. 258

MILLER, D. H. (ed.). *Treaties and Other International Acts of the United States.* 8 vols. Washington: U.S. Government Printing Office, 1931.
231, 232

MILLER, J. C. *Crisis in Freedom.* Boston: Little, Brown and Co., 1951.
253, 258

POUND, ROSCOE. *Introduction to the Philosophy of Law.* New Haven: Yale University Press, 1922. 244

POUND, ROSCOE. *The Spirit of the Common Law.* Boston: Marshall Jones Co., 1921. 240

PRATT, LAWRENCE S. "Present Disabilities under New York State Law in Real Property," 12 *Brooklyn Law Review* 1 (1942). 231

RICHARDSON, JAMES (ed.). *Messages and Papers of the Presidents.* 10 vols. Washington: U.S. Government Printing Office, 1897. 246, 261

ROBERTS, KENNETH L. *Oliver Wiswell.* New York: Doubleday, Doran and Co., 1940. 230

RUTHERFORD, LIVINGSTON. *John Peter Zenger.* New York: Dodd, Mead and Co., 1904. 255

SELDEN, JOHN. *Table Talk,* ed. Sir Frederick Pollock. London: Quaritch, 1927. 239

SUTHERLAND, ARTHUR E. "British Trials for Disloyal Association during the French Revolution," 34 *Cornell Law Quarterly* 303 (1949). 246

SUTHERLAND, ARTHUR E. "Due Process and Disestablishment," 62 *Harvard Law Review* 1306 (1949). 232

SUTHERLAND, ARTHUR E. "Restricting the Treaty Power," 65 *Harvard Law Review* 1305 (1952). 233, 236

"The Supreme Court, 1961 Term," 76 *Harvard Law Review* 75 (1962).
223

U.S. *Annals of Congress.* Vols. 3–9. 572

U. S. House of Representatives, Committee on the Judiciary. *Amendments to the Constitution With Respect to Treaty Ratification.* H. R. Rep. No. 139, 79th Cong., 1st Sess., 1945. 233

U. S. House of Representatives, Committee on the Judiciary. *Hearings on H. Jt. Res. 6.* 78th Cong., 2d Sess., 1944. 233

VAN TYNE, CLAUDE HALSTEAD. *The Loyalists in the American Revolution.* New York: Peter Smith, 1929. 230

WARREN, CHARLES. "The Mississippi River and the Treaty Clause of the Constitution," 2 *George Washington Law Review* 271 (1934). 233

WARREN, CHARLES. *The Supreme Court in United States History.* 3 vols. Boston: Little, Brown and Company, 1922.

220, 222, 225, 226, 228, 234, 247, 248, 253, 260

CHAPTER 11

COBB, SANFORD H. *Rise of Religious Liberty in the United States.* New York: Harper and Brothers, 1950. 265, 276, 287, 288, 289, 291, 295

Colonial Laws of New York. 5 vols. Albany: James B. Lyon, State Printer, 1894. 280, 281, 282

FORD, P. L. (ed.). *Writings of Thomas Jefferson.* New York: G. P. Putnam's Sons, 1893. 290

HENING, W. W. (ed.). *Statutes at Large; Being a Collection of All the Laws of Virginia.* 13 vols. Philadelphia: Thomas DeSilver, 1823.

288, 289, 290

HUNT, GAILLARD (ed.). *The Writings of James Madison.* 9 vols. New York: G. P. Putnam's Sons, 1900–1910. 290

HUTTON, W. H. *The English Church.* New York: Macmillan, 1903. 282

The Laws and Liberties of Massachusetts. Introduction by Max Farrand. Cambridge: Harvard University Press, 1929. 267, 268, 269, 271

LECKY, W. E. H. *History of the Rise and Influence of the Spirit of Rationalism in Europe.* Rev. ed. 2 vols. New York: D. Appleton and Co., 1886.

274, 300

LINCOLN, CHARLES Z. *Constitutional History of New York.* Rochester: Lawyers Cooperative Publishing Co., 1906. 280

PARRINGTON, VERNON L. *Main Currents of American Thought.* New York: Harcourt, Brace and Co., 1930. 274

RIVES, WILLIAM C. *Life and Times of James Madison.* 3 vols. Boston: Little, Brown and Co., 1859–1868. 289

SAUNDERS, W. L. (ed.). *Colonial Records of North Carolina.* 10 vols. Raleigh: P. M. Hale, State Printer, 1886. 291, 295

SHURTLEFF, NATHANIEL B. (ed.). *Records of the Governor and Company of the Massachusetts By in New England.* Boston: Commonwealth Printer, 1853. 267, 268

SPENCER, HERBERT. *Social Statics.* New York: D. Appleton and Co., 1872. 266

STOKES, ANSON PHELPS. *Church and State in the United States.* New York: Harper and Brothers, 1950. 265

SUTHERLAND, ARTHUR E. "Due Process and Disestablishment," 62 *Harvard Law Review* 1306 (1949). 301

SUTHERLAND, ARTHUR E. "Establishment According to Engel," 76 *Harvard Law Review* 25 (1962). 290, 301

SUTHERLAND, ARTHUR E. "The Tenantry on the New York Manors," 41 *Cornell Law Quarterly* 620 (1956). 291

THORPE, F. N. *Federal and State Constitutions, Colonial Charters and Other Organic Laws.* 7 vols. Washington: Government Printing Office, 1909.
265, 278, 280, 284, 285, 286, 291, 292, 296–9

TREVELYAN, G. O. *The American Revolution.* London: Longmans, Green and Co., 1915. 282

WERTENBAKER, THOMAS J. *The Puritan Oligarchy.* New York: Charles Scribner's Sons, 1947. 267, 268, 274

WHITMORE, W. H. (ed.). *The Colonial Laws of Massachusetts.* Boston: City Council, 1890. 267, 269, 273

CHAPTER 12

CORWIN, EDWARD S. *Constitutional Revolution, Ltd.* Claremont, California: Claremont Colleges, 1941. 305

RICHARDSON, JAMES (ed.). *Messages and Papers of the Presidents.* 10 vols. Washington: U.S. Government Printing Office, 1897. 303

SCHLESINGER, ARTHUR M. *The Rise of the City, 1878–1898.* New York: Macmillan, 1933. 304

STORY, JOSEPH. *Commentaries on the Constitution.* Boston: Hilliard, Gray and Co., 1833. 303

CHAPTER 13

ADAMS, HENRY. *History of the United States during the Administration of Thomas Jefferson.* 4 vols. New York: Charles Scribner's Sons, 1889.
383

ALLEN, GARDNER W. *Our Navy and the West Indian Pirates.* Salem, Mass.: The Essex Institute, 1929. 315

Association of American Law Schools. *Selected Essays on Constitutional Law.* 5 vols. Chicago: The Foundation Press, 1938. 330

BALDWIN, HENRY. "A General View of the Origin and Nature of the Constitution and Government," Philadelphia, 1837. Reprinted in 9 *Lawyers' Edition of the Supreme Court Reports* 869. 364

BASSETT, J. S. *Short History of the United States.* New York: Macmillan, 1923. 313, 384

BEVERIDGE, ALBERT J. *Life of John Marshall.* 4 vols. Boston: Houghton Mifflin and Co., 1916–1919. 307–311, 325, 326, 343

BLACKSTONE, WILLIAM. *Commentaries on the Laws of England.* 3rd ed. 4 vols. Oxford: Clarendon Press, 1768. 323

BURKE, EDMUND. *Speeches and Letters on American Affairs,* ed. Ernest Rhys. London: J. M. Dent and Sons, 1908. 323

CARMAN, H. J., and SYRETT, H. C. *History of the American People.* New York: Alfred A. Knopf, 1952. 309, 316, 372, 384

COOK, EUGENE, and POTTER, WILLIAM I. "The School Segregation Cases: Opposing the Supreme Court," *American Bar Association Journal* (1956).
364

CORWIN, EDWARD S. "The 'Higher Law' Background of American Constitutional Law," 42 *Harvard Law Review* 149 (1928–1929). 322, 323

EASTLAND, JAMES. Address to the Senate. *Congressional Record*. Vol. 101, p. 7119. 322

ELLIOT, JOHNATHAN (ed.). *Debates in the Several State Conventions*. 2nd ed. 5 vols. Washington: Elliot, 1836–1845. 309, 328

FINKELSTEIN, MAURICE. "Judicial Self-Limitation," 37 *Harvard Law Review* 338 (1924). 334

FISKE, JOHN. *The Critical Period of American History*. Boston: Houghton Mifflin and Co., 1888. 357

FLICK, ALEXANDER C. "Loyalism in New York." *Fourteen Studies in History, Economics and Public Law*. New York: Columbia University Press, 1902. 317

FRANKFURTER, FELIX. "Marshall and the Judicial Function." *Government Under Law*, ed. Arthur Sutherland. Cambridge: Harvard University Press, 1956. 312, 318, 369

FRUEND, PAUL, SUTHERLAND, ARTHUR E., HOWE, MARK DEWOLFE, and BROWN, ERNEST J. *Constitutional Law; Cases and Other Problems*. 2nd ed. 2 vols. Boston: Little, Brown and Company, 1961. 378

GREELY, HORACE. *The American Conflict*. 2 vols. Hartford: O. D. Case and Co., 1864–1866.

GRIGSBY, H. B. *History of the Virginia Federal Convention of 1788*. 2 vols. Richmond: Virginia Historical Society, 1890–1891. 309

HAMILTON, ALEXANDER, JAY, JOHN, and MADISON, JAMES. *Federalist*, ed. Ernest Rhys. London: J. M. Dent and Sons, 1934. 328

HAMMOND, BRAY. *Banks and Politics in America from the Revolution to the Civil War*. Princeton: Princeton University Press, 1957. 365, 367, 370

HART, HENRY. "Processing Taxes and Protective Tariffs," 49 *Harvard Law Review* 610 (1936). 334

HOLMES, OLIVER W. "The Law and the Court," *Collected Legal Papers*. New York: Peter Smith, 1952. 330

JENKS, EDWARD. *Law and Politics in the Middle Ages*. 2d ed. London: J. Murray and Co., 1913. 322

Journals of the Continental Congress. 34 vols. Washington: U.S. Government Printing Office, 1904–1937. 366

KLINGELSMITH, M. C. "James Wilson and the So-called Yazoo Fraud," 56 *University of Pennsylvania Law Review* (Old Series) 1 (1908). 358

LAFOLLETTE, ROBERT. Address before the American Federation of Labor on June 21, 1922, at Cincinnati, Ohio. Reprinted in *Congressional Record*. Vol. 62, p. 9077. 321

MCGOVNEY, DUDLEY O. "The British Origin of Judicial Review of Legislation," 93 *University of Pennsylvania Law Review* 1 (1944). 323

MCILWAIN, C. H. *The High Court of Parliament and Its Supremacy*. New Haven: Yale University Press, 1910. 322

MITCHELL, J. D. B. *Constitutional Law*. Edinburgh: Green and Son, Ltd., 1964. 322

MORGAN, DONALD G. *Justice William Johnson, the First Dissenter.* Columbia: University of South Carolina Press, 1954. 312, 360

PHILLIPS, HOOD. *The Constitutional Law of Great Britain and the Commonwealth.* London: Sweet & Maxwell, 1952. 322, 323

POUND, ROSCOE. *Introduction to the Philosophy of Law.* New Haven: Yale University Press, 1922. 338

RICHARDSON, JAMES (ed.). *Messages and Papers of the Presidents.* 10 vols. Washington: U.S. Government Printing Office, 1897. 372, 373

ROSENMAN, S. I. (ed.). *Public Papers and Addresses of Franklin Delano Roosevelt.* 13 vols. New York: Random House, 1938–1950. 335

ROSTOW, EUGENE V. "The Democratic Character of Judicial Review," 66 *Harvard Law Review* 193 (1952). 339

SMITH, J. H. *Appeals to the Privy Council from the American Plantations.* New York: Columbia University Press, 1950. 323

STERN, ROBERT L. "The Commerce Clause and the National Economy, 1934–1936," 59 *Harvard Law Review* 645 (1946). 342

SUTHERLAND, ARTHUR E. *The Law and One Man Among Many.* Madison: University of Wisconsin Press, 1956. 347

SUTHERLAND, ARTHUR E. "The Nation's Economy and State Frontiers," 8 *Stanford Law Review* 26 (1955). 377

SUTHERLAND, ARTHUR E., and VINCIGUERRA, STEPHEN. "The Octroi and the Airplane," 32 *Cornell Law Quarterly* 161 (1946). 377

THAYER, JAMES B. *Cases on Constitutional Law.* Cambridge: George H. Kent, 1895. 324

THAYER, JAMES B. "The Origin and Scope of the American Doctrine of Constitutional Law," 7 *Harvard Law Review* 129 (1893). 323, 324

WARREN, CHARLES. *The Supreme Court in United States History.* 3 vols. Boston: Little, Brown and Co., 1922.
316, 317, 325, 329, 346, 358, 379, 380

WEBSTER, DANIEL. *Works.* Boston: Little, Brown and Co. 6 vols. 1851.
361

WRIGHT, BENJAMIN F. *The Growth of American Constitutional Law.* Boston: Houghton Mifflin and Co., 1942. 331

CHAPTER 14

Anonymous pamphlet. *The Boston Slave Riot and Trial of Anthony Burns.* Boston: Fetridge & Co., 1854. 399

BOWEN, CATHERINE DRINKER. *The Lion and the Throne.* Boston: Little, Brown & Co., 1957. 403

BRADLEY, JOSEPH P. *Miscellaneous Writings,* ed. Charles Bradley. Newark, New Jersey: L. J. Hardman, 1901. 427

BRAUCHER, ROBERT, and ARTHUR E. SUTHERLAND. *Commercial Transactions.* 3rd ed. Brooklyn: The Foundation Press, 1964. 422

CARMAN, HARRY J., and HAROLD C. SYRETT. *History of the American People.* 2 vols. New York: Alfred A. Knopf, 1952. 386

CUSHMAN, ROBERT E. *"Ex parte* Quirin *et al.*—the Nazi Saboteur Case." 28 *Cornell Law Quarterly* 54, 1942. 419

FAIRMAN, CHARLES. *Mr. Justice Miller and the Supreme Court, 1862–1890.* Cambridge: Harvard University Press, 1939. 427

FAIRMAN, CHARLES. "The Law of Martial Rule and the National Emergency," 55 *Harvard Law Review* 834 (1942). 421

FAIRMAN, CHARLES. "The Supreme Court on Military Jurisdicitio: Martial Rule in Hawaii and the Yamashita Case." 59 *Harvard Law Review* 834 (1946). 421

FAIRMAN, CHARLES, and STANLEY MORRISON. "Does the Fourteenth Amendment Incorporate the Bill of Rights?" 2 *Stamford Law Review* 5 (1949). 442, 448

FLACK, HORACE EDGAR. *The Adoption of the Fourteenth Amendment.* Baltimore: Johns Hopkins University Press, 1908. 448

GARDINER, S. R. *Constitutional Documents of the Puritan Revolution, 1625–1660.* 3rd ed. Oxford: Clarendon Press, 1906. 403

GRAHAM, H. J. "The Conspiracy Theory of the Fourteenth Amendment," 47 *Yale Law Review* 371 441

HOPKINS, VINCENT C. *Dred Scott's Case.* New York: Fordham University Press, 1951. 399

HURST, WILLARD. "Treason in the United States," 58 *Harvard Law Review* 226, 395, 806 (1944, 1945). 419

MASON, ALPHEUS THOMAS. "Inter Arma Silent Leges: Chief Justice Stone's Views," 69 *Harvard Law Review* 806 (1950). 419

PERRY and COOPER. *Sources of Our Liberties.* Chicago: American Bar Foundation, 1959. 387

RANDALL, J. G. *Constitutional Problems under Lincoln.* Urbana: University of Illinois Press, 1951. 402, 408, 411

RICHARDSON, JAMES P. (ed.). *Messages and Papers of the Presidents.* 10 vols. Washington: U.S. Government Printing Office, 1897. 402, 403, 404, 409, 421, 443, 445, 450

ROSSITER, CLINTON. *Constitutional Dictatorship: Crisis Government in the Modern Democracies.* Princeton: Princeton University Press, 1948. 402

ROSSITER, CLINTON. *Supreme Court and Commander in Chief.* Ithaca: Cornell University Press, 1951. 402

SANDBURG, CARL. *Abraham Lincoln: The War Years.* 4 vols. New York: Harcourt, Brace and Co., 1939. 415

Senate Document 263, 67th Cong. 2d Sess., *Federal Aid in Domestic Disturbances.* Washington: Government Printing Office, 1922. 449

SWISHER, CARL BRENT. *Roger Brooke Taney.* Hamden, Conn.: Anchor Books, 1961. 398

WARREN, CHARLES. *The Supreme Court in U.S. History.* 3 vols. Boston: Little, Brown & Co., 1922. 400, 418, 427, 428

CHAPTER 15

ALLEN, FREDERICK LEWIS. *The Big Change,* quoted by George F. Baer. New York: Harper & Brothers, 1952. 456

CUSHMAN, ROBERT E. "The Independent Regulatory Commission," 24 *Cornell Law Quarterly* 13, 163 (1938–1939). 459

DARWIN, CHARLES. *Origin of Species*. 1859.   461
FAIRMAN, CHARLES. "The So-called Granger Cases," 5 *Stanford Law Review*
    587 (1953).   462
GRAHAM, H. J. "The Conspiracy Theory of the Fourteenth Amendment,"
    47 *Yale Law Journal* 371 (1938).   463
HOUGH, JUDGE CHARLES. "Due Process of Law Today," 1918 Irvine Lecture.
    32 *Harvard Law Review* 218 (1919).   463
SPENCER, HERBERT. *Social Statics* (1851).   461

CHAPTER 16

ALLEN, ROBERT S., see Pearson, Drew, and Robert S. Allen.   493
DE RUGGIERO, GUIDO. "Liberalism," *Encyclopedia of Social Sciences*, ed.
    E. R. A. Seligman and Alvin Johnson. New York: Macmillan, 1930–
    1934.   469
FRANKFURTER, FELIX. "Mr. Justice Roberts," 104 *University of Pennsylvania
    Law Review* 311.   496
HOLMES, JUSTICE O. W. "Natural Law" in "Collected Legal Papers," New
    York: Peter Smith, 1952.   468
LA FOLLETTE, ROBERT. *Speech before the American Federation of Labor.*
    Congressional Record, vol. 62, p. 9077.   470
PEARSON, DREW, and ROBERT S. ALLEN. *Nine Old Men*. Garden City, N. Y.:
    Doubleday, Doran and Co., 1937.   493
ROSENMAN, S. I. (ed.). *Public Papers and Addresses of Franklin Delano
    Roosevelt*, Vol. IV. 13 vols. New York: Random House, 1938–1950.
                                                                            490
ROUSSEAU, JEAN JACQUES. *Du Contrat Social*, Book II, Chapter 3.   468
SELLAR, W. C., and R. J. YEATMAN. *1066 and All That*. London: Methuen
    & Co., 1931.   471

CHAPTER 17

CAHN, EDMOND. *Sense of Injustice.*   535
CARTER and STRONG. *Reports of the Proceedings and Debates in the Con-
    vention of 1821*. Albany, N. Y.: E. & E. Hosford, 1821.   508
FAIRMAN, CHARLES, and STANLEY MORRISON. "Does the Fourteenth Amend-
    ment Incorporate the Bill of Rights?" 2 *Stanford Law Review* 5 (1949).
                                                                            531
Federalist Papers: "Publius," published 1777–1788 in several New York
    newspapers, written by Hamilton, Madison, and Jay. New York: Modern
    Library, 1937.   505, 533
HOUGH, CHARLES M. "Due Process of Law Today," 32 *Harvard Law Re-
    view* 218 (1919).   535
LEHUËROU, JULIEN MARIE. *Histoire des Institutions Carolingiennes*. 2 vols.
    Paris: Joubert, 1843.   527, 547
MYRDAL, GUNNAR. *American Dilemma*. New York: Harper & Row, 1944.
                                                                            536
PEASLEE, AMOS J. *Constitutions of Nations*. 3 vols. Concord, N. H.: Rum-
    ford Press, 1950.   549

PEASLEE, AMOS J. *International Governmental Organizations.* 2 vols. Hague: M. Nighoff, 1956. 549

POUND, ROSCOE. *Interpretations of Legal History.* Cambridge: Cambridge University Press, 1923. 534

Race Relations Law Reporter, edited by the Vanderbilt Law School. Published quarterly. Southern Education Reporting Service. 536

ROUSSEAU, JEAN JACQUES. *Du Contrat Social.* 533

SUETONIUS. *Lives of the Caesars,* translated by J. C. Rolfe. Cambridge: Harvard University Press, 1944. 528

SUTHERLAND, ARTHUR E. "Due Process and Disestablishment," 62 *Harvard Law Review* 1306 (1949). 524, 545

SUTHERLAND, ARTHUR E. "Establishment According to Engel," 76 *Harvard Law Review* 25 (1962). 540

SUTHERLAND, ARTHUR E. "The Law and One Man among Many," Madison: University of Wisconsin Press, 1956. 535

SUTHERLAND, ARTHUR E. "Private Government and Public Property," *Yale Review,* Spring, 1952. 529

WECHSLER, HERBERT. *Principles, Politics and Fundamental Law.* Cambridge: Harvard University Press, 1961. 511

WECHSLER, HERBERT. "Toward Neutral Principles of Constitutional Law," 1959. 73 *Harvard Law Review* 1 (1959). 511

INDEX

583

ABOUT THE AUTHOR

Arthur Eugene Sutherland has been Bussey Professor of Law at Harvard University since 1955. He received his A.B. degree from Wesleyan University, L.L.B. degree from Harvard University. In 1927–28 Professor Sutherland was secretary to Justice Oliver Wendell Holmes of the United States Supreme Court. He taught at Cornell University from 1945–50 before appointment to the Harvard faculty. In 1956 Professor Sutherland was a Fulbright Lecturer at Oxford University; in 1958–59 he was designated Purington Visiting Lecturer of Political Science at Mount Holyoke College. Professor Sutherland is author of *The Law and One Man Among Many* and co-author of *Constitutional Law Cases and Other Problems* and *Cases and Materials on Commercial Transactions*. In addition he has published many articles in various legal journals.

THIS BOOK WAS SET IN

CALEDONIA AND PALATINO TYPES

BY ATLANTIC LINOTYPE CO., INC.

IT WAS DESIGNED BY THE STAFF OF

BLAISDELL PUBLISHING COMPANY

DATE DUE

OCT 8 '71	OCT 8 71		
OCT 2 9 '71	NOV 1 71		
GAYLORD			PRINTED IN U.S.A.